SCHOOLS OF THOUGHT

Schools of Thought

TWENTY-FIVE YEARS OF INTERPRETIVE
SOCIAL SCIENCE

EDITED BY

Joan W. Scott

Debra Keates

PRINCETON UNIVERSITY PRESS

PRINCETON AND OXFORD

Library of Congress Cataloging-in-Publication Data

Schools of thought : twenty-five years of interpretive
social science / edited by Joan W. Scott, Debra Keates.
p. cm.
Papers presented at a conference.
Includes bibliographical references.
ISBN 0-691-08841-1 (alk. paper)
ISBN 0-691-08842-X (pbk. : alk. paper)
1. Social sciences—Congresses. I. Scott, Joan Wallach. II. Keates, Debra.
H22 .S36   2001
300—dc21   2001019856

PUBLICATION ACKNOWLEDGMENTS

Peter Galison's essay, "Material Culture, Theoretical Culture, and Delocalization," was
published in *Science in the Twentieth Century*, ed. John Krige and Dominique Pestre (OPA
[Overseas Publishers Association] N.V., 1997). It is reprinted here with permission from
Gordon & Breach Publishers.

Joan Scott's essay, "After History," appeared in *Common Knowledge* 5:3 (winter 1996).

Anna Tsing's essay, "The Global Situation," appeared in *Cultural Anthropology* 15:3
(August 2000): 327–60. It is reprinted here with permission from the American Anthropological Association.

Michael Walzer's essay, "International Society: What Is the Best that We Can Do?" was
given as the Multatuli Lecture at the Catholic University of Leuven and published in the
journal of the European Ethics Network, *Ethical Perspectives*, December 1999. A different
version appeared in *Dissent*, fall 2000.

CONTENTS

ACKNOWLEDGMENTS

SCHOOLS OF THOUGHT developed out of a conference held at the Institute for Advanced Study in May 1997 to celebrate the twenty-fifth anniversary of the Institute's School of Social Science and organized by the School's faculty: Clifford Geertz, Joan W. Scott, Michael Walzer, and Albert Hirschman. Invited scholars were asked to consider changes in their fields in the context of the social and political transformations that took place over the last quarter of the twentieth century. The papers in this collection reflect the wide variety of responses elicited by that challenge. Some participants do not have papers included in this collection. They did, however, make crucial interventions for which we are grateful. They are George Marcus, Laura Engelstein, Geoffrey Hawthorn, Fred Inglis, Carl Kaysen, Michael McPherson, Claus Offe, Sherry Ortner, Orlando Patterson, Richard Sennett, and Elliott Shore. The conference was generously funded by the Russell Sage Foundation and the Gladys Krieble Delmas Foundation. We would also like to express our appreciation for the crucial support of Deborah Koehler, Lucille Allsen, Phillip Griffiths, James Barbour, Julianne Kmiec, Michael Ciccone, Michael Campton, Michelino Antenucci, and the maintenance and kitchen staffs of the Institute.

SCHOOLS OF THOUGHT

School Building

A RETROSPECTIVE PREFACE

Clifford Geertz

As JUST ABOUT everyone understands by now, dividing history into bounded periods, named, characterized, and placed within an imagined larger order, is a far from innocent business. The Long Nineteenth Century, The Sixties, The Brown Decades, The Gilded Age, Scoundrel Time, The Guns of August all frame arguments, reflect somebody or other's desire to put a particular spin on things that on their surface are but temporally connected. Similarly, to take twenty-five years of free-form, cross-cutting social, political, economic, and historical writing growing out of work at a single, unstandard, American institution and isolate it as an "era" in such writing—a stage, a phase, a line of thought—is to pursue an agenda, take a position, state a case. Finding either an inward connection or a general direction in work ranging from "The Global Situation," "Science as Alchemy," "The Moral Uses of the 'Prisoner's Dilemma,'" and "Retrotopia" to "Economic History as a Cure for Economics," "Structure, Contingency, and Choice," "Whatever Happened to the 'Social' in Social History," and "Can the 'Other' of Philosophy Speak?" (to say nothing of "Interdisciplinarity at New York University," some sort of terminus, surely, of particularized analysis) would seem to take some doing. If "interpretive social science"—much less Interpretive Social Science—is up to that, it should be up to just about anything.

The fact is, it is. Rather than a program to follow, a faction to join, or a theory to celebrate, it is very much an ad hoc post hoc business. First you do it, then you name it, then you try to determine what sort of "family resemblance," if any, holds it intelligibly together, such as "recreation," or "criticism," or, in some ways a closer parallel, "tropical forest." And to do that, you need to go into what Marxists used to call "the material conditions of production"—the place, time, and social environment in which it was constructed. And in the present case, that means you need to go into the School of Social Science at The Institute for Advanced Study between 1970 and 1995 and look at what thing went on there then. The spread, the diversity, the complexity of direction, of at least this sort of interpretive social science, as well as what, in general, it comes to as a way of describing the shapes of what happens, can only be made plain, if it can be made plain at all, by determining (to recycle an old slogan) Who made it, When, Where, Why, and How. An "Effort After Meaning" (to recycle another one), it is the nature of that effort that at base defines it, not its topics or its arguments, which remain dispersed and unreconciled.

For all practical purposes, the School got under way in 1970, when I, at that time professor of anthropology at the University of Chicago, was invited to become its first professor. (There had been a small experimental program for a couple years prior to that, but formal establishment did not come until 1973, after a great deal of uncertainty about whether to proceed.) The originator of the notion that there should be such a school, and the driving force behind its formation, was the Harvard economist Carl Kaysen. Kaysen had become Director of the Institute in 1966, following the retirement of Robert Oppenheimer, with the understanding that he would undertake to organize some sort of effort in the social sciences. Faced with bitter and unappeasable opposition from most of the faculty in the already existing Schools—Mathematics, Natural Science, and Historical Studies—he was required to raise all the money to endow the new school externally, off budget. Rather to the surprise of his adversaries, and certainly to their dismay ("this will be your Vietnam," one *enragé* had assured him), he promptly did so, tapping a wide range of sources, large and small, including, most critically, the Ford Foundation, which initially funded my chair. After an attempt to appoint a second professor failed in 1973, leading to public uproar, private rancor, and institutional near-death, Kaysen, reduced to fending off personal attack, resigned to take a post at MIT, and the task of keeping the enterprise afloat until help arrived was left largely in my hands. Amidst an at least a somewhat chastened, but still generally hostile, faculty and with the backing (more or less) of The Board of Trustees, I somehow contrived do so. In 1974, Albert Hirschman, then professor of economics at Harvard, was appointed as the second professor. In 1980, Michael Walzer, professor of government, also at Harvard, became the third. And in 1985, Joan Scott, professor of history at Brown, joined as the fourth. What began as a fragile and imperiled enterprise—suspect, maligned, and ill-defined—became, over the course of a quarter century of the eternal vigilance that is the price of liberty, a firmly established, if still controversial, presence, both at the Institute and on the social science scene overall.

But, again, it didn't just happen: it was made to happen. Pure possibility is not the sort of thing your average professor, buried in the smothering routines of university life, where, as Francis Comford famously remarked in his *Guide for the Young Academic Politician*, "nothing should ever be done for the first time," is used to confronting; and when it does appear it turns out to be about as unnerving as it is exhilarating. Sheer option and a free hand are fine as prospects. It is only when one is obliged actually to exercise them, especially in a maelstrom, that things get complicated. When there are so many directions in which to move, moving, or even deciding to move, in any one of them seems particularly fateful.

Some guidance was, of course, provided by the general operating procedures of the Institute, as they had evolved, more or less informally, since its foundation in 1930 as an American haven for Albert Einstein, Hermann Weyl, and other scholar refugees from Hitler's Europe to pursue any research they wanted to pursue in any way they wanted to pursue it. The professors, or, as they were then called, "permanent members," in each School were empowered to invite, either directly or via application, a number of visiting, or "temporary," members. These members were usually appointed for a year (longer or shorter stays were sometimes granted), awarded a stipend, and provided with an office, housing, secretarial support, and the like, on the understanding that they would pursue a suitably "advanced" program of study and research, and then return, enriched and upgraded, to their academic posts. By 1970, there were perhaps 150 of these visitors a year, almost all of them mathematicians, physicists, classicists, or medievalists, plus an occasional off-line intellectual celebrity—Jacques Maritain, Arnold Toynbee, T. S. Eliot. Beyond this, the organization of the Schools, their mode of operation, the direction of their research, and even the allocation of their budgets were left, more or less, to the permanent members to determine. The point, as Oppenheimer—he of that other intellectual forcing house, the Manhattan Project—is supposed to have phrased it, was to leave no one with an excuse for not getting his or hers (but there were not many hers involved then) work done.

As essentially nothing else than the funding and these skeletal outlines were in place so far as the new School was concerned, a number of matters had immediately to be decided, if not precisely by fiat—"Let there be social science! "—at least precipitously, and from a standing start. What sort of visiting members (or as we came to call them, "fellows") was the School to have? How many? For how long and at what stipends? Of what seniority, from which fields, with what sort of credentials from what sort of institutions? Would they work separately, in informal groups, in organized teams? What facilities beyond an office, a desk, paper, and a typewriter would they need and could we provide? And, of course, most consequentially, what was to count as "social science?" What, after all, were we trying to do? Extend a tradition? Strengthen an elite? Establish a beachhead? Find a niche? Launch a revolution?

Kaysen's original idea was that the School would consist of two "wings." One of these wings would be centered in the New Social History movement, just then at the peak of its influence, with the work of Fernand Braudel and Emmanuel Le Roi Ladurie in France; E. P. Thompson and Peter Laslett in Britain; Lawrence Stone and Charles Tilly in the United States; and the cliometricians Robert Fogel, William Aydelotte, Michel Vovelle, and E. A. Wrigley, among others. The other would concern itself with the just emerging "cognitive sciences": linguistics, computer studies, artificial intelligence, experimental psychology. But he was unable to raise the money to fund the second, which to the faculty was, if anything, even more dubious than the first, bad experiment and worse mathematics, so the people he had assembled to launch it—George Miller, Duncan Luce, and David Rumelhart, a remarkable cohort—drifted away. And as I came out of a background of area studies, political development, symbolic anthropology, and the comparison of cultures, whose connections with the new social history were (at that time anyway) not particularly strong, and as we were unsuccessful in inducing Wrigley to join us, the first wing never quite flew, at least as originally conceived, either. With Kaysen's departure, the School, pushed by my anxieties and inclinations—both intense—moved off in less settled directions, trying to find out what a "social scientist" was by inviting as broad a range of people claiming to be such as we could find to be fellows and seeing what, if anything, save the label, set them apart.

The main anxiety was simply to escape from the eye of the storm into a calmer, more "normal" existence, whatever that might turn out to be; the main inclination, which in the long run was much more consequential, was to break away somehow from the prevailing paradigms in the social sciences, poor imitations, mostly, of misunderstood physics, and to adapt those sciences to the immediate peculiarities of their supposed subject matter: the human way of being in the world. The aim was and (reworked, revised, reconsidered, and reasserted) still is, not just to measure, correlate, systematize, and settle, but to formulate, clarify, appraise, and understand. A small off-line enterprise in a glamorous up-market place, the loosening up of things, not their solidification seemed the way to go.

• • •

IT HAS BEEN, in any case, the way we have gone. Unable even to try to match the infrastructural resources of the great universities, we could neither support extramural research or sustained programs of collective study, nor could we subsidize travel or publication; and, of course, we provide no formal teaching. (The Institute is not formally connected to Princeton University—"We have separate deficits," as Kaysen put it—though relations have generally been cordial, and we have library privileges there.) The School is, and doubtless will continue to be, whatever substantive directions it moves in, primarily a place for planning research, for reflecting upon it, or for writing it up, rather than a place for carrying it out. The anthropologist is either back from the field or preparing to go into it; the survey sociologist has already conducted his interviews or is designing his instrument; the social historian is either getting ready to enter the archives or just emergent from them; the economist must bring most of her data with her; the sociologist of science, likewise. The division between "thinking" and "doing" is difficult to make in the social sciences; "pure" and "applied" do not separate out into kinds and vocations.

TABLE 1
Fellows, Social Science, IAS 1970–95

Field	No.	%
History	97	20.3
Politics	90	18.8
Anthropology	82	17.2
Sociology	80	16.7
Economics	47	19.8
Philosophy	32	6.7
Psychology	17	3.6
Literature	14	2.9
Linguistics	9	1.9
Law	4	0.8
Art	4	0.8
Religion	2	0.4

But to the degree that they can be distinguished, the Institute location was, and is, clearly on the "thinking"—writing, discussing, criticizing—"pure" side. (That is, I take it, what "advanced" is supposed to mean.) This, as much as any single consideration, sorts out the kind of scholar most likely to profit from a stay in the School: someone who wants to discuss, order, and reflect upon either something he or she has already done or something he or she is getting ready to do.

There were, apparently, enough of these. Between 1970 and 1995, the years celebrated in this volume, 478 scholars (that is, about nineteen a year, though it has gone as low as fifteen and as high as twenty-one), chosen from about fifteen times that many applicants, from about twelve disciplines, broadly defined, were fellows, research assistants, or special visitors at the Institute (see table 1).

As for other characteristics of the population, the "international" ethos of the Institute and the comparative interests of the School made for a very wide geographical spread in terms of the origins of the scholars as well as their areas of research concentration (see table 2).[1] So far as distribution according to region and institution, it, too, has been very broad. [2] And, finally, 23 percent (13 1) of the fellows were women, about 32 percent (15 1) "junior."[3]

Given the population—fifteen to twenty scholars, from all sorts of backgrounds, all sorts of specialties, and all sorts of interests, and, of course, all sorts of personalities, from the saintly to the impossible—how should we (or should we?) try to organize the common life of the School? We have been, and continue to be, minimalist in this regard. Scholars come to the Institute to do their work, and should be left alone to do it. Yet a simple collection of

TABLE 2

Origin of Fellows and Area Focus of Research
(1970–95)

	Origins	*Area*
U.S.	276	54
Canada	7	5
Germany	28	18
France	26	31
Great Britain	25	8
Italy	18	7
Other Western Europe	7	55[a]
Eastern Europe[b]	11	16
Russia[c]	2	7
Latin America	17	28
Middle East[d]	10	14
Israel	11	5
North Africa[e]	6	12
Sub-Saharan Africa	7	22
India	8	18
Other S. Asia	2	2
Japan	7	5
Korea	0	2
China	4	8
S.E. Asia[f]	3	17
Australia	3	3
Non-Area[g]	—	141
Totals	478	478

[a] Composite category; includes those working on Europe generally.
[b] Poland, Hungary, Romania, Balkans.
[c] Including Soviet Union.
[d] Egypt, Turkey, Jordan, Iran.
[e] Morocco, Algeria, Tunisia.
[f] Indonesia, Malaysia, Philippines.
[g] Topical focus only.

isolate eminences, geniuses in cubicles, seems contrary to the very idea of social science, where both geniuses and loners are rare, and it is social processes that are the object of study. Some kind of community, some sort of ordered interaction, with luck, even some sort of cooperation, ought, if delicately, as though it were not actually happening, to be encouraged. Otherwise, where is the School? And what are the professors for? Our first move in this regard was a decision to have only yearlong fellows. So extended a stay, combined with the fact that virtually all of the fellows were in residence in subsidized housing on the campus, made the formation of an at least temporary community—"a year," with at least something of a shape and character—practicable in a way a more fluctuating population, with people entering and leaving at irregular intervals, would not. Second, we instituted a weekly "School Seminar." All fellows were expected to attend and to give, in turn, an account of his or her work, after which it would be discussed. As the seminar is open to the Institute generally, and to the university as well, it has also served to stimulate interchange beyond the borders of the School. But perhaps the most effective measures for giving some overall form to the school were the establishment, after awhile, of yearly "themes," and the appointment, also after awhile, of a few "longer-term," three-to-five-year fellows.

The themes, which began in 1972, when I organized one on "Islamic Societies," and have continued since, are but generally (even vaguely) formulated, so as not to constrain research concerns too sharply, and are designed to involve from about a third to about a half (i.e., seven to ten) of the year's fellows, the others being focused on their various projects. The themes are announced in advance, are organized and led by one or another of the professors in turn, and, mainly for funding purposes, planned in three-year blocks. The fellows associated with the theme, as well as others who discover themselves to be interested, are urged to form a second, smaller research seminar at which, rather than formal presentations, readings on the subject, suggested by the members, are circulated to form the basis for extended discussion.[4] As for the three-to-five-year fellowships, they were designed to provide the School with a "junior faculty," and, as they participated in the selection process and in the planning of the year's work, to broaden our representation generally. William Sewell, a social historian from the University of Chicago, served in such a capacity from 1975 to 1980; Quentin Skinner, an historian of political thought from Cambridge University, served from 1976 to 1979; and Wolf Lepenies, a sociologist and intellectual historian from the Freie Universität in Berlin, served from 1979 to 1980, and 1982 to 1983. Their contribution to the establishment of the School as a going concern, to its finding a form in which to exist, was critical. They broadened it, stabilized it, and propelled it at the same time.

The overall structure of things (professors, seminars, long- and short-term fellows, themes, office staff), as minimal and indefinite as it was, it remained only to see how, and whether, it would work. How would it connect itself to the ferocious swirl of theory, method, action, and partisanship that marked the social sciences everywhere following the adventures and insurrections of the 1960s? What would it mean to innovative at a time when just about everything in academia and in the life of the mind was up for grabs? A few years after Paris, Berkeley, Columbia, and Chicago exploded, and the very idea of disinterested scholarship grew suspect, what on earth could "advanced study" be?

• • •

IT WOULD be idle to attempt to review here all the developments in the Social (or Human, or Behavioral, or Cultural) Sciences that appeared and took hold during the last quarter of the last century—the period in which the School was formed and whose un-centeredness this collection reflects. A mere listing of some labels gives a sense of the wealth, the variety, the ambition, and the incoherence: structuralism, sociobiology, cultural studies, gender studies, evolutionary psychology, dependency theory, science studies, game theory, ethnomethodology, subaltern studies, deconstruction, symbolic anthropology, critical legal studies, feminism, environmental studies, discourse analysis, cultural psychology, human rights. And, of course, there were all the post-s, neo-s, new-s, turns, and revolutions: post-structuralism, post-colonial studies, post-modernism, neo-Marxist, neo-Weberianism, neo-liberalism, the new historicism, new social movements, the linguistic, the hermeneutic, the semiotic, the textual turn, the cognitive revolution. The talismanic names, blazoned like war whoops and banderoles, were as numerous and, if anything, even less reconcilable, one with the next: Lévi-Strauss, Lacan, Derrida, Althusser, and Foucault from France; Gramsci from Italy; Stuart Hall, Raymond Williams, D. H. Winnicott, and Wittgenstein from Britain; Adorno, Habermas, Benjamin, and Gadamer from Germany; Goffman, Chomsky, Kuhn, Rawls, and Edward Said from the United States; Guha from India; Henrique-Cardoso from Brazil; Fanon from Algeria; Bakhtin and Vygotsky from the Soviet Union, Roman Jakobson from Moscow, Prague, Paris, and Harvard. Simply to survive in this abundance was taxing enough; to lay a path through it seemed impossible altogether.

Fortunately, the School had only to accommodate it, not to straighten it up or beat it into shape. And for that, what was needed was an attitude, not a program—*another* program—and certainly not a paradigm. As "interpretivists," self-declared and self-understood, we were interested in work that reached beyond the narrowed confines of a fixed and schematized "scientific method," one that connected up with moral, political, and spiritual concerns. We were interested in empirical work, conceptually informed, not (or not particularly) in methodology, system building, punditry, or policy formation. And we were interested in careful, at least reasonably dispassionate argument, not in ideological ax grinding. This left room for just about everyone but the zealous and the terminally pretentious. And even a few of them (names available upon request) slipped in.

All this is not to say that the adoption of an "interpretive," or "hermeneutical" stance, one that, in the words of Charles Taylor, "attempts to make sense of an object of study" in some way "confused, incomplete, cloudy . . . contradictory . . . unclear," to render "matters on their surface strange and puzzling . . . no longer so, accounted for," did not lend a certain tone and direction to the School's work.[5] Openness is one thing, insipidness another, and there is hardly much point in going to the trouble of setting up such an enterprise if one does not want to influence somehow the way things are going. "Interpretive social science," may be an intellectual style, a general outlook, even a mood and a temper, but as such it has a weight of its own.

There are a number of ways in which this weight (the thumb on the scale) is reflected in the sort of work the School has in general supported, and in the contributions to this volume intended to represent it. Foremost among these is the tendency to reach out rather more toward the humanities—to philosophy, literature, history, art, religion—than is generally common in social science, anxious as so many of its practitioners are to improve their claims to objectivity, precision, and positive knowledge by casting their work in mechanistic terms. (As one last approximate statistic, somewhere around a third of the fellows have come from the humanities.) When you conceive of your task as making the confused, the incomplete, the cloudy "clear," "accounted for," the concepts and techniques developed by literary criticism, philology, iconography, political theory, or the history of ideas become relevant in a way they are not when one's central activity is constructing causal hypotheses and trying to verify them. One would not expect to encounter discourses on "Political Theory and Moral Responsibility," "International Society: What Is the Best that We Can Do?" or "Prelude to a Political Economy: Norms and Law in Economics" in most surveys of social scientific work. Second, since the social sciences are undoubtedly, whatever we might wish or think appropriate, still predominantly a European and American enterprise descended from and located within "Western," "Enlightenment," and, some would say, "colonial" modes of thought, we have tried, with some deliberateness, to bring Asian, African, and Latin American—"non-Western"—voices into the discussion, to deprovincialize things. Not an easy task, but an essential one, as Anna Tsing, Renato Rosaldo, and Nicholas Dirks in their different ways all argue here. And third, there is something of a stress on the particular, even the odd or irregular, case— German sociology, railway travel, the New York Institute of the Humanities, the economics of slavery—as a means to broader conclusions. Few of the fellows followed all of these directions, and many followed none at all. But as general, diagnostic tendencies in the otherwise vastly miscellaneous body of work the school has supported, they are visible enough, marks of place, time, and intellectual climate, of the material conditions of production.

The papers collected in this volume, a selection from the School's twenty-fifth anniversary symposium, held at the Institute for Advanced Study in 1997, with some pieces added afterward by invitation to round things out, are not intended as a complete and unbiased sample of its work. It should be clear that such a thing is impossible. Instead, these papers are intended, by the organizers of the symposium anyway, to look like a not-untypical "year," organized around the theme of "twenty-five years of social science and social change." Various disciplines, various backgrounds, various ages, various subjects, various approaches, various prose styles, all "somehow linked" to a common concern: Where have we been? Where might we be going?

The authors are, naturally enough—being scholars not seers—more comfortable with the first question than with the second. The future, as usual, lies ahead. Nothing assures it will be much like the past, nothing assures it will be less contentious and less troubled. (Although one hopes that institutionally it will be at least a little less besieged.) Nothing assures, either, that a quarter century on we—whoever "we" will be then—will be able to present so impressive a set of examples of our work. But the groundwork for that, and more, is there. We proceed with a wary confidence, a tempered assurance, appropriate both to the sort of thing we are trying to do and the sort of experience we have had in trying to do it.

NOTES

1. This classification is even more casual than that in table 1, which is casual enough. I have simply assigned "origins" and "areas" according to my judgments of the individuals concerned and of the direction of their work. Such judgments are surely contestable in particular cases, but the general pattern is clear enough. Origins are assigned according to where the individual's undergraduate education occurred, even for people— a fair proportion—now working in Europe or the United States. Area focus indicates the part of the world on which, at the time they were at the Institute, they concentrated. Those without such an areal focus (Models of Perception, Welfare Economics, The Crisis of Empiricism, Biographical Research, Entrails and Ticker Tape, Does History Permit a Philosophical Interrogation of Sexual Difference? Envy and Equality, The Theory of Slavery) are categorized as "Non-Area." Grouped into larger blocks, the percent origin (N = 478)/percent area (N = 337) are: North America, 59.8/17.5; Europe (including Australia and Russia), 24.5/42. 1; Latin America, 3.6/8.3; Middle East (including North Africa and Israel), 5.7/9.2; sub-Saharan Africa, 1.5/6.5; Asian 5.0/15.4.

2. I have calculated these figures only for the 88 U.S. and Canadian institutions, because the "extra-North American" institutions are even more dispersed. (There are 77 of them from 26 countries.) By region, about 32% of the institutions are in the mid-Atlantic states, 19% in New England, 17% Midwest, 17% West, 8% South, and 6% Canada. In "rank" terms, the top ten universities (Princeton, Harvard, Chicago, Berkeley, Yale, Michigan, Penn, MIT, Stanford, UCLA) account for 38% of the fellows, the other 78 for 62%.

3. "Junior" includes individuals under about 40 and/or untenured, and so, even more than the other statistics, it is but a ballpark figure. All fellows are postdoctoral, except for a handful of predoctoral "research assistants," and almost all, upwards of 90%, were in residence for a year. "Visitors," a few individuals who come without a stipend, often stay for shorter periods ranging from a month to a semester.

4. Among the other themes treated over the years (some of them more than once): Authoritarianism and Democracy in Latin America; Science Studies; Political Theory of the State; New Approaches in Economic Analysis; Symbolic Anthropology; The Sociology of Art; Equality and Inequality; The Cognitive Sciences; Gender Studies; Post-Communist Transitions in Eastern Europe; Modernity and Postmodernity; Biographical Methods in the Social Sciences; Hermeneutic Approaches in Law, History, Anthropology, and Philosophy; Globalism; Human Rights. Fellows are, of course, also free to organize smaller seminars on subjects that interest them, and a fair number have—on trauma, on class and race, on ritual, on postcolonialism.

5. C. Taylor, *Philosophical Papers* (Cambridge: Cambridge University Press, 1985), vol. 2, pp. 15, 17.

PART ONE

Blurred Genres: Reflections on Disciplinary Practices

CHAPTER 1

Political Theory after the Enlightenment Project

Quentin Skinner

THIS ESSAY was originally presented at a conference honoring the twenty-fifth anniversary of the School of Social Science at the Institute for Advanced Study. When revising it for the less celebratory occasion of this collection, I discovered that to excise all specific references to the School of Social Science at the Institute would do damage to the view of changes in my field that I, in fact, hold. The small size of the school belies its enormous influence; I hope I shall be forgiven for leaving my references to it intact.

• • •

I HAVE been asked to say something specifically about changes in the study of political theory during the past quarter of a century. But I must begin by explaining that I am not myself a first-order political theorist but merely (or at least mainly) an historian of the subject. I revere the talents of such political philosophers as Michael Walzer and Charles Taylor; they have shown us how to combine historical scholarship with fundamental philosophical enquiry into the concepts and assumptions that shape our contemporary political world. By contrast, I have mainly confined myself to tracing some of the processes by which our contemporary political world came into being. Were I to try to say anything about that world itself, I would I think have little hope—especially in the face of such a dauntingly well-informed audience—of telling you anything you don't already know or, alternatively, don't already know to be strongly contestable.

This being so, what I should like to do instead is to invite you for a moment to enter the particular neck of the academic woods in which I live and move. I inhabit a province remote in space and time from the United States today, so I hope it will not strike you as merely alien and strange. It is far removed in space, in that I am a student exclusively of western European traditions of reflection about political life. And it is still further removed in time, in that I am a student of the European tradition only during its most formative days, which I take to have been the sixteenth and seventeenth centuries.

My focus in what follows will, however, be somewhat broader than these limitations may suggest. Taking this admittedly narrow perspective, what I plan to do is to look at two massive social and political movements that have both been accelerating during the past twenty-five years. One has been the feminist movement, the diversified but continuing progress of which profoundly affects us all. I am not, of course, going to say anything about this movement itself, but I do want to say something about the transforming influence it has exercised on the academic subdiscipline within which I work.

True to my desire to welcome you into my corner of the Academy, I should like to examine this influence in the case of one specific topic on which I have myself tried to write, namely the moral and political theory of Renaissance Europe. Let me begin by casting my mind back twenty-five years and asking what scholarly studies would have been widely regarded in the early 1970s as classic contributions to this particular subject. A small number of works stand out, but one that would undoubtedly have been cited by every expert in the field would have been the study that Felix Gilbert published in 1965, when he was already a member of the School of Historical Studies here at the Institute, a post from which he retired in 1975. I am referring to his book *Machiavelli and Guicciardini* in which he provided an analysis, as his subtitle puts it, of politics and history in sixteenth-century Florence.

As Gilbert emphasised, one of the pivotal concepts around which the political theory of the Renaissance was organized was that of virtue—*virtus* in Latin, *la virtù* in Italian. As he also indicated, however, this concept was not employed merely to refer, as it later was in the philosophy of Kant and his followers, to a range of allegedly desirable qualities. It is true that the term *virtus* was used in the Renaissance as a shorthand for the so-called cardinal virtues of wisdom, courage, temperance, and justice. But I take it to have been part of Gilbert's thesis to argue that there had been an excessive readiness, perhaps especially prevalent in the German historiography, to read the political theory of the Renaissance through the lens later supplied by Kant, thereby failing to see that the concept of virtus had previously borne a much more complex and potentially ambiguous character. One of the insights to be gained from Gilbert's contrasting analysis is that, among Renaissance political writers, the concept was also used as the name of a distinctive causal power. To cite the ambiguity we still invoke when speaking of the virtues, it was taken to be the name of the power by virtue of which we are alone capable of attaining our highest and most characteristically human goals.

If we ask about the nature of those goals, we find ourselves led to speak, Gilbert went on to show, about some of the most profound and defining values of Renaissance culture. The specific ends that the political theorists of this era invite us to pursue are those of attaining honor and fame for ourselves and our community by way of seeking glory in the public sphere. This sphere was in turn taken to include the theater of war as well as politics, and the question whether civil or military glory should be assigned the higher value continued to be debated throughout the bloodstained history of Renaissance Europe.

With this portrait of the virtuoso, we are presented with a vision of morality as a series of hypothetical imperatives, and hence in effect as a practical skill. We are asked to become adept at reasoning about the relations between individual virtues and our chosen goals, learning how to calculate on each particular occasion which particular quality of virtù will best enable us to achieve what we desire. At the same time, we are offered a powerful explanation of why we have an interest in behaving morally. If and only if we learn to act virtuously, it is suggested, can we hope to attain the goals that, as a matter of fact, we chiefly desire.

Felix Gilbert's account of Renaissance virtù was a study of exceptional subtlety, and in many ways it remains an unsurpassed guide to the very different moral terrain traversed by Machiavelli and his contemporaries. But at the same time Gilbert's analysis contained a lacuna that now seems astonishing. Although he wrote so perceptively about virtus as the name of a causal power, he made little of the fact that virtus was also viewed by the neoclassical writers of the Renaissance as the eponymous attribute of the figure known as the vir. And when the moralists of the Renaissance spoke of the vir, what they were referring to—as our own word *virile* is there to remind us—was the figure of the truly manly man.

Once we add this ingredient, the organizing categories of Renaissance political theory jump to life with a vengeance. Let me single out two specific implications of this way of thinking about the moral and political world. The first stems from the claim that the exercise of virtus presupposes a capacity for sustained practical reasoning. When we add to this the claim that virtus is the quality of the vir, we find ourselves confronting a syllogism of which the conclusion affirms that reason is an inherently male attribute. Nowadays the implications for the gendering of public life hardly need spelling out. But I know of no historical study that brought these implications fully to the surface before Genevieve Lloyd published her pioneering book *The Man of Reason* in 1984. As she indicated, it was at the historical juncture of which I have been speaking that the opposition began to be constructed between the preempted male quality of rationality and the supposedly contrasting ideal of feminine intuition. Once this distinction took firm root, male domination of the public sphere came to be seen as nothing less than a part of the natural order of things.

The other implication I want to single out is arguably of even greater importance. The quality of virtus, according to the ideology I am here considering, is the name of the congeries of attributes required for success in political life. Once again, however, virtus is at the same time held to be a specifically male set of qualities. But these premises yield the conclusion that women inherently lack the attributes requisite for operating effectively in the public sphere. It is, of course, acknowledged that they may have appropriate goals of their own, and thus that an ideal of female virtus can undoubtedly be assigned a sense. But at the same time it is argued that the only appropriate arena for the display of such *virtus* must be private and domestic, by contrast with the specifically male domain of politics. Again, the implications for the gendering of public life hardly need spelling out. But I know of no historical study that brought them center stage before the publication of Jean Elshtain's book *Public Man, Private Woman*, a study I recall as eye-opening in the literal sense when it first appeared in 1981.

I have mentioned some pioneering contributions of feminist scholarship to the intellectual history of the Renaissance. If I had been speaking about the nineteenth century, however, I should certainly have wanted to mention the work published at the same time by Joan Scott here at the Institute. But whatever historical period we examine, the moral of the story remains the same. No one writing the history of political theory, nor any other kind of intellectual history, would nowadays write with the kind of blinkered vision that limited even the most perceptive historians of a generation ago. The impact of feminist scholarship has transfigured the intellectual landscape. Everyone has been given the means to see how far these intellectual traditions were also discourses of power, discourses that served to legitimize certain hierarchical arrangements, to marginalize conflicting possibilities and thereby to hold in place a pervasively masculine construction of the social and political world.

• • •

I NOW turn to the other social and political movement of recent years whose impact on my corner of the Academy I want to discuss. The transformation I have in mind here might be called, in defiance of Max Weber, the reenchantment of the world. Again, this is proving to be something of a global phenomenon, but in this case it is even more important for me to stress that I view it only from the standpoint of western Europe.

I am partly thinking of the growing sense that there are more things in heaven and earth than were ever dreamt of in the philosophies inherited from the Enlightenment. An increasing number of people assure us, at least in Great Britain, that Western medicine is an oppressive fraud; that they have been abducted by aliens; that they know for a fact that there is a prehistoric monster living in Loch Ness. They go on to demand our respect for these and a range of comparable beliefs that would have been widely and confidently stigmatized a quarter of a century ago as little better than magical in character.

This is sufficiently interesting in itself. But I am more concerned with an explicitly political movement that might appear, from the point of view of an apostle of the Enlightenment, to have some connections with the evidently increasing prevalence of such beliefs. I am thinking of the drift toward the whole-scale rejection of the values of the modern secular state in the name of religious faith, something that would, I think, have seemed almost unimaginable only twenty-five years ago. We are now witnessing, at least in Europe, the utter breakdown of the liberal consensus whereby religious belief was considered to be paradigmatically a private matter. The world religions, in Europe as in the Middle East, are instead seeking once more to seize the political arena as the best means of furthering their own purposes.

The most obvious example is usually taken to be that of Islam. The rule of the Mullahs continues in Iran, while a fundamentalist Islamic government was in 1996 democratically installed in Ankara. I have promised, however, to limit myself to unequivocally European instances, and there it is hard to avoid reflecting on the continuing rivalries between different versions of the Christian faith. The divisions between Orthodox and Catholic Christianity undoubtedly played some role in the recent tragedy in Bosnia, while the struggles between the Protestant and Catholic Churches continue to separate the communities in Ireland. Let me add one further example that, from my point of view, is even closer to home. The Saudi Arabian ambassador to London stated in an interview early in 1997 that one of the gravest mistakes made by Europeans was ever to believe that the march of civilization depends on the withdrawal of religion from public life. It is obvious, he declared, that civilizations decline as soon as they cease to organize their common life around a shared religious faith.

Among contemporary political philosophers, Charles Taylor has been one of the leading students of the relations between religion and multiculturalism, and I hope he may have something further to say about these crucial questions today. But in the meantime, the point I wish to make is similar to the one I made before. The increasing prominence and fervent commitment of these religious confessions is changing the sensibility of us all. It is even changing the sensibility of those who, like myself, remain so much the children of the Enlightenment that, in our Weltanschauung, all the world religions appear more or less equally magical in character. This in turn is having the effect of altering not merely how we think about our own political world, but also how as cultural historians we approach and write about the religious life of the past.

To illustrate my point, let me take, as before, an example from the field in which I work. One of the books I wrote while I was here at the Institute in the 1970s was a study of the ideologies underlying the religious wars of post-Reformation Europe, especially in France. Suppose that, as before, I cast my mind back to the period when I was writing that book, and ask myself what scholarly works were regarded at that time as classic contributions to that particular theme. One study that would, I think, have been cited by everyone would have been Emmanuel Le Roy Ladurie's two-volume work, *Les paysans de Languedoc*, originally published in 1966 and translated into English in 1974 (*Les paysans de Languedoc* [Paris: Mouton, 1966]; *The Peasants of Languedoc*, trans. John Day [Urbana: University of Illinois Press, 1974]). This was widely hailed, a quarter of a century ago, as the most important investigation of social conflicts and popular religious *mentalités* in the era centring on the Reformation. I recall Bob Darnton telling me (when I first met him here at the Institute in 1974) that he thought it the greatest historical work of the age.

One of the phenomena that interested Ladurie was the increasing prevalence of witchcraft beliefs in the half-century following the Reformation. What, he asked, could account for this feature of what he called "the peasant consciousness"? Ladurie opened his analysis by assuring us that the beliefs to be explained—including as they did the claim that witches swore homage to the Devil incarnate—were of course false, and amounted to little more than "demonic superstitions." But Ladurie went much further, adding that the beliefs in question were not merely mistaken but were such that no one could ever have had adequate grounds for holding them. They were an instance of "mass delirium," a reflection of "a surge of obscurantism." They belonged to a period in which the peasants were "slipping savagely back into the irrational" in thought and action alike.

When Ladurie turns to ask what might account for this feature of the peasant mentalité, he accordingly takes himself to be looking for a strongly causal form of explanation. As he sees it, the historical task is that of discovering what social conditions could have affected the peasantry and their leaders in such a way that, as he puts it, "the peasant consciousness suddenly broke loose from its moorings" and "fell prey to the ancient deliriums."

One explanation Ladurie suggests is that, at the time of the Reformation, many people in remote areas felt abandoned by their spiritual mentors and expressed their resulting terrors in a displaced form. "Far from their priests, the peasants found themselves alone with their anxieties and their primordial fears—and abandoned themselves to Satan." But Ladurie's controlling hypothesis is that the peasants felt collectively frustrated at the failure of the Reformation to improve their lot. Due to their lack of "an enlightened elite" with "a modern conception of man," they found themselves unable to engineer any "reasonable confrontations" with the privileged orders of society. As a consequence, their hope of bettering themselves was forced to take on a "mythical dress" and finally to express itself in "demonic forms of escape."

Ladurie's study may have been viewed as a classic work a quarter of a century ago, but any historian or ethnographer who nowadays wrote about popular religion in this way would I think be fortunate not to be run out of town. As I have intimated, one basic reason is surely that the children of the Enlightenment, among whom Ladurie clearly numbers himself, have been obliged in the meantime to come to terms with multiculturalism as a cognitive as well as a political force. They have been obliged to recognize that a number of present-day beliefs which they might feel inclined to dismiss as no less obscurantist than the belief in witchcraft are not only held by millions of people with passionate sincerity, but are proving capable of mobilizing political forces strong enough to pull down principalities and powers.

This is not to say that I wish to offer you a socially reductionist argument to the effect that our changing experiences necessarily transform our sensibilities. On the contrary, it is always possible to insist on holding on to our existing theories more or less in spite of everything. This was certainly what happened, at least in western Europe, at the time when the current demands of religious and ethnic minorities first began to be vehemently heard. When, for example, the present state of conflict in Ireland broke out in the late 1960s, the uprising in the North was at first classified straightforwardly as a civil rights movement. As for the religious language in which it was couched, this was either dismissed as an instance of false consciousness, or even more commonly regarded as a mask behind which the combatants were prudently hiding their real political interests.

If we no longer find it helpful to think in such terms, this must be due to the fact that, in the meantime, we have been forced to reflect on our experiences in new ways, and especially to filter them through new interpretative schemes. If, to take an obvious example, we feel no disposition to accuse the Iranian Mullahs of false consciousness, this must be due in part to our having acquired some new willingness to acknowledge that other people may profoundly believe, and be capable of argumentatively defending, not merely propositions but entire worldviews that may be incommensurable with our own most cherished beliefs.

What has persuaded so many children of the Enlightenment over the past generation to embrace this change of heart? Here we cannot avoid referring to the deepening influence of those philosophers of the human sciences who have been deconstructing our inherited assumptions about truth and rationality, and thereby undermining the comfortable assumption that there is just one cognitive world that all reasonable persons may be said to inhabit and share. The history of how these philosophies have evolved over the past generation, and come to acquire their present hegemonal hold, is one that remains to be written. When the intellectual historians get round to this task, however, it seems to me that, among the great names that will have to be singled out, there are two that are very close to us here today. They are the names (in alphabetical order) of Clifford Geertz and Thomas Kuhn.

Thomas Kuhn was an unforgettable presence here at the Institute in the 1970s, and his premature death tragically robbed us of a philosopher who still had much of importance to say, especially about the problems of meaning-change and incommensurability. By contrast, I am happy to emphasize, Cliff Geertz is as much present as ever, and seems to range with the same breadth and energy over the world of learning and the world itself. Age has not withered him, nor custom staled his infinite variety.

Although I want to say a word about these two thinkers, there are some serious pitfalls to be avoided. I am naturally anxious not to misinterpret Cliff Geertz's philosophy in his presence. And I am equally anxious not to assimilate Geertz and Kuhn, not only because they address very different issues, but also because they do so in their own distinctive and highly original ways. There is one crucial juncture, however, at which they seem to me to have entertained the same liberating thought. To put it negatively, both of them utterly repudiate the contention that, if we come upon some proposition or body of beliefs that strikes us as delusory, we are entitled to assume that we must be dealing with some failure of reasoning, and that the right explanatory question must be to ask what social mechanism may have caused the falsity of the beliefs in question to be disguised. To put the point positively, they have both insisted that the question of what it makes sense for you to believe about any given issue depends on what else you believe; that what it makes sense to believe will vary with the totality of your beliefs.

These are exactly the thoughts that a scholar like Le Roy Ladurie gives himself no space to think. I am not of course assuming that Ladurie still approaches the study of religious belief in the way I have described, and I do not know what opinion he currently holds of the work he published in the 1960s. Looking back at the historical method he employed at that time, however, it is hard not to feel that something vital was missing from it. Confronted with the beliefs of the French peasantry about witchcraft, Ladurie made no attempt to discover whether they held a range of other beliefs that could have given them good grounds, by their lights, for holding their specific views about witches and their alleged power to do harm. The possibility that someone else's view of the world might strike us as delusory, and might nevertheless be the most appropriate view for them to hold, is never even entertained. For Ladurie, the manifest falsity of the peasants' beliefs is sufficient evidence that they must have been suffering from some lapse in normal reasoning capacities. Like Durkheim, whose theories about religion seem so strongly present in Ladurie's account, the peasants' ideas about witches are accordingly treated as expressions of something else, as displaced reflections of social anxiety. The explanatory task is accordingly taken to be that of identifying the social mechanisms that generated their delusions while preventing them from seeing the world as it really is.

Few theorists of the human scientists nowadays talk about the world as it really is, and this has had a profound effect on the practice of the subdiscipline within which I work. I promised at the outset to limit myself to illustrating that point, and this I have now tried to do. But it is obvious that historians of social and political theory cannot at this juncture insulate themselves from political philosophy itself. If we accept that the social and political world is interpreted through and through, and that there may be many conflicting yet defensible interpretations circulating at any one time, we must apply that thought to ourselves as well. We cannot consistently speak about different defensible perspectives while uniquely privileging our own particular body of beliefs. We have to see ourselves as one tribe among others. But this is to say that we are committed—as political philosophers are increasingly emphasising—to the most wholehearted multiculturalism, to the fullest attempt to deconstruct hegemonal ideologies and make it possible for those with different cognitive as well as social allegiances to be heard with equal respect.

I nowadays find this very easy to manage, so long as I carefully confine myself to writing about the history of social and political thought. But one of the most troubling questions in contemporary political philosophy is whether we can hope to manage the same feat at an existential level as well. The demand upon our tolerance is certainly unparalleled. We are being called upon to cultivate a genuine respect for various beliefs that, from our perspective, we may be unable to see any good reason for holding; and we are further being called upon to allow those beliefs to have a potentially equal voice in the organization of our common world.

Many people, for example, believe in complete freedom of speech. They ask us to respect their right to give voice to their thoughts and imaginings as they choose. But many people deny that there can be any right to use this freedom to insult and ridicule the deepest susceptibilities of their fellow citizens. The novelist Salman Rushdie found himself placed under sentence of death for having committed exactly this offense. The British Muslim community may not have agreed with the fatwa against him, but many who claim to speak for that community ask us to respect the view that Rushdie ought never to have published what he wrote.

Where ought the liberal state to stand on such issues? On the one hand, we can hardly imagine asking the state to intervene in such cases to suppress the freedom of expression of its own citizens. But on the other hand, it hardly seems sufficient for the state to shrug its shoulders in the face of the new sensitivities—and in consequences the new demands for recognition—being voiced by ethnic minorities, many of whom have good reason to fear that the promise of the liberal state to offer equal respect to all its citizens amounts to little more than a pious fraud. The implications of the dilemma are disquieting. So far, political theorists have assumed that the legitimate demands of multiculturalism can be accommodated within the structure of the modern liberal state. But it is becoming clear that, if we are genuinely committed to multiculturalism, it is the structure of the modern liberal state that may have to change.

• • •

I SHOULD like to end by trying, very briefly, to meet the second requirement of the brief given to those speaking at this conference. Besides looking at changes in our disciplines over the past twenty-five years, we were asked to say something about the coming quarter century.

I must begin by frankly avowing that I have rarely encountered anyone, even here at the Institute, who seems capable of using the materials of history to extrapolate future trends while continuing to sound sane. Nevertheless, I do want to risk one prediction arising out of my observations about multiculturalism and its impact on historians and political theorists alike.

Unfortunately, my prediction is a somewhat gloomy one. I foresee a risk of our becoming less interested in each other, and in each other's political arrangements and philosophies. This form of parochialism already seems to me on the rise in Europe. There we are beginning to try to do justice to the complex subcultures out of which, we are coming to see, our so-called national identities were in fact very loosely formed. At the same time we are trying to reconsider the character of Europe itself, asking ourselves about the new political groupings that are beginning to emerge. Is Turkey part of Europe? Is the Ukraine? Is the United Kingdom? For us these are leading questions for politicians and political theorists alike. But they are of course local questions, and the inevitable effect of focusing on them is that other intellectual traditions appear less relevant, and perhaps less interesting as a result.

Similar forms of parochialism seem to be developing elsewhere. Certainly I have felt this myself when teaching in recent years far from where I normally live. When I talk to students in England and other parts of western Europe about the dead white European philosophers from the era of the Renaissance to the Enlightenment, I continue to feel the utmost confidence that these philosophies can and ought to be brought alive. I do not in truth think of them as dead, since they played such an obvious role in shaping the values and assumptions still prevailing in the communities in which we live. The further I move outside these local boundaries, however, the more I feel my confidence ebbing away. When I lately found myself as far away as Australia, the fact that we were still conversing in the English language did little to disguise the fact that Australia now sees itself as an Asian country in which it is becoming increasingly important, as it consolidates its new identity, for the cultural traditions of Europe to be firmly left behind.

I am bound to say that I regret these developments, partly because an exclusive interest in our own origins and identities strikes me as boringly self-absorbed, but also because a more demanding but more rewarding form of multiculturalism is available to us. I first encountered this alternative form here at the Institute, and for me it is incarnated in the two great scholars who supplied the intellectual leadership in the School of Social Science throughout the period when I was here between 1974 and 1979. I mean, of course, Albert Hirschman and Clifford Geertz. Both continue to move between different cultures, different languages, different continents. But both do so without embracing the Hegelian heresy that some nations are world-historical while others are not. They appear to be equally interested in all cultures, remaining internationalist in outlook while dedicating themselves at the same time to the uncovering of local knowledge (to coin a phrase).

Reflecting on the example of these presiding spirits, I feel able to end not with the anxiety I have been expressing, but rather with a bias for hope (to coin another phrase). I hope that this more strenuous and inclusive form of multiculturalism may be carried forward. And I hope that, in the coming generation, the Institute for Advanced Study will remain as much a leading center and a leading patron of this approach as it has been over the past quarter of a century.

CHAPTER 2

Twenty-five Years of Social Science and Social Change

A PERSONAL MEMOIR

Wolf Lepenies

WHEN I WROTE the talk that was the germ of this essay for the twenty-fifth anniversary conference of the School of Social Science, I took my direction from the question it posed. Speakers were asked to reflect on their own work, on how their research, discipline, and world had changed in the last twenty-five years, and what the critical task of the next twenty-five might be. I found myself responding to these questions in an unashamedly autobiographical manner; in the last twenty-five years my world has changed more than my discipline, and a lot more than my research. My other guide to writing was the way my talk was announced on the program: as an "interlude." According to Webster's Dictionary, interlude is defined as "entertainment of a light or farcical character introduced between the acts of an old mystery or morality play . . . any irrelevant change or happening in a course of events." I will try my best to fulfill what this definition promises.

When I left the School of Social Science in 1984 (a very reluctant farewell indeed), I almost left the social sciences. But then, I have never been a social scientist in the strict sense of the term. I almost managed to write myself out of the discipline with my first book.[1] Professional sociologists could not forgive me for not writing about status, class, or role theory—the favorite topics of the time in German sociology. I had not even done empirical research on large organizations or small groups. Instead, I had written an essay on melancholy in which La Rochefoucauld figured much more prominently than any of my fellow professionals. I can still remember how puzzled and pleased I was to get a letter from a famous American sociologist with some nice comments on my book. From that time on I have nurtured a deep appreciation of the shoulders of giants and of serendipity, of theories of the middle range, of the unintended consequences of social action and, though to a somewhat lesser degree, of the Matthew principle.

At the beginning of the sixties it was almost impossible for a student of the social sciences who had done her homework properly not to become a professor at some German university. I don't remember many of the classes I attended, but I do remember that most of my classmates got tenure some years later. I know that this says more about the selectivity of my own memory than about the German economy or our university system. But those were times indeed that reminded me of P. G. Wodehouse, who once described New York City as a haven for literature where no desperate author could jump out of a window without landing on the shoulders of a publisher.

Those were the heydays of the student revolt in Germany, and especially in Berlin. I remember vividly when Herbert Marcuse came to Berlin and roused some four thousand students to stormy applause by denouncing American imperialism in the splendid Auditorium Maximum of the Free University that had been built by the Ford Foundation. I would not have been surprised if the revolution had broken out the very next day.

What kind of revolution? Our revolutionary ideas were vague; but despite— or maybe even because of—their vagueness, we defended them ferociously. We were all socialists of sorts. What else could one be? The problem was that this socialist movement of the nonworking class was a mass movement of individuals and very small groups indeed; in most of the communist parties that flourished on campus the majority of members were also in the Central Committee. Still, chances for unprecedented structural changes were suddenly beginning to open up, and I enthusiastically joined a group that supported the candidacy of an assistant professor of sociology for the post of university president. Eventually, he was elected. A friend of mine who had just graduated in economics became Chancellor of the university. I felt happy for both of them, but was also glad that I had completed my own Ph.D. under the ancien régime. All this happened in Berlin—West Berlin, to be precise.

These two appointments may actually have been the greatest achievement of the social sciences during the student revolt. Sociology once again was associated with socialism. We were rather proud of this. The big books by Karl Marx are still the most heavily annotated volumes on my library shelves. As true connoisseurs, we referred to them simply as the "blue books," *die blauen Bände*, because blue was the color of the countless volumes of the Collected Works of Karl Marx and Friedrich Engels published in the German Democratic Republic under the auspices of the SED, East Germany's ruling communist party. We referred to the blue books wherever possible by number; everyone knew the "mid-twenties" (i.e., volumes 23 through 25: *Das Kapital*). Number 3 was probably the most popular because *The German Ideology*, where polemics prevailed over theory, was such great fun to read. But only true aficionados knew that Marx's and Engels' writings on the war in Italy and Hungary were to be found in volume 6. All this sounds rather amusing today, and there was indeed something playful about it; Marxism became very much part of an academic quiz culture. Where does Marx first mention the bonuses and increased dividends of the Bank of England as stated before the Lords' Committee in 1817? In *Das Kapital*, volume 3, chapter 33, p. 560, footnote 1. Where else?

At the same time, all this was deeply serious. The German university had changed—I still cannot say whether for better or worse, nor is it my topic here. The social sciences were to remain rather parochial for some time to come. We did read French sociology, for instance, but much later than we read Michel Foucault. It was hard for us to understand what American sociology was all about. As an undergraduate I had studied sociology in Munich. We were given a proper introduction to the methodology of the social sciences and we read the classics: Max Weber, Georg Simmel, and Talcott Parsons—a lot of Parsons. We were expected to cheer at the announcement that the author of *The Structure of Social Action* was coming to give a talk on the invitation of the Sociology Department. He came, he spoke—and we didn't understand a word. The joke went around that one of our professors complained that Parsons's English pronunciation had been too difficult for him to follow, and was told that the great man, the renowned translator of Max Weber, had spoken in German as a matter of courtesy. I cannot confirm or deny this. But I didn't understand anything either.

Parsons must have come to Munich in 1964, the year that the famous *Soziologentag* in Heidelberg restored Max Weber to the rank of a classic. It was three speakers from abroad who carried this off: Herbert Marcuse (who had taken on American citizenship), Raymond Aron, and Talcott Parsons. It is impossible to imagine the same thing ever happening to Emile Durkheim in France. But Max Weber's aura was enhanced in our eyes because he was presented more as a cosmopolitan author than a German one. He really did become a classic for us.

So it came as a shock to me several years later to see how unfairly Max Weber was being treated in my own department in Berlin, where a compulsory course on *Das Kapital* had been introduced. We had to attend a three-hour lecture and an equally long seminar every week. This course, however, was not nearly as popular as a similar one in the department of philosophy, which involved studying the "mid-twenties"—volumes 23 through 25, if you remember—for three full days a week in two successive semesters. Shortly afterward, because some of us had objected, the lecture course in the department of sociology was changed somewhat to become a seminar on Marx and Max Weber. The latter, however, never had a chance in this play-off, which invariably and predictably ended with the same score: Marx 5, Max Weber nil. I had read too much of Max Weber to accept this outcome, so I suggested changing the rules of the game to make it more exciting. I didn't dare say that Max Weber should win once in a while, but I thought that a rather more even score, maybe with the faint chance of a draw between the two, might be more appropriate. When this suggestion was rejected, I proposed an alternative introductory course on Max Weber, which was also rejected. That was the moment I began losing faith.

Some of my colleagues displayed much more astuteness. Since Parsons and the structural-functional school had been denounced as nothing other than American imperialism in sociological disguise, my colleagues presented ethnomethodology as the deadly enemy of functionalism—and got away with it, at least for a while. In Berlin, the cultural or linguistic turn in the social sciences thus came quite early, by virtue of political correctness. When Harold Garfinkel and Aaron Cicourel came to Berlin, followed sometime later by Erving Goffman, they were a huge success, at least with a minority of us.

Today it is hard to conceive the extent to which Marxist beliefs shaped the study of the social sciences in the sixties and well into the seventies, in Berlin and some other places, though certainly not everywhere in Germany. For us, economics was political economy, *Völkerkunde* was a Nazi discipline, anthropology was an intellectual slave, history was historical materialism, and dialectical materialism was philosophy.

We had lost touch with reality before ever entering the real, i.e., the nonacademic world. Leaving aside my personal admiration for authors like Robert Merton or Daniel Bell, we were not interested in theories of the middle range or in cultures of compromise; we were only interested in grandeur and clearcut causes. We were always fighting about principles and presuppositions. The so-called *Positivismusdebatte* was a case in point. It was a time of big books with sweeping titles. I have just been asked to describe the personal impact on me of Adorno and Horkheimer's *Dialectics of Enlightenment*, whose fiftieth anniversary of publication we are currently celebrating. The title alone was more than welcome; it provided my generation with an all-purpose catchword. It also led to an all too facile denunciation of bourgeois culture and liberal democracy, as did Herbert Marcuse's notorious attack on what he maliciously called "repressive tolerance."

Since I had to carve a niche for myself in my department, I opted for the sociology of literature. I liked *belles lettres* anyway, and applauded Marx's and Engels's comment that Balzac was a much better social scientist than those professionals who they contemptuously dismissed as "*Guizot e tutti quanti.*" I thought it might be fun to apply to literature what I had gleaned from the sociology of knowledge. But there seemed to be something intrinsically wrong with the subject. Faced with the intellectual options, I found myself unable to choose between a clear yet disturbing alternative. On the one hand there was an author who could give you a precise recipe for how to proceed both methodologically and theoretically. But for all his painstaking efforts, his results were disappointing. The other author, however, produced marvelous results. You knew instinctively he was right. Yet, he could not tell you how he had achieved these results. The first author you could imitate; the second you could not help admiring. The first was a dull instructor, the second was a true artist. You would have liked to be able to learn from the first how the second thought and worked, but this was impossible. They hated each other. The first was Georg

Lukàcs; the second was Theodor Adorno. I continued to read Adorno, but I gave up the sociology of literature.

Reading Adorno, of course, did not merely mean reading the coauthor of *The Dialectics of Enlightenment*, but reading all those who were grouped together under the somehow too-universal label "Critical Theory" or the too-parochial heading "Frankfurt School." At least to my ears, this always sounded as if intellectual options could be classified into various *appellations controlées* like some select wines and cheeses. Only later did we learn that this allusion was not so far-fetched, since from its inception intellectual control did indeed play a much greater role in the Frankfurt School than we had imagined. Critical Theory arrived at exactly the right time. It enabled many of us to sneak out of socialism without expressly abandoning it and at the same time to deceive ourselves about this defection, because for some time to come we would continue to use a jargon that sounded moderately Marxist.

Being an adherent to, or at least a sympathizer, of the Frankfurt School implied, at least for me, a switch from the purely moralistic or ideological side to the aesthetic side of the social sciences. Though we probably did not understand what we were doing then, we did not study theoreticians as much as admire great authors. Eventually, and almost inevitably, Siegfried Kracauer became more important than Herbert Marcuse, and Theodor W. Adorno always mattered more than Horkheimer. The most influential of them all, the loner Walter Benjamin, regarded as an outsider by the gatekeepers of Critical Theory as well, became an icon—not least because he had written some of the best German prose of this century. It is somewhat ironic that Adorno, who had written a pamphlet against Heidegger entitled *The Jargon of Authenticity* (*Der Jargon der Eigentlichkeit*),[2] probably initiated more young authors into the use of jargon than anyone else. The Frankfurt School furnished a good example of the danger that a too-faithful imitation may pose for those trying to establish a tradition. It is no coincidence that the second-generation author who succeeded best in emancipating himself from the jargon of the founding fathers of the Frankfurt School has had the greatest influence on a national as well as international scale: Jurgen Habermas. Yet he remained close enough to his teachers to become a key intermediary in intellectual commerce who translated Anglo-Saxon attitudes into a language more familiar in a German context.

At that time, genres had already become blurred, though Clifford Geertz had not yet written his famous essay. One of the *topoi* of Frankfurt School discourse was its denunciation of academic departmentalization. The tone of this was a trifle too pathetic, as was always the case, especially where Adorno was concerned. Rather than seeing departmental structures and intellectual specialties as the result of academic power games, sometimes with a lengthy history, the drawing of academic boundaries—especially the separation of sociology from philosophy—was seen as yet another indicator of the decline of the West. I should point out here that West Germany was a country whose intellectual scene had turned a moral disaster to intellectual advantage. After the war, it did not take long for denazification to fail, reeducation to be rejected, and the old cultural élites to be largely rehabilitated. As a result, the tension between émigrés and fellow travelers, between active opponents of the Nazi regime and fascist collaborators produced works of literature and scholarly books that were both provocative and bursting with innovative energy. In philosophy, an awesome intellectual tension was created by a constellation of thinkers including Martin Heidegger and Karl Jaspers, Karl Löwith and Hannah Arendt. In sociology the intellectual fabric of the discipline was shaped on the one hand by the fascinating confrontation of the Frankfurt School with the émigré Karl Popper, and on the other by authors like Arnold Gehlen and Helmut Schelsky.

Philosophical Anthropology, a rather offbeat intellectual field that cannot really be called a discipline, also played an important role. It has remained a German specialty, if not a German peculiarity. To an outsider, Philosophical Anthropology could best be described as Existentialism without the smart set, which was so important and so attractive in postwar France. We had no café like the Deux Magots, nor any singer like Juliette Gréco. The only thing we had were magazines that came close to the *Temps Modernes*. We did not have a reigning couple like Sartre and Simone de Beauvoir, but it might be an interesting project to retrace the development of French and German philosophical thought in the period before and after the war by comparing and contrasting the *couple infernal* with Martin Heidegger and Hannah Arendt.

Philosophical Anthropology referred to a general science of man, a deep if not brooding reflection on the human condition that was invariably presented with a tragic undertone—a follow-up to the nineteenth-century German cultural pessimism that Fritz Stern had analyzed in such a masterly fashion. Max Scheler and Heidegger had done much to create Philosophical Anthropology, but the two authors who became most influential in the social sciences after the war were Helmuth Plessner and Arnold Gehlen. It was the old, all too German, all too European confrontation between an émigré and a fellow traveler. Arnold Gehlen, who is still unknown outside Germany, was perhaps the most interesting of the authors mentioned. In the first place, he was a follower of the Nazis, but if we apply Hippolyte Taine's triad, Gehlen's theory of human action was not, as we might initially suspect, a theory of race, but a theory of milieu and of moment. Second, Gehlen shied away from the tragic essentialism of Heidegger as well as the cosmic speculations of Max Scheler, and tried to develop what he called, tongue in cheek, an "empirical philosophy." This meant that he tried to incorporate into his theory the results of ethology and other biological disciplines, along with the findings of French and Anglo-Saxon anthropology.

When a friend of mine who had read everything, Henning Ritter, and I founded our own publication series, *Hanser Anthropologie*, we used the term *anthropology* in the broadest possible sense, yet with an implicit distancing from its all too German connotations. We just wanted to publish the books we liked, mainly translations of authors who were as yet unknown or not sufficiently renowned in Germany. We were the first to publish German-language editions of Philippe Ariès and Georges Canguilhem, Georges Devereux and Marcel Mauss, Edmund Wilson (*Apology to the Iroquois*) and Gaston Bachelard. We also published a translation of what I still regard as Michel Foucault's best book by far: *The Birth of the Clinic*. Suspicious of what we regarded as over-professionalization of the humanities and the social sciences, we longed for a free-floating atmosphere of intellectual commitment and academic adventure. We loved outsiders and delighted in publishing Philippe Ariès, who called himself *l'historien du dimanche* and was certainly no socialist. We also had great pleasure in numbering among our authors the psychoanalyst and anthropologist Georges Devereux, who had written such a wonderfully idiosyncratic *Discours de la Méthode* with his *Anxiety and Method in the Behavioral Sciences*; and Georges Canguilhem, who died last year and whom I still regard as one of the most underrated authors in the recent history of science.

All this was done in an atmosphere of vague rebellion against the academic establishment, enhanced by the youthful leadership of the Free University. Those were the days when Paul Feyerabend was given an appointment at Jacob Taubes's Institute for Hermeneutics, in addition to the two others he already held in London and Berkeley. Feyerabend immediately ordered a dozen computers, which neither he nor anyone else ever used. These computers, too new then and too ancient now, are still to be found, I am told, in the attic of the institute villa.

What the social sciences meant to me before I came to the School of Social Science at the Institute is best summed up by verses from the "hermetic dialogue" in Wystan Hugh Auden's "Under Which Lyre: A Reactionary Tract for the Times," written at Harvard in 1946 (and which can be found in his *Collected Poems*, ed. Edward Mendelson [New York: Vintage Books, 1991], page 339):

> Thou shalt not do as the dean pleases,
> Thou shalt not write thy doctor's thesis
> On education,
> Thou shalt not worship projects nor
> Shalt thou or thine bow down before
> Administration.
>
> Thou shalt not answer questionnaires
> Or quizzes upon World-Affairs,
> Nor with compliance
> Take any test. Thou shalt not sit
> With statisticians nor commit
> A social science.

I had pretty much followed these prescriptions—with one exception. Like most members of my generation, I had been engaged in quizzes upon World-Affairs without knowing much about the world.

When I was invited to join the School of Social Science and arrived for the first time in 1979–80 at what was then still called *The* Institute, I was surprised to learn immediately that what had been an attitude of protest at home had become an institutionally established intellectual program here. Only later did I learn about the fights that had preceded the introduction of this program. After years of ideological fights, whether in agreement with, or in opposition to, a reigning dogma, at the School of Social Science I found a world of academic tolerance, trust, and extensive intellectual possibilities. Only later did I read what Albert Hirschman had written about his belief in possibilism. I did not yet know the word then, but the thing was already there. I also began to understand what Abraham Flexner had meant by saying that the Institute should gather together the best minds, minds that teach best by not teaching at all. The School of Social Science, where nothing was being taught, became the place where I learned a great deal.

It is only in retrospect that I realize how important the three Thursday luncheon talks I gave at the school were to be, not only for my research and my academic work but also for my involvement in academic policy and in establishing institutions—long after I had left Princeton. My first talk dealt with the "Transformation and Storage of Scientific Traditions in Literature." This talk was developed into a book that described the social sciences as a kind of third culture between the humanities on the one hand and the sciences on the other. I wanted to show that from the middle of the nineteenth century, literature and sociology rivaled in their claims to offer the key orientation for modern civilization and to constitute the guidelines for a good life in industrial society. Sociology, for me, has always been and still is a discipline oscillating between a scientific orientation, which has sometimes led it to imitate the natural sciences, and a hermeneutic attitude, which has shifted the framework of discourse toward the realm of literature.

In my second talk, "Pride and Forgetfulness: Sociology in Weimar Culture and under the Nazi Regime," I tried to describe how German sociology failed to achieve its due cultural standing in the Weimar Republic and how this failure affected the fate of sociology under the Nazi regime. Contrary to everything I had been told then, it did not disappear but became a discipline whose proponents for the most part actively supported or at least tolerated the regime. And yet both emigrants and fellow travelers were agreed that sociology had disappeared in Nazi Germany. Obviously, differing reasons were given for the vanishing of an entire discipline. Most of the emigrants speculated that sociological research, which they held to be a discipline of great inherent morality, would inevitably have exposed the lies of the Nazi leaders to the German people and was therefore seen as a tremendous threat to the totalitarian regime, a threat that had to be suppressed immediately. On the other hand, those who remained in Germany pretended that the Nazi regime could not and did not expect much from a discipline that had already become intellectually obsolete by the end of the Weimar Republic.

According to these analyses, sociology had destroyed itself before 1933. In the history of sociology the Nazi regime was regarded as a period of too little interest to be remembered. This rather odd consensus was shaken at the beginning of the eighties. The first contours of a puzzling and appalling picture began to emerge. There was no region of innocence under a totalitarian regime. That was the lesson the new historiography of the social sciences taught us. It was a lesson we should have recalled once again after the fall of the Berlin wall and, more recently, during the debate on Goldhagen's book about ordinary Germans and the Holocaust.

In my third talk at the Institute, "The German Connection: A Chapter in the History of French Sociology," I tried to solve, at least partially, the Durkheim-Weber puzzle to which Edward Tiryakian of Duke University had first drawn our attention: the seemingly mutual ignorance displayed by the two giants of the discipline. I tried to argue that the relationship between French and German social science had always been overshadowed by political conflicts. I argued further that to take sides in a national context of intellectual life and learning, to take sides, albeit innocently, with a theoretical or methodological position that was not regarded as specifically "German," or even specifically "French," would result in serious contempt, if not prosecution. Thus the Durkheimians simply could not take any notice of Max Weber. When Raymond Aron gave his inaugural lecture at the Collège de France, he caused an intellectual scandal by almost forgetting to mention Durkheim, the founder of the French school of sociology, and admitting that he felt much closer to Max Weber. This was a piece of pure historical research, yet it had some practical consequences later when, in the process of several attempts to create new scholarly institutions in Central and Eastern Europe, I made it almost a prerequisite to act, wherever possible, on the basis of French-German consensus, if not formal cooperation.

I left Princeton in 1984. In 1986 I was elected Rektor of the *Wissenschaftskolleg zu Berlin*, an Institute for Advanced Study where the humanities, the social sciences, and the natural sciences are not divided into different schools but combined to form a relatively close-knit academic community. My world changed, but not dramatically. The "great transformation" occurred only much later, in the year 1989, the *annus mirabilis* of recent European history. It also affected my view of the social sciences.

After 1989, I was struck by the asymmetry between the social role and public recognition of the intellectual in Western Europe as opposed to Central Eastern Europe. In the West we had become well aware that the Common Market would foster the Europe of the expert, not the Europe of the intellectual. There was not much need for what Paul Valéry at the beginning of the century had called *politique de l'esprit*. The end of communism, however, saw the renewed rise of the intellectual—in the East. One would have to go back to the days of the Dreyfus scandal to relocate a constellation of public issues and private concerns in which intellectuals played a similar role to that played in Eastern Europe by György Konrad, Vaclav Havel, Bronislaw Geremek, Milan Kundera, and Czeslaw Milosz.

Eastern Europe? By using the term *Central Europe* (*Mitteleuropa*) instead, these intellectuals had succeeded in turning a semantic opposition against the term *Eastern Europe* into a political issue. The vagueness of the term *Central Europe*, which sounded like the name for a very distant utopia indeed, was turned to considerable advantage. Central Europe is much less, if at all, a geographical territory than a cultural model. It was a political idea in need of constant reinterpretation. The never-ending necessity of this genuinely herme- neutical task explains in large measure why poets, essayists, novelists, artists, some social scientists, and ideographically minded historians had played a leading political role. With an eminently visible helping hand from Mikhail Gorbachev, they were able to create a culture of quarrel and complaint that finally became strong enough to overthrow the old regimes. Their fight for human rights, the classic ideal of the modern European intellectual, endowed the intellectuals of Central Eastern Europe with certain inalienable rights and with a degree of political credibility that no intellectual in the West had been able to acquire. The revolutions in the East, so it seemed, had also been a victory of culture over power. The Prague Autumn of 1989 was a particularly wonderful example of how aesthetics could turn into morality.

In 1989, it became clear to me that in the years to come, we were likely to witness the clash of two political cultures whose members would consist on the one hand of the economic poor in the East, of intellectuals with high moral credit but a rather low level of expertise, and on the other hand of economically wealthy people in the West, professionals with a high degree of expertise but without much concern for moral issues. The clash between the political culture of the expert and the political culture of the moralist was to become a major confrontation on the European political stage.

In this picture, German intellectuals played a very odd role. With very few exceptions indeed, the heroes of the revolution in the German Democratic Republic were not intellectuals but ordinary people who courageously took to the streets of Leipzig and Dresden. Germany—East Germany, to be precise— became the only country in Central and Eastern Europe where the estrange- ment of the literary and scientific intelligentsia from the majority of the popula- tion was so patently obvious. This was due to the specific conditions under which intellectuals in East Germany had lived and worked for over forty years. What they had learned most of all was, to quote Wyndham Lewis, the art of being ruled. Unlike Poland or Czechoslovakia, the GDR had neither an intellectually or politically influential samizdat nor a catacomb culture, and unlike Hungary, for instance, it did not produce a circle of engaged émigrés. Intellectuals who fled the country or were expelled from it and lost their citizenship mainly went to West Germany, where they could continue to publish in their own language. Those who remained in the GDR found ways and means to arrange themselves with the powers-that-be. Of course, not all intellectuals were fellow travelers, but almost all of them enjoyed the social security and subsidies awarded to the literary and scientific intelligentsia by a communist regime that merely leveled but never equalized. This is one reason why, per capita, seven times more poets and novelists lived in the GDR than in the Federal Republic.

After 1989, intellectuals in both Germanies were forced to realize that the decayed moral and spiritual environment in the GDR was part and parcel of a common past. Watching the intellectual decay of the GDR was, for any German intellectual, like looking into a mirror after a very long time. All of a sudden we all remembered or reminded our parents of the lack of civil disobedience, the lack of empathy with the oppressed, the tricks of adaptation and self-deception that characterized intellectual life in Germany from 1933 to 1945. In the GDR, things were even worse, for the existence of the Federal Republic prevented the formation of another émigré culture that might have been able to contribute to the intellectual recovery of East Germany.

At the time of these momentous changes, the Wissenschaftskolleg, the German Institute for Advanced Study, could easily have become—as some people still think it should have—the Institute for the Study of the Advancement of German Unification. Instead, it took another intellectual and institutional turn that I shall now describe, because it is relevant to the situation of the social sciences after 1989. The intellectual climate in which we found ourselves could best be described as a mixture of complacency and confusion. Two episodes may illustrate my point.

In 1989, we were preparing a conference for the 100th birthday anniversary of Ernst Reuter, the legendary Social-Democratic mayor of West Berlin. The foundation, of which the Wissenschaftskolleg is a part, is named after him. We asked Willy Brandt whether he would be willing to come to the Kolleg in December and give the memorial address in honor of Ernst Reuter. Brandt agreed, and in the spring of 1989 I flew to Bonn to discuss the details of his visit with him and, most important, the topic of his talk. Willy Brandt hesitated for a moment, then said: "You know, I don't want to commit myself to a subject that might be somewhat out of fashion by the time I give my talk. Let's choose a rather vague topic that leaves me free to react spontaneously to anything that might be happening around me at the time of my speech." So we decided that Willy Brandt should talk about "political reactions to unforeseen historical events."

Willy Brandt gave this speech in Berlin on December 11, 1989, almost exactly one month after the fall of the Berlin wall. When I introduced him, I had to explain that we had not chosen the title of his speech just a few weeks earlier but more than half a year previously. In a highly memorable speech that none of us present will ever forget, Willy Brandt naturally spoke about the fall of the Berlin wall, the end of communism, the history of the two Germanies, and the prospects of unification. He managed to cover all this in no more than twenty minutes. In the most important part of his speech, he warned his audience not to let this moment of joy make them forget Europe, not to forget the non-Western world. Brandt had been a member of the Brundtland commission, and to our amazement, he talked more about North-South than about East-West problems. He warned us that even with unification, our greatest problems did not lie behind, but were still to come.

About a year later, when it had become clear that German reunification was inevitable, notwithstanding Margaret Thatcher's open resentment and François Mitterand's barely concealed opposition, we gathered together a group of politicians and practitioners, businesspeople and economists, to discuss the political and economic future of Germany after reunification. It was indeed a distinguished group, including board members of General Motors and Coca Cola, Thyssen and Krupp and the Deutsche Bank, and a group of distinguished American and German economists, as well as Detlev Rohwedder, who would later become director of the Treuhand privatization organization and was murdered by terrorists from the RAF, the Red Army Fraction. It could very easily have turned into a boring debate, because the consensus was so unanimous and so strong: in a few years—some said two years, others said four and were immediately labeled pessimists—the German economy would be thriving in both East and West, and the differences between the two former states would not be visible anymore.

It could very easily have been a boring debate were it not for the presence of Thomas Kuczynski, son of veteran GDR economist Jurgen Kuczynski and an economic historian who had been running his own institute in the East German Academy of Sciences. He contradicted everyone else's prognoses and predicted that East Germany would rapidly become deindustrialized and deteriorate into nothing but a market for the West, with high unemployment and growing social unrest. Thomas Kuczynski was right, but for the wrong reasons: what he predicted was more the result of his ideological beliefs than his economic reasoning. Still, he was indeed right. Two years later everyone else was proven wrong, but they were all still in office or had even been promoted. Only one of our group had lost his job: Thomas Kuczynski.

This was the period of great complacency, reflected in Francis Fukuyama's prediction of the end of history, the final victory of capitalism and Western democracy. Much to the gratification of the State Department, this dire prediction had a significant influence on foreign affairs, and not just in the United States. Arnold Toynbee's childhood memories of Queen Victoria's Diamond Jubilee in 1897 come to mind: "I remember the atmosphere [Toynbee writes].

It was: well here we are on the top of the world, and we have arrived at this peak to stay there—forever! There is of course a thing called history, but history is something unpleasant that happens to other people."

Nineteen eighty-nine was the moment when the social sciences were severely criticized and much sought-after at the same time. Social scientists were blamed because they had not been able to predict the end of the communist regime—with very few but notable exceptions. *Voir pour savoir, savoir pour prévoir, prévoir pour prévenir*: Auguste Comte's words were mischievously quoted and many a jest was made about the social scientists who never see anything coming, but always know everything better with hindsight. Yet blame did not prevent the social sciences from being looked to with great expectations. They had missed a revolution but they were still useful for conducting the business of "normal science," to use the terminology of yet another Princetonian, Thomas Kuhn. Perhaps never before in their history had the social sciences faced a similar challenge or had a better chance to prove their applicability than in the vast laboratory of German reunification and the spread of the market and democracy all over Europe.

This expectation led to the boom in transformation studies, arguably the biggest industry that has ever existed in the social sciences. This is not the time and place to deliver a final verdict on transformation studies, but its industry reminds me of a story told by Sören Kierkegaard about his trip to Berlin to hear Hegel lecture. One day he was walking through an unfamiliar street when he spotted a sign on the front of a little shop: Laundry. He rushed back to his apartment, grabbed his dirty linen, and returned to the shop—only to learn that the sign was for sale. That's what most of transformation studies are about: they are pretending to clean the linen but are really only trying to sell the sign.

During those times of turmoil, the discipline I probably learned most from was the history of mentalities as developed by the *Annales* School. I had the advantage of not encountering the *Annales* School in the famous Sixième Section of the École des Hautes Études in Paris, but of being able to follow its work closely from a safe distance in the Maison des Sciences de l'Homme, which was housed in the same building on the Boulevard Raspail. It was first headed by Fernand Braudel and Clemens Heller, and then by Heller alone. It was he who had been so instrumental after 1945 in rebuilding the social sciences in Europe with the help of the Ford Foundation, and who had become in my eyes the undisputed master of weak—and therefore successful institutionalization—strategies. A lot of things Clemens Heller did while he was still active at the Maison seemed chaotic at first sight, but in the long run they turned out to have been deliberately planned, always with the aim of preserving maximum institutional flexibility for whatever intellectual program was to be inaugurated, amended, or strengthened.

I saw mentality gaps and changes in mentalities as the greatest challenge for both European politics and European scholarship after the fall of communism. This led me to coin the term "Politics of Mentalities" to emphasize that our problem was not the short-term application of what we already knew but long-term change in cherished patterns of thought and behavior—the "wheeles of custome" as Bacon had called them.

In the spirit of this Politics of Mentalities, the Wissenschaftskolleg has helped to establish new scholarly institutions in Central Eastern Europe and given extra support to existing institutions. These include Collegium Budapest, the New Europe College in Bucharest, the Graduate School for Social Sciences in Warsaw, and the Bibliotheca Classica in St. Petersburg. The intention was to strengthen local cultures of knowledge. We did not go there to teach; we went to learn from each other. We did not want to lay down rules; we wanted to give examples of a new, commonly shared policy for science and scholarship. For instance, to avoid the temptation of intellectual colonizing, we never engaged in bilateral projects; all these institutions were founded by at least three European partners and, wherever possible, partners beyond Europe as well. Our funding policy always involved finding both private and public sources of support. This demonstrates one essential element of a democratic culture; cooperation between the state and institutions of civil society.

The institutions we have created and/or supported are multidisciplinary ones where the social sciences naturally play a pivotal role. We learned very quickly that under the communist regime there had not simply been a void in the social sciences but that scholars had developed ingenious compensatory strategies to cope with the lack of contact, cooperation, and information. Fresh, innovative cultures of reasoning and novel strategies of writing and publishing had been developed; we had much to learn from them. In Budapest we found out that there were different European visions of Islam from those we knew; in Bucharest we learned that the study of Orthodoxy and the intellectual presence of Byzantium could give a new direction and spirit to the study of religion and of secularization; and in S. Petersburg we discovered, to our amazement, that Latin was not only far from being a dead language but had been a medium of communication that had fulfilled life-saving functions for intellectuals in Russia.

Conscious of the wealth of different local cultures of knowledge and relatively immune to the brutal adaptive strategies of transformation ideologies, our experience of setting up institutions in Central Eastern Europe has made us aware of the very peculiar situation we are all in. Almost overnight, the first transformation has been superseded by a second transformation of a much more dramatic kind.

The modern world was molded primarily by four processes: secularization, the rise of science and technology, industrialization, and democratization. These processes unfold at varying speeds and take locally specific forms, but they intertwine and influence each other worldwide. If we define modernity as the result of these processes, we can see that we are indeed at a turning point. When the increase in knowledge produced by science is no longer unquestioningly accepted as cultural enrichment but seen as a possible threat, when the core value of the labor-based society begins to weaken with the erosion of traditional patterns of work, when participation and involvement are no longer self-evident motives for action in the political sphere and participatory democracy is transformed into a democracy of absence, and finally, when fundamentalist creeds spread while established religions lose ground, then we are indeed in a crisis of orientation that affects all the guiding principles of our economic and social activity.

But it is still not clear exactly what this crisis is about. We can debate, for example, whether religious belief is really vanishing today or whether it is merely the official churches that are losing their appeal while an invisible Church is steadily growing. We can diagnose the shrinking capacity of our system of scholarship and higher education to provide directions for a "good life," while pointing at the same time to alternative forms of knowledge that are increasingly being taken as guidelines in our society. We can balance the growing disillusion with political parties against the anarchic pleasure of free-floating political mobilization, and we can accept the crumbling of traditional structure of industrial labor in the recognition that new working patterns are emerging today in the service industry. In short, we can confront each catastrophic prediction with a scenario of compensation. But we are nonetheless faced with the necessity of rethinking modernity. In Europe we are in a very peculiar situation indeed: we have entered the era of the second transformation—the transformation of modernity—before the completion of the first transformation—the transformation of many societies *into* modernity. We had asked our neighbors to join our markets and our democracies, and now, just as they start arriving, the traditional market is no longer there and a great debate has begun on how the social and spiritual fabric of democracy can be preserved or renewed. This is the challenge the social sciences face today.

It was only after 1989 that I realized how much what I had learned at the School of Social Science—on "this side of paradise"—mattered in the outside world. In the work being done there I found the kind of economic, anthropological, and political reasoning that we have needed more than ever before after 1989, a social science that does not pretend to predict but is able to think about possibilities; a social science that does not indulge in the rhetoric of globalization but continues to take heed of local contexts; a social science that, very much against the mainstream, preserves a moral awareness in everything it does. The school has shaped my own scholarly work and at the same time has deeply influenced the way in which I tried to help create new institutions— my main occupation since 1989. I regard it as the most important institution for the reorientation of social thought in the last twenty-five years. So let me make a suggestion. Some years ago we were all informed that, for reasons of historical accuracy, *The* Institute for Advanced Study had to be renamed the Institute for Advanced Study. But to be strictly accurate, a history of the social sciences in the past twenty-five years would require us to rename the School of Social Science at the Institute *The* School of Social Science.

NOTES

1. *Melancholie und Gesellschaft* (Frankfurt Am Main: Suhrkamp, 1969).
2. Theodor W. Adorno, *Der Jargon der Eigentlichkeit; zur deutschen Ideologie* (Frankfurt am Main: Suhrkamp Verlag, 1964).

CHAPTER 3

Economic History as a Cure
for Economics

Gavin Wright

ECONOMICS seems to be in a state of crisis at the present time. It may well be that economics has always been in a state of crisis; but the current volume of critical and even hostile public commentary seems to be particularly intense. A *New Yorker* article by John Cassidy (2 December 1996) was entitled "The Decline of Economics," and Cassidy in turn cited publications with titles such as "Economists Can Be Bad for Your Health," "The Crisis of Vision in Economic Thought," and even "The Death of Economics." Although nearly all the economists with whom I have spoken believe "Decline" to have been both poorly informed and misguided in its characterization of the state of the discipline, it would be difficult to deny that it exposed a raw nerve. My colleague John Taylor says that some reference was made to the article at every session he attended at the annual meetings of the American Economic Association in January of 1997. And when John organized a roundtable discussion devoted to this topic a few weeks later at Stanford, the crowd was SRO. What is this new round of economics-bashing all about? Much of what one hears is in fact not new at all but reflects caricatures and stereotypes that have been familiar to me for as long as I have been teaching introductory economics and collecting economics jokes—most of which are probably much older than I am. Economists are said to love abstract mathematical models but to lack realistic knowledge of the real world. Economists are accused of adhering to a crude conception of human psychology, assuming the universality of behavior based on calculated self-interest. And perhaps in imitation of their own assumptions regarding the rest of humanity, economists are seen to offer unappetizing and unrealistic policy advice to real-world problems, assuming that everything important can be reduced to costs and benefits, which really means, to money. Environmentalists are particularly hard on economists along these lines, as suggested by this quotation from an article entitled "What Good Is a Forest?" in the nature magazine *Audubon* (May/June 1996):

> Let's assume, for the duration of this article, that to you trees are vertical stalks of fiber, that a forest carries no more spiritual or aesthetic value than a parking lot, that woodland creatures are uninteresting sacks of calories, and that the smell of sunbaked pine needles on a breezy June afternoon

merely matches the scent that comes from those conifershaped air fresheners that dangle from your rear-view mirror. Let's assume, in other words, that you've done something rotten and God has turned you into an economist.

It is tempting, and it would be easy, to join this chorus of dissent and dismay. But in this presentation, I choose not to. For one thing, much of the criticism is poorly informed about developments in economics. The critiques apply better to caricatures than to the reality, or at best they pertain to textbook economics rather than the intellectual frontiers. Virtually all over the map of economics, one can point to vigorous new developments that belie the image of an encrusted bastion of intellectual orthodoxy. Without trying to be exhaustive, I am thinking particularly of work coming out of the economics of information and risk; of collaborative research with psychologists on the role of cognitive processes in economic decisions; of the renewed interest in the roles of *institutions* and *culture* in economic life, which are closely related to the efforts to adapt evolutionary selection models to economics; and to the theoretical rediscovery of the significance of *increasing returns* for economic dynamics, leading to the possibility of multiple equilibria, lock-in effects, tipping phenomena—all examples of systems that may exhibit path *dependence*, a piece of jargon that may be summarized by the expression, "history matters."[1] Economics today suggests a new variation on Hegel's dictum about the owl of Minerva flying at dusk: Public criticism of economic orthodoxy has peaked, just as modes of thought in the profession are undergoing fundamental change. These remarks are not intended as a clean bill of health for the present state of economics, only to observe that much of the popular criticism is misplaced and beside the point. But economists would not be sensitive to this criticism if they were not also aware of the discipline's glaring failure to shed informative light on some of the most noteworthy economic trends of the past twenty-five years. Two of these are the slowing of productivity growth and the rise of inequality in the United States and other advanced countries over roughly the same period. Despite its new and welcome openness to diverse intellectual strategies, economics has not succeeded in consolidating a body of evidence and interpretation supporting a professional consensus on these and other important developments in contemporary economic history.

That last phrase offers a clue to where I will be going in my attempt at diagnosis and a suggested remedy: Economics needs to become a more historical social science, but this advice clashes with some of the discipline's deepest intellectual tendencies. I could devote the remainder of this presentation to delineating all of the ways in which economics is unhistorical; if the subject were the sociology of the profession, or the efficacy of economics education, that is precisely what I would do. But our topic is social science and social change, and in this arena my view is that insights from economics are not only relevant, but are systematically avoided or neglected by other disciplines.

Perhaps the most fundamental is the notion that interactions of purposeful individuals can generate outcomes very different from what any one of them really wants. In a sense this is *the* basic proposition of economics, dating at least as far back as Adam Smith, and restated regularly within the discipline, in countless variations and contexts and theoretical clothes.[2] As a working presumption, it is very different from the emphasis one finds in historical literature on "agency," the idea that some class or interest group drives the historical narrative.

To me, the internal tendencies of economics are no more distressing than the structural situation that allows these tendencies to persist and caricatures to fester, namely the isolation of economics from the most active currents of the rest of the intellectual community—and vice versa. As one of a relatively few half-breed economist-historians, I can testify to the rigidity of the prevailing cultural and intellectual segregation between those two camps. I often feel like an emissary between hostile tribes, trying to develop a kind of cross-cultural pidgin language through which to inform each one that the other guys are not as bad as they think, and in fact they might actually learn something useful from hearing (or even reading) what they have to say. Although these attempts are often politely applauded, the truth is that neither side takes them to heart, and one begins to feel that deeper historical and/or economic forces must be working against me.

But hope springs eternal, and the invitation to contribute to this collection was enough to induce me to try once again, in a modest way, to show the value of intermarriage between economics and history. Since preaching and exhortation generally get you nowhere in this enterprise, the remainder of this chapter will be devoted to two illustrations: the institution of slavery as an object of study in economic history, and the analysis of technological change as a problem for contemporary economics.

WHAT WAS SLAVERY (ECONOMICALLY SPEAKING)?

Some economists (the late George Stigler was one) say they are all in favor of economic history, but they don't see the need to support a group of economic history specialists in economics departments. It is perfectly true that if economists specializing in industrial organization, labor markets, public finance, economic development, and other applied fields were to take a more historical view of their subject matter, the demand for economic historians would be much reduced. But if that day were to arrive, who would study slavery? It is the one major topic in economic history that seems safely historical; yet it was also an institution (important both for the rise of long-distance commerce and in the shaping of economic thought) whose economic nature has long been in dispute. Slavery has been a prime topic for research by historical economists, yet today's historians of slavery have little time or regard for what economic historians have had to say about it. This has been the case at least since the storm in the 1970s over Robert Fogel and Stanley Engerman's *Time on the Cross: The Economics of American Negro Slavery*,[3] an event that played a small part in bringing about the current divide between the two disciplines. Having returned to this topic after some years, as a result of an invitation to give the Fleming Lectures at LSU, I have had occasion to rethink the issue. A brief synopsis follows. Nothing stated here should be taken to imply that slavery should be conceived of and analyzed exclusively in economic terms; what is implied is that an account of slavery will not be complete unless its economic dimensions are adequately covered.

I asked my listeners to distinguish three dimensions of slavery as an economic institution: (1) slavery as a *system of work organization*, which has to do with issues of incentives, punishments, and effort levels; (2) slavery as a set of *property rights* (a form of wealth, a basis for credit, a form of property that could be carried to remote locations and assigned to any tasks); and (3) slavery as a *political regime*, referring to the need for an apparatus of enforcement to prevent running away or rebellion. In a nutshell, my main point was that category 1, work organization, has been vastly overemphasized in the study of slavery, relative to categories 2 and 3, property rights and politics. Perhaps contrary to intuition, there are few if any robust historical generalizations about slavery as a system of work organization—the level of effort, the degree of supervision, the quality or skill of the labor. Indeed, we now know enough about the varieties of experience to say that it is positively misleading to refer to "slavery" as though it were a single well-defined labor relationship, no more so than "free labor" usefully describes the full range of non-slave labor relationships in the world.

What was slavery, then, economically speaking? I argue that the enduring and historically significant features of slavery fall under the heading of property rights, the opportunity for slave owners to arbitrage wide geographic gaps in the value of labor productivity, by carrying involuntary laborers to remote locations and assigning them to disagreeable tasks. Because of these property rights, "the wealthiest and most dynamic regions of the Americas" were slave regions, prior to the nineteenth century.[4] The transatlantic sugar trade would have been no more than a pale shadow of itself if planters had been required to attract labor through voluntary migration from Europe or Africa. The same could be said for the rapid westward spread of the American cotton belt in the first half of the nineteenth century, catapulting that vital industrial raw material into world-class export status well in advance of anything produced by the free-labor states. In this view, there is real validity in the controversial propositions advanced by Fogel and Engerman: that American slavery was a profitable and effective economic system, operating in many respects at a more "advanced" level of financial and organizational sophistication than its free-labor counterparts. But it is out of place, and indeed pointless, to analyze this record as they did, primarily in terms of work discipline and gang-labor methods. The notable feature of the high payoffs to slavery is that they derived crucially from the historical context, specifically a context in which transportation costs were high, trade was based largely on exotic goods that produced in locations that were remote and unhealthful, and institutions to facilitate the voluntary migration of free laborers and family farmers were poorly developed.

Now an interesting feature of this contrast between two alternative views on the economics of slavery is that it does not turn on acceptance or rejection of the traditional tools or assumptions of economics. The idea of gains from trade and the expansion of markets is at least as old as Adam Smith. And what could be more "economic" than the proposition that a more complete set of property rights in productive assets will generate a more complete exploitation of potential gains from trade? The distinction between property rights and politics is precisely the distinction between the individual incentives of slave-holders and the collective interest of slave owners as a class. Yet for some reason, economic interpretations have overlooked these types of insights about the role of slavery. Since this oversight has persisted for over two hundred years, it might be timely to speculate about possible reasons. The notion that slavery was backward because of poor work incentives was not, after all, an invention of Fogel and Engerman. Adam Smith himself argued that because a slave could not own property, he "can have no other interest but to eat as much, and to labour as little as possible. Whatever work he does beyond what is sufficient to purchase his own maintenance, can be squeezed out of him by violence only. . . ."[5] The motivation of the slave owner in perpetuating this brutality was attributed by Smith to "the pride of man" that "makes him love to domineer," and slavery persisted only where crops were sufficiently profitable to "afford the expence of slave cultivation." Although elsewhere Smith was careful to analyze the interaction between individual motives and social outcomes, when it came to slavery he did not even ask how such self-indulgent enterprises could survive in a competitive world. It seems clear to me that Smith had little real knowledge of slavery, indeed may not have thought about it deeply; but he had absorbed the prevailing eighteenth-century image of slave societies as "social and cultural wastelands blighted by an obsessive pursuit of private profit,"[6] and saw clearly enough that slavery was contrary to the somewhat idealized vision that he wished to present of a free society.

But does this sort of wishful self-image of a free society still influence the thinking of economic historians in our own day, more than a century after the demise of slavery? Eugene Genovese argues that yes, indeed it does. Slavery remains one of the untouchables of American history, even in an age with little sympathy or respect for any number of other long-entrenched orthodoxies. Since the Civil War was a formative moment in shaping the American national self-image, it is perhaps not really surprising that historical writing has been shaped by the national consensus that emerged from that conflict. But these forces influence almost everyone, at least any American working in this area, while my focus here is on economics. Economists have had special problems in coming to grips with slavery as an economic institution, not mainly because of the internal logic of economic theory, but because of certain traditions that the discipline has maintained over the years but rarely acknowledged explicitly, professional inhibitions that Veblen called "learned incapacities." Two in particular come to mind.

The first is that the institution of slavery forces us to recognize that what we call "free labor" is in fact a restriction on the right of free contract, and hence constitutes a contradiction in the very idea of a society organized around free markets and free choice. The modem association between individual freedoms and market-based economies is by no means as obvious historically as it seems to us today. The first generation of antislave trade activists had to confront the allegation that *they* were the hopelessly unrealistic idealists trying to repeal the laws of supply and demand, a project as futile as King Canute's commands against the tides. The fact that the abolitionists were politically successful does not mean that their critics were wrong about the economics, only that slavery was in the end brought down by political rather than purely economic forces—a conclusion now widely accepted among historians.

A second learned incapacity is, in my view, even more difficult for economists, namely the problem that comprehending the economics of slavery requires a form of analysis in which historical context really does matter, in an integral rather than merely a formalistic way. As I see it, slavery was crucial at a certain historical phase, because it overcame the absence or underdevelopment of certain markets and complementary institutions, which later did emerge and thus made slavery economically inessential. (This way of stating the argument may seem to imply a commitment to an autonomous logic of progressive institutional evolution under capitalism, which I certainly do not mean to imply but may have to for the sake of this desperately rushed summary.) Thus there are, after all, some essential grains of truth in the long-dismissed "Eric Williams thesis" that slavery played a pivotal role in the rise of Western capitalism, even if many of the particulars of that 1940 formulation have not stood up to subsequent research.[7] But this kind of thinking rubs against the grain for economists, who still aspire to emulate what they take to be the timeless laws of natural science. The bias in their thinking is not really an intrinsic problem in the concepts of economic analysis, but rather a deep reluctance to accept a view of economic life as genuinely historical, shaped by both the contingencies of the moment and by the evolutionary pulses of the times. Fortunately, slavery is history, in the sense of the colloquial expression meaning "finished," and the failure of economists to get it right may have no great consequences for today's world. But the bias against historical thinking is more serious in the second of my two illustrative topics, the economics of technological change.

TOWARD A MORE HISTORICAL APPROACH
TO TECHNOLOGICAL CHANGE

The economics of technology may seem to be light-years removed from slavery, but I see the two topics as closely related. Just as slavery has been too troublesome for most economists, the same has been largely true for the study of technological change. The dominant tradition has been to treat technology as exogenous, one of the two fundamental determinants of economic allocations, along with individual tastes or preferences. Not that technology was assumed to be constant and unchanging; it was just that understanding the reasons for technological change was not considered part of the economist's purview, but someone else's department. The division of labor was: You tell us how technology changes, and we will trace the economic implications.

But now we know that technology is not exogenous to the economy, and never was. In a market economy, changes in methods of production typically result from the purposeful acquisition of new knowledge, by inventors, by individual producers, or by profit-seeking firms. Because growth-accounting studies have shown that a large fraction of long-term productivity growth is attributable to technological change (which is to say, is not accounted for by conventional capital), practitioners of the so-called new-growth or endogenous growth theories have advocated a broadening of the definition of capital to include the accumulation of technological knowledge and human capital. This may sound like a simple step forward, but therein lies a problem for the internal logic of economics.

As laid out most clearly by Kenneth Arrow,[8] the problem is that investment in research for the purpose of generating new technology differs in two fundamental ways from conventional investment: high uncertainty and lack of appropriability. Those economic sectors that exhibit high rates of technological progress over extended periods are those that have "solved" these two problems in one way or another. Private market power, government procurement programs, legal protection for intellectual property, cooperative and nonprofit research arrangements, and diversified risk portfolios have all been important in one or another instance, but one does not find many stable empirical regularities with respect to any subset of these variables. Further, at any point, a number of more fundamentally innovative ideas may be spreading through the economy, typically without explicit public or private sponsorship, their potential as yet incompletely realized in practice. This is another broad lesson of studies in this area: No matter how successful we may be in accounting for purposeful investments in the generation of knowledge, the historical record persistently reflects the impact of forces that are not readily accounted for in this way, something like "technological opportunities," which we may describe (eschewing the now-forbidden term *exogenous*) as having historical trajectories of their own.[9] Technological opportunities for a particular sector are related to its proximity to what are known as "general purpose technologies," new schemes or conceptions of broad potential import, such as the steam engine, the electric motor, and semiconductors.[10] Identifying and tracing the course of general purpose technologies should be central to the research agenda of economics. But the appropriate research will be historical in character, that is to say, specific to the technologies and institutions in question; as such, it will not necessarily look or feel like conventional applied economics. This sort of assignment makes economists nervous. Despite its importance, the economics of technology is still not a recognized specialty within economics, and the volume of good-quality research to date is disappointingly small.

What does this discussion have to do with slavery? The connection may seem far-fetched, but the trajectories of technology are surely affected by the *absence* of property rights in human beings in our society. Technological change is fundamentally a form of learning, and learning is a network phenomenon. Profit-seeking firms may invest in R&D because they anticipate positive net private returns, but the accumulation of learning over extended periods is implicitly a collective endeavor; new discoveries typically start from and extend the previously existing body of knowledge. To engage in these activities, you first have to gain access to the network, by learning its language, its formulas, its measuring instruments and machinery, perhaps even its culture and folkways. The crucial step in the rise of the United States to world economic leadership at the end of the nineteenth century was the emergence of a national technological network, an "invisible college" of technical people implicitly engaged in collective learning. Broadly speaking, we can characterize this project as the adaptation of what were originally European technologies to fit the distinctive features of the U.S. economic environment: high wages, abundant natural resources, and a large, rapidly growing domestic market. At that historical juncture the learning network had a strong national character, because the "problem-solving environment" was increasingly national, and this unity of focus reflected the growing integration of national product markets and the high level of internal population mobility across state lines.

Nobody owned the American labor force, but for more than a century an important feature of American technological evolution was the adaptation of jobs to the American labor *market*, which is to say, to the characteristics (the experience, the work norms, the educational background) of the most rapidly growing segments of the national labor force. Perhaps it would be more appropriate to say that American technology and the American labor market were coevolutionary. The important point is that although it has never been routinely possible to call forth fundamental new technologies through the conventional operation of market forces, historical studies suggest that the *detailed* labor requirements of basic technologies are remarkably malleable.[11] They are rarely dictated by technical imperatives.

Despite this historical record, economic studies of the labor market have primarily focused on demonstrating that the widening gap between skilled and unskilled labor is attributable to "technology," and most economists seem to feel that this constitutes a satisfactory explanation.[12] The main alternative candidate, growing international trade, is typically dismissed as quantitatively implausible, despite reasonably strong statistical correlations across countries.[13] What is troubling about this research is not so much the conclusion itself, which has more empirical focus and policy relevance than many others one could name, but the absence of professional curiosity about why technology should have this particular polarizing impact at this particular historical phase. Because it seems intuitively self-evident that modem, high-tech, electronic information based technologies should require skilled labor, economists and many others seem to feel that this is all that can be said. A century earlier, however, American engineers were devoting their talents to techniques that could absorb and make *more* use of young, untrained laborers. Surely the more flexible and sophisticated technologies of the 1990s could do the same, if the institutional structures of the economy gave them an incentive to do so. But these questions are rarely asked.[14]

Because the study of technological networks has not been a primary research area in economics, suggestions about the structure and properties of these networks are necessarily speculative. But there is reason to believe that the "technology of technological change" has not been constant through history, that today's firms make greater use of general and abstract knowledge than they formerly did, and that the greater universality of technological knowledge has reduced the correspondence between technology and nationhood.[15] Between 1870 and 1930, more than 90 percent of U.S. patents were assigned to U.S. residents. Between 1963 and 1968, the figure fell to 80 percent, and by the late 1970s to 60 percent. In the 1990s it has stabilized at just over 50 percent. The trend toward internationalization seems to be strongest in those fields characterized by the existence of a strong science base and the presence of large managerial companies.

Such figures should not be understood as measures or symptoms of national economic decline; far from it. In today's world, any successful economy has to learn to monitor and absorb innovations originating all over the world. The question is, however, does any part of the collective learning process internalize the skills, experience, and potential of the existing American labor force? At the present juncture, the U.S. economy is riding high in the world, and its productive dynamism in recent years has indeed been impressive. But its success in utilizing the productive potential of its population is far more questionable.[16] It is at least a plausible hypothesis that a linkage exists between widening inequality and the changing "technology of technological change," that is, the institutional arrangements and the geographic scope of the learning networks from which new technologies emerge and diffuse.

In general, economists are far too ready to attribute rising inequality to technological change, and to infer as a corollary that nothing much can be done about it, all the while acknowledging that little is really known about the nature of these technological forces. Exactly what if anything should be done, I do not know. I do not have a policy agenda to offer, but I do have a research agenda for the discipline of economics, namely, to study the locus and evolution of technological learning networks over extended historical periods and their implications for the scope and direction of technological change. The broader message is that if economics really wants to take technology seriously—and it will have to if it hopes to command an understanding of productivity and inequality—economics will have to become a more historical discipline.

NOTES

1. A now-standard citation on path dependence is Paul A. David, "Understanding the Economics of QWERTY: The Necessity of History," in *Economic History and the Modern Economist*, ed. William N. Parker (Oxford: Blackwell, 1986). A recent collection of theoretical essays (some technical, some readily accessible) is W. Brian Arthur, *Increasing Returns and Path Dependence in the Economy* (Ann Arbor: University of Michigan Press, 1994). A recent article on bargaining citing numerous disciplinary interactions between psychology and economics is Linda Babcock and George Loewenstein, "Explaining Bargaining Impasse: The Role of Self-Serving Biases," *Journal of Economic Perspectives* 11 (winter 1997): 109–26. Incidentally, this article appears in the official publication of the American Economic Association mandated to concentrate on ideas rather than technique. The *JEP* regularly publishes nontechnical surveys of recent research in various branches of economics.

2. In tracing the idea to Adam Smith, I am simply referring to the idea that competitive markets serve the social function of determining resource allocation, even though the individual producers are motivated primarily by the search for profit. One can also cite the related concept that the competitive search for profit drives the level of profits down to a minimum, which is surely not the intention of the competitors involved. But as Jane Mansbridge has suggested, there are many analogies in social and political contexts. A good collection of examples may be found in Thomas Schelling, *Micromotives and Macrobehavior* (New York: W.W. Norton, 1978). A formalized extension to political preferences is Timur Kuran, "Preference Falsification, Policy Continuity and Collective Conservatism," *Economic Journal* 97 (September 1987): 642–65.

3. Robert William Fogel and Stanley L. Engerman, *Time on the Cross: The Economics of American Negro Slavery* (Boston: Little, Brown, 1974).

4. David Eltis, *Economic Growth and the Ending of the Transatlantic Slave Trade* (New York: Oxford University Press, 1987), p. 24.

5. Adam Smith, *An Inquiry into the Nature and Causes of the Wealth of Nations*, vol. 1 (1776; reprint, Oxford: Clarendon Press, 1976), pp. 411–12.

6. David B. Davis, "American Slavery and the American Revolution," in *Slavery and Freedom in the Age of the American Revolution*, ed. Ira Berlin and Ronald Hoffman (Charlottesville: University Press of Virginia, 1983), p. 80.

7. Eric Williams, *Capitalism and Slavery* (Chapel Hill: University of North Carolina Press, 1944).

8. Kenneth J. Arrow, "Economic Welfare and the Allocation of Resources for Invention," in Universities-National Bureau Committee for Economic Research, *The Rate and Direction of Inventive Activity* (Princeton: Princeton University Press, 1962).

9. On this point, see particularly Alvin K. Klevorick, Richard C. Levin, Richard R. Nelson, and Sidney G. Winter, "On the Sources and Significance of Inter-industry Differences in Technological Opportunities," *Research Policy* 24 (1995): 185–205.

10. See Timothy Bresnahan and M. Trajtenberg, "General Purpose Technologies: 'Engines of Growth'?" *Journal of Econometrics* 65 (1995): 83–108.

11. The division of labor by gender has received most attention. A case study showing the importance of gender lines established early in a technology's evolution is Ruth Milkman, *Gender at Work* (Urbana: University of Illinois Press, 1987). Saxonhouse and Wright show the wide dispersion of gender composition among national textile industries (ca. 1900), within a common technology from an engineering standpoint: Gary Saxonhouse and Gavin Wright, "Two Forms of Cheap Labor in Textile History," *Technique Spirit and Form in the Making of the Modem Economies* (Greenwich, CT: JAI Press, 1984). Evidence for Britain is presented in Sara Horrel and Jane Humphries, "Women's Labour Force Participation and the Transition to the Male Breadwinner Family, 1790–1865," *Economic History Review* 48 (1995): 849–80.

12. Examples include Alan Krueger, "How Computers Have Changed the Wage Structure," *Quarterly Journal of Economics* 108 (February 1993): 33–60; and Eli Berman, John Bound, and Zvi Griliches, "Changes in the Demand for Skilled Labor within U.S. Manufacturing Industries," *Quarterly Journal of Economics* 109 (May 1994): 367–97.

13. See the symposium in the *Journal of Economic Perspectives* (1995), involving Richard Freeman, J. David Richardson, and Adrian Wood.

14. A notable exception is Goldin and Katz, which offers a brief sketch of a project to track the long-term trajectory of complementarity between capital and human skills; see Claudia Goldin and Lawrence F. Katz, "Technology, Skill and the Wage Structure: Insights from the Past," *American Economic Review* 86 (May 1996): 252–55.

15. See Ashish Arora and Alfonso Gambardella, "The Changing Technology of Technological Change: General and Abstract Knowledge and the Divison of Innovative Labor," *Research Policy* 23 (1994): 523–32.

16. Robert Haveman, Lawrence Buron, and Andrew Bershadker, "The Utilization of Human Capital in the United States, 1975–1992," Jerome Levy Institute Working Paper, no. 180 (1997).

CHAPTER 4

Can the "Other" of Philosophy Speak?

Judith Butler

I WRITE THIS paper as someone who was once trained in the history of philosophy, and yet I write now more often in interdisciplinary contexts in which that training, such as it was, appears only in refracted form. So for this and surely for other reasons as well, what you will receive from me is not a "philosophy paper" or, indeed, a paper in philosophy, though it may be "on" philosophy, but from a perspective that may or may not be recognizable as philosophical. For this I hope I will be forgiven. What I have to offer is not exactly an argument, and it is not exactly rigorous, and whether or not it conforms to standards of perspicacity that currently reign in the institution of philosophy is difficult for me to say. This may well have a certain importance— even philosophical importance—that I did not originally intend. I do not live or write or work in the institution of philosophy and have not for several years, and it has been almost as many years since I have asked myself the question, What would a philosopher make of what I have to offer?

I understand that this question, what would a philosopher think of this or that piece of writing, is one that troubles those who work within that institution, especially doctoral candidates and junior faculty. We might pause to note that this is a perfectly reasonable worry, especially if one is trying to get a job within a department of philosophy and needs to establish that the work one does is, indeed, properly philosophical. Philosophers in the profession must, in fact, make such judgments, and those of us outside philosophy departments hear those judgments from time to time. The judgment usually takes one of these forms: "I cannot understand this," or "I do not see the argument here" or "All very interesting, but certainly not philosophy." These are all voiced by an authority who adjudicates what will and will not count as legitimate knowledge, one who seems to know and acts with the full assurance of knowledge. It is surely impressive to be in such a situation and to be able to know, with clarity, what counts and what does not count. Indeed, some might even say that it is one of the responsibilities of philosophers to make such decisions and abide by them.

Well and good, but I would like to suggest that a certain embarrassment has been introduced into this institution, into what Bourdieu has called the "ritualized institution of philosophy," because the term *philosophy* has ceased to be in the control of those who would define and protect its institutional parameters. Surely, those who pay their dues to the American Philosophical Association and enter into that committee structure at various levels of power have been surprised, perhaps even scandalized, by the use of the word *philosophy* to designate the kinds of scholarship that in no recognizable sense mirror the academic practice they perform and that they understand to be their duty and privilege to define and protect. Philosophy has doubled itself. It has, in Hegel's terms, found itself outside itself, lost itself in the Other, and wonders whether and how it might retrieve itself from the reflection of itself that it finds travelling under its own name. Philosophy, in its proper sense, if it has a proper sense, wonders whether it will ever return to itself from this scandalous appearance as the Other. It wonders, if not publicly, then surely in the hallways and bars of Hilton Hotels at every annual meeting, whether it is not besieged, expropriated, ruined by the improper use of its proper name, haunted by a spectral doubling of itself.

I do not mean to introduce myself as that spectral double, but it may be that my own talk, which is on philosophy but not of it, will seem somewhat ghostly as a result. Let me reassure you that the perspective from which I speak is one that has been, from the start, at some distance from the institution of philosophy. Let me start, then, in the spirit of Edmund Husserl, who claimed that philosophy was, after all, a perpetual beginning, and refer to my own beginnings, humble and vexed as they surely were. When I was twelve, I was interviewed by a doctoral candidate in education and asked what I wanted to be when I grew up, and I said that I wanted either to be a philosopher or a clown, and I understood then, I think, that much depended on whether or not I found the world worth philosophizing about, and what the price of seriousness might be. I was not sure I wanted to be a philosopher, and I confess that I have never quite overcome that doubt. Now, it may be that having doubt about the value of a career in philosophy is a sure sign that one should not be a philosopher. Indeed, if you have a student who contemplates that bleak job market and says, as well, that he or she is not sure of the value of a career in the field or, put differently, of being a philosopher, then you would, as a faculty member, no doubt be very quick to direct this person to another corner of the market. If one is not absolutely sure about the value of being a philosopher, then one should surely go elsewhere. Unless, of course, we discern some value in not being sure about the value of becoming a philosopher, unless a resistance to its institutionalization has another kind of value, one that is not always marketable but that nevertheless emerges as a counterpoint to the current market values of philosophy. Could it be that not knowing for sure what should and should not be acknowledged as philosophy has itself a certain philosophical value? And is this a value we might name and discuss without it thereby becoming a new criterion by which the philosophical is rigorously demarcated from the nonphilosophical?

In what follows, I hope to show how I was introduced to philosophy in a fairly deinstitutionalized way, and to show how this distance from the institutionalized life of philosophy has in some ways become a vocation for me and, indeed, for many contemporary scholars who work in the humanities on philosophical topics. I want to argue that there is a distinctive value to this situation. Much of the philosophical work that takes place outside of philosophy is free to consider the rhetorical and literary aspects of philosophical texts and to ask, specifically, what particular philosophical value is carried or enacted by those rhetorical and linguistic features. The rhetorical aspects of a philosophical text include its genre (which can be varied), how it makes the arguments that it does, and how its mode of presentation informs the argument itself, sometimes enacting that argument implicitly, sometimes enacting an argument that is contrary to what the philosophical text explicitly declares.

A substantial amount of the work done in the Continental philosophical tradition is currently done outside of philosophy departments, and it is sometimes done in especially rich and provocative ways in conjunction with literary readings. Paradoxically, philosophy has received a new life in contemporary studies of culture and the cultural study of politics, where philosophical notions inform both social and literary texts that are not (generically speaking) philosophical, but that nevertheless establish the site of cultural study as a vital one for philosophical thinking within the humanities. I hope to make this clear by narrating my own engagement with philosophy, my turn to Hegel and to his place in contemporary scholarship on the question of the struggle for recognition within the project of modernity.

My first introduction to philosophy was a radically deinstitutionalized one, autodidactic and premature. This scene might best be summed up by the picture of a young teenager hiding out from painful family dynamics in the basement of the house where her mother's college books were stored, where Spinoza's *Ethics* (the 1934 Elwes translation) was to be found. My emotions were surely rioting, and I turned to Spinoza to find out whether knowing what they were and what purpose they served would help me learn how to live with them in some more manageable way. What I found in the second and third chapters of that text was rich indeed. The extrapolation of emotional states from the primary persistence of the *conatus* in human beings impressed me as the most profound, pure, and clarifying exposition of human passions. A thing endeavors to persist in its being. I suppose this signaled to me a form of vitalism that persists even in despair. In Spinoza, I found the notion that a conscious and persistent being responds to reflections of itself in emotional ways according to whether that reflection signifies a diminution or augmentation of its own possibility of future persistence and life. This being desires not only to persist in its own being, but to live in a world of representations that reflect the possibility of that persistence, and finally to live in a world in which it reflects the value of others' lives as well as its own. In the chapter entitled "On Human

Bondage, or the Strength of the Emotions," Spinoza writes, "No one can desire to be blessed, to act rightly and to live rightly, without at the same time wishing to be, to act, and to live—in other words, to actually exist."(Proposition XXI).[1] And then again, he writes, "Desire is the essence of a man, that is, the endeavor whereby a man endeavors to persist in his own being."

I did not know at the time that this doctrine of Spinoza's would prove essential for my subsequent scholarly work on Hegel, but this is the early modern precedent for Hegel's contention that desire is always the desire for recognition, and that recognition is the condition for a continuing and viable life. Spinoza's insistence that the desire for life can be found nascent in the emotions of despair lead to the more dramatic Hegelian claim that "tarrying with the negative" can produce a conversion of the negative into being, that something affirmative can actually come of the experiences of individual and collective devastation even in their indisputable irreversibility.

I came upon the Spinoza at the same time that I came upon the first English publication of Kierkegaard's *Either/Or*, skirting Hegel until I arrived at college. I tried in Kierkegaard to read a written voice that was not exactly saying what it meant; in fact, this voice kept saying that what it had to say was not communicable in language. Thus, one of my first confrontations with a philosophical text posed the question of reading, and drew attention to its rhetorical structure as a text. As pseudonymous, the author was unforthcoming, never saying who it was who was speaking, nor letting me escape the difficulty of interpretation. This extraordinary stylistic feat was compounded by the fact that *Either/Or* is two books, each written in a perspective that wars with the other perspective, so whoever this author was, he surely was not one. On the contrary, the two volumes of this book stage a scene of psychic splitting that seemed, by definition, to elude exposition through direct discourse. There was no way to begin to understand this work without understanding the rhetorical and generic dimensions of Kierkegaard's writing. This did not mean that one could first consider the literary form and rhetorical situation of the text and then cull from them its philosophical truth. On the contrary, there was no way to extricate the philosophical point, a point that has to do with the insuperability of silence when it comes to matters of faith, without being brought, through the language, to the moment of its own foundering, where language shows its own limitation, and where this "showing" is not the same as a simple declaration of its limits. For Kierkegaard, the direct declaration of the limits of language is not to be believed; nothing less than the undoing of the declarative mode itself will do.

Kierkegaard and Spinoza were, for me, philosophy, and they were, interestingly, my mother's books, books bought and perhaps read for some undergraduate course at Vassar in the early fifties. The third I found was Schopenhauer's *The World as Will and Representation*, which belonged to my father and appeared to have traveled with him to Korea, where he worked on the dental staff of the army during that strange and suspended state of war. The book was apparently given to him by a lover who preceded my mother, her name was engraved on the first page. I have no way of knowing how she came upon this book, why she gave it to my father, what having it or reading it might have meant to him. But I assume that my father's lover took a class in "philosophy," or perhaps a friend of her's did, so that the book travelled from the institution of philosophy to me in my adolescent suffering at a time that allowed me to think of the world as having a structure and meaning larger than my own, that placed the problem of desire and will in a philosophical light, and exemplified a certain passionate clarity in thought.

These books came to me, we might say, as byproducts of the institution of philosophy in a deinstitutionalized form. Someone decided they should be translated and disseminated, and they were ordered by someone for courses that my parents took or that their intimates took, and then they were shelved, only to emerge as part of that visual horizon that graces the smoke-filled basements of the suburban home that was mine. I sat in that basement, sullen and despondent, having locked the door so that no one else could enter, having listened to enough music, and somehow I looked up through the smoke of my cigarette in that darkened and airless room and saw a title that aroused in me the desire to read, to read philosophy.

The second route by which philosophy arrived for me was the synagogue, and if the first route arose from adolescent agony, the second arose from collective Jewish ethical dilemmas. I was supposed to stop taking classes at the synagogue before high school, but I somehow decided to continue. The classes tended to focus on moral dilemmas and questions of human responsibility, on the tension between individual decisions and collective responsibilities, and on God—whether God existed and of what use "he" might finally be, especially in light of the concentration camps. I was considered a disciplinary problem of sorts and given, by way of punishment, the task of taking a tutorial with the rabbi, which focused on an array of Jewish philosophical writings. I found several passages that reminded me of Kierkegaard's, where a certain silence informed the writing, where writing the could not quite deliver or convey what it sought to communicate, but where the nonetheless mark of its own foundering illuminated a reality that language could not directly represent. Thus, philosophy was not only a rhetorical problem, but was tied in rather direct ways to questions of individual and collective suffering and whether transformations were possible.

I entered my institutionalized philosophical career from the context of a Jewish education, where the ethical dilemmas posed by the mass extermination of the Jews during World War II, including members of my own family, to set the scene for the thinking of ethicality as such. It was thus with difficulty that, upon arriving at college, I agreed to read Nietzsche; my disdain for him lasted through most of my undergraduate years at Yale. A friend of mine brought me to Paul de Man's class on *Beyond Good and Evil* and I found myself at once compelled and repelled. Indeed, as I left his class for the first time, I felt myself quite literally lose a sense of groundedness. I leaned against a railing to recover my balance. In alarm, I pointed out to my friend that de Man did not believe in the concept, that he was unraveling concepts into metaphors, destroying the very presumption of philosophy, and stripping its powers of consolation. I did not, needless to say, return to that particular class. Instead I copped an attitude and decided that those who attended his seminars were not really philosophers (thereby enacting the very gesture that I am thinking about today). I resolved that they did not know the materials, that they were not asking the serious questions, and I returned to the more conservative wing of Continental philosophy thirty yards away, in Connecticut Hall, acting for the moment as if the distance that divided Comparative Literature from Philosophy was much greater than it could possibly be. I refused and rejected him, and yet found myself sitting in the back of the room. I've been asked since why I wasn't there in his classes? I wasn't *there*, but sometimes I was there without appearing to be. And sometimes I left very early on.

Moving from high school to Bennington College and then to Yale was not easy. In some ways I never became acclimatized to the profession of philosophy. As a young person, I came upon philosophy as a way of posing the question of how to live, and I took seriously the notion that reading philosophical texts and thinking philosophically might give me necessary guidance on matters of life. I myself was scandalized the first time I read Kierkegaard's remark that one could make out of philosophy a queer comedy if a person were to act according to its teachings. How could there be this ironic and inevitable distance between knowing a thing to be true and acting in accordance with that knowledge? I was taken aback again when I heard the story about how Max Scheler, when pressed by his audience to explain how he could have lead such an unethical life at the same time that he pursued the study of ethics, responded by saying that the sign that points the way to Berlin does not need to go there to offer the right direction. That philosophy might be divorced from life, that life might not be fully ordered by philosophy, struck me as a perilous possibility. And it wasn't until several years later that I came to understand that philosophical conceptualization cannot fully relieve a life of its difficulty, and it was with some sadness and loss that I came to reconcile myself to this post-idealist insight.

But whether or not my belief about the relation of philosophy to life was right, it was still a belief that referred philosophy to existential and political dilemmas, and my disillusioned idealism was not as shocking finally as my entrance into the disciplinary definitions of philosophy. That happened in high school when I attended an introduction to philosophy class at Case Western Reserve University in 1977. My teacher was Ruth Macklin, who has now assumed a post as an ethicist at the Hastings Institute. She taught us Plato and

Mill and an early essay on justice by John Rawls; the approach was distinctively analytic, something I did not understand or even know how to name at the time. I stumbled through that first course and then, determined, took another one with her on moral philosophy in which I read mainly British analytic thinkers from Russell and Moore through Stevenson and Phillipa Foot, interrogating the various senses of the word *good* as it is employed in ethical argument and expression. Although I finally triumphed by the end of that year, my senior year, I knew as I entered college that I might not find my version of philosophy mirrored in any institutional form.

After I traveled to Germany on a Fulbright to work with Hans Georg Gadamer and study German Idealism, I returned to Yale as a graduate student and began to become politically active within the university, to read books by someone named Foucault, to ask after the relation between philosophy and politics, and to inquire publicly whether something interesting and important might be made of feminist philosophy and, in particular, a philosophical approach to the question of gender. At the same time, the question of alterity became important to me in the context of Continental philosophy. And I was interested in the problem of desire and recognition. Under what conditions can a desire seek and find recognition for itself? This became for me an abiding question as I moved into the area of gay and lesbian studies. This and the question of the Other seemed to me, as it did for Simone de Beauvoir, to be the point of departure for thinking politically about subordination and exclusion. I felt myself to occupy the term that I interrogated—as I do today in asking about the Other to philosophy—and so I turned to the modern source of the understanding of Otherness: Hegel himself.

My dissertation work on desire and recognition in Hegel's *Phenomenology of Spirit* took up some of the same issues that had preoccupied me at a much earlier age. In *The Phenomenology*, desire (Paragraph 167) is essential to self-reflection, and there is no self-reflection except through the drama of reciprocal recognition.[2] Thus the desire for recognition is one in which desire seeks its reflection in the other. This is at once a desire that seeks to negate the alterity of the other (it is, after all, by virtue of its structural similarity to me, in my place, threatening my unitary existence) and a desire that finds itself requiring that very Other whom it fears to be and to be captured by; indeed, without this constituting and passionate bind, there can be no recognition. Thus, recognition begins with the insight that one is lost in the other, appropriated in and by an alterity that is and is not oneself, and it is motivated by the desire to find oneself reflected there where the reflection is not a final expropriation. Indeed, consciousness seeks a retrieval of itself, a restoration to an earlier time, only to come to see that there is no return from alterity to a former self, but only a future transfiguration premised on the impossibility of any such return.

Thus, in "Lordship and Bondage" (Paragraphs 178–96) recognition is motivated by the desire for recognition, and recognition is itself a cultivated form of desire, no longer the simple consumption or negation of alterity, but the uneasy dynamic in which one seeks to find oneself in the other only to find that that reflection is the sign of one's expropriation and self-loss.

It may be that institutionalized philosophy finds itself in this strange bind at the moment, though I know that I cannot speak from its perspective. It has before it something called "philosophy," which is emphatically "not philosophy" and does not follow the protocols of that discipline or measure up to apparently transparent standards of logical rigor and clarity. I say apparently transparent only because I sit on several committees that review grant applications from the humanities, and the practice of clarity that many philosophers espouse and enact is one that often leaves other humanities scholars quite confused. Indeed, when standards of clarity become part of a hermetic discipline, they are no longer communicable, and what one gets as a result is, paradoxically, a noncommunicable clarity. This institutionalized philosophy, which is not itself, produces another paradox as well: it proliferates a second philosophy outside the boundary that philosophy itself has set, and so seems to have unwittingly produced this spectral double of itself. Further, it may be that what is practiced as philosophy in most of the language and literature departments in this country has come to constitute the meaning of "philosophy," so the discipline of philosophy must find itself strangely expropriated by a double. The more it seeks to dissociate itself from this redoubled notion of itself, the more effective it is in securing the dominance of this other philosophy outside the boundary that was meant to contain it. Philosophy can no longer return to itself, for the boundary that might mark that return is precisely the condition by which philosophy is spawned outside of its institutional place.

There are, of course, more than two versions of philosophy, and here the Hegelian language no doubt forces me to restrict my characterizations to a false binary. Institutionalized philosophy has not been at one with itself for some time, if ever it was, and its life outside the borders of philosophy takes various forms. And yet, there is some way that each is haunted, if not stalked, by the other.

At the point where I started lecturing for the Department of Philosophy at Yale on feminist philosophy, I noticed a few rather disturbed figures at the back of the hall, adults pacing back and forth, listening to what I had to say and then abruptly leaving, only to return again after a week or two to repeat a disturbing ritual similar to the one I enacted when I tentatively attended de Man's seminars. Thus auditors turned out to be political theorists who were enraged that what I was teaching took place under the rubric of philosophy. They couldn't quite come in and take a seat, but neither could they leave. They needed to know what I was saying, but they couldn't allow themselves to get close enough to hear. It was not a question of whether I was teaching bad philosophy, or not teaching philosophy well, but whether my classes were philosophy at all.

I don't propose today to answer the question of what philosophy should be, and to be quite honest, I no longer have definite views on this matter, not because I have left philosophy, but because I think that philosophy has, in a very significant way, departed from itself and found itself scandalized by the wandering of its name beyond its official confines. This became clear to me as I practiced feminist philosophy. I was appalled to learn that just two years ago, graduate students at the New School for Social Research held a conference entitled "Is Feminist Philosophy Philosophy?" That had been the question posed by the skeptics of feminist thought, and it was now being quoted by the young practitioners of feminism in earnest. Some may want to argue that yes, feminist philosophy is philosophy, and proceed to show all the ways that feminist philosophy poses the most traditional of philosophical problems. But my own view is that such a question should be refused because it is the wrong question. The right question, as it were, has to do with how this redoubling of the term *philosophy* became possible such that we might find ourselves in a strange tautological bind in which we ask whether philosophy is philosophy. Perhaps we should simply say that philosophy, as we understand the institutional and discursive trajectory of that term, is no longer self-identical, if it ever was, and that its reduplication plagues it now as an insuperable problem.

For a while I thought I didn't have to deal with this issue because once I published on gender theory, I received many invitations from literature departments to speak, and to speak about something called "theory." It turned out that I had become something called a "theorist," and though I was glad to accept the kind invitations that came my way, I was somewhat bewildered and began trying to understand what sort of practice this enterprise called "theory" was supposed to be. "Ah yes, the state of theory," I would say at the dinner table on such occasions, sipping my Chardonnay and looking around anxiously to see whether there might be a kind soul there who might tell me precisely what this "theory" was supposed to be. I read literary theory and found my own work lodged on shelves under that rubric. I had understood from my earlier days that there was such a practice (I thought of Wellek, Fletcher, Frye, Bloom, de Man, Iser, Felman), but it wasn't clear to me that what I was doing was "theory" and that that term could and should take the place of philosophy. At this point, it no longer bothered me that I wasn't doing philosophy, because the world of literature allowed me to read for rhetorical structure, ellipsis, and metaphorical condensation, and to speculate on possible conjunctions between literary readings and political quandaries. I continued to suffer bouts of anxiety every time that word *theory* was used, and I still feel something of an uneasiness about it, even as I now know that I am part of it, that I am perhaps indissociable from that term.

I have come to see, however, that this confusion is not mine alone. It is now with some surprise that I pick up the catalogues of various publishers and see under the heading "Philosophy" several writers whose work is not taught in philosophy departments. This includes not only large numbers of Continental philosophers and essayists but literary theorists and scholars of art and media studies as well, scholars in ethnic and feminist studies. I note with some interest the number of dissertations on Hegel and Kant that have emerged from the Humanities Center at Johns Hopkins or the Department of English at Cornell or German Studies at Northwestern, and the number of young scholars in humanities departments who have traveled to France in the last ten years to work with Derrida, Levinas, Agamben, Balibar, Kofman, Irigaray, Cixous, or those who continue to travel to Germany to learn the tradition of German Idealism and the Frankfurt School. The most interesting work on Schelling and the Schlegels is being done by cultural and literary theorists at the moment, and the extraordinary work by a scholar like Peter Fenves on Kant and Kierkegaard emerges from comparative literature and German studies. And some of the most philosophically important work on Foucault is produced by scholars such as Paul Rabinow, the philosopher of anthropology.

Consider the extraordinary interdisciplinary life of a figure like Walter Benjamin, who in many ways epitomizes the excessive travels of philosophy outside the gates of its containment. One might expect to find him taught under the rubric of the Frankfurt School in philosophy departments that offer such courses (I would imagine there are about a dozen such departments by now), but the difficulty of his language and his aesthetic preoccupations often lead to the excision of his work from philosophy courses and its reemergence in English, Comparative Literature, French, and German departments. I noted a few years ago with some interest that *New Formations*, the leftist British journal, published a volume on his work at the same time as the ostensibly post-ideological *Diacritics*, and now the most recent issue of *Critical Inquiry* joins the fray. Is it that his writing is not philosophical? The philosopher Jay Bernstein has argued passionately to the contrary. Or is it the way that philosophy appears here, precisely in a contentious and scattered form, through cultural analysis, through the consideration of material culture and failed or inverted theological structures, in a language that moves from the aphoristic to the densely referential in the manner of literary readings and theory. The multidisciplinary trajectory of Benjamin's work makes a presumption about where one might look to find the question of the meaning of history, the referentiality of language, the broken promises of poetry and theology intrinsic to aesthetic forms, the conditions of community and communication. These are all clearly philosophical concerns, but they are pursued through a variety of means, forms of analysis—of reading and writing—irreducible to argumentative form and which rarely follow a linear style of exposition. There are those who will say that Benjamin can become philosophical if someone would write a book that transmuted his writing into a linear exposition of arguments. And there are others who claim that the very challenge to linear argumentation carries its own philosophical meaning, one that calls into question the power and appearance of reason, the forward motion of temporality. Unfortunately, most of the people willing to make the second argument belong to humanities departments outside of the field of philosophy.

If we look at the work of Luce Irigaray, for instance, we read a feminist interrogation of the problem of alterity that draws upon Hegel, Beauvoir, and Freud, but also Merleau-Ponty and Levinas, one that is profoundly immersed in the history of philosophy even as it counters philosophy's exclusion of the feminine, and forces a rearticulation of its most basic terms. This work cannot be read without philosophy, for that is its text, and yet including it in the canon of philosophy is not possible for most philosophy departments, (although publishers have no problem with that move and have been largely responsible for keeping a robust and inclusive notion of philosophy alive (here the Stanford University Press is especially to be commended on their excellent list in philosophy and critical theory).

The question of what belongs to philosophy and what does not sometimes centers on the issue of the rhetoricity of the philosophical text, whether it has any, whether those rhetorical dimensions must or should be read as essential to the philosophical character of the text. But we can see as well that certain ways of extending the philosophical tradition to touch upon questions of contemporary cultural politics and questions of political justice as they emerge in the vernacular or contemporary social movements also pave the way for an exit from institutional philosophy into a wider cultural conversation.

What do we make of the enormously influential philosophical work of Cornel West, for instance, whose utopian pragmatism and commitment to Du Bois's vision has brought philosophical concerns to the forefront of African-American politics in this country? He finds his home in a divinity school and in religion, and does it say something about the limitations of institutional philosophy that he finds no home there? In some ways, his work shows the continuing relevance of the tradition of American pragmatism for contemporary struggles for racial equality and dignity. Is it the transposition of that tradition onto the context of race relations that renders the philosophical dimension of that work impure? And if so, is there any hope left for philosophy unless it actively engaged precisely such an impurity?

In a similar vein, almost every feminist philosopher I know is no longer working in a philosophy department. When I look at the roster of the first anthologies of feminist philosophy in which I published (*Feminism as Critique*,[3] *Feminism/Postmodernism*,[4]) the names were Drucilla Cornell, Seyla Benhabib, Nancy Fraser, Linda Nicholson, Iris Marion Young—all students of scholars like Alasdair MacIntyre and Peter Caws and Jurgen Habermas. None of them are in philosophy departments anymore. We have all found more auspicious homes in other disciplines: law, political science, education, comparative literature, English. And now this is true of Elizabeth Grosz as well, perhaps the most important Australian feminist philosopher of our time, who has recently joined the ranks of comparative literature in this country. This has been remarkably true as well of the many feminist philosophers of science who work in women's studies or science studies or education departments. Some, if not many, of the most influential people in these fields are no longer affiliated with philosophy as their institutional home. The problem here is not simply that philosophy as practiced by these individuals remains outside the discipline of philosophy, creating once again the specter of "philosophy outside of philosophy." Awkwardly, these are the philosophical contributions that are constantly in contact with other fields, that establish the routes by which interdisciplinary travel of philosophy into the other humanities takes place. These are the philosophers who are in the conversations across disciplines, who are producing interest in philosophical work in French and German departments, in English and comparative literature, in science studies and women's studies. Of course, philosophy has pursued interdisciplinary contacts in cognitive science, computer science, and in those areas of medical ethics, law, and public policy that are so essential to the field of applied ethics. But with respect to the humanities, it has been for the most part a loner—territorial, protective, increasingly hermetic. There are, however, exceptions to this rule, and one sees in the work of Rorty, Cavell, Nehamas, Nussbaum, Appiah, and Braidotti, for instance, active ways of engaging with the arts, with literature, with cultural questions that form a common set of concerns across the disciplines. And I would suggest that none of these individuals have crossed the border into the wider conversation without paying some price within their own discipline.

The presence of philosophy in the humanities disciplines is not simply the effect of trained philosophers having, as it were, become derailed. In some ways, the most culturally important discussions of philosophy are taking place by scholars who have always worked outside the institutional walls of philosophy. Indeed, one might say that what emerged after the days of high literary theory, what John Guillory understands to be literary formalism, was not the dissolution of theory but the movement of theory into the concrete study of culture, so that what one now confronts is the emergence of theoretical texts in the study of broader cultural and social phenomena. This is not the historicist displacement of theory; on the contrary, it is the historicizing of theory itself that has become the site of its new life. I've made that theory/philosophy conflation again, but consider that philosophical texts have a central place in many of the most trenchant of recent cultural analyses. Indeed, I would suggest that as philosophy has lost its purity, it has accordingly gained its vitality throughout the humanities.

Take the work of Paul Gilroy, a British sociologist and cultural studies practitioner, whose book *The Black Atlantic*,[5] has made a profound impact on both African-American and diaspora studies in the last five years. The first ninety pages of that book are concerned with the Hegelian notion of modernity. He argues there that the exclusion of people of African descent from European modernity is not a sufficient reason to reject that modernity, for the terms of modernity have been and still can be appropriated from their exclusionary Eurocentrism and made to operate in the service of a more inclusive democracy. At stake in his subtle historiography is the question of whether the conditions of reciprocal recognition by which the "human" comes into being can be extended beyond the geopolitical sphere presumed by the discourse of equality and reciprocity. And though Hegel gives us the strange scene of the lord and bondsman, a scene that vacillates between a description of serfdom and slavery, it is not until the work of W.E.B. Du Bois, Orlando Patterson, and Paul Gilroy that we start to understand how the Hegelian project of reciprocal recognition might be renarrated from the history of slavery and the effects of the subsequent diaspora.

Gilroy writes that the perspective of slavery "requires a discrete view not just of the dynamics of power and domination in plantation societies dedicated to the pursuit of commercial profit but of such central categories of the Enlightenment project as the idea of universality, the fixity of meaning, the coherence of the subject, and, of course, the foundational ethnocentrism in which these have all tended to be anchored." (55) Less predictably, he then argues that it would be a great mistake to dismiss the project of modernity. Citing Habermas, he notes that even those who have been most radically excluded from the European project of modernity have been able to appropriate essential concepts from the theoretical arsenal of modernity to fight for their rightful inclusion in the process. "A concept of modernity worth its salt," he writes, "ought, for example, to have something to contribute to an analysis of how the particular varieties of radicalism articulated through the revolts of enslaved people made selective use of the ideologies of the western Age of Revolution and then flowed into social movements of an anti-colonial and decidedly anti-capitalist type." (44)

Gilroy takes issues with what he calls postmodern forms of skepticism that lead to a full-scale rejection of the key terms of modernity and, in his view, a paralysis of political will. But he then also takes his distance from Habermas, because Habermas fails to take into account the relationship between slavery and modernity. That failure, he notes, can be attributed to his preference for Kant over Hegel: "Habermas does not follow Hegel in arguing that slavery is itself a modernising force in that it leads both master and servant first to self-consciousness and then to disillusion, forcing both to confront the unhappy realisation that the true, the good, and the beautiful do not have a shared origin." (50)

Gilroy proceeds to read Frederick Douglass, for instance, as "lord and bondsman in a black idiom" and then to read the contemporary black feminist theorist, Patricia Hill Collins, as seeking to extend the Hegelian project into that of a racialized standpoint epistemology. In these and other instances, he insists that the Eurocentric discourse has been taken up profitably by those who were traditionally excluded from its terms, and that the subsequent revision carries radical consequences for the rethinking of modernity in non-ethnocentric terms. Gilroy's fierce opposition to forms of black essentialism, most specifically, Afrocentrism, makes this point from another angle.

One of the most interesting philosophical consequences of Gilroy's work is that he provides a cultural and historical perspective on current debates in philosophy that threaten to displace its terms. Whereas he rejects the hyperrationalism of the Habermasian project, even as he preserves certain key features of its description of the Enlightenment project, he also rejects forms of skepticism that reduce all political positioning to rhetorical gesture. The form of cultural reading he provides attends to the rhetorical dimension of all sorts of cultural texts and labors under the aegis of a more radically democratic modernity. Thus, his position, I would suggest, is worth considering as one rehearses the debates between the defenders and detractors of the Enlightenment project.

But how often do we see job advertisements that emanate jointly from philosophy and sociology departments looking for someone versed in the philosophical and cultural problems of modernity in the context of slavery and its aftermath? My example will probably not be compelling to most philosophers, since Hegel is, in many departments throughout this country, not taught as part of any listed course, and in some instances, he is explicitly excluded from the history of philosophy sequence. The resistances to Hegel are, of course, notorious: his language is ostensibly impenetrable, he rejects the law of non-contradiction, his speculations are unfounded and, in principle, unverifiable. So it is not within the walls of philosophy that we hear the question, According to what protocols that govern the readability of philosophy does Hegel's writing become unreadable? How is it that so many have, in fact, read him, and that he continues to inform so much contemporary scholarship? What is the argument that he offers against the law of non-contradiction, and what rhetorical form does that argument take? How are we to read that argument once we understand the rhetorical form by which it is structured? And what is the critique of verifiability that emerges in the course of his work? Because the standards that these questions seek to interrogate are taken for granted by those philosophers who invoke those standards in dismissing Hegel, we find the questions pursued elsewhere: in the humanities, in German and history and sociology departments, in English and comparative literature, in American studies and ethnic studies.

Similarly, when was the last time you heard of a philosophy department joining with a German department in a search for someone who works in German romanticism, including Kant, Hegel, Goethe, Holderlin? Or when did you hear of a philosophy department joining with French to hire someone in twentieth-century French philosophical thought? Perhaps we have seen a few instances of philosophy departments joining with African-American studies or ethnic studies, but not often, and surely not often enough.

This is but one way that philosophy enters the humanities, redoubling itself there, making the very notion of philosophy strange to itself. We should, I suppose, be very thankful to live in this rich region that the institutional foreclosures of the philosophic have produced such good company and better wine, so many more unexpected conversations across disciplines to be had, and such extraordinary movements of thought that surpass the barriers of departmentalization, posing a vital problem for those who remain behind. The bondsman scandalizes the lord, you will remember, by looking back it him, evincing a consciousness he or she is not supposed to have had, and thus showing the lord that he has become other to himself. The lord is perhaps out of his own control, but for Hegel this self-loss is the beginning of community, and it may be that our current predicament threatens to do no more than bring philosophy closer to its place as one strand among many in the fabric of culture.

NOTES

1. What I read at the time was the Elwes translatio of Spinoza: *The Chief Works of Benedict de Spinoza*, translated with an introduction by R.H.M. Elwes, 2 volumes (New York: Dover Publications, 1951). Any edition of Spinoza can, however, be consulted.

2. See G.W.F. Hegel, *Phenomenology of Spirit*, trans. A.V. Miller, foreward by J.N. Findlay (Oxford: Clarendon Press, 1970), pp. 104–05. But, as with the Spinoza references above, any edition of the *Phenomenology* can be consulted, hence no further page numbers will apear.

3. *Feminism as Critique: Essays on the Politics of Gender in Late-Capitalist Societies*, ed. Seyla Benhabib and Drucilla Cornell (London: Polity Press, 1987).

4. *Feminism/Postmodernism*, edited and with an introduction by Linda J. Nicholson (New York: Routledge, 1989).

5. Paul Gilroy, *The Black Atlantic: Modernity and Double Consciousness* (Cambridge, Mass.: Harvard University Press, 1993). Page number of citations appear in the body of the text.

CHAPTER 5

Reflections on Interdisciplinarity

Renato Rosaldo

THIS PAPER is a reflection on interdisciplinarity both as a contemporary cultural conception and as a form of life within the institutions of modern thought in the late twentieth century. My method is ethnographic, more properly autoethnographic,[1] in that I use my own experiences of interdisciplinarity to sketch the connections between ideas and social relations, between thought and social formations. What I lose in systematic mapping I hope to gain in knowledge of the terrain. Not unlike the informal economy, interdisciplinarity as a social form thrives in intersticial spaces relatively beyond the reach of institutional norms. These human communities, characterized less as formal organizations than as loose aggregates or networks of thinkers who are in conversation with one another, produce and sustain the modes of thought that have come to be called interdisciplinarity. The term of art for the social aspirations central to interdisciplinarity concerns the "need" to have someone to "talk with." Intellectual conversation and the reading group are key forms of sociality for interdisciplinarity as a form of thought today.

Awkward and difficult to pronounce, the term *interdisciplinarity* came into vogue, at least in my circles, during the late 1970s. It referred to a style of thought and forms of collaboration that the speaker regarded with favor. It was better to be interdisciplinary than department-bound. Yet it was puzzling as a cultural conception because it referred only to certain, but not to all, forms of intellectual collaboration, which included members of different disciplines or departments. It referred more to conversations than to interdepartmental research teams, encompassing newly convergent areas that brought together, say, the analysis of culture and the study of social history. It also included turns of thought called interpretivist or historicist, whatever their departmental homes, and involved select members of different departments within the human sciences, such as philosophy, history, legal studies, literature, cultural anthropology, and sociology. The term referred to distinctive modes of thought and forms of sociality among like-minded people who happened to inhabit different departments.

Interdisciplinarity as a form of social life tends to be dissident and critical of modes of thought in department-based disciplines. It often embodies research agendas and intellectual currents at odds with work done within conventional discipline-based paradigms of research. Hermeneutics and the new historicism unite such scholars as the cultural anthropologist Clifford Geertz and the literary critic Steven Greenblatt, who probably feel that they have more in common with one another than with the more positivistic members of their own disciplines or departments. Within their own fields, they are dissident intellectual leaders. Their scholarship is critical of departmental business-as-usual. Feminist thought and critical race studies probably enable Judith Butler and Patricia Williams to find more grounds for discussion with one another than with many members of their own departments. One could say much the same of Raymond Williams and E. P. Thompson in relation to cultural studies and social history.

Arguably, then, the ethnographic exploration of interdisciplinarity as a series of overlapping communities of thought requires one to map personal networks rather than to study such established units as departments or annual meetings of discipline-based units. Such networks flow along interpersonal lines of collegiality and friendship. Thought and mutual influence move through informal personal visits, correspondence (phone, letters, or e-mail), and episodic encounters at professional conferences.

Seen from another angle, one less celebratory, it bears saying that younger scholars committed to interdisciplinarity may find it difficult to be hired or granted tenure in their own fields because conventional disciplinary scholars either do not recognize the value of their work or fail to recognize how it fits within their department. Members of interdisciplinary communities often seek alliances outside their departments as a means of sheer survival in hostile academic environments structured around departments. The urgency of interdisciplinarity and its affiliations derives from intellectual choices, political commitments, and gender, sexuality, and racialized identities. The primary intellectual reference group of such scholars extends beyond departmental bounds.

OUT OF BOUNDS: LUNCH WITH A MATHEMATICIAN

Perhaps my autoethnography of interdisciplinarity should begin with what seems an especially clear example of where its outer limits lie. Not every interdepartmental contact, I shall argue, should be regarded as an instance of interdisciplinarity as the term is currently used. The outer boundaries of interdisciplinarity were made especially clear to me in 1975–76 when I was a member of the Institute for Advanced Study in Princeton. I recall meeting a mathematician who sat down at lunch with me and immediately announced, "I won't understand a word you say." Thinking his remark foolish, I protested that what I did was actually quite simple. I was certain he would understand the basics about my work. After I explained that I conducted nearly three years of field research among a group of hunter-horticulturalists in northern Luzon, Philippines, he asked me if their language was grammatical, meaning, was it spoken in accord with rules of grammar. He did not mean to ask whether or not there was a published book of Ilongot grammar. For me, that was a conversation stopper. It was well known, I believed, that all human languages were grammatical in the sense of being rule-governed, although their grammars might be immensely various. I felt I had no choice but to concede his point: he would not be able to understand anything I said.

In a second meeting at lunch, we tried to make small talk as a means of evading the disciplinary borders yawning between us. This time he surprised me by saying, "I speak fluent Russian." He then portrayed himself at the blackboard, chalk in hand, doing equations with a Russian colleague. He later explained, however, that he lacked the technical vocabulary to read Chekov. Once again, we had strayed beyond the outer limits of interdisciplinarity. We held incompatible ideas of what it meant to speak a language as opposed to the ability to use a technical vocabulary. For me, technical vocabulary was what he used in talking with his fellow mathematician in Russia; it worked well in a restricted speech context. What he called technical vocabulary, I would call the linguistic competence required for meaningful human dialogue. We finished our lunch by ignoring the evident fact that we were not communicating.

Note well that my criterion for the outer boundaries of interdisciplinarity is the impossiblity of significant dialogue. I simply could not imagine a conversation between the mathematician and myself about how we think, feel, or what we do at work. On the other hand, perhaps there exists a project where we could collaborate by making rather different contributions—perhaps he, equations; me, words. Such a form of collaboration, however, would not comprise what I understand to be interdisciplinarity.

THE BORDERLANDS: A VIEW FROM AN EARLIER ERA

The borders of present-day interdisciplinarity, what it is and is not, can be explored though comparison and contrast with a distinguished thinker of an earlier era. The anthropologist Clyde Kluckhohn, a man prominent during the 1940s and 1950s, shows revealing similarities and differences from current interdisciplinary intellectuals. To begin, Kluckhohn was noted for working across disciplinary boundaries. He published, among other places, in *Education and Human Values*, *Journal of Philosophy*, *Sociometry*, *American Journal of Orthopsychiartry*, and *Harvard Theological Review*. A classics major as an undergraduate, he was, in the immediate post-World War II era, a cofounder of the Harvard Department of Social Relations, an uneasy union of sociology, anthropology, social psychology, and clinical psychology. Kluckhohn sought out and appeared to thrive in interdisciplinary contexts; in this literal sense, the term *interdisciplinarity* at first glance might seem appropriate as a description of his work.

In Kluckhohn's essay "Education, Values, and Anthropological Relativity,"[2] he at times sounds like a dissident interdisciplinary thinker of the present. In the following passage, for example, he moves from his argument that cultural relativity overlooks human ethical universals and asserts that cultural differences at times involve what are little more than matters of taste. There is, he argues in the following, no rational basis for saying that certain features of the lifeways of one culture are morally superior or inferior to those of another:

> There are many values that are a question of taste, and the fact that the taste of other people does not coincide with our own does not make them stupid or ignorant or evil. Moreover, in a world society each group can and must learn from other cultures, can and must familiarize itself with divergent value systems even when it prefers, in the last analysis, to hold in the main to its own traditional norms. Hence, the "Great Books" of Mr. Hutchins are a gigantic piece of cultural impudence. The Harvard report on General Education, published in 1945, is in many respects a wise and, indeed, a noble document; yet not one word is said of the need of the educated citizen to know something of the great religions of Asia nor of the aesthetic values of non-European languages. Africa remains the completely dark continent in spite of Benin bronzes and Bushmen paintings. The significant values of human culture are taken as limited to the Mediterranean Basin, Europe, and America. A peaceful revolution must dethrone such parochialism. (293)

Kluckhohn attacks Eurocentrism before the term came into existence, and he sounds ahead of his time, like a combatant in the so-called Culture Wars of the 1980s. Indeed, his interdisciplinary predilections are at play as he mixes a cultural anthropologist's convictions about the educational value of knowing different cultures and a humanist's feeling for what is at stake in teaching the Great Books or in the General Education Program at Harvard. Neither a pure humanist nor a strictly disciplinary anthropologist could have Kluckhohn's foresight about an intellectual issue that would become vital and vexed some three decades after he wrote.

Not unlike Kluckhohn, I have a home base in cultural anthropology and a commitment to the humanities. For reasons that partially do and do not coincide with Klukhohn's, I found myself involved in what came to be called the Western Culture Controversy at Stanford.[3] I found Stanford's Great Books course, with its restrictive reading list and the implication that anything not on the list was of lesser value, an indefensible form of ethnocentrism in an increasingly multicultural world. In addition and unlike Kluckhohn, I was concerned as a Chicano about the impact of such a course on the first-year undergraduates of whom it was required. It simply would not do to begin the course, as a number of teachers did, by asserting that the list of Great Books is "our heritage." Who, one might wonder, is the "we" in such a statement? Students of color, women, and significant numbers of white male students did not feel included in the "we" and saw matters much as I did. They mobilized in a "Rainbow Coalition" that advocated making the course more inclusive in its readings.

The differences between Kluckhohn's and my engagement with the issue of the Great Books resides not only in distinctive perceptions or convictions but also in distinctive social contexts. My context involved social movements and changes in the human composition of universities brought by affirmative action for women and racialized minorities. Unlike Kluckhohn, I had the opportunity to participate in changing the frosh culture course. Furthermore, Kluckhohn did not mention an issue I found compelling, that of including appropriate writings by women and people of color in the United States. Instead, he addresses only the significant cultural achievements of Africa and Asia, and neglects to address diversity within the United States. Put differently, social context is substantive, not something added on; it shapes thought. Social forms and modes of thought cannot easily be separated.

If Kluckhohn's remarks on the Great Books and General Education seem, in certain respects, quite up-to-date, his essay, "Ethical Relativity: Sic et Non,"[4] argues in a way that appears dated. He bases his argument for and against ethical relativity on reviews of the fields of sociology, psychology, and anthropology; he uses each discipline as a corrective or supplement to the others, and he seeks a consensus among the three. He describes, for example, the consensus of psychologists and psychiatrists in the following manner:

[T]here appears to be a growing trend toward agreement on two fundamentals:
 1. Psychological fact and theory must be taken into account in dealing with ethical problems.
 2. There are pan-human universals as regards the needs and capacities that shape, or could at least, rightly shape, the broad outlines of a morality that transcends cultural difference. (270)

He treats statements from various practitioners of the Behavioral Sciences as if their opinions on ethical universals were facts or findings rather than, as I see them, as a consensus of opinions at best weakly supported by evidence and argumentation. Kluckhohn concludes by discussing the "ethical universals or near-universals [that] have been documented by behavioral science." (278) Most of the universals Kluckhohn arrives at are so general as as to be banal, such as the notion that "all cultures have moral systems." (276) The content of these moral systems is remarkably varied. Kluckhohn's universal is like observing that all human beings have the capacity to speak a language without either offering any notion of the mechanisms that linguists or cognitive scientists might postulate as underlying the production of universals or attempting to analyze the remarkable differences among the vast array of mutually unintelligible languages.

Where Kluckhohn diverges from contemporary interdisciplinarity is in his notion that he can master the knowledge of different disciplines and that each discipline contains truths of findings that do not require critical assessment.

Increased specialization since the post–World War II period makes the posture of multidisciplinary mastery more and more difficult to sustain. Arguably, today's interdisciplinarity posits that people share assumptions that overlap sufficiently for them to engage in meaningful conversations and arguments. In order to disagree productively about certain issues, debaters need to agree on a significant range of other issues. Interdisciplinarity, as the term is used today, is a historically specific cultural conception, probably of the last twenty-five years, that finds its community of thought across different disciplines in certain journals, conferences, reading groups, and personal networks. In other words, the limits of possible dialogue comprise the outer limits of interdisciplinarity as the term has come to be understood in the academy today.

POLICED BORDERS: A DEPARTMENTAL SPLIT

Let me explore a case of policed borders that revealed intradepartmental limits on meaningful conversation among colleagues. This was the case of an anthropology department, my own department at Stanford, that split in two over the period of 1996 to 1998. One might expect that anthropologists would be especially gifted at getting along in spite of our intellectual differences. After all, we seek out the alien wherever we find it across the globe. We have become known for judiciously extolling the uses of diversity.[5] We believe that learning about different cultures can be enlightening, and that cultural differences should not be taken as signs of insanity, immorality, or stupidity. It would seem that such broadmindedness could begin at home, within departmental confines, such that anthropologists of different stripes—interpretivist and positivist, cultural and sociobiological—would, if not embrace, at least tolerate one another's existence. Surely, one might think, sociobiologists or interpretivists are no more difficult to converse or live with than are cannibals or headhunters.

One could tell a long story about my department—its ingredients being, from my partisan position, brutal interventionist deans pouring gasoline on smoldering departmental tensions that enabled born-again positivists and evangelical sociobiologists to barge through the window of opportunity thereby opened—but I will not. Suffice it to say that the anthropological amalgam of the so-called four subfields (cultural, linguistic, archeological, and biological) could not hold together in a group that once was purely sociocultural. Our department emerged from a sociology department in the 1960s and not, as did others, from a capacious museum that housed the four subfields. In my view the possibility of meaningful collegial dialogue across the subfields had been killed by the specialization of knowledge. Four-field departments that have remained unified have often done so through a separate-but-equal holding operation, where disparate units operate under a single umbrella. The separate units, in certain cases known as wings, function as de facto autonomous units, particularly in relation to such matters as graduate admissions and faculty appointments. In my department, pressures from the dean opened an irreparable chasm between particularizing interpretive ethnographers and universalizing biological evolutionists. A cautionary tale may be found here, indicating that departments are not always, perhaps not even often, unified communities of thought. There are other cases (one is the erosion between analytic and continental philosophy) where it has in fact proved more difficult to bridge the divisions within than between departments.

The striking thing about the eventual outcome of this intradepartmental conflict is that modes of sociality—what I have called the conversation and the division of labor—determined the lines of fission in an unambiguous way. The fission occurred along internal borders that were policed vigorously, not to say viciously. The Department of Anthropology split into two departments in a remarkably successful divorce, where all participants agreed that the "bad guys" went to one department and the "good guys" remained in the other.

Conflicting models of collegiality were an unacknowledged source of the conflict. Some followed the model of interdisciplinarity with its notion of meaningful dialogue, and others followed the notion of the social division of labor within research teams. Arguably, distinct modes of sociality and their concomitant modes of thought were at the heart of the conflict. Each side accused the other of being narrow, and each side felt wrongly accused and proudly pointed to its own multiple extradepartmental affiliations.

THOUGHT AS PROCESS AND THOUGHT AS PRODUCT

The division in my department is but a local manifestation of a broader, unrefined but pervasive divide between what Clifford Geertz has called thought as process and thought as product.[6] This distinction, a rough and ready one that I do not wish to reify, I find useful for thinking about interdisciplinarity. Arguably, interdisciplinarity, as the term is used today, refers broadly to intellectual communities that bridge different departments but are unified in considering thought as product rather than process.

Geertz argues that the notion of "thought as process" finds its home in certain fields, such as psychology, linguistics, and computer science, where scholars tend to hold the position that the ways humans think are governed by the same kinds of mechanisms in all times and in all places. Their project is to understand precisely what those mechanisms are and how they work. Such forms of cognitive science explore the bases of what anthropologists once called the psychic unity of humankind. One thinks further of such areas as game theory, rational choice theory, and sociobiology as part of this field of inquiry.

In these areas, research is often conducted by teams comprised of members of different departments. The mode of operation in such teams involves a collaboration based on a division of labor whereby each person or group has particular skills or expertise to offer a larger project. The mode of cooperation could be compared with a potluck dinner, where one person brings the main course and another the salad. Both together help produce the dinner, but neither has to know how the other prepares his or her contribution. The range of researchers thus brought together in projects on environmental studies or cognitive science is often admirable, as are the human relations among the members of such research teams. For them, terms such as *interdisciplinary team* or *interdisciplinary program* would apply, but the term *interdisciplinarity*, as I have heard it used, does not apply to such groups.

The "thought as product" school finds its home, according to Geertz, in cultural anthropology and in certain areas of history, philosophy, literature, and sociology. It covers fields that have taken a historicizing or a hermeneutic turn. These fields also include law (critical legal studies, critical race studies), social history, the new historicism, science studies, and cultural studies. In my view, if the paradigmatic social unit for culture as process is the research team based on the division of social labor, the primary social unit for culture as product is the seminar constituted by meaningful conversation.

Arguably, a term of art within this school of thought is "the social construction of . . . ," a phrase that can end variously with such terms as *motherhood*, *sexuality*, or the *fact*. Such a phrase assumes that the cultural meanings and social practices of, say, sexuality change through time and vary from place to place; they are diverse in their construction, more the products of historical vicissitudes than of an invariant biological foundation. It is from the social constructivist perspective that terms such as *essentialism* and *Orientalism* have become markers of opprobrium. It is also from this perspective that one studies change as historical processes in ways that specify and contextualize rather than seeking invariant universal mechanisms.

In effect, the process and product views have different objects of knowledge (universal processes of thought versus diverse products of thought). They operate with different assumptions about the phenomena they study and about how to go about studying them. These two schools are complementary, not contradictory. The fact, for example, that all human languages are grammatical and that human grammars have certain universal features does not contradict the equally obvious fact that human languages are enormously various and mutually unintelligible. At the same time differences in the process and product modes of thinking about human thought tend to be quite different as forms of sociality.

In what follows I attempt to describe the processes of crossing the borders from one discipline to another. The issues thus raised concern both modes of thought and informal modes of sociality. Not unlike the sociology of knowledge, my notion is that ideas emerge from the forms of life that generate and sustain them and not from the mind as an abstract entity.

STUDIED DIALOGUE: SOCIAL HISTORY AND
CULTURAL ANTHROPOLOGY

I can now embark on an autoethnographic account of border crossing. It is the tale of a cultural anthropologist who, in an exercise of studied interdisciplinarity, learned to converse with social historians. The process began in 1975–76 when I was a member at the Institute for Advanced Study and participated in a seminar on symbolic anthropology that included a number of social historians of about my age. I had majored in history and literature as an undergraduate but had not learned about social history. Within a short time I found myself saying that I was working on a social history about a hill people in northern Luzon, Philippines. I often added that I hoped to write the history of a people who were not supposed to have one. It had taken me two and a half years to sort out the chronology of the Ilongots. They had no calendrical dates, but they had a precise way of reckoning time by naming their place of residence. The complexity of unraveling their chronology had to do with the fact that they reckoned place in multiple ways—the nearest named rock, hill, stream, or the place where they went for water. A single place could thus have five or six names. In any case, I was proud of having developed a chronology and yet was far from sure of how to write it all up.[7]

My encounters with interdisciplinarity as a form of life were marked by surprises, by the sorts of things that happened when I was hanging out with social historians—attending parties, playing ping pong, sitting on the porch, and talking into the night. We were, as I now see in retrospect, building friendships that have lasted into the present. Even in these activities we found ourselves bound as much by differences as by similarities between us. Late in the year, for example, a social historian and I planned to roast a lamb for a social gathering, but we had forgotten how to do it. I recalled that an article on how to roast a lamb had appeared in *Sunset Magazine*. The day before the party we rushed to the local library. The disciplinary difference between us became apparent when, in searching for *Sunset Magazine*, I went straight to the librarian to ask, and the social historian headed directly for the card catalogue. The anthropologist, as we said after the fact, sought out the knowledgeable native and the historian burrowed into the local archive.

Early in that year I was working on what I regarded as a historical paper, so I promptly showed it to my social historian colleagues. My colleagues found the paper interesting, but politely put me in my neophyte place by saying that the paper was an example of anthropology not history. My paper studied an enduring ideology, which I called the rhetoric of control, that was evident through both the Spanish and the American periods of colonial rule in the Philippines. Patiently they explained to me that for an analysis to be historical it had to show how something had changed. Instead, my paper showed how an ideology persisted through time without change.

As I began to write about change through time I found narrative a useful tool for analysis. Coached by historian friends, I avidly read theoretical studies on the nature of narrative as well as exemplary cases of narrative histories. The former I read with excitement (though historians assured me they were of no practical value) and the latter I read studiously (historians highly recommended these, especially Garret Mattingly)[8] to see what techniques I could steal for my ethnographic history of the Ilongots. My dilemmas as a trespasser into social history were most probably not those of a trained historian. I found it difficult to break out of my narrative frame (to give an overview, make theoretical observations, or say what else was happening in the meantime). In my studious reading of histories, I found that the most narrative of narrative historians had multiple artful ways of breaking out of their narrative flow.

What most took me aback was that my historical narratives were readily comprehensible to historian friends and colleagues, but anthropology colleagues often could not "follow" them. Had I "gone native?" Compared with social historians, most anthropological readers brought rather different habits of reading, background knowledge, and expectations to my ethnography. They needed to be given more "signposting" to follow a narrative analysis than did historians. My sense of social history deepened in subsequent years as I taught a graduate seminar on history and anthropology with a congenial colleague, a historian of East Africa.

BORDER CROSSING: EXPLORATIONS IN ANTHROPOETRY

In the fall of 1996 I suffered a life-threatening illness. In the process of recovery I found poems coming to me, both in English and in Spanish, and I began to write them down. A few months after the illness, my partner, Mary Pratt, noticed that a group of local poets were going to read at a church near our home. I went to the reading and learned that their group met for open-mike readings on the first Friday evening of every month. I began to read at the group meetings and sought out a tutor for writing poetry and eventually participated in a monthly workshop of eight group members. I now am on the group's steering committee and have on occasion helped coedit their photocopied poetry magazine.

Not unlike my border-crossing excursion into social history, I found myself learning through mistakes, bumps, and surprises. Although I had criticized the ethnographic practice of concluding a case study with what I called "detachable conclusions" because they invite the reader not to peruse the case itself, I found my early poems criticized on virtually the same grounds. Poems, I was told, should not end with a statement saying what the poem said. If the reader did not understand the poem itself, it was too late. In poetry one must not follow the journalist's motto, "Tell 'em what you're gonna tell 'em, tell 'em, then tell 'em what you've told 'em." On the other hand, I found the principle of showing rather than telling (of finding concrete particulars through which to express one's perceptions and feelings) challenging and full of insight for a person committed to using the examples of ethnography as not only the object of thought but also the material through which one thinks new thoughts.

The context of publication for writing poetry has proven challenging. I learned that most poets speak of publishing in magazines, not journals. The acceptance rate of these magazines is mind-boggling for an anthropologist who believes that an acceptance rate of one article out of four submitted is too low. To take a pair of the most extreme instances, the magazine *Poetry* accepts 300 of the 80,000 unsolicited poems it receives in a year; *The American Poetry Review* publishes 60 of the 14,000 unsolicited poems it receives in a year. Most other poetry magazines accept 1–5 percent of the poems that they receive. Clearly the meaning of publication for poets is quite different from what it is in most academic fields. Popular venues where local poets make their work known are the open-mike reading with the occasional opportunity to be a featured reader. They also participate in workshops given by poets of local or national reputation, and they even speak of this process of rewriting as "workshopping" a poem.

Participation in the local poetry community has transformed my sense of the issues raised in doing ethnography by introducing me to discussions I would not otherwise have known. A recent issue of *Poets and Writers*, for example, is devoted to the truth claims of creative nonfiction. The term *creative nonfiction* could apply, I would have thought, to ethnographic writing, particularly to much ethnography of the past decade. As it happens, creative nonfiction workshops have begun to proliferate, but the term seems to focus on such forms as memoirs and travel writing, not ethnography. The conventions that govern truth claims in creative nonfiction are unsettled and now in question; similar issues have erupted in cultural anthropology as evidenced by the controversy surrounding the truth-claims of Rigoberta Menchu's *"testimonio."*

In certain cases, the conventions of making truth claims in creative nonfiction are precisely the opposite of those in ethnography, although in neither creative nonfiction nor ethnography are such notions well codified. One writer on creative nonfiction categorically said that composite characters—those constructed as an amalgam of two or more actually existing people—were not allowed in creative nonfiction.[9] To construct a composite character would be to distort the truth. Yet without regarding it as a distortion, ethnographers have long created composite characters, sometimes explicitly and sometimes not so, particularly in analyses of the life cycle or the developmental cycle of domestic groups. At the same time a writer of creative nonfiction, Kat Meads, says that one can alter the sequence of events as long as each event actually happened.[10] To my ears, attuned as they are to the conventions of writing ethnographic history, tampering with sequence distorts vastly more than the creation of a composite character. When sequence is changed a reader is likely to make mistaken inferences about what led to what or what caused what (the *post-hoc-ergo-propter-hoc* fallacy).

My categories were most shaken by an essay in the same issue of *Poets and Writers* in which a professor teaching at a prominent school of journalism explains why she wrote a novel rather than a true story about a Dominican-American teenage mother. She says that books of interviews she surveyed told about why teenage mothers became pregnant, but they said nothing about "feeling loneliness, despair, rage, or even irritation with her baby, let alone neglecting or abusing the child."[11] Her novel enabled her to address the matters that the books of interviews remained silent about. Anthropologists were the fall guys in her account; they could not fathom that she had written a work of fiction and insisted, even when told otherwise, that she was "exploiting" her protagonist, her "informant." One of the key lessons, for me, of such disciplinary boundary crossing (into social history and local poetry) has been the experience of being shaken to rethink certain unquestioned assumptions in my home field of cultural anthropology.

THE READING GROUP: A PARADIGM OF INTERDISCIPLINARITY

Arguably, the best example of interdisciplinarity is the reading group, a voluntary association brought together on an occasional basis with a relatively informal, open-ended project. Usually, the members of such groups participate on their own time without any institutional compensation. They participate because they want to be there, not because it is part of their job description. Such groups do not have the burdens of institutional reproduction, such as hiring and promotions, graduate student admissions, and hiring and promoting staff members. There is no store to mind. On the other hand, these groups are ephemeral and have difficulty maintaining continuity through time; they face problems comparable to those embodied in the nearly paradoxical Weberian notion of the routinization of charisma. They are usually made up of faculty members from more than one department. Indeed, the reading group is in part defined by what it is not. It is not a department. Interdisciplinarity in this sense is less a union among disciplines than a space at the interstices between departments. Its relations are relatively egalitarian as contrasted with the hierarchical structures of departments.

In the late 1970s, a group of Stanford faculty from the law school, literary studies, cultural anthropology, and history came together to form a reading group called the Interpretation Seminar. We began by reading Michel Foucault. Most of us had read Foucault but had had little opportunity to discuss his work because his books were too long to assign in classes. When Foucault visited our campus we found him to be a remarkable interlocutor.

Most of us in the reading group were excited to talk with colleagues about books and ideas rather than about shop. The Interpretation Seminar continued for over a decade, longer than most voluntary associations where members are working overtime without compensation. Signs of the imminent demise of the group appeared. In part, the group was killed by its own success; it became known as the happening place in the human sciences. Over the years initial annual attendance soared from about fifteen to over fifty. Discussions became more like a performance arena than the dialogue among peers they once had been. Other signs of trouble appeared. An ethnographic film about a southern white snake-handling cult provoked a split in the group between those who felt challenged to comprehend and those who felt disgusted by activities they regarded as beyond the pale of proper human behavior. It appeared that, as one group member put it, "the tyranny of the enlightenment" was about to split the group. Shortly thereafter Ursula LeGuin's *The Word for World Is Forest* provoked a similar division from those who discussed an allegory for the Vietnam War and imperialism versus those who decided this was not a rich and complex text (that is, not a great book) and therefore not worth talking about. These were early warnings of what at Stanford would become the Western Culture debate and what elsewhere came to be called the Culture Wars.

Certain members of the Interpretation Seminar split off and formed a separate group, the Cultural Studies Seminar. They kept their numbers small in order to enhance dialogue, even if it meant being at odds with their democratic impulses to have an open group. They subscribed to the principles of community, dialogue, and like-mindedness. They tended to be age-graded, with a critical mass of younger scholars. The Cultural Studies Seminar emphasized diversity of race and gender both in its membership and in its intellectual agenda. In time the group went into decline not because of increasing size or because of intellectual lines of disagreement but rather because administrative duties began to consume much of the participants' time.

A number of members of the Cultural Studies Seminar gravitated toward an outstanding interdisciplinary program called Modern Thought and Literature, whose characteristics echo those of the Reading Group as a Social Form. All the faculty on the Committee-in-Charge volunteer their time. Indeed, a staff person commented that it is a happy place to work because the faculty get along so well precisely because they are volunteers. This program has no capacity to appoint faculty and therefore relies on faculty appointed in departments; it is a Ph.D. program, not an undergraduate major, and its primary administrative burden is the admission of graduate students. There is a relaxed sense of hierarchy compared with regular departments.

The program of graduate study begins with a core course that is required of all the Ph.D. students in their first year of graduate work. Students also take nine advanced courses in literary studies of the modern era as well as eight courses outside of literature departments in a coherent interdisciplinary program. The interdisciplianry component can either come from a minor in an existing department (such as anthropology, art, communications, history, philosophy, political science, religious studies, or sociology) or from an inter-departmental concentration (such as ethnic studies, feminist and gender studies, popular culture, and science and technology studies). The advisor's role is critical in devising a coherent set of courses. Thus the program combines literary and cultural studies either by bringing together the methods of existing disciplines or by working at the boundaries of existing disciplines.

SUMMARY

Although this paper does not begin there, I began thinking about interdisciplinarity by considering the case of an individual moving between two disciplines. The two cases of studied interdisciplinarity I have presented—cultural anthropology and social history; cultural anthropology and local poetry—depict border-crossings that contain elements of "going native" or virtually becoming a member of another discipline. I suggested that such processes often lead to changes within disciplines as a number of seemingly secure assumptions become unsettled and as certain conventions of writing and understanding are called into question. In part it is these excursions that make interdisciplinarity a dissident form of knowledge that is critical of business as usual within departmental confines.

I have argued that interdisciplinarity as a cultural conception, refers to more and to less than the collaboration of a group of people from different departments. Interdisciplinarity has a distinctive mode of sociality, the seminar as a meaningful conversation. Other forms of interdisciplinary collabration to the best of my knowledge are not referred to, either by participants or by outsiders, as interdisciplinarity. They bring together people with different skills and expertise in the sevice of a larger project in which the model of sociality is the division of labor. In such contexts I have heard people speak of being interdisciplinary, but not of interdisciplinarity.

Even if my knowledge of the term *interdisciplinarity* proves to be parochial, it nonetheless reveals a pervasive divide between the seminar and the division of labor as modes of sociality that are at play in interdisciplinary forms of collaboration. I have argued that the seminar roughly corresponds with the notion of "thought as product," whereas the division of labor has affinities with the notion of "thought as process." Neither form of collaboration presupposes that an individual has a mastery of multiple disciplines. The seminar derives from certain shared assumptions and elements of a common language that allow for meaningful conversation; the division of labor builds on the assumption that people need one another precisely because they differ so deeply in their skills and knowledge. It is like a form of collaboration between people who speak different languages and therefore need one another to carry out their project in a multilingual world.

If I could do further autoethnographic research, I would further explore the problem of the institutionalization of interdisciplinarity. At one extreme I have heard the term *interdisciplinarity* applied to programs (often cultural studies) within single departments of literary studies (usually English).[12] I am puzzled by such usage, and it bears investigation for deepening the understanding of the term *interdisciplinarity* as a cultural conception. At another extreme I am relatively unfamiliar with the departmentalization of interdisciplinarity under a variety of names that differ from those of the established disciplines. As I have posed the issue with the reading group as the paradigmatic instance of interdisciplinarity, the departmentalization of interdisciplinarity would seem a contradiction in terms. The crux of the matter is the dilemma of ensuring continuity through time (including the ability, for example, to make faculty appointments) without losing the capacity to work flexibly with changing intellectual projects that have failed to develop and flourish within departmental confines. The paradox is that the very informality of institutional support (including the absence of departmental status, annual meetings, and national organizations) for programs that support interdisciplinarity leaves them vulnerable to being dismantled in a way that departments are not.

Interdisciplinarity will, I think, be a persistent presence in universities. Faculty and students will find like-minded colleagues as often outside as within their departments. Conferences and journals will gravitate around emergent fields because innovative and productive intellectual agendas often emerge in the spaces between established disciplines and their relatively codified ways of doing things. The enduring tension will be between the desire for institutional supports of continuity into the future and the effort to maintain a more spontaneous capacity to work at the edges of thought.

At the same time, one should keep in mind that most forms of interdisciplinarity are not on the path to becoming departments, nor should they be regarded as having failed if they do not. The work of conversations across departments is to invent and develop distinctive projects that will not thrive in more established institutional settings. This task, as I see it, is by its very nature unending and constantly changing.

NOTES

1. On this concept, see Mary Louise Pratt, *Imperial Eyes: Travel Writing and Transculturation* (New York: Routledge, 1992).

2. This can be found in his *Culture and Behavior*, ed. Richard Kluckhohn (New York: The Free Press of Glencoe, 1962) pp. 286–300.

3. See Mary Louise Pratt, "Humanities for the Future: Reflections on the Western Culture Debate at Stanford," in *The Politics of Liberal Education*, ed. Darryl J. Gless and Barbara Herrnstein Smith (Durham, N.C.: Duke University Press, 1992) pp. 13–

31; and Renato Rosaldo, *Culture and Truth: The Remaking of Social Analysis* (Boston: Beacon Press, 1989).

4. This essay can also be found in Kluckholn's *Culture and Behavior*, pp. 265–85.

5. Clifford Geertz, "The Uses of Diversity," in *Available Light: Anthropological Reflections on Philosophical Topics* (Princeton: Princeton University Press, 200) pp. 68–88.

6. Clifford Geertz, "The Way We Think Now: Toward an Ethnography of Modern Thought," in *Local Knowledge: Further Essays in Interpretive Anthropology* (New York: Basic Books, 1983) pp. 147–63.

7. See here my *Ilongot Headhunting, 1883–1974: A Study in Society and History* (Stanford: Stanford University Press, 1980).

8. Garrett Mattingly, *Catherine of Aragon* (New York: Vintage, 1941); and *The Armada* (Boston: Houghton Mifflin, 1959).

9. Sarah Heekin Redfield, "Surveying the Boundaries: An Inquiry into Creative Nonfiction," *Poets and Writers* 27:5 (1999): 36–41.

10. Cited in Redfield, "Surveying the Boundaries," p. 40.

11. Helen Benedict, "Fiction vs. Nonfiction: Wherein Lies the Truth?" *Poets and Writers* 27:5 (1999): 46–49.

12. See my "Whose Cultural Studies?" *American Anthropologist* 96:3 (1994): 524–29.

PART TWO

The State of the Art: New Methods and New Questions

CHAPTER 6

After History?

Joan W. Scott

HISTORY IS in the paradoxical position of creating the objects it claims only to discover. By creating, I do not mean making things up, but rather constructing them as legitimate and coherent objects of knowledge. Construction is a complex process that takes place according to standards of coherence and intelligibility that are widely diffused and usually unarticulated (they function as a kind of disciplinary "common sense") except in moments of crisis. In these moments—when intense conflict breaks consensus, when change threatens or is accomplished, when public scrutiny intensifies—historians feel called upon to justify their standards, not always an easy task.

The paradoxical position of history has long been acknowledged by historians, even when they write history as if it existed "as it was" in the form they recount it. Leaving aside the abundant observations of philosophers of history (who, because of their penchant for systematic thinking and abstraction, were placed outside the domain of the discipline at its inception in the late nineteenth century), there is no absence of commentary by historians themselves about this aspect of their craft. In 1954 the *Harvard Guide to American History* warned against a simple belief in objectivity this way: "If a time machine were available to carry the historian back through the past at will, he would confront, on stepping off the machine, the very problems of interpretation he thought he left behind."[1] Earlier, Crane Brinton rejected the "metaphysical overtones" of the belief in "a reality that lay altogether outside . . . thinking." "We can now admit," he wrote in 1939, "that the past . . . is forever lost to us; that the historian must relate his facts to a pattern, a conceptual scheme of which he can require only that it prove useful."[2] More recently, Neil Harris, reflecting on the Enola Gay controversy at the Smithsonian Institution, dismissed the idea that a once value-free history had been only recently corrupted. "It was all interpretive," he said—by which we might say he meant "always already" interpretive.[3] The futility of separating fact from interpretation was captured by the wry definition that Merle Curti offered to his graduate seminars at the University of Wisconsin in the 1960's. You knew it was a fact, he told them, when there were identical accounts from two independent witnesses not self-deceived.

In a recent paper, historian of science Peter Galison has tracked the changing definition of the concept of objectivity among scientists, and his work reminds us that the terms I have been using—history, reality, interpretation, objectivity—must themselves be historicized. (Galison shows that objectivity in the early nineteenth century dealt not with human perception, but with the mechanical transmission of images. Later, when objectivity referred to the activity of scientists, it included, first, qualities of morality and, then, the training of judgment.)[4] I think Galison's project is one we could undertake in relation to history; rather than treating the "objectivity question" as a static question whose meaning was fixed once it was posed, it would be interesting to analyze the changing meanings historians have attributed to terms such as objectivity. That, however, is not my purpose here.

Instead, I want to remind us of the fact that there is a paradox at the heart of the historian's practice: the reality to which the historian's interpretation refers is produced by that interpretation, yet the legitimacy of the interpretation is said to rest on its faithfulness to a reality that lies outside, or exists prior to, interpretation. History functions through an inextricable connection between reality and interpretation that is nonetheless denied by positing reality and interpretation as separate and separable entities. The historian's inevitable dilemma consists in the need simultaneously to avow interpretation and to disavow the productive role interpretation plays in the construction of knowledge. This dilemma is not a new discovery, neither the product of the ravings of radical relativists nor the by-product of some nihilistic "deconstructionism"; it inheres in the practice of history itself.

To say that historical reality is produced by the interpretive practice called history is not to deny the seriousness or the usefulness of the enterprise. It just calls analytic attention to the interpretive operations of the discipline, to the various ways it achieves its authority. I find Roland Barthes' structuralist dissection of some of these operations extremely useful; it is unsurpassed in its clarity and constructiveness and so provides me with a framework for thinking about our contemporary debates on these issues. Barthes points out that historical discourse claims merely to report what, in fact, it constructs and it does this in a number of ways. It suppresses the subjective or emotive presence of the historian, substituting for him (or her) an "objective" person; then, since there is no "sign referring to the sender of the historical message, history seems to *tell itself.*"[5] This Barthes calls the "referential illusion" because it establishes the (false) impression that what is being referred to exists entirely apart from the story being told about it: "[F]act never has any but a linguistic existence (as the term of discourse), yet everything happens as if this linguistic existence were merely a pure and simple 'copy' of *another* existence, situated in an extra-structural field, the 'real'" (138). Not only must the voice of the historian be rendered neutral or silent to achieve this effect, his writing also employs a "two-term semantic schema" that equates referent and signified. In this way the troubling intervention of language (the presence of the signified) in the representation of the real is denied. The signifier is taken as a faithful reflection of the referent; signified and referent thus become one: "[I]n 'objective' history, the 'real' is never anything but an unformulated signified, sheltered behind the apparent omnipotence of the referent. This situation defines what we might call the *reality effect*" (139).

Barthes' use of the terms *referential illusion* and *reality effect* have often been taken as debunking measures, aimed at undermining history's authority to tell us what happened in the past. But this negative impact would be so only if we took the naive philosophical position that external reality has the power to imprint itself directly on the human mind. If we do not believe that that is the case, then we cannot avoid the questions Barthes poses about representation and signification. By problematizing the ways in which signification shapes the past, we can critically examine the knowledge we are being given and the knowledge we ourselves produce.

But there is more to it than that. Barthes' analysis of historical discourse has the virtue, for me at least, of describing not only how historical knowledge is produced and how it achieves its authority, but also why reinterpretation and revision are such troubling, vital, and contested issues. What is at stake is "reality itself":

> The extrusion of the signified outside the 'objective' discourse, letting the "real" and its expression apparently confront each other, does not fail to produce a new meaning, so true is it, once more, that within a system any absence of an element is itself a signification. This new meaning—extensive to all historical discourse and ultimately defining its pertinence—is reality, itself . . . (139)

One of the assets of this process is its openness to change: The pursuit of an ever-elusive "real" leads to new objects of knowledge and new interpretations that reorganize reality. The reorganization alters not only our understanding of the past, but also our sense of possibility for the future. (This is surely the import of the Adage Every generation writes its own history.) If the opening to the future is an asset, it is also a liability because it exposes the instability of reality, its dependence, finally, on the discourse that signifies it. Even when change comes in "scientific" form with the discovery of new evidence or with the introduction of new documentation to support a new interpretation, the fact that historical knowledge can be revised is unsettling. How much evidence is required to challenge a prevailing understanding of the past? What is the test of validity that will prove the superiority of the new story? There are no ready answers to these questions. What then is the appeal against false revisionism and misinterpretation? The answers given by some historians—those I cited at the beginning of this essay—are not definitive; they recognize the complexity involved in establishing facts; they live with plausibility instead of truth; they make judgments according to changing disciplinary standards of procedure and coherence.

But complexity of this kind is not easy to live with at moments of heated political debate about the past and the future. At those moments—and we are in one of them now—the quest for truth becomes a way to banish the paradox at the heart of historical knowledge. In response to the paradox that cannot be resolved ("This discourse is doubtless the only one in which the referent is addressed as external to the discourse though without its ever being possible to reach it outside this discourse" [138]), some historians have sought ways to install truth—in its many guises as objectivity, reality, experience, authenticity, human nature, or transcendent morality—as the guarantor of the knowledge they in fact produce. This effort not only does violence to historical practice by repressing the interpretation that makes sense of the past and links it to a future we might have a hand in making, it also substitutes dogma for open-ended inquiry. When the "reality effect" is either dispensed with entirely or offered as incontestable truth, we have reached the end of history.

THE END OF HISTORY?

In 1989, Francis Fukuyama published an article in *The National Interest* whose title asked whether the triumph of the principles of liberal democracy and free-market capitalism (most recently in the former Soviet Union and Eastern Europe) meant "the end of history." By 1992, he had expanded the article into a book whose title no longer posed a question, but stated a fact. It was called *The End of History and the Last Man*.[6] In the language of Christian evangelicalism, Fukuyama announced the "good news" that liberal democracy was the "end point of mankind's ideological evolution" and "the final form of human government" (xi); technological progress had also guaranteed the "increasing homogenization of all societies" (xiv). Mankind was now at the gates of the "Promised Land," and so History, "understood as a single, coherent, evolutionary process," was at an end (xii).

Of course, Fukuyama conceded, events large and small would continue to occur, and not every country would achieve "stable liberal democracy," while "others might lapse back into other, more primitive forms of rule like theocracy or military dictatorship." Nonetheless, "the *ideal* of liberal democracy could not be improved on" (xi); the future was now. His vision of history, rooted in Hegelian idealism, looked not to empirical evidence for validation, but to "a permanent, trans-historical standard": "man as man." Man's truth had been read in nature by a variety of philosophers. It included a desire for "recognition" as better than others, a need to strive and struggle purposively, and a need for spiritual comfort in some form of community. Excesses of equality and tolerance undermined this nature, creating the complacent, soft bourgeois citizen Nietzsche called "the last man." Fukuyama's point is that the end of history need not produce "the last man." Liberal democracy, market capitalism, social hierarchy, inequality and injustice, family and religion are the conditions that permit "the first man"—natural man—to thrive.

If that sounds like a description of the status quo, it is. But Fukuyama relieves himself from the charge of special pleading by invoking a higher truth. History as it is normally practiced cannot make his case, for it is always fraught with uncertainty: " 'History' is not a given, nor merely a catalogue of everything that happened in the past, but a deliberate effort of abstraction in which we separate out important from unimportant events" (138). The relativism this might imply must be avoided, he warns, because the "historicist approach" cannot protect us from illusion, cannot guarantee that our assessments are right. Instead, we need a transhistorical measure, a "Universal History" as a guarantee of intelligibility. Christian history is an example of what Fukuyama has in mind:

> The first truly Universal Histories in the Western tradition were Christian. . . . Christianity, moreover, introduced the concept of a history that was finite in time, beginning with God's creation of man and ending with his final salvation. . . . As the Christian account of history makes clear, an "end of history" is implicit in the writing of all Universal Histories. The particular events of history can become meaningful only with respect to some larger end or goal, the achievement of which necessarily brings the historical process to a close. This final end of man is what makes all particular events potentially intelligible. (56)

Armed with some form of indisputable knowledge, "the Universal Historian must be ready to discard entire peoples and times as essentially pre- or nonhistorical, because they do not bear on the central 'plot' of his or her story" (139). When the plot has been foretold, it is the only reality; events, facts, contingent actions, anecdotes need not be given the status of referents whose prior existence grounds the plot. There is no "referential illusion" necessary here. Rather, allusions to events and facts are recognized as signifiers, the demonstration or illustration of Divine or Universal truth:

> Without an underlying concept of human nature that posited a hierarchy of essential and non-essential human characteristics, it would he impossible to know whether an apparent social peace represented true satisfaction of human longings, rather than the work of a particularly efficient police apparatus, or merely the calm before a revolutionary storm. (137)

The "underlying concept of human nature" provides enormous comfort and certainty. It is immune from both empirical and ethical challenge. That is because empirical matters only become significant within a preordained scheme (objective reality is nothing but the realization of the concept) and that scheme rests on its own morally absolute foundations:[7]

> We do not want to he sidetracked by objections . . . for example, by pointing to this or that social group or individual which is demonstrably dissatisfied by being denied equal access to the good things of society due to poverty, racism, and so forth. The deeper question is one of first principles—that is, whether the "good things" of our society are truly good and satisfying to "man as man." (*EHLM*, 139)

When truth is the standard, historians are relieved of the dilemma of evaluating competing interpretations, or of justifying their principles of selection. In fact, their practice becomes irrelevant: "Neither the diplomatic historian nor the social historian can evade the choice between important and unimportant, and hence reference to a standard that exists somewhere 'outside' of history (and, incidentally, outside of the sphere of competence of professional historians *qua* historians)" (*EHLM*, 139). That last parenthetical comment ("and, incidentally . . .") suggests an additional meaning for the "end of history"—with the hour of our salvation at hand, there is no role for professional historians. Universal standards are outside of history; historians are not trained to see them. Universal truth comes from elsewhere, the higher place of religion or philosophy. The work of historians then becomes a kind of biblical exegesis, discerning signs of the present in the past. No longer do they write with an eye to the future; instead (in the words of one critic of these developments), they furnish "the society of the victors with the encyclopedia of its prehistory."[8]

This approach places outside of consideration what Fukuyama refers to as "popular discontent in the real-world societies of, let us say, Britain or America" (*EHLM*, 138). The histories of the discontented would be a distraction since they signify nothing in relation to Universal History; they are referents without significance, that is, without signifying power. But they also pose a challenge Fukuyama feels he must address. He takes the example of feminism to make his point. Some contemporary feminists, he says, argue that matriarchy would be a more consensual and peaceful form of society than patriarchy. This cannot be proven by reference to the past, since there seem to have been no such societies, and "yet, the possibility of their future existence cannot be ruled out, if the feminist understanding of the possibilities for the liberation of the female side of the human personality proves to be correct. And if it is so, then we clearly have not reached the end of history" (137–38). Leaving aside the question of the accuracy of Fukuyama's representation of feminist arguments, it is important to ask how he or we would know they were any more "correct" than his arguments about "man as *man*." Fukuyama's answer is that his position is based on "first principles" and thus is "transhistorical" and universal; presumably, by contrast, feminism is secondary, transient, and particularistic. Feminist interpretation is at best uncertain, in contrast to the incontrovertability of (Fukuyama's) truth. Its uncertainty undermines both the plausibility of the feminist critique (and for that matter any form of "discontent") and the possibility of imagining a future (by definition different from the present). That history's role has been to furnish resources by which futures can be imagined—precisely through the plurality and confusion of its interpretations—is acknowledged by Fukuyama when he links discontent, the future, and history. If the future can be imagined and brought into being, he reminds us, "then we have not reached the end of history."

Fukuyama's proclamation of "the end of history" can be read as a conservative (if not reactionary) document. It disqualifies politics as a constructive force in the world, since the end of history is also the end of politics. (Here I think of the English historian Edward Freeman's comment, repeated tirelessly by the founders of the American Historical Association, that history was "past politics and politics present history.") Or at least the end of history reduces politics to a second order of activity aimed not at fundamental change but at working out the best way to cross the threshold to the Promised Land. Yet it is too easy to dismiss the book because it is a polemic by a conservative publicist passing as a public intellectual. I think Fukuyama's book has to be taken as symptomatic of a more general belief that has developed in late twentieth-century American society, one that—whether it is associated with the joyous anticipation of the arrival of the Redeemer or with a sense of deep despair—no longer looks to the possibility of a different and better future. If we take the "end of history" to mean a loss of futurity, then the book exemplifies one consequence of that loss: When time stops, truth can be declared.

WHO OWNS HISTORY?

The connection between truth and the cessation of time is evident in a whole series of recent conflicts that some have dubbed the "history wars." These conflicts pit matters of fact against interpretation, but not as concerns susceptible to differences of opinion or approach. Rather, taking history to be a finite legacy, these debates are about proprietary rights in the stories historians tell.

"Who Owns History?" asked the critics of the National History Standards as they denounced the "negativism" and "politically correct" multiculturalism that threatened to undermine "our" collective sense of national identity. Former NEH director Lynne Cheney charged that the standards had been "hijacked" by feminist and minority scholars with a "great hatred for traditional history."[9] The notion of a sacrosanct "traditional" history implied that "the Nation" was not Benedict Anderson's "imagined community," but an established being with clearly discernible attributes, attitudes, and behaviors.[10] To own this history meant both to possess it and to avow it, to acknowledge it as fact or truth.[11] "We are a better people than the National Standards indicate," Cheney declared, "and our children deserve to know it."[12]

The issue of ownership has come up repeatedly on all sides of the political spectrum. When veterans groups protested the Smithsonian Institution's plans to commemorate the dropping of the A-bomb on Hiroshima, they did so in the name of the rights of ownership their firsthand experience conferred. Against "revisionist" curators and historians who seemed to be casting doubt on "commonly accepted viewpoints,"[13] the veterans and their supporters in the Senate argued that only they knew "what really happened during that war" (1138). Senator Wendell H. Ford of Kentucky put it this way: "Let me tell you what bothers me right now. I have five great, wonderful grandchildren and before me is history, personal, real, you can put your hand on it. I think our responsibility is to be sure that this real reflection on what actually happened—and I underscore real and personal—is projected onto the future and not sanitized . . . (1139). The sense of history as palpable ("you can put your hand on it") came in part from the fact that the Smithsonian display was to feature the fuselage of the Enola Gay, the plane from which the bomb was dropped. This artifact was taken to be transparent; in its concrete embodiment of history it was as transparent as the facts of veterans' memories (they were referred to as "facts proven at the time of the decision"). Together, fact and artifact constituted the only acceptable evidence for a "fair and unbiased" history (1138). (This is a reversal of Fukuyama's "speculative historicism." Here we have operating "empiricist historicism" instead; concepts inhere in real objects and so are determined by them.)[14] Senator Ford's notion of "projecting history onto the future" meant something like the transmission of a fixed legacy or perhaps the entailment of a large estate. The point was to place this story outside of time, to preserve it against "erosion" and "interpretation" (sometimes equated with "something that a historian dreamed up") (*JAH*, 1100). The owners would determine the meanings and uses of their property forever. Patriotism required nothing less.

On the other side of the great political divide, there is no less concern with ownership as a way of preventing the appropriation and distortion of our histories, and therefore of our selves. On 16 January 1995, the *New York Times* reported on a dispute between the family of Martin Luther King and the National Park Service about the monument to be built in honor of the slain civil rights leader. The issue, according to King family spokesman Dexter King, was "who will interpret the people's history." Maintaining that the story of the civil rights movement was "too important, to be controlled by a Government agency," he insisted instead that its history and "the legacy of Dr. King shall forever remain in the care and custody of the King family." In the same article, a former civil rights activist described the creation of the Mississippi Community Foundation in reaction to the movie *Mississippi Burning*, which glorified the role of the FBI in the events of the 1960s. To prevent future distortions of their experience, activists had transferred the legal rights to their life stories to the foundation, stipulating that it had final say in the approval of anything written about them. "The issue is ownership and control of our history," said former CORE leader David Dennis. "If we don't tell the story or have some control over the telling, then it is no longer about us."[15]

In these examples, and the many others that have erupted over the past months (the most recent of which was about who had the right to depict the story of Irish Americans at an exhibition at the Museum of the City of New York), the ostensible issue has been the limits of interpretation. Historians have been accused of "revisionism" (no longer the neutral or even positive term it once was, now it evokes an association with those who would deny the Holocaust), of tampering with "commonly accepted viewpoints" (*JAH*, 1100), and of imposing esoteric academic speculation on popular audiences. During the Enola Gay hearings, Senator Dianne Feinstein of California went so far as to blame interpretation itself. When she was an undergraduate history major at Stanford, she recalled, history was "essentially a recitation of facts. . . . Now what you see is a writer's interpretation. . . . I wonder about the wisdom in presenting an interpretation" (*JAH*, 1141). I think it would be granting too much sophistication to Feinstein's comment to read it as a criticism not of interpretation per se, but of its visibility ("now what you *see* is a writer's interpretation"), and therefore as a call to contemporary historians to follow disciplinary rules of procedure and stick to the rhetoric of fact and reality. It may well be that historians have become more self-conscious, more willing to call attention to the interpretive moves in their work. But I do not think this self-consciousness has been the source of the current controversies. After all, debates about historians' interpretations have a long history, and not just among professional historians. It has been almost a commonplace that different histories served different political interests, not necessarily crudely, but implicitly. Indeed, a typical form of argument (and an exercise graduate students were often asked to undertake) involved exposing the investments historians and others had in the stories they told. The importance of factual evidence was, of course, not discarded in these debates; they involved complex negotiations between interpretation and fact. So questions about the status and validity of interpretation are not new; it may be that their very familiarity moves us—too quickly—to understand recent debates in those terms. The new twist I find remarkable is the way in which ownership is invoked as the authority for truth claims, as if possession were the ultimate antidote to the ceaseless revisiting of the past that we associate with interpretation.

And perhaps it is. Perhaps it is the sense that we have reached the "end of history" that provokes the desire to claim final knowledge of our collective and individual selves. This certainly is the implication political theorist Wendy Brown draws from her analysis of identity politics in the United States. Brown sets her topic in a broad field: "I consider politicized identity as both a production *and* contestation of the political terms of liberalism, disciplinary-bureaucratic regimes, certain forces of global capitalism, and the demographic flows of postcoloniality that together might be taken as constitutive of the contemporary North American political condition."[16] She continues, "It is shaped as well by the contemporary problematic of history itself, by the late modern rupture of history as a narrative, history as ended because it has lost its end—a rupture that paradoxically gives history an immeasurable weight" (71). The effect that this rupture has is contradictory:

> We know ourselves to be saturated by history, we feel the extraordinary force of its determinations; we are also steeped in a discourse of its insignificance, and, above all, we know that history will no longer (always already did not) act as our redeemer. (54)

In this large, general context, the desire for ownership of one's past becomes a way of asserting agency. But it is an agency that consolidates the present in terms of the past, an agency that has no future. History offers redemption only to the extent that it fixes identity. When politics are contested in terms of enduring identities rather than historically variable statuses or positions, when the goal is to redress the pain of exclusion rather than to reform the structures of power that produce exclusion, then we have lost our sense of time and therefore of the possibility of difference and change. "Time," writes Michel de Certeau, "is precisely the impossibility of an identity fixed by a place."[17] Being able to grab a piece of the past as our own enables us to hold a meaningful space in the present; there is no future to imagine or behold. History then becomes the expression and the guarantee of identity; to revise or reinterpret it is to threaten the very being (the authenticity, the truth, the essence, the reality) of a national or racial or ethnic or sexual or individual self.

Is There History after the "End of History"?

Much has been written lately about history after the "linguistic turn"—can it exist without foundations? Are the referents really real? In these debates, historians have spent a good deal of time fruitlessly trying to sever the inseparable connection between reality and interpretation by defending truth, facticity, and objectivity, or seeking to specify limits to interpretation. The far more troubling question—about the practice of history after the "end of history"—has been given decidedly less play. Perhaps that is because there has been no shortage of demand for the services of historians as providers of birth certificates and titles of ownership for politicized identities. Perhaps that is because the heightened public interest in history (theme parks, specialized magazines, museums, local societies, a television cable channel, and even the debates about interpretation and ownership) has been misread as a confirmation of the vitality of a history that still looks to the future. Perhaps it is simply because we have taken every invocation of "history" to mean the same thing.

What would it mean to think about our practice in the face of the declared "end of history"? How might we rescue time (and so some sense of futurity) without reintroducing teleology? How can we argue for the validity of one account over another? How can we work with the "referential illusion" without repressing interpretation in the name of truth? There have been answers offered to these questions, but because they make interpretation (the production of knowledge and its categories) the object of historical inquiry, they have often been rejected as themselves causing the end of history. I want to argue a contrary proposition: It is precisely by reconceptualizing the object of historical inquiry that we can maintain (in the current discursive context) the connection between history and time.

There are at least three aspects to such a reconceptualization. The first takes *discontinuity*, not continuity or linear development, to be the operative principle of history. The second is concerned not with lineages for difference, but with *processes of diffierentiation*. And the third *historicizes interpretation*, understanding it not as a shameful distortion of objectivity, but as the very source of knowledge itself.

Discontinuity

If teleology implies an "end of history," discontinuity keeps it forever open. The present is understood to have resulted from its break with the past (however many elements or traces of the past are sedimented into contemporary actions and behaviors). Historical investigation locates the breaks, describes them as the deviations they are from established norms, and attempts to account for their emergence—not in terms of general principles of development, but in terms of the specificity of their occurrence. This is what Foucault called "effective history":

> "Effective" history . . . deals with events in terms of their most unique characteristics, their most acute manifestations. An event, consequently, is not a decision, a treaty, a reign, or a battle, hut the reversal of a relationship of forces, the usurpation of power, the appropriation of a vocabulary turned against those who had once used it, a feeble domination that poisons itself as it grows lax, the entry of a masked "other." The forces operating in history are not controlled by destiny or regulative mechanisms, but respond to haphazard conflicts. They do not manifest the successive forms of a primordial intention and their attraction is not that of a conclusion, for they always appear through the singular randomness of events.[18] (154–55)

For Foucault, "randomness" is a replacement for determination; it introduces contingency into history: "We want historians to confirm our belief that the present rests upon profound intentions and immutable necessities. But the true historical sense confirms our existence among countless lost events, without a landmark or a point of reference" (155). The absence of inherent meanings does not plunge us into an abyss; rather, it makes the production of meaning a human, albeit historically variable and contested, activity. If there is nothing inevitable about the direction of change, it nonetheless happens and it does so because of human intervention, understood not as an assertion of autonomous will, but as a discursively situated challenge to prevailing rules and as a disruption of existing hierarchies. If there are no inherent landmarks or points of reference, this has not prevented humans from establishing them. Indeed the "lesson of history" is that human agency consists in imposing sense, differently and mutably, upon our worlds.

Discontinuity posits fundamental ruptures and, therefore, profound differences between present and past. These are not differences that function (as do any relations of contrast) simply to establish the present as a distinctive time. They are more decisive, more disruptive differences. There is no continuous transmission imagined from the past to the present—whether of identity, ancestors, or humanness: "'Effective' history differs from traditional history in being without constants. Nothing in man—not even his body—is sufficiently stable to serve as the basis for self-recognition or for understanding other men" (153). Foucault's histories showed that differences in the knowledges of madness, illness, sexuality, and illegality made for differences in the phenomena themselves, as they were perceived by observers and subjectively experienced. The madmen and delinquents of the past had nothing (but a name, perhaps) in common with those of the present. By depriving us of the comfort of self-recognition, "effective" history not only establishes the difference of the past, its remove in time, it also severs its connection—as direct antecedent or precedent—to the present. That which we take most for granted loses its universal or transcendent dimension. It depends only on current time. In this way, the present is historicized.

This historicizing of the present opens the way for a future. Not one that is foreordained or whose dimensions are predictable, but one that will exceed—in undetermined and contingent ways—the limits of the present. The difference of the past challenges the certainty of the present (its understanding of itself as the culmination of evolution, for example) and so introduces the possibility of change. If neither sentiments, nor instincts, nor bodies have always been as we believe them to be now, then Fukuyama's claim to know "man as man" cannot be sustained as a universal insight. It must be read instead as a political gesture taking place at a particular time. "Effective" history's insistence on the temporality of our conceptual categories denies the totalizing power of any system of thought, any regime of truth. The result does not guarantee progress; but it does support belief in futurity.

Certeau ties such a belief to history's ethical project, a project in which time establishes the difference not only between past and present, present and future, but also between "what is and what ought to be":

My analysis of historiography (that is, of history writing or historical practice) must be situated in the context of a question too broad to be treated fully here, namely the antimony between ethics and what, for lack of a better word, I will call dogmatism. Ethics is articulated through effective operations, and it defines a distance between what is and what ought to be. This distance designates a space where we have something to do. On the other hand, dogmatism is authorized by a reality that it claims to represent, and in the name of this reality, it imposes law. Historiography functions midway between these two poles: but whenever it attempts to break away from ethics, it returns toward dogmatism. ("HSF," 199)

To get from "what is to what ought to be" does not require that we equate history with inevitable progress, but that we understand that limits and rules (in all conceptual spheres: political, economic, aesthetic, religious, sexual, etc.) have always been, and still are, susceptible to change. From this perspective, "discontent" is not (as Fukuyama wanted to treat it) a distraction; it is, as he also recognized, a sign that motion in space (time) is still possible, that, in other words, history has not come to an end.

Processes of Differentiation

In contrast to histories that establish the roots of politicized identities in their distinctive cultures and experiences and so essentialize those identities, I am suggesting we produce histories that focus on the production of identity as a process both of homogenization and differentiation.

Although such a focus most obviously applies to marginalized groups, it also pertains to the study of dominant identities, including national identities. To assume that Americanness or Frenchness consists only in an enduring set of traits or beliefs established (say) in 1776 or 1789 is to accept the ideological terms of national identity rather than to write the history of the repeated and changing ways in which the imagined community was consolidated. With the first approach, historians collude in a nationalist project by abstracting the Nation from the processes that continually produce and reproduce it; with the second approach, they demystify national identity and expose the various differences it has been used to balance and contain.

In the case of so-called marginal groups, history has been used to mobilize protest, but it has often had an effect analogous to celebrational national histories; it makes identity static and invests it in the past. In these histories of marginal groups, the pain of the present is shown to be long-standing, hence that much more intense, that much more immoral. Their demands become more legitimate in the light of their long history. At the same time, past and present are conflated and identity is reified as a universal, ahistorical story of exclusion and suffering. When identity becomes synonymous with exclusion and suffering, inclusion and the end of suffering portend the end of identity. From this perspective, the future is unimaginable. Brown describes the operations of contemporary identity politics this way:

> In its emergence as a protest against marginalization or subordination, politicized identity thus becomes attached to its own exclusion. . . . [I]t installs its pain over its unredeemed history in the very foundation of its political claim, in its demand for recognition as identity . . . Politicized identity . . . enunciates itself, makes claims for itself, only by entrenching, restating, dramatizing, and inscribing its pain in politics; it can hold out no future—for itself or others—that triumphs over this pain. The loss of historical direction, and with it the loss of futurity characteristic of the late modern age, is thus homologically refigured in the structure of desire of the dominant political expression of the age: identity politics. (*SI*, 73–74)

To the extent that histories of different groups both produce and reflect contemporary identity politics, they contribute to what Brown calls a politics of resentment (in which the expression of victims' anger substitutes for strategic interventions aimed at structural reform) and also to the "end of history." Of course, these histories, importantly, give enormous visibility to the diversity and difference we associate with multiculturalism. But they also naturalize differences, making them appear to have always existed in the way they do now, depriving them as well of their specific political significance. Jacques Rancière offers an alternative to this naturalizing of difference by calling for histories that attend to the enunciation of social subjects, to the specificity of their political expression:

> The identity of social combatant is . . . not the expression of the "culture" of some group or subgroup. It is the invention of a name for the picking up of several speech-acts that affirm or challenge a symbolic configuration of relations between the order of discourse and the order of states of affairs. (*NOH*, 97)

Rancière suggests that the alternative to the universalization of difference (in the culture of a group or subgroup) is the historicization of identity. If instead of asking how women were treated in some former time, we ask how and in what circumstances the difference of their sex came to matter in their treatment, then we have provided the basis for an analysis of "women" that is not a rediscovery of ourselves in the past.[19] The examples can be multiplied. If we ask not how African-Americans—as a universal category—were treated under slavery, but how and under what circumstances race came to justify forced labor, we understand the oppression of slaves but have to ask different questions about how racism constructs black identity today. Or if we document not the long history of homophobia, but the ways and times and terms in which certain sexual practices were pathologized and others normalized, we histori-cize rather than naturalize both homosexuality and heterosexuality. Or, to take up the question of national identity again, if we ask not what it means to be an American, but how Americanness has been defined—and by whom—over time, we can write the history of the United States not as the realization of an essence, but as the story of ongoing political contestation around terms and practices that are at once durable and changeable.

This kind of history requires a certain disidentification with the objects of our inquiry, a deliberate effort to separate ourselves from others who seem to be like us. The relationship between identity and identification changes. Mak-ing identity a contingent, historical event, not a fixed property, creates analytic distance not only between ourselves and our objects, but also on our own sense of self—"History becomes 'effective' to the degree that it introduces discontinuity into our very being. . . . It will uproot its traditional foundations and relentlessly disrupt its pretended continuity" ("NGH," 154). Identity, in other words, is not a fixed set of attributes into which one is born; rather, it has multiple and contradictory aspects that are contextually articulated and that change. And this reconceptualization of identity problematizes the question of identification by complicating the terms of (self-)recognition. If "women" have not always been the same, what aspects of myself can I find in "women" of the past?

The analysis of processes of differentiation is not a matter of applying a predetermined grid to events of the past—not a matter of assuming that the differences (national, ethnic, racial, religious, class, sexual, etc.) that order our social relationships always have been or will be the same. For this reason, it is necessary to historicize the terms of difference themselves. This historicization refers us back to the question of discontinuity (of the different meanings of apparently similar words) and it brings us to the question of interpretation. For if the historical analysis of differentiation I am proposing is premised on discontinuity, it takes interpretation as one of its objects. Interpretation is the means by which we participate in shaping reality.

Historicizing Interpretation

What if instead of thinking of interpretation as something historians (and others) do to the facts of history, we thought of interpretation as a fact of history? By this I do not mean simply that no fact can be known without interpretation (that, to put it in other terms, historians produce knowledge), but that interpretation inheres in social phenomena—in institutions, relationships, political systems, markets, as well as in various forms of written texts. The study of the history of these phenomena is, at its most profound, an analysis of changing interpretations. As Foucault puts it:

If interpretation were the slow exposure of the meaning hidden in an origin, then only metaphysics could interpret the development of humanity. But if interpretation is the violent or surreptitious appropriation of a system of rules, which in itself has no essential meaning, in order to impose a direction, to bend it to a new will, to force its participation in a different game, and to subject it to secondary rules, then the development of humanity is a series of interpretations. The role of genealogy is to record its history: the history of morals, ideals, and metaphysical concepts, the history of the concept of liberty or of the ascetic life; as they stand for the emergence of different interpretations, they must he made to appear as events on the stage of historical process. ("NGH," 151–52)

This kind of history understands facts to be objects of knowledge brought into view or granted importance in a conceptual system; they are the data that provide insight into particular interpretive operations. Of course, the insight gained from "genealogical" analysis is no more fixed than any other. Nor does it dispense with the "reality effect" since interpretations are treated as "facts" of history, even as they produce other kinds of facts. There will also continue to be debates about how systems of knowledge are to be read as well as about their causes and effects. Making interpretation an object of inquiry precludes neither judgment nor the need for standards of evaluation; the discipline will continue to have to furnish ways to distinguish persuasive from unpersuasive readings. The shift of focus to interpretation does, however, entail at least two other consequences. It means that attention to "facts" involves attention to signification as the means by which subjects and their objects of knowledge are constituted. (I will return to this point later.) It also makes visible historians' interpretations, for we cannot read for conceptual differences without distinguishing them from our own.

Historical consciousness is in this approach always double; it is a process of confrontation between or among interpretations. It recognizes that recounting the "facts" of another age without analyzing the systems of knowledge that produced them either reproduces (and naturalizes) past ideologies or dehistoricizes them by imposing present categories. It recognizes that the "discovery" of new materials is actually an interpretive intervention that exposes the terms of inclusion and exclusion in the knowledges of the past. (Women's history, from this perspective, is not the simple addition of information previously ignored, not an empirical correction of the record, but an analysis of the effects of dominant understandings of gender in the past, a critical reading that itself has the effect of producing another "reality.")

Historical consciousness takes responsibility for its interpretations, for the place from which it speaks. "Connecting history to a place is the condition of possibility for any social analysis," writes Certeau.[20] And by that he means less an avowal of the individual political commitments of a historian than an examination of the social (or discursive) relationships of the production of history in which he or she is enmeshed. These relationships determine not the immediate political impact of interpretations (are they good or bad for some constituency or another?), but how they do or do not serve to protect time from ideological foreclosure and thus keep open possibilities for change. For Certeau, a history that loses the dimension of time is no history at all. And a history committed to time is necessarily a critical history:

> [T]aking (the historian's) place seriously is the condition that allows something to be stated that is neither legendary (or "edifying") nor atopical (lacking relevance). Denial of the specificity of the place being the very principle of ideology, all theory is excluded. Even more, by moving discourse into a non-place, ideology forbids history from speaking of society and of death—in other words, from being history. (69)

Assuming responsibility for one's interpretations also means acknowledging their place in evaluations of other interpretations, other histories with which one does or does not agree. I do not mean here applying a test of political correctness, but recognizing the part that interpretation (according to systems of knowledge, standards of coherence) plays in assessment. This recognition makes it no harder than before to refuse revisionist claims about the nonexistence of the Holocaust even if it does not make knowledge dependent upon truth. Instead, accuracy is established in accord with agreed-upon historical procedures. And there can then be a critical reading of the ideological investments of revisionists, a set of questions about the discursive sites of their interpretations and the effects they seek to produce. Similarly, Mississippi civil rights workers can contest the effects of accounts that give heroic agency to government operatives, offering their own readings of what happened, without claiming sole possession. If this means historical accounts are forever contestable, so be it. The alternative (to return to the comment from Certeau I cited earlier) is dogmatism. Only a history that is both the study and practice of interpretation enables the "effective operations" Certeau called "ethics": "It defines a distance between what is and what ought to be. This distance designates a space where we have something to do" ("HSF," 102-3).

The historicizing of interpretation is necessarily the historicizing of signification, and this is the link back to discontinuity and differentiation. For it is through attention to signification that historians practice history, that they bring past, present, and future into being as functions of time. In his recent critique of cultural history and of the Annales school in particular, Rancière offers "poetics" as the alternative to the "scientistic belief" he associates with the "end of history." He recommends that history become interested in

> the exploration of the multiple paths at the unforeseen intersections by which one may apprehend the forms of experience of the visible and the utterable,

which constitute the uniqueness of the democratic age and also allow the rethinking of other ages. It becomes interested in the forms of writing that render it intelligible in the interlacing of its times, in the combination of numbers and images, of words and emblems. To do this it consents to its own fragility, to the power it holds from its shameful kinship with the makers of histories and the tellers of stories. (*NOH*, 102–3)

In response to those who fear an invasion of literary techniques into history's domain, Rancière replies in terms more eloquent than any I could supply as an end for this essay. I will therefore give him the last word:

[N]othing threatens history except its own lassitude with regard to the time that has made it or its fear before that which makes its material sensitive to its object—time, words, and death. History doesn't have to protect itself from any foreign invasion. It only needs to reconcile itself with its own name. (*NOH*, 103)

After history? History!

NOTES

1. Cited in Robert F. Berkhofer, Jr., *Beyond the Great Story: History as Text and Discourse* (Cambridge, Mass.: Harvard University Press, 1995), p. 64.

2. Cited in Peter Novick, *That Noble Dream: The "Objectivity Question" and the American Historical Profession* (Cambridge: Cambridge University Press, 1988), p. 141.

3. *New York Times*, 11 February 1996, sec. 2, p. 26.

4. Peter Galison, "Judgment Against Objectivity," unpublished paper, June 1995.

5. Roland Barthes, "The Discourse of History," in *The Rustle of Language*, trans. Richard Howard (New York: Hill & Wang, 1986), p. 131.

6. Francis Fukuyama, *The End of History and the Last Man* (New York: Avon Books, 1992), hereafter cited as *EHLM*. For an important reading, see Jacques Derrida, *Specters of Marx: The State of the Debt, the Work of Mourning, and the New International*, trans. Peggy Kamuf (New York: Routledge, 1994), pp. 49–76.

7. See Christina Crosby, "Dealing with Differences," in *Feminists Theorize the Political*, ed. Judith Butter and Joan W. Scott (New York: Routledge, 1992), pp. 130–43, esp. p. 134.

8. Jacques Rancière, *The Names of History: On the Poetics of Knowledge*, trans. Hassan Melehy (Minneapolis: University of Minnesota Press, 1994), p. 102 (hereafter cited as *NOH*).

9. Cited in Karen J. Winkler, "Who Owns History?" *Chronicle of Higher Education, 20* January *1995*, A1.

10. Benedict Anderson, *Imagined Communities: Reflections on the Origin and Spread of Nationalism* (London: Verso, 1983).

11. See under "own," *American Heritage Dictionary* (1992), p. 1294.

12. Lynne V. Cheney, "The End of History," *Wall Street Journal*, 20 October 1994, A22.

13. "History After the *Enola Gay* Controversy," special issue of the *Journal of American History* 82:3 (December 1995): 1100 (hereafter cited as *JAH*).

14. See Crosby, "Dealing with Differences."

15. *New York Times*, 16 January 1995, A1, A10.

16. Wendy Brown, *States of Injury: Power and Freedom in Late Modernity* (Princeton: Princeton University Press, 1995), 54 (hereafter cited as *SI*).

17. Michel de Certeau, "History: Science and Fiction," in *Heterologies: Discourse on the Other*, trans. Brian Massumi (Minneapolis: University of Minnesota Press, 1986), 218 (hereafter cited as "HSF").

18. Michel Foucault, "Nietzsche, Genealogy, History," in *Language, Counter-Memory, Practice: Selected Essays and Interviews*, ed. Donald F. Bouchard (Ithaca, NY: Cornell University Press, 1977), 154 (hereafter cited as "NGH").

19. This is the project of Denise Riley, *"Am I That Name?" Feminism and the Category of "Women" in History* (London: Macmillan, 1988). See also Riley, "A Short History of Some Preoccupations," in Butler and Scott, *Feminists Theorize the Political*, pp. 121–29.

20. Certeau, *The Writing of History*, trans. Tom Conley (New York: Columbia University Press, 1988), p. 69.

CHAPTER 7

The Global Situation

Anna Tsing

CLICK ON worldmaking.interconnections. Your screen fills with global flows.

Imagine a creek cutting through a hillside. As the water rushes down, it carves rock and moves gravel; it deposits silt on slow turns; it switches courses and breaks earth dams after a sudden storm. As the creek flows, it makes and remakes its channels.

Imagine an Internet system, linking up computer users. Or a rush of immigrants across national borders. Or capital investments shuttled to varied off-shore locations. These world-making "flows," too, are not just interconnections but also the recarving of channels and the remapping of the possibilities of geography.

Imagine the landscape nourished by the creek. Yet even beyond the creek's "flows," there are no stable landscape elements: Trees sprout up, transforming meadows into forests; cattle browse on saplings, spreading meadows past forest edges. Nor are forests and meadows the only way to divide up the landscape. Consider the perspective of the earthworm, looking for rich soils, or the weed, able to flourish in both meadow and forest, though only when each meets certain conditions. To tell the story of this landscape requires an appreciation not only of changing landscape elements but also of the partial, tentative, and shifting ability of the storyteller to identify elements at all.

Imagine ethnic groups, corporations, refugees, nongovernmental organizations (NGOs), nation-states, consumers, social movements, media moguls, trade organizations, social scientists, international lawyers, and bankers, all swarming alongside creeks and earthworms to compose the landscape, to define its elements, carve its channels of flow, and establish its units of historical agency. We live in a time of self-consciousness about units and scales: Where shall we draw the boundaries of regions? How are local communities composed? And, most important for this essay, what is this thing we call the globe? If social scientists have had a lot to say about these questions of late, so have other people. Contestants form themselves in shifting alliances, mobilized for reasons of power, passion, discipline, or dis-ease and mounting campaigns for particular configurations of scale. Some of the most excited campaigning in the last twenty-five years has concerned the globe, that planetwide space for all humanity and its encompassing habitat. Moreover, in the last ten years, talk about the globe has heated up to the point that many commentators imagine a global *era*, a time in which no units or scales count for much except the globe. "Globalization," the process taking us into that era, has caught up enthusiasts ranging from corporate managers to social activists, from advertisers to cultural theorists.

For many years, the creek makes only gradual changes in the landscape. Then a storm sweeps the flux beyond its accustomed boundaries, shifting every bank and eddy. Trees are uprooted, and what was once on the right side is now on the left. So, too, the social world has shifted around us. Market enthusiasms have replaced communism; national governments prostrate themselves before international finance; social movements market "culture" on a global scale. How should social scientists analyze these changes? This question is muddied by the fact that social science changes too. "Global" practices challenge social scientists to internationalize their venues, as North American and European scholars are brought into discussion with scholars from the South. Social science theories no longer take Western genealogies for granted but, rather, require fluency with a wider range of perspectives, from Latin American dependency theories to South Asian subaltern studies. The excitement of this internationalization of scholarship encourages many of us to throw ourselves into endorsements of globalization as a multilayered evolution, drawing us into the future. Sometimes our critical distance seems less useful than our participation. And yet, can we understand either our own involvement or the changing world without our critical skills? This essay argues that we cannot.

IS GLOBALIZATION LIKE MODERNIZATION?

Consider another moment in which social science was remade together with the world: the period after World War II, when social scientists were called on to participate in the international project of modernization and development. Modernization frameworks brought together scholars, policymakers, politicians, and social activists in a common program for social betterment. It offered the hope of moving beyond the colonial segregation of Europeans and natives to a world in which every nation could aspire to the highest standards of livelihood and culture. Even social scientists who feared its destructiveness or despised its imperiousness thus came to imagine modernization as the world-making process of the times. The charisma of the notion of an era of globalization is comparable in many ways to the charm of modernization in that postwar period. Like modernization theory, the global-future program has swept together scholars and public thinkers to imagine a new world in the making. Do globalization theories contain pitfalls for engaged social scientists similar to those of modernization theory?

Modernization, like globalization, was seductive. It was many years before social scientists moved beyond endorsements, refusals, and reforms of modernization to describe modernization as a set of *projects* with cultural and institutional specificities and limitations. Only when the shine of modernization began to fade did scholars ask how it managed to capture the hopes and dreams of so many experts, how its formulas were communicated to such a variety of social groups and within such a diversity of situations, and how its features were transformed in the process for multiple uses. Recent literature on modernization in its guise as "development" for the Third World is exemplary in this regard. A number of analysts, including Escobar and Ferguson, have shown the discursive specificities of development, which often thrived more through the coherence of its internal logic than through any insight into the social situations in which it was expected to intervene.[1] The commitment of experts to development drew material and institutional resources to its programs even when they were quite obviously destructive of the human well-being that formed its ostensible goal. Meanwhile, development was also reformulated through its constant negotiation and translation within particular settings, and it assumed multiple forms. Recent studies have shown how development policies diversified as they become entangled in regional political struggles and as they were reinterpreted in varied cultural settings.[2] This rich literature has inspired new attention to the making of modernization. Its example can stimulate attention to the multiple projects of imagining and making globality.

Studies of modernization as a set of projects look in at least three directions. First, analysts attend to the cultural specificity of commitments to modernization. They may make these commitments seem exotic to remove them from the reader's common sense. (How odd, the analyst might say, that sitting in uncomfortable chairs is considered more modern than squatting.) Analysts explore the elements through which modernization projects make assumptions about the world. For example, modernization projects create notions of time through which groups and activities can be situated in relation to stories of progress. Second, analysts attend to the social practices, material infrastructure, cultural negotiations, institutions, and power relations through which modernization projects work—and are opposed, contested, and reformulated. Modernization projects do their work through educational practices, military coercion, administrative policies, resource entitlements, community reorganization, and much more; these arenas and practices both make and are transformed by modernization. To examine the effects of modernization commitments requires attention to the social worlds both of and beyond modernization visions. Third, analysts use the promise of questions and dilemmas brought up in modernization programs without becoming caught in their prescriptions for social change. For example, through its emphasis on critical reflection as a mode of "modern" thought, modernization draws attention to the awkward relationship between representation and its object and to the craft and creativity through which social life must be described. Analysts of modernization projects make use of this insight without assuming the framework of progress that helped generate it.

These directions of analysis seem equally useful to understanding projects of imagining and making globality. Certainly, commitments to globalism are strange enough to warrant cultural analysis. Furthermore, as globalization becomes institutionalized as a program not only in the academy but also in corporate policy, politics, and popular culture, it is important to attend to these sites to understand what projects of globalization "do" in the world—and what else goes on with and around them. Finally, I think there is enormous analytic promise in tracing global interconnections without subsuming them to any one program of global-future commitments. A global framework allows one to consider the making and remaking of geographical and historical agents and the forms of their agency in relation to movement, interaction, and shifting, competing claims about community, culture, and scale. Places are made through their connections with each other, not their isolation: This kind of analysis seems too important to relegate only to studying the best-promoted "global" trends; indeed, among other uses, we can employ it to specify the uneven and contested global terrain of global promotion.

In this essay, I use these three directions of analysis to learn something about social science commitments to the newly emerging significance of a global scale. First, I examine the charisma of social science globalisms. By "globalism," I refer to endorsements of the importance of the global. I want to know how the idea of the global has worked to excite and inspire social scientists. I pick out a number of elements that add to this charisma and argue for their obfuscating as well as enlivening features.

Second, to see how this charisma produces effects in the world, I examine reading and discussion practices in the field of anthropology, as these produce and reproduce commitments to globalization. As an observer, I try to track the excitement of my students and colleagues; yet, as a participant, I want to argue for a *better* use of the charisma of global frameworks.

Thus, third, I show how questions about global interconnections might be detached from the most problematic globalist commitments to offer a more nuanced and critical analysis of culture and history, including recent shifts that have turned attention to the global. I argue that we can investigate globalist projects and dreams without assuming that they remake the world just as they want. The task of understanding planetwide interconnections requires locating and specifying globalist projects and dreams, with their contradictory as well as charismatic logics and their messy as well as effective encounters and translations.

Globalization draws our enthusiasm because it helps us imagine interconnection, travel, and sudden transformation. Yet it also draws us inside its rhetoric until we take its claims for true descriptions. In the imagery with which I began, flow is valorized but not the carving of the channel; national and regional units are mapped as the baseline of change without attention to their shifting and contested ability to define the landscape. We lose sight of the coalitions of claimants as well as their partial and shifting claims. We lose touch with the material and institutional components through which powerful and central sites are constructed, from which convincing claims about units and scales can be made. We describe the landscape imagined within these claims rather than the culture and politics of scale making. This essay suggests approaches to the study of the global that seem to me to hold onto the excitement of this endorsement of planetary interconnection without trading our critical stance for globalist wishes and fantasies.

Hurtling through Space

To invoke the global at the turn of the second millennium is to call attention to the speed and density of interconnections among people and places. In this imagery, the planet overwhelms us in its rush toward the future; we must either sit on top of it or be swamped and overcome.[3] It seems worth hesitating for a moment to consider the difference between this aggressive globe, hurtling through space, and an only slightly earlier fragile planet, floating gently in its cloud cover. This fertile yet vulnerable green planet was conjured by the global environmentalism that emerged in the United States and Europe at the end of the 1960s and blossomed in the 1970s, 1980s, and early 1990s. As Yaakov Garb has shown, the global environmentalists' globe gained its power from the visual image of the earth first seen in photographs from space in the 1960s; this awe-inspiring image was repeated in many forms and contexts to mobilize sentiment for the kind of nature that most needed our respect, love, and protection.[4] It became possible to imagine this nature as extending across the planet because global environmentalism brought together the universalist morality of 1960s social justice politics and the transboundary expertise of an emergent ecological science.[5] Politics and science, working together, conjured an earth worth studying, managing, and fighting for at multiple but compatibly stratified scales and levels of advocacy and analysis. Global environmentalism also participated in building another image of the global, in which globality represented the goal of a *process* of building transnational political and cultural ties. Beginning most intensely in the 1980s, social movements—including environmentalism, human rights, indigenous rights, and feminist causes—extended themselves through NGOs; they sought to work around the restrictions of nation-states by forging transnational lines of financial, scientific, and political support.[6] Activists put pressure on their respective governments with these resources; national policies were also pressed to respond to international agreements. The global here is a never-ending process of "networking" and building lines of support. Annelise Riles has shown how the aesthetics of global network formation developed such charisma within NGOs that it became a major objective in itself.[7] Global process here encourages participants to speak up, to learn from each other, and to extend themselves. But it does not yet push us over the edge of an evolutionary abyss.

It was only at the beginning of the 1990s that the process of "globalization," as the definitional characteristic of an *era*, became popular in the media and advertising. The triumph of the capitalist marketplace had been proclaimed with the dismantling of the Soviet Union, and enthusiasm ran high for national economic deregulation and privatization in the North and more thorough forms of structural adjustment in the South. In this atmosphere, "globalization" came to mean an endorsement of international free trade and the outlawing of protected or public domestic economies.[8] Yet the term came to encompass much more. Corporate reorganizations required not just markets but also the ability to transfer operations and finances transnationally to find the most profitable conditions; these kinds of corporate transfers, although reaching several decades back, became caught up in the talk of globalization. Furthermore, social commentators reminded the public that the new mobility of labor was tied to capital mobility and global market guarantees.[9] Cosmopolitan connoisseurs have delighted in the new availability of West African music, Brazilian martial arts, and Thai cuisine, as Southern arts blossomed in wealthy Northern cities.[10] A variety of public debates and discussions came to be seen as "globally" interconnected: not only labor-and-capital-oriented fights about immigration, unionization, downsizing, subcontracting, and impoverishment but also debates about the worldwide spread of U.S. media productions, the role of national governments, the dangers and promises of multiculturalism, and the growing influence and proper management of new computer-based communications technologies. Indeed, the popularity of "global" terms and approaches drew from their evocation of multiple causes, agendas, and historical layers of imagery.[11]

At the turn of the century, then, globalism is multi-referential: part corporate hype and capitalist regulatory agenda, part cultural excitement, part social commentary and protest. Within this shifting agenda, several features attract and engage an expanding audience for imagining the globe: first, its futurism, that is, its ability not only to name an era but to predict its progress; second, its conflations of varied projects through which the populist and the corporate, the scientific and the cultural, the excluded margins and the newly thriving centers, all seem wrapped up in the same energetic movement; and third, its rhetoric of linkage and circulation as the overcoming of boundaries and restrictions, through which all this excitement appears positive for everyone involved. These elements are worth examining separately.

Futurism

Globalization is a crystal ball that promises to tell us of an almost-but-not-quite-there globality. This is powerful stuff for experts, politicians, and policy-makers. Social scientists are particularly caught by the force of this charisma. The rush of prescience returns social science to the period after World War II, when the field charted the development of the new nations of the South and, in the North, the welfare state. Since then, social scientists—like economists and sociologists—have been better known as technicians of the present or—like anthropologists and geographers—as collectors of ancient survivals. Now the opportunity has come to look forward with a new expertise. The crystal ball inspires us to rush anxiously into the future, afraid to be left behind.

The future orientation of this discussion of the global requires the assumption of newness. If global interconnections do not define the contemporary era, setting it off from the past, to examine these interconnections shows us complexity rather than direction. Analysts of globalization force attention to the break that differentiates the present from the past because in the context of that break they can see forward.[12] The assumption of newness has other benefits. It can help us see the distinctiveness of a historical moment. It can inspire a "bandwagon" effect whereby unexpected and creative alliances among different kinds of analysts may be forged.[13] In this spirit, it can break up too-comfortably established fields, inspiring new forms of discussion.[14] However, the assumption of newness can also stifle other lines of inquiry and disallow questions about the construction of the field for which it forms the starting line. In history and anthropology, for example, the idea that global interconnections are *old* has only recently been revitalized, muffled as it was for much of the twentieth century by the draw of nationally contained legacies, in history, and functionally contained social worlds, in anthropology; it seems unfortunate to lose this insight so quickly.[15]

Perhaps the worst fault of the assumption of global newness is that it erects stereotypes of the past that get in the way of appreciating both the past and the present. This fault has been particularly glaring in the discussion of the nation inspired by talk of globalization.[16] In interpreting the defeat of various national attempts to control financial capital, analysts have imagined an unprecedented world-historical defeat of the nation, as if nations, until now, were unquestioned, consistent, and everywhere hegemonic. Yet national control of finance may itself have been a recent, ephemeral product. After World War II, economic regulations emerging from the Bretton-Woods agreement made it possible for nation-states to control domestic financial capital, providing funding for welfare states. An earlier free-flowing internationalization of finance was cut off, as national capitalisms were set in place.[17]

Similarly, political commitment to national territorial boundaries and the importance of regulating population movements across national borders has a particular history. The new nation-states that emerged after World War II in Africa and Asia, for example, developed special concerns for territorial sovereignty to declare their autonomy from the colonial condition; their national histories and geographies stress self-development, not regional and transregional flow.[18] To turn nationalist visions from this period into a description of a homogeneous past seems likely to lead to distortions. Given long-term commitments in the humanities to tracing intellectual lineages and civilizational commitments, it is perhaps surprising that literary critics have embraced the assumption of era-making global newness to put together anthologies on "the cultures of globalization."[19] The anthologies they have created are in many ways extremely exciting: Here are a variety of themes, a breadth of places discussed, and a diversity of scholars that form a striking intervention into the narrowly Western, textual orientation of most humanities. This is not scholarship as usual; it has the political energy and passion of cultural studies. This development is so important that it is awkward to say anything else. But I am suspicious of cultural stage theories, with their determinations of who is at the peak of human evolution and who will be left behind. Without denying their contribution, it may be useful to question how the articles in these anthologies are connected to each other. To discuss globalization, the editors make the a priori assumption of a cultural political era.[20] The era must have a cultural logic, and the descriptions of culture gathered in the book must form part of that logic.[21] I think we can discuss global projects, links, and situations with a better frame: one that recognizes the making and unmaking of claims about the global, even as it examines the consequences of these powerful claims in the world we know, and one that recognizes new and surprising developments without declaring, by fiat, the beginning of an era.[22]

Yet global futurism is seductive. It can be conjured equally by a technical mathematics or by an enthusiastic and suggestive vagueness. Frederic Jameson is perhaps the most up-front about all this, claiming that questions about the definition of the global era to which he devotes his book are not only premature but decidedly uncool.[23] Surely we will find that the disparate cultural and political processes we investigate in these times will turn out to be the trunk, limbs, and tail of that elephant not recognized as a single beast by the blind men. He disarms critics: Anyone who has questions about the elephant must certainly be a curmudgeonly old elephant hater who believes that there is nothing new under the sun; this exhausts, for him, the options for dissent.[24] And yet, might it not be a *newly* productive strategy to pay close and critical attention to these different limb-like global projects and agendas, to appreciate their articulations as well as their disengagements and mismatched encounters?

Conflations

In "Notes on Globalization," Jameson argues that globalization is best understood through the Hegelian dialectic: Its ideological logic produces both a dark and a light side. This is a useful reminder that the global developments that we, as social commentators, find promising are often deeply connected to those we find dangerous. But why jump quite so quickly into the assumption that the vast array of transcommunal and transnational ideas and activities around us form a single ideological system? There are some important advantages. Overlaps among ideological projects produce an added intensity all around. When the machinery of corporate and state publicity has converged on a single image, it is doubly hard to avoid the sense of complicity, for better or worse. In analyzing recent developments, it would be silly to argue for autonomous institutional, regional, or political-cause domains. It is clear that the appreciation of synergy among varied globalist projects is at the heart of the new enthusiasm about the globe. My point is that this very search for overlaps, alliances, collaborations, and complicities is one of the most important phenomena we could study. We might look at how particular projects become formulated, how they are tied and transformed in the process, and how they sometimes interrupt each other despite themselves. The "globalization" that is formed from these hit-and-miss convergences would be considerably more unstable, and more interesting, than the one posited by any single claimant as a world-making system. One step in looking for this kind of globalization must be to recognize that there are varied agendas, practices, and processes that may or may not be deeply interconnected at a given historical moment.

Two recent studies of the cultural logic of global "network" formation are useful to compare in this regard. Roger Rouse analyzes a series of advertisements produced for the telephone company MCI that promote the company's ability to build an interactive multimedia communications network.[25] This communication network is advertised as part of a world-changing, future-making revamping of space and time, in which instantaneous communications within a personalized web of ties will replace geographically grounded routes and central-place hierarchies. The "network" MCI promotes is simultaneously the material technology of telephones, computers, and the like, and the individualized, flexible, transnational set of contacts and associates that citizens of the future will be able to maintain through these technologies.

A similar but contrasting global network-in-the-making is analyzed by Annelise Riles, who studied women's organizing in Fiji in preparation for the United Nations–sponsored international conference on women in Beijing in 1995.[26] The women she studied had formed NGOs addressing gendered concerns; these organizations were connected to sister organizations, funders, and other kinds of political supporters all over the world. What they learned from this system of ties, Riles shows, is the importance of "networks," that is, webs of imagined interconnection through which groups in one area were to exchange information and support with other groups on what was seen as an egalitarian, voluntary basis. Riles argues that networks took on a formal aesthetic value and, through this formalism, the Fijian women organizers saw themselves as part of an emergent global process.[27]

These two globe-making projects have a lot in common. Both have educational goals to teach people to visualize a future globalism in which "networks"—rather than nations or bureaucracies—will be the organizing aesthetic. Both value personal contacts over long distances and individual initiative over the recognition of preset roles. Yet it is also clear that each project has come into being along a different historical trajectory, with different material and political resources and objectives, and their convergence is broken by those differences. As Rouse shows, MCI's presentation of its product as a "network" separates wealthy professionals (i.e., those in the network) from the underpaid workers and other poor people to whom they have some responsibility in the public space of the nation. Only through this separation can they build a constituency for the global mobility of corporate resources and the wealthy niche marketing of corporate products. The globalization this network promotes, then, is one that ties privileged consumers and their corporate sponsors in a self-conscious forgetting about the rest of the world. In contrast, the NGO networks discussed by Riles are intended to build a transnational women's solidarity that brings women's rights *into* particular national contexts rather than excluding network builders from participation in nations. Attention to national and regional "levels" of network building is supposed to strengthen the call of public responsibilities within these units rather than eviscerate them. Even as they bypass state bureaucracies, the women are called on to act as national representatives; in this capacity, Riles argues, the Fijian women bring national cultural sensibilities to the imagination of global network activities by focusing on a formal aesthetics grounded in other Fijian cultural work.

One further striking contrast between these two images of the network is their differential gender content. MCI's network, as Rouse explains it, rescues vulnerable young girls through the patriarchal security of a privatized globe. The Fijian women's NGO network creates new arenas of all-female sociality that draw on but extend local forms in transnational translations. The contrast provides rich grounds for thinking about emergent forms of subjectivity and agency in varied global projects. There is a lot going on, and it does not all match up. Were we to limit ourselves to one of these visions as a description of the new global landscape, we would miss the pleasures and dangers of this multiplicity. Furthermore, we might over-valorize connection and circulation rather than attending to the shifting, contested making of channels and landscape elements.

Circulation

Interconnection is everything in the new globalisms. And interconnection is created through circulation. Many things are said to circulate, ranging from people to money, cultures to information, and television programs to international protocols to the process called globalization itself. "Circulation" is in global rhetoric what the "penetration" of capitalism was in certain kinds of Marxist world-systems theory: the way powerful institutions and ideas spread geographically and come to have an influence in distant places. The difference is significant; where *penetration* always evokes a kind of rape, a forcing of some people's powerful interests onto other people, *circulation* calls forth images of the healthy flow of blood in the body and the stimulating, evenhanded exchange of the marketplace.

Both bodies and markets as models for understanding social process have been much criticized in social theory in the twentieth century. Images of society as organically interconnected like a body were important in establishing the social sciences, but they have been largely discredited as disallowing the study of power, meaning, conflict, disjuncture, and historical change. Images of society as a market have had a different kind of lasting power. Caught up in the endorsement of capitalism as an economic system and free trade as its ideal political context, they have been revived and given new authority in celebration of the end of communism and the Cold War. Marxist scholarship, however, continues a substantial record of criticism of these images. Market models assume a "level playing field" of exchange that erases the inequalities of property and the processes of labor exploitation. Market models appear to be inclusive, but they privilege social actors who, because of their economic resources, are able to participate in markets. Most important in the context of the post–Cold War enthusiasm for market models, Marxist scholars have shown how bourgeois governments and social institutions have promoted market thinking to naturalize class and other social distinctions. By training the attention of citizens on the equalities and opportunities of circulation and exchange, they justify policies of domination and discrimination. Recent endorsements of "global circulation" as one process for making the future partake in the obfuscations of inequality for which market models are known.

Global circulation is not just a rhetoric of corporate expansion, however. Leftist social commentators often find as much good use for circulation models as capitalist apologists. Circulation is used to discuss the breaking down of oppressive barriers among cultures, races, languages, and nations, including immigration restrictions and segregation policies. Diasporas circulate, bringing the wealth of their cultural heritage to new locations. Authoritarian regimes prevent the circulation of information, inspiring democratic movements to create underground channels of flow. The circulation of film inspires creative viewing practices. Circulation is thus tapped for the endorsement of multicultural enrichment, freedom, mobility, communication, and creative hybridity.

In part, the acceptability of circulation rhetoric among liberal and leftist social scientists derives from a self-conscious rejection of the Marxist emphasis on capitalist production and its consequent deemphasis on market exchange and consumption.[28] Leftist critics of corporate globalization point to the importance of marketing and consumption in contemporary corporate strategies for reaching out to new fields of operation (Jameson is one example); these are topics that need to be discussed. The growth of managerial and service professions also calls out to critics to abandon an exclusive analytic focus on factory production to attend to the variety of economic forms of contemporary capitalism.[29]

The form and variety of capitalist economic activities are not, however, the only issues to raise about the use of the rhetoric of circulation as a ruling image for global interconnections. There are hidden relations of production here that may have nothing to do with labor in factories: the making of the objects and subjects who circulate, the channels of circulation, and the landscape elements that enclose and frame those channels. A focus on circulation shows us the movement of people, things, ideas, or institutions, but it does not show us how this movement depends on defining tracks and grounds or scales and units of agency. This blindness may not be inherent in the idea of circulation itself but, rather, may be caused by the kinds of circulations that have delineated the model. For historically layered political reasons, the model has been closed to attention to struggles over the terrain of circulation and the privileging of certain kinds of people as players. We focus on the money—the *ur* object of flow—instead of the social conditions that allow or encourage that flow. If we imagined creeks, perhaps the model would be different; we might notice the channel as well as the water moving.

In this spirit, Saskia Sassen has addressed channel making in relation to global circulations of corporate communications as well as labor. She argues that "global cities" have developed as centers for transnational corporate operations because of the density of corporate real estate, professional service workers, and telecommunication connection grids. Corporate rhetoric aspires to an infinite decentralization and deterritorialization of management operations, but this rhetoric ignores the material requirements for dispersed communication, for example, telephone and computer connections, as well as the specialized labor of advertising, finance, and other services, all of which is concentrated in particular cities. The much touted mobility of information, capital, products, and production facilities depends on these coordinating centers. Similarly, Sassen shows that immigration, often discussed as the mass product of individual mobility, requires the creation of institutional ties linking sending and receiving areas. Histories of direct foreign investment or military intervention, for example, have predictably produced flows of immigrants from the targeted regions to the United States. "Flow" is movement stimulated through political and economic channels.

Sassen's work shows that the alternatives to conventional models of circulation are not just to close off our attention to travel and trade. Analysts can also examine the material and institutional infrastructure of movement and pay special attention to the economic coercions and political guarantees that limit or promote circulation. In order to do this, however, we would need to redefine the common distinction between the "local" and the "global." Most commonly, globalist thinkers imagine the local as the stopping point of global circulations. It is the place where global flows are consumed, incorporated, and resisted.[30] It is the place where global flows fragment and are transformed into something place bound and particular.[31] But if flow itself always involves making terrain, there can be no territorial distinctions between the "global" transcending of place and the "local" making of places. Instead, there is place making—and travel—all around, from New York to New Guinea.[32]

Place making is always a cultural as well as a political-economic activity. It involves assumptions about the nature of those subjects authorized to participate in the process and the kinds of claims they can reasonably put forth about their position in national, regional, and world classifications and hierarchies of places. The specificities of these subjects and claims contradict and misstate those of other place makers, even as they may form overlaps and links imaged as "flows." The channel-making activity of circulation, then, is always a contested and tentative formation of scales and landscapes. To avoid letting those who imagine themselves as winners call all of the terms, we need to attend to the missed encounters, clashes, misfires, and confusions that are as a much part of global linkages as simple "flow."

Culture, specificity, and place making have conventionally been the domain of the discipline of anthropology, particularly as practiced in the United States. Because these kinds of issues are so often missing from discussions of the global, the stakes are particularly high in seeing their incorporation into global questions in anthropology. Yet it is not these issues that first chaperoned globalism into U.S. anthropology. Instead, the charisma of the global was introduced to forward a disciplinary transition away from an overzealous and nonreflective localism. It is from the perspective of this trajectory that it is possible to examine the specific disciplinary practices through which globalist frameworks are being read by U.S. anthropologists.

READINGS IN ANTHROPOLOGY

Social science globalisms take particular forms in relation to disciplinary reading and discussion practices. They gain their influence not only because they are adopted in the work of articulate practitioners but, equally important, because they enter local trajectories of disciplinary momentum. They are rebuilt to speak to disciplinary challenges as these, in turn, are understood in relation to specific social locations of scholarly practice. In the process, social science globalisms pick up regional and disciplinary frameworks and assumptions, even as they throw themselves as objections against others.

Anthropologists do not merely mimic the understandings of globalism of other experts, even as they are influenced by them. No anthropologist I know argues that the global future will be culturally homogeneous; even those anthropologists most wedded to the idea of a new global era imagine this era as characterized by "local" cultural diversity. Disciplinary concern with cultural diversity overrides the rhetoric of global cultural unification pervasive elsewhere, even though, for those in its sway, globalism still rules: Diversity is generally imagined as forming a reaction or a backdrop to the singular and all-powerful "global forces" that create a new world. (Globalisms are not themselves regularly regarded as diverse.) Politically progressive anthropologists sometimes show how this kind of circumscribed, reactive, self-consciously "local" diversity is a form of resistance to the proliferation of globalist capitalism and hypermodernist governmentality; however, the possibility that capitalisms and governmentalities are themselves situated, contradictory, effervescent, or culturally circumscribed is much less explored. Anthropologists who have argued against simplistic models of "global culture" have also, then, naturalized globalist ideologies of the global.

In the United States, the excitement of this globalism for anthropologists draws from a rather "local" disciplinary heritage: a more than twenty-five-year journey away from analyses of "cultures" as autonomous, self-generating, and bounded entities. In the 1960s and 1970s, U.S. anthropologists criticized the discipline's complicity with colonial projects of conquest and administration. Historical, anticolonial, and world-systems frameworks moved to the discipline's center, ousting functionalism, and interpretive accounts of national and nationalist commitments replaced descriptions of isolated cultures. In the 1980s, ethnographic research and description were interrogated for their role in making cultures appear isolated, and U.S. anthropologists recommitted themselves to more open, reflexive, and textually responsive ways of approaching the inequalities and interconnections among people and places. The recent turn to the global takes its alignment within this pathway of disciplinary self-criticism. Globalism within this trajectory renews stereotypes of the anthropological past in order to confront them. The "old" anthropology imagined here describes cultures so grounded that they could not move out of place. This anthropology imprisons its objects in a cell; interconnection and movement in the form of "global flows" are thus experienced as a form of liberation. Furthermore, these flows fit most neatly inside the discipline when, in deference to past teachers and conventions, the boundedness of past cultures goes unchallenged; global flows can then take the discipline, and the world, into a freer future.

This "freeing up" variety of globalism is both exhilarating and problematic. On the one hand, it shows us new dreams and schemes of world making; on the other, as an aspect of its liberatory project, it also turns attention away from the quirky eccentricities of culture and history that have perhaps been U.S. anthropology's most vital contribution to critical thought. In the process, too, anthropologists tend to endorse the globalist dreams of the people they study, and thus we lose the opportunity to address the located specificity of those globalist dreams.

The three features I have discussed as creating the charisma of social science globalisms are prominent in U.S. anthropology. Each has been endorsed for good "local" reasons. Yet the very enthusiasm that each of these features has provoked has made it easier to erase specificities to create a misleading portrait of a single global future. It is hard not to universalize a globalist framework. But let me see if I can locate these globalisms—and in the process get them to do some very different work.

FUTURISM

U.S. anthropologists come to an endorsement of a singular global future from their interest in the macroeconomic context of cultural diversity. An important part of the disciplinary trajectory away from the study of isolated cultures has been attention to the capitalist world system. Anthropologists have been able to show how even out-of-the-way and exotic cultures respond to capitalism's challenges. This is crucial work. At the same time, risks and dilemmas remain in this analysis: In turning one's gaze to the systemic features of world capitalism, it is easy to lose track of the specificity of particular capitalist niches. In coming to terms with the transnational scope of contemporary finance, marketing, and production, it is easy to endorse globalism as a predictive frame. Indeed, it is in this context that anthropologists most commonly imagine singular global futures. Even as critics, we are caught in the hyperboles imagined by advocates of neoliberalism, structural adjustment, and transnationalization. Particularly in its critical versions, this global future forms part of a narrative of the evolution of capitalism. Furthermore, most anthropologists attracted by this narrative take their model from a single source: David Harvey's *The Condition of Postmodernity*.[33] Within much globalist anthropology, Harvey's book establishes the fact of epochal change, laying the ground for global futurism. Yet I find this a particular, peculiar reading of Harvey, and it is worth considering in its own right: For anthropologists, Harvey provides the evidence for a new era. As readers, they pick out "flexible specialization" and "time-space compression"as the characteristics of this new era.[34]

Yet when I turn to Harvey's book, it seems to me that the central argument is that the "cultural aesthetic" of postmodernism is related to the economic logic of flexible accumulation. The first section of the book reviews modernism and postmodernism as trends in the arts and letters, including architecture and philosophy. This is "capital C" culture: a genealogy of great men and their ideas. The second section of the book turns to the economic "regimes of accumulation" of Fordism and post-Fordist "flexible accumulation." The book's original idea is to juxtapose these two bodies of literature and to argue that postmodernism mirrors post-Fordism. It takes a certain amount of economic determinism to make this argument, in which Culture acts as a mirror of economic realities.[35] But in this gap, space and time come in. For Harvey, the "experience" of space and time mediates between Culture and the (nonculturally organized) economy.

For me the space and time section is the least satisfying section of the book. Harvey describes categories for understanding human encounters with space and time, representations of space and time in the arts and letters (and, in one chapter, in two films), and anecdotes about space and time in the capitalist workplace. No ethnographic sources for understanding spatial and temporal texture or diversity are consulted. The concept of "experience" is never explained. Because the mirror relation between arts and letters and the economy has already been established, their mediation by experience is a formal requirement, needing no substantiation.

In this context, it is strange that anthropologists so often pick only "the acceleration of space-time compression" along with "flexible accumulation" out of this book. In the process of citation, too, the book's tone changes. Harvey's book is polemical. He ranges over a wide variety of scholarship to criticize postmodern aesthetics. This is not a science experiment but, rather, a book-length essay. Yet somehow Harvey's description of economic evolution comes to have the status of a fact when drawn into globalist anthropology. Harvey has the ability to read economics, a skill few anthropologists have developed. It may be that anthropologists ignore the discussion of aesthetics, thinking they know more about culture than he does, and are drawn to the accumulation strategy and associated space-time requirements because they believe that macroeconomic facts are outside of their knowledge base. The result is that a selection of Harvey's terms is used to build a noncultural and nonsituated futurist framework, "beyond culture."[36] This poses certain immediate problems. One set of problems derives from the attempt to make this future global; as anthropologist Michael Kearney admits, Harvey's thesis is "not dealing with globalization per se"(1995: 551). Indeed, Harvey has a distinct blindness to everything outside dominant Northern Cultures and economies; to make his story applicable to North-South articulations is not impossible, but it is a challenge. Another set of problems seems even more intractable. If we drop Harvey's discussion of aesthetics (as Culture) but still ignore the ethnographic sources through which anthropologists identify culture, just how do we know the shape of space and time? The pared-down Harvey readings preferred by anthropologists have lost even literary and filmic representations of temporal and spatial processes; we are left with economic facts. Without "Culture" or "culture," we must assume rapid circulation, fragmentation, compression, and globality; certainly, we cannot consult either popular or official representations, discourses, or cultural practices. Anthropological analysis, which could look at scale-making claims and representations in conjunction with the social processes that support and result from those claims and representations, becomes reduced to building starships on millennial fantasies. Another way Harvey's work could be used is to scale back its epochal claims to look at some limited but powerful alliances between aesthetics and economics. Harvey's claim that postmodernism and flexible accumulation have something to do with each other could be pursued by locating patterns and players more specifically. This kind of project, however, diminishes the excitement of another globalist reading practice, which I have called "conflations." Let me examine how this practice both brings to life and impoverishes the anthropology of global interconnection.

CONFLATIONS

Not all anthropological globalism is engaged in understanding the systemics of capitalism; another significant sector attempts to hold onto "culture" as an anthropological object while showing its increased contemporary mobility and range. In this genre, anthropologists have done exciting work to specify modes of cultural interconnection that tie people in far-flung locales or travel with them across heterogeneous terrains. This work offers the possibility of attention to regionalisms and histories of place making within an appreciation of interconnection. However, to the extent that this work has been harnessed for the search for a singular anthropological globalism, it has blurred the differences among places and perspectives to emphasize the break from past localisms. This anthropological globalism renaturalizes global dreams instead of examining and locating them ethnographically. Moreover, it leads readers to assume that all globalisms are at base the same; thus, most readers read globalist anthropologists as an undifferentiated crowd.

Might a different kind of reading practice reestablish the potential for appreciating multiple, overlapping, and sometimes contradictory globalisms? Consider, for example, contrasts among the globalisms of Ulf Hannerz, Michael Kearney, and Arjun Appadurai.[37] I choose these authors because each has elaborated his ideas about globalism in a book-length exposition. Each sees his work as advancing the disciplinary trajectory of anthropology beyond the anthropology of separate, segregated cultures and societies. Each is concerned with migrants and travelers and the worlds they make and are made by. Each argues that new analytic tools are necessary for new times.

Yet they conjure different global geographies. The globality of Hannerz, the "global ecumene,"[38] is a space of interaction among once-separate cultures now growing in dialogue and mutual acknowledgment. Its creolization is created by cultural flows, particularly flows from powerful centers to less powerful peripheries; it is carried and extended by cosmopolitans who, of necessity, acknowledge and extend European and North American cultural frameworks even as they incorporate and remake non-Western cultures. Center-periphery relations thus organize world culture.

In contrast, Kearney's postmodern globality is a critique of center-periphery frameworks, which Kearney identifies with the classificatory modernist era that has passed away as we have entered transnational hyperspace and nonteleological, postdevelopmental time. The key feature of the global era is the "implosion" of center and periphery, as distinctions between rural and urban as well as South and North disintegrate. Spatial and cultural discriminations become impossible in a world of global flows, as nonunitary migrant subjects are formed in the interstices of past classificatory principles. In the unruly "reticula" Kearney conjures, however, he retains a dialogue with Marxian political economy that gives his multiplicity of identities and geographies its shape. The organization of the transnational economy creates differences of class, power, and value that forge subaltern and dominant social niches of identity and agency.

In contrast, again, Appadurai evokes a globality of contested "scapes" in which no single organizing principle rules. "Financescapes,"which include capital flows, are only one of several imaginative geographies that compete to make the globe; Appadurai finds that "ethnoscapes" and "mediascapes"—the cultural worlds conjured by migrants and in movies, respectively—are more decisive features in the "rupture" of the global era, with its heightened dependence on the imagination. Like Kearney's, Appadurai's globalism refuses center-periphery frames, but, like Hannerz, he situates it squarely in modernity's worldwide cultural spread rather than postmodernism's epistemological disruptions. Appadurai's globalism refuses Kearney's sociology of migrants to foreground their cultural worlds; indeed, these kinds of cultural terrains, although ungrounded in space, are those criticized by Kearney as modernist classificatory tricks.

Different subjects are at the center of each of these understandings of the global. In the best spirit of anthropology, one might read each account, indeed, in relation to the author's ethnographic experience. Appadurai imagines global scapes from the perspective of his attention to the Indian diaspora and its cultural world. Kearney theorizes from his encounter with Miztec "postpeasants": Mexican Indian farmers who have become migrants selling crafts in San Diego parking lots. Hannerz is concerned about cosmopolitans, world travelers, journalists, and city people everywhere; he returns often to his knowledge about Africa. These varied subjects assist the authors in evoking different globalisms. If, instead of assuming a single global trajectory, we attended to varied globalist claims and perspectives, what might we see?

Diasporas, almost by definition, conjure deterritorialized areas, worlds of meaning and "home" feeling detached from original territorial boundaries— like Appadurai's scapes. This kind of self-consciousness about the making of cultural worlds contrasts sharply with the cultural commitments of cosmopolitans and poor migrants, as these create focal knowledges for Hannerz and Kearney, respectively. Both cosmopolitans and poor migrants erase the specificity of their cultural tracks, although for different reasons: Poor migrants need to fit in the worlds of others; cosmopolitans want more of the world to be theirs. Cosmopolitans, like diasporas, promote projects of world making, but, as Hannerz stresses, the projects they endorse enlarge the hegemonies of

Northern centers even as they incorporate peripheries. In contrast, neither the world-making projects of Southern diasporas nor those of poor migrants fit into a center-periphery frame. They limit, rather than spread, Northern hegemonies. In this spirit, Appadurai and Kearney implicitly criticize Hannerz's center-periphery approach. Yet it is also the case that Kearney's and Appadurai's actors diverge. Poor migrants, like those at the center of Kearney's globalism, are particularly aware of their need to survive—politically, economically, and culturally—in worlds that others have made; the imagination is never enough for them to create autonomy and self-determination. Thus, Kearney (1995: 553) refuses Appadurai's imagination-ruled scapes, while Appadurai and Hannerz, thinking through diasporas and cosmopolitans, respectively, stress the world-making power of imaginative perspectives.

The regional specificities of these focal knowledges may also be relevant to the globalisms imagined through them: I think of the strength of the culture and media industries of India and its diaspora, the self-consciousness about Northern cultural impositions of cosmopolitan Africans, and the centrality of transnational capitalism in Latin American studies. It also may be suggestive to compare all these knowledges with other angles for thinking about contemporary culture. Consider, for example, U.S. minority groups who have demanded protection from the nation-state against discrimination; thinking through U.S. minority culture provides a less fertile ground than diasporas, poor migrants, and cosmopolitans to imagine an inclusively postnational era.[39] These differences do not make these perspectives wrong; my point is to show that these are differences that matter theoretically. The next step for readers—and future researchers and writers—is to think about that world in which the respective focal knowledges on which they draw could *all* exist, whether in competition or alliance, in mutual acknowledgment or erasure, in misunderstanding or dialogue.

This task requires that we study folk understandings of the global, and the practices with which they are intertwined, rather than representing globalization as a transcultural historical process. With some modifications, each of the perspectives I have been describing can be used for this task. However, we would have to resituate the authors' theories in relation to histories of their respective knowledges of and experiences with specific people and events. We would have to abandon the search for a single global future.

Appadurai's stress on disjunction as well as on the importance of the imagination is well suited for thinking about the interplay of varied globalist perspectives. Yet imaginative landscapes come in many kinds, and this diversity is more useful to understanding disjunction than a division into functional domains of ethnicity, technology, finance, media, and ideology, for these posit a singular formula for "society." If, instead of hegemonic domain divisions, we turned to the social and cultural struggles through which imaginative visions come to count as "scapes" at all, we might be able to incorporate disjunction not only among domains but also among varied and contested kinds of imaginative landscape making in this framework. We might contrast the cultural world of the Indian diaspora with other globalist scapes. For example, Paulla Ebron (1998, 1999) has described the regional and global claims of African American history and memory landscapes; she traces these landscapes through many formats of discussion, which both enter and interrupt Appadurai's "mediascape" domain.[40] Moving beyond a list of globally settled "scapes," we need to study how scales, geographies, eras, and other imaginative terrains are differentially and dialogically negotiated, refused, or erased.

Hannerz's attention to the cultural specificity of cosmopolitanisms is important to assess the power and limitations of claims about scale, era, and geography without subsuming one's own analysis under the truths these claims promote. Hannerz also usefully reminds us of the power of certain imaginative landscapes, especially those that "make people from western Europe and North America feel as much at home as possible" (107). Yet these powerful perspectives do not necessarily determine the cultural evolution of the whole world; the key is to *situate* them in relation to the political economies that make them possible and the struggles over meaning in which they participate.

In the process of putting global perspectives in situated dialogue, the political economy engaged (if not often endorsed) by Kearney is essential. Imaginative landscapes mobilize an audience through material and institutional resources. Yet, as discussed in the previous section, it is difficult to give full attention to such mobilizations with a theory of the singular evolution of a monolithic capitalism.[41] As J. K. Gibson-Graham argues, models that predict the stages of capitalism bow to the ideology of a single world-capitalist system rather than investigating its heterogeneous complexities.[42] Instead, Kearney's concern with political economy, like that of Harvey, might point us toward an investigation of shifting cultural developments among surprisingly diverse capitalisms. The innovations of these approaches are not served well, however, by an overreliance on a vocabulary of "flows."

CIRCULATION

"Circulation" has a deep genealogy in anthropology. I keep waiting to find an author who takes me through this legacy, perhaps tracing his or her thoughts from French structuralist "exchange" through global "flows." But I have not yet found that author. Instead, it has become easy for anthropologists to talk about global circulations as a sign of everything new and of future making.

Circulations are said to be what we are able to study as global. George Marcus is informative and clear about this in the introduction to the series of essays he edited as *Rereading Cultural Anthropology*.[43] Under the heading "Circulations," he says:

The other major related trend that concerns contemporary global transformations is a move out from local situations to understand how transcultural
processes themselves are constituted in the world of the so-called "system"
(modern inter-locking institutions of media, markets, states, industries, universities—the worlds of elites and middle classes) that has encapsulated,
transformed, and sometimes obliterated local cultures. This work examines
the circulation of cultural meanings, objects, and identities in diffuse time-
space. *It shows how the global arena is itself constituted by such circulations.* (xiii, emphasis added)

Circulations define the newness of the global epoch. Kearney's review "The
Local and the Global: The Anthropology of Globalization and Transnationalism" offers a useful statement of this. His field is the study of movement, both
population movement and "the movement of information, symbols, capital,
and commodities in global and transnational spaces. . . . Special attention is
given to the significant contemporary increases in the volume and velocity of
such flows for the dynamics of communities and for the identities of their
members" (547).

Newness is defined by increased flow. Because authors and readers focus
on the excitement of this newness, there has been almost no discussion about
the implied dichotomies here: circulation versus stagnation, new versus old.
Does the newness and globality of movement mean that once-immobile "local"
places have recently been transcended by "global" flow? If analysts must
"move out of local situations" to find circulation, there must be some local
folks who are still stuck inside them, being stagnant. These imagined stagnant
locals are excluded from the new circulating globality, which leaves them outside, just as progress and modernity were imagined as leaving so many behind.
Here we must consider which new Orientalisms will define who is in and who
is out of circulation, just as frameworks of race, region, and religion defined
those excluded from the idea of progress. Furthermore, if circulation is new,
does that mean that the old order was static and segregated? Were there really,
after all, isolated autonomous cultures out there until the circulations of the last
few years? Each of these misleading dichotomies would encourage analysts to
resurrect that very anthropology that has been criticized and reworked for the
last twenty-five years: the anthropology that fixed and segregated cultures. But
in each case, it would be resurrected only for special cases: the marginal, the
past. A globalist anthropology of movement would reign at the center.[44] This
will not do. To move beyond the contrast between past and local stability and
present/future global flow, we need to examine different modes of regional-
to-global interconnection.

The new attention to global circulation responds to real changes in the
world—and in anthropology as practiced in the United States. Anthropologists
once set out to study "communities"; they thought they could find society and

culture within a relatively narrowly defined social sphere. For some years, it has seemed difficult to do anthropology without paying attention to much wider-ranging objects of study: national visions, elite networks, popular culture, social movements, state policies, histories of colonial thinking, and much more. One piece of the excitement of contemporary anthropology involves new ideas about how to do fieldwork on these complex objects. We rush into interdisciplinary social theory to find innovative, project-oriented suggestions. In this process, it is easy to endorse frameworks of globalization that transcend the limitations of site-oriented local research. Instead, I am arguing that we can study the landscape of circulation as well as the flow. How are people, cultures, and things remade as they travel?

SCALE AS AN OBJECT OF ANALYSIS

Understanding the institutional proliferation of particular globalization projects requires a sense of their cultural specificities as well as the travels and interactions through which these projects are reproduced and taken on in new places. In thinking about where one would begin a globally informed investigation of local and global processes that avoids the pitfalls I have been discussing, I might begin with two analytic principles. First, I would pay close attention to *ideologies* of scale, that is, cultural claims about locality, regionality, and globality; about stasis and circulation; and about networks and strategies of proliferation. I would track rhetorics of scale as well as contests over what will count as relevant scales. Second, I would break down the units of culture and political economy through which we make sense of events and social processes. Instead of looking for world-wrapping evolutionary stages, logics, and epistemes, I would begin by finding what I call "projects," that is, relatively coherent bundles of ideas and practices as realized in particular times and places. The choice of what counts as a project depends on what one is trying to learn about, but, in each case, to identify projects is to maintain a commitment to localization, even of the biggest world-making dreams and schemes. The various instantiations of capitalism can be regarded as projects; so can progressive social movements, everyday patterns of living, or university-based intellectual programs. Projects are to be traced in relation to particular historical travels from one place to another; they are caught up in local issues of translation and mobilization; although they may be very powerful, we cannot assume their ability to remake nature and society according to their visions. Projects may articulate with each other, creating moments of fabled stability and power.[45] They may also rub up against each other awkwardly, creating messiness and new possibilities. Through joint attention to ideologies of scale and projects of scale making, it is possible to move into those cracks most neglected by unself-conscious reliance on global futurism, globalist conflation, and global circulation.

To illustrate such cracks, I turn to scholarship on the making of projects of environmental modernization. Although the rhetoric of globalization has much affected the reconstruction of cities, it is the rhetoric of modernization that continues to make rural hinterlands into the kinds of places that global capital and globalist planning can best use for their projects. Talk of national and international development still dominates the reshaping of the countryside; yet it is the complement of globalization talk. Global dreams require these rural modernization projects, and, thus, globalist strategies can be studied within them. Indeed, there are certain advantages of tracking the importance of globalism in an arena where this rhetoric does not amass a difficult-to-question hegemony.[46] It is easier to see the exotic particularities and the grounded travels of scale-making commitments where these are not the only goal of the scholarship. It is possible to read against the grain of analyses of modernism to make scale an object of analysis. I offer four examples of such starting points.

Scale Making.   Certainly, a key issue in assuming a critical perspective on global claims and processes is the making of scales—not just the global but also local and regional scales of all sorts. Through what social and material processes and cultural commitments do localities or globalities come, tentatively, into being? How are varied regional geographies made real? Globalism's automatic association of particular scales with particular eras makes it very difficult to notice the details and idiosyncrasies of scale making—thus, more the reason to foreground this issue. And, because the globe is a region made large, asking about the making of global scale brings forward questions of the various forms of region making that both facilitate and interrupt global claims.

Critical studies of environmental modernization offer a number of useful examples about how social scientists might approach the investigation of regional and global scale making. "Bioregions" have been a central feature of environmental policy; how are they made? I think of Warwick Anderson's research on the hygiene-oriented experiments that helped define "the tropics" as a zone of challenge for scientific modernism, or of Peter Haas's discussion of the transnational strategies of scientists in shaping the cross-border political treaties that made "the Mediterranean" a zone in which issues of water pollution could be addressed.[47] And what of the making of the global superregion? Richard Grove's research on the construction of global environmental science is particularly exciting in thinking about the makings of globality.[48] Grove shows how the imperial placement of scientists in botanical gardens and research stations across the European colonies inspired continent-crossing correspondence in the late eighteenth century. Through this correspondence, informed by widespread fears of climate change caused by colonial deforestation, colonial scientists formulated notions of a "global" climate. This commitment to planetwide environmental process allowed further developments in imagining both science and policy on a global scale. Obviously, this is not the only global scale that matters. But in tracing its specificity, Grove offers a model for thinking about the many kinds of globality that have become important in the contemporary world.

Close Encounters. Where circulation models have tended to focus only on message transmission, one might instead investigate interactions involving collaboration, misunderstanding, opposition, and dialogue. Attention to these processes provides an alternative to the conflation of varied scale-making claims, projects, and agents. One literature that has become unusually attentive to mixed encounters is the literature on transnational social movements, which require coalitions among extremely various kinds of people, with disparate goals and perceptions of the issues at hand.[49] Thus, for example, the coalitions that have been built for rain forest protection have brought together tribal leaders, union organizers, college professors, wildlife lovers, rural workers, cosmetic entrepreneurs, and activists for democratic reform, among others.[50]

To understand even momentary successes of this kind of motley coalition, analysts must attend to the changing definitions of interests and *identity* that both allow and result from collaborative activities. They must focus on the historical specificity of the events that resulted in alliance and the open-ended indeterminacy of the regional processes stimulated by that alliance.[51] These are useful reminders in rethinking transnational interactions.

It is not just in transient and defensive social movements, however, that it is important to look for social processes sparked by coalitions, dialogues, missed messages, and oppositional refusals. In considering developments in transnational capitalism, this kind of attention can offer an alternative to the blindfolded dedication to a singular unfolding economic logic that has characterized so much globalist analysis. If we investigate the series of historically specific collaborations that create distinctive cultural forms of capitalism, we might better appreciate global heterogeneity.

Peter Dauvergne, for example, has shown how Japanese trading companies, requiring a mass scale of transactions, were able to form productive coalitions with national political leaders in Southeast Asia, who were seeking the support of powerful clients; together they created the distinctive features of the Southeast Asian timber industry, which has devastated regional rain forests for cheap plywood.[52] The cultural and economic specificities of both Japanese trading companies and Southeast Asian national political regimes created a particular and peculiar capitalism that cannot be reduced to the playing out of a singular transnational capitalist logic. Instead, Dauvergne argues, it created economic and ecological "shadows" between Japan and Southeast Asia that redefined and reformulated their separate and combined regional agency. This kind of analysis should prove useful in understanding the many forms of capitalism that help to create regional and global scales.

Definitional Struggles. Circulation imagery can draw attention away from the transformation of actors, objects, goals, perspectives, and terrains that characterizes regional-to-global interaction. Instead, we might pay special attention to the roles of both cultural legacies and power inequalities in creating the institutional arenas and assumptions of world-making transitions. Every globalization project is shaped from somewhat unpredictable interactions among specific cultural legacies. Furthermore, the cultural frames and assumptions of globalization projects cannot be understood without attention to multiple levels of political negotiations, with their idiosyncratic and open-ended histories. "Definitional struggles" call attention to how these arenas are designed and the politics of their development. They can remind us that globalization both requires and exceeds the work of particularly positioned and repositioned globalizers.

Critical studies of environmental modernization can also provide illustrative guidance here. Consider, for example, how agribusiness came to power in the western United States. Donald Worster's study of the building of the great irrigation projects that stimulated the emergence of agribusiness offers a wealth of detail on the interacting cultural legacies that made the scale and design of these massive irrigation projects possible.[53] The wide streets of Mormon aesthetics inspired irrigation design, breaking it away from Hispanic community water control; the legal precedence of California gold rush mineral claims allowed the fluorescence of water law that privileged state-private coalitions; the opportunity for water engineers to tour the irrigation canals of British colonial India created a parallel vision for the western United States in which the landscape should properly be managed by alien experts. Compromises between populists and business advocates congealed center-oriented land allocation policies. These, and more, legacies shaped the design of the great water apparatus that transformed the U.S. economy, bringing profitable farming from east to west and helping to build U.S. imperial strength. Not just definition but also struggle is at issue in the formation of projects of world transformation. Studies of the formation of the "frontier" in Amazonia, for example, could be told as the classic story of modernization, with its replacement of native traditional living spaces with cosmopolitan modern economies. But critical histories by scholars such as Hecht and Cockburn and Schmink and Wood have shown that the cultural assumptions of property and resource management that modernizers might want us to take for granted have been established unevenly, awkwardly, and tentatively, in the midst of passionate and unfinished struggles.[54] Hecht and Cockburn stress the historically shifting wielders of power who have worked so hard, with varied success, for particular programs of frontier making. Schmink and Wood stress the uncanniness of the frontier, in which the best laid plans produce results opposite to their predictions. The works show varied histories at community, regional, and national scales; their components do not fit easily into a single story. Together, they highlight definitional struggles involved in making the frontier.

Concrete Trajectories and Engagements. In contrast to the abstract globe conjured by social science globalism, the scholarship I am imagining would stress the concreteness of "movements" in both senses of the word: social mobilizations in which new identities and interests are formed and travels from one place to another through which place-transcending interactions occur. These two senses of *movement* work together in remaking geographies and scales. Tracing them concretely offers more insight into planetary complexity than the endorsement of a heterogeneous globalism whose features ricochet helplessly between an imagined spreading global dynamism and its contained local Other. How might this be done? A number of scholars have followed modern forestry, as developed in Europe, to examine its deployment in colonial regions. Here I am less interested in the metropole-to-colony transfer and more in the movement from one particular place to another, say of British forest science to India. Ramachandra Guha, Ravi Rajan, and K. Sivaramakrishnan (1996) have all done important research on this movement, as it made and transformed forestry experts, forest-dwelling human communities, and forests themselves.[55] Each tells of the effects of this movement: the development of colonial authority relations, involving dissent and opposition as well as compliance, between forest experts and forest peasants; the importance of reaffirming cultural and scientific standards in empire-wide conferences; the incorporation of local knowledges into Indian forestry policy; and the changing practices of foresters as they learned the Indian landscape and its social and political conventions. The concrete sites of encounter and engagement among people as well as trees shape the trajectories of the forestry project. This kind of attention to particular "routes" of travel is equally important in tracing contemporary social and cultural processes around the globe.[56]

In globalization theories, we have confused what should be *questions* about the global ramifications of new technologies and social processes into *answers* about global change. Each of the starting points I have suggested offers an attempt to reverse this globalist thinking to turn concerns about the global back into researchable questions.

RELEASE

Let me return for a moment to the parallels between modernization and globalization. Many anthropologists are able to look at the dreams and schemes of modernization with a critical distance. We need this critical distance, too, in studying globalization. Globalization is a set of projects that require us to imagine space and time in particular ways. These are curious, powerful projects. Anthropologists need not ignore them; we also need not renaturalize them by assuming that the terms they offer us are true. At this point, some readers may say, "Why not throw out 'the global' completely, since it exists as a fantasy?" My answer is that even fantasies deserve serious engagement. The best legacies of ethnography allow us to take our objects of study seriously even as we examine them critically. To study ghosts ethnographically means to take issues of haunting seriously. If the analyst merely made fun of beliefs in ghosts, the study would be of little use. Several other steps would be needed: a description of ghost beliefs; an examination of the effects of ghost beliefs on social life; and, in the spirit of taking one's informants seriously, a close attention to the questions that ghosts raise, such as the presence of death and its eerie reminders of things gone. In the same spirit, an analyst of globalism cannot merely toss it out as a vacant deception. Instead, an ethnographic study of the global needs careful attention not only to global claims and their effects on social life but also to questions of interconnection, movement, and boundary crossing that globalist spokespeople have brought to the fore. To take globality as an object of study requires both distance and intimate engagement.

Other readers may object that it is important to reify globalization because of the terrible toll it promises to take on cultural diversity and human well-being. Their endorsement of a self-consciously paranoid vision of total transformation involves the choice to glimpse the terrors of the new world order it promises. Yet I would argue that by reproducing this totalizing framework of social change, critics bind themselves within the assumptions and fantasies of those they oppose. If we want to imagine emergent forms of resistance, new possibilities, and the messiness through which the best laid plans may not yet destroy all hope, we need to attune ourselves to the heterogeneity and open-endedness of the world. This is not, however, an argument for "local" diversity; if anything, it is an argument for "global" diversity and the wrongheadedness of imagining diversity—from an unquestioning globalist perspective—as a territorially circumscribed, "place-based," and antiglobalist phenomenon. (Since when are globalists not place based?) Unlike most anthropologists working on "global" issues, I have tried to examine some basic assumptions of globalism, using them to form a critical perspective rather than a negative or positive endorsement of projects for making a future imagined as global.

Most global anthropologists embrace the idea of diversity. Anthropologists have been critics of theories of global homogenization; at the same time, those who have joined the argument with globalization theorists have been influenced by the terms of debate to accept most of the premises of these theories in order to join the conversation. The debate about global cultural unification has encouraged anthropologists to agree that we are indeed entering an era properly called global, although that era, according to anthropologists, is characterized by local cultural divergences as much as unification. In the embrace of the argument, the cultural divergence we find must be part of the globalist phenomenon.[57]

This is not, I think, a useful place to be stuck. To get out of its grip, analysts need to give up several of the tools and frames we have found most easy to work with, perhaps because they resound so nicely with popular "common sense," at least in the United States. First, we might stop making a distinction between "global" *forces* and "local" *places*. This is a very seductive set of distinctions, promising as it does to give us both focused detail and the big picture, and I find myself slipping into this vocabulary all the time. But it draws us into globalist fantasies by obscuring the ways that the cultural processes of all "place" making and all "force" making are *both* local and global, that is, both socially and culturally particular and productive of widely spreading interactions. Through these terms, global "forces" gain the power to cause a total rupture that takes over the world.

Second, we might learn to investigate new developments without assuming either their universal extension or their fantastic ability to draw all world-making activities into their grasp. International finance, for example, has surely undergone striking and distinctive transformations in the last thirty years. Certainly this has effects everywhere, but what these effects are is unclear. It seems unlikely to me that a single logic of transformation is being produced, or a singular moment of rupture.[58]

Third, globalisms themselves need to be interrogated as an interconnected, but not homogeneous, set of projects with their distinctive cultural commitments and their powerful but limited presence in the world. Critical studies of modernization projects provide some thought-provoking examples of analytic direction here.

Freed up in these ways, it might be possible to attend to global visions without imagining their world hegemony. Outside the thrall of globalization, a more nuanced and surprising appreciation of the making and remaking of geography might yet be possible.

NOTES

This essay began as a thought paper for the 1997 Histories of the Future Seminar at the University of California Humanities Research Institute. I thank the participants of that seminar for their suggestions and encouragement. It was resurrected for a University of California at Santa Cruz environmental politics study group in 1998; my thanks also go to the members of that group. I rewrote the essay for both this volume and *Cultural Anthropology*. In that long process, I am particularly thankful for the comments of Arjun Appadurai, Kathryn Chetkovich, Timothy Choy, James Clifford, Paulla Ebron, Donna Haraway, Celia Lowe, Vicente Rafael, Annelise Riles, Lisa Rofel, Roger Rouse, Shiho Satsuka, Joan Scott, Dan Segal, Sylvia Yanagisako, and the anonymous reviewers of *Cultural Anthropology*. Their criticisms and suggestions have invigorated my writing even when I have not been able to fully incorporate them.

1. See Arturo Escobar, *Encountering Development: The Making and Unmaking of the Third World* (Princeton: Princeton University Press, 1995); and James Ferguson, *The Anti-Politics Machine: "Development," Depoliticization, and Bureaucratic Power in Lesotho* (Cambridge: Cambridge University Press, 1990).

2. On regional political struggles, see Pauline Peters, *Dividing the Commons: Politics, Policy, and Culture in Botswana* (Charlottesville: University Press of Virginia, 1994). On culturally influenced interpretation, see Stacey Pigg, "Constructing Social Categories through Place: Social Representations and Development in Nepal," *Comparative Studies in Society and History* 34(3): 491–513.

3. The image of sitting on top of the globe, either with one's body or one's technology, has become a mainstay of advertising. As I write this, for example, I have just received two telephone company advertisements: one, from a local telephone company (US West), features a woman sitting in an office chair on top of the globe while talking into the telephone and typing on her personal computer; the other, from a long-distance telephone company (MCI), shows a telephone receiver resting on top of the globe. This globe is a field to be mastered, managed, and controlled.

4. Garb argues that the image of the globe also brought with it political understandings about white male mastery and control; environmentalists have fought against these understandings in stressing the fragility of the earth but have also been influenced by them. See Yaakov Garb, "Perspective or Escape? Ecofeminist Musings on Contemporary Earth Imagery," in *Reweaving the World: The Emergence of Ecofeminism*, ed. Irene Diamond and Gloria Orenstein (San Francisco: Sierra Club Books, 1990), pp. 264–308.

5. See Peter Haas, *Saving the Mediterranean: The Politics of International Environmental Cooperation* (New York: Columbia University Press, 1990). See also Peter Taylor and Frederick Buttel, "How Do We Know We Have Global Environmental Problems? Science and the Globalization of Environmental Discourse," *Geoforum* 23:3 (1992): 405–16.

6. On this see Margaret Keck and Kathryn Sikkink, *Activists beyond Borders* (Ithaca, NY: Cornell University Press, 1998).

7. Annelise Riles, "Infinity within Brackets," *American Ethnologist* 25:3 (1998): 1–21.

8. On this, see Noam Chomsky, "Free Trade and Free Market: Pretense and Practice," in *The Cultures of Globalization*, ed. Frederic Jameson and Misao Miyoshi (Durham, NC.: Duke University Press, 1998), pp. 356–70.

9. See, for example, Saskia Sassen's *Globalization and Its Discontents* (New York: The New Press, 1998); and the essays in *Towards a Transnational Perspective on Migration: Race, Class, Ethnicity, and Nationalism Reconsidered*, ed. Nina Glick Schiller, Linda Basch, and Cristina Blanc-Szanton (New York: New York Academy of Sciences, 1992).

10. This is documented in *The Dictionary of Global Culture*, ed. Kwame Anthony Appiah and Henry Louis Gates (New York: Knopf, 1997).

11. A fuller genealogy of the idea of globalization—whether in corporate policy, social commentary, or academic analysis—is beyond the scope of this essay. New books and articles appear on the subject every week. The inclusively imagined *Globalization*

Reader [ed. Frank Lechner and John Boli (Oxford: Blackwell, 2000)] reprints a number of social science contributions to the conversation, offering a sense of its heterogeneity and breadth. Of the recent anthologies I have seen, I find *Globalisation and the Asia Pacific* [ed. Kris Olds, Peter Dicken, Philip Kelly, Lily Kong, and Henry Wai-chung Yeung (London: Routledge, 1999)] the most sensible and insightful.

12. Saskia Sassen nicely articulates this analytic choice, necessary to make globalization a significant field-defining process: "My approach entails . . . constructing 'the difference,' theoretically and empirically, so as to specify the current period." She adds, frankly, "I do not deny the existence of many continuities, but my effort has been to understand the strategic discontinuities" (*Globalization and Its Discontents*, pp. 85 and 101).

13. I take the notion of the building of a "bandwagon" effect from Joan Fujimura's work on cancer research: "The Molecular Biological Bandwagon in Cancer Research: Where Social Worlds Meet," *Social Problems* 35:3 (1988): 261–84.

14. For example, discussion of globalization has stimulated a rethinking of area studies scholarship in the United States; research and teaching programs are being revamped not only at many universities but also at many of the major research institutes and funding foundations. (On this, see for example, Abraham and Kassimir on the Social Science Research Council and Volkman on the Ford Foundation: Itty Abraham and Ronald Kassimir, "Internationalization of the Social Sciences and Humanities, *Items* 51: 2/3 [1997]: 23–30; Toby Volkman, "Crossing Borders: The Case for Area Studies," Ford Foundation Report, winter 1998, pp. 28–29.) This rethinking allows promising new configurations of training and scholarship. At the same time, the national discussion about area studies illustrates the problems I refer to in describing the limitations of the dogma of global newness. Too many participants, asked to rethink areas in the light of globalization, jump to the conclusion that "areas" are archaic forms beset and overcome by newly emergent global forces. Scholarship, many conclude, should either position itself with the winners, studying global forces, or with the losers, attending to regional resistance. In this configuration of choice, no attention is paid to the continually shifting formation and negotiation of "areas," the consideration of which might have been the most exciting product of the rethinking of area studies.

15. Mintz argues in this spirit, reminding anthropologists that massive transcontinental migrations have occurred in past centuries. He suggests, provocatively, that scholars find global migration new because large waves of people of color have recently turned up in the "big white societies" of Europe and its diaspora, where, in the nineteenth century, they were refused: Sidney Mintz, "The Localization of Anthropological Practice: From Area Studies to Transnationalism," *Critique of Anthropology* 18:2 (1998): 117–33, esp. 123.

16. In their first waves of enthusiasm about globalization, many scholars, social commentators, and policymakers argued that it was forcing nations to disappear. This remains perhaps the most popular argument (see, for example, Arjun Appadurai, *Modernity at Large: Cultural Dimensions of Globalization* [Minneapolis: University of Minnesota Press, 1996]; and Misao Miyoshi, "A Borderless World? From Colonialism to Transnationalism and the Decline of the Nation-State," in *Global/Local: Cultural Production and the Transnational Imaginary*, ed. Rob Wilson and Wimal Dissanayake

[Durham, NC: Duke University Press, 1996], pp. 78–106). More recently, a number of scholars have argued that the nation-state takes new forms in the context of rapid international transfers of capital and labor (e.g., Aiwha Ong, "Chinese Modernities: Narratives of Nation and of Capitalism," in *The Cultural Politics of Modern Chinese Transnationalism*, ed. Aihwa Ong and Donald Nonini [New York: Routledge, 1997], pp. 171–202; and Saskia Sassen, *Globalization and Its Discontents*). Even the most rapidly mobile of corporations depends on the apparatus of the nation-state to guarantee its property and contracts; in this context, national deregulation reregulates the economic domain in the interest of global capital (see Philip Cerny, "The Deregulation and Re-Regulation of Financial Markets in a More Open World," in *Finance and World Politics*, ed. Philip Cerny [Hants, UK: Edward Elgar, 1993], pp. 51–85). Nation-states have also been instrumental in forging niches of ethnic and national privilege through which the new "global" entrepreneurs secure their advantage. For these kinds of arguments in particular, an appreciation of the shifting histories of the nation and of the hegemonies of particular nation-states—as I advocate here—seems essential.

17. On this, see Eric Helleiner, "When Finance Was the Servant: International Capital Movements in the Bretton Woods Order," in *Finance and World Politics*, pp. 20–48.

18. This set of post–World War II nationalist commitments was brought to my attention in the insightful comments of Malaysian economist Jomo K.S. at the conference "Public Intellectuals in Southeast Asia," held in Kuala Lumpur, May 1998. As an example, he pointed out that histories in which nationalism in Southeast Asia was stimulated by conversations with overseas Chinese (e.g., Pramoedya Ananta Toer, *Child of All Nations*, trans. Max Lane [New York: Penguin, 1996]) were suppressed by post–World War II Southeast Asian nations.

19. See Jameson and Miyoshi, *The Cultures of Globalization*. See also *The Politics of Culture in the Shadow of Capital*, ed. (Durham, NC: Duke University Press, 1997); and Wilson and Dissanayake, *Global/Local*.

20. Why is globalization a new era (rather than, say, an object of reflection or an approach to appreciating culture) for these humanists? Some have come to their acceptance of cultural evolutionary stages from a slightly earlier exploration of "postmodernism" as the latest stage of cultural development; for them, globalization is a variation on postmodern culture. For some, too, the appeal of imagining globalization as a stage of cultural politics is drawn from Marxist evolutionary histories of capitalism; the cultural era is generated by the economic era as superstructure to base. For others, the main appeal seems to be the intervention into earlier civilization-bound humanities studies: the opportunity to draw together a diverse group of scholars who can talk to each other across lines of nation, language, and cultural background. Indeed, I see little evidence that most of the contributors to these volumes are themselves particularly invested in positing a singular global era; even the editors, in their separate articles, contribute to a much more nuanced approach. It seems there is something about introductory material that stimulates era making. There is also an admirable political goal in gathering a diverse group under a common banner: Perhaps a politically united front against unregulated corporate expansion can be formed. However, this political cause can only be aided by building an appreciation of the multiple and conflicting agendas of globalization.

21. Jameson and Miyoshi's, *The Cultures of Globalization* does not include an editors' introduction. In lieu of an introduction, the preface and the contributions by the two editors, however, offer the reader a sense of the editors' stakes and stand in that regard.

22. A number of the contributors, including the editors themselves, offer insightful descriptions of the coming together and coming apart of varied agendas of "globalization"; they describe the scope and the exclusions of varied transnational projects; they ask about the legacies and transformational possibilities of various global interconnections. But these kinds of insights are lost in those parts of the editors' introductions that condense this richness into the definitional homogeneity of a new era.

23. Preface to *The Cultures of Globalization*, pp. xi–xvii.

24. "Notes on Globalization as a Philosophical Issue," *The Cultures of Globalization*, p. 54.

25. Roger Rouse, "'There Will Be No More There': Globalization, Privatization, and the Family Form in the U.S. Corporate Imaginary, unpublished manuscript, Department of Anthropology, University of California at Davis, 1997).

26. Annelise Riles, "The Network Inside Out: Designs for a Global Reality" (paper presented at the Department of Anthropology, University of California at Santa Cruz, 1998).

27. Riles's analysis is not a naive celebration of the possibilities of networks for global feminism. In fact, she emphasizes the strangeness of the object the women she studied called a "network." It did not, for example, include their ordinary collegial social relationships; it was a formal design more suited for documents and diagrams than for everyday living. My goal in contrasting Riles's NGO networks and Rouse's corporate ones is not to show what Jameson would call the light and the dark side of globalization. Instead, from my perspective these are both curious ethnographic objects, and I am interested in how they are produced and maintained, separately and together, in the same world.

28. See, for example, Arjun Appadurai, "Introduction: Commodities and the Politics of Value," in *The Social Life of Things*, ed. Arjun Appadurai (Cambridge: Cambridge University Press, 1986), pp. 3–63; and Jean Baudrillard, *The Mirror of Production*, trans. Mark Poster (St. Louis: Telos Press, 1975).

29. See Aihwa Ong, *Flexible Citizenship: The Cultural Logics of Transnationality* (Durham, NC: Duke University Press, 1999); and Sassen, *Globalization and Its Discontents*.

30. Allan Pred and Michael Watts, *Reworking Modernity: Capitalism and Symbolic Discontent* (New Brunswick, NJ: Rutgers University Press, 1992).

31. See Wilson and Dissanayake, "Introduction: Tracking the Global/Local," in *Global/Local*.

32. My comments are not meant as a criticism of the kind of analysis that shows how cosmopolitan ideas and institutions are translated and specified as they come to mean something in particular communities. To the contrary, I would like to see the extension of this kind of work to show the cultural specification of the cosmopolitan.

33. David Harvey, *The Condition of Postmodernity* (Cambridge, Mass.: Blackwell, 1989).

34. George Marcus makes Harvey's argument about accumulation the basis for his call for new research methods in anthropology: "For those across disciplines interested

in placing their specific projects of research in the unfolding of new arrangements for which past historical narratives were not fully adequate, a firm sense of a world system framework was replaced by various accounts of dissolution, fragmentation, as well as new processes—captured in concepts like "post-Fordism" [Harvey], "time-space compression"[Harvey], "flexible specialization" [Harvey], "the end of organized capitalism" [Lash, Urry], and most recently "globalization" [Featherstone, Hannerz, Sklair]—none of which could be fully understood in terms of earlier macro-models of the capitalist world system"; see George Marcus, "Ethnography in/of the World System: The Emergence of Multi-Sited Ethnography," *Annual Review of Anthropology* 24 (1995): 95–117. (I have substituted the names of authors for the numbered references included in the original.)

Michael Kearney brings up time and space: "The most cogent and comprehensive analysis of changing images of time and space associated with globalization is Harvey's [1989]. Although not dealing with globalization per se, Harvey's thesis is that a marked acceleration in a secular trend of time-space compression in capitalist political economy is central to current cultural change": Michael Kearney, "The Local and the Global: The Anthropology of Globalization and Transnationalism," *Annual Review of Anthropology* 24 (1995): 547–65. Kearney usefully calls it a thesis; more often Harvey is mentioned to establish a fact.

35. There is also the suggestion that Culture can provide an aesthetic blueprint for the economy, see Harvey, *The Condition of Postmodernity*, p. 345.

36. Akhil Gupta and James Ferguson, "Beyond 'Culture': Space, Identity, and the Politics of Difference," *Cultural Anthropology* 7:1 (1992): 6–23.

37. Appadurai, *Modernity at Large*; Ulf Hannerz, *Transnational Connections* (New York: Routledge, 1996); Michael Kearney, *Reconceptualizing the Peasantry: Anthropology in Global Perspective* (Boulder, Co: Westview Press, 1996).

38. See Hannerz, "Notes on the Global Ecumene," *Public Culture* 1:2 (1989): 66–75.

39. Appadurai begins this comparison in his chapter "Patriotism and Its Futures." However, he is interested in convergences between multicultural and postnational commitments. His goal is to mobilize a forward-looking form of postnationalism, not to assess the contrasts among groups with varied histories of dependence on and opposition to nation-states.

40. See Paulla Ebron, "Regional Differences in African American Culture," *American Anthropologist* 100:1 (1998): 94–106; and "Tourists as Pilgrims," *American Ethnologist* 26:4 (1999): 910–32.

41. While Kearney appears to draw on a theory of capitalist stages in his review article, in his book he refutes the centrality of capitalist accumulation strategies as producing historical stages. Yet his arguments are completely dependent on the eras he posits, which neatly join scholarly theory and world history. Because he rejects forms of economic, cultural, and historical logic that might generate these all-encompassing eras, I am not sure how they might appear in such a world-hegemonic form.

42. J. K. Gibson-Graham, *The End of Capitalism (As We Knew It)* (Cambridge, Mass.: Blackwell, 1996).

43. George Marcus, *Rereading Cultural Anthropology* (Durham, NC: Duke University Press, 1992).

44. Some globalist anthropologists conflate the excitement of new postlocal approaches in anthropology and that of new developments in the world. But, thus, they weaken the case for each. Global interconnections are not just a new phenomenon, although they certainly have important new features and permutations. If older anthropological frameworks were unable to handle interconnection and mobility, this is a problem with the frameworks and a reason for new ones but not the mirror of an evolutionary change in the world.

45. See my "Notes on Culture and Natural Resource Management,"Berkeley Workshop on Environmental Politics, Working Paper WP 99–4, 1999, Institute of International Studies, University of California at Berkeley; and my "Inside the Economy of Appearances," *Public Culture* 12:1 (2000): 115–44.

46. Environmental studies has generated its own local globalism. Unlike the globalisms I have been describing, it is not focused on the distinctive features of a future-making epoch. Instead, the most commonly promoted environmental globalism endorses a technical and moral "global" unit. The goal of this environmental globalism is to show the compatibility of all scales into the "global" across all time. (There has been some interest in the kinds of globalisms I have been describing here among environmental scholars, especially social scientists. But to trace the encounter between "globalization" and the technical-moral "global environment" is beyond the scope of this essay.) That "global" domain into which all other scales can be collapsed, across all time, is the domain of agency for global environmental science and activism. Social scientists and historians have been rather disruptive of this global domain, although not always self-consciously, when their descriptions establish the incompatibility of various socially defined spatial scales and historical periods, as nature is made and remade in diverse forms that evade simple conflations. The critical literature on environmental modernization, which I tap here, contributes a sense of the historical and spatial rupture of projects of making nature's modernity. Through this distinctive anti-globalism, it can perhaps offer possibilities for non-globalist global analyses in a different scholarly conversation, in which we might begin to get around blinding endorsements of futurism, conflation, and circulation.

47. See Warwick Anderson, "The Natures of Culture: Environment and Race in the Colonial Tropics," in *Imagination and Distress in Southern Environmental Projects*, ed. Paul Greenough and Anna Tsing (forthcoming); and Haas, *Saving the Mediterranean*.

48. Richard Grove, *Green Imperialism* (Cambridge: Cambridge University Press, 1995).

49. See Keck and Sikkink, *Activists beyond Borders*.

50. See Peter Brosius, "Green Dots, Pink Hearts: Displacing Politics from the Malaysian Rain Forest," *American Anthropologist* 101:1 (1999): 36–57; "The Forest and the Nation: Negotiating Citizenship in Sarawak, East Malaysia," in *Cultural Citizenship in Southeast Asia*, ed. Renato Rosaldo (Berkeley: University of California Press, in press); Margaret Keck, "Social Equity and Environmental Politics in Brazil: Lessons from the Rubber Tappers of Acre," *Comparative Politics* 27:4 (1995): 409–25; Anna Tsing, "Becoming a Tribal Elder, and Other Green Development Fantasies," in *Transforming the Indonesian Uplands*, ed. Tania Li (London: Harwood Academic Press, 1999), pp. 159–202; and Terrence Turner, "Indigenous Rights, Indigenous Cultures, and Environmental Conservation: Convergence or Divergence? The Case of the Brazilian

Kayapo," in *Earth, Air, Fire, Water*, ed. Jill Conway, Kenneth Kenniston, and Leo Marx (Amherst: University of Massachusetts Press, 1999), pp. 145–69.

51. I have developed this idea further in "Finding Our Differences Is the Beginning Not the End of Our Work," in *Culturally Conflicting Views of Nature*, Working Paper Series, Discussion Paper 3, ed. Kent Redford (Gainesville, FL: Conservation Development Forum, 1999).

52. Peter Dauvergne, *Shadows in the Forest: Japan and the Politics of Timber in Southeast Asia* (Cambridge: MIT Press, 1997).

53. Worster's overriding theoretical interest in framing this book is the relationship of irrigation and state power. My discussion here turns instead to his fascinating account of irrigation history. See Donald Worster, *Rivers of Empire* (New York: Oxford University Press, 1985).

54. Suzannah Hecht and Alexander Cockburn, *The Fate of the Forest: Developers, Destroyers, and Defenders of the Amazon* (New York: Verso, 1989); and Marainne Schmink and Charles Wood, *Contested Frontiers in Amazonia* (New York: Columbia University Press, 1992).

55. Ramachandra Guha, *The Unquiet Woods* (Berkeley: University of California Press, 1989); Ravi Rajan, "Imperial Environmentalism" (Ph.D. diss., Oxford University, 1994); and K. Sivaramakrishnan, "Forest Politics and Governance in Bengal, 1794–1994" (Ph.D. diss., Yale University, 1996).

56. On "routes," see James Clifford, *Routes: Travel and Translation in the Late Twentieth Century* (Cambridge: Harvard University Press, 1997).

57. The power and dilemmas of arguing for diversity are illustrated in Paolini's insightful review of the intersections between postcolonial literary studies and globalization in sociology. Paolini argues provocatively that the overhomogenization of the Third World in postcolonial studies has led to the ease with which globalist sociologists formulate unitary frameworks of modernist progress. But he cannot give up on these frameworks even as he argues against them—despite the fact that they turn Africa into a "nonplace." His alternative involves recognition of agency and ambiguity in African cultural formation. This seems right, but to avoid separate, segregated arguments for every neglected nonplace, we could demand, instead of worldwide modernist globalism, an examination of when, where, and how such frameworks hold sway. See Albert Paolini, "The Place of Africa in Discourses about the Postcolonial, the Global, and the Modern," *New Formations* 31 (summer 1995): 83–106.

58. In my "Inside the Economy of Appearances," I explore one case of the specificity of international finance in relation to other "scale-making" claims.

CHAPTER 8

Modernity and Identity

Charles Taylor

THE THREE AXES OF IDENTITY

Why do people nowadays talk so much about identity? Or, to consider the question from a different angle, why would our ancestors have found it hard to understand our constant preoccupation with it? Any attempt to answer this question will have to explore the links between modernity and identity.

To arrive at a better understanding of the discourse of identity I should like to distinguish three contexts in which the word is commonly used, but with a slightly different meaning in each. This is not, however, a genuine case of polysemy, still less of confusion of meaning, because the three contexts (or axes, as I shall also call them) are closely linked.

• • •

FIRST of all, we have identity in the sense given to it by certain psychologists: I am thinking particularly of Erik Erikson. An "identity" is a definition of oneself, partly implicit, which a human agent must be able to elaborate in the course of becoming an adult and (according to Erikson) must continue to redefine through his or her life. This is not an optional project. Without a stable identity, one is in a critical condition, and not only very unhappy, but almost incapable of functioning normally. The moments in which one's identity is threatened are defined as moments of crisis; so, for example, Erikson explains some disorders of adolescence by means of the concept of an "identity crisis."

What exactly is the identity that is referred to in this type of theory? While this is not easy to pin down, one might say that my identity in some way defines the horizon of my moral world. It is through my identity that I know what is truly important to me, and what is less so; I know what affects me profoundly, and what is less significant for me. What is terrifying about an identity crisis is precisely the loss of these landmarks: One no longer knows what is truly important; instead, one teeters on the edge of a gulf in which absolutely nothing is important—like the central character of Camus's *L'Étranger.*

In a sense, it is my identity that situates me in moral space. That it situates me somewhere is what justifies Erikson's use of the term. In a common sense, my identity is "who I am"; to show an identity document is to reveal who I am. But "identifying" myself in that way means positioning myself in social space. My identity card gives you my name, perhaps where I come from, my social insurance number, and so on, situating me in a family, a region, or the catalogue of employable citizens of the Ministry of Manpower, et cetera. Erikson's use of the word follows the same logic. My identity situates me in the moral sphere; it accords me one position among all possible positions; it fixes me somewhere, rather than in some bewildering, unbearable "nowhere."

"Identity" as a moral horizon is one parameter of the discourse about identity. But to consider it only from this point of view would mean a failure to grasp the full force of the word, particularly its peculiarly modern character. This emerges from the celebrated use of the term by Erikson in his remarkable psychobiographical study of Martin Luther.[1] There Erikson describes the spiritual crisis from which the young Luther emerged by means of a conversion to the radical theology of salvation *sola fide*, as an identity crisis. It is immediately obvious why the use of the expression is justified: What was involved was a matter of the ultimate moral horizon. Luther found it impossible to live within the horizon of Catholicism (as he understood it) because it appeared to doom him to eternal damnation, being as he was incapable of ever satisfying the demands of salvation through good works. Thus the doctrine of salvation by faith alone had a liberating effect on him.

Despite the obviousness of this usage, however, the word *identity* in Erikson's book remains an anachronism. Luther could never have understood himself in such terms. Why? Because he could never have understood the definition of the ultimate horizon as a personal one. It was not in any way a matter of defining oneself, but of defining the condition of every human being as depraved by sin and saved by divine grace. Before such a crisis and such spiritual struggles could be described in terms of identity, it was necessary to conceive the ultimate horizon of each individual as being in some sense personal. This transformed relation is what defines the extraordinary practice (as most human beings at most times in history would find it) of us moderns: speaking of the ultimate spiritual horizon as if it were an answer to the question "who am I?"

To arrive here, it was necessary (among other things) to accept, or to invent, the idea that every human being has his or her own way of being human, and that consequently questions about the ultimate horizon can be asked not only in the register of the universal—a universal that is either strictly human or a universality of class, rank, or status—but that these questions also confront individuals in all their individuality.[2]

THIS brings us to the second context of discourse about identity, which understands it as something personal, potentially eccentric or original, and consequently to some extent something invented or assumed. It is in this context that we can see clearly the relationship between identity and modernity. While we casually attribute an identity to premodern people because they too lived—

and could only live—within a moral or spiritual horizon, their horizons were very far from being identities as we understand them. They were not an attribute of individuals, as our term *identity* implies, for the three reasons suggested in the previous section.

Let us expand on that discussion. We said, first, that identities belonged to the province of the universal rather than the personal. It might be a question of the universal in the strict sense—that which affects all human beings—as was the case with Luther. But distinctions were also made between horizons, particularly in a society of ranks. Here, too, the horizon was not something that belonged to individuals, but to their group, class, rank, or sex, among other possible classifications.

Second, the horizons were understood as already defined. There was no question of innovation or exploration; originality had no place in this understanding except as a source of error or deviancy. This leads us to a third difference, namely that the horizon was entirely preset; it existed in the same manner as a destiny or an objective fact. A modern identity, on the contrary, although composed of given elements, is thought of as something taken on by the individual. For it to be mine, my identity must be accepted, which in theory opens a space for negotiation with my surroundings, my history, and my destiny. Of course, the individual may remain passive and unhesitatingly comply with the horizon offered by those around him. But even in a case such as this, his identity will count as his own, as the result of a tacit agreement of the kind spoken about by Locke: To speak of identity means no longer conceiving my horizon as fated.[3]

And this is why identity discourse is an integral part of modern civilization. It was necessary for the individual's social destiny, dictated by rank, to lose its hold over him in an increasingly egalitarian society. Henceforth, in theory, human beings could become whatever they wished or whatever they were capable of becoming. But more than this egalitarian revolution was required to bring about our modernity. The expressivist revolution I earlier associated with Herder was also necessary. It recognized in each individual his or her own mode of being human, and thus, entreated them to realize this state in all its originality rather than conform to a pattern imposed from outside. A new and more radical meaning to the ideal of authenticity and fidelity to oneself emerges.

It is this turning point that subtends our discourse of identity, because an expressivist conception of the human being not only introduces us to a terrain in which every individual can be an innovator, but for that very reason attributes an ineluctable role to the individual in the process of self-definition. If I have to discover an original way of being, and not conform to a pattern predefined for everybody, then my identity is first and foremost an object of inquiry. It has to be invented, and if anyone has an inalienable part to play in that, it is myself. But saying that I participate as of right in this process of invention means saying that any solution should satisfy me before I accept it. If I do not recognize it as the form of my own originality, then it cannot be called mine. To all intents and purposes, however, this means that an identity must be assumed, taken on. The fundamental notion that we collaborate, at least in theory, in the definition of our own identity is only comprehensible against the background of this expressivist revolution. In the end, it was this revolution that resulted in the discarding of fixed and predetermined horizons in favor of personal identities that have to be invented.

This turn may seem to give absolute power to the individual, and many commentators do indeed speak of modern culture as a freeing of the individual in relation to society, some to hail it, some to deplore it. But this vision is a little too simple.[4] The individual takes part in the definition of his or her own identity; it could be said that she negotiates it with those around her. But she does not enjoy complete freedom to do this. It is no accident that the period of the expressivist revolution should witness the birth of another discourse, which is that of recognition.

I mean by this the theme of recognition by others as a condition for achieving a successful identity. To be himself, the individual needs to be recognized. As Hegel stated in a well-known passage, he *requires* recognition.[5] Hegel is often identified as the originator of this discourse but, leaving aside the fact that Fichte preceded him down the same road, I think the modern discourse of recognition originates with Rousseau. Indeed, people start to talk about recognition at the moment in which the expressivist foundations of a modern concept of identity are being laid down. This coincidence is testimony to the basic non-self-sufficiency of the human being in this field. We cannot define ourselves by ourselves; we need the cooperation of "significant others" (while naturally being able within certain limits to redefine who may enjoy this status for us).[6]

Of course, this non-self-sufficiency was always our human lot. If at a particular moment we start to talk about recognition, this is not because no one needed it before then. On the contrary, it is because fixed and predetermined horizons could not be otherwise than confirmed by their world. The "identity" bestowed on us by belonging to a particular rank was inevitably reflected by the whole of society. It was because "recognition" was certain to take place that it was not spoken about.

But as soon as one attempts to define oneself, especially in an original way, it becomes possible for there to be a gap between what we claim to be and what others are prepared to accord us. This is the space occupied by a recognition that can be asked for but refused, and hence the space that gives rise to the discourse and theories of recognition.[7]

I have talked about two parameters of the discourse of identity: first, identity as a moral horizon, which allows us to define what is significant. This is identity in the sense used by Erikson and those who define it as a condition of the individual's health and integrity. Then I spoke about identity as something personal, something that the individual takes on as his or her own, which is not to say that it is something arbitrarily chosen by this same individual. This is the identity that arises from the expressivist revolution, shifting the moral horizon from the register of destiny to that of negotiation and a struggle for recognition.

BUT there is also a third axis, which brings us to a crucial theme in modern politics: What does a group identity consist of? We need not only to explore this theme, but to trace the different relations between the key terms already delineated as they would appear on this axis.

Let us first make clear the parallel relation between this and the previous axis. When one looks at the expressivist foundations of the concept of identity, one notes that Herder developed at the same time two discourses: one about the originality of individuals and one about the differences between peoples. Just as every individual had his own standard against which he had to conduct his life, so every people had its own genius, which should form the basis of its culture. Thus Herder's protest against the tendency of many Germans from the intellectual classes—including Frederick II of Prussia—to prefer writing in French, at that time the language of a universal culture. In Herder's opinion, every *Volk* had a duty to develop the spirit implicit in its language and in the spontaneous creations of its historical culture rather than imitate, in pale and imperfect copies, the achievement of other peoples.

The individual and the *Volk* are consequently two entities in search of identity, whose task is to define what makes up their originality, and then to hold on to it. They are, similarly, two agents among others, in a field of exchanges inside which they need recognition from others. *Völker*, like individuals, are required to extend mutual recognition to one another of their inevitable but complementary differences, because together they make up the whole chorale of humanity.

From what we call today a group identity for peoples, there arose almost immediately the phenomenon we nowadays call nationalism. One can see how closely parallel this "identity" was to its equivalent on an individual level. It belonged to the group, both distinguishing its original character and requiring, in order to be defined, the cooperation of the group that was to take it on.

But the two levels do not simply run parallel, they are at the same time interrelated. On the one hand, individuals often identify themselves by their group relationships. If identity constitutes a moral horizon that allows them to situate themselves in the register of what is significant, people will predictably define themselves, in part, in terms of universal moral commitments (I am Catholic, Communist, Liberal, and so on). But it is also normal that they should align themselves with their membership in historical communities. A historical community does offer a horizon, through its culture and its way of life, inside which things acquire differential values. On the other hand, like the identity of an individual, a group identity must be accepted. This involves the individuals who make up the group: The group can only live with an identity to the extent that many of its members define themselves in such terms. Otherwise, the collective identity becomes a sort of fiction, like the identities deriving from the idea of a "socialist motherland" on which communist regimes used to pride themselves. Most of our contemporaries have complex identities, made up of both universal allegiances and particular attachments to the groups or communities they belong to historically. It is all the more normal that the latter should play an important role in a person's identity, if one considers that identity is defined through exchanges with significant others, who are often fellow members of the group in question.

Moreover, since a modern identity is thought of as what differentiates me from my peers, it cannot reside solely in a universal allegiance, which could belong to anybody. I must particularize myself, and this often drives me to identify with one historical group among others. In fact, the term *identity* is often restricted to this differential component, at the expense of universal elements, which sometimes ultimately count for more in our moral horizon. This is a point where "identity" in the Eriksonian tends to diverge from "identity" in the Herderian sense.

Consequently, there is an interchange between the two levels of identity. Membership in a group supplies the individual with important "identity documents." At the same time, when enough individuals identify strongly enough with a group, it acquires a collective identity that underpins some joint action in history.

This is clearly the case with nations. But this is where the particularities of this third axis begin to emerge. Other factors intervene, making some identity almost obligatory at this level. By nations, I mean nation-states; and when I say that an identity is almost obligatory for them, I am thinking of the requirements for legitimacy in the modern world. I am, of course, speaking of democratic states, which are consequently founded, in theory, on popular sovereignty. For the people to be sovereign, they need to form an entity and have a personality. This need can be expressed in the following way: The people are supposed to rule; this means that the members of this "people" make up a decision-making unit, a body that takes joint decisions. Moreover, it is supposed to make its decisions through a consensus, or at least a majority, of agents who are deemed equal and autonomous. It is not "democratic" for some citizens to be under the control of others. It might facilitate decision making, but it is not democratically legitimate.

In addition, to form a decision-making unit of the type demanded here, it is not enough for a vote to record the fully formed opinions of all the members. These units must not only decide together, but deliberate together. A democratic state is constantly facing new questions, and it should aspire to a consensus on the issues, not merely to a reflection of diffuse opinions. Moreover, a joint decision emerging from joint deliberation requires that everybody vote according to his or her opinion. It is also necessary that each person's opinion have taken shape or been re-formed in the light of discussion, that is to say, by the exchange of ideas with others.

This necessarily implies a degree of cohesion. To some extent, the members must know one another, listen to one another, and understand one another. How can they otherwise engage in joint deliberation? This is a matter that takes us to the very conditions of legitimacy of democratic states.

If, for example, a subgroup of the nation decides that it is not being listened to by the rest, or that its point of view is not being understood, it will immediately consider itself excluded from joint deliberation. But popular sovereignty requires that we should live under laws that derive from such deliberation: Anyone who is excluded can have no part in the decisions that emerge, and these consequently lose their legitimacy for him. If a subgroup is not heard, it is in some respects excluded from the nation. By the same token, it is no longer bound by the will of that nation.

For it to function legitimately, a people must thus be so constituted that its members are capable of listening to one another, and should effectively do so. It should, at a minimum, come close enough to that condition to ward off possible challenges to its democratic legitimacy from subgroups. In practice, more is normally required. It is not enough for us to be able to listen to one another now. Our states aim to last, so we want an assurance that we shall continue to be able to listen to one another in the future. This demands a certain reciprocal commitment. In practice, a nation can only ensure the stability of its legitimacy if its members are strongly committed to one another by means of their common allegiance to the political community. Moreover, it is the shared consciousness of this commitment that creates confidence in the various subgroups that they will indeed be heard, despite the possible causes for suspicion implicit in the differences between them.

In other words, a modern democratic state demands a people with a strong collective identity. Democracy obliges us to show much more solidarity and much more commitment to one another in our joint political project than was demanded by the hierarchical and authoritarian societies of yesteryear. In the days of the Austro-Hungarian Empire, the Polish peasant in Galicia could be altogether oblivious of the Hungarian country squire, the bourgeois of Prague, or the Viennese worker, without this in the slightest threatening the stability of the state. On the contrary, this condition only becomes untenable when ideas about popular government begin to circulate. At this moment, subgroups that will not, or cannot, be bound together are demanding their own states. This is the era of nationalism, of the breakup of empires.

I have been discussing the political necessity of a strong common identity for modern democratic states in terms of the requirement of forming a people, a deliberative unit. But this necessity is also evident in a number of other ways. Thinkers in the civic humanist tradition, from Aristotle to Arendt, have noted that free societies require a higher level of commitment and participation than despotic or authoritarian ones. Citizens must do for themselves, as it were, what otherwise the rulers do for them. But this process will only occur if these citizens feel a strong bond of identification with their political community, and hence with those who share with them in this.[8]

From another perspective, because these societies require strong commitment to do common work, and because a situation in which some carried the burdens of participation and others simply enjoyed the benefits would be intolerable, free societies require a high level of mutual trust. They are therefore extremely vulnerable to the mistrust among citizens as expressed by the belief that others are not really assuming their commitments: not paying their taxes, cheating on welfare, or (as employers) benefiting from a good labor market without assuming any of the social costs. This kind of mistrust creates extreme tension and threatens to unravel the whole skein of the mores of commitment that democratic societies need to operate. A continuing and constantly renewed mutual commitment is an essential basis for taking the measures needed to renew this trust.

The relation between nation and state is often considered from a unilateral point of view, as if it were always the nation that sought to provide itself with a state. But the opposite process also occurs. In order to remain viable, states sometimes seek to create a feeling of common belonging. This is an important theme in the history of Canada, for example. To form a state, in the democratic era, a society is forced to undertake the difficult and never-to-be-completed task of defining its collective identity. This involves all three of the parameters mentioned above: a moral horizon, freely adopted by many and constantly open to redefinition by them; the demand for recognition from others; and the binding together of individuals so as to form a joint agent.

STRUGGLES FOR RECOGNITION

I have been discussing group identity exclusively in the context of modern political society, something we usually call the "nation." It is obvious, moreover, that these issues of identity also arise elsewhere. Indeed, within most contemporary nations there are contestations that come from different nonstate identities—ethnic, religious, racial, gender, sexual—the whole field that we often refer to as "multiculturalism." And some identity struggles—at least some of those that appear to be battles over the self-definition of a group—also exist on a transnational basis; we have only to think of the Islam in our day.

The discussion of collective identity plainly has to be enlarged. And yet there was a point in starting with the political. In a sense it provides the framework in which the struggles of group identity are carried on in our time. I don't just mean that these struggles occur within modern political societies and often employ political means. I mean that the development of modern society has in many ways set the terms of these battles. The evolutions that brought about modern society have shaped the challenges that the contemporary identity definitions strive to meet.

Let us examine this transformation more closely. Premodern societies in Europe were based on a principle that might be called "hierarchical complementarity." They were societies composed of different ranks or orders: Nobility, bourgeoisie, and peasants are examples of these ranks. In some cases, such as the Austro-Hungarian Empire or the Ottoman Empire bordering Europe, there were ethnic or religious differences in addition to these differences of social orders. These were societies of complementarity, because the different orders were necessary to one another, and they were thought of as such. But at the same time, they were hierarchical because no one pretended that mutual interdependence made them equal. On the contrary, some possessed greater prestige or dignity than others.

I have just spoken of "dignity," but they preferred to speak of "honor." In its original sense, this is a hierarchical concept. As Montesquieu said, "It is in the nature of honor to demand preferences and distinctions."[9] The egalitarian revolution means that we now more often speak of dignity, but in the sense suggested by Kant, among others. In theory, this is a status enjoyed by all human beings: The dignity of modern man, the dignity of the citizen, project an egalitarian world in the context of which they acquire their meaning.

Now, the transition from "honor" to "dignity" in this sense is precisely the one that informs the modern discourse of identity. In a society of ranks, the criteria of honor are distinguished from one another. They are relative to one's rank and may not even exist at all for some of the very lowest orders. They are perceived as fixed and immutable. It follows from this that the arena of recognition is limited in two respects. First, since the criteria are fixed, the judgment of others about me is limited to the question of deciding to what extent I do, or do not, fulfill these criteria. Second, those who are in a position to judge me in this way are the fellow members of my rank or class. If I belong to the nobility, what comprises my honor seems beyond any discussion or negotiation; and those who have the right to judge me honorable or no are those of my rank and will not be anyone from the rank of the common people.[10]

In the era of egalitarian dignity, these two boundaries disappear. To start with, in theory, the category of possible judges of my state of worthiness extends to infinity. The basis of any restriction disappears with a society of ranks. But at the same time the egalitarian universe is one of moral contention among equals. Human beings are only equal within a certain moral vision, for example, as citizens possessing rights. And the meaning and nature of this moral vision is always open to challenge. The criteria of true dignity are not automatically laid down; they have to be constantly discussed and renegotiated. The Herderian revolution merely accentuates this lack of closure in the modern concept of identity.

Henceforth, the recognition that I need to assert a sense of my own value can in theory come from anywhere, even, at the limit, from the whole human race. In practice, however, my position of strength or prestige in a given common field means that I do not have to take account of the opinion of those who are weaker. And at the same time, the criteria for this recognition will very often be a matter for dispute between me and those whose support is essential to me.

It is this essential contestability that has given rise to a discourse of identity as something that can be redefined and assumed by the subject. We can see that this discourse is linked internally to that of recognition, as something that one seeks and that might be lacking, not for the simple, familiar reason that we are considered wanting with regard to fixed and undisputed standards, but for the more fundamental and disturbing reason that our standards themselves are not accepted by others.

In other words, the conditions of being recognized in one's self-worth are fundamentally different in modern egalitarian society whose development has eroded the barriers between hierarchically ranked orders, classes, ethnicities, or status groups. The very nature of this society forces us, in all sorts of ways, to see ourselves, at least normatively, as equal individuals, regardless of origin or historical differentiating marks. In these circumstances, it is less and less possible to restrict one's interlocutors, the people whose recognition counts, to a limited historical group.

Of course, if our society really succeeded in abolishing all these distinctions, if it lived up to its vocation of making everyone really equal in esteem, then this wouldn't matter. One would still be judged by one's peers, albeit in a group that now extended to the whole of society. The pathos of modern society is that differences in esteem, power, and values do not disappear, they only lose the greater part of their legitimacy. Any group that is living, or wants to live, according to its own standards (even if only in part) nevertheless may need recognition from outsiders, that is, from people who are outsiders to these group standards but who, from another very important standpoint in modernity, are supposedly peers because they are, for instance, co-citizens. And, as mentioned above, this recognition no longer measures whether I live up to a fixed code (the principle issue within hierarchical enclaves), but rather focuses on the worthiness or validity of the standards themselves.

In practice, nonacceptance by others may not matter very much to us. Here we come to another important aspect of the matter: that the de jure egalitarianism of modernity covers a de facto hierarchy. This is based in part on differential social, economic, or military power. But these are in turn closely tied up with the process of "modernization." By this term I mean to gesture toward a set of changes in institutions and practices—the development of a dynamic, market-oriented industrial economy, a bureaucratically organized state, organized military forces, and (in some versions) modes of stable popular rule. The first three changes, if not the fourth, are in a sense irresistible. Whoever fails to adopt them, or some functional equivalent, will fall so far behind in the power stakes as to be conquered and forced to undergo these changes anyway. There are good reasons in the relations of forces for the onward march of modernization so defined.

From this point of view, modernization is like a wave, flowing over and engulfing one "traditional" culture after another. This wave moves either from one region to another, via colonization or preemptive imitation, or from one subgroup to another, as a "modernizing elite" makes over a whole society, turning "peasants into Frenchmen."[11]

But modernization as lived from the inside, as it were, is something different. The institutional charges just described always shake up and alter traditional culture. They had this effect in the original development in the West, and they continue to have it elsewhere. But outside of those cases where the original culture is quite destroyed and the people either die or are forcibly assimilated—and European colonialism has a number of such cases to its discredit—a successful transition involves a people finding resources in their traditional culture with which to take on the new practices. In this sense, modernity is not a single wave. It would be better to speak of alternative modernities, as the cultures that emerge in the world to carry the institutional changes turn out to differ in important ways from each other. Thus a Japanese modernity, an Indian modernity, various modulations of Islamic modernity will probably enter alongside the gamut of Western societies, which are themselves far from uniform.

Seen in this perspective, we can see that modernity—which I have been calling "the wave"—can be felt as a threat to a traditional culture. It will remain an external threat to those deeply opposed to change. But another reaction can be found among those who want to take on some version of institutional changes. While, unlike the conservatives, they don't want to refuse change, but they do want to avoid the fate of those aboriginal peoples who have been engulfed and utterly transformed by these changes. What they look for is a creative adaptation, and they draw on the cultural resources of their tradition, which would enable them to take on the new practices successfully. In short, they want to do what has already been done in the West. But they see, or sense, that they cannot simply copy the West's adaptations; that would bring them perilously close to engulfment. Creative adaptation, because it makes use of traditional resources, has by definition to differ from culture to culture; each has to invent its own modernity.

Now this wave, whether moving across different regions or across different milieus within one society, is the dynamic context in which contemporary struggles for identity occur. It accounts, to a great extent, for the de facto hierarchy I mentioned above. Societies, or milieus within societies, that have more successfully carried out these changes—which means, of course, having adapted their "traditional" cultures to this end—enjoy greater power and prestige. This is true for the United States—and G-7 or perhaps OECD countries on the world scene—as well as for certain groups within these societies (e.g., in the recent past, WASPs in the U.S.).

In general, societies or strata high on this totem pole care little for the esteem or recognition of those who are lower. But the reverse is not the case. Western modernity has been a conquering culture, because the changes described above confer tremendous power on the societies that adopt them. In the relations derived from conquest, there come to be presumptions of superiority and inferiority, which the conqueror accepts and the conquered resist. These presumptions pose a challenge to dignity. To the extent that traditional elites can remain insulated from the relationship, they feel the challenge less. But those involved in "being moderninzed," whether they be in a colony or in a country overshadowed and threatened or in a subaltern milieu within a developing society, have before them constantly what they also see as a state of backwardness that concerns them and that they would like to remedy. The issue is whether they can.

Thus, the urgency on the part of elites in a culture to find their own modernizing path is more than a matter of concern for their compatriots. It is also a matter of how they will stake their own claims to dignity. Until they can find their own creative adaptation, and take on institutional changes while remaining recognizably themselves, the imputation of inferiority leveled against the culture with which they identify remains unrefuted. Such imputations are liberally made by members of dominant societies whose word tends (irrationally but understandably) to have weight, if only because of their success and power. They become, in a sense, important interlocutors whose recognition would count for a great deal if ever they gave it. In the face of nonrecognition, this importance will frequently be denied, but often with a vehemence that makes it suspect.

This brings us to a second important consequence of the wave. The desire to adapt a traditional culture is what puts the issue of identity on the agenda. I said earlier that we speak of our horizon as an "identity" in part because we moderns are aware that it is properly defined, and also assumed, by those who live within it. But now we can see that it also arises from a situation in which redefining tradition can be an urgent need. We live in an age where such redefinitions are acknowledged as a possibility, perhaps especially by those who want to resist them with all the power at their disposal, the so-called fundamentalists. The very fact that they are "remaining the same" only by dint of a vigorous fight means that they are condemned to innovate in relation to the real past, where such issues didn't arise.

But we can also see why the drama of recognition can be so poignant and deeply felt. The redefinition of a group's values is always attended with tension, conflict, disagreement, uncertainty, and division, both within and between peoples. When, on top of that, one is open to the gaze of prestigious and powerful others, whose depreciatory views on one's new definitions can deeply undermine one's confidence, the disturbing and destabilizing effects can be very great. No wonder that nonrecognition is very often experienced as a kind of aggression.

IDENTITY IN THE MODERN PUBLIC SPHERE

All this gives us some idea why group identity is often so important an issue for people today. And, conversely, why the definition of the group's basic values is so readily described as an "identity." For in fact it shares the features I mentioned earlier in my discussion of the second axis: It concerns not a universal identity, but one among many, living and relating to interlocutors, open in part to redefinition such that, as a consequence, it has to be actively assumed by those who will live under it.

The drama of recognition is played out at an individual level, but also at the level of groups. We are very aware of the struggle around "multiculturalism" within today's democratic societies. But something like the issue of recognition can and does arise at the level of the nation in relation to other nations. One can only understand nationalism, as a modern phenomenon, in relation to this drama. Modern nations have to build a common identity, as I explained earlier; but in the era of dignity, they cannot be content to define themselves solely among their compatriots. Every people knows that it exists in an international sphere made up of other peoples, who in principle have the same rank and dignity. For nations, as for individuals, the arena of recognition extends, in theory, to infinity. This is not to say that certain interlocutors—for example, those who are successful in the military or economic field—do not become crucial, while others are sometimes ignored.

The international public sphere is an arena in which the identities of nations often have to struggle to survive. Even those who pretend to stand aside from it are affected, as one can see from the reaction of various authoritarian governments to criticism by Amnesty International. Even those who would like, in principle, to reject Western modernity, and a public international space dominated by the values of Western modernity, find themselves drawn into its sphere of influence. Consider the Islamic fundamentalist movements, whose appeals to mobilization are often launched against a West that seems to despise them. This kind of mobilization is too often expressed in the register of honor, or of some sense of humiliation, or of recognition refused, for declarations of an exclusive allegiance to an internal religious tradition to be entirely credible. While Salman Rushdie may have committed a crime by insulting the Prophet, this crime was infinitely aggravated by the fact that the blasphemy was published in English for a Western audience. This is what earned him a death sentence, which was as much a media event as the act that provoked it. A *fatwa* pronounced in front of television cameras, breaking with certain procedures of the *sharia* itself, is no longer a "traditional" act, in any simple sense. The international public sphere, and the politics of identity that it contains, invade every corner of our world.[12]

The discourse of identity, struggles for recognition, and public spaces—national and international—which are in theory egalitarian, constitute three profoundly interrelated elements of modern civilization.

The Limits of Identity Discourse

And we have seen, not only subnational groups, ethnicities, and genders but also transnationally existing religions can be caught up in this kind of struggle. This is why it may seem natural to speak of "Islamic identity," or "Theravada Buddhist identity," and so forth.

The above discussion also indicates a possible limit on this language. "Identity" offers us a language in which to speak of the basic horizon of individuals or groups. Talk of defining, or defending, this identity relates also to this basic horizon. But this talk is given its immediacy by the context of modern antihierarchical society, and in the face of challenges raised by the wave of modernization and the adaptations it calls for.

People have fought over the definition of their common faith before. Luther, after all, engaged in such a struggle with the Catholic Church of his day. But we noted above how absurd and anachronistic it would be to see this as a struggle about identity. The terms of that battle were quite alien to identity discourse. The idea that the faith was one among many and related to other faiths as interlocutors was entirely lacking, as was the sense that *the* faith could be redefined. For Luther, it could only be "reformed," returned to its pristine apostolic purity. Beyond this, there lacked altogether the sense of an agenda of redefinition imposed by inescapable exogenous change and, along with this, the idea that the redefinition would have to be ratified to count as the new identity. Above all, in Luther's time there would have been no overlap between the stakes of the definition and the register of dignity, of recapturing or safeguarding a sense of self-worth. While this dimension has never been absent from any important battle in human history, it has no real historical precedent.

This difference is not simply a warning not to export our language backward into the past; it may also tell us to discriminate between some of the controversies of the present. All faiths today are caught in unprecedented circumstances; all have change thrust upon them as a practical challenge; all find themselves drawn into a world public sphere and must exist in some sense as one among many. This can provoke a crisis of dignity and self-worth. But not all questions raised by the specter of change are those that relate to the world public sphere, at least not in the register of dignity. Gandhi did something to redefine Hinduism in full ecumenical awareness of the other great faiths and their points of convergence and divergence. It's not at all clear, however, that the language of identity redefinition suits the Gandhian enterprise (though it often seems appropriate when talking about the program of the contemporary B.J.P.). It is not my intention to delegitimate identity talk. I wish only to pose a question about the limits of identity discourse, for we can be certain that limits are needed if we are to gain insight into the complex and confusing struggles proceeding in the world today.

NOTES

The editors are grateful to Ruth Abbey for her help in the preparation of this essay.

1. See his *Young Man Luther* (New York: W.W. Norton, 1958).

2. This is the revolution that I identify with Herder, one of the most important articulators of this new understanding of the individual. "*Jeder Mensch hat ein eigenes Maasz*" Each Human Being Has Its Own Measure); see *Ideen*, vol. 8 of *Sämtliche Werke*, ed. Bernard Suphan, 15 vols. (Berlin: Weidmann, 1877–1913), p. 291. For a more extensive discussion of this topic, see my *Sources of the Self* (Cambridge, Mass.: Harvard University Press, 1989), chap. 21. I will return to Herder's expressivist revolution later in this text as well.

3. See here Locke's argument about tacit consent to the social contract in his *Second Treatise on Civil Government (An essay concerning the true original, extent and end of civil government) and A letter concerning toleration*, ed. with a rev. introd. by J. W. Gough (New York: Barnes & Noble, 1966).

4. I make a similar argument in *The Ethics of Authenticity* (Cambridge, Mass.: Harvard University Press, 1992).

5. This is, of course, a reference to the master-slave dialectic in his *Phenomenology of Spirit*, trans. A.V. Miller (Oxford: Oxford University Press, 1977), chap. 4.

6. For a fuller discussion of these issues, see my article "The Dialogical Self," in *The Interpretive Turn: Philosophy, Science, Culture*, ed. David Hiley, James Bohman, and Richard Shusterman (Ithaca, NY: Cornell University Press, 1991).

7. I have discussed this further in "The Politics of Recognition," in my *Philosophical Arguments* (Cambridge, Mass.: Harvard University Press, 1995).

8. I discuss this in "Why Democracy Needs Patriotism," in *For Love of Country: Debating the Limits of Patriotism*, ed. Joshua Cohen (Boston: Beacon Press, 1996).

9. "*La nature même de l'honneur est de demander des préférences et des distinctions*." Montesquiere, *De l'Esprit des lois*, Livre III, chap. vii (Paris: Garnier, 1973).

10. This is discussed at length in my "Politics of Recognition."

11. Eugen Weber, *Peasants Into Frenchmen* (London: Chatto & Windus, 1979).

12. I discuss this in "The Rushdie Controversy," *Public Culture* 2:1 (autumn 1989): 118–22.

CHAPTER 9

The Role of Norms and Law in Economics:
An Essay on Political Economy

Kaushik Basu

THE THREE-HOUR stretch of road between Hazaribagh and Dhanbad in eastern India is as desolate as it is beautiful. One winter evening, some half a dozen years ago, as I was traveling this route by taxi to catch a train from Dhanbad to get to Calcutta, I was lucky—or, I suppose, unlucky, depending on one's point of view—to be stopped by a road block created by a gang of youngsters wielding *lathis*[1] and swords. In front of us, also stopped by the ramshackle road block, was a truck, and some of the youngsters were talking to the truck driver. From the sight of some distant lanterns I figured that we were close to a village. My taxi driver looked very nervous as he waited for the youngsters to come to our car. He told me that they were hoodlums, collecting illegal money by threatening to beat up passengers and drivers. He asked me not to speak and to leave it all to him. Eventually, a bearded young man walked up to our car regally and asked me to lower my window glass. He spoke courteously and explained that he was collecting *rangdari* tax. He had a wad of papers in one hand (the other held a *lathi*) and he explained that after we paid the money, which, he added firmly, we would have to, he would even give us a receipt.

I had read about the institution of *rangdari* tax found to occur in some parts of India. The "tax" is an illegal collection made by gangs in remote rural areas where the hand of the law is lax. The reason I felt lucky about the incident was that this experience is very rare for an urban Indian, and it subsequently made me think hard about the meaning of law and norms, and I owe a part of this paper to the incident.

This is unimportant for my present paper, but I must finish the story. My taxi driver, despite the cold sweat, was not one to give up. He got into an argument and was soon asked to get down from the car and talk to the boss, who stood with others a little farther away. Several minutes passed before he returned, the bamboo road block was removed, and as we sped away toward Dhanbad, he explained how we got away without paying. His arguments in the beginning fell on deaf ears he said. Then he suddenly changed tack and explained that I was a visitor from Delhi who had come to see rural Bihar, and it would create a very bad impression on me if I were forced to make a payment. This appeal to regional pride clicked and, like some visiting ambassadors, we were allowed to go without paying local dues.

There are several features of this little incident that shed light on the functioning of an economy and also cast shadows on our textbook models. First, what the youngsters were offering us was, at a certain level of abstraction, like any exchange. If we wanted our arms intact and heads not bruised, we would have to pay them some money. In other words, they were *selling* nonviolence. And most people, like the trucker ahead of us (and I, for that matter), thought it was a good bargain. A small sum of money in exchange for no bodily harm seemed well worth it. But note that what they were selling was what in most societies is treated as belonging to the buyer's endowment. If I wanted *my* arm unharmed, I would have to pay him. In textbook economics we usually treat individual endowments as beyond the reach of others. But in reality, individuals often encroach on each others endowments, selling to *i* what in most societies would be considered as belonging to *i*. This happens between powerful landlords and poor serfs; between big countries and small countries; between big corporations and small companies. Evidently, the theorem that individuals, left to themselves, lead to an efficient society, is predicated on the *assumption* that agents respect each other's endowments. But to the extent that they do not do so in reality, this claim that individual rationality is enough to create an efficient society is false or, at best, remains to be established.

The other matter on which the incident sheds light is the meaning of the law. Virtually all accounts in the Indian press have described the *rangdari* tax as illegal extortion. Yet it is impossible not to notice how analogous it is to a regular tax. It is not paid by people voluntarily but needs the threat of punitive action. The fact that the extortion was taking place so close to a village makes it plausible that it has some legitimacy in the eyes of the villagers.[2] In all likelihood a part of the money is spent on local village welfare, with the remainder being used by the tax collectors on themselves. This is analogous to the uses to which government tax revenue is put. In brief, the institution that I had chanced upon that evening was pretty much like a local government. It is considered illegal only because it commits acts that, in the eyes of what we consider the real government, are illegal, though in essence the actions are similar to the real government's own actions. Hence, as per common usage, the institution of the *rangdari* tax cannot be thought of as supported by the law and the threat of state penalty; it is supported by norms and informal threats. But what, really, is the difference between a law and a norm? There are several differences to be sure, but at some level they are indistinguishable from each other. The latter is a nontrivial claim and is one of the central theorems of this paper. It will be called the *core theorem*. It expresses a viewpoint that can have important influence on the way we conceptualize the role of law in economics, as will be argued in a later section. It is not a theorem in the sense of geometry or even axiomatic economics, which can be mathematically proved, but a point of view to which I aspire to convert the reader through examples, arguments, and persuasion. It is formalizable, but only potentially so.

The core theorem and the discussion around it are related to the research in economics often called the new or positive political economy,[3] and is part of the older "institutional economics." My method of analysis, relying on game-theoretic constructions, is similar to the method used in this new literature. But at the same time my central claims, embodied in and stemming from the core theorem, diverges from the view that is taken in the literature on political economy. Moreover, I do not share the confidence of this new literature, with which economists—ready with their median voter theorems and techniques of optimization—have rushed to explain the rise and fall of nations: why some dictators ruin nations and others bring prosperity, why one government loses the election and another one does not, and why democracies appear when they do and why they do not when they do not (hindsight being never too far away from these analyses). I do not think we are in a position to answer such large questions. But I know that a group of people all praising one another for their understanding of these questions and at the same time trying to outdo one another can create a "cult effect," where knowledge is replaced by illusion. This essay has a much more limited objective: to expose some flaws in our thinking that lie at the base of conventional economics and even the new political economy, and to provide the preliminaries for a large program that lies mostly ahead.

If I owe a part of my interest in this area of research to rural Bihar, I also owe a part to the Institute for Advanced Study, Princeton. I came to the Institute with a fledgling interest in power and the politics of oppression. I had argued in my paper "One Kind of Power" that we needed to move away from traditional dyadic economics to the economics of triads if we were to incorporate the role of power and influence in our models.[4] During the year that I spent at the Institute, 1985–86, I was fortunate to have been able to collaborate with two remarkable economists, Eric Jones and Ekkehart Schlicht. We brought our respective skills to write a critique—in the original sense of the word "critique," that is, as evaluation—of the new institutional economics. In writing the paper that came out of this collaboration,[5] I learned a lot about historical methods and institutional economics. We were touching on several issues of political economy, which was then far from being a discipline in vogue.

In the next two sections I shall comment on social norms, and law and economics. Finally, I shall try to present what I believe is a new approach to the study of political economy.

SOCIAL NORMS

Assumptions in economics have been at the receiving end of a lot of attention. They have been reviled for their unrealism, admired for their elegance, the mainspring of jokes, appreciated for their explanatory powers, and dismissed as untenable. All this attention, however, has been directed at the *explicit* assumptions, such as the transitivity of preference, or the convexity of technology. What has gone virtually unnoticed and therefore eluded criticism are the *implicit* assumptions. Yet the most untenable assumptions often belong to this category. One such assumption is the existence of social norms. Much of economics has been written up as if social norms do not matter. This is empirically false, as virtually all economists and certainly other social scientists will agree. What is more interesting is that it is, in all likelihood, *analytically* flawed as well. That is, a norms-free economics may not be possible. Hence, when we write up a model with no reference to norms and institutions, we are nevertheless using norms and institutions, but doing so unwittingly.

This is best illustrated by the act of exchange. According to the first principles of economics, two agents will exchange or trade goods if the following assumptions are true: (a) each individual prefers having more goods to less; (b) each person satisfies the law of diminishing marginal utility;[6] and (c) the initial endowment of goods is lopsided, for example, one person has all the butter and the other all the bread. To many economists, (a), (b), and (c) are indeed sufficient conditions for trade to occur. What they do not realize is that these are sufficient only when the agents are already embedded in a certain institutional environment and characterized by adequate social norms.[7] For one, exchange is greatly facilitated by the ability to communicate or, even better, to speak a common language. And given that language is after all an evolved social convention,[8] trade and exchange are predicated on social conventions.

The importance of these implicit requirements for trade can be inferred from some experiments in economics, which were conducted for a different purpose. Experiments have shown that rats do prefer more to less—a fact that I suspected well before I read experimental economics. Furthermore, experiments have established that rats also satisfy the law of diminishing marginal utlity or, more precisely, have convex preference. This was established by some innovative experiments conducted by Kagel et al. on white albino rats, belonging to the—this for the connoisseur—Wistar and Sprague-Dawley stock.[9] So, rats do satisfy our assumptions (a) and (b). All that remained to be done to check the exchange hypothesis was to give different kinds of food to different rats, which would fulfill assumption (c), and see what the rats did. It seems some relentless researchers did just that.[10] They presumably placed two rats at some distance, with each possessing a different food item. The researchers discovered that, though these rats satisfied assumptions (a), (b), and (c), they did not, alas, indulge in trade and exchange. I feel I could have predicted this from my occasional encounter with rats, but it is anyway good to have these things experimentally confirmed.

Facetious though it may sound, the above account does amount to a very substantial critique of traditional economics. It shows that even in models which seem transparently free of any requirements of norms and institutions, that is not the case. Market-related activity, trade, and other economic functionings have to be embedded in institutions and social norms.[11] If we refuse to embed our models consciously, we will still be doing so, only unwittingly. And given that the latter is not such a wise approach, it is important that we recognize the role that social norms play and try to build these in consciously and in keeping with reality.

Before venturing to discuss different kinds of norms and critiquing mainstream economics, I want to put in a word of caution. That mainstream economics has ignored social norms is quite evident; one has simply to browse through a few random books of economics to verify the claim. That social norms are an important part of reality is also obvious enough. But these two facts are not reason enough for criticizing mainstream economics. Something can be an important part of life but not important for the research one is involved in. Indeed, for some of the core concerns of mainstream economics the social norm was not germane. Moreover, economists were wary of using a concept that was so vaguely defined that it could be used to explain almost everything, thereby falling into a tautological trap, a danger that has been pointed to by Solow.[12]

This justification for keeping norms out of our analysis, however, has grown weaker over the years. As economists have reached out to addressing larger questions, concerning political economy and law and economics, the silence on social norms has become less defensible. Moreover, with the rise in game theory, we have within our ambit methods for formalizing and giving more rigorous definition to different concepts of norms.

For the purposes of economic analysis, norms are best divided into three kinds: rationality-limiting norms, preference-changing norms, and equilibrium-selection norms.[13] By a "rationality-limiting norm" I mean a norm that stops us from doing certain things or choosing certain options irrespective of how much utility that thing or option gives us. Thus most individuals would not consider filching another person's wallet even if it were lying unattended, not by speculating about the amount the wallet is likely to contain, the chances of getting caught, the severity of the law, and so on, but because they consider stealing wallets as something that is *simply not done*.

In traditional economics, the "feasible set" of alternatives facing an individual (from which the person can pick one) is defined in terms of technological or budgetary feasibility. Thus a consumer's feasible set is the collection of all the combinations of goods and services that the consumer can purchase given his or her income. From the above discussion it should be evident that a rationality-limiting norm further limits the feasible set, because now certain alternatives may be infeasible to an individual not just because it is technologically infeasible (like walking on water) or budgetarily infeasible (like buying a Jaguar car) but because it is ruled out by the person's norms. Indeed, a person with norms may let go on options that could have enhanced his utility,[14] and thus such a person would be considered irrational in terms of traditional economics. Basically, such norms limit the domain over which the rationality calculus is applied.

Elsewhere I have taken the line that we can, at least partially, understand why some norms exist and some do not, in terms of *evolutionary* stability.[15] According to this argument, we do not see any society with the norm that one must not eat proteins simply because such a society would perish along with its norm. Similarly, we do not find any society where stealing anything from anyone is considered legitimate because such a society would soon be in complete chaos, become impoverished, and wither away.

On Forest Home Drive in Ithaca there is a bridge on which two cars cannot cross at the same time. When we were small we were told how in the Andes there are pathways along steep mountains that are so narrow that two persons cannot cross; and so when two persons found themselves face to face on one of these paths, the one with the quicker draw survived by shooting the other person and continued on his journey. In Ithaca a different norm is used. Cars pass in little convoys, three or four at a time, and the convoys from the two directions alternate. That is, after the third or fourth car ahead goes, one just stops and waits for an oncoming convoy and then starts once again. This stopping and waiting is against one's self-interest, so it is indeed a rationality-limiting norm, but the reason we find some norm of this kind and not the Andean custom of a shoot-out is that it is evolutionarily more stable. This is also the reason that the "Andes custom" probably exists nowhere. A society practicing this norm would not survive and so neither would the norm.

Some may argue that instead of thinking that such norms limit individual rationality, we can simply redefine our utility function so that what I described above as normatively infeasible is described as an option that gives a very low utility, perhaps negative infinity. But that would reduce utility theory to a sterile tautology. In reality, moreover, there are certain things we would love to do but our norms get in the way. We would not have to ask the lord to deliver us from evil if the evil gave us such disutility that it was no temptation to start with.

This does not mean that norms never change our preference or utility function. Certain norms do get internalized. There are many individuals whose religion requires them to be vegetarian, and they tell you that they find nonvegetarian food revolting anyway. More often than not, this is no coincidence; a religious norm adhered to over a stretch of time often gets internalized so that one begins to actually prefer what the norm requires one to do. This can explain why one finds systematic variations in taste across regions and nations. What starts out as a norm or a custom can, over time, become part of one's preference. Such a norm may be referred to as a "preference-changing norm."[16] Since such a norm works through an individual's preference, it can be ignored by traditional economics, which treats preferences as primitives. The only reason for being aware of this kind of a norm is that it can give us an understanding of how some of our preferences are formed.

This essay, however, is concerned with neither rationality-limiting norms nor preference-changing norms but rather with norms that have no effect on individual preference nor the feasible set from which a person chooses, but those that help coordinate actions across human beings. Consider the norm of driving on the right in the United States. It is true that this norm is additionally fortified by the law; but it is arguable that even if this were just a norm or custom and not the law, people would still drive on the right.[17] This is because this norm, once it is in place, happens to be entirely compatible with self-interested behavior. In the absence of such a norm, there are at least two possible equilibriums—everyone drives on the left or everyone drives on the right. The norm simply helps people to *select* an equilibrium. It is for this reason that I call such a norm an "equilibrium-selection norm."

According to this terminology, Akerlof's conception of caste is that of an equilibrium-selection norm.[18] In my model of totalitarian states,[19] people mimic loyalty to the totalitarian regime not because that is their preference but because the expression of loyalty is an equilibrium-selection norm. If others show loyalty to the regime it is in your self-interest to also show loyalty to the regime. Since this can be true for all individuals, the entire display of loyalty in some totalitarian states can be superficial, an exercise in mimicry from which no *individual* would want to deviate.

David Lewis's idea of a "convention" is also close to this kind of social norm. More recently, Cooter,[20] in discussing the connection between norms and law, has identified norms entirely with equilibrium-selection norms. He describes a "social norm" as an "effective consensus obligation," and he goes on to identify a consensus obligation with an equilibrium of a game.[21]

Since most of this essay will focus on norms of this kind, from here on the term *norm* should be taken to mean an equilibrium-selection norm, unless explicitly stated otherwise.

LAW'S ECONOMY

The standard view of law in economics and related social sciences is of something that changes the set of strategies open to an individual, or the "payoff function" of the individual. If the law does not permit emitting pollutants into the atmosphere, then the payoff that I expect when I build a factory that freely emits pollutants into the atmosphere will be different from the payoff I would expect from the factory if the law of the land had nothing against pollutants. In the former case, in addition to the profits from sales, I would have to calculate the probability of being caught and fined and adjust that against my expected profit in order to get to the expected payoff.

This view is predicated on a conception of the economy as a game. In other words, each individual in the economy is supposed to have a (feasible) set of "strategies," or actions, open to him or her. The payoff that each individual, or "player," receives depends on the strategies chosen by all the players—often referred to as a "tuple of strategies." The payoff is a number that expresses the net utility that a player receives from the state of the world that emerges when every player has picked a strategy from his or her set of strategies. The rule that summarizes the payoff received by each player for every possible tuple of strategies is called a "payoff function." This is the view taken, implicitly or explicitly, in virtually all works of law and economics. It is an idea often associated with Pigou and referred to as the "Pigovian view"[22] and is quite explicit in, for instance, Baird, Gertner, and Picker[23] and Benoit and Kornhauser.[24] It is possible to contest this view of the economy, but that is not my purpose here; indeed, it seems to me to be an adequate model for most purposes.[25] What I want to focus on is the role of law in such an economy.

As just explained, according to the traditional view, a law is something that changes the "economy game" by altering the payoff functions of players (or by limiting the set of strategies open to a player[26]). In other words, according to this view, a new law typically alters the payoff that a person expects from certain actions. Thus Baird, Gertner and Picker observe, "We can capture the change in the legal rules by changing the payoffs."[27] And given that the payoffs are an integral part of a game, a law is treated as something that changes the game.

This has an immediate appeal. Consider a new law that raises the income tax rate. The payoff that one now expects to earn from eight hours of work will be less than what one would have earned from the same action or strategy earlier. Likewise with the example of the pollution law above. I shall, however, argue that, while this ubiquitous view of law serves well for some limited purposes, it is fundamentally flawed. The law needs to be understood very differently if we are to get a better grip on reality while building models of economics.

LAW AND ECONOMICS: CRITIQUE AND A NEW APPROACH

The standard view of the role of law in an economy would be right if it were the case that the economy game is one that is played only by the "nongovernmental" individuals in society. That is, if the police, the tax collectors, and the judges were agents exogenous to the game, who mechanically went about doing what the law required them to do, then indeed for the other people in the society (that is, for the players of the game) a law would be something that determined the game by fixing the payoff function; and so a change in the legal regime would amount to a change of the game.

But in reality those who work for government—the police, the district judge, the tax collector, the bureaucrat, the individuals in the pollution control department, and so on—are also individuals with their own motivations, dreams, striving, and cunning. Hence they are also players and should not be treated as exogenous to the economy game. This fact, in itself, is now recognized in the new literature on economics and government.[28]

What is not always recognized is that this throws a wrench in the traditional models of law and economics. Morever, even those economists who recognize the significance of endogenizing the "law enforcer" balk at taking this idea all the way to its natural conclusion; and they tend to err on the side of the traditional approach in their instinctive moments.

Note that whether a particular law is there or not, the policeman's, the tax collector's, and the judge's sets of strategies remain the same. And if everybody behaves the same way, whether or not the law is there, everybody must get the same payoff. Hence, the law cannot change the payoff function either.

Consider, for example, the case of antipollution law. *Whether or not the law is there*, the strategies open to the policeman include (a) arrest a person who emits pollutants and (b) not arrest a person who emits pollutants; the strategies open to the judge include (1) punish the policeman who arrests a person who pollutes the atmosphere and (2) punish the policemen who does not arrest a person who pollutes the atmosphere.[29] Now if—whether or not the law is there—the person, the policeman, and the judge behave the same way, then the person, the policeman, and the judge will get the same payoff. Hence, the game played by *all the individuals* in the economy is unaffected by the law.

If the enforcers of the law or the agents of the state automatically enforce the law, then a new law does affect the payoff function and therefore the game *played by the rest of the citizens*. But once everybody, including the enforcers of the law, are included in the game (as they should be), a law is nothing but some ink on paper. There being or not being such ink on paper cannot alter the game. This rather unusual conclusion, which is elaborated upon later in this section, is baffling at first sight. But this merely reflects the fact that the standard approach, though flawed, is deeply ingrained in modern social science thinking.

To digress for a moment, consider the new literature on rights and liberty, which expresses rights as game forms.[30] There has been much controversy about whether this is the correct way to describe rights. I would argue that, according to this conception of rights, a change in the structure of rights changes the sets of actions open to individuals and therefore changes the game.

But it is not clear why a new rights assignment will change what I *can* do, even though it may well change what I *will* do. I argue that granting a person, i, a right to do something, call it x, must mean that if i does x, then another person, j, will not have the right to do something (for instance, punch i's nose). Of course, j's not having the right to do something, in turn, must mean that if j does do that thing, then others will acquire the rights to certain actions (typically punitive actions against j) to which they otherwise would not have had a right.[31] This is discussed in greater detail in Appendix B.

The above discussion may give the impression that law does not have any effect on society, that it is a chimera, but such an impression would be wrong. The law does not affect the payoff functions of the individuals or of the game, but it can influence the *outcome* of the game. It does so by creating focal points, and by giving rise to beliefs and expectations in the minds of the individuals.[32] Thus, in the above example, the policeman can choose between (a) and (b) and the judge between from among (1) and (2), but the policeman may *believe* that the judge will choose (1) if there is no antipollution law in the state and (2) if there is an antipollution law in effect. Hence, this may prompt the policeman to choose (a) if, and only if, the law is there. This in turn may mean that no one will pollute the atmosphere if, and only if, there is an antipollution law in effect. Hence, the outcome of the game may well get influenced by the law. But note that the law works here entirely through its influence on people's beliefs and opinions. A central thesis of this essay is that it cannot be otherwise. Law's empire, tangible and all-encompassing as it may seem, is founded on nothing but beliefs.

Of course, we will need to check that a particular outcome is self-enforcing (that is, an equilibrium solution) before we can say that the outcome will occur given the law. But the important point is that a law *can* affect the *outcome*, and that in the final analysis, the law and the state are simply a self-supporting structure of beliefs and opinions. Hence, the order that one finds in very different kinds of collectivities—ranging from the totalitarian state to what anthropologists, in their zoological moments, call the acephalous society—are *self-enforcing* outcomes.

What is a self-enforcing outcome or a reasonable equilibrium solution for a game is itself a controversial question. Over the last two decades solution concepts have proliferated rapidly.[33] But it would be foolish to get drawn into that debate here. Hence, without further justification, we shall treat the set of *Nash equilibrium* outcomes[34] as the self-enforcing set.[35] So from here on, a reference to an "equilibrium" outcome is always to a Nash equilibrium.

Many games have the problem of there being too many Nash equilibriums. Consider a game in which you and another player will each have to choose one number (without letting the other player see what you are choosing) from among 3, 7, 9, and 100. If both of you choose the same number, each of you gets $1,000; if you choose different numbers, neither gets anything. In this game the following pairs of choices are the only Nash equilibriums: (3,3), (7,7), (9,9), and (100,100). If you were playing this game, your essential problem is to try to guess what the other player will do. What complicates the guess is that what the other player does will depend on what she guesses you will do. One way of guessing is to try to see if a particular strategy is salient or "focal," and to employ it in the expectation that the other player will do the same. If such a salient outcome exists, it is called a *focal point*,[36] and predicting a focal outcome often turns out to be a good prediction. This method has no rigorous explanation but works through human psychology. In the above game, for instance, most human beings would choose 100. It is a large number, it is well-rounded, and somehow it stands out.

Nebulous though this method is, it works fairly well and has been used to great convenience. At Heathrow Airport there is an arbitrary place with a large sign above it saying Meeting Point. If you plan to meet a friend at Heathrow Airport and fail to decide in advance where to wait for the friend, then in this game there are millions of Nash equilibriums. As long as both of you choose the same place you have a Nash equilibrium. It does not matter where that place is. The value of the sign is that it creates a focal point among all the possible Nash equilibriums. You would typically choose to wait under the sign and so would your friend. There is no hard reason for doing that, but you would expect the other player to do so, and that becomes reason enough. Putting up the sign Meeting Point does not change the game that you and your friend are forced to play by virtue of having forgotten to decide where you will meet, but it nevertheless influences the outcome. The writing on the paper that constitutes law is like the signboard in Heathrow. In itself it is quite a vacuous thing, but it creates expectations in the minds of individuals as to what the others will do; it creates focal points, and thereby influences the outcome.

Suppose now the airport authority at Heathrow, in trying to be helpful and not have people walk too far, puts up twenty signboards saying Meeting Point at different locations in the airport. You may then decide that it is futile to wait under one of these (since it is not clear which one you should wait under), and remembering that your friend is a bookworm, and he knows that you know that he is a bookworm, and you know that he knows that you know that he is a bookworm, and so on, you may go to the store, Books Etc., and wait for him there. In anticipation of this, he may also choose to go the bookstall. Whether he does so or not, in this case the well-meaning signboards fail to influence behavior and the outcome of the game. This can happen with the law as well. Poorly drafted legislation or legislation that takes inadequate cognizance of individual incentives can fail to have effect on people's behavior or can have unintended effects by actually causing confusion. To avoid such poor quality legislation, we have to first understand how and when the law works in the first place. For that we have to cast aside the widespread view that law changes the payoff functions and, hence, the game.

Recall that social norms (of the equilibrium-selection variety) also are simply a mechanism for players to coordinate onto an equilibrium (or some outcome within a certain set of equilibriums). It follows that actions and behavior (and therefore outcomes) that are enforceable by law are also enforceable by social norms. Since an outcome that is enforceable by the law is an equilibrium, we can always imagine norms (which lead to beliefs) that sustain the same actions, behavior, and outcome.[37]

To take an example, consider a society in which the law allows you to drive on any side of the road, but the norm is to drive on the left. Since we have seen that if such a law were there it would be enforceable, it follows that this norm is also enforceable. This is an easy example because it is empirically transparent. In some remote parts of India, the hand of the law is so weak that it is indeed the case that, in effect, there is no law about which side of the road to drive on. Yet people do drive on the left because once the norm is in place, there is no reason for one to violate it.[38]

Obedience to a tyrant also is best explained along these lines, since no one really fears the hurt the tyrant can *himself* bring upon one. I have previously made use of a triadic model explaining this.[39] The subordinate's fear of the tyrant, based on what the subordinate expects other subordinates to do to him should he disobey the tyrant, is what Hume was talking about when he wrote: "No man would have any reason to *fear* the fury of a tyrant, if he had no authority over any but from fear; since, as a single man, his bodily force can reach but a small way, and all the farther power he posses *must be found on our own opinion, or on the presumed opinion of others.*"[40] (The second set of italics is mine.)

This brings us to the central proposition of this paper, which I've called the "core theorem."

> CORE THEOREM: *Whatever behavior and outcomes in society are legally enforceable are also enforceable through social norms.*

This theorem has two immediate implications or corollaries.

> FIRST COROLLARY: *What can be achieved through the law can, in principle, also be achieved without the law.*
> SECOND COROLLARY: *If a certain outcome is not an equilibrium of the economy, then it cannot be implemented through any law.*

Let us begin with the first corollary and, in particular, with some examples. In India till fairly recent times, and in some parts even now, a widow was expected to lead a life of general abstinence: do not eat nonvegetarian food, wear black and white clothes, avoid close relationships with men, and so on. This social norm used to be adhered to very strictly in many parts of India. To an outside observer, unfamiliar with India, this would appear to be a practice enforced by law, just like in some Islamic states where the women are required by law to wear the *chador*. But this appearance would be deceptive because there is no law that achieved this remarkable conformity in India. The conformity was achieved entirely through a system of sanctions and threats of ostracism, the threats themselves being given by individuals who feared that if they did not give such threats, they themselves would be ostracized. So this an example of behavior that we would expect to be caused by the law but is actually the result of social norms. The rules of caste are another example. The core theorem, in particular, the first corollary, challenges the myth that norms are somehow spontaneous and natural, while laws are intrusive and unnatural.

Turning to a different setting, consider a researcher who is given the task of finding out the extent to which the press is free in different countries. The typical thing this person will do is find out what kinds of legal restrictions each country places on its scribes. She may also check on more general laws and statutes, such as the First Amendment in the United States, which guarantees freedom of speech to individuals and, therefore, also to the press. It has been found that in some countries the state persecutes its critics even when the law does not disallow criticism; and so this researcher may go a step further and check the record of state persecution of journalists and television commentators. She would then somehow combine all this information to decide in which nations the press is the most free and in which nations the least. To most of us, at least at first sight, this seems like a reasonable procedure.

In light of the core theorem, however, it turns out that this method of research can yield seriously flawed results, because the method presumes that the only curb on press freedom can come from the nation's laws and the state. But the theorem tells us that what the state can do, individual citizens, going about their daily chores, can also achieve. So it is not enough to observe the law and state or governmental action.

One may try to rebut this criticism by arguing that there are practical limits to what we can study; so when we look for whether certain freedoms are guaranteed in a certain nation, it is only natural to study the nation's law and governmental behavior. Suppose we agree to this rebuttal. Then, of course, we have to use this criterion for all studies of a similar nature. Now suppose the researcher were asked to study the amount of freedom that the widow has in different nations. She would then have to say that the Indian widow is no less free than widows elsewhere in the world because she faced no legal or governmental restrictions on her behavior. This would then also be true of India several decades ago, when in some parts of the country the widow was expected to commit *suttee*—burn herself on the dead husband's pyre. Most of us would agree that the woman climbing on to the pyre was not, typically, committing a voluntary act. The voluntary act conclusion would be a folly stemming from the erroneous presumption that it is only the state that can curb individual voluntariness.

Newspapers and magazines come under all kinds of social—and in particular nongovernmental—pressures. If a newspaper criticiz es a wealthy business lobby, it can face debilitating cuts in advertisements, and so it may feel compelled not to criticize the lobby. If it criticizes its government during an international crisis and the people of that nation are sufficiently nationalistic, it may face a boycott by general readers, and fearing this, it may decide not to criticize the government. Once these extralegal constraints are taken into account, certain rankings become ambiguous. Between, for instance, China and the United States, it may be relatively easy to conclude that the latter has a more free press, even without studying social control, because the state is *so much* more repressive in China; but between the States and India, the answer is less obvious. In terms of the *law*, the U.S. media are probably more free than the Indian ones; but the social and business sanctions seem to be greater on US newspapers and television channels. This is not just because of the pressures of political correctness, but there seems to be a wide recognition among corporations, lobbies, and power brokers in the United States that the control of opinion and information is an important ingredient for profit and survival. Even if my empirical conjecture about China, the U.S. and India is false, it still remains true that merely studying legal controls may be inadequate, not just for determining press freedom but the freedom of the widow or the low caste.[41]

Freedom of speech is similarly problematic. When you say that you believe that individuals should have the freedom to say what they want or what they believe in, the main problem, to my mind, is not the moral status or appeal of that statement but to understand what it means. If by the above declaration you mean that the set of feasible actions available to an individual should include his ability to make different speeches, then your commitment to free speech is pretty meaningless. It is based on the same flawed view of an economy that underlies some of the literature on rights that I have discussed above and examine in greater depth in Appendix B. Having a freedom or a right must be interpreted as other people not having certain freedoms or rights after you have exercised that freedom.[42] And unless it is made at least partly clear what restriction one is willing to put on other people's freedom when guaranteeing a certain freedom to one person, the declaration that you believe in that freedom remains ambiguous.

An individual's freedom of speech can be curbed by the state; but it can also be curbed by the voluntary, atomistic actions of ordinary citizens.[43] Some societies are temperamentally more prone to sanctioning one another's speech and behavior, of being less tolerant of what one considers to be deviancy. If we are committed to maximizing the freedom of speech and recognize that such freedom is not just a matter of law but also social norms, we may have to contend with the even more difficult problem that arises from the possibility that one person's exercising of his or her freedom of speech can result in the curtailment of another's freedom.[44]

Another example of how the meaning of "freedom" can quickly become complicated occurs in the context of labor markets. Most people believe that slavery is coercion but that modern labor markets are voluntary. Those who study developing societies agree that bonded labor is unfree but that wage labor is voluntary. But once one goes beyond contemporary, industrialized society to consider examples of labor markets from primitive societies or bygone eras, the dividing line between what is free and what is not is not so clear, as one encounters institutions that appear strange to the modern observer.[45] Morever, on returning to contemporary markets, after such a journey, the dividing lines that had earlier seemed obvious also appear less sharp. It is true that in the light of the core theorem, individual freedoms become vastly more difficult to compute. But that cannot be reason enough for confining our attention to the law and the behavior of government when studying individual freedom.

Let us now turn to the second corollary. According to this, if we have a law, the adherence to which entails out-of-equilibrium behavior on the part of some individual, then such a law is doomed to failure; it can never be enforced. This is because according to the core theorem, the law can achieve only what a social norm can achieve. And since a social norm simply selects an equilibrium, no law can induce a non-equilibrium outcome.[46] Attempts to induce such an outcome would either result in the law being inconsequential or have unintended effects on the economy. Ellickson's claim that there can be "order without law" is now easy to understand, as is the converse of that claim: disorder despite law.[47]

Considering the core theorem, the question must arise, in what way is the law different from norms, since up to now we have shown how, in certain important respects, they look very similar? To answer this we have to recognize that the economy, described as a game, ignores a lot of information concerning prior beliefs and histories, which is a part of the real economy. In reality, even before a specific law is enacted there exists a predefined set of roles for various players concerning the way they should relate to the law, *whatever the law is*. The players are, of course, free to violate these rules, but they are nonetheless there. Thus the traffic policeman is supposed to follow the rule that he should stop drivers who violate the traffic laws. This instruction to the traffic police remains in force *no matter what the traffic laws are*. The ordinary citizen is supposed to follow the rule that he or she respects the orders of the traffic police.[48] The judge is supposed to follow the rule that he should punish the person who violates the law, and this remains valid no matter what the law is. Even if the speed limit is changed, the judge's rule remains the same. These prior rules and institutions may be referred to as "quasi-laws," "quasi-norms," or as "standing orders." The qualifier *quasi* reminds us that on their own they may not have any bite. The rule that the policeman should stop a car that breaks the speed limit is not an operational law till the speed limit is specified.

But once the speed limit law is specified, the quasi-laws come to life. The speed limit law thrown in with the preexisting quasi-laws is much more than a law that simply says that a driver must not cross 65 mph. It is a law (or a set of laws, if we want to emphasize its reach) that specifies behavior rules for various people—the driver, of course, but also the policeman, the magistrate, and also, frequently, the ordinary citizen (who, for instance, may not obstruct a policeman carrying out his duty). The role of quasi-laws is illustrated with an example in Appendix A.

Given that all modern societies have predefined rules or standing orders for people with respect to the law, which are independent of what the actual law is, this means that when new laws are enacted, the set of supporting activities and behavior by the various citizens do not have to be specified separately each time. It is this preexisting structure of rules and instructions, along with the expectations in people's mind, that these will be adhered to as long as they are not against the adherer's self-interest, which make it possible for the laws to be implemented. For any law, the full ramification of what it implies for individual behavior is enormous. Suppose Montana enacts a new speed limit legislation. This does not ask just drivers to behave in a certain way; it also asks traffic wardens to behave in a certain way, judges to behave in a certain way, and so on.[49] The existence of preexisting rules (and, therefore, expectations) for laws is what makes a law different from a norm. If the Montana speed limit were to be introduced as a *norm*, all the supporting behaviors by the various agents would have to be specified, since norms do not have the advantage of preexisting rules and expectations. So, though for each implementable law there is also a norm that would yield the same outcome, the full statement of that norm would be enormously complicated.

The histories of norms and laws are also different.[50] Usually (though not always) social norms appear through long processes of evolution. Similar acts repeated over time can become a norm. To quote Ullmann-Margalit: "Norms as a rule do not come into existence at a definite point in time, nor are they the result of a manageable number of identifiable acts. They are, rather, the resultant of complex patterns of behavior of a large number of people over a protracted period of time."[51] Even some very sharply defined social norms and customs, such as the caste system or eating habits of different peoples, have such distant and diffused origins that there may be no agreement among historians as to where they came from. The law, on the other hand, is normally a product of deliberate choices, with dates of their enactment frequently known. Of course there are exceptions. The laws that certain tribes follow often merge into what we think of as norms; even in modern societies there are laws that emerged from common customs. This is true, for instance, of English common law, and the U.S. practice of relying on interpretive principles and judicial rulings.[52] Conversely, there are some norms which are deliberate decisions.

But norms are difficult to change, since norms do not have the paraphernalia of preexisting rules, which can be used to usher in a new norm. On the other hand, norms may well be more robust than the law, because just as most norms were not deliberately instituted, it is difficult to deliberately discard them.

CONCLUDING REMARKS

In the previous sections I have discussed how to correctly model the role of law in an economy. There are, however, situations where we may willfully choose to reject the correct method, just as economists often do a partial equilibrium analysis where, strictly speaking, they should be doing a general equilibrium analysis. Indeed, it is possible to view the standard literature on law and economics as something akin to partial equilibrium analysis. It *presumes* law-abiding behavior on the part of the law enforcement officers. Even in more sophisticated models that allow for bribery and other kinds of lapses, ultimately (and often implicitly) there is a layer of enforcement that is assumed to be automatic. This can work within limits, and if we are lucky, those who are assumed to do the job automatically actually find it in their interest to do so. But surely, instead of working with models that rely on our keeping our fingers crossed, it would be better to approach modeling law and economics as suggested here.

If one does adopt this approach to law and economics, it will have implications for several related areas of research, notably, the study of government and the state. In general, economists have been quite cavalier in modeling government. It has usually been treated as an exogenous agent or a puppet organization, carrying out the advice of economists (thereby providing a raison d'être for policy economists). Even when economists have gone beyond this, they have generally taken a simplistic or mechanical view of government.[53] This essay draws our attention to the fact that both the enforcers of the law and, for want of a better word, the enforcees need to be modeled together, as strategic agents, having volition and choice. Such a construction will not be easy and will not happen all at once, but it is a target worth keeping in mind.

THIS APPENDIX illustrates formally some of the principles discussed in the main text. I proceed here entirely through an example.

For most games that economists talk about, it is possible to define a larger game by adding on to it the possibility of punitive actions after the end of the main game. Thus chess is a game, but at the end of a game of chess, I can sock my opponent in the nose, he can sock me back, and so on. So for every game G, we can define an "expanded game" G_E, which appends to G a string of punitive actions.

I shall consider a very simple game G. This game consists of one player, called player 1, who has to choose any action from the set [0,1]. His payoff function is as follows. If he chooses $x \in [0,1]$, then he gets a payoff of x. We could think of an action as the amount of pollution generated by him. This takes a value between 0 and 1. The more he pollutes the more profit he earns. Call this game G. If this was all there was, player 1 would pollute up to level 1.

Now consider the expanded game G_E. In period 0 of G_E, player 1 plays the above game G. In period 1 player 2 can choose between P (punish the other player) and N (not punish the other player). In period 2 player 1 chooses between P and N; in period 3 player 2 chooses between P and N; and so on ad infinitum. Suppose in period t (≥ 1), player i has to move. Then if i plays P, player j ($\neq i$) earns $-B$ (where $B > 0$) in that period and i earns 0; and if i plays N, both earn 0. In other words, punishment hurts and inflicting a punishment is costless and joyless (it will be interesting to modify this assumption). Both players have a discount factor of $\delta \in (0,1)$.

What we are interested in checking is how much pollution can be controlled through legislation. To keep the analysis simple, we shall assume that there is the following "preexisting quasi-law." This is simply a contingent definition.

At any time period $t \geq 1$, agent i's chosen action will be called *illegal* if he chooses P (i.e., punishes the other player), though player j's move at time $t - 1$ was legal (i.e., not illegal) or he chooses N, though j's move at $t - 1$ was illegal.

In words, what we are saying is this: (a) It is illegal to punish someone who has done nothing illegal and (b) it is illegal to not punish someone who has violated the law. We can think of other kinds of quasi-laws—for instance, we may think of dropping (b).

This preexisting quasi-law has no bite till we specify a law regarding what constitutes an illegal move in game G, and that is the reason I refer to it as quasi-law. Consider a possible law, which I will call "the pollution law." In period 0, if player 1 chooses any action greater than α, where α is a given number in $[0,1)$, then 1's action is *illegal*.

The pollution law, coupled with the preexisting partial law, is a well-defined law—let us call it a "legal system"—which allows us to classify every action in every play of the game as either legal or illegal. Given a play of the game, a person is described as law abiding if he or she makes no illegal moves.

Note that the legal system that we are considering is parameterized by α. We want to investigate for which α's is the legal system enforceable in the sense that there exists a Nash equilibrium outcome where everybody is law abiding.

Observe that a new pollution law or, for that matter, a new legal system, leaves the strategy sets and payoff functions (and therefore the game) unchanged. As in the main text, the legal system *can* nevertheless influence behavior by affecting everybody's expectation about everybody else's behavior, as long as it is enforceable.

To check this, suppose both players are law abiding. In particular, let us suppose that 1 decides to play α in period 0 (i.e., the highest possible legal move) and be law abiding throughout. To check if this is an equilibrium, we have to verify that no one stands to benefit by deviating unilaterally.

If both are law abiding, 1 gets a payoff of α and 2 gets a payoff of 0. Clearly, 2 cannot do better through any deviation since 0 is the highest she can earn in this game. Consider 1's strategy if 1 decides to deviate from being law abiding. It is easy to see that the best deviation is to play 1 in period 0 and from then on to make only legal moves. That will of course invite punishment from player 2 (since she is law abiding) in period 1. After then, it is not worthwhile for player 1 to play P because that, and only that, will prompt player 2 to play P in the following period. Hence, if 1 deviates from being law abiding, 1's highest possible payoff is $1 - \delta B$. Thus, 1 will not deviate if, and only if,

$$\alpha \geq 1 - \delta\beta$$

It follows that the only pollution laws that are enforceable are ones that permit people to pollute up to some level at least as high as $1 - \delta B$. If $1 - \delta B > 0$ and the pollution law sets $\alpha \in [0, 1 - \delta B)$, then a behavior in conformity with the law cannot be enforced in any way. Since the law cannot change the game, a pollution level below $1 - \delta B$ is impossible in this society.

THE LITERATURE on liberty and rights that emerged from social choice theory[54] has gradually moved to a representation of rights as game forms.[55] This representation of rights has been the source of some controversy. The discussion of norms and law undertaken here suggests a new line of criticism of this approach. According to the rights-as-game-form approach, every assignment of individual rights translates into a game; thus a change in rights is represented by a change in the game being played by the players, since rights determine the strategies available to a player. Thus if i does not have the right to steal j's wallet, that option is typically omitted from i's available strategies or actions.

It is arguable, however, that i's not having a right to do something does not mean i *cannot* do that thing, so a change in rights should not be thought of as causing a change in the feasible set of actions. Stepping back from these academic debates, let us ask ourselves what it means to say: "Person i does not have the right to steal j's wallet." It means that if i does steal j's wallet, then someone else (j or a policeman) has the right to take some punitive action (y) against i, which otherwise that person would not have the right to do. Thus, i having a right to action z means that if i chooses z, then someone else j will not have a right to some action y that punishes i. This interdependent character of rights is very similar to the law described in Appendix A. Hence, a rights structure can influence what happens in the game, but it does not do so by influencing the game itself.

The above idea of interdependence of rights has been stressed by several writers. Hart writes that "to have a right entails having a moral justification for limiting the freedom of another person and for determining how he should act."[56] More pertinently, Lyons argues: "When others are under an obligation to me and threaten to default, there are actions I might appropriately take which I would not otherwise be justified in taking."[57]

To illustrate a rights structure of this kind, consider the game G_E in Appendix A. Think of action P as punching the other person in the nose or some such action to which no one has a right normally, but could acquire a right by virtue of the person in question doing something wrong or hurting one's right in the first place. Think of the two players in the game as neighbors and the actions open to player 1 in period 0 (given by the set [0,1]) as different levels of pollution from some activity in his backyard, which has a negative externality for player 2 but gives happiness to 1.

A *rights structure* can be defined by a basic right parameterized by α and other (contingent) rights. Let us suppose that by this society's values, 1 has the *right* to choose pollution levels up to α; but no more. If he chooses a pollution level s $> \alpha$, then in period 1 player 2 acquires the right to choose P.

If, however, in period 0, 1 chooses s ≥ α and in period 1, 2 chooses P, then in period 3, 1 acquires the right to choose P, and so on. More formally, this may be stated as follows.

At time $t ≥ 1$, if it is player i's move, we shall say that i chooses an action to which he or she *does not have a right* if that action happens to be P and if in period $t - 1$ agent j ($≠ i$) had chosen an action to which he or she had a right (i.e., did not choose an action to which he or she did not have a right). This, coupled with the initial assumption that 1 in period 0 does not have a right to choose s > α, where $α ∈ [0,1]$, defines a rights structure.

Now when the game is played we can evaluate the *outcome* as one that does or does not respect the rights structure. So in this formulation, it is not a game that can satisfy or violate rights, but it is the outcome that can be put to this test. And, as with equilibrium-selection norms and law, a rights structure can potentially be enforced only if it is such that the intersection between the set of outcomes that satisfy the rights structure and the set of equilibrium outcomes is nonempty. No amount of policing or state intervention can change this fact, since the enforcers are already a part of the game and cannot do anything that was not already a part of their strategy sets.

NOTES

This essay draws on my forthcoming book, *Prelude to Political Economy: A Study of the Social and Political Foundations of Economics*. In writing the essay I have benefited from the comments and criticisms of Patrick Emerson, Michael McPherson, Andy Rutten, Eduardo Zambrano, and an anonymous referee.

1. Rods, iron or wooden—I did not manage to find out which.

2. This fits in well with the "self-help" view of law so perceptively described by D. Black in "Crime as Social Control," *American Sociological Review* 48: 34–45. Thus while at one level collecting money by issuing threats is criminal, we must remember that "there is a sense in which conduct regarded as criminal is often quite the opposite." (p. 34) Black goes on to provide a variety of examples from different societies of "moral" crimes. A similar view from a historical perspective emerges from E. P. Thompson's classic essay on the moral economy of the crowd: "The Moral Economy of the English Crowd in the Eighteenth Century," *Past and Present* 50 (1971).

3. This is not to be confused with the "political economy" of the nineteenth century, which was the older name of economics till the advent of neoclassical economics.

4. This was later published in *Oxford Economic Papers* 38 (1986): 259-82.

5. K. Basu, E. Jones, and E. Schlicht, "The Growth and Decay of Custom: The Role of the New Institutional Economics in Economic History," *Explorations in Economic History*, vol. 24 (1987): 1–21.

6. Strictly speaking, what we need is the convexity of preference. But since that turns out to be equivalent to the law of diminishing marginal utility, if the utility function happens to be additively separable, I shall here use the more familiar condition.

7. See M. Granovetter, "Economic Action and Social Structure: The Problem of Embeddedness," *American Journal of Sociology* 91 (1985): 481–510.

8. This view of language, which I adhere to, is not undisputed, but it has the respectability of age, dating at least as far back as to the writings of David Hume. Warneryd has formalized this point of view in terms of evolutionary game theory; see K. Warneryd, "Language, Evolution and the Theory of Games," in *Cooperation and Conflict in General Evolutionary Processes*, ed. J. L. Casti and A. Karlquist (New York: John Wiley, 1995).

9. J. H. Kagel et al., "Experimental Studies of Consumer Demand Behavior using Laboratory Animals," *Economic Inquiry* 8 (1975): 22–38.

10. Warneryd, "Language, Evolution and the Theory of Games."

11. I argue in my article "On Misunderstanding Government: An Analysis of the Art of Policy Advising," *Economics and Politics* 9 (1997): 231–50, that this is an implicit assumption in standard general equilibrium theory; and that once this is recognized it becomes possible to interpret the first fundamental theorem of welfare economics quite differently from what is usual.

12. R. M. Solow, "Mass Unemployment as a Social Problem," in *Choice, Welfare and Development*, ed. K. Basu, P. K. Pattanaik, and K. Suzumura (Oxford: Clarendon Press, 1995), p. 318.

13. See my "Social Norms and the Law," in *The New Palgrave Dictionary of Economics and the Law*, ed. Peter Newman (London: Macmillan, 1998). A more elaborate, though similar classification occurs in R. A. Posner, "Social Norms and the Law: An Economic Approach," *American Economic Review* 87 (1997): 365–69.

14. The norm of reciprocity, as described by R. Sugden, which involves self-interested behavior subject to some moral constraints, is a rationality-limiting norm; see his "Reciprocity: The Supply of Public Goods through Voluntary Contributions," *Economic Journal* 94 (1984): 772–87.

15. See K. Basu, "Civil Institutions and Evolution: Concepts, Critiques and Model," *Journal of Development Economics* 46 (1995):19–33; and K. Basu, "Notes on Evolution, Rationality and Norms," *Journal of Institutional and Theoretical Economics* 152 (1996): 739–50.

16. An example of a preference-changing norm, along with its implications for economic policy, occurs in A. Lindbeck, S. Nyberg, and J. W. Weibull, "Social Norms and Economic Incentives in the Welfare State," mimeo, Stockholm School of Economics, 1997.

17. This explains why the police have to be vigilant in enforcing the Stop-sign rule or the speeding rule but not about drive-on-the-right rule. The first two are laws that are not in peoples' self interest (they may, of course, be in their *group* interest).

18. G. Akerlof, "The Economics of Caste and of the Rat Race and Other Woeful Tales," *Quarterly Journal of Economics* 90 (1976): 599–617.

19. K. Basu, "One Kind of Power," *Oxford Economic Papers* 8 (1986): 259:–82.

20. R. D. Cooter,"Law from Order" (University of California, Berkeley, 1997, mimeographed).

21. Greif constructs an equilibrium-selection explanation of certain kinds of cultures and cultural beliefs that can explain different trading institutions: A. Greif, "Cultural Beliefs and the Organization of Society: A Historical and Theoretical Reflection on Collectivist and Individualist Societies," *Journal of Political Economy* 102 (1994).

22. J. M. Buchanan, "The Coase Theorem and the Theory of the State," *Natural Resources Journal*, 13 (1973): 580–94.

23. D. G. Baird, R. H. Gertner, and R. C. Picker, *Game Theory and the Law* (Cambridge, Mass.: Harvard University Press, 1995).

24. J. P. Benoit and L. A. Kornhauser, "Game-Theoretic Analysis of Legal Rules and Institutions," Economic Research Reports, #96–30 (1996), C. V. Starr Center for Applied Economics, New York University.

25. Dixit in his recent work on the political process in an economy also views the interaction between agents as a game. While not going into such a formal contruction, Bhagwati and O'Flaherty nevertheless adopt a game-theoretic approach in which individuals who constitute government are also players with their own objective functions: A. Dixit, *The Making of Economic Policy: A Transaction-Cost Politics Perspective* (Cambridge, Mass.: MIT Press, 1996); and B. O'Flaherty and J. Bhagwati, "Will Free Trade with Political Science Put Normative Economists Out of Work?" *Economics and Politics* 9 (1997): 207–20.

26. One way of limiting the strategies open to a player is to assume that all the strategies are still available, but some of them give a payoff of negative infinity and thus would never be adopted. Hence, once we allow for the payoff function to be altered, there may be no need for separately assuming that the strategy set can be shrunk.

27. D. G. Baird, R. H. Gertner, and R. C. Picker, *Game Theory and the Law*, p. 15.

28. See J. Bhagwati, R. Brecher, and T. N. Srinivasan, "DUP Activities and Economic Theory," in *Neoclassical Political Economy*, ed. D. Collander (Cambridge: Ballinger, 1984); D. Friedman, "A Positive Account of Property Rights," in *Property Rights*, ed. E. F. Paul, F. D. Miller, and J. Paul (Cambridge: Cambridge University Press, 1994); R. L. Calvert, "Rational Actors, Equilibrium and Social Institutions," in *Explaining Social Institutions*, ed. J. Knight and I. Sened (Ann Arbor: University of Michigan Press, 1995); A. Dixit, *The Making of Economic Policy*; K. Basu, "On Misunderstanding Government: An Analysis of the Art of Policy Advising," *Economics and Politics* 9 (1997): 231–50; and R. Gibbons and A. Rutten, "Hierarchical Dilemmas: Social Order with Self-Interested Rulers" (Cornell University, 1997, mimeographed). An interesting attempt to apply some of these theoretical ideas to political events and phenomena occurs in R. H. Bates and B. R. Weingast, "Rationality and Interpretation: The Politics of Transition" (Harvard University, 1996, mimeographed). For an endogenous but evolutionary view of institutions, see A. Schotter, *The Economic Theory of Social Institutions* (Cambridge: Cambridge University Press, 1981).

29. The game, properly defined, would require specifying what the remaining strategies are, the sequence of moves, and other such details, but since I do not aim to analyze the game in any detail, it is all right to leave the description at this level of generality.

30. W. Gaertner, P. K. Pattanaik, and K. Suzumura, "Individual Rights Revisited," *Economica* 59 (1992): 161–78; A. Sen, "Minimal Liberty," *Economica* 59 (1992): and R. Deb, "Waiver, Effectivity and Rights as Game Forms," *Economica* 61 (1994): 167–78.

31. More formally, a "rights structure" is simply a specification of a subset of actions from among all the actions open to the relevant player at that information set. The interpretation is that the player has a *"right"* to choose an action only from the specified subset.

32. This point of view builds on the legacy of David Hume. In his essay "Of the First Principles of Government," Hume had puzzled about the sources of state influence on social and economic outcomes. Thus he wrote: "Nothing appears more surprising to those who consider human affairs with a philosophical eye, than the easiness with which the many are governed by the few." And he reaches the remarkable conclusion that those who rule do so only by the force of opinion: "It is therefore on opinion only that government is founded; and this maxim extends to the most despotic ... governments, as well as to the most free and most popular." David Hume, *Essays: Moral, Political and Literary* (reprint, Indianapolis: Liberty Fund, 1987), p. 32.

33. See, for instance, M. J. Osborne and A. Rubinstein, *A Course in Game Theory* (Cambridge, Mass.: MIT Press, 1994).

34. A *Nash equilibrium* outcome of a game is a choice of strategy by each player (that is, a tuple of strategies) such that no individual can do better by *unilaterally* deviating to some other strategy. Thus, once a Nash equilibrium outcome is expected by all players, the outcome becomes self-enforcing.

35. Left to myself, I would prefer to use the coarser solution concept of "rationalizability," but for the present purpose it is simpler to rely on the much more widely used solution of Nash equilibrium. It is worth noting that in some situations, despite there being a rationalizable equilibrium and even a Nash equilibrium, there may be no reasonable way of predicting the outcome. See my "On the Nonexistence of a Rationality Definition for Extensive Games," *International Journal of Game Theory* 19 (1990): 33–44; and "The Traveler's Dilemma: Paradoxes of Rationality in Game Theory," *American Economic Review* 84 (1994): 391–95.

36. See T. C. Schelling, *The Strategy of Conflict* (Oxford: Oxford University Press, 1960).

37. For a real-life illustration of how norms and beliefs translate into action and policy, see P. Katzenstein, "Coping with Terrorism: Norms and Internal Security in Germany and Japan," in *Ideas and Foreign Policy*, ed. J. Goldstein and R. O. Keohane (Ithaca, N.Y.: Cornell University Press, 1993).

38. In this case, the norm is imported from the cities where it is the law and is enforced.

39. K. Basu, "One Kind of Power."

40. Hume, *Essays*, p. 34.

41. Bernstein's engaging study of the diamond industry makes it amply clear that the advice carries over even to the more microeconomic domain of specific industries and markets; see L. Bernstein, "Opting Out of the Legal System: Extralegal Contractual Relations in the Diamond Industry," *Journal of Legal Studies* 21 (1992): 115–57.

42. I am fully aware that this is a circular definition. But it is not meaningless for that reason, as is demonstrated in Appendix B.

43. G. Loury, "Self-Censorship in Public Discourse: A Theory of 'Political Correctness' and Related Phenomena," *Rationality and Society* 6 (1994): 428–61.

44. O. M. Fiss, *The Irony of Free Speech* (Cambridge, Mass.: Harvard University Press, 1996).

45. S. L. Engerman, "Coerced and Free Labor: Property Rights and the Development of the Labor Force," *Explorations in Economic History* 29 (1992): 1–29.

46. Following Leibnitz, Steiner has argued that for a set of rights to be implementable, it is necessary that the rights be "compossible," that is, that the set of social

outcomes or states where each of these rights are satisfied be nonempty. By the same argument, he would no doubt argue that for a set of laws to be implementable, a necessary condition is that they be compossible. Viewed in this light, the second corollary can be thought of as simply taking this argument further and claiming that for a set of laws to be implementable, the intersection of the set of outcomes that satisfy these laws and the solution set of the economy game must be nonempty. A similar extension is possible for rights, as illustrated in Appendix B. See H. Steiner, *An Essay on Rights* (Oxford: Blackwell, 1994), pp. 2–3.

47. R. C. Ellickson, *Order without Law: How Neighbors Settle Disputes* (Cambridge, Mass.: Harvard University Press, 1991).

48. Ask yourself why you would not stop driving if an ordinary civilian (perhaps mad), pretending to be a traffic warden, asked you to stop. The reason is not what we expect this person to do to us; neither the traffic warden nor the civilian would do anything directly to us. Moreover, both may report the license plate number to the police department. The difference is not in that. The difference is in how we expect others to react to this person. When the licence plate number is reported to the police department, we expect very different kinds of actions on the part of the police, depending on who the report comes from, a traffic warden or a mad person.

49. Some of these preexisting rules may not even have the status of quasi-*laws*. They may be more in the nature of norms. Thus, for the successful implementaion of a law, it may be important for the law to be embedded in a certain structure of norms. Cooter's claim that "state law builds upon preexisting social norms," though based on a different kind of argument, has some parallels to the position being taken here; see Cooter, "Law from Order," p. 2.

50. See Ellickson, *Order without Law.*

51. E. Ullmann-Margalit, *The Emergence of Norms* (Oxford: Clarendon Press, 1977), p. 8.

52. See J. Ferejohn, "Law, Legislation, and Positive Political Theory," in *Modern Political Economy*, ed. J. S. Banks and E. A. Hanushek (Cambridge: Cambridge University Press, 1995).

53. R. Hardin, "Economic Theories of the State," *Perspectives on Public Choice*, ed. D. C. Mueller (Cambridge: Cambridge University Press, 1997).

54. Among others, see A. Sen, "The Impossibility of a Paretian Liberal," *Journal of Political Economy* 78:1 (January–February 1970): 152-57.

55. Gaertner, Pattanaik and Suzumura, "Individual Rights Revisited," Deb, "Waiver, Effectivity and Rights as Game Forms."

56. H. L. A. Hart, "Are There any Natural Rights?" in *Rights*, ed. D. Lyons (Belmont, CA: Wadsworth Publishing, 1979), p. 19.

57. D. Lyons, introduction to *Rights*, p. 5.

CHAPTER 10

Material Culture, Theoretical Culture, and Delocalization

Peter Galison

IT WAS 1993, and superstrings, the "theory of everything" was the rage. Arthur Jaffe, a senior member of the physics department at Harvard and for several years chair of the mathematics department, along with Frank Quinn, a mathematician at Virginia Tech, penned the following in the pages of the *Bulletin of the American Mathematical Society*:

> Theoretical physics and mathematical physics have rather different cultures, and there is often a tension between them. Theoretical work in physics does not need to contain verification or proof, as contact with reality can be left to experiment. Thus the sociology of physics tends to denigrate proof as an unnecessary part of the theoretical process. Richard Feynman used to delight in teasing mathematicians about their reluctance to use methods that "worked" but that could not be rigorously justified.[1]

Jaffe and Quinn quickly added that mathematicians, unsurprisingly, retaliated: as far as they were concerned, physicists' proofs carried about as much weight as the person who claimed descent from William the Conqueror . . . with only two gaps. Nor has tension between cultures been restricted to the axis of theory/mathematics. Albert Einstein and Paul Dirac famously derided putative experimental refutations of major theories, and experimentalists have never hesitated to mock what they considered to be the aimless speculation of theorists. One cartoon, widely circulated in the physics community during the 1970s, portrayed a balance scale with thousands of offprints labeled "theory" heaped on one side, outweighed by a single paper marked "experiment" on the other. Beneath these cross-currents of jibes and jests lie substantive disagreement about what constitutes an adequate demonstration, and, ultimately, a clash over whose pilings sink sufficiently deep to stabilize further construction. What vouchsafes knowledge, and for whom?

Like Jaffe, I find it useful to talk about the difference in cultures between the interacting groups that participate in physics. In fact, as we look around the national and international laboratories—now and throughout the last two centuries—the diversity of such cultures is striking: there are electronic engineers, cryogenic engineers, experimenters, computer programmers, field theorists, phenomenologists, just to name a few.

What motivates talk of "cultures" or, perhaps better, the subcultures of physics? Part of the appeal of the distinction between cultures is driven by historical concerns. To address the question Why does this happen there and then? we want to identify affiliations between certain activities inside the walls of the laboratory and others outside, all the while being careful not to exaggerate the distinction between "inside" and "outside." The world of the electrical engineer fashioning circuitry for the central tracking detector at a major colliding beam detector is a world apart from that of the theorist who may eventually be a consumer of its data. By contrast, the electrical engineer may well share a world with other electrical engineers also concerned with shielding their delicate printed circuits from massive pulses of X-rays—engineers, for example, preparing electronic devices to survive a nuclear battlefield. A condensed matter theorist may have more to say to a quantum field theorist than to his own condensed matter experimentalist colleagues as they struggle to lay atom-thin films of metal, or build new ceramics.

Anthropologists generally understand the cultural to embrace not only social structures per se, but crucially the values, meanings, and symbols associated with them. Now it is true that the term *culture* has always been, and continues to reside, in disputed anthropological territory. Clifford Geertz, Marshall Sahlins, Gananath Obeyesekere, for example, sharply disagree on how constraining, how overarching a "culture" is. But the important point for the historico-philosophical characterization of the production of science is that we cannot pretend that meanings, values, and symbols are mere window dressing. When a mathematician derides a computer-based demonstration as a horrendous violation of the very idea of mathematics; when a theoretical physicist recoils from renormalization, pronouncing it a "trick"; when an experimenter asks, in shocked tones, if future generations of experimentalists will get their data from "archives" rather than through the concerted application of screwdrivers, soldering irons, and oscilloscopes—at these and other moments like them, *values*, always present, have surfaced. Meanings too can differ: when theorists speak about a particle, say an electron, they may, through usage, deploy a concept quite distinct from the usage of "electron" spoken of by an experimenter.

It is useful to separate subcultures of physics on more philosophical, specifically epistemic grounds. We can ask: What is it, at a given time, that is required for a new particle or effect to be accepted among theorists (in contrast to the requirements that must be satisfied among experimentalists)? This can be stated more precisely: What, at a given time and place, are the *conditions of theoreticity*? What is it that a theory must exhibit for it to count as reasonable even before it faces new experiments? From time to time these requirements change, and we can specify the circumstances of these alterations. A theory in many branches of physics is not out of the starting gate if it is not relativistically invariant, if it does not conserve charge. Such constraints may not be forever. For generations, *conservation of parity* was such a rigid requirement. (Conservation of parity is the demand that any process allowed by physical law ought also to allow a mirror-reflected image of the same process.) Parity, along with time reversibility, fell as absolute demands, leaving behind only approximate conservation laws. Renormalizability (the demand that a theory be constructed with a fixed and finite set of parameters that can then be used to predict to arbitrary precision) was another such broken constraint. Thought to be a rigid and exact stricture on theory in the early 1970s, by the 1980s renormalizability too reappeared as an approximate constraint.

In a similar way, we can speak of *conditions of experimentality*, focusing on the constraints that allow (or disallow) forms of laboratory argumentation. How are probabilistic arguments to be treated? Would a single instance of an event be considered a persuasive demonstration? Are witnesses necessary to secure experimental closure? Do experimental results without error bars count? Or, if results do include errors, how much statistical power is demanded? How much and what kind of knowledge can be deferred to other fields, literally or figuratively "black-boxing" component parts of the experiment?

Conditions of instrumentality can also be distinguished as those constraints that delimit the allowable form and function of laboratory machines themselves. These conditions governing the material culture of physics may be of different temporal structures: there are broad, long-lasting classes of instruments (picture-producing instruments or statistic-producing instruments). Such classes provide constraints of the *longue durée*, as they set out the conditions under which (for example) picture-producing apparatus will be judged distortion free, or by which statistics-producing instruments will be assessed as having a certain loss rate. Then there are middle-term conditions on "species" of instruments that may achieve legitimacy as knowledge facilitating objects (bubble chambers or optical telescopes or spark chambers). And at the short-range of temporality there are the individual tests and conditions that certify individual instruments, *this particular* bubble chamber, or even more specifically this particular bubble chamber and its production of *this particular* bubble chamber photograph. All such conditions of possible theorizing, experimentation, and instrumentation are temporal: they change with time; the dynamics of those changes constitute some of the most interesting and difficult questions facing the study of science.

Taken together, the historical, anthropological, and philosophical concerns suggest that periodization is a far more complicated business than might be suspected from older models of the philosophy of science. We ought at least look to see if the rhythms of change in one domain (experiment, for example) are the same as that of another (theory, for example). That is, instead of assuming that theory, instruments, and experiments change of a piece in one great rupture of "conceptual scheme," "program," or "paradigm," we would do better to see how the various practice domains change, piece by piece. Dates of conceptual breaks such as 1905 (special relativity), 1915 (general relativity), 1926 (non-relativistic quantum mechanics), and 1948 (quantum electrodynamics) may have been points of discontinuity in theory; they were not so in the development of the material culture that surrounded instrumentation and experimentation. And while there may be good reasons not to jettison widely accepted experimental practices at precisely the same moment the community is entertaining the radical reformation of theoretical practice, none of this is to say that co-periodization *cannot* occur. But it is to say that co-periodization ought be shown, not assumed to follow from the dictates of antipositivist philosophy of science in any of its forms.

An objection springs to mind. The separation of theory and experiment holds good in many branches of twentieth-century physics. Certainly this sociological division is so in atomic, cosmic-ray, nuclear, and particle physics, but also astrophysics, planetary physics, plasma physics, condensed matter physics. In each of these domains separate societies, meetings, and reprint exchange networks have long existed. But what of areas of inquiry where the separation is incomplete or nonexistent? What of the physics of the broad middle of the nineteenth century where a James Clark Maxwell, a Heinrich Hertz, or a Lord Kelvin could hardly be classified as a pure theorist or a pure experimentalist? And what of whole domains of other kinds of science, biology, to take perhaps the most powerful example? Does it make sense to speak of separate cultures of experimentation and instrumentation in such instances? The question could be rephrased: are there clusters of practices in experimental work tied to practices outside the laboratory differently from the way theory is situated? An example might be found in the introduction of nuclear magnetic resonance just after World War II. At least for Robert Pound and Edward Purcell, though they worked both theory and experiment, their theoretical efforts drew on classical electrodynamics and basic quantum mechanics—both long since established—while their instruments and procedures drew heavily on then-recent wartime radar developments. I would argue this: there is no universal answer to the question of whether it pays to speak of distinct cultures of theory and experiment in the absence of sharp sociological lines between the groups. Everything rides on how bundled together certain practices are—and that cannot be settled in advance, but only in the thick of historical inquiry.

The periodization picture sketched here might be represented by figure 1, designating *intercalated* practice clusters. Looked at more finely, even "theory" ought to be broken up in a similar arrangement, with some forms of theoretical practice lasting for the long term, while others are of shorter duration. These same considerations hold good for instruments and experiments. Such a scheme contrasts directly with two others. In one (figure 2), denoted in a too-rough designation as "positivist," the view is that observations build aggregatively and continuously, while the level of theory breaks seriatim. Because observation builds cumulatively and intertheoretically, many followers of logi-

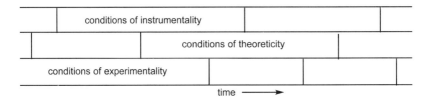

FIGURE 1: Intercalated Periodization.

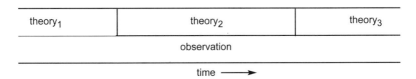

FIGURE 2: Positivist Periodization.

cal positivism and logical empiricism held it in special esteem.[2] Theory in a sense builds on the foundation of observation, and numerous metaphorical systems have designed to capture this primacy of the neutral observation language. In the other metaphorical scheme—designated (also crudely) as "antipostivist"—the scheme of figure 2 is stood on its head: now instead of viewing a neutral observation language as primary and theory as secondary, the reverse is true (see figure 3). "Theory" is everywhere, as Benjamin Whorf, Thomas Kuhn, Paul Feyerabend, N. R. Hanson, and so many others taught us. To enforce the notion of a conceptual scheme, antipositivists assumed the equivalent of the co-periodized picture of figure 2. When theory changed, it precipitated a break in meaning that extended "all the way down."

Suppose we stay with the argument presented so far, conservatively focusing on that sector of twentieth-century physics in which the separation of cultures of theory, experimentation, and instrumentation are reasonably well defined. Still, a new and more serious objection arises: if the culture of theory, for example, is really all that distinct in its contextualization, meaning, values, and argumentative structure from that of experiment, how do the domains relate at all? Reformulating the problem we could say this: to escape from the problems of noncommunication that arise from the confrontation of various block-periodized "conceptual schemes" we moved to specify more local, intercalated subcultures of physics. Doesn't this just multiply the original problem, leaving us with hundreds of incommensurabilities, ruptures, revolutions, or epistemic breaks where before we had a few?

Behind this objection is a picture of language that is fundamentally holistic. 'Mass', 'time', and 'space', are thought of as fixed terms, fully specified along with their connotations in one conceptual scheme (the "paradigm of classical or Newtonian physics") and carrying with them a particular set of instruments

observation$_1$	observation$_2$	observation$_3$
theory$_1$	theory$_2$	theory$_3$

time ──────▶

FIGURE 3: Antipositivist Periodization.

and experimental procedures that are only understandable in terms of that conceptual scheme. Equally fully specified, or so goes the argument, is another,
incompatible conceptual scheme (the "paradigm of Einsteinian physics") in
which 'mass', 'time', and 'space' have utterly different meanings. Because
Einstein and Newton and their respective followers "speak different languages," any putative communication between them amounts to little more
than puns, a homophonic happenstance. Out of this picture come some of the
most famous metaphorical structures used to capture the radical untranslatabil-
ity of languages: Gestalt shifts and systematic visual-perceptual misconstruals
on the basis of prior conceptions. If Gestalt shifts or total shifts of conceptual
scheme are the model for what happens at the boundary between languages,
then, indeed, the repartition of schemes like the positivist periodization of figure 3 into the antipositivist periodization of figure 1 may be of use historically,
but analytically we advance not one inch.

What does happen at the boundary between cultures, where peoples face one
another? Do people, in fact, translate with the sudden, Gestalt-like character
of the duck-rabbit switch? Here we can learn from the burgeoning field of
anthropological linguistics, a field that at least in one of its forms has dealt
extensively with the historical and structural development of *trading languages*, highly specific linguistic structures that themselves fit between two or
more extant full blown languages. Very roughly, a "trading jargon" or "for-
eigner talk" designates a few isolated terms used to facilitate interlinguistic
communication; "pidgin" refers to a more developed language, with sufficient
structure to allow more complex modes of exchange between speakers. Generally, pidgins are characterized by more regularized phonetic, syntactic, and
lexical structure than the "parent" languages that the pidgin links. For example,
while one of the parent languages may carry multiple consonant clusters
(CCC), pidgins tend to be routinized into consonant-vowel-consonant (CVCV)
form. Pidgins may—but do not necessarily—develop into full-fledged creoles,
where "creole" designates a language with sufficient structure to allow people
to "grow up" within it. Creoles, unlike pidgins, can be a *first* language. Intrigu-
ingly, it seems to be the case that among our linguistic capacities is the ability
to shift the register of the language we speak: we are able to restrict vocabulary
and regularize syntactic as well as phonetic form.

On this view, linguistic borders are not the thin-line mathematical idealizations that they appear to be in the Gestalt-switching picture of the antipositivists. Instead, linguistic borders appear as thick and irregular, more like the creoles one in fact finds in border regions in many areas of the world. So it is, I argue, in the *trading zones* between theories or between experiment and theory, or between a physics subculture and an engineering subculture grounded in the industrial or military traditions in contact with physics. Here I would suggest that we drop the attempt to gloss the interaction among the electron theorists Lorentz, Abraham, and Poincaré with Einstein in the early twentieth century as "Classical" physicists "talking past" "Relativistic" physicists, a forced Gestalt switch between old and new notions of 'mass', 'space', and 'time', with language shifting as a whole. Instead, we ought to examine the ways in which each of these physicists actually went about coordinating their theories with the results of experimenters like Kaufmann and Bucherer. For despite these philosophical protestations about incommensurability, these laboratory ventures were precisely aimed at comparing the various electrodynamic theories. How, they asked, did the deflection of fast electrons as a function of velocity come into contact with (for example) Abraham's and Einstein's specific theoretical proposals? Or consider the interaction of experimenters and theorists around track images in bubble chambers. While each may have very different ideas about adequate demonstration, or even about the nature of particles, it is nonetheless often possible for both groups to come to common ground of "interpretation" (e.g., "this particle decays here to two lighter particles, one of which escapes and the other is absorbed"). The point is that some meaning gets stripped away in the trading zone where theory meets experiment, where engineering meets theory, where, in general, the scientific subcultures encounter one another. What thrives in the interstitial zones is neither trivial nor purely instrumental; it is a form of scientific exchange language.

In the interstitial zone I have not distinguished sharply between locally shared terms and mathematical-syntactic relations on one side, and the material objects on another. This is deliberate: we ascribe meaning to machines as surely as we do to mathematical symbols. And in new material and functional contexts, the meaning of machines can alter as well. We need only look around the laboratory to see a myriad of technologies now performing functions (and carrying meaning) a long way from their site of origin. For this reason, it may be helpful to think of the process by which a computer logic circuit, vacuum tube, or clock mechanism becomes modularized as a form of pidginization. But because this process is not, at least in the first instance, purely linguistic, it is helpful to think of the production and elaboration of such common objects as "wordless pidgins" and "wordless creoles." Wordless grammar corresponds to the rules of combination allowed for these objects—circuit design rules, for example. Similarly, an element in such a wordless interlanguage (should we call it the analog of a noun?) corresponds to the useful notion advanced by Leigh Star and James Griesemer of the "boundary object," an entity participating simultaneously in two or more fields of inquiry.[3] Here a cautionary note is worth sounding. To speak of wordless creoles is not to commit oneself to a position in which concepts can be extricated from language altogether; I mean to emphasize that pieces of scientific objects are often transferred without words.

Throughout this discussion, I intend the pidginization and creolization of scientific language to be treated seriously just the way one would address such issues for language more generally (that is, not as a "model" or "metaphor"). First, physicists themselves regularly refer to problems of language in terms of idioms, meaning compatibility, and translation. There are books such as *Computers as a Language of Physics*, and physicists characteristically speak about "putting this current algebra argument into the language of field theory" or ask "can you express that relation in the language of effective field theory?" Second, the standard account of science in terms of "conceptual schemes," "epistemic breaks," and "paradigm shifts" presupposes and relies on talk of meaning change between terms; the argument presented here simply says that the account of linguistic work at the boundary is oversimplified and unhelpful. For example, "translation" as used by Kuhn to describe scientific change explicitly borrows from notions of translation from ordinary language: "In time," says Kuhn's expositor Paul Hoyningen-Huene, "the members of one group will be able to translate (in the everyday sense of 'translate') portions of their counterparts' theory."[4] Finally, "model" and "metaphor" talk presupposes a radical break between scientific and ordinary use of language, and philosophical attempts to enforce such a dichotomy have notoriously foundered. The point I want to make is this: the characterization of different registers (such as jargons, pidgins, and creoles) is helpful in distinguishing between different modes of scientific and nonscientific uses of language. My intention is to expand the notions of interlanguages to include both the discourse of scientific and nonscientific utterances, and both material and abstract systems. It is not to "apply" the results of one field to another.

How literal is the notion of a "trading zone"? At one level, I have in mind the most literal sorts of spatialized scientific practice. Laboratories, scientific campuses, often reflect architects' and scientists' expectations of intellectual proximity and meeting points in the walls, hallways, and stairwell landings. Conferences, informal meetings, visits, present other transient sites for face-to-face interactions. If one is trying to understand the development of the bubble chamber one would do well to register the circumstance that in the 1950s cryogenic engineers from the air force were meeting with staff from Lawrence Berkeley Laboratory. If one is trying to understand the development of computer simulations, it is essential to track the direct encounter of mathematicians, physicists, weapons designers, and statisticians with one another in a series of conferences from UCLA to Endicott, New York. In the end, however, the issue is one of the coordination and regularization of different systems of values and practices; if that takes place outside of any spatial configuration, this too is of interest. In a typical colliding beam experiment, the full set of 500 or so experimenters may never be in the same place at the same time. Many will never meet at all. Webs and computer links bind interlocking laboratories and subgroups together, and conventions, standards, and procedures are often established with no single point of authority or geographical center. Exchange zones are written into architectures, but the architectures may not be physical or spatial.

As such considerations suggest, there are many avenues opened up by the less restrictive image of substantive as opposed to mathematically thin boundaries between the subcultures of physics. And in the conceptual sphere, the stripped-down view of shared, specific meanings as opposed to total translation between full languages may offer a better vision of how knowledge moves in and across boundaries. Other questions arise as well. One could follow the development of a highly restrictive interfield into a full-fledged "creole," as in the gradual articulation of physical chemistry or biochemistry out of highly localized shared techniques.[5] Or one could examine instances in which the interlanguage more or less died off, as did the eighteenth-century boundary field of iatromechanics—or, in more recent times, the myriad unification schemes such as those that would (à la Millikan) join cosmic ray physics to the genesis of higher elements in deep space; or Einstein and Weyl's notion that they would be able to unify *directly* electrodynamics with general relativity. As in linguistic boundaries, there is nothing to block the attempt to put languages together, but at the same time there is no guarantee that either social or intellectual coherence will follow. Some pidgins get resorbed back into one of the "parent" languages, some stabilize as pidgins, and some grow into full-fledged creoles, and then ultimately into a language, full stop.

Here I would like to explore a different point: *delocalization*. The problem is this. Over the past years, we have again and again seen how tied specific laboratory practices are to their conditions of origin. An instrument made in one spot is often difficult to replicate in another without the bodily transport of things and people. Paper instructions are often not enough. We have learned from scholars like Harry Collins how necessary it is to attend to the site-specificity of particular materials, skills, and resources available at a given time and place: the little tricks of the trade that made one group of people able to build a certain kind of laser where others could not. Eventually, though, these objects do travel, the lasers, prisms, accelerators, detectors, tubes, and films—hence the problem. If the original production of scientific knowledge is so reflective of local conditions, whether they are craft techniques or religious views, material objects or forms of teamwork, how does *de*localization take place?

One solution, referred to by Simon Schaffer as the "multiplication of con-texts," accounts for delocalization by a process in which the original context is imposed elsewhere. Methods are devised that "distribute instruments and values which make the world fit for science."[6] One pictures maps of imperial expansion, the dark black arrows of distributed context radiating outward like the footsteps of a conquering army from Oxford, Cambridge, London, or Paris to newly acquired sites elsewhere. To be replicated, air pumps required a par-ticular set of machines, facticity, and witnessing to be in place. To be enforced, values and methods of standardization stamped their mark on distant sites. Multiplying *these* contexts was a precondition for replication, and the lines of power that designate the creation of those conditions extend from center to periphery. Similarly, Bruno Latour focuses on ways in which the world is modified to make it possible for an instrument, even one as simple as a clock, to "travel very far without leaving home."[7]

A different solution, building on the notions of discursive and wordless pidginization within trading zones of limited exchange, would put greater em-phasis on two features of the "transfer." First, it would stress the *activity* of interpretation that takes place on the receiving end of the objects, techniques, or texts. Varying Latour's apt phrase, scientific practices can also travel to very *different* homes. However imposed the more powerful set of techniques might be, the site of their application fundamentally alters the way those technologies manifest themselves. Many creolists insist, for example, that French creoles can only be understood if one abandons the attempt to view them as merely simplified French, and instead considers the combination of the lexical French structure with a variety of syntactic elements from African languages. Just such a nuanced view is needed in the domains of material and theoretical cultures—pieces of apparatus can circulate without the whole, devices can move without their scientific contexts, functional specifications can move without a trace of their original material form. An abbreviated example: work-ing against low-flying attack fighters, radar engineers during World War II designed a "memory tube" that would store radar returns and cancel out the signal of any stationary object—leaving only the plane. In traveling to a differ-ent context not long afterward, the tube became a recirculating memory to store information for the early computers. Again, cut loose from its "meaning" the device is then appropriated by particle physicists who want to use it to locate the position of a passing particle (by measuring the time it takes for a particle-induced pulse to reach the end of the tube). We have, in a sense, a hermeneutics of material culture. At every stage of such multiple transfers, we need to ask *both*: How does the stripping-down process occur by which local circumstance is removed? And then how does the reintegration into a *new* context take place?

If the first feature pointed to is *activity*, a second is *locality*. Elements of the meaning of a scientific practice are pared away. Theoretical physicists drop many properties that they ascribe to an electron or quark before they bring those notions to the bubble chamber scanning table at which they meet the experimentalist. The embedding of "electron" in a quantum field theoretical description, or a particular unified theory might be deleted altogether. Conversely, before encountering the theorists, the experimentalists bracket many of the concerns about the nature of the film, the optics, and compression pattern of the liquid hydrogen. The tracks being discussed carry, in this interaction, a shared local meaning. Experimentalist and theorist can pore over the scanning table, gesturing at the tracks and arguing interpretations: ". . .this kaon here into two unseen gammas, which then produce these two electron-positron pairs over here. . . ." But such exchanges, though widely shared, are not pieces of a universal protocol language interpretable in *any* epoch of physics. Against the positivists: there is no "neutral observation language" in the activity of track interpretation—what goes on in the process of sorting out the particle decay scheme does not in any way, shape, or form constitute a "pure" observation to be positioned against "hypothesis." Against the conceptual-schemers: we do not find a homogenized amalgam in which experimentation and theory become a single, undifferentiated whole in which every experimental statement is utterly fixed by the theory to which it is inseparably attached. The pidginized hybrid of the language of track interpretation has *both* elements of theory and of experiment, while recognizing the self-maintained distinct identity of each. A pidgin is neither a linguistic passe-partout nor a subset "baby-talk" of a "full" language; it facilitates complex border interactions. Coordination around specific problems and sites is possible even where globally shared meanings are not.

The history of physics can be profitably seen as a myriad of such productive, heterogeneous confrontations. Field theorists met radio engineers in the American radar laboratories of World War II. British cosmic ray experimentalists encountered colloidal chemists in the production of nuclear emulsions sensitive enough to "photograph" all known elementary particles. Such heterogeneity continues. One collaboration joining mathematics and physics expertise began a 1980 article in *Physics Reports* by recalling the halcyon days in which Newtonian mathematics and Newtonian physics could develop together, only to separate under the pressures of specialization:

> a formidable language barrier has grown up between the two. It is thus remarkable that several recent developments in theoretical physics have made use of the ideas and results of modern mathematics. . . . The time therefore seems ripe to attempt to break down the language barriers between physics and certain branches of mathematics and to reestablish interdisciplinary communication.[8] (215)

This exchange was bilateral: physical techniques from field theory were solving problems in algebraic geometry, and mathematical tools were at the root of the "string revolutions" that, for many late-twentieth century physicists, promised a final unification of gravity and the short-range forces that held matter together. When algebraic geometry "traveled" to the physicists, it was often precisely by *shedding* many of the values with which it was practised in mathematics departments. To the horror of many mathematicians, "speculative," "intuitive," and "physical" argumentation were supplanting the hard-won rigor of mathematics proper. When these practices traveled, some of the mathematically constitutive values associated with them stayed behind.

This observation—that meanings, values, and symbols often stay home or switch identities when scientific theories and instruments travel—lies at the heart of the alternative (exchange language) picture of delocalization I have in mind. Donald Glaser, inventor of the bubble chamber, desperately hoped the device would "save" small-scale physics (and the life that went with it) from the onslaught of Luis Alvarez's factory laboratory. But substantial portions of Glaser's original device—stripped of those material components that were tied to the small-scale—were reappropriated into the massive chambers that became the very symbol of Big Physics, Alvarez's sector of the Lawrence Berkeley Laboratory. This is not to say that values played an inessential role in the constitution of particle physics at any stage; it is, instead, to say that the particular guiding values altered radically as they shifted from a defense of individual craft-style work to a form of scientific life that emerged from the massive nuclear weapons and radar projects of World War II.

What then is the relation between these two accounts of delocalization— "multiplication of contexts" and "exchange language"? Let us return briefly to the relation of algebraic geometry to quantum field theory in string theory. For there the practitioners of both sides were of roughly equal stature; such an exchange did not resemble (for example) the relation between technicians in Alvarez's laboratory to the Nobel Prize–winning physicists who ran various groups. And perhaps here lies a clue. In examining situations in which the balance of power was maximally unequal, it might well be the case that one group could impose a fuller set of contextualized values along with specific practices on the other. In other words, we might keep in mind that in terms of power relations, there are two interesting limits to the confrontation of languages. At one extreme, the two languages enter into contact in states of roughly equal power. Linguistically, such situations typically result in pidgins in which the lexical admixture of the two languages is markedly heterogeneous. This is of great interest from the scientific standpoint, because we are often faced with situations of this type. String theory, for example, puts quantum field theorists on one side and algebraic geometers on the other—a situation in which the balance of power is roughly equal. At the other extreme, in which one group is far more powerful than the other, very different linguistic structures might be expected. For instance, in very unequal balance of power, it is common to find that the lexicon emerges overwhelmingly from the superordinate language and a regularized, restricted syntactic structure from the less powerful language. It is also well documented that in very unequal situations, pidgin languages can be reabsorbed back into the superordinate language. Such instances occur in the domain of science and technology. In large-scale collaborative ventures, such as the Manhattan Project, one sees sectors of almost every possible power relation, from the Du Pont (engineer run) effort in Chicago to the Los Alamos (scientist run) laboratory.

We are now in a position to understand the relation between the interlanguage and context-multiplying accounts of delocalization. Context multiplication is the limit case of interlanguage coordination just when the power imbalance is so pronounced that the recipients' constitutive values and technical practices were thoroughly subordinated, or where relevant local values did not enter.

Let me end with one final thought. In a sense, the last fifteen years of studies in the history and sociology of science have left us with a powerful set of tools for understanding the local origins of scientific ideas, practices, and methodological precepts. But awkwardly we have grafted to this local description a picture of language (broadly conceived) that remained global, rigid, and holistic. No wonder we often end with a peculiarly bad set of choices. At one extreme we anchor our notion of science in a global picture of language, imagining that moving machines and ideas is automatic, completely ignoring the contextualized circumstances in which scientific work originates. At the other, we imagine that practices are so tied to local circumstances that we either descend into a radical nominalism in which no one is "really" talking to anyone else, or we wrongly conclude that the full context of origin is packed off, kit and caboodle, to every distant site of application. If, as the anthropological linguists are trying to teach us, meanings don't travel all at once in great conceptual schemes, but rather hesitantly, partially, albeit efficaciously, then perhaps, for those studying the development of science, there is an exit from this impasse.

FURTHER READING

I have developed the view discussed here of periodization, constraints, trading zones, and exchange languages in numerous places including the following, with the most extensive development in the first item: Peter Galison, *Image and Logic: A Material Culture of Microphysics* (Chicago: University of Chicago Press, 1997); *How Experiments End* (Chicago: University of Chicago Press, 1987); "Introduction: The Context of Disunity," and "Computer Simulations in the Trading Zone," in *The Disunity of Science*, ed. P. Galison and D. J. Stump, (Stanford: Stanford University Press, 1996); "Context and Constraint," in *Scientific Practice*, ed. Jed. Z. Buchwald (Chicago: University of Chicago Press, 1995); "History, Philosophy, and the Central Metaphor," *Science in Context* 2 (1988): 197–212; and "Multiple Constraints, Simultaneous Solutions," *PSA* 2 (1988): 157–63.

For more on logical positivism, especially the centrality of observation, see Rudolf Carnap, *The Logical Structure of the World and Pseudoproblems in Philosophy*, trans. Rolf George (Berkeley and Los Angeles: University of California Press, 1967); and Carnap, "Intellectual Autobiography," in *The Philosophy of Carnap, Library of Living Philosophers*, vol. 11, ed. Paul Arthur Schilpp (La Salle, IL: Open Court, 1963), 3–84.

For more on antipositivism, especially on the primacy of theory over observation, see T. S. Kuhn, *Structure of Scientific Revolutions* (Chicago: University of Chicago Press, 1970); N. R. Hanson, *Patterns of Discovery* (Cambridge: Cambridge University Press, 1958); Hanson, *The Concept of the Positron* (Cambridge: Cambridge University Press, 1963); P. Feyerabend, *Problems of Empiricism: Philosophical Papers*, vol. 2 (Cambridge: Cambridge University Press, 1981); and Feyerabend, *Realism, Rationalism and Scientific Method: Philosophical Papers*, vol. 1 (Cambridge: Cambridge University Press, 1981). My own view is that the split between positivists and antipositivists was somewhat exaggerated by the antipositivists and their followers, but the impact of this perceived dichotomy was registered strongly among historians, sociologists, and subsequent philosophers of science.

To get a sense of how these antipositivist ideas are used within social constructivism, see B. Barnes, *T. S. Kuhn and Social Science* (New York: Columbia University Press, 1982); and A. Pickering, *Constructing Quarks: A Sociological History of Particle Physics* (Chicago: University of Chicago Press, 1984).

For ideas linked to the multiplication of contexts, see S. Shapin and S. Schaffer, *Leviathan and the Air Pump*: Hobbes, Boyle and the Experimental Life (Princeton: Princeton Univsity Press, 1985); Schaffer, "Glass Works: Newton's Prisms and the Uses of Experiment," in *The Uses of Experiment*, ed. D. Gooding et al. (Cambridge: Cambridge University Press, 1985), pp. 67–104; Schaffer, "A Manufactory of Ohms," in *Invisible Connections: Instruments, Institutions, and Science*, ed. Robert Bud and Susan E. Cozzens (Bellingham, Washington: SPIE Optical Engineering Press, 1991); and Bruno Latour, *Science in Action* (Cambridge: Harvard University Press, 1987), esp. 251ff.

Literature on the culture of experimentation is sufficiently large that the reader is referred to the above works and other essays in this volume for an extensive bibliography. Literature on theoretical culture that takes into account the work done on experiment is more sparse. See, for example: Andrew Warwick, "Cambridge Mathematics and Cavendish Physics: Cunningham, Campbell, and Einstein's Relativity 1905–1911 Part I: The Uses of Theory," *Studies in the History and Philosophy of Science* 23 (1992): 625–56; and Peter Galison, "Theory Bound and Unbound: Superstrings and Experiment" in *The Laws of Physics*, ed. Friedel Weinert (Berlin and New York: Walter de Gruyter, 1995), 369–408.

NOTES

1. Arthur Jaffe and Frank Quinn, "'Theoretical Mathematics': Toward a Cultural Synthesis of Mathematics and Theoretical Physics," *Bulletin of the American Mathematical Society* 29 (1993): 1–13.

2. Peter Galison, "Aufbau/Bauhaus: Logical Positivism and Architectural Modernism," *Critical Inquiry* 16 (1990): 709–52.

3. Peter Galison, "The Trading Zone: The Coordination of Action and Belief," paper presented at TECH-KNOW Workshops on Places of Knowledge, Their Technologies and Economies, UCLA Center for Cultural History of Science and Technology, 1989; and Susan Leigh Star and James R. Griesemer, "Institutional Ecology, 'Translations' and Boundary Objects: Amateurs and Professionals in Berkeley's Museum of Vertebrate Zoology, 1907–39," *Social Studies of Science* 19 (1989): 387–420.

4. Paul Hoyningen-Huene, *Reconstructing Scientific Revolutions* (Chicago: University of Chicago Press, 1993), p. 257.

5. John W. Servos, *Physical Chemistry from Ostwald to Pauling* (Princeton: Princeton University Press, 1990); and Robert E. Kohler, *From Medical Chemistry to Biochemistry* (Cambridge: Cambridge University Press, 1982).

6. Simon Schaffer, "A Manufactory of Ohms," in *Invisible Connections: Instruments, Institutions, and Science*, ed. Robert Bud and Susan E. Cozzens (Bellingham, WA: SPIE Optical Engineering Press, 1991), p. 23.

7. Bruno Latour, *Science in Action* (Cambridge: Harvard University Press, 1987), p. 251.

8. Tohru Eguchi, Peter B. Gilkey, and Andrew J. Hanson, "Gravitation, Gauge Theories and Differential Geometry," *Physics Reports* 66 (1980): 213–393.

CHAPTER 11

Science as Alchemy

Andrew Pickering

A SKELETON history of science studies might go like this. For much of the twentieth century, the dominant positions in history and philosophy of science have been broadly positivist, concerned in the main with scientific theory and its control by reason, and evidence. Even the path-breaking work of Thomas Kuhn and Paul Feyerabend in the 1960s remained within this space, retaining an overall theory-centeredness even while arguing that relations between theory, reason, and evidence were much more complicated and interesting than was usually thought.[1] Since the 1980s, though, ethnographic and historical studies of scientific practice—of scientific work, of the doing of scientific research—have suggested a need for rebalancing our image of science. Instead of putting scientific theory, knowledge, and representations of the world at the center of our accounts, these studies suggest that we should be sensitive to the interplay of the material and social as well as representational aspects of science, without necessarily giving center stage to any of them. My idea in this essay is to clarify what is entailed in this rebalancing and to indicate some interesting directions in which it can lead.[2]

We can begin with Marx's aphorism: "Production not only creates an object for the subject but also a subject for the object." Two things appeal to me about this. First, the reference to production conjures up, among other things, an image of material agency—of steam engines and factories full of machines, all acting to effect transformations in the material world, from raw materials to finished goods. Though Marx's referent is technology, one message from science studies is that we should think of science, too, in this "performative idiom"[3] rather than being obsessed with its representational aspects. We should recognize that struggles with the agency of the material world (in the field of instruments, say, and devices) are integral to the doing of science. Second, Marx points here to a constitutive interconnection between people and things: In production, we make things what they are, but at the same time they make us what we are. This is the point I want to worry away at. Back in the 1970s, the Strong Programme in the sociology of scientific knowledge helped us to see that the things of science are socially constituted.[4] The most important subsequent development in science studies has been to recognize the reciprocal flow: the fact that people are scientifically and technologically constituted as well.[5]

So, how can we connect Marx's aphorism to the interrelation of subjects and objects in science? As a small example, we can start with Ludwik Fleck's long-neglected masterpiece, *The Genesis and Development of a Scientific Fact*.[6] Fleck's book is about the establishment early this century of the so-called Wassermann reaction as a blood test for syphilis. He describes the historical development of this test as a process of the *reciprocal tuning* of people and things. The Wassermann reaction was a material—here, chemical and biological—procedure performed on human blood, which issued in a diagnosis of whether the patient had syphilis or not. And, on the one hand, Fleck shows that this procedure emerged from a process of trial and error, exploring a space of material performativity, "adding now 'a little more,' now 'a little less' of a reagent," letting the reaction proceed for a little longer or shorter time, and so on, until the success rate of the test increased from 15–20 percent to 70–90 percent. (72–73) At the same time, and on the other hand, Fleck emphasizes that in this process of material tuning a new and specific social community came into being. This was a community of people possessing the "serological touch": the specific skills, competences, and disciplines that were required for successful performance of the Wassermann reaction, skills that only came into being in the historical development of the reaction and that could only be exhibited in its successful performance, competences that were socially differentiated and distributed and came together in the "quasi-orchestral" (97) performance of the blood test. Going back to the aphorism, then, the Wassermann reaction as a material procedure was the *object* for the community of practitioners, and the practitioners were the *subject* for the object: Each developed and took on a particular shape in relation to the other.

This reciprocal becoming of people and things, of the human and the nonhuman, is the theme of this essay. It is not easy to get to grips with, partly, at least, because established disciplinary patterns of thought get in the way. The hard sciences and engineering offer us a technological-determinist picture of science and technology as something absolutely other than the human world, linked to the social only in their effects. The social sciences either ignore the material world completely, or they accept the technological-determinist story of the relation between people and things, or, more imaginatively, they invert it, in a social-determinist story of scientific knowledge and technological artifacts as symptoms of the play of social forces.[7] But the processes that interest me conform to neither of the determinist stereotypes, which is why I am drawn to the alien imagery of *alchemy*. Think of alchemists transforming their inner being in one and the same process of transforming base matter into the philosopher's stone, and you've got the idea. The transformations of subject and object hang together; you can't imagine one without the other, but neither does the one cause or explain the other. I think that this alchemical image is the most important contribution to the scholarly imagination to emerge from science studies in a long time.[8] It is still dawning on me how widely applicable it is—

to what extent it illuminates the construction of the world we live in—so my idea here is to run through some examples, to indicate the kinds of things I have in mind. I think that, above all else, what we need are examples.

• • •

WE CAN start with the macro. My idea here is that one can periodize the overall history of the West in terms of a series of big alchemical transformations and discontinuities. For instance, I have recently been looking into the nineteenth–century origins of the synthetic dye industry as one of the sites of emergence of the industrial-scientific complex that has become increasingly central to the modern world ever since. And the dye story goes, crudely, like this.[9]

William Henry Perkin's 1856 discovery of the first synthetic dye, aniline purple, was followed by a period of intense material tinkering, which resulted in the production of a continuing series of new syntheses, new industrial technologies, and new dyes. This tinkering, itself, intertwined with major scientific developments, including Kekulé's structure theory of 1859 and his benzene-ring theory of 1865, the latter forming the basis of modern organic chemistry. And the first point I want to stress is that here we have one of those processes of mutual becoming just mentioned. Organic chemistry did not first evolve according to its own autonomous dynamics and then find application in the dye industry. Instead, its history is better understood as a continual reflection upon the existing accomplishments of the industry—material processes and products of synthesis—a reflection that continually fed back into further industrial achievements, and so on. The dye industry and the science of organic chemistry grew together.[10]

To get people into the story, we have only to note that scientific and technological developments here intertwined with a remarkable range of social developments. The history of azo dyes after 1877 can stand as our example. Within contemporary chemical theory, the so-called coupling reaction promised to generate an indefinite series of new azo dyes in "an endless combination game" of different ingredients (van den Belt and Rip, 151). And the response to this recognition was the establishment within the German dye industry of a *new social institution*, the industrial research laboratory. From this point on, chemists appeared in the history of synthetic dyes in the new role of "scientific mass-labour," located within industry itself, and running through the endless combination game of dye syntheses as quickly as they could. The industrial research laboratory thus represented a device through which the dye industry could, as it were, wrap itself around scientists, paying, controlling, and *enfolding* them, as a tactic in the optimization of its own performativity.[11] And the industrial research laboratory was, of course, the key social innovation that geared science into industry in the developing scientific-industrial complex that has become central to modern economies and states.

We thus see how, in classically alchemical fashion, the material, the conceptual, and the social all evolved together in the history of the synthetic dye industry. The establishment of new material technologies and products (the coupling reaction and azo dyes, for example), new bodies of knowledge (modern organic chemistry), and topological transformations of social institutions (the enfolding of science by industry in the industrial research laboratory) hung together, reinforced one another, and reciprocally structured each other's development. To return to Marx, we see how "production not only creates an object [synthetic dyes] for the subject [industry, science, the universities, the consumer] but also a subject [an industry with science now socially enfolded within it] for the object."[12]

The development of technoscientific industries, including the electrical as well as the synthetic dye industry, is sometimes referred to as the second industrial revolution, to mark its significance in the overall history of the West, but other equally important historical breaks have had the same alchemical character. The industrial revolution itself is surely best seen as the mutual becoming of a novel set of machines (steam engines, spinning jennies), sciences (thermodynamics, electromagnetism, microbiology), and social arrangements (a new class structure, the factory, industrial towns, etc). Moving the other way in time, the intersection of scientific and military enterprise in World War II set in motion major constellations of scientific, technological, and social development that contributed significantly, in all sorts of ways, to the construction of the postwar world. And it is clear that this coming together of science and the military had much the same structure as the nineteenth-century gearing of science into industry, but now involving (a) new machines such as radar sets and their powers, (b) interlinked transformations in scientific and military practice (the coming of big science and technoscientific warfare), (c) new social relations (the NDRC and OSRD as new institutions linking science and the military), and (d) the emergence of new sciences like operations research (as enfolded, again, by the military hierarchy).[13]

On an even more macro scale, we might think about Bruno Latour's book *We Have Never Been Modern*. There Latour tells a story of the emergence of modernity itself as an episode in the history of thought and ideas, led by the emergence of purified and separate discourses of people and things, the natural sciences taking the things, and humanist philosophy taking the people.[14] Latour's narrative is very seductive, but the alchemical perspective suggests that it might be worth paying attention to the material as well as the conceptual correlates of this break. The modern is, after all, an era that can be characterized not only by new patterns of thought, but also in terms of novel regimes of production and destruction, central to which have been what I call "free-standing machines," machines that display a certain kind of autonomous agency. Think, for example, of cannons. The human soldier lights the fuse, but the cannon itself throws the cannonball at the enemy, with a force that no combination of unaided humans could equal. Such free-standing machines thus exemplify a kind of *practical dualism*, a striking separation of the worlds of human and nonhuman agency, which surely invites the dualist split in the realm of thought that Latour brings to our attention (and which continues to dominate the academic disciplines): To the physicist go the material agents, to the philosopher the human and social ones. And this, in turn, invites the speculation that the modern obliteration of the nondualist alchemical cosmos was itself an alchemical process, in which, again, the worlds of machines, people, and ideas all evolved in relation to one another. The dualist philosopher was a new kind of subject for a new kind of object: mechanized warfare and production.[15]

So, the alchemical strain of science studies leads us straight into the heart of the modern West along quite a different axis from those usually followed by the academic disciplines. The alchemical account helps us to see that the human race cannot and need not bear the awful weight of its history alone. Who we are now is a function of specific historical encounters with the material world, encounters that have remade us at the same time that they have delineated the emergent powers of material agency and our scientific and technical knowledge of those powers.

What I have just said is, of course, very crude—but that is just another way of saying there is a lot of absorbing and important work that remains for the future. Now I want to elaborate my theme from a different angle.

So FAR, I have been talking about a kind of social alchemy, the transformation of social classes and relations, and so on, as reciprocally coupled to transformations in science and technology. Real alchemy, however, was about inner transformation of the alchemist's being. Such inner transformations have not been a central concern of the science-studies literature, at least not until recently (see, for example, Gomart and Hennion's article),[16] but inspiration can be found outside elsewhere. I turn to Wolfgang Schivelbusch's great work, *The Railway Journey*.[17]

Schivelbusch's intent in that book is to explore what he calls the new industrial consciousness that grew up during the nineteenth-century industrialization of Europe, focusing especially on phenomena connected with railway travel. One straightforward example of his way of proceeding concerns the development of what he calls panoramic seeing (chapter 4). His suggestion is that the railway journey made possible a new way of perceiving the landscape quite different from earlier modes of apprehension, associated, say, with horse-drawn carriages or walking. Where the latter foster a detailed (and multisensual) sequential engagement with the specifics of the local environment, rail supports a panoramic (and purely visual) grasp of the terrain, in which the immediate foreground vanishes while the background is seen synthetically, and translations between towns, countryside, and villages are grasped as a whole. As we can now say (but could not have said then), in the railway journey the landscape appears like a movie projected onto the screen of the carriage window.

With panoramic seeing, Schivelbusch offers us a rather different take on the reciprocal production of subjects and objects from that discussed earlier. Now inner experience is part of the construction of a subject (the panoramic voyeur) for the object (the railway landscape). And it is worth emphasizing that panoramic seeing was not envisaged in the construction and use of the railways, nor was it something actively at stake (subject to tinkering and tuning) in the evolution of railway travel. In this sense, panoramic seeing was an *emergent phenomenon*—a new way to perceive—which just happened to manifest itself in a new material situation.[18]

I should note that a certain frustration can arise here as elsewhere in Schivelbusch's discussions of industrial consciousness. On the one hand, he certainly does seem to get at the specificity of what it's like to be in an industrial society; on the other hand, no special language of inner states is involved. Somehow, Schivelbusch gets at the inner by describing the outer: The train rushes along, so of course the foreground becomes an unreadable blur, while the landscape unfolds like a map in the distance. One suspects some sleight of hand. But I think this suspicion is misplaced. The point to note is that while there are many ways of describing the motion and relation of bodies and objects in railway travel, Schivelbusch describes outward circumstances from a certain perspective or *subject-position*—the embodied position of the fast-moving traveler. The railway journey, then, made available the new subject-position at which panoramic seeing emerged.

Though Schivelbusch's declared focus is on industrialized consciousness, he also explores somatic and psychosomatic phenomena—new ways for bodies (or bodies-and-minds) to be. Railway accidents, perhaps by virtue of their unprecedented violence and lack of forewarning, precipitated the construction of the new psycho-medical category of victims of shock—persons showing no severe bodily injuries, but exhibiting unusual mental or physical symptoms some time after the event. Shock was thus a new form of bodily performance— another truly emergent phenomenon—made possible by the new subject-position created by rail.[19] Here, then, is another, inner, sense, in which production creates a subject for its object as the reverse.

There is one further aspect of Schivelbusch's work to which I can draw attention. While the traditional academic disciplines strive to conceal the alchemical coupling of people and things, Schivelbusch makes clear that this same coupling and its human/nonhuman interface has long been at the center of attention of engineers, architects, and designers. I can give three examples.

First, furniture. Schivelbusch argues that heavily upholstered furniture appeared on the railways as a solution to the problem of matching flesh to metal—specifically, as a response to the discomfort of vibrations induced in the human body by railway travel. And he suggests that upholstery thus concealed the truly industrial nature of railway travel, functioning, in effect, as an equivalent in the material world to ideology in the world of thought. I like the idea of comfy chairs as ideology very much. It reminds me of the Monty Python Spanish Inquisition sketch; now I understand what that sketch was about!

Second, station architecture. In the nineteenth century, major railway stations exhibited a peculiarly schizophrenic structure, with grandiose street facades concealing the industrial landscape of steam, smoke, and geometrical tracks to their rear. And in the early days of rail, waiting rooms constituted a kind of air lock (or decompression chamber, or buffer), with travelers being held there en route to their journey, slowly making the inner transit from the known world of the street to the unknown world of rail. Stations thus processed subjects architecturally, re-attuning them from the familiar urban to the unfamiliar industrial environment.

Third, the department store. The railways speeded up immensely the flow of people and things, and Schivelbusch has a brilliant analysis of the creation of the department store as an architectural zone of turbulence, in which the human and nonhuman flows were slowed down again and made to intermingle—a space in which desire could be unleashed and channeled, in which subjects and objects were reframed to establish new relations between them. Here we can begin to see how to complete the loop and connect an alchemical analysis of production to its necessary counterpart in the realm of consumption. The department store was, for example, the destiny of the synthetic dyes I talked about earlier. The age of mass consumption was, then, constituted in reciprocal becomings of people and things in shopping as much as in the factory, and in railway translations between the two.

So, MY suggestion is that one can grasp the history of the West and the construction of our present as a series of continuing alchemical transformations: outwardly and socially in production, warfare, and so on; inwardly in the experience of new subject-positions, including that of mass consumers. The contrast here is with the traditional determinisms I mentioned at the beginning: the technological determinism that would have us believe that science and technology are beamed down from outer space; and its inverse, a social determinism that would credit everything to us, to reason, class struggle, or whatever. These determinist reductions obscure much more than they reveal, and we need to think about the mutual becoming and interdefinition of people and things, not to ignore them or sweep them under the scholarly carpet.

And here I cannot resist adding a theoretical remark. Though I have been talking about the history of modernity and the West, I cannot imagine why a similar alchemical analysis would not also apply to cultures of other eras, an observation that leads us to a position I think can be fairly described as relativist. Our science is *our* science, proper to our own historical trajectory through time, space, and matter. Other trajectories would entrain other knowledges.

What needs to be emphasized, however, is that such a relativism does not entail scepticism.[20] To note that organic chemistry grew up as the science of the synthetic dye industry in an age of industrial capitalism, is not to deny a constitutive and productive connection between chemical knowledge and its material objects. Nor is it to reduce the science to the play of social forces. Clearly the social was itself at stake in the engagement of organic chemistry with the dye industry; my argument is precisely that a new form of scientific-industrial capitalism emerged from that engagement, with the industrial research laboratory as its nexus. So there is no reason to fear this kind of relativism: it will not sap the moral fiber of American youth by teaching them that all propositions are equal and that "anything goes." It might, however, stimulate our atrophied imaginations, which would be no small thing.

To CLOSE, I want to return to the history of science, and to mention one further topic that I find absorbing. It concerns what I call the cyborg sciences. I have complained, several times now, that the mainstream disciplines obscure the reciprocal becoming of people and things. The natural sciences have a pure ontology of things; the social sciences have a pure ontology of people. But cyborg sciences, by which I mean sciences of impure ontology, have always lurked in the margins of Western thought. Marx, I suppose, was the first great modern alchemist, which is why I quote him. I am struck, however, by the explosion of cyborg thought that took place in and after World War II.[21] Ergonomics and operations research, systems analysis and systems dynamics, are all literally, in my terms, alchemical sciences concerned with optimizing the joint performances of human and nonhuman agents. Operations research, for example, began as the science of military operations, of radar sets and radar operators, planes, pilots, flight patterns, depth charges, and submarines. And there are even sciences of transcendence and transubstantiation: information theory, game theory, cybernetics, artificial life, artificial intelligence, and cognitive science more generally. In a project I call the attack on the mind, dating back to the early days of the industrial revolution, many of these have sought to detach the last remnant of human uniqueness, the mind, from its bodily home and to reinstall it in formalisms and machines (e.g., computers).

These strange sciences fascinate me for several reasons. On the one hand, going back to the theme of World War II as a historical discontinuity, they have been part and parcel of intensely practical projects: fighting the Second World War, constituting the Cold War, precipitating a certain discourse of globality (which arguably marks a new phase of, if not the end of, modernity), and, needless to say, feeding into the progressive automation of ever-widening circles of activity. To grasp the specificity of the second half of the twentieth century, then, one has to understand the history of the cyborg sciences.[22] On the other hand, I strongly suspect we could draw theoretical inspiration from them, and this in two respects. Most obviously, as science of people-and-things (or people-as-things) engagement with them might serve to thicken up our discourse on the kinds of alchemical couplings I have been discussing. But also they speak directly to a theoretical concern with time and change that I have so far left in the background.

Very briefly, the traditional disciplines are not good on time and change. They have no real sense of time. The social sciences, for example, are often content to ignore change in favor of this exploration of atemporal correlations between this variable and that. When change is on the agenda in social theory, one typically finds that, in fact, discussion centers on that which does not change, constant parameters of change: causes, contexts, constraints, and so on.[23] In contrast, the alchemical vision I have attempted to conjure up here is of change in itself. I have tried to look change in the face. The basic image is of genuine becoming, as I have been calling it (Pickering "Units of Analysis")—the alchemist becoming in relation to becomings of matter in an essentially temporal process that cannot be understood as a function of any external and unchanging givens. Here, too, I want to emphasise, one finds a resonance with the cyborg sciences. Especially, a tradition of work on self-organizing systems, running from postwar cybernetics to current research on complexity, has been devoted to the surprising inner dynamics of complex systems and their strange, often disturbingly lifelike, becomings.[24]

My suggestion is, therefore, that in the elaboration of an alchemical vision, social theory might productively engage with these lines of development in the cyborg sciences. The argument, I should stress, is not that we should simply transplant their results into social theory en masse. It is rather that a critical engagement with these sciences can serve to enliven and give substance to our presently impoverished discourses, not only on the human and the nonhuman, but also on time and change, chance and order.[25]

AND THAT, I hope, is enough. What I have been trying to get across is that the alchemical thread has led at least one wing of science studies out of the claustrophobic space of arguments about representation, scientific theory-choice, and allied topics, into an unexplored garden (or perhaps a jungle, or a new world), and perhaps to a whole new take on social theory and social change. What remains for the next twenty-five years is to elaborate the theory and enjoy the garden.

NOTES

I am very grateful to Debra Keates for her insightful comments and suggestions on an earlier draft of this essay.

1. T. S. Kuhn, *The Structure of Scientific Revolutions*, 2d ed. (Chicago: University of Chicago Press, 1970); and P. K. Feyerabend, *Against Method* (London: New Left Books, 1975).

2. On the shift from accounts of science-as-knowledge to science-as-practice, see the contributions to A. Pickering, ed., *Science as Practice and Culture* (Chicago: University of Chicago Press, 1992). Sewell (this volume) suggests that we need to undo, or go beyond, the linguistic turn in social science; what follows points to one principled way of doing so. P. Galison, *Image and Logic: A Material Culture of Microphysics* (Chicago: University of Chicago Press, 1997) is a major contribution to the literature on scientific practice, though his emphasis on the "pidgins" and "creoles" that arise in scientific "trading zones" (see also his essay in this volume) echoes the fascination with language and representation of the positions he otherwise opposes. Galison's idea is that the positivists and their Kuhnian critics were not very good on language (and I'm sure he is right about that).

3. See A. Pickering, *The Mangle of Practice: Time, Agency, and Science* (Chicago: University of Chicago Press, 1995).

4. The Strong Programme elaborated the Kuhnian and Wittgensteinian insight that knowledge production is open-ended: nothing within an existing body of knowledge dictates what it will become in the future; see B. Barnes, *T. S. Kuhn and Social Science* (London: Macmillan, 1982). The central argument of the sociology of scientific knowledge was, then, that "closure" in knowledge production—fixing on one vector of extension rather than another—is determined by the social, often conceived in terms of social interests. The two centers of development of the Strong Programme in the 1970s were the Universities of Edinburgh and Bath. The Edinburgh line was macrosociological, and is carefully presented in B. Barnes, D. Bloor, and J. Henry, *Scientific Knowledge: A Sociological Analysis* (Chicago: University of Chicago Press, 1996). The Bath line was more microsociological, and its canonical text is H. M. Collins, *Changing Order: Replication and Induction in Scientific Practice*, 2d ed. (Chicago: University of Chicago Press, 1992 [1985]). Both variants remain within the "representational idiom": They take it for granted that science should be considered, above all, a body of knowledge and representations; their problematic is to explain why particular facts or theories were produced and collectively accepted.

5. The key paper here was perhaps Bruno Latour's essay on Pasteur, "Give Me a Laboratory and I Will Raise the World," published in 1983, though I first began to get the hang of what was going on in the autumn of 1986 while I was at the Institute for Advanced Study. I had been thinking about language and representation, and I had begun an essay in which I accused Kuhn and Feyerabend of what I called global linguistic holism (in a paper, "Positivism/Holism/Constructivism," that I presented at the weekly Colloquium of the Institute for Advanced Study, Princeton, 8 January 1987), when I started to think not so much about representation per se as about the relation between representations and material performances, and about how experimental practice in science could be understood as an uncertain process of aligning the two. I remember coming down from my office for lunch, and someone asking me the usual question—"How's it going?" To which I replied, "I just had an idea." Everyone laughed, but, anyway, the idea eventually grew into my book, *The Mangle of Practice* (Chicago: University of Chicago Press, 1995).

6. L. Fleck, *The Genesis and Development of a Scientific Fact* (Chicago: University of Chicago Press, 1979).

7. These dualist determinisms have been the dominant tropes in academic discourse on science, technology, and society. In my paper, "The Objects of the Humanities and

the Time of the Cyborg," given at a conference on "Cyborg Identities: The Humanities in Technical Light," at the University of Aarhus, Denmark, 21–22 October 1999, I attempted a more nuanced (but still crude) survey of disciplinary resources for getting beyond these positions, including Hegelian and pragmatist philosophy and evolutionary theory, before arriving at the "cyborg sciences," which reappear at the end of the present essay.

8. Some canonical works in science studies: M. Callon and B. Latour, "Unscrewing the Big Leviathan, or How Do Actors Macrostructure Reality?" *Advances in Social Theory and Methodology: Toward an Integration of Micro- and Macro-Sociologies*, ed. K. D. Knorr-Cetina and A. V. Cicourel (Boston: Routledge & Kegan Paul, 1981), 277–303; D. Haraway, "A Manifesto for Cyborgs: Science, Technology, and Socialist Feminism in the 1980s," *Socialist Review* 80 (1985): 65–107 (reprinted as "A Cyborg Manifesto: Science, Technology, and Socialist-Feminism in the Late Twentieth Century," in *Simians, Cyborgs, and Women: The Reinvention of Nature* [London: Free Association Books, 1991], pp. 149–81); B. Latour, *Science in Action: How to Follow Scientists and Engineers through Society* (Cambridge: Harvard University Press, 1987) and *The Pasteurization of France*, trans. Alan Sheridan and John Law (Cambridge: Harvard University Press, 1988); and J. Law, "Technology and Heterogeneous Engineering: The Case of Portuguese Expansion," in *The Social Construction of Technological Systems: New Directions in the Sociology and History of Technology*, ed. W. E. Bijker, T. P. Hughes, and T. J. Pinch (Cambridge: MIT Press, 1987), pp. 111–34. I should say that while these authors all emphasize the coupling of subjects and objects, the idea to thematize this coupling by reference to alchemy is my own. (Latour [1988] refers to "microcosms" and "macrocosms" but does not develop the metaphor; Latour's [1993] thought that "we have never been modern" also invites the present line of development: B. Latour, *We Have Never Been Modern*, trans. Catherine Porter [Cambridge: Harvard University Press, 1993]). I could also add that different people have different ideas of what alchemy was. I need to make it clear, however, that I am *not* following Jung here in thinking of alchemy as a purely symbolic field relating exclusively to inner, psychic processes (see C. G. Jung, *Alchemical Studies* [Princeton: Princeton University Press, 1967]), nor am I interested in any ultimate telos of alchemy as material and spiritual purification.

9. For an excellent brief introduction to this topic, see H. van den Belt and A. Rip, "The Nelson-Winter-Dosi Model and Synthetic Dye Chemistry," in *The Social Construction of Technological Systems: New Directions in the Sociology and History of Technology*, ed. Wiebe E. Bijker, Thomas P. Huges, and Trevor J,. Pinch (Cambridge, Mass.: MIT Press, 1989). For more history and analysis, see my "Alchemical Wedding of Science and Industry: Synthetic Dyes and Social Theory" (in preparation).

10. In Sewell's terms (this volume), this is an instance of the coevolution of the discursive and the nondiscursive.

11. For more on enfolding, see the discussion of operations research and military enterprise in World War II in my "Cyborg History and the World War II Regime," *Perspectives on Science* 3(1995): 1–48. Recent historical work by Carsten Reinhardt challenges the hitherto accepted centrality of the azo dyes to the rise of industrial research and emphasizes, instead, research in industrial chemistry aimed at securing patents on new or improved syntheses of existing dyestuffs. Reinhardt also emphasizes the creativity of industrial research. Neither of those points disturb the overall image

of the intertwined transformation of scientific knowledge, industrial technologies, and social relations. See C. Reinhardt, "An Instrument of Corporate Strategy: The Central Research Laboratory at BASF, 1868–1890," in *The Chemical Industry in Europe, 1850– 1914: Industrial Growth, Pollution and Professionalization*, ed. E. Homburg, A. S. Travis, and H. G. Schröter (Kluwer: Dordrecht, 1998), pp. 239–59.

12. The transformation of the social in this instance had many interesting aspects beyond those just discussed. The very content of German patent law was mangled in the process of developing azo dyes (see van den Belt and Rip, "The Nelson-Winter-Dosi Model," pp. 148–55). New career structures also emerged, linking advanced academic training in scientific research to secure positions within industry, and the expansion of such career paths led progressively to the changes in scientific curricula and in the balance of power in the universities (scientists vs. humanists) that culminated in the twentieth century in the distinctive form of the American "research university."

13. A. Pickering, "Cyborg History and the World War II Regime."

14. This is Latour's reading of S. Shapin, and S. Schaffer, *Leviathan and the Air Pump: Hobbes, Boyle and the Experimental Life* (Princeton: Princeton University Press, 1985). In Latour's image of the "modern settlement," natural science is personified by Robert Boyle, political philosophy by Thomas Hobbes.

15. For more on transformations of science, technology, and society that have centered on warfare, see W. H. McNeill, *The Pursuit of Power: Technology, Armed Force, and Society since A.D. 1000* (Chicago: University of Chicago Press, 1982); and M. De Landa, *War in the Age of Intelligent Machines* (New York: Swerve Editions, 1991).

16. E. Gomart and A. Hennion, "A Sociology of Attachment: Music Amateurs, Drug Users," *Actor Network Theory and After*, ed. J. Law and J. Hassard (Oxford: Blackwell, 1999), pp. 220–47.

17. W. Schivelbusch, *The Railway Journey: The Industrialization of Time and Space in the 19th Century* (Berkeley: University of California Press, 1986). Schivelbusch acknowledges debts to Walter Benjamin (e.g., Benjamin's *Illuminations*, edited and with an introduction by Hannah Arendt, trans. Harry Zohn [New York: Harcourt Brace Jovanovich, 1968]), and Schivelbusch's work can stand here as a marker of a potentially fruitful intersection between science studies and Benjamin-style cultural studies.

18. One way to appreciate the significance of panoramic seeing is to reflect upon satellite imagery of the earth as a recent instance of the trend that began with the railways. Elichirigoity argues that satellite images of the earth as an isolated body floating in space were crucial to the emergence of a distinctive "discourse of globality" (or "planet management") in the late 1960s and early 1970s: I. Elichirigoity, *Planet Management: Limits to Growth, Computer Simulation, and the Emergence of Global Spaces* (Evanston, IL: Northwestern University Press, 1999). Schivelbusch notes that panoramic and dioramic shows and gadgets appeared in the decades just prior to the opening of the railroads (62), but their existence did not imply that a related form of seeing would appear in rail travel. Schivelbusch also characterizes the commodity-aesthetic of the department store (see below) as a kind of panoramic seeing (192–94).

19. Strictly speaking, "shock" was not novel to rail; it was a phenomenon already recognized on the battlefield (Schivelbusch, 150–58). But that similar phenomena might be connected with rail travel was unexpected; and, of course, the connection with the battlefield is interesting in itself. Schivelbusch thematizes what is at stake here in a nice alchemical metaphor, comparing shock with metal fatigue (132–34): just as metal

cracked unexpectedly on the railways (a phenomenon subsequently explained in terms of novel and specifically dynamical stresses), so human beings cracked unexpectedly in railway accidents. "Fatigue" itself, as an attribute of human labor, emerged as an important concept along with the nineteenth-century industrialization of production: see A. Rabinbach, *The Human Motor: Energy, Fatigue, and the Origins of Modernity* (Berkeley: University of California Press, 1992). Schivelbusch (163ff) makes a connection between shock and Sigmund Freud's theory of the "stimulus shield" as an account of the battlefield neuroses of World War I, and then turns Freud's theory around so that the stimulus shield is seen as incorporating nonpsychic material elements like panoramic seeing and the interfaces mentioned below.

20. For more on this, see chapter 6 of *The Mangle of Practice.*

21. See "Cyborg History and the World War II Regime," and my article "History of Economics and the History of Agency," in *The State of the History of Economics: Proceedings of the History of Economics Society,* ed. J. Henderson (London: Routledge, 1997), pp. 6–18. For discussion of the continuing marginalization of the postwar cyborg sciences within the university, see Pickering (forthcoming article), "Units of Analysis: Notes on World War II as a Discontinuity in the Social and Cyborg Sciences," under consideration for a volume to be edited by Esther-Mirjam Sent and Albert Jolink, *Economists at War: The Influence of the Practice of World War II and the Cold War in the Culture of Economics.*

22. In "A Manifesto for Cyborgs," Haraway emphasizes this; it is why she thinks that reference to "cyborgs" should be confined to the postwar period. On the cyborg sciences and the construction of the Cold War, see P. N. Edwards, *The Closed World: Computers and the Politics of Discourse in Cold War America* (Cambridge: MIT Press, 1996); on planet management and the discourse of globality, see Elichirigoity, *Planet Management.* For further angles on this topic, see N. K. Hayles, *How We Became Posthuman: Virtual Bodies in Cybernetics, Literature, and Informatics* (Chicago: University of Chicago Press, 1999), and P. Mirowski, *Machine Dreams: Economics Becomes a Cyborg Science* (Durham, NC: Duke University Press, forthcoming).

23. As with my earlier comments on the dualism of the disciplines, these remarks on time need to be more nuanced—a task I take up in "The Objects of the Humanities and the Time of the Cyborg."

24. In cellular automata, for example, random sequences of zeros and ones often evolve under very simple transformation rules into unexpectedly beautiful quasi-organic patterns. For more on the "monstrous" becomings of self-organizing systems, see A. Pickering, "A Gallery of Monsters: Cybernetics and Self-Organization, 1940–1970," talk presented at the Dibner Institute for History of Science and Technology, MIT, weekly seminar, 1 December 1998.

25. And here, some pointers might be G. Deleuze and F. Guattari, *A Thousand Plateaus: Capitalism and Schizophrenia,* trans. and foreword Brian Massumi (Minneapolis: University of Minnesota Press, 1987); M. De Landa, *Deleuze and the Question of Science* (New York: Zone Books, forthcoming); and I. Stengers, *Power and Invention: Situating Science* (Minneapolis: University of Minnesota Press, 1997). Drawing, instead, primarily on the writings of Alfred North Whitehead, see also N.V. Hansen, "Process Thought, Teleology and Thermodynamics: A Reinterpretation of the Second Law of Thermodynamics," in *Time, Heat and Order,* ed. Niels Viggo Hansen, forthcoming.

PART THREE

Thick Description: Field Overviews and Institutional History

CHAPTER 12

Whatever Happened to the "Social" in Social History?

William H. Sewell, Jr.

SOCIAL HISTORY as an intellectual project is in crisis. After rising to a position of hegemony in the historical profession in the United States and in most other countries by the end of the 1970s, social history has since been displaced as the leading edge of historical scholarship by cultural history. Many established social historians, myself included, have effectively stopped doing social history and taken up cultural history instead. More important, perhaps, current graduate students don't show much interest in social history. At the University of Chicago, at least, most history graduate students would count it an insult to their intelligence and dignity if their professors so much as intimated that they might construct data bases, plot out graphs, and analyze statistical distributions. In this chapter I will attempt to diagnose social history's crisis, to indicate why I think the project of social history is worth saving or revising, but also to sketch out how it might be rethought and made more vital in the current intellectual context.

My reflections on social history have a strong biographical basis, one that makes them seem particularly appropriate for a book inspired by the twenty-fifth anniversary of the School of Social Science at the Institute for Advanced Study. My own turn from social to cultural history was largely effected during the years I was connected with the Institute. In 1971, when I spent my first year at the Institute, I was a fresh Ph.D. and a practitioner of what we then called "the new social history"; when I left the Institute after a five-year appointment stretching from 1975 to 1980, I had taken the "linguistic turn" and was writing in the style that later came to be dubbed "the new cultural history."[1] Although I could not have known it at the time, my own transition anticipated the path of historical scholarship more generally. This chapter is at once a somewhat disillusioned reflection on what I and my fellow cultural historians have wrought over the past quarter century and an argument for a form of historical scholarship that might revive some of the lost virtues of social history without abandoning the tremendous intellectual gains attendant upon history's linguistic turn.

THE RISE AND DECLINE OF SOCIAL HISTORY

It is worth remembering why social history seemed so exciting during its heyday in the 1960s and 1970s. These were heady times for social historians, who were young, numerous, and moving toward hegemony in the history profession.[2] But the rise of social history was more than just a generational transition. It effected a profound intellectual transformation of the field of history—in subject matter, in methods, and in intellectual style. One of social history's most important achievements was a vast double enlargement of the scope of historical study. First, social history studied categories of people who had previously been ignored by historical scholarship. Rather than political leaders and great intellectuals, who had been the prime subjects of previous scholarship, social historians tended to work on the obscure and downtrodden: servants, workers, criminals, women, slaves, shopkeepers, peasants, or children. And second, rather than concentrating on politics, social history attempted to capture the whole range of ordinary people's life experiences: work, child rearing, disease, recreation, deviant behavior, kinship, sociability, procreation, consumption, popular religion. Social history not only studied new categories of people but asked new questions about them. In order to answer new questions about new categories of people, social historians used new forms of evidence. All sorts of records previously not thought to contain information relevant to historical research suddenly became documentary gold mines. Old census manuscripts, tax registers, wills, advice books, inventories of estates, popular songs, statutes of mutual aid societies, building permits, records of marriages, baptisms, and deaths—all these and many other kinds of documents yielded evidence about the social structures, institutions, and life experiences of millions of ordinary people.

These new forms of documentation were also subjected to new methods of analysis. A characteristic mark of the new social history was the systematic use of quantitative methods. The kinds of people social historians studied were often illiterate, and even those who could read and write rarely left papers that revealed much about their lives. But such people came into contact with public authorities when they paid taxes or tithes; when they were drafted; when they registered births, marriages, and deaths; when they got counted by the census or were arrested by the police. It was largely by aggregating the rather thin and stereotypic information contained in the records of such encounters between ordinary people and the state that social historians were able to reconstruct the patterns of their lives. Quantification as a method of analysis was thus intimately linked to social history's radical expansion in subject matter. It was from the social sciences that historians borrowed the quantitative methods they applied to these novel data sources. One of the new social historians' distinctive characteristics was that we self-consciously modeled ourselves on the social sciences. We tended to regard what we called "traditional narrative history" as intellectually bankrupt and turned for guidance to sociology, political science, economics, or geography, whose claims to methodological rigor and theoretical sophistication we tended to accept quite uncritically. Like the mainstream of the social sciences in the United States, the new social history was profoundly empiricist and objectivist.

These various changes introduced by social history were mutually reinforcing; they made up a fairly coherent package, constructing a distinct epistemic object for social history—what I am calling "the social." The new social historians' "social" was composed above all of what we (following our social scientist friends) called "social structure." Social structures were objective and transpersonal patterns or forces of which actors were at best incompletely aware and which tightly constrained their actions and thoughts. These structures—occupational distributions, economic structures, demographic patterns, inheritance systems, urban settlement patterns, systems of land tenure, and the like—left palpable traces in historical records, especially in the quantifiable records that supplied what we called "hard data." We thought of social structures as essentially autonomous from political or intellectual history; indeed, we argued that they formed the underlying conditions for, perhaps even the determinants of, the political or intellectual developments that historians had previously taken as primary. In short, the rise of social history entailed a redefinition of the very object of historical knowledge, from politics and ideas to anonymous social structures, as well as the discovery of new means of gaining knowledge about this object.

This is, of course, a vastly oversimplified sketch of the new social history, which was never a fully unified intellectual project. It combined, in sometimes unstable mixtures, the traditions of the French *Annales* school, British Marxism, and American quantitative empiricism and could therefore be riddled with tensions or contradictions.[3] I would cite as examples both Joan Scott's book on the glassworkers of Carmaux or my early articles on the workers of nineteenth-century Marseille, which were inspired simultaneously by E. P. Thompson's Marxist "history from below" and by the quantitative "bourgeois sociology" that Thompson so despised.[4] Indeed, there was a subterranean fault line within social history between the objectivist epistemology that defined social structures as the object of study and the powerful desire—fueled ultimately by sixties leftism—to resurrect in a more personal and palpable way the lives, sufferings, and struggles of the oppressed. This fault line became more glaringly evident when social history, under the influence of anthropology, underwent its "linguistic turn."

I can testify from personal experience that by the mid-1970s a significant minority of American "new social historians," myself included, had grown increasingly frustrated by the limits of quantitative history. Although our methodology enabled us to understand more and more about the structural constraints and social forces that shaped people's lives, they offered no guidance for understanding how people actually made sense of and grappled with these forces and constraints. The persistent objectivism of the new social history's practicing epistemology—the mode of thinking that C. Wright Mills brilliantly dubbed "abstracted empiricism"—virtually ruled out asking some of the most interesting questions about the past.[5] Like the quantitative sociologists or political scientists who were their primary models, the new social historians were fixated on "hard data" about objective "social structures" and tended to dismiss questions of meaning or motivation as unscientific, and evidence derived from "literary sources" as "soft" or "impressionistic."

One prominent path out of the new social history's abstracted empiricism was a turn to anthropology, a field that had been largely ignored during the new social historians' orgy of borrowing from the social sciences. It was in the mid-1970s that an intense interchange between history and anthropology emerged, and Princeton and the Institute for Advanced study were an epicenter of the dialogue. The miracle year was 1975–76, when Clifford Geertz assembled at the Institute a particularly talented group of "symbolic anthropologists," including Victor Turner, Hildred Geertz, James Fernandez, David Sapir, Michelle and Renato Rosaldo, and Keith and Ellen Basso. The anthropologists magnanimously invited a group of interested historians to join their "symbols seminar," including Robert Darnton, Thomas Kuhn, William Reddy, Ralph Giesey, and myself. An intense discussion of the relationship between anthropology and history ensued, not only in the meetings of the symbols seminar, but in the social science luncheon seminar, the seminar of the Shelby Cullom Davis Center at Princeton University, and endless conversations over lunch, coffee, tea, and dinner.[6] At least in the vicinity of Princeton, these conversations attained a kind of critical mass in 1975–76, enabling a sustained intellectual interaction that was still going strong when I left Princeton in 1980.

What the discussions with anthropology offered was, above all, a means of restoring to social history the dimension of meaningful human action, which had been largely eliminated by the new social history's pervasive objectivism. Of course, questions about the history of meaning already had a significant place in the field of intellectual history. But cultural anthropology made it possible to pursue such questions not only in the texts of great thinkers, but in the rituals, conventions, language, and everyday conduct of ordinary people. It made possible, one might say, a kind of intellectual history of precisely the poor, marginalized, oppressed, illiterate or semiliterate groups whose study was the bread and butter of social history. In this respect, then, social history's turn to anthropology was perfectly consistent with the field's frankly expansive ethos. Just as the use of quantitative methods enabled social historians to grasp the social, economic, or geographical structures of the poor, the marginalized, and the oppressed, so the use of anthropological methods could enable us to grasp such people's cultural systems. Adopting anthropological methods was therefore a means of enriching our conception of the social.

Yet in another respect, the turn to anthropology had unsettling epistemological consequences. This was because anthropology—or at least the kind of hermeneutical "symbolic anthropology" that was practiced by Clifford Geertz or Victor Turner—conflicted with the objectivist epistemology and ontology that the new social history had absorbed in its earlier round of borrowing from sociology, political science, economics, and geography.[7] Cultural anthropology not only posited that interpretive methods were necessary to grasp the shape and workings of cultural systems. More fundamentally, it rested on a very different conception of the social. Unlike the new social history's presumption that social structures were analytically prior to social action, cultural anthropology implied that the social world was constituted by the interpretive practices of the actors who made it up. Rather than scientists whose analysis of "hard data" revealed the structures of an objective social world, social historians who made the anthropological turn had to recast themselves as interpreters of the inevitably interpretive practices that produced intersubjective cultural patterns.

Taking on the anthropological study of culture was therefore an exciting but also profoundly troubling step for an adept of the new social history. In my case (and I think in others as well) taking this step amounted to a sort of conversion experience, a sudden and exhilarating reshaping of one's intellectual and moral world.[8] I can also testify that going over to anthropological methods and theories could attract considerable hostility from one's erstwhile new social history colleagues—especially in my subfield of labor history, where anything smacking of "idealism" was taken as evidence of political as well as intellectual apostasy.[9] But the anthropologists' vivid and persuasive ethnographies contained a double promise: first, that interpretive methods could uncover structures or systems of meaning no less real or far reaching in their implications than the social structures uncovered by quantitative research and, second, that by doing so they could restore to history the dimension of meaningful human action that had been marginalized in the new social history. Anthropological history, in short, seemed a risky but also an irresistible intellectual adventure.

The importation of cultural anthropology into social history did not create a stable form of sociocultural history. Instead, it helped to initiate a dynamic transformation of the field toward a more thoroughly culturalized history. For the "anthropological turn" that affected social history in the 1970s was but one episode in a much broader "linguistic turn" that swept through most of the human sciences between the 1960s and the 1980s. Especially in the course of the 1980s, additional streams of cultural or discursive analysis began to flow into history. Hence, arguments for the significance of culture launched by anthropological historians in the late 1970s were fortified, supplemented, and sometimes disputed or displaced by arguments from a variety of other cultural perspectives. Most significant were the assorted poststructuralisms. Michel Foucault's influence has been particularly notable, in part because his interest in marginalized groups and in the links between discourse, power, and inequality fitted with—but also challenged—the preoccupations of social historians.[10] But increasingly in the 1980s, historians also began to be influenced by literary critics, whose own field had been massively transformed during the 1970s by poststructuralist theory. Thanks to the literary connection, Derrida and Lacan, in addition to Foucault, became names to conjure with in historical circles in the 1980s. Powered by the confluence of all these theoretical streams, cultural history became the major growth area in the profession, soon attracting the best students in the major centers of graduate training. The publication of an influential collection entitled *The New Cultural History* in 1989 might be said to mark cultural history's claim to have usurped the hegemonic position occupied by social history at the end of the 1970s.[11]

The radicalism and the rapid success of the linguistic turn in the American historical profession owed much to the parallel rise of another former subfield of social history: women's history (or, under the new dispensation, the history of gender). Women's history was easily the most politically intense and intellectually creative field in historical studies during the 1980s. Through the 1970s, women's history looked much like other subfields of social history, focusing on the familiar tasks of documenting the experiences of a previously ignored category of the population and specifying the structural sources of women's particular social and economic burdens. But during the 1980s, women's historians—increasingly influenced by feminist philosophers and literary scholars—began to explore the intrinsically radical epistemological consequences of the modern feminist movement. Feminism had, after all, challenged the supposedly most natural of social distinctions, the difference between male and female, arguing that its meaning was contingent and susceptible to fundamental redefinition. Hence the problem for historians, stated most influentially by Joan Scott, became not to document the distinct historical experiences of women but to decipher the processes by which gender difference—indeed sexual difference itself—has been established, maintained, and transformed.[12] In this effort the resources provided by literary theory have proved tremendously valuable. This critical and deconstructive historical analysis of central cultural categories (sex and gender) has unquestionably radicalized and energized cultural history as a whole.

Finally, this steeply rising interest in culture has by no means been confined to history. The emergence of the new cultural history is but one facet of a widespread culture mania that has swept through the human sciences since the early 1980s. In literary studies, the key move has been to use the now dominant poststructuralist theoretical categories to analyze a wide range of texts previously considered outside the canon of literature: popular fiction, science writing, film, journalism, advertising, hip-hop—in short, culture in general. The new trans-disciplinary (some would say a-disciplinary) field of cultural studies has grown explosively in English, American, and Australian universities over the past fifteen years. Even fields like sociology, political science, and psychology, whose dominant scientism long made them highly resistant to taking culture seriously, now have burgeoning subfields devoted to the study of culture. Indeed, culture has become a buzzword of American popular discourse as well. You can't turn on television news or National Public Radio these days without hearing some commentator pontificate about the "business culture of Silicon Valley" or the "culture of the Senate." And political claims about the importance of cultural difference, especially in issues of race and ethnicity, are ubiquitous. In the current intellectual and political context in the United States, it is hardly surprising that cultural history has emerged as the hegemonic form of historical scholarship.

THE THINNING OF THE SOCIAL

As a pioneer in the field of cultural history, one might think I would be thrilled by its rise to intellectual hegemony. But I have increasingly come to worry that the rise of cultural history has been accompanied by—indeed has resulted in—an effective *thinning* of the social in historical scholarship. This thinning of the social has been, I think, largely inadvertent. Many would probably dispute that it has happened at all. Let me briefly state my case about what I think has happened and speculate about why.

To make culture or discourse the central object of study is to orient historical research toward a semiotic approach to documents. Documents are read not so much as a means of gaining information about the practices they describe or allude to but for the assumptions, tropes, narrative forms, or symbolizations embodied in the text of the document itself. This new orientation is nicely exemplified by a paper of Joan Scott's that was incorporated into *Gender and the Politics of History*, in which she subjects a statistical inquiry into work in Paris in 1847 and 1848 to a brilliant cultural reading, treating statistical categories themselves as discourse rather than taking the numbers they produced as objective data about social life.[13] In principle, of course, any cultural artifact produced in any social location can be "read" semiotically. Nevertheless, I think that the natural preference of cultural historians for symbolically rich artifacts—usually texts—has tended over time to displace our gaze from the poor and powerless, who were the favorite subject of the new social history, to those more favored, who were likely to commit their thoughts to paper and whose papers were more likely to be conserved. In European history, at least, there has been a clear trend from studies of workers and peasants in the sixties and seventies to studies of the bourgeoisie in the eighties and nineties. Lest it seem that I am chiding others for abandoning the poor and downtrodden, let me cite my own exemplary trajectory, which began with a study of the working class of Marseille, then moved to what might be characterized as a study of literate artisans and their political and intellectual relations with the radical intelligentsia, and most recently to a study of the Abbé Sieyes, one of the leading constitutional theorists of the French Revolution.[14]

This subtle but palpable drift toward intellectually rich forms of evidence and toward studies of higher classes of the population has been compounded by the epistemological radicalism that entered cultural history along with poststructuralism and literary theory. Poststructuralism, especially in its Derridean form, has made the unreflective realism that underlay social history's evidentiary practices seem utterly naive. It has taught us that all the texts and text analogs we use as evidence must be subjected to an acute critical reading and that much of what once passed for direct evidence of past "realities" might better be thought of as a textual reference to yet another level of textuality. The "undecidability" of texts and the potentially endless play of intertextuality has, understandably, made cultural historians extremely reticent about referring to social structures, social forces, modes of production, or class relations as facts standing outside of textual logics. The pasts that cultural historians feel comfortable making claims about, therefore, tend to be the pasts of discourse, and above all of those forms of discourse readily available in textual form. This reticence about naming an "extratextual" social places many of the questions and problematics that were central to the new social history beyond the pale of the new cultural history: questions, for example, of the distribution of wealth, the dynamics of industrial development, changing patterns of landholding or employment, demographic structures, or patterns of geographical concentration and dispersion. Indeed, one sometimes feels that it makes such questions seem downright uncouth.

I worry that the emergence of the current form of exclusively cultural history is extremely inopportune, coming as it does in a period of fundamental transformation of capitalism on a world scale—of decreasing ability of states to control their own destinies, of growing income disparities all over the world, of ubiquitous declines in state welfare provision, and of sharp demobilizations of labor and the Left. Somehow, at the very time when particularly powerful changes in social and economic structures are manifested ever more insistently in our daily lives, we cultural historians have ceased not only to grapple with such structures but even to admit their ontological reality. If the initial breakthrough to cultural history might be thought of as an important phase in a struggle against the social scientific version of "Fordism," I fear that the current vogue for cultural studies merely abets the emerging capitalist phase of "flexible accumulation." I worry that we have disarmed ourselves for what I see as the great political and therefore historical battle of the coming years: attempting to reclaim effective political and social agency from the juggernaut of world capitalism and the hegemony of so-called free-market economics. I don't see how historians can play an important part in this struggle unless we regain a more robust sense of the social.

RETHICKENING THE SOCIAL

I am not advocating a return to social history as it was practiced in the 1970s. I have no desire to revive the new social history's uncritical objectivism, its presumptive preference for quantitative data, or its blindness to questions of meaning. I continue to believe, as I did in the late 1970s, that the linguistic turn is in itself an immensely positive intellectual development for historical studies. What we need, in my opinion, is the development of a more robust sense of the social on the terrain that the linguistic turn has opened up. This is, obviously, not a simple problem, nor can I claim to resolve it in this essay. But I can at least sketch out some possible approaches to grappling with it. I shall begin very much on the terrain opened by the linguistic turn, asking how the social might be rethickened *within* the logic of a radically cultural history, under the assumption that the world is constituted by discourse all the way down.

In this effort it seems useful to begin with a particularly clear statement of the radically discursive approach: that of Keith Baker in *Inventing the French Revolution*. Baker begins by defining politics in linguistic terms. Politics is, he writes,

> the activity through which individuals and groups in any society articulate, negotiate, implement, and enforce the competing claims they make upon one another and upon the whole. Political culture is, in this sense, the set of discourses or symbolic practices by which these claims are made . . . [P]olit- ical authority is, in this view, essentially a matter of linguistic authority: first, in the sense that political functions are defined and allocated within the framework of a given political discourse; and, second, in the sense that their exercise takes the form of upholding authoritative definitions of the terms within that discourse.

He then proceeds to answer the anticipated objection that such a definition "denies the relevance of social interests to political practice." His response is formulated on a distinctly ontological terrain. He denies categorically the existence of "social realities independent of symbolic meanings," asserting that what we see as social realities or social interests are themselves entirely constituted by discourse.

> [C]laims to delimit the field of discourse in relation to nondiscursive social realities that lie beyond it invariably point to a domain of action that is itself discursively constituted. They distinguish, in effect, between different discursive practices—different language games—rather than between dis- cursive and nondiscursive phenomena.[15]

In Baker's formulation, putative social interests or social realities are in fact reducible to discourse and should be thought of as "discursive practices" or "language games." The implication is that "the social" is an illusion and that invoking it is actually an analytical error; what appear to be "social" influences on discourse are in reality a form of intertextuality, links between different language games. And if all of human reality is discursive in character, it follows that the study of human history must be the history of human discourses—of interlocking language games. All the world is a text, and the appropriate methods of historical research are linguistic.

But what sort of text is the world? Baker is an expert on what one might call "high" political culture—political theory and formal political argument. He asserts that *all* human practices are discursively constituted, but he actually has had relatively little to say about the sorts of practices that are usually evoked by the term *social*—such matters as work relations, consumption, modes of sociability, kinship, institutional dynamics, status hierarchies, or material culture. We must, therefore, take on faith his claim that such arenas of practice are best understood as "language games" and can therefore be analyzed adequately by means of linguistic methods. Roger Chartier, another leading cultural historian of Early Modern France, has sharply challenged Baker's claim that language is the appropriate model for all spheres of human practice. He insists that even within the realm of cultural practices, the textual model is of strictly limited applicability. "Experience," he warns, "is not reducible to discourse," and historians therefore "must guard against unconstrained use of the category of the 'text'—a term too often inappropriately applied to practices . . . whose tactics and procedures bear no resemblance to discursive strategies."[16] There is, he argues, "a radical difference between the lettered, logocentric, and hermeneutic rationality that organizes the production of discourses and the rationality informing all other realms of practice."[17]

Yet on closer inspection, many of the analyses of "non-discursive practices" that Chartier singles out as exemplary have a surprisingly "textual" quality—for example, those of Michel de Certeau on practices of daily life and Michel Foucault on the microtechnologies of discipline.[18] It is true that their works focus on practices whose logics are not, strictly speaking, linguistic—practices such as urban strolling or meticulous bodily training. But practices of this kind might be thought of as "textual" in a more extended or metaphorical sense, that is, they are "based on signs whose meaning is fixed by convention and they constitute symbolic systems inviting to elaboration and interpretation."[19] Chartier does not deny that all social life is symbolically constituted. He merely insists that such symbolic practices cannot be reduced to forms of *discourse* . Chartier reminds us that many of the practices studied by cultural history are not governed by the specific semiotic logics of language but by a great variety of other quite distinct semiotic logics: iconic, ludic, spatial, technical, gestural, ritual, disciplinary, and the like. I actually agree with him that use of the linguistic term *discourse* as the general signifier for semiotic practices is misleading. But Chartier's observations do not so much refute Baker's point about the "discursive"—I would say semiotic—constitution of all human practices. Rather, they complicate and enrich his point, reminding us that the world of meaning is much wider than the world of speech and writing.[20] The world, then, might really be a text, but it's a text of tremendous diversity and complexity.

Another way of grasping the complex nature of the world's "textuality" is to consider further Baker's Wittgensteinian reference to "language games." Baker uses the metaphor to suggest that the various practices we think of as "social" are actually constituted by language. But Wittgenstein's usage of "language games" could be read as pointing in quite the opposite direction; the metaphor indicates that in order to know what words mean, we have to understand the system of structured and purposive activities, the "game," within which they are used. The meanings of words are not intrinsic; they are given by the place of the words in the activity being carried out, or, as Wittgenstein also puts it, in the "form of life" of which they are a part. These language games, or forms of life, are (as I read Wittgenstein) constituted by language but not by language alone.[21] This implies that we need to think as seriously about the "games" aspect of Wittgenstein's metaphor as about the "language" aspect.[22]

Here it might be useful to think about the many games—most obviously competitive athletic games—in which the role of linguistic utterance per se is distinctly secondary. There are, of course, linguistic terms for the various moves and meaningful objects in, for example, the game of basketball: *free-throw*, *rebound*, *backboard*, *point guard*, *jump shot*, *power forward*, *pump fake*, *fast break*, and so on. The rules of the game are written down in language; strategies are developed and explained verbally; coaches instruct players partly by telling them in words what they are doing wrong; and the notion that teams somehow represent schools or cities and compete within organized leagues is elaborated above all in language. But much of the knowledge and strategy that makes a basketball game work and that distinguishes a skillful player or team from a mediocre one is not constituted primarily by language—it is above all bodily or kinesthetic. The jump shot or the dunk is communicated from one player to another visually rather than linguistically, and it is mastered by physical emulation and repetition. It may be argued that this kinesthetic knowledge itself constitutes a semiotic system. Players with kinesthetic competence give off and respond to each others' bodily cues and are capable of making meaningful kinesthetic innovations that lead to responding innovations by teammates and opponents. The resulting interplay of moves and countermoves is interpreted and evaluated by knowledgeable spectators. One indication that kinesthetic basketball competency is at least in part semiotic is that strategies are often based on bodily deception—like the pump fake, which mimics the beginning of a jump shot, thereby making the defender leave his or her feet to disrupt the expected shot, after which the shooter can go up for an unhindered jump shot while the defender is on the way down. But I do not think this system can be said to work by linguistic rules. It might be possible to analyze the kinesthetic dimension of basketball as having a syntax and semantics, or as system of signs whose meanings are determined by their relations of contrast with other signs. Yet efforts to apply a discursive or linguistic model of this sort would probably result in misconstruing the dynamics of the game and missing the distinctive logics that actually do characterize basketball, and perhaps kinesthetic systems of knowledge in general.

Thinking about basketball reinforces Chartier's argument against the linguistic reductionism implicit in much current cultural history and potentially revalues the import of Baker's invocation of language games. It suggests that we might make considerable progress toward thickening the social by extending radically the range and ambition of cultural history. We could do this by shifting our focus from discourses in the strict sense—that is, linguistic performances—toward meaningful practices that seem resistant to linguistic analysis and that might conventionally be thought of precisely as the sort of "nondiscursive social realities" that causally limit or shape discourses. Important examples of such efforts already exist: Richard Biernacki's study of how largely implicit and practical conceptions of wage labor structured work experience in nineteenth-century British and German factories, Loic Wacquant's ethnographic studies of the bodily practices of boxers, or Peter Galison's studies of the material culture of experimental physics.[23] Rather than making it appear that we can easily make sense of the relationships between different language games by already available discursive methods—for example, those of literary criticism or "Cambridge School" intellectual history— this radicalization of cultural history would imply the search for a much wider variety of semiotic methods. And it would also imply close attention to the question of how semiotic practices carried out in such different media and according to such different logics are articulated to one another.

I believe that this question of the articulation of very different semiotic practices is far-reaching, profound, and terribly underinvestigated. Among other things, the problematic of articulation makes possible an argument for the potential value of objectivist methods and rhetoric in historical analysis— and to do so without adopting an objectivist ontology. From the point of view of one realm of semiotic practice, the activities of another realm of practice to which it is articulated may take on the appearance of objective limits. From the perspective of currency traders, Mexican pesos or Korean yuan are counters in a high-stakes game, a self-contained semiotic system with its own rules, strategies, categorical distinctions, signals, and motivations. But from the point of view of Mexican or Korean politicians or auto workers, fluctuation in the exchange rate of the national currency is an exterior fact, a highly constraining limit on the possibilities of political rhetoric or strategies of unionization. These different semiotic practices or language games go on at such different spatial scales—the world currency market in the case of currency trading, the nation-state in the case of politics, and the plant or the industry in the case of auto workers' unionization efforts—that their articulation may take the form of dull compulsion rather than the intersubjective understanding posited by linguistic models. Even though the world currency market really is a semioti-cally structured language game, it is also true that the market's workings are often symbolized as a matter of objective facticity in the political language of developing countries. This suggests that historical analysts might themselves be justified in treating such processes as objective or structural constraints, at least strategically. Thus, a study of shop floor union politics in Korea might well represent exchange rates of the yuan against the dollar as an objectively calculated statistical series and argue that exchange rates act as a structural constraint on the nature of union demands on management, rather than make a long detour from shop floor practices to decipher the very different logic of currency trading as a semiotic practice. Even within the procedures of a cultural history that assumes semiotics all the way down, strategic methodological resort to objectivism—as a useful abbreviation of semiotic processes going on outside one's sphere of intensive research—is not only justifiable, but, I would suggest, virtually impossible to avoid.

But I think there are also good ontological reasons for not abandoning objectivist research strategies. Here let me circle back to Keith Baker's argument against the reality of extradiscursive social constraints. I actually accept the ontological argument that everything human is symbolically constituted, which I take as an axiom widely shared among cultural historians. But I would object that from the axiom that everything human is symbolically constituted, it does not necessarily follow that human social existence is constituted by symbols alone, that it is exhausted by its discursivity. I would argue, to begin with, that although the social world is discursively or symbolically constituted, actors are also constrained and enabled by certain physical facts of existence: for example, that they are born, age, and die; that they cannot be in two places at the same time; that they must eat to live; and that they are subject to sexual desire, sickness, pain, and fear of bodily harm. These physical facts are themselves discursively shaped; everything human, I am assuming, passes through symbolization and is assigned a place in a meaningful order. But at the same time, the discursive shaping of, say, aging and death, is also subject to important nondiscursive constraints.

That this has important consequences for thinking about the place and limits of discourse in the social world may be illustrated by an example. Consider a premodern, predominantly rural population in which a mutation of the plague bacillus extends the average life span by several years. This will significantly raise the age at which children can expect to inherit their parents' assets, which inheritance, I am assuming, is normally a precondition for marriage and the foundation of a new family. This deferral of inheritance will almost certainly result in significant changes in the society's forms of life. It might, for example, lead to later marriages; to increased rates of lifetime celibacy; to a burgeoning of bandit gangs, monasteries, and nunneries; to changes in the amount or composition of dowries or bride prices; or to increased migration to cities where excess labor can be employed in manufacturing. It seems obvious that we could not hope to understand which of these possible changes might actually result from the lengthening of the life span without understanding the cultural or discursive milieu in which it took place. But equally, it would be absurd to claim that such a discursive reconstruction alone would be a sufficient account of the change, or to disdain the use of objectivist demographic theory and methods to determine the effects of rising life expectancies on the age structure of the population. In short, such banal and undeniable facts as that we age and die or that we cannot be in two places at the same time have far-reaching effects on the shapes and possibilities of human social life and discourse, effects that cannot be fully accounted for by discursive analysis.

My second claim is that discursive processes have extensive *nondiscursive effects*, that they create processes, forces, or structures whose shapes and dynamics cannot be fully explained in discursive terms. Again, an example might be helpful. The stigmatization of dark skin is a deeply entrenched semiotic fact in contemporary American society. One widespread effect of this semiotic fact is massive housing discrimination against African-Americans. But housing discrimination, even if discursively caused, has nondiscursive (as well as discursive) effects; for example, it physically restricts African-Americans to certain urban neighborhoods. In the 1970s, 1980s, and 1990s, this geographical constraint has had powerfully negative effects on African-American economic well-being over and above the continuing direct effects of the racial stigmatization that restricted blacks to urban ghettos in the first place. Thus, when job opportunities moved outward into the suburbs, African-Americans found themselves physically removed from potential sources of employment and unable to follow them. This resulted in an intensification of certain pathologies of ghetto life: higher rates of unemployment, lower incomes, increasing appeal of criminal careers, and a rise in single-parent households.[24] In this case, a discursive fact had enduring spatial or geographical effects, effects that were sedimented into the urban physical landscape and that operated with some autonomy from the initial discursive fact. But the point I mean to illustrate is general: I claim that discursive or semiotic processes regularly give rise to *emergent* structures or forces—spatial, or economic, or technical, or demographic, or political—that are governed at least in part by extradiscursive logics. And I further contend that tracing out such extradiscursive logics authorizes, indeed requires, recourse to something more than discursive methodologies.

What this points to is a conception of the social in which every sphere of life—from production, to art, to family life, to the state—is constituted by both discursive and extradiscursive logics that are always tightly intertwined in social practice. Although one of the tasks of sociocultural historians is to disentangle these logics, to assess their autonomous pressures and dynamics, it is also important to remember that they are always merged in practice, that, for example, questions of meaning, spatiality, relative scarcity, and coercion are conjoined in the world in a dance of mutual and simultaneous determination. According to this social ontology, the economic, the political, the cultural, and the geographic are not distinct institutional spheres of social existence; they are distinguishable but mutually constituting dimensions of social life, dimensions that are present in all institutional spheres.

This leads to a final point. Although this conception of the social implies the use of a variety of analytical methods, it also implies that such methods should be subjected to mutual confrontation, interrogation, and testing in the context of the practices whose logics the historian is attempting to disentangle. If, for example, economic and cultural determinants are tightly intertwined in the practices of a given sphere of activity, it seems somehow implausible that the methods used to explicate the cultural determinants should be divided from those used to explicate the economic determinants by an unbridgeable epistemic chasm. It has long seemed to me that the accounts typically given of quantitative and discursive methodologies exaggerate the real differences between them. Although it is common to speak of methods used to analyze discourse (or semiotic practices) as "interpretive," the actual techniques used in such analyses vary enormously, from relatively intuitive to highly formalist. Structuralists of the Levi-Straussian stripe are every bit as objectivist as quantitative historians, and quantitative analyses of the use of lexemes is a common practice among historical lexicographers.

Quantitative research has, by its very nature, a formalist character. But there is a hermeneutic element in much quantitative research that is rarely acknowledged, let alone highlighted or theorized. Scholars who have worked with complex quantitative data sets know that part of the process is something often expressed as "getting to know your data." Rather than simply deciding a priori on the categories into which cases will be placed and the kinds of analytic techniques that will be used, quantifiers usually engage in a good deal of preliminary probing that—except for the fact that what one "reads" is statistical tables, graphs, or indices—seems quite similar to the "hermeneutic circle," as described, for example, by Paul Ricoeur.[25] The investigator formulates guesses or hypotheses about the categories appropriate to the data set, produces a set of statistical measures based on them, finds anomalies in the results, refines or alters the hypotheses, uses these altered hypotheses to interrogate the data set again, and so on, until he or she is satisfied that the categories used in the analysis are true to the data set's internal structure. In the course of this hermeneutical interrogation of the data set, the investigator may also turn to nonquantitative sources of information, in an attempt, for example, to learn from apprenticeship contracts whether plumbers should be classified with other builders or other metal workers. None of this "quantitative hermeneutics" ever finds its way into print in books or articles. I think positivist social scientists fear that if they admitted they worked this way, they would be accused of "cooking their data" when, in fact, they are simply gaining enough sense of the inherent structures of their quantitative "texts" to be able to "read" them effectively, to plumb their depths. In short, the real procedures of quantitative researchers have more in common with interpretive methods than the official methodologists would ever suspect.

In short, I wish to argue that, on closer inspection, the conventional methodological divide between social and cultural history does not hold up very well. I think we do need to rethicken our histories by making them more social, but I think that doing so will require both the selective use of some of the classical research procedures of social history and the sort of radicalization and extension of cultural history that I have suggested in my paragraphs on language games and basketball. I personally see the development of appropriate non-schizophrenic rhetoric and methods for rethickening the social—on a terrain that has been permanently redefined by the linguistic turn—as one of the most important tasks currently confronting historians.

NOTES

1. I do not know who coined the term "the new social history," but it was certainly in widespread use by the end of the 1960s. "The new cultural history" is the title of an important collection of essays published under the editorship of Lynn Hunt in 1989: *The New Cultural History* (Berkeley and Los Angeles: University of California Press). My early work in the new social history style is represented in, for example, William H. Sewell, Jr., "The Working Class of Marseille under the Second Republic: Social Structure and Political Behavior," in *Workers in the Industrial Revolution*, ed. Peter Stearns and Daniel Walkowitz (New Brunswick, NJ: Transaction Publishers, 1974), 75–115; "Social Change and the Rise of Working-Class Politics in Nineteenth Century Marseille," *Past and Present* 65 (November 1974): 75–109; and "Social Mobility in a Nineteenth-Century European City: Some Findings and Implications," *Journal of Interdisciplinary History* 7:2, (autumn 1976): 217–33. My turn to cultural history is best represented by *Work and Revolution in France: The Language of Labor from the Old Regime to 1848* (Cambridge: Cambridge University Press, 1980).

2. An essay that recaptures much of the excitement of the era is E. J. Hobsbawm, "From Social History to the History of Society," *Daedalus* 100 (1971): 43.

3. On the *Annales* school, see Peter Burke, *The French Historical Revolution: The Annales School, 1929–89* (Stanford: Stanford University Press, 1990). On the British Marxists, see Harvey J. Kaye, *The British Marxist Historians* (Oxford: Polity Press, 1984).

4. Joan Wallach Scott, *The Glassworkers of Carmaux: French Craftsmen and Political Action in a Nineteenth-Century City* (Cambridge: Harvard University Press, 1974); Sewell, "Social Change"; E. P. Thompson, *The Making of the English Working Class* (London: Victor Golancz, 1963).

5. C. Wright Mills, *The Sociological Imagination* (Oxford: Oxford University Press, 1959), pp. 50–75.

6. Three works of historical anthropology/anthropological history were unquestionably born out of the ferment of this year: William M. Reddy, *The Rise of Market Culture: The Textile Trade and French Society, 1750–1900* (Cambridge: Cambridge University Press, 1984); Renato Rosaldo, *Ilongot Headhunting, 1883–1974: A Study in Society and History* (Stanford: Stanford University Press, 1980); and Sewell, *Work and Revolution.* A fourth was surely at least strongly influenced by the ferment: Robert Darnton, *The Great Cat Massacre and Other Episodes in French Cultural History* (New York: Basic Books, 1985).

7. Clifford Geertz, *The Interpretation of Cultures* (New York: Basic Books, 1973); Victor Turner, *The Forest of Symbols: Aspects of Ndembu Ritual* (Ithaca, N.Y.: Cornell University Press, 1967); and *The Ritual Process: Structure and Anti-Structure* (Oxford: Clarendon Press, 1969).

8. In my case, the "conversion" took place at the University of Chicago in 1973–74, largely under the influence of my history department colleague Ronald Inden. For me the "miracle year" of 1975–76 in Princeton was a deepening and confirmation of a turn I had already taken. The published evidence of my initial conversion is "État, Corps and Ordre: Some Notes on the Social Vocabulary of the French Old Regime," in *Sozialgeschichte Heute: Festschrift für Hans Rosenberg zum 70 Gebürtstag*, ed. H.U. Wehler (Göttingen: 1974), 49–68.

9. For a concise account of a hostile interchange centering on the anthropological turn, see Geoff Eley, "Is All the World a Text? From Social History to the History of Society Two Decades Later," in *The Historic Turn in the Human Sciences*, ed. Terrence McDonald (Ann Arbor: University of Michigan Press, 1996), pp. 197–98.

10. See, especially, Michel Foucault, *Discipline and Punish: The Birth of the Prison*, trans. Alan Sherridan (New York: Vintage Books, 1979).

11. Hunt, *New Cultural History.*

12. Joan Wallach Scott, *Gender and the Politics of History* (New York: Columbia University Press, 1988).

13. Joan Wallach Scott, "A Statistical Representation of Work *La Statistique de l'industrie à Paris*, 1847–1848," in *Gender and the Politics of History*, pp. 113–38.

14. See the works cited in note 1 and William H. Sewell, Jr., *A Rhetoric of Bourgeois Revolution: The Abbé Sieyes* and *What Is the Third Estate?* (Durham, NC: Duke University Press, 1994).

15. Keith Michael Baker, *Inventing the French Revolution* (Cambridge: Cambridge University Press, 1990), pp. 4–5.

16. Roger Chartier, *On the Edge of the Cliff: History, Language, and Practices*, trans. Lydia G. Cochrane (Baltimore: Johns Hopkins University Press, 1997), pp. 18–19, 20.

17. Chartier, *On the Edge*, p. 77.

18. Michel de Certeau, *The Practice of Everyday Life*, trans. Steven F. Rendall (Berkeley: University of California Press, 1984); and Foucault, *Discipline and Punish.*

19. This definition of textuality is actually taken from Chartier, *On the Edge*, p. 81.

20. For a more extensive critical evaluation of Chartier's position, see William H. Sewell, Jr., "Language and Practice in Cultural History: Backing Away from the Edge of the Cliff," *French Historical Studies* 21 (1988): 241–54.

21. Ludwig Wittgenstein, *Philosophical Investigations*, 3d ed., trans. G.E.N. Anscome (New York: Macmillan, 1985).

22. Here I am following up a suggestion made in conversation by Stuart Hall.

23. Richard Biernacki, *The Fabrication of Labor: Germany and Britain, 1640–1914* (Berkeley: University of California Press, 1995); Loic Wacquant, "The Pugilistic Point of View: How Boxers Think and Feel about Their Trade," *Theory and Society* 24 (1995): 489–535; and Peter Galison, *Image and Logic: A Material Culture of Microphysics* (Chicago: University of Chicago Press, 1997).

24. William Julius Wilson, *The Declining Influence of Race: Blacks and Changing American Institutions*, 2d ed. (Chicago: University of Chicago Press, 1980); *The Truly Disadvantaged: The Inner City, the Underclass, and Public Policy* (Chicago: University of Chicago Press, 1987); and *When Work Disappears: The World of the New Urban Poor* (New York: Knopf, 1996); and Douglas S. Massey and Nancy Denton, *American Apartheid: Segregation and the Making of the Underclass* (Cambridge: Harvard University Press, 1993).

25. Paul Ricoeur, "Meaningful Action Considered as a Text," *Social Research* 38 (autumn 1971): 529–62.

CHAPTER 13

Postcolonialism and Its Discontents: History, Anthropology, and Postcolonial Critique

Nicholas B. Dirks

> For a man who no longer has a homeland, writing becomes a place to live.
> —Theodor Adorno

WRITING

Writing is hardly a neutral space. In the last fifty years we have learned anew how much it matters from where we write, to whom we write, and more generally how writing is positioned: geo-politically, socio-historically, and institutionally. The crisis of writing has been ushered in by many factors, among them decolonization, a rising chorus of new nations, and the dispersal through migration and relocation of once colonized peoples. It is thus that postcolonial critiques have become necessary features of all the new landscapes we inhabit or survey. Postcoloniality is neither some new, faddish, trend, nor an abandonment of the real, whether constructed in relation to positivist or Marxist inclinations. And although postcoloniality is related to current developments in identity politics, multiculturalism, poststructuralism, and postmodernism, it is both far more and far less than these particular terms imply. In a general sense, I would argue that postcoloniality signifies those places and histories (rather than general theories) that resist (whether by active resistance or the mere memory of exclusion) the universalization of position and perspective, even as it underscores the extraordinary power of the forces of universalization. Postcoloniality reminds us of the fact that culture and modernity were always flawed, invariably predicated on violence and domination, the terms of seduction and conquest for colonization itself. Postcoloniality both embodies the promise of the West—the promise that flows from the enlightenment and the birth of nations—and reminds us that the promise is always flawed, the present always an impossible time and place in which to live. Postcoloniality is the epic story of seduction and betrayal.

Postcolonial studies are usually seen as having originated in the critique launched by Edward Said in his brilliant polemical work, *Orientalism*.[1] The central tenets of this argument are by now well known: colonial histories—the historical relations of domination between West and East—produced, and in turn were produced by, a range of discursive formations in which the colonial other was essentialized, inferiorized, feminized, and ultimately naturalized as the always already colonized. The East was constituted as something that could be known, indeed could only be known, through tropes that reproduced relations of domination, even as domination became increasingly seen as the natural condition of the world rather than the result of specific geo-political forces. Thus students of colonialism have uncovered the myriad discursive sedimentations of histories of domination, the complicities of literary, philological, cartographic, historical, anthropological (to mention just the obvious) forms of representation in the project of colonial rule, the ways the categories of knowledge have both been shifted by and done much of the work of colonial domination. Said took his principal theoretical inspiration from the work of Michel Foucault, whose insistence on the mutually constituting character of knowledge and power did for the domain of epistemology what earlier Marxist thinkers such as Lukàcs, Adorno, and Gramsci had done for culture. Despite recurrent and often vociferous critiques of Said, his work has been enormously influential in literary, cultural, and historical studies; since Said's account of Orientalism, it has been difficult to study the "West" without remembering the extent to which both its economic and its cultural identities have been enabled, if not produced, by the history of colonialism.

Since 1978, when *Orientalism* was published, the field of postcolonial studies has achieved a canonic measure of autonomous status, while influencing in a variety of ways fields from imperial and "third world" history to most of social and cultural anthropology, and from modern literary criticism to classics and cultural studies. Postcolonial studies has been defined in relation to a number of theoretical positions: the historicism of Said; the Derridian or Lacanian poststructuralism invoked in the remarkable theoretical corpus of Gayatri Chakravorty Spivak[2] and Homi Bhabha;[3] or at times the undifferentiated postmodernist celebration of difference and multiplicity, even as it has become at times a vehicle for identity politics. In my view, postcoloniality has been at its best when it has constituted a position that has insisted on the importance of historical critique from a multiplicity of historical (and so epistemological) perspectives. Thus academic knowledge practices in Europe and America have been scrutinized for their silences, exclusions, and complicities, providing serious and sometimes devastating critiques of fields such as area studies, anthropology, and comparative literature. And thus novel historical movements, from subaltern studies to new versions of historical anthropology or literary study, have been animated by a variety of postcolonial critiques. Postcolonial studies, however, has not always been absorbed happily into older paradigms, questioning the identities of all who write even as it privileges certain kinds of voices over others. In turn, postcolonial studies has been attacked both by traditional disciplinarians (the old and the new right) and by partisans of an old left that see American (multi)culturalism and academic poststructuralism as agents of global capitalism. In ensuing debates, we have had to confront questions about the future of disciplines, and the fundamental ethics of much academic knowledge, in ways that bear only a few traces of their original histories. In a recent essay, I wrote that the field of cultural theory has literally become a minefield, that the Florentine Villa of Michael Ondaatje's prize-winning novel, *the English Patient*, might be taken as a metaphor for the state of theory today.[4] What follows here is a personal reflection about this turn of events, both an endorsement of and a critical reaction to the current state of postcolonial critique. But let me begin with a little history.

HISTORY

No American of my generation who has committed an academic career to the study of a place like India has been unaware of the question of identity. Both at home and abroad, I have been repeatedly asked why *I* do the things I do. Whether at village rituals in southern India or cocktail parties in New York City, people ask how I came to be interested in the history of South Asia. I am usually expected to tell some anecdote about why my singular, North American path crossed India's. Because of the colonial connection, the British did not have to explain an interest in India in the same way, or had to explain themselves for rather different reasons. The generation of American scholars of South Asia before me often pointed to military service or missionary backgrounds; my own generation often points to an experience in the Peace Corps, or perhaps to world travel occasioned by the extraordinary opportunities and confusions of the late 1960s and early 1970s. I have my own story, which underscores the serendipity of my choice. For reasons as specific as they were accidental, I found myself doing research for an undergraduate Honors thesis in southern India, on a topic that still animates a part of my research project almost thirty years later. While my story satisfied most of my interlocutors, it has on occasion fallen short. I have often noted a look of residual bafflement on the part of many villagers in southern India, too polite to accuse me of being a U.S. spy, too self-deprecating to believe that my interest could be both so contingent and so disinterested. I have on occasion been told that American scholars used the research and materials of Indian academics to advance their careers and attain great wealth. And in the wake of *Orientalism*, I have asked myself why the conceit of accident has seemed to be so critical to the self-representation of American academics like myself, who are fully aware of the implication of U.S. area studies in cold war geo-politics and new forms of American imperial power. More recently, I have wondered about the personal implications of the current struggle over questions of authenticity and identity, rights of representation, and the impossibility of disinterested, disengaged, neutral inquiry. I assume neither that individual accidents are unconnected to structures of power nor that forms of knowledge are unrelated to the locations of power. But I will not disavow my right to speak or my capacity to know, even if I can no longer claim that my identity is either accidental or incidental. Indeed, I occupy locations of knowledge that have now become as much the objects of critique as certain questions around identity. The personal reflections that follow in this paper are in part about these questions of identity and location, and the crises that have come to circulate around them in debates over knowledge in the academy today.

I chose to do my graduate work in South Asian history at the University of Chicago, but when I arrived there learned that my advisor had in fact been trained as an anthropologist. South Asian history in the United States was then a fledgling field, as indeed was South Asian studies more generally, still dominated by the first generation of post war practitioners. South Asian studies only began after the Second World War, established first at the University of Pennsylvania by the Sanskritist W. Norman Brown, who had earlier recruited a first generation of South Asianists to assist him in advising the U.S. government about India in the last years of the war.[5] Brown, who went on to write an important treatise on contemporary South Asia, hired Holden Furber, an imperial British historian, to teach South Asian history at Penn. It seemed the logical choice, given the reach of imperial history to things subcontinental. However, it was perhaps no accident that when the University of Chicago wished to tenure a South Asian historian to begin a graduate program in line with the accomplishments and understandings of postwar American area studies, it recruited Bernard Cohn, an anthropologist who had done work as part of a village India project in the 1950s. Cohn played a major role in the development of social history for South Asia, experimenting with quantitative as well as anthropological methods in the study of history, training a new generation of students required to have extensive language skills and to engage in a unique combination of field and archival research work. Along the way, Cohn charted a new kind of relationship, supplementary and occasionally dialectical, between history and anthropology. Before Marshall Sahlins claimed to discover history, and before a new generation of post-Braudelian European historians discovered the uses of anthropology to fill in the vacuums created by quantitative data collection and analysis, Cohn argued for and demonstrated the contours of a new kind of historical anthropology.

The two decades of the 1970s and 1980s seem in retrospect a kind of heyday for historical anthropology. In anthropology, Cohn, Wolf, and Mintz were joined by Sahlins and Geertz; each of these major figures, in his own way, echoed Evans-Pritchard's earlier call for the recognition that contemporary analysis required historical context.[6] Cohn increasingly turned to the study of colonialism as a site both for understanding the history of contemporary anthropological assumptions and for historicizing the contingent character of caste structure, village organization, and religious affiliation in South Asia.[7] Wolf demonstrated in a series of magisterial studies that history, in at least its two major senses of historical records and historical writing, had systematically denied access to peasants and other subaltern groups. Mintz showed us that a history of commodities could both reanimate our understanding of material culture and chart out global connections that linked colonial forms of labor control to the rise of European and American capital and the formation of bourgeois society.[8] Sahlins discovered history on the shores of the Sandwich Islands in the fatal encounter between Captain Cook and Hawaiian mythic consciousness.[9] And Geertz demonstrated how rich his semiotic version of cultural theory could be when projected backwards onto the precolonial Javanese or Balinese state.[10] In history, Natalie Davis, Keith Thomas, Emmanuel Le Roi Ladurie, Carlo Ginsburg, Robert Darnton, Hans Medick, Caroline Bynum, David Sabean, William Sewell, Lynn Hunt,[11] among many others, used anthropological ideas of ritual, witchcraft, structure, ethnographic description, and semiotic analysis to enliven social historical investigations that ran aground against the limits of formal archival sources and quantitative analysis. The comparative aspirations of historical sociology gave way to the theoretical originality and excitement of new explorations in historical anthropology that promised for a time to collapse the borders of two disciplines that had previously demarcated the difference between the worlds of the colonizers and the colonized.

It was no accident that many of the historians seduced by the lure of anthropology were writing about premodern history. This was before modernity had become a primary interest in anthropology, and at a time when the idea that history and anthropology shared a common interest in alterity was rooted in shared understandings of "distance" in both time and space. And it strikes me, once again, that Bernard Cohn was way ahead of his peers. Cohn's critical historical interest in colonialism both collapsed some of the formal distinctions between metropolitan and colonial domains and helped pave the way for understanding that the anthropological other was in large part produced by the historical self. In the first instance, Cohn began to show us how the modern state in places like Britain was itself fashioned in places like India, for example, through technologies of rule represented by land settlements, grammars and dictionaries, cartographic explorations, ethnographic and statistical reports, and so on. In the second instance, Cohn was the first to suggest that institutions such as caste and the village were themselves radically transformed by the colonial encounter. When Cohn cited F. W. Maitland's famous line—that anthropology would have to choose between being history and being nothing— he meant something rather more radical than was intended either by Maitland or by Evans-Pritchard, who had earlier used the citation to advocate a more historical form of anthropology in his classic *Marret* lecture of 1951.[12] Cohn instructed us that the history of anthropology was deeply tied in its historical origins and mission to colonial rule; he insisted that the study of the colonizer and the colonized could not be separated; and he demonstrated how the contemporary categories, and assumptions, of anthropological analysis still bore the traces of colonial history. Perhaps even more significantly, Cohn did all of this in a voice of irony and humor rather than of anger and self-distancing critique. Of course his own work bore many of the contradictions found in the very critiques he mobilized against others, such as when he used a strictly anthropological notion of culture to talk about both cultural misunderstanding and cultural transformation under colonial traditions.

ANTHROPOLOGY

In my own training, then, anthropological debate was permeated by a concern with colonial history, and there was no contradiction in thinking of the project as part of a larger ethnography of the colonial state. Anthropology was a way of relativizing the cultural certainties of the colonizers, even as it usefully privileged the colonial rather than the metropolitan world. History for me was thus anthropologized through my immersion in anthropological theories and debates and through my sense that the universal narrative of Europe's self-realization was disrupted when one paid attention to other cultural "logics" and "systems." But history was also anthropologized through an insistence on method. Not only did I travel to archives that scarcely concealed the institutional histories that render most Western archives monuments of historical method and truth rather than contingent depositories of political process, I traveled beyond them, enjoined by the methods of "ethnohistorical" engagement to create new archives by using oral traditions, village records, mythical texts, and ethnographic encounters as part of my historical quest. Ethnohistorical projects did not simply take one to archives, it implicated one in the production of new archives. I found myself engaging the archive ethnographically. It was the field within which I conducted my research, prodding me by its recurrent recalcitrance, limiting me by its aggravating absences, fascinating me by its own patterns of intertextuality, seducing me by its appearance of the real. The official archive was the primary site of state monumentality: it was the very institution that canonized, crystallized, and classified the knowledge required by the state even as it made this knowledge available for subsequent generations in the cultural form of a neutral repository of the past.

But even as I write this, I remember that in those earlier days, history and anthropology merged together rather too seamlessly. Anthropology's conceit that it could know and represent the culture of the "other" within the academic spaces of the postcolonial metropole was not in fact seriously interrupted either by history or colonial studies. Indeed, this was the conceit that served as the epistemological justification for area studies programs. The leading Western interpreters of India were the anthropologists Louis Dumont and McKim

Marriott, both of whom used classical texts and village traditions to understand modern India, both of whom wrote about caste and Hinduism as the essential institutions of India. Dumont's celebrated work, *Homo Hierarchicus*,[13] chastised Western sociology for approaching Indian ideologies and institutions of hierarchy through the prejudicial lenses of egalitarianism and individualism. But in fact the work is resolutely situated within a Western, and colonial, view of India. When Dumont postulated a religious domain that, at least in the Indian case, transcended (or, in his terms, "encompassed") the political or material domain, Dumont countered Western sociology with its own Orientalist assumptions about the East. And when Marriott countered Dumont by insisting on a "monistic" rather than a "dualistic" sociology, one in retrospect can only hear the sound of one hand clapping. Dumont's structuralism and Marriott's culturalism shared extraordinary confidence in the epistemological project of a universal social science, and at the same time both defined the cultural domain as knowable in ways that were continuous with colonial and Orientalist understandings about India. Despite blistering attacks, on each other as well as against earlier anthropological and sociological approaches to India, Western anthropology was untroubled and largely unchanged by the furor of the times, and anthropology continued, even when proclaimed as the mouthpiece for the "native" point of view, to be unapologetically a Western science.

When anthropology had its major crisis in the 1980s (like all the disciplines, it is perpetually in crisis), it was less over its implication in colonial history than it was over its relationship to science. James Clifford made an eloquent case that the professionalization of anthropology—and thus its attendant trajectories and anxieties—took place within a colonial history, but the attention of the discipline seemed much more trained on the questions of writing, objectivity, and authorial responsibility (and style) in relation to the critique of science than it was on colonial, or neo-colonial, issues.[14] Questions of colonial history were relegated to the general virus of postmodernism by critics of the new reflexive moves in anthropology. Indeed, most critiques of the classic scientific ambitions of anthropological social science were lumped together as postmodern, poststructuralist, and relativistic. While cultures were relative one to another, they could not be relative to anthropological knowledge itself. Interestingly, materialists who always had problems with the idea that culture as a concept was at least partially autonomous (at least from universal forms of apprehension to material determinations) tended to join hands with die-hard culturalists in ways that led to odd coalitions between political positions both on the left and the right. The "writing culture" critique was seen by many anthropologists as having been problematic because it lost sight of the "other," even as its emphasis on the self was said to be narcissistic and ethnocentric.[15] In another context, I myself critiqued the "writing culture" message by suggesting that the emphasis on "writing" took away from a more proper emphasis on reading, specifically on the pre-histories of "fieldwork" that constituted the historical conditions for anthropological knowledge (including the epistemo-logical conceits of ethnography itself). My point was that the crisis of anthro-pology should lead to a heightened incorporation of genealogical critique in relation to historical contexts and colonial questions, rather than to the hyper-aestheticization of the anthropologist as "writer."[16]

History need not lead to critique. And for many anthropologists there are alternative histories, in which anthropology was more often critical of the colo-nial state than not, and in which anthropology has championed the people left out of history (along with their agency and their resistance) rather than itself jettisoning the people from history.[17] For other anthropologists, the problem was not so much the account of the past but its effects, the sense of guilt that the past provoked and the paralysis (a deficit of agency all around) produced by that guilt. Guilt may be a classic liberal dodge, but it has led many to argue that critique, whether driven by historical or other epistemological concerns, stands firmly in the way of progress or, in the artisanal language of the acad-emy, "getting on with the job at hand." And indeed, history alone is neither the problem nor the solution, at least so long as history is incorporated into anthropology merely as critical genealogy or interdisciplinary method. Instead, we must recall that the postcolonial critique raised the issue of location: the core historical as well as contemporary investments of a system of knowledge predicated on the "self" and the "other." Postcolonial perspectives have on occasion been as troubling for history as they have been for anthropology.

INDIA

Since 1978, it has been impossible to engage in the study of the colonial (or postcolonial) world without either explicit or implicit reference to Said's charge that not only our sources but our basic categories and assumptions have been shaped by colonial rule. The power of the Saidian critique lay precisely in linking colonial knowledge to contemporary scholarship. Orientalism, whether in the guise of colonial cultures of belief or of more specialized sub-cultures of scholarship, shared fundamental premises about the East, serving to denigrate the present, deny history, and repress any sensibility regarding contemporary political, social, or cultural autonomy in the colonized world. The implications of Said's critique have been challenging both for anthropol-ogy and history, as for area studies more generally. In a review essay first published in 1990 considering the question of what a post-Orientalist history would look like, Gyan Prakash attempted to specify the challenge in the con-text of South Asian history: "The attention to the historicity of knowledge demanded by the invitation to chart post-Orientalist historiography, therefore, runs counter to those procedures that ground the third world in essences and see history as determined by those essential elements. It requires the rejection of those modes of thinking which configure the third world in such irreducible essences as religiosity, underdevelopment, poverty, nationhood, non-Westernness; and it asks that we repudiate attempts to see third-world histories in terms of these quintessential principles."[18] Prakash went on to propose what he called a post-foundationalist history in which attempts to grapple with the fundamental historicity of modernity in South Asia would necessarily entail critical attention to the historical formation of basic categories for the representation of South Asia.

In calling for a new kind of history, Prakash reviewed various genres of nationalist and Marxist history in and about India, arguing that much of this history worked against Orientalism both as a structure of rule and a source of authority but found itself implicated nevertheless in some of the key categories and problematics of Orientalist knowledge.[19] In the end, he advocated a kind of critical post-Orientalist historiography, historical work that interrogated its own categories and assumptions in relation to a genealogical critique of colonialism. Examples of this work included new forms of historical anthropology that sought to blend the critical history of Cohn and the critical theory of Said. Prakash also advocated the importance of a new school of South Asian historiography—Subaltern Studies. Founded as a collective of historians under the leadership of Ranajit Guha, Subaltern Studies brought out its first volume of historical writings on South Asian history and society in 1982, motivated in part by an interest in critiquing two forms of historiographical elitism: colonialist and bourgeois-nationalist. By the first form of elitism, Guha implied the kind of "Cambridge school" history that characterized nationalism as "the sum of activities and ideas by which the Indian elite responded to the institutions, opportunities, resources, etc., generated by colonialism," not through "lofty idealism," but rather with the "expectation of rewards in the form of a share in the wealth, power and prestige created by and associated with colonial rule," the drive for such rewards creating collaboration and competition as the core ingredients of Indian nationalism. By the second, Guha meant to describe the story of the "freedom struggle" as a "phenomenal expression of the goodness of the native elite with the antagonistic aspect of their relation to the colonial regime made, against all evidence, to look larger than its collaborationist aspect." Guha wrote further that the study of the "historic failure of the nation to come to its own" would constitute for the collective "the central problematic of the historiography of colonial India."

As Prakash told the story, post-Orientalist historiography and Subaltern Studies history shared similar influences, and at the same time stressed different kinds of critical visions and historiographic locations. The former analyzed "power relations in the context of academic disciplines and institutions"; the latter saw itself "disrupting and derailing the will of the powerful." Both, however, were aligned in various ways with Said's critical concerns about Orientalism, as well as with new tendencies in poststructuralism that critiqued all "solidly grounded existence and identities." Prakash's critique, and his celebration of post-Orientalist historiography in connection with poststructuralism, was not universally admired. Two English historians of India, David Washbrook and Rosalind O'Hanlon, wrote a spirited reply to Prakash, sparking a debate on such matters as the importance of Subaltern Studies, the status of Marxism in Indian historiography, the place of cultural analysis and reflection in the American academy, and the implications of poststructuralist theory and post-modernist dispositions in the writing of history and anthropology. In a polemical flurry that anticipated a variety of impassioned attacks on postcolonial perspectives (see below), the authors pilloried Prakash's advocacy of postfoundational history for its endorsement of poststructuralism as well as its internal contradictions.[20] Indeed, we were told that politics can only be preserved by taking class, and historical materialist analysis, as foundational for any historical project, and that postcolonial critics such as Prakash ignore class so as to disguise their own position as victors rather than victims in a world capitalist system that produces both the ideological underpinnings of American academic political culture and the global elites who benefit—now more than ever—from that culture.

What was really at stake in this debate was the place of colonialism in the historiography of South Asia. Washbrook and O'Hanlon only referred to British colonialism in their piece once, to disparage the writing of James Clifford about American anthropology. If, as they suggested, the great sin of colonialism was to develop the idea of culture, the great sin of the American academy was to take a colonial idea and embrace it as amounting to anything more than mystification. Historiographical attention to colonialism, rather than identifying key political dynamics behind the exercise of capitalist domination in India, merely licenses postcolonial anxiety about cultural rather than economic matters, allowing a postcolonial (and now American based) elite to masquerade as the oppressed rather than the oppressors. If only the workers of the world would unite, they seem to be saying, the oppressed would have nothing to lose but their (cultural, national, racial) mystifications. A history focusing on world capitalism would instead underscore the weight of global forces that in fact differentiate among peoples based on access to the means of production rather than the epiphenomenal questions of cultural identity. And here is where a foundational Marxism seems to blend seamlessly with Cambridge school history, for the latter used networks of materialist analysis and so-called class analysis to disparage nationalism and ultimately deny the historical reality of either colonialism or nationalism.

Anxiety without Ambivalence

This debate was hardly unique. While subalterns may still not speak loudly, or frequently, about the causes of their oppression, an unprecedented number of academics are speaking and arguing on their behalf. Indeed, many of these academics are speaking very loudly. Recent critiques by Arif Dirlik,[21] Sumit Sarkar,[22] Neil Lazarus,[23] Harry Harootunian,[24] and most insistently and stridently by Aijaz Ahmad,[25] have argued that postcolonial studies is bankrupt because it has sold the Marxist agenda down the river, replacing materialist analysis and critique with poststructuralist idealism and literary free play, drawing upon the identity claims of American multiculturalism to mystify the continuing and increasingly insidious operations of class and capital, in particular the newly constituted relations of late industrial/global capital. Ahmad has emerged as a new voice in the wilderness, exposing the hypocrisy and self-aggrandizement (and self-enrichment) of a new breed of postcolonial critic, reiterating time and again the need to write materialist histories of capitalism and of literary production in different and historically specific regions of the world. Characteristically, Ahmad cannot quite free himself from the allure of the postcolonial debate to set about these important tasks, instead writing polemic after polemic against the devious villains of postcolonial studies. At base is his concern that Marx has been abandoned, usually in the disguise of Foucault. "Polemical dismissals of Marxism, without any detailed engagement with Marx's thought, are now a fairly common feature of French poststructuralism and of the straightforwardly right-wing ideas which have arisen in its wake."[26] Unlike some critics, Ahmad does not separate off the good Said from his bad followers, instead blaming the father for the sins of his sons (and daughters).

The debate often claims to be about politics but it is in fact far more frequently about truth, which is why the critics of postcolonialism spring so promiscuously from different political positions. Arif Dirlik, like Ahmad, finds the new postcolonial criticism highly troublesome, asserting that "the denial of capitalism's foundational status also reveals a culturalism in the postcolonialist argument that has important ideological consequences. . . . By throwing the cover of culture over material relationships, as if the one had little to do with the other, such a focus diverts criticism of capitalism to the criticism of Eurocentric ideology, which not only helps postcolonialism disguise its own ideological limitation but also, ironically, provides an alibi for inequality, exploitation, and oppression in their modern guises under capitalist relationships."[27] The Cold War might not so much be over as simply shifted to a new locale. The level of polemic in many of these exchanges seems particularly explosive given the fact that many of the victims of the new polemic would not only place themselves on the left, but unabashedly acknowledge various kinds of debts to Marxism. Prakash writes that the emerging historiography he applauds "can be located at a point where poststructuralist, Marxist, and feminist theories converge and intersect." And certainly there seems little contradiction between noting Marx's general acceptance of at least certain key components of Britain's own narrative of imperial progress and acknowledging Marx's life-long critique of the capitalist system that he knew was complicit in, as well as productive of, the history of imperialism. However, a new iron curtain is being policed by polemicists who tend to parody the contemporary influences of poststructuralist thought, link it mechanically to an overdetermined theoretical conception of global capital, and maintain the claim that politics can only be legitimated by an unmodulated declaration of the primacy of an unreconstructed sense of the material and the economic. The American academy has not only lost its capacity to identify the real, so the charge goes, it has undermined the real in order to mystify its own complicity in the inequalities and oppressions of world capital.

There are, however, reasons to question the motivations behind the debate over truth claims. The critique has not only resurrected the unreconstructed antinomies of culture and practical reason, it has done so on a ground that is fundamentally about identity politics; so it is perhaps not surprising that the greatest concern seems to be about the identities of the postcolonial crowd. Both Ahmad and Dirlik, from their respective locations, seem equally concerned about the salaries and notoriety of a handful of postcolonial theorists.[28]

For example, H. D. Harootunian has recently published an impassioned critique of postcolonial studies in which he argues that postcolonial theory has reinscribed the unfortunate history of area studies. Harootunian provides a lively critique and a detailed history of area studies, with special reference to East Asian Studies. He then observes that postcolonial theory is "the natural successor of area studies by virtue of both genealogy and geography."[29] He explains this by noting that whereas area studies traditionally privileged the region and national location, postcoloniality has "valorized the formation of subjectivity and a politics of identity rooted in location."[30] The argument is based on the rhetoric of "risk." On the one hand, area studies, "owing to its own desire to identify with native knowledge . . . has strangely run the risk of forming a link with all those more recent efforts to elevate identity and cultural difference as the true vocation of a cultural studies."[31] On the other hand, Harootunian suggests that there are moments when postcoloniality, "in discourses like subaltern studies, risks resembling earlier plaints protesting the loss of native culture and knowledge before the eroding assault of capitalist modernization."[32] Harootunian puts this point more baldly later in his article: "In mapping this image of authentic knowledge on to an earlier moment—the colonial era—postcolonial proponents such as the subaltern historians risk becoming seekers of the authentic, yearning for the silent cultural space of an unaffected interior accessible only to native sensibility and everything else that such a gesture implies politically. Moreover, this return to the pursuit of cultural authenticity loops back to form a symmetry with the desire of an earlier area studies programme to stand in the place of the native."[33] We could paraphrase Harootunian to imply that the problem here is that the native, in the guise of the postcolonial subaltern historian, seeks to occupy the place of the native that was charted out for him/her by area studies programs. Clearly, the native does not know his place, or rather does not know enough to avoid the place of exoticized essentialism that Western Orientalism through area studies has produced. In these terms, Said's argument has become a parody of itself.

Harootunian is arguing in part that the appeal to native culture reiterates the degree to which much traditional culture is in fact a sign of capitalist modernity and risks rehearsing appeals of a kind that were made in prewar Japan, with all the complicities between fascism, ultranationalism, and appeals to tradition. However, his blanket denunciation of postcolonial theory, and in particular his polemical effort to consign such scholars as subaltern historians—"Guha's stable"—to the sins of U.S. area studies, makes one wonder about his real intent. In Harootunian's rhetoric, modernization theory is equated with literary theory (because they are both antihistorical), subaltern historians don't really do history (because they don't acknowledge the global hegemony of capital), and natives are part of the problem, hardly the solution. Had Harootunian actually read Chatterjee's work (he alludes to it in a general way), he would have realized, for example, that Chatterjee has argued that what he calls the rule of colonial difference was fundamental to colonial forms of rule, and that both nationalism itself—and the importance of various cultural formulations to anticolonial nationalism—were deeply implicated in a history of colonial modernity.[34] What makes it possible to so radically misread the work of subaltern historians (and, for that matter, poststructuralist critics) as being fundamentally about a politically suspect yearning for cultural authenticity? What unites cultural historians like Harootunian, economic historians like Dirlik, and Marxist literary critics like Ahmad? Indeed, their angry reaction to postcolonial critique is reminiscent of older concerns about who can speak on behalf of universal reason, and where indeed universal reason is genuinely located. The anxiety is palpable.

THE RETURN OF THE NATIVE

Anthropology, at least since Malinowski, has been committed to the "native" point of view. As Milton Singer once wrote, "Malinowski's axiom that a major aim of ethnology is to understand the "native" from his point of view, his relation to his world, has been accepted by anthropology since the 1920s."[35] Singer was one of the few in earlier anthropological days for whom the "native" was genuinely in scare quotes; one of his first anthropological essays took on the idea of American character. However, until recently, anthropologists supposed that natives were generally others. As a result, studying their own society made them nervous: that was thought to be a topic for sociologists, armed with modern techniques of analysis. Anthropological assumptions were of course mapped onto the colonial world—first-world anthropologists studied third-world natives, while the few third-world anthropologists either renamed themselves sociologists after returning home or struggled to justify their anthropological practice. When M. N. Srinivas began his fieldwork, under the supervision of E. E. Evans Pritchard, he was sent off to study a "tribal" group in India, in part because of prevailing anthropological commitments to the study of primitive society, in part because the position of the native anthropologist was felt to be awkward. When Srinivas went on to study his own society, in the form of fieldwork in a Mysore village just a few miles away from his ancestral village, some anthropologists thought he was in fact uniquely situated to do the work, being as it were both a native informant and an Oxford-trained anthropologist. But worries that these two subject positions could not be united were expressed in a number of places. The Cambridge anthropologist Edmund Leach, in a review of *Caste in Modern India*, complimented Srinivas for his insider's knowledge of India, but questioned whether this was fully an advantage or not "from the viewpoint of sociological analysis." In particular, Leach was referring to Srinivas's proposals about the concept of sanskritization, in which "there is a long term tendency for caste groups which are low in the social hierarchy to imitate the style of life of high caste Brahmins, thus introducing a certain fluidity into the total hierarchy of castes." As Leach put it in his review: "That such fluidity exists has been clearly demonstrated, but that it should be seen as arising from an emulation of the Brahmins seems to me odd—a specifically 'Brahminocentric' point of view!"[36]

Srinivas responded by writing an epilogue for his next book, *Social Change in Modern India*, a chapter entitled "Some Thoughts on the Study of One's Own Society." He began by noting, wryly, that his work had been repeatedly evaluated outside of India in reference to his being "an Indian sociologist engaged in the study of my own society." While many observed that this gave him a great advantage, there were those who asked, "How far can any sociologist understand his own society?" as well as others who felt he was at his best when he wrote about India forgetting the technical apparatus of social anthropology. Srinivas decided to take these questions seriously, without raising obvious questions about the relationship of Western anthropological views about India to colonial concerns, let alone Western claims about the possibilities of self-knowledge.[37] Indeed, he used the opportunity of this essay to raise critical questions about his own position, noting for example that his views on the effects of reservations could not but be related to his sensitivity regarding the distress of many Mysore Brahmins, many of them his friends and relatives, over the "steady deterioration in efficiency and the fouling of interpersonal relations in academic circles and the administration—both results of a policy of caste quotas."[38] But when he defended himself against Leach, he did so by adducing empirical evidence from his fieldwork to support his case.

In fact, Leach was not wrong to raise questions about the ideological presuppositions of the theory of sanskritization. But what is remarkable in retrospect is how he felt licensed to make a critique of "native" anthropological analysis on the grounds of identity, when such questions were not asked of British anthropologists either during the colonial era or its immediate aftermath. Srinivas could have written, as did an earlier writer on caste, S. V. Ketkar, that only a Hindu who felt the burden of the civilizational history of caste could write about it properly, as, "they cannot afford to enjoy the absurdities as an Englishman would."[39] Or Srinivas could have responded in kind that Leach's particular form of structural functionalism was perfectly at home in the colonial office, conveying forms of analysis that were motivated by issues of colonial control. Instead, Srinivas wrote one of the first reflexive essays in anthropology, and was taken seriously in the West not least because of his modest and subdued self-scrutiny.

Why is it that natives are so frequently the targets of concerns about identity and interested knowledge, and that whether or not "natives" claim privilege for "insider" knowledge they provoke serious professional anxiety when they engage in theoretical reflection and critique? The recent controversies over postcolonial studies have made it clear that things have not changed, even if they now take a new, and angrier, form. Indeed, one can find other examples of anxiety well within the current heart of anthropology that show the problem to be pervasive even outside the specific genre of postcolonial criticism. As only one example, we could turn to the recent—already classic—debate over the death of Captain Cook between Marshall Sahlins and Gananath Obeyesekere.[40] The debate appears at first glance to be a familiar one, another example of the contest between culture and practical reason. But the level of vitriol distinguishes it—how often have scholars written book-length rejoinders?—and the claims about native knowledge give this debate a particular edge. Take Sahlins's suggestion that he originally thought to entitle his book *How 'Natives' Think* as: "Natives versus Anthropologists; Or, How Gananath Obeyesekere Turned the Hawaiians into Bourgeois Realists on the Ground They Were 'Natives' Just Like Sri Lankans, in Opposition to Anthropologists and Other Prisoners of Western Mythical Thinking." What upset Sahlins most was that Obeyesekere had used his own identity as a Sri Lankan native to predicate a part of his critique of Sahlins, "invoke[ing] his native experience, both as a theoretical practice and a moral virtue, claiming on both scores the advantage over the "outsider-anthropologist."[41] According to Sahlins, "The underlying thesis is crudely unhistorical, a not-too-implicit notion that all natives so-called (by Europeans) are alike, most notably in their common cause for resentment." For Sahlins, the stakes return to the question of cultural particularity, the delineation and interpretation of which is anthropology's one epistemological raison d'être. As Sahlins puts it, "In negating Hawaiian cultural particularity in favor of a universal practical rationality, Obeyesekere subverts the kind of ethnographic respect that has long been a condition of the possibility of a scholarly anthropology."[42]

To be sure, Obeyesekere predicated the suspicion that led him to reexamine the sources for the debate on both South Asian data and his experience as a

South Asian native. But rather than thereby claiming exclusive insight or moral virtue, he set about to reexamine the evidence adduced by Sahlins, but with different presuppositions about how natives might think about Europe. His book is an exhaustive, compelling if not always persuasive, inventory and analysis of the same sources used by Sahlins rather than an assertion that any native would be in a position to reject his thesis out of hand. In my view, Obeyesekere succeeds less in making a new argument of his own than in suggesting that the sources are far more complicated than Sahlins makes them out to be, situated as they are in cultural logics of their own, determined in part by the propensity of Europeans to believe in myths about how natives believe Europeans to be gods. Obeyesekere wrote his book to make a general point: that the theories of culture used by anthropologists such as Sahlins make simplistic assumptions about native modes of thought, mistaking the universal capacity to make myths for a native alterity that requires a science (anthropology) predicated on the suspension of disbelief, one that these same anthropologists would never use on their own culture. However, Obeyesekere hardly dismisses the significance of cultural analysis, despite his abiding concern with the way Eurocentric ideas of culture have distorted anthropological efforts to understand myth and meaning.

An interesting alignment emerges from this debate. For even as Sahlins is ostensibly most concerned by Obeyesekere's critique of culture, he would doubtless take umbrage at Harootunian's critique of culturalism. Harootunian—like Dirlik, Ahmad, Washbrook, and O'Hanlon—was concerned precisely with claims about cultural particularity, whether these claims emerged from area studies, anthropology, or the mouths of natives. And while Harootunian and Sahlins would seem to be on opposite sides concerning the power of global capital to produce and contain all forms of cultural difference/autonomy, they are on the same side when it comes to nativism. Harootunian's universal history aligns itself resolutely, if curiously, with Sahlins's anthropology, at least in opposition to the right of natives either to reject cultural difference or to celebrate it. Of course, the natives in question—whether the anthropologist Obeyesekere or the subalternist historians—hardly claim unmitigated cultural difference or unconditional universal rationality. They are, rather—and this is where Sahlins perhaps sensed the core issue—united only in the claim that the colonized world has historical reason(s) to feel a certain resentment about both the colonial past and the ways that past lives on in, among other places, the knowledge practices of the Western academy. Ergo the postcolonial critique.

I would suggest that this resentment (and this is Sahlins's phrase) seems to be in part a response to the relentless linking of postcolonial critique with identity politics by the critics of both, and the affiliated identification of the identities (and personal conditions) of postcolonial writers as part of the problem. Whether it is Leach raising issues of anthropological bias in regard to Srinivas, Sahlins fuming about Obeyesekere's invocation of native knowledge to critique anthropological knowledge about natives, Dirlik questioning the salaries of postcolonial theorists, Ahmad carefully concealing his own past as an American academic while dripping resentment about those who can't or don't, Harootunian risking the comparison of subaltern historians to prewar Japanese fascists, or Washbrook and O'Hanlon directing their greatest ire at the embrace of the liberal American academy by postcolonial theory and identity politics, we have to wonder why it is that the native's identity is always the question. And we may now understand that when Prakash responded to his critics by noting that he felt himself in the predicament of the Bengali babu being told he didn't know his proper place, he was not the one to raise the issue of identity. Instead, Prakash was reacting to the echoes of earlier critiques in contemporary attacks, the policing of issues of authenticity, cultural analysis, and universal reason: in short, the colonial genealogy of the debate. And when Prakash defended his position by insisting on the necessity of ambivalence, he both made an implicit argument about the multiple locations of knowledge and brought stark attention to the nature of the assault on "native" critiques in literary theory, history, and anthropology.[43]

HISTORICAL ANTHROPOLOGY AND POSTCOLONIAL CRITICISM

Issues of identity became critical to the delineation of difference in relation both to the justifications and mechanisms of colonial rule. In the period of the Spanish colonization of the New World, difference was categorized in terms of religion and purity of blood.[44] In Asia, difference became both cultural and racial, though racial categories were used to subsume cultural ones as empire entered the latter part of the nineteenth century. In Africa, ideas of race seemed for the most part to obliterate culturalist thinking in imperial thought and policy. Ideas of difference thus carry with them a deep colonial history that complicates efforts both to overcome the essential(izing) character of difference and to accept the residual force of difference as a necessary and occasionally strategic category of thought as well as identity. Questions of difference will no more disappear of their own accord than will issues of identity be submerged in some new universal logic of global capital. But neither should postcolonial theory be mistaken as a reductionist claim about the transhistorical status of identity and difference. And, indeed, I am hardly defending all iterations of postcolonial theory, even as I am not attacking all the grounds that have served for its critical engagement elsewhere. I have myself criticized the substitution of highly aestheticized textual analyses for intertextual and rigorously historical studies of the ways colonial discourse has been empowered in and by institutional histories that work to reveal the contradictions as well as the particular power of these discursive forms and sites. I too am concerned about the generalization of the postcolonial into a transhistorical and global category of the same level of uniformity and generality as the global capital of the old core

Marxists. I too worry about the inflation of claims about the political implications of postcolonial critique. While much postcolonial criticism has been very specific in its delineation of academic disciplines as the principal target of critique, this field has also been the scene of grand pronouncements about the stakes in the battles being waged. And how can one not be concerned about the subordination of some social categories in the generalization of claims about the universal character of postcoloniality? There are major differences between political exiles, the migrant poor, and middle-class immigrants; forms and patterns of hybridity do not swirl about in some undifferentiated diaspora, even if a core connection between modern hybridity and colonial history seems irrefutable. Perhaps most worrisome of all is the recognition of the dangerous borderlands inhabited by critiques of the enlightenment narrative of progress and reason, given the extent to which these borderlands are also inhabited by critiques from many forces on the right, from religious fundamentalists to political fascists. But this is not to yield to the arguments of Ahmad, Harootunian, and others who insist that these positions are fundamentally the same, for even the most basic attention to location, context, and genealogy demonstrates basic differences. Indeed, despite a necessary wariness about the way some critiques can be appropriated to other ends, and that can be appropriated all the more easily when they are unaccompanied by positive social and political commitments and theories, the point of the postcolonial critique is precisely about the importance of location, not its elision.

I will conclude with two examples of ethnographic translation, both of which pose the dilemma I have tried to characterize just now, though in rather different registers. Much of my recent work has been devoted to critiquing colonial and anthropological constructions of caste in India. I have argued that under colonialism caste became the foundational basis of Indian society, the anthropological substitute for civil society that could be used both to explain how Indian civilization survived its history of despotisms and political failures and to justify British colonial rule. Even as caste became the central trope for India, it was made into a unitary social form that could be recognized as fundamentally religious rather than political, as not only autonomous from but opposed to the "state." When H. H. Risley—writing as Census commissioner and colonial anthropologist in 1909 shortly after the swadeshi movement had introduced the political implications of mass agitational politics—he was clear that caste opposed nationality and would oppose the growth, and the possibility, of nationalist politics. The colonial utility of caste was clear, even as the postcolonial importance of critiquing caste, as a major impediment to modernity and as the sedimented marker of traditional privilege and oppression, seemed self-evident.

Within anthropology, the project of joining this critique in the postcolonial period was more complicated; figures as various as Dumont and Marriott argued that a simpleminded dismissal of caste was ethnocentric and elitist. In my own work, once I could establish that the contemporary form of caste had in fact been produced by a combination of forces (from British rule, nationalist reaction, the colonial depoliticization of Indian society, to Western anthropology), I was able to argue simultaneously against Western knowledge and contemporary forms of inequality. But my satisfaction about the character of this critique has now yielded to a sense of the much greater volatility and complexity of the issues at hand.[45] Within India, the debate over the report of the Mandal Commission—which recommended a vast expansion of the system of quotas and policies of affirmative action using caste identity—has highlighted some of the contradictions in the contemporary politics of caste. It has created conditions that made it possible—and frighteningly compelling—for BJP (Hindu nationalist) party ideologues to assert that a newly defined notion of Hinduism might be less divisive than caste as a focus for national politics. Caste is now being turned into a symbol of traditional decadence by the Hindu right, who wish to replace it with other forms of tradition—chief among which seem now to be the equation of Hindu-ness with Indian nationality. As a result, any attempt today to critique caste finds itself in possible ideological alliance with forces of communalism that change the stakes of academic argument in violent and unexpected ways.

We all know the dangers here; we know we cannot control the political appropriations of our writing any more than we can contain their interpretive readings. Academic commentators who have either opposed or been extremely wary of Mandal, not members of the Hindu right by any means, often now argue that the effect of Mandal will be to exacerbate the colonial construction of caste groups as primordial, rendering caste even more divisive and involuted than it already is. Indeed, I have recently discovered that critiques of colonialism (such as my own) have been used to argue against progressive politics (as compromised as the progressivism of these politics might be).

The issues here become even more complicated if we can shift to the contemporary writing of the important intellectual and social critic Ashis Nandy. Nandy has conjoined powerful critiques of colonialism and insightful interrogations of the enlightenment project and modernity; he has further linked critiques of the group he calls the secular elite in India to a call for a new version of "traditionalism," with appropriate gestures to the inner truths of Indian culture.[46] While his critique of secularism—of how the ideology of universally enlightened desacrilization masks its own hierarchies and exclusions, and works to empower an indigenous elite and an affiliated set of international forces—not only helps explain the rise of middle-class *ressentiment* and religious fundamentalism, but links a powerful theoretical critique of the forces of modernity with a plea for Indian particularism. However, it accepts too readily a hegemonic notion of Indian tradition that itself was produced in large part in reaction to colonial modernity. It also works to justify and, so it would seem, support forces of reaction and repression. If Nandy identifies the dynamics of India's postmodern predicament better than many other social critics, he also reveals the dangerous relationship between calls for cultural and social recuperation and political movements that attack enlightenment ideologies (and institutions) for very different reasons, with very different goals. There is real danger here. Nevertheless, it is important not to lose sight of how even the terms of this discussion have been framed by colonial history.[47]

The angel of history speaks with sadness not just about the atrocities of the past, but about the atrocity of history itself, propelled as he is into the future by the terrible storm called progress. Colonial encounter not only provided the wealth for the consolidation of European power but enabled the formation of fundamental notions, not just of nation, race, ethnicity, and gender, but also of democracy, liberalism, cultural pluralism, and even internationalism. The delineation of modern divisions between private and public spheres, church and state, ultimately the justificatory rhetoric for the principle of secularism, are also deeply rooted in the history of colonialism, and by implication Judeo-Christian assumptions about the domains of religious belief and practice. Even as Hegel's allegory of the master and the slave can remind us that the colonizing self was in large part produced through this violent encounter with the colonized other, Europe would not have been, indeed could not have been, quite itself without colonial history. Thus it is that the anthropological idea of culture was in large part produced out of the colonial experience. Culture was what colonialism was all about: it emerged as the science of the colonial laboratory and the means of colonial governmentality. Culture was the gift to the colonized that rendered difference both essential and inferior, resistance either impossible or inauthentic, development derivative or doomed. And yet difference was not merely an unfortunate European invention, even as it can hardly be wished away, either by European desire or regret.

The critique of modernity began in the colonized world, where the contradictions of the modern—its exclusions and exceptions, its deceptions and displacements—were first recognized, exposed, and interrogated. It must be in the space of memory around this past that the disciplinary rapprochement between history and anthropology proceeds to address the past and engage the *post*colonial future. Reason must henceforth accept the ambivalence of its postcolonial condition.[48] I conclude therefore with the heightened realization that the critique of colonialism (and colonial anthropology) in which I have been engaged is far more perilous than I at first thought. Neither politics nor truth occupy universal ground.

We have only just begun to consider how multiple the regime of politics can be,[49] and what might happen when we engage politics "ethnographically," with all the ambivalence that the oxymoronic locution "participant observation" implies. Rather than assuming that some specter of postcolonial, postmodern, poststructural, or postnational perspectives will jettison the foundations of genuine criticism, or throwing our hands up in mock horror at our incapacity to control the meanings of our work, we need to pay far better attention to, and implicate ourselves much further within, the multiple readings and global uses of our own scholarly interventions. A revitalized attention to the cultural and historical specificity of the conditions of knowledge, the locations of contexts, as well as the multiplicities of politics, suggests the possibility both for a different kind of critical engagement and for a new kind of historical ethnography in the post–Cold-War world in which reflexivity is always inflected by the particularities of location. It is in this sense that politics turns out to be relentlessly anthropological. Despite all the genealogical nightmares of the past, anthropology is perhaps at last in a position where it might help show how a fundamental concern with difference, when situated in historical critiques that engage the ways difference itself has grown out of the colonial past, can continue to muddy and complicate the abstractions of the new world order. In a postcolonial anthropology, I would suggest, all knowledge must be conceived as native knowledge, at once empirically based, theoretically animated, locationally situated, and reflexively engaged. Only then will anthropology find not just history, but a sustainable future.

Notes

1. Edward Said, *Orientalism* (New York: Pantheon Books, 1978).

2. For an extraordinary contribution to various postcolonial debates, see her recent *Critique of Postcolonial Reason* (Cambridge, Mass.: Harvard University Press, 1999).

3. See *The Location of Culture* (New York: Routledge, 1994).

4. See my *In Near Ruins: Cultural Theory at the End of the Century* (Minneapolis: University of Minnesota Press, 1998).

5. That area studies emerged out of Cold War interests and concerns is now widely accepted and much documented. South Asian Studies emerged directly out of World War II in its initial formation at the University of Pennsylvania. Subsequently, South Asian Studies both flourished at Penn and developed into major knowledge complexes, paralleling the history of other area studies programs, at universities such as Chicago, Berkeley, and Wisconsin. The Ford Foundation pumped millions of dollars into the formation of active area studies programs, endowing faculty positions and graduate fellowships, before the U.S. Government regularized funding, first in the Defense Department and then in Education, through Title VI and other allocations. For the story of South Asian Studies in the U.S., see my "Futures Past: South Asian Area Studies in the United States," forthcoming in David Szanton, ed., *Rethinking Area Studies*.

6. E. E. Evans-Pritchard, *Social Anthropology and Other Essays* (New York: Free Press), pp. 139–54.

7. See Cohn's essays in his two major collections: *An Anthropologist among the Historians and Other Essays* (Delhi: Oxford University Press, 1987); and *Colonialism and Its Forms of Knowledge* (Princeton: Princeton University Press, 1995).

8. Sidney W. Mintz, *Sweetness and Power: The Place of Sugar in Modern History* (New York: Viking, 1985).

9. Marshall Sahlins, *Islands of History* (Chicago: University of Chicago Press, 1983).

10. Clifford Geertz, *Negara: The Theater State in Nineteenth-Century Bali* (Princeton: Princeton University Press, 1980).

11. See Natalie Davis, *Society and Culture in Early Modern France* (Palo Alto: Stanford, 1965); Keith Thomas, *Religion and the Decline of Magic* (London: Weidenfeld & Nicolson, 1971); Emmanuel Le Roi Ladurie, *Montaillou*, trans. Barbara Bray (New York: G. Braziller, 1978); Carlo Ginzburg, *The Cheese and the Worms*, trans. John and Anne Tedeschi (Baltimore: Johns Hopkins University Press, 1980); Robert Darnton, *The Great Cat Massacre* (New York: Vintage, 1984); Caroline Bynum, *Holy Feast and Holy Fast: The Religious Significance of Food to Medieval Women* (Berkeley: University of California Press, 1987); David Sabean, *Power in the Blood: Popular Culture and Village Discourse in Early Modern Germany* (Cambridge: Cambridge University Press, 1984); William Sewell, *Work and Revolution in France* (Cambridge: Cambridge University Press, 1981); Lynn Hunt, *Politics, Culture, and Class in the French Revolution* (Berkeley: University of California Press, 1984).

12. E. E. Evans-Pritchard, "Social Anthropology: Past and Present," in *Social Anthropology and Other Essays* (New York: The Free Press of Glencoe, 1963, c1962).

13. Louis Dumont, *Homo Hierarchicus: The Caste System and Its Implications* (Chicago: University of Chicago Press, 1980). See also M. Marriott, ed., *India Through Hindu Categories* (New Delhi: n.p., 1990), and Marriott and Inden, "Caste Systems," *Encyclopedia Britannica* (Chicago, 1974).

14. James Clifford, *The Predicament of Culture* (Cambridge, Mass.: Harvard University Press, 1988).

15. See James Clifford and George Marcus, *Writing Culture: The Poetics and Politics of Ethnography* (Berkeley: University of California Press, 1986). Others thought of course that the writing culture folks had not gone far enough, concerned as they were with the problem of the modernist author, rather than the surrealist possibilities and dimensions of anthropological writing and representation. See, for example, Michael Taussig, *The Magic of the State* (New York: Routledge, 1997).

16. See "Reading Culture: Anthropology and the Textualization of India," in *Culture/Contexture: Explorations in Anthropology and Literary Study*, ed. E. V. Daniel and J. M. Peck (Berkeley: University of California Press, 1995).

17. See Eric Wolf, *Europe and the People without History* (Berkeley: University of California Press, 1982).

18. Prakash, "Writing Post-Orientalist Histories of the Third World: Perspectives from Indian Historiography," *Comparative Studies in Society and History* 32 (April 1990), p. 384.

19. Here echoing the suggestions of Partha Chatterjee in his provocative book, *Nationalist Thought and the Colonial World: A Derivative Discourse?* (London: Zed Books, 1986).

20. David Washbrook and Rosalind O'Hanlon, "After Orientalism: Culture, Criticism, and Politics in the Third World," *Comparative Studies in Society and History* 34 (January 1992). For example, they said that Prakash's interest in Derrida, whose positions they found disabling and hardly emancipatory, was politically self-serving, his

endorsement of Said contradictory, his approval of Subaltern Studies history puzzling, and his praise of American-based historical anthropology revealing, all because he focused on the relationship between culture and power only to obscure and conceal questions concerning class and capital.

21. Arif Dirlik, "The Postcolonial Aura: Third World Criticism in the Age of Global Capitalism," *Critical Inquiry* 20 (Winter 1994).

22. Sumit Sarkar, *Writing Social History* (New Delhi: Oxford University Press, 1997).

23. Neil Lazarus, *Nationalism and Cultural Practice in the Postcolonial World* (New York, Cambridge: Cambridge University Press, 1999).

24. H. D. Harootunian, "Postcoloniality's unconscious/area studies' desire," *Postcolonial Studies* 2:2 (1999): 127–47.

25. Aijaz Ahmad, *In Theory* (London: Verso, 1992).

26. Ibid., p. 14. Ahmad makes this pronouncement in connection with my own work, suggesting that my use of Foucault in my book, and my opening invocation of the fact that Marx wrote about India through the same fundamental Orientalist lens as Weber and Dumont, was intended to dismiss Marx, and Marxist concerns altogether. I must confess that I hardly thought my book an exercise in right-wing politics; debates about Foucault and Marx aside, this kind of polemic is slanderous.

27. Dirlik, "The Postcolonial Aura," pp. 346–47.

28. "Postcolonial intellectuals in their First World institutional location are ensconced in positions of power not only vis-à-vis the 'native' intellectuals back at home but also vis-à-vis their First World neighbors here. My neighbors in Farmville, Virginia, are no match in power for the highly paid, highly prestigious postcolonial intellectuals at Columbia, Princeton, or Duke." Dirlik, "The Postcolonial Aura," p. 343.

29. Harootunian, "Postcoloniality's unconscious/area studies' desire," p. 141. Given his argument, this implies, among other things, that postcolonial studies has benefitted from enormous state and foundation investment. Thus the putatively high salaries of a few academic stars stand in for the millions of dollars of support for area studies; in this context, is it irrelevant that the stars in question are from the "third world?"

30. Harootunian, "Postcoloniality's unconscious/area studies' desire," p. 131.

31. Ibid., p. 139.

32. Ibid., p. 130.

33. Ibid., p. 145.

34. Partha Chatterjee, *The Nation and Its Fragments: Colonial and Postcolonial Histories* (Princeton: Princeton University Press, 1993).

35. Singer, *When a Great Tradition Modernizes* (Chicago: University of Chicago Press, 1972), p. 3.

36. E. R. Leach, *The British Journal of Sociology* XIV: 4 (December 1963): 377–78.

37. M. N. Srinivas, *Social Change in Modern India* (Berkeley: University of California Press, 1973). He chose not to raise issues around the difficulties of proper sociological analysis in the face of what was usually massive ignorance about language, history, and culture, let alone the fact that this question had never been posed to Weber, Durkheim, or other major Western sociologists.

38. Srinivas, *Social Change in Modern India*, p. 152.

39. See S. V. Ketkar, *History of Caste in India: Evidence of the Laws of Manu on the Social Condition in India During the Third Century A.D., Interpreted and Examined, with an Appendix on Radical Defects of Ethnology* (1909; reprint, Jaipur: n.p., 1979).

40. See Marshall Sahlins, *Islands of History*; Gananath Obeyesekere, *The Apotheosis of Captain Cook: European Mythmaking in the Pacific* (Princeton: Princeton Univeristy Press, 1992); Marshall Sahlins, *How "Natives" Think: About Captain Cook, For Example* (Chicago: University of Chicago Press, 1995).

41. Sahlins, *How "Natives" Think*, p. 5.

42. Ibid., pp. 5 and 9.

43. Indeed, while Prakash did not claim that he stood in the place of the Bengali babu, he did make clear the resonance of the contemporary attack with earlier rhetorics of colonialist dismissal. See his "Can the Subaltern Ride? A Reply to Washbrook and O'Hanlon," *Comparative Studies in Society and History*, 1992.

44. See Walter Mignolo, *The Darker Side of the Renaissance* (Ann Arbor: University of Michigan Press, 1995).

45. I am referring to my forthcoming book, *Castes of Mind: Colonialism and the Making of Modern India.*

46. For example, see Ashis Nandy, "The Politics of Secularism," *Mirrors of Violence*, ed. Veena Das (Delhi: Oxford University Press, 1992). Colonial studies, postmodern criticism, and old anthropological representations of Indian civilization become aligned and even mutually sustaining in ways that appear at first view uncanny in the extreme, especially perhaps given their simultaneously psychoanalytic registers and their political blindnesses.

47. Indeed, the secular state in India directly inherited both ideas of secularism and constitutional mandates concerning the protection of minorities from the colonial state, and even the most utopian visions have been compromised by the colonial past. In an even more general and pervasive sense, the emergence of a self-evident and now nearly universal idea (at least in the abstract) of the reality of some form of "pre-modern" tradition may be the most extraordinary bequest of colonial modernity for the postcolonial world. While some of the worries of postcolonial critics are very real indeed, the causes for worry are deeply implicated in the very contradictions of colonial history, to which the postcolonial theorists in question direct persistent attention. The ethical and political issues are not resolved by simple resort to reflexive criticism of one's "class-position in global capitalism," nor by appeals to universal (read metropolitan) reason, whether Marxist or conservative, culturalist or materialist. The predicament is precisely a postcolonial predicament: modernity was born of the colonial encounter.

48. Although I do not in fact agree with all that Prakash writes in his "reply," as I am far more skeptical of the contributions of poststructuralist thought than he is (at least in this particular exchange), I endorse his gesture toward ambivalence, for the way it allows one both to emphasize the discipline of context, and the geopolitical implications of most efforts to insist on universals.

49. For a thoughtful and critical consideration of the ethical status of postcolonial criticism, see David Scott, *Refashioning Futures: Criticism after Postcoloniality* (Princeton: Princeton University Press, 1999). Scott begins his work by taking for granted that the "antifoundationalist claim that the philosophical anthropologies that have sought to provide criticism with a Final Ground in relation to which its purposes

are to be secured and its appeals guaranteed are in fact no more than local (European) stories backed up by the power to authorize what counts as truth and what does not."(4) But he too worries about the loss of the political ground of critique, suggesting that the "anti-essentialists show themselves unable to put away or suppress their own desire for mastery, for certainty, for the command of an essential meaning." His book is a sustained reflection on the problem space posed by postcolonial criticism in relation to some specific conditions raised by postcolonial politics.

CHAPTER 14

Structure, Contingency, and Choice: A Comparison of Trends and Tendencies in Political Science

David E. Apter

"Then" and "Now"—An Overview of the Field[1]

In this essay I want to examine certain changes in political science by tracing their relation to three major emphases. The first is *structural*. In the study of politics, the first structural form of analysis was constitutionalism: constitutions were analyzed according to the different ways they awarded and distribute power(s), established boundaries around social life, and represented publicly approved principles. These criteria were then used to establish and compare taxonomies of regimes and political systems, and the principles they instituted. The extent to which structure actually configures, that is, establishes limits on or to behavior is, of course, a matter of considerable debate. Which suggests the importance of a second emphasis in political analysis: *choice*, both individual and collective. As a focus in political analysis, it assumes a greater emphasis on experience, empirical events, and rationality. No matter what the configuring system in place, it provides analysis of the opportunities which affect, change, and indeed, determine structure.[2] Structure then is subject to contingencies of choice and choosing which, as phenomena in themselves, represent, as Gellner puts it, "a complex symbiosis of conceptual styles."[3] The third emphasis is *behavioral*. It analyzes the actions of individual actors, less for their choices than for their motives, perceptions, commitments, belief systems, and ideologies which it takes to be the factors that influence, if not determine, political activity.[4] Behavior suggests that the interplay between individual predispositions and political structures be studied in terms of socialization, performance, institutionalization, and the internalization of values and beliefs.

What these three tendencies suggest is that no structure is fixed or permanent, that choice is always inter-subjective, and no behavior is random. The differences lie in how the first elevates structure over contingency, the third elevates contingency over structure, and choice—particularly in the forms of game and rational choice theory—lies somewhere in between.[5]

Obviously any selection will vary with purposes. No claims are made to judicious equity. By phrasing this discussion in terms of structure, choice, and behavior we in effect elevate certain analytical and comparative emphases over others, tempered by a sense of how historically the field of political science has evolved. The three approaches remain central to political science, despite changes in meaning, interpretation, and theoretical emphases. Common to all of them, especially in the United States, is the focus on democracy and the state, to which all other problems are subordinate. This focus helps to explain the continuing preoccupation with the configuring capacity of the state, particularly as embodied in institutions which distribute and exercise power, and public political action which is often in tension with prescribed limits. Democracy serves as the basis of comparison between different constitutional forms; authority, power, institutions, and political action constitute the central and ongoing concerns of political science. Of the particular approaches selected here, institutionalism was and remains the fundamental focus, if not the primary subject, of politics and political analysis. Pluralism has been hospitable to a variety of methodological and theoretical approaches.[6] Structuralism is included because it became a framework for interdisciplinary case materials, especially those directed at social implications of developmental changes. Behavioralism, and its key components, political psychology, and political sociology (not to speak of its strong methodological emphasis, although perhaps not given the distinct attention it deserves, will be reviewed in part because they came to represent a revolution of sorts against the more formal-legal aspects of institutionalism. And the study of political economy has perhaps become the most widely accepted way to explain most forms of political activity.[7]

For practical purposes, this essay will take a half century as its time frame. Two major analytical trends stand out sharply. One is the revival of political philosophy, which has redefined the moral discourse of political science. The other is rational choice theory which restores a certain intellectual order on the chaos of events. These in turn open one possible future tendency that I will discuss only very briefly in the conclusion: a form of theory emphasizing discourse, with a focus on communicative action, how people interpret events and by so doing create other forms of power, not least symbolic capital.[8] This last attempts to account for how people talk themselves into action through interpretation. It is an approach which, in effect, configures contingency and by so doing provides a context for the analysis of choice.

Disputes about and changes in approaches, theories, and methods are mostly decided by practical considerations rather than academic rivalries and ideological preferences. Those that stand are generally speaking, the ones which prove the most useful in making sense of actual conditions of political life. In the last half century, extraordinary changes have taken place, some of which had to force their way into the consciousness and corpus of what was then the conventional practice of political science. These include problems of development, decolonization, nationalism, populism, the Cold War, not to speak of changes in administration and politics in terms of the extraordinary varieties of power outside the normal sphere of political understanding. These changes led to a period of often bitter conflicts within political science departments. "Institutionalists" were pitted against "behaviorists," the latter widely regarded by the former as subverting the field. Today the passions and internal politics of the field have long cooled and the institutionalists are returning to prominence. Behaviorism, or what Heinz Eulau called "the behavioral persuasion," can be said to have so penetrated the field, both in its emphasis on quantitative method and its reliance on political psychology,[9] that as a term it has lost its relevance. One lesson is clear: if social science is to mean anything at all as science, it should be sensitive to problems ahead, whether on the basis of a projective logic or empirical probabilities.[10]

This was the predicament facing the institutional approach of the 1950s such that in the years that followed this preeminent position suffered considerable erosion. It took some time for scholars to realize that downgrading it excessively left something of a hole at the center of the discipline—one eventually to be filled by so called neo-institutionalist approaches. In the interim, the focus of the field shifted and new topics became relevant. Political scientists "borrowed" ideas from other disciplines,[11] for example, they tried to emulate science by plundering biology, physics, and mechanics, mining them for suitable metaphors. The more they did so, the more impatient they became with traditional philosophical reflections and moral teleologies. Concepts like evolution, development, system, structure, model, feedback, vectors, and equilibrium became a significant part of the political science vocabulary rather than social contract, or the rule of law.[12]

There was a similar innovation in techniques. Although fear of intellectual thinness accounted for at least some of the resistance to quantitative methods, few objected to applied statistics as an adjunct to the main lines of inquiry. As the range of subjects amenable to such analysis enlarged, it sometimes appeared as if methods were becoming the basis for research design rather than the questions to which such methods were put. Nor have concerns over this matter disappeared. It remains a matter of debate whether or not political science should be methods- or problems-driven. Things have instead become more complex with the quickened pace of methodological innovation. New quantitative methods have altered the style, character, and nature of research. What was formerly an activity for individual scholars has become more a matter of collaborative if not team research. With such developments has gone a remarkable expansion of facilities, centers, institutes, programs, and other such venues. As these have increased, so too the discipline has become fragmented. Groups form around different methodological techniques, the more robust of these having their own journals, which today have proliferated to include virtually every sub-speciality. Nor is this situation likely to change;

new possibilities are offered by the digital future with as yet unknown effects on the way research will be conducted.

Indeed, one might say that political science has broadened its scope only to become more differentiated according to sub-specialities, a situation which—in the name of precision—encourages intellectual sterility.[13] To a surprising extent, the stuff of daily politics and power has become the property of semi-academic journals and intellectual periodicals.[14] Only the return to "roots" in the form of neo-institutionalism and the virtual rebirth of political philosophy (as philosophy rather than a history of ideas), save this situation from being worse than it is. Equally important has been the extension of liberal political economy into politics which follows the same logic as the rationalist enlightenment model. Paradoxically enough, this model is the basis of both Marxism and modern rational choice theory.[15]

INSTITUTIONALISM AS AN ORIGINAL POSITION

The main components of institutionalism were drawn from history, philosophy, political philosophy, law, and economics. Their singularly coherent synthesis constituted a frame for political ideas, moral sensibilities, and institutions. It invoked an evolutionary history of the instruments and mechanisms of the state; stages of this evolution were defined by property and status relations, the changing balance and role of natural law and positive law, and both were embodied in the progressive development of political ideas from corporation to enlightenment. In England, these took the form of liberal ideals of freedom and accountability; on the continent they more often took a Kantian turn in which the refinement of moral sensibilities found their way into an evolution of political institutions.[16] Institutionalism in this sense belongs in part to a larger *Staatslehre* tradition and became the dominant approach to political science before the Second World War in Europe as well as the United States.[17]

It was this synthesis which began to fray in the fifties and sixties when history was rejected in favor of structure, political philosophy marginalized in favor of science,[18] while law gave way to culture, norms, and values. Economics shifted from concern with business cycles to growth and development. Interest in political philosophers declined in favor of the philosophy of science or with its various systems of assumptions. Hypotheses were now subjected to "scientific" tests (based on validity and falsifiability), and this affected methodological strategies of research. Not that the study of institutions disappeared entirely: institutionalism remained a central focus for research, analysis, and teaching. But it found its rich analytical and historical pedigree—one by no means American in origin, deriving as it did from French and German continental traditions as well as English Common Law—displaced.

Also lost to this new scientific fervor was its view of democracy as the result of an emergent historical teleology. In the beginning were the Greek polities and such ancestral figures as Plato and Aristotle credited with the creation of the discourse of politics. Roman law, then Salic Law were incorporated in an ecclesiastical framework, evolving through medieval corporations to conciliarism—the critical point of transition to secular law and legislative government. Since each stage of the transition was accompanied by confrontation and conflict, certain kinds of legitimizing theories—social contract is one example—became essential and loomed large in the jurisprudential constitutional corpus (Hobbes, Locke, Mill, in political philosophy; Bracton, Blackstone, Main, Maitland, Vinogradoff, and Kelsen in jurisprudence; Gierke, Dicey, Barker, and Austen in English institutional analysis; Duguit, Renard, and Hauriou, in French institutionalism, to name only a few).[19] Sharing two different intellectual traditions, one deriving from political philosophy and the other from jurisprudence, the original institutionalist emphasis was on the evolution of relationships between political principles and the legal forms and instrumentalities of power and political accountability using theories of contract, conciliarism, corporations, and parliamentary institutions.[20]

In its American incarnation, institutionalism spoke less of the state than the government. It had a practical bent and an unending project: how best to realize, improve, and enrich democracy. Democracy was, as indeed it remains, the default system; all other types are judged deviant cases or lost opportunities.[21]

With its emphasis on the unique properties of democracy, American institutionalism defined its system aspects as a balance of principles embodied in institutions that worked instrumentally to realize them. In these terms, libertarian principles establish the basic rules of the game while leaving ends open; rules and laws guaranteeing fundamental rights and the institutional forms which effectuate them enable choice, itself a continuous pursuit of changing ends. Some sustained level of reasonable political performance by incumbents in office is required, as is sufficient self-restraint on the part of the citizenry in keeping with a government of laws rather than of men and women. The result represents a self-rectifying political system which depends on and reinforces higher and prior rights.[22]

Such a system contains all the ingredients for an equilibrium theory, one in which there is a perpetual tension, and balance, between liberty and efficiency. This is manifest in the opposition between those favoring libertarian and equity formulas. Such "liberal" and "radical" tendencies can, of course, appear in many different programmatic guises and doctrinal alternatives, examples of which can be found in practical party competition which tends to divide between efficiency versus equity claims no matter how such issues are phrased. Public preferences are understood to be shaped as much by public discourse as by government policies and more formal institutions. So too individual choice and discretion play off against public responsibility and collective obligation.[23] Among the virtues of such an approach to political analysis, besides its high degree of coherence, is a heavy emphasis on the role of principles and of institutions themselves, and a system based on the mutual responsiveness of rulers and ruled. But its "system" also suffered from ethnocentrism and a corresponding elitism. Democracy, so institutionalism seemed to say, was not for everyone—at least not yet.[24]

Thus it is not surprising that, in its view, the instruments of democracy were limited to presidential or parliamentary, unitary or federal alternatives. Democracy was understood to be a self-limiting method of rule and jurisdictionally mimetic. Just as each actual democracy was required to recapitulate the broad historical and analytical evolution of rights, representation, and accountability, so too it had to replicate in lower organs of state and local government those more ramified forms that obtained at the national levels. Furthermore, this notion of democracy in its modern form was inextricably linked with economic growth. Development was the evolutionary process that would accompany the evolution of constitutionalism. Capitalism was crucial to democracy because opposing equity claims and doctrinal solutions—especially those emerging in the nineteenth century calling for greater re-distributive justice—needed to be reconciled according to some rough approximation of public demand.[25] With its premise and promise of unlimited growth, capitalism offered the prospect of re-distributive rather than retributive justice, the more disadvantaged making gains without the more advantaged incurring losses.[26]

But, as suggested above, institutionalism had all the disadvantages of its advantages. It ignored entire regions of the world. After the Second World War, the emphasis of development could not be restricted to Western reconstruction, but had to be expanded to the moral debts incurred by the West toward other parts of the world, chiefly the then colonial territories. The notion of "subject" people began to lose its rationale. Political independence and racial equality became linked, their solidarity manifesting itself in various pan-African, pan-Asian movements as well as the internationalization of nationalism as a unifying force. This latter not only signaled the end of empire but the opening of a belief that the "third" world would now be a source for new ideas as well as economic vitality. This excitement could not help but be infectious; to undertake fieldwork in such a political climate was morally exciting. The frontiers of research expanded as hitherto closed or exotic parts of the world became accessible. A new worthiness was attributed to research in and of itself, as well as to the establishment of necessary conditions which could best render development and democracy mutually compatible and reinforcing.[27] New opportunities and expectations arose that were unparalleled in the field, but those opportunities took political scientists far beyond the confines of the more traditional corpus of political science. The quality of the configuring powers of political systems in underdeveloped and former colonial countries—where development and economic growth became more urgent concerns than democracy and its future possibilities, and where there were newly organized political forces, often militant, nationalist, and radical—posed policy questions that could not be theoretically ignored. As the concept of development as an extension of economic principles now became relevant, the significance of cultural differences became so obvious that economists began to concern themselves with noneconomic factors relevant to economic growth.[28]

In addition to such concerns a host of other questions became central to the study of politics, most of them involving situations of real urgency. What were the best political solutions to be applied to an occupied and defeated Japan, a divided Germany, and prostrate Italy? How to comprehend the explosive and murderous mass killings that accompanied partition in India and Pakistan? How would Burmese independence fare under a "socialist" constitution? How would militant and radical regimes compare with countries following more conventional political and economic routes? What would be the impact of nationalist discontent in colonial territories in Asia and Africa and elsewhere and what institutional variations would be required to make democracy work in the absence of normal supportive social and societal factors? On such matters institutionalism had little to suggest about appropriate and inappropriate relationships between Western and non-Western political forms, the role of tradition in social and political life, especially in their juxtaposition within the framework of developmental growth.[29] Moreover, in situation after situation, those who had been ruled, administered, and controlled from afar, were gaining agency. More and more they were able to act for themselves, taking initiatives many of which the West did not approve. Actions spoke louder than systems. Not only did political leaders in the West have to learn how to respond in terms not always their own, but forms of government and ideologies hostile or alien to those favored both by politicians and to the principles embodied in institutional approaches to government, required alternative approaches. While accepting the eventual universality of parliamentary institutions and democratic practices, the fundamental question was whether such institutions and practices could serve as appropriate vehicles for both devolution and democracy and whether, by hastening the end of empire and the acquisition of national independence, they could be made to work instrumentally.[30] The new emphasis on development led to what might be called a sociological moment, wherein political science became more hospitable to psychological, sociological, and anthropological theories and concerns.[31]

The protagonists of the "old" institutionalism resisted amendments in part out of fear that by so doing the moral basis of democracy would be undermined: too much emphasis on public opinion, or how belief systems and ideologies were formed, or even on basic questions of economy and politics was thought to be detrimental to the civic purpose of political science.[32] But whatever the arguments, it soon became apparent that the gap between formal legal institutions and what happened on the ground was too great. Concern with descriptive trivia obscured underlying processes and actual behavior. Citizens exhibited irritating propensities to ignore, undermine, or overthrow democratic constitutions. Institutionalists had never been particularly interested in popular opinion, attributing insufficient importance to anti-democratic forms of populism. They did not attend to the ways and means by which parliamentary institutions could so easily be converted into parliamentary dictatorship. Worst of all, institutionalists were too often surprised by unanticipated events and circumstances and were unable to keep up intellectually with the multiplicity and speed of changes occurring in the world. Institutionalist explanations were so inadequate that, at best, one could conclude only that democracy worked when it worked and failed when it failed.

THE BEHAVIORAL REVOLUTION

The so-called behavioral revolution was a direct response, and intellectual challenge, to the narrowness of institutionalism. It was above all a product of ideas drawn from outside the discipline, such as psychoanalysis (Lasswell), the concern with voting and mass publics (Merriam), and administrative reform (White). A good deal of the pressure for change came from outside the academy altogether.[33] Behaviorism consisted mainly of two components: political sociology and political psychology. For the first time quantification was recognized as crucial to the science of political science, as were the organizational and motivational aspects of politics, voting, and coalition formation. As for its intellectual pedigree, while there were many diverse sources, among its more important and formative influences was the work of Graham Wallas and Arthur F. Bentley and their concerns with psychological and group politics. The group most associated with its development is the so-called "Chicago School" and such figures as Charles Merriam. Later influences would include V. O. Key, David Truman, and Earl Latham.

If the starting point for behaviorism was found in discrepancies between the presumed configuring power of institutions and how people actually conducted themselves, behaviorally minded political scientists concerned themselves not only with voting, attitude formation, socialization, value commitment, and change, but the relationship between different sources of political and social stimuli and public responses generally not least of all the role of the press and the impact of electoral campaigns. Theoretical inspiration came from psychological studies of motivation, perception, cooperation, and competition, much of it the result of small-scale group observation or survey work on public opinion. Many of its early studies were analyses of factory work and the conditions which made for improved productivity; much of it was stimulated by the analysis of the efficacy of wartime propaganda. Survey research and voting behavior became its most dominant modes. To behaviorists, "grand" theory was unwieldy at best and teleological at worst; in any case, it did not easily mesh with on-the-ground research.

• • •

POLITICAL psychology was critically important. Where prevailing social psychology differentiated class, political psychology broke down class into roles. Indeed, role became the most important operational concept in political psychology. Defined as a functionally specified position in a social system, where the latter was composed of role networks, role became crucial to personality formation, socialization, and political relationships.[34] Institutionalization, the incorporation within the individual of norms of performance and obligation, became more analytically important than institutions—as did interaction between roles in role networks. Here the influence of such diverse psychologists and psychoanalysts as Theodore Newcomb, Kurt Lewin, David C. Mclelland, Abram Kardiner, and Erik Erickson overlapped with anthropologists such as Ralph Linton, and political scientists like Robert Lane and Fred I. Greenstein.[35] The specific links between personality, role and role networks, behavior, influence, preferences, and social mobility, voting, political participation and nonparticipation, and ideological predispositions became the object of both experimental research in small groups, and more general survey analysis.[36]

Political sociology became important at the same time as political psychology. Its founding fathers might be said to have been Michels, Pareto, and Mosca.[37] Among its central concerns was the comparative analysis of social stratification, the ability of political democracy to facilitate social mobility. It combined developmental considerations with social consequences in terms of political implications. Posing differentiated gradients of class in opposition to more Marxist emphases, and resisting class cleavage approaches (as represented, for example, in the work of Barrington Moore[38]) mobility replaced class conflict as the dynamic factor, making possible the mediation between contending parties and opening up political hierarchies by means of multiple forms of access and power. One crucial instrument of such mediation is voting, and with it the variable shifts in public opinion and ideologies the consequences of which are measured in the interplay of coalitions, group formation, party organization, and their effects on policy. Using both historical comparisons of whole societies and as well available statistics based particularly on survey work, more original concerns with the United States and Europe progressively broadened to what was then called, somewhat hopefully, the "developing" world.[39]

But while political behaviorism (the field constituted by the combination of political psychology and political sociology)[40] was essentially interdisciplinary, it remained concerned primarily with American politics. And some argued that the empirical tools it developed—instruments from survey analysis to roll-call voting, the examination of legislative behavior, coalition formation, belief systems, and ideology—were merely raw empiricism designed to demonstrate the more evolved nature of social democracy when compared to communism.[41]

PLURALISM AS POLITICAL SCIENCE

If on the whole institutionalists resisted "behaviorism," pluralists incorporated it with traditional institutionalist approaches so successfully that it was not long before pluralism displaced institutionalism and virtually shaped a generation of political scientists occupying the middle ground between 1965 and 1980.[42] Pluralism did not only combine the institutional analysis of democracy, and the need for greater equity; pluralists were influenced in their empirical work by the behavioral emphasis on statistical and quantitative data. Shifting political emphasis away from formalist aspects of institutionalism to behavioral ones, it emphasized factors such as the role of interests, popular and public opinion, and changing social mobility. It also accepted the principles of a market model of the political system modified for political purposes but preserving rationality assumptions. Hence as pluralism evolved as a political system, it both sustained and transcended individual choice. Indeed, while pluralists tended to reject an equilibrium theory based on a neo-utilitarian calculus of costs and benefits, they accepted the principle of a political system that balanced public policy and leadership preferences, electoral systems serving as the critical instrument. So persuasive was this synthesis that pluralism provided the new focus for political analysis.

Like political behavior, which to a considerable extent it expropriated, pluralism was a peculiarly American concern, especially in its preoccupation with diversity, public differences, and their incorporation into a common polity. Perhaps its accomplishment was to argue the virtues of diversity. One important influence was Joseph Schumpeter's *Capitalism, Socialism and Democracy* which not only showed how social democracy might work in conjunction with socialism, but offered a non-Marxist alternative to how this might occur, thus opening the way for different political modalities favoring compensatory social and economic policies, and social democratic forms of welfare.[43] From its inception pluralism made explicit questions of the relations between equity and social democracy.[44]

If pluralist theory replaced institutionalism as the framework for the study of politics it did so felicitously. British and American political institutional history took on a quite different appearance when seen from the standpoint of behaviorism. For example, the political sociology component of the latter broke up conventional ideas of class and power rigidities embodied in older sociological theories of society, emphasizing instead the fluidity and mobility of American social life. But by emphasizing a group rather than individualistic approach to coalitional action, pluralists could see politics in terms of its diversity; indeed, this perspective on democracy (changing access by differential groups in the political process) provided a very different view of community politics than had prevailed, particularly in terms of its consequences for democratization. It was a view that gave an exceptionally defining role to political economy and rationality. The two constituted the basis for interest competition, itself the motiving element in pluralist politics.

By the same token, pluralism framed the political economy in terms of equity principles. It emphasized the importance of the latter systemically: without some agreed and plausible standard of equity, political democracy would not only be faulty but political order prejudiced. The central concern was how best to strengthen the institutions of democracy, in both systemic and empirical terms.[45] Dahl in particular established new rules and conditions for appropriate equity, while the political psychological dimension of pluralism (especially learning, beliefs, motivation, and socialization) was provided by scholars like Robert E. Lane, who were explicitly concerned with political participation and ideology.[46] Indeed, so effectively did pluralism combine political psychology, political sociology, political behavior, and institutionalism, around the problem of moral and distributional proportionalities that it became *the* American approach to democracy, at least for a time.

Perhaps the main problem with pluralism (and this includes polyarchy) is that it assumes as self-evidently reasonable a certain degree of political toleration, in the Lockean sense. That is, it starts from the assumption, common to economics, that since people are more alike than different in their basic wants and desires, similarities will outweigh differences as long as the political framework is accessible. Citizens will form multiple majorities which in turn favor compromise and tolerance; different identities and cultures could be incorporated because they offered diversity and therefore richness to the political culture. Not anticipated was the hardening of these identities into restrictive clienteles, or the rise of intolerance and prejudice which became the basis of single-issue politics, posing a challenge to any robust conception of the public good. Nor was pluralism prepared for the disaffiliation from the state that has occurred not only in the United States but particularly in so-called less developed societies. Moreover, pluralism, especially when confronted with problems like massive immigration, was never able to deal with the problem of how tolerant to be of intolerance nor with the ways in which cultural "tipping" arouses kinds of social antagonism which intensify political and social conflict. In other words, insofar as pluralism implied a prior assimilationism, it could not account for groups that wished to preserve their differences.

SYSTEMS ANALYSIS AND STRUCTURALISM

Pluralism introduced a new realism into the study of politics without thereby losing the moral purposefulness of democracy. But in the end, it lacked a tightly integrated general "systemic" framework. That was left to what has been called "general systems theory."

General systems theory emphasized certain properties of all systems, from micro-biological organisms to galaxies. It was inspired by such figures as Ludwig von Bertalanffy, Anatol Rappaport, and others and from fields as different as mathematics, physics, engineering, and organizational behavior.[47] Where pluralism and behaviorism led to refinements in the technique of quantitative methods, general systems analysis developed logical and comprehensive models which in effect became meta-theories that preferred deductive forms of logical propositions.[48] They thus removed politics from the system. Systems theorists took the properties of empirical systems and analyzed their components into types according to certain salient properties or systems problems such as adaptation, innovation, and self-maintenance. One strand of systems theory then treated the system according to a mechanistic metaphor derived from engineering, emphasizing feedback and equilibrating mechanisms; cybernetics was its most celebrated form.[49] The other major form of general systems theory was a derivative of functionalism. Although its model originated in anthropology and sociology, it uses "requisite" or system maintenance approaches derived from biological models.[50] While this approach was very different from the input-output approach of the mechanical model, both understood system maintenance as a form of equilibrium. As it evolved, the systems approach to functionalism came to focus on a structural and closed network of variables using "viability" tests.[51]

General systems analysis stimulated a good deal of discussion about the nature of science in relation to social science, the evolution of classificatory into comparative and quantitative concepts, the relationship between technical terms, concept formation, and empirical referents. It was strongly influenced by various efforts to develop a theory of unified science which combined philosophical with empirical analysis, and the physical and natural sciences with the social sciences.[52]

The functionalist approach lent itself to comparisons of developmental changes in whole societies in relation to developmental change, even though it had a half-life in the social sciences and little direct impact on the study of politics. As developed in particular by Malinowski, it was recognized as useful for comparative theories, particularly for examining the impact of "modernism." It was also employed by anthropologists studying so-called primitive societies who emphasized culture, ritual, belief, and their interpretive significance.[53] From Radcliffe Brown (under the influence of Durkheim), it elaborated a science of society modeled after the study of living organisms.[54] On this basis, formal functional attributes were found common to all communities in a single period of time—as they might be to all organisms of a similar type—no matter the structural differences or the ways those structures were performed. This familiarization of functions allowed observers to identify functional equivalents in the midst of varied practices, and facilitated the comprehension and comparison of unfamiliar societies.

It was to systematize these attributes even further that functionalism was elaborated and indeed changed almost beyond recognition by Talcott Parsons, his associates, and collaborators in the Social Relations Department at Harvard, who developed it in the form of "structural-functionalism."[55] Structural-functionalism remained quite limited in terms of application in empirical work, but had great influence in debates over the proper study of social science. In general it might be said that in its modified form, functionalism provided a discourse for discussing not only comparative categories but in effect tried to become a discipline in and of itself.[56] Its political focus was on how to manage societal changes, functionally identified as significant, by weakly legitimized states using parliamentary institutions as frameworks for authoritarian or one-party rule. Oddly enough it was in these terms that the very conventionality of political science became its advantage. For, wedded to the more unconventional approach of structural-functionalism, it afforded an interesting framework for doing fieldwork and empirical comparative analysis.[57] Like its predecessor, structural-functionalism was particularly useful for the analysis of the "systems problems" development and modernization posed for state formation, governance, and the future prospects of democracy. This, for example, was the underlying theme of *Old Societies and New States*, a book edited by Clifford Geertz in 1963, a good representative of the interdisciplinary work going on at the time.[58]

It also brought into play questions of theory qua theory: what were the rules of the game, specifically in terms of research and the language of norms?[59] It attempted to bring societal and state components together systemically rather than heuristically or eclectically.[60] To this end, it purported to be as scientific with respect to social life as biology was to human life—indeed, it stressed the importance of scientific neutrality.[61]

But for all that it put the language of norms into question, structural-functionalism had a fairly normative account of economic development: it argued that the more appropriate government action promoted "modernized" role sets, the greater the opportunities for growth; the more growth, the greater the spread of functional roles and the opportunities for appropriate role performance. In the long run then, because rather than in spite of greater diversity resulting from economic differentiation, societies all over the world would come to look structurally more like each other—in terms of roles and role networks, if not classes. Normatively, the dominant values and beliefs of Western societies—particularly those associated with secularism and rationality—would come to predominant over more provincial ones; behaviorally, through schools and work places, such norms would be learned and internalized. Individuals would learn to perform in new roles germane to and creating opportunities for more modernization and economic growth. This integrative tendency would not only establish order, it would enhance the societal conditions for development—and possibly democracy as well.[62]

Therefore, functionalists focused on how best to control deviant behavior, measured in terms of discrepancies in role performance. Solutions were sought for how to deal structurally (and remedially) with groups and individuals who might dilute the power of the collectivity, or the establishment of new political orders.[63] Indeed, it is in his focus on such threats to power that Parson's concern with politics can be distinguished. For him, political power is "relational" and integrative.[64] It was perhaps a measure of Talcott Parson's sociological imagination that he believed he could synthesize such complex processes within a single theoretical embrace, taking a diagnostic view of dysfunctionalities the removal of which would lead to greater functional integration. He thought he could locate the critical factors that allowed for the maintenance and adaptation of modern societies undergoing developmental change through his extraordinarily ambitious efforts to incorporate and abstract components drawn from all fields of the social sciences, plundering the full range of available theory.[65]

The application of Parsonian functionalism, albeit in very adaptive ways, took several different forms. One general approach was that of case studies such as Robert Bellah's *Tokugawa Religion*.[66] Another was my own *The Politics of Modernization*.[67] Perhaps the most concerted effort was that of Gabriel Almond and his associates in the Comparative Politics Sub-Committee of the Social Science Research Council, which considerably influenced the way in which comparative politics and contemporary theories could be brought together. Almond combined pluralism with a heuristic form of functionalism— restructured in the form of input-output analysis similar to that used by general system theorists (David Easton in particular)—borrowing certain Parsonian ideas as well as conventional institutional categories.[68] The deliberations of the Committee also provided problematic and analytical criteria for evaluating particular development problems which contributed to larger debates about the nature of comparison and the demands of research. Perhaps the classic early study of democracy and pluralism was Gabriel Almond and Sidney Verba's *The Civic Culture*,[69] but there were many others who took up the question of political culture and values.[70]

Although heuristic functionalism gained considerable momentum in political science, like structural functionalism more generally it began to lose its relevance for research. Attacks on functionalism came from within and without. Among the more significant challenges from within and as a critique was that of Harold Garfinkle (a former Parsons student), and his theories of ethnomethodology. From without it was attacked by those who preferred conflict to equilibrium theory, as for example Ralf Dahrendorf.[71] Perhaps the final indignity: even the term structuralism became expropriated by French and continental versions, from the linguistically oriented concern of Levi-Strauss and his emphasis on the relationship between kinship, language, myth, and rationality, the philosophical Marxism of Althusser with its condemnation of bourgeois science as ideology, and the inversionary theories of Foucault which turned social science into another form of hegemony. It was regarded by a radical generation as conservative if not reactionary, not least because, in emphasizing role rather than class, stratification rather than equality, and integration rather than conflict, it paid little attention to real-life activities.[72] At best one could claim that as a framework for interdisciplinary and comparative theory, it led to lively discussions about scientific method in the social sciences, particularly positivism, and other comparisons based on paradigmatic change.[73] But even in these terms it was analytically unwieldy and difficult to apply in empirical work. Above all it became politically vulnerable—indeed, the reaction to it may have been more important than the thing itself.[74]

THE RADICAL INTERLUDE

What can be called the radical interlude had a moral moment. It never became a fully fledged alternative system of political analysis, and had far less impact on political science than it did on sociology, among other fields. But for a time it exerted considerable influence on the kinds of questions that could be examined and on how the subject of politics should be taught. Its moral claim lay in rubbing political scientists' noses in problems of race, poverty, domination, hegemony, colonialism, and imperialism. It attacked virtually all that represented "bourgeois" social science, including Parsons and his "school," while ridiculing the special subjects of pluralism—socialization, political learning, and adaptation—as well as the multiple forms of stratification and role favored by social and political scientists. Radicalism went beyond ordinary conflict theory and attacked all forms of equilibrium analysis and integrative emphases, on grounds of the failure of democratic political systems to recognize class dynamics and their source in capitalist market systems.[75] Structuralism and behaviorism were excoriated for their role in the American hegemonic "project." Doubt was cast on the "disinterested" nature of social science as science and the neutrality of the outside observer; these were said to be methods for the development of false consciousness. It considered political science an ideology favoring establishment elites, their institutions, and the capitalism with which establishment scholars were by definition complicit. It attacked liberal political economy for being equilibrium (and therefore status quo) oriented. Above all, liberal developmental dynamics were judged to be wrong.

Despite the diversity of radical approaches, the common denominator of radical political economy was its critique of the capitalist state and its affirmation of some kind of socialism. Its logic shared certain characteristics with systems theory: it tended to be monopolistic in that it constituted a highly generalized system of thought that was configurational and totalizing.[76] But in contrast to general systems theories, Marxism supplied independent variables:

socially and politically in terms of class struggle; economically in the contradictions between capitalist modes of production and relations of production; and philosophically in a unilinear dialectical logic.

It is very difficult to put the diverse and often warring offshoots of this period under one umbrella. There were of course several different radical revivals ranging from classical Marxism to a variety of offshoots, neo-Marxism, dependency theory, and in a very different vein, the Frankfurt School and critical theory. There were several forms of Marxism pure as well as Marxism adapted. Some traced the pedigree to Marx himself, others to Hegel, a few to Alexandre Kojève and Alexandre Koyré and the College of Sociology, and others to the Frankfurt School not least of all Walter Benjamin.[77] The revival took many forms and expressions. Some combined Marxism with Freudianism and language theory to create a post-Freudian framework for political as well as other forms of analysis (Lacan). Virtually every field had its Marxists or neo-Marxists: history (E. P. Thompson, Eric Hobsbawm, Perry Anderson); literature (Williams, Jameson, Eagleton); linguistics (Chomsky); critical sociology (Goldmann, Bourdieu); inversionary discourse (Foucault); post-structuralism (Lyotard); deconstruction (Derrida); not to speak of political science itself (Benedict Anderson, Walter Rodney), all of whom influenced the radical study of politics.

In both the United States (where there was little Marxist tradition) and Britain (where Marxism was only one strand in a more general working-class radicalism), the rediscovery of Marxism seemed to strip away the political facade of democracy.[78] Not only Eric Hobsbawm and E. P. Thompson, but radical economists like Paul Baran and Andre Gundar Frank, political scientists like Gavin Kitching, Colin Leys, and Benedict Anderson, and sociologists like Immanuel Wallerstein gained in stature. All connected historical studies of capitalism and the hegemonic bourgeoisie to the spread of neo-imperialism, neo-colonialism, globalization, marginalization, and the role of the "negativized other" (Edward Said). The persuasiveness of their arguments, if momentary, left little space for institutionalism, behaviorism, pluralism, and structuralism. Instead, Neo-Marxism also came to include neo-dependency theory, and the work of Huber, Rueschemeyer and Stephens, Fernando Enrique Cardozo (in a much earlier incarnation), as well as concern with participatory democracy following the work of Pateman and others. Powerful sources for Marxist theory were found in philosophers and social philosophers, beginning perhaps with Sartre, but including Althusser, Lefevre, Poulantzas, Foucault, and Baudrilliard. Behind much of this were particular concrete New Left movements, some serious, some more rocambolesque. But the issues they raised were mostly serious enough: in the United states these included the civil rights movement and the Vietnam War; in France the Algerian war; and in Britain, the last dying gasp of leftist working-class trade unionism.

What can be called post-Marxism incorporated several meta-theories partic-ularly active around topics such as race, gender, and sexuality. When connected to psychoanalytical theories, it sponsored detailed neo-Marxist case studies of underdevelopment and dependency that attacked social and political problems from a very different perspective than that of conventional political economy (Cardozo, Kitching).[79] Less fortunately perhaps, most such ideas subscribed to notions of world system developmentalism that, if not unilinear, partook of those kinds of improving solutions that invoked higher stages and modalities of growth such as socialism (Wallerstein).[80] For Touraine, for example, it was new social actors who would lift the weight and oppressiveness of bourgeois education, arts, and social style.[81] For Bourdieu, one had to transform the *habi-tus*. For E. P. Thompson, the moral economy of capitalism was its fundamental fault. Perhaps the greatest effect of the period was that it enabled scholars from very different disciplines to intersect between literary, artistic, architectural, and theatrical discourses.[82] It created a new kind of intellectual arena—cultural studies—in which political analysis became common property of public intel-lectuals in general.[83] In this way it gave license to scholars in virtually every field to engage directly in political analysis.[84]

Such brief a description can hardly even begin to give justice to a movement which in the scope of its concerns and the diversity of those involved in it was international both in its protagonists and in its chosen subject matter. But while it would be a mistake to regard the undoubtedly lively radical interlude as a dominant one, it was nonetheless intellectually polarizing. There was, for ex-ample, an enormous difference between liberal and radical political economy. The Marxist understanding of capitalist contradictions led to a theory of social and political rupture, confrontation, and transformation; the liberal belief in market mechanisms led it to pursue the mediating effects of competition and rationality in a context of quantity, price, supply, and demand.

Radical theory, in its efforts to unmask bourgeois social and political science by showing how it had in effect "commodified" itself along with all other aspects of social life, created its own discrepancies. One could argue that ap-parent and negative consequences of development were the reason why social conditions eroded in the so-called underdeveloped parts of the world, but on closer inspection this appeared to happen in spite rather than because of capital-ist enterprise. Indeed, only by denying agency to local principals was it possi-ble to explain why government and state were part of the problem in both socialist and non-socialist systems. Even if democracies were mostly facades, the claim of capitalism's sole responsibility was, to say the least, an inadequate explanation for why none of the obvious solutions were particularly successful in socialist countries. Nor were radical "socialist" political regimes in various parts of the world, Africa, Asia, or Latin America any more immune to bureau-cratic authoritarianism and corruption than so-called capitalist ones. Marxism and neo-Marxist persuasions failed as configuring theories; they ignored agency, the actual exercise of power within countries supposedly victimized by capitalism.

What remains of the radical interlude falls to a considerable extent under the rubric of cultural studies which has considerable influence in various university departments but not political science. Still there lingers, not far under the surface, a nagging if residual radicalism, an echo of the critique resulting from the growing disparities between rich and poor, as well as from critical social issues such as gender politics, racial politics, and ethnicity with their implications for changing conventional social and political roles. Such residual radicalism manifests itself in social movements and confrontational politics whose issues and arenas have changed from transformational to protest politics in the context of globalization and the universalization (and triumphalism) of market principles, a concern of those studying social movements as in the work of Tarrow, Tilly, McAdam, and Apter.[85]

POLITICAL ECONOMY AND THE STATE

Liberal political economy has, in contrast, prospered, particularly after the demise of socialism. One could argue that it has become universalized in an equilibrium model of the political system, a model always at least implicit in institutionalist interpretations of democracy. In this model, choice is the central problematic, based on market principles and applied to a dual market (economic and political). Each market articulates and ranks in schedules wants, needs, and preferences; the first caters to consumers, the second to citizens. The first establishes its ranking in terms of money, the second in terms of votes. The economic market, based as it is on private ownership of the means of production, dilutes political power; the political market, based on public equity preferences, rectifies inequities resulting from the first. The mutual penetration of the two markets sustains equilibrium. The liberal market model underlies the "third way" proposed by Anthony Giddens and is more or less favored in a pro-social democratic Europe which increasingly deals only tangentially with equality, while remaining primarily concerned with the dynamics of marketization and how to maximize the flow of innovative enterprise. Of course the political economy literature on such subjects is enormous. Liberal and market approaches have effectively pushed aside the more specifically socialist treatments of democracy, such as the work of, for example, Ralph Miliband or in a different vein, Claus Offe, both of whom favor social democratic over social welfare and social solutions.[86]

Of course, political economy by no means names a single approach but covers several very different lines of inquiry. One, Weberian in origin but not in method, works on what is called political culture; it emphasizes the connection between values, culture, economic growth, and democratization.[87] Many have used this focus for comparative studies, the political economy literature on such subjects is enormous.[88] This kind of study has effectively pushed aside the more specifically socialist treatments of democracy.[89] Speaking broadly, what political economy approaches share is an analysis of how fluctuations in the overall economy can be differentiated in terms of their impacts on various groups, and how these influence political perceptions of interests. Over time its approaches have become more methodologically sophisticated. Its studies have served as the basis for theories about appropriate expenditures in relation to party and other forms of organization, monetary and fiscal policy, the money supply, and the effects of World Bank and IMF policies on developing countries.

At the same time there has been a virtual explosion of work linking political economy to institutional political analysis. In fact, in its original incarnation it was that part of economics considered to be "institutional economics." Lijphart, for example, who compares thirty-six different countries in terms of parliamentarian and consensus models perhaps most personifies the importance of institutional analysis which combines quantitative and statistical analysis with analytical judgments.[90] The comparative study of the international economy's effects on class and other interests—as found in the works of Cameron, Katznelson, Gourevitch, and Hall—and connections between nationalism, identity, elites, corporatism, and democratic state formation—the focus for the work of Schmitter, O'Donnell, Stepan, and Linz—remain central concerns.[91] Political economy remains central to case studies of both country and regional evolution, particularly to the European Community, whether in the framework of a modified Keynesianism or of more classically liberal market traditions.

Whatever else that can be said about political economy, it is neither abstract nor systemic. It tries to define interests, particularly self-interests, in terms of market models. The link between cause and effect, hypothesis and general propositions is based on statistical analysis and probabilities rather than the logical, mathematical, and deductive traditions of modern-day economics. These same traditions do however make themselves felt as the final trend in political science that I shall discuss here: rational choice theory. This last is also currently the dominant paradigm in the field.

POLITICAL PHILOSOPHY/RATIONAL CHOICE

One might think that these two subjects occupy diametrically opposite places in the spectrum of ideas and in many ways this is so. But, linked by political economy and the renewal of institutionalism, they join in what one might call a political hermeneutic circle. Because liberal political economy now also incorporates the political and social impact of developmentalism and globalization, tracking their political effects within the state itself has required greater knowledge about how political institutions work, thus stimulating a revival of institutionalism.[92] Depending on one's point of view, institutionalism has either been incorporated within the broader framework of political economy, or it has incorporated political economy.

Something similar has happened to political philosophy. Though at first glance political philosophy and political economy have almost nothing to do with one another, political economy—in part because of the Rawlsian revolution—has come to emphasize the importance of state welfare functions, especially their role in social welfare and social democratic states.[93] In this sense political economy has become part of the larger debate within political philosophy about the theoretical goal of equality, a debate that includes Walzer, Pocock, Nozick, Barber, and Ackerman.[94] Suddenly too the classical liberal thinkers are being reinterpreted with due regard for a pluralism newly informed by contemporary, post-polyarchy ideas of the proper role of government, the politicization of virtue, and the reconsideration of moral context. One might say that Rawls's emphasis on fair shares is particularly susceptible to the kind of thinking characteristic of game theory.[95] Political principles and a how-to account of trade-offs between liberty, justice, and equality have become both more formalized, in terms of rational choice theory, and more institutional.[96] All of this suggests that we are presently at a new interpretative crossroads— a moment in political philosophy coinciding with the neo-institutionalist "re-rediscovery" of the state, and using political economy as the strategy that leads to rational choice theory as the overarching theoretical framework.[97]

The point of departure for rational choice theory might be said to be Kenneth Arrow's *Social Choice and Individual Values*.[98] Like political economists, his book emphasized the role of rationality in consumer preferences and extended such principles to individuals as voters. This differentiated it from classical liberalism which, while also assuming a universalized notion of rationality, distinguished strongly between citizens and consumers—and what was expected of each. The same individual occupied both roles, but citizenship was thought to carry with it some presumed degree of mutual obligation, civic consciousness, and moral responsibility. Rational choice extends the classic principle of the maximization of utilities into the political marketplace without reference to constraints other than those rules which govern choice. In other words, the theory assumes the equivalence of the economic and political marketplaces, a system of rules governing market behavior, and a common and rational maximizing public acting less as citizens in relation to some sense of civic virtue, or even consumers seeking goods and services, than as customers for whom exchange constitutes the focal point of all activity. As Chong puts it, "Rational choice theory builds on the assumption that people choose, within the limits of their knowledge, the best available means to achieve their goals. They are presumed to be instrumentally rational, meaning they take actions not for their own sake, but only insofar as they secure desired, typically private ends."[99]

This kind of analysis, with its use of a mathematical discourse and the logic of preferences, has been found particularly useful in studies of the institutional rules of politics. It becomes possible to identify discrepancies between the way institutions are supposed to work and the confounding consequences of the way they actually work, for example, to thwart collective goals in favor of private gains. How this works in terms of principles and agents is itself an interesting point of entry in case studies and comparative analysis.[100] Within this very broad characterization one can find a great variety of emphases, from Mancur Olson's concern about the efficiency of group action to realize its goals to Fearon and Laitin's examination of identity and ethnic politics in Africa, Eastern Europe, and elsewhere not in terms of group actions as such but as information exchanges which form patterns of social matching according to a calculus of punishment, gain, and gratification.[101]

Applied by Shepsle to reform in American politics, Gauthier to the rational basis of moral beliefs, and Przeworski to economic and political development, rational choice has thus colonized the field. It has become a kind of meta-theory which applies to economics, economic sociology, organizational behavior, as well as anthropology. In its own terms, rational choice has been able to make non-rational choice approaches to political economy seem essentially ad hoc in their explanations.[102] Today, too, if one looks for major figures in political science, more can be found in political philosophy and rational choice than any other fields within the discipline (and here one thinks of, for example, Fiorina, Ferejohn, Ordeshook, Schofield, and Taylor).

This monopolistic ambition has, not surprisingly, led to attacks on its presumptions. Green and Shapiro, for example, argue that rational choice theory suffers from too many methodological flaws to make sweeping claims: they point to both its inability to derive generalized theory and its lack of significant empirical findings—that indeed it is not even much interested in empirical work. If this is correct, rational choice theory might be said to suffer from some of the same defects as structuralism. But where structuralism came out of a tradition of case studies and intensive empirical fieldwork—and, as a result, developed both a comparative framework and propositions about developmental change in normative, structural, and behavior terms—rational choice theory lacks for any basis of explanatory power.[103] Rational choice theory also leaves aside the question of what happens to political institutions when citizenship declines and "the public" comes to consist of customers: what effect does it have on political behavior, on civic consciousness, on institutions when electoral systems become advertising campaigns? Or when there seems to be a pay-off and pay-out system of allocational politics? One might well argue that rational choice models for political analysis disguise rather than expose the very phenomena they are designed to examine. And if it is the case that rational choice theory tends to state a problem in the form of a conclusion and if, in the course of a specific situation, principle agents and institutions fail to operate as rational choice deems appropriate, its explanations for the success or failure of institutions and programs cannot really be valuable. Nor does it query the rationality of the overall context. Rational choice can occur under conditions of collective non-rationality (if not downright madness) and give the irrational the illusion of rationality.

THE FUTURE

If rational choice is debunked, we arrive at the question of the future of theory in political science. On this score one can only speculate. Four quite different directions seem possible. One will be the further development and formalization of rational choice as it struggles to engage empirical problems and tried to account for its own inadequacies. A second will be the method-ological fine tuning of theories that break up larger questions of equality, lib-erty, institutions, and the role of the state, comparative evolution and develop-ment, and political economy into components amenable to more detailed analysis.[104] This path may lead to ever more method-driven empirical work where the design rather than the context determines the significance of a prob-lem. What may save this potential devolution is the persuasiveness of contem-porary political philosophy, which serves as a fund of ethical and moral prob-lems. But the danger remains that methodological strategies will become too central to the definition of appropriate research questions. Political science in general has been relatively un-reflexive in such matters.[105]

A third path will be a return to field studies and depth analysis. Indeed, if rational choice theory should subject itself to the bright light of empirical studies, its level of explanation will come to be seen as overkill or—to use Ferejohns's term—thin. One will then wish for in-depth studies which reveal multiple networks and systems at play in systemic and structural terms, but which refer to a form of structuralism that uses narrative, discourse, and sym-bolic density to get beyond superficial notions of "rationality."[106] This latter form of structuralism is, in fact, the final possible direction that political theory may take. Its next ascendent tendency may likely be discourse theory.

Discourse theory in general is a kind of theorizing that contextualizes the meaning of intentionality, establishes the multiple dimensions even of rational-ity itself, and attends to the uses of language in communication (and in a way that opens the door to far more interesting research than is implied by say, Habermas's rather clumsy formulations of discourse in a context of communi-cative action). What began with Geertz in this country and took a linguistic turn in French structuralism and post-structuralist approaches, is again of use to political science. This newer form of discourse theory draws on several different perspectives, chiefly sociological and linguistic, but grounded in the context of work on political violence and democratic theory.[107] In the context of political science, discourse theory begins by studying situations that can be regarded as politically significant. It emphasizes the aspects of political activity that are connected—by those involved or by designated interpreters—to narratives (or other kinds of texts) linking those events to personal or collective histories. In this manner, specific circumstances are both located in relation to a retrieved past and translated into critical signifiers that provide logical explanations for future choices.[108] The past becomes "real" in the events of the present. Texts so produced appear to embody truth values; they are widely distributed, or passed around, and begin to take on iconographic properties so as to serve as a source of instruction or a frame of reference for the more general understanding. Symbolic capital is generated; grounded in events, myth—which reconstitutes experiences validated as theories—creates forms of power particularly relevant to the examination of the politics of confrontation. In effect, discourse theory is an approach which examines how people try to transcend the limitations of their predicaments through reinterpretation. If and when such reinterpretation becomes inter-subjective, capable of forming new codes and tropes, the consequence is a form of political chemistry that can be called collective individualism: political discourse comes to possess performative consequences, changing the world by reinterpreting it.

One cannot go into such theory here. However, whatever the approach to be favored there is a clear need for a theoretical framework capable of probing more deeply into the intentions, meanings, actualities, and ambiguities of political and social life under conditions which challenge theories and lead to new forms of explanation, and applicable to field studies (Bates and other proponents of rational choice theory to the contrary).[109] Such a paradigm would return to the broader questions of language, meaning, and science, bringing to bear on the empirical study of political science that intellectual dimension which professionalism has undermined. Alas, such changes remain, at this stage, only wishful thinking.[110]

NOTES

1. I am particularly indebted to Joseph LaPolombara for detailed comments on an earlier version of this article.

2. In this view structure is a function of choice even though the latter is constituted by the space between structure and contingency. The latter enables an escape from presumed limits and established options. In this sense no matter how "rigoristic" a regime or depleted of freedom, members of a political community, whether citizens or subjects, define and make available for themselves alternatives and preferences both within and without structurally defined boundaries and constraints. See K. R. Popper, *The Open Society and Its Enemies* (London: Routledge and Kegan Paul, Ltd., 1945).

3. In this regard, see Ernest Gellner, *Legitimation of Belief* (Cambridge: Cambridge University Press, 1974), p. 193.

4. Behavioral analysis has mainly been applied to the study of American politics.

5. See, for example, Philip E. Converse, "The Nature of Belief Systems in Mass Publics," in *Ideology and Discontent*, ed. David E. Apter (New York: The Free Press of Glencoe, 1964), pp. 206–61.

6. Indeed, pluralism constitutes a particularly hospitable combination of both institutionalism and behaviorism, incorporating a variety of methodological and theoretical approaches centered by a preoccupation with the historical grounding and internal logic of democracy as a system. See Bernard Crick, *The American Science of Politics* (London: Routlege and Kegan Paul, 1957), p. 245.

7. I should add that my own concerns are among those which on the whole I am excluding from the present analysis, namely, social and political movements, discourse theory, and confrontational politics.

8. See Pierre Bourdieu, *Esquisse d'une theorie de la pratique* (Paris: Droz, 1972).

9. See Heinz Eulau, *The Behavioral Persuasion in Politics* (New York: Random House, 1963).

10. For a classic early review of the field, see Bernard Crick's *The American Science of Politics* (London: Routledge and Kegan Paul, 1959). My own effort along these lines is David E. Apter, *Introduction to Political Analysis* (Cambridge, Mass.: Winthrop Publishers, 1977). More recent combinations of review with critique include Anthony Giddens and Johathan Turner, *Social Theory Today* (Stanford: Stanford University Press, 1987). See also Craig Calhoun, "Sociology, Other Disciplines, and the Project of a General Understanding of Social Life," *Sociology and Its Publics*, ed. Terence C. Halliday and Morris Janowitz (Chicago: University of Chicago Press, 1992). For recent discussions of the field, see Robert E. Goodin and Hans-Dieter Klingemann, "Political Science: The Discipline" and Gabriel Almond, "Political Science: The History of the Discipline," both in *The New Handbook of Political Science*, ed. R. Goodin and H.-D. Klingemann (Oxford: Oxford University Press, 1996). For a more European perspective, see Madeleine Grawitz and Jean Leca, *Traité de Science Politique*, 4 vols. (Paris: Presses Universitaires de France, 1985).

11. If it can be said that political science constitutes a corpus it is in terms of its subject matter even more than its theories. In terms of the latter it has always been a "borrowing" discipline, whether from history, law and jurisprudence, economics, sociology, anthropology (e.g., political culture), psychology, organizational behavior, etc. To the extent that it has had internal cohesion this has been provided by the examination of state, its power, and its institutions.

12. If it was at some point pushed off its perch by the more "behaviorally" inclined, political philosophy has come back and moral issues are now central to political inquiry.

13. While political analysis has certainly broadened in scope, there is widespread unease in the profession that perhaps the currency of its ideas has become debased. There is a tendency to back away from bigger issues of politics. Or they are broken up into smaller and more manageable units and subjects, narrowing the results and putting a premium value on validity tests rather than interpretive power. To be sure this can make for some interesting collaboration, as, for example, between political theorists working on, say, equality, and those doing particular studies on the subject. But so much do methods take precedence that serious debate about the nature of politics qua politics is more likely to be undertaken by public intellectuals (whose ideas are likely to be more stimulating than valid).

14. Political scientists, while they may read specialized journals in their narrow areas of specialization, are more likely to favor *The Economist*, or even *The New York Review of Books*, while on the whole ignoring *The American Political Science Review*.

15. See Jon Elster, *Making Sense of Marx* (Cambridge: Cambridge University Press, 1985).

16. For a discussion of this distinction, see Gellner, *Legitimation of Belief*.

17. Its subject matter included all things pertaining to the state, constitutional structures, codified rules, usages, structures and procedures, the role of the speaker of the house, clerks, administrative departments, and agencies. Its concerns extended to details of government and administration, including bylaws of legislative and executive committees, to the role of the Great Seal in British parliamentary practice. David Truman called it his "institutional description." See his *Research Frontiers in Political Science* (Washington, D.C.: Brookings Institution, 1955). See also, for example, W. Ivor Jennings, *Cabinet Government* (Cambridge: Cambridge University Press, 1947); Gilbert Campion, *An Introduction to the Procedure of the House of Commons* (London: Macmillan, 1930); and A. V. Dicey, *The Law of the Constitution* (London: Macmillan, 1959). For an excellent commentary, see Harry Eckstein, "On the Science of the State," in *Dateless* 108:4 (Fall 1979): 1–36.

18. Indeed, political philosophy was treated so dismissively (wrongly in my view) that in some departments steps were taken to separate it from political science and make it a department of its own.

19. An emphasis on law, the juridical personality, the state, and the "common good" was a centerpiece of French institutionalism. See Albert Broderick, ed., *The French Institutionalists* (Cambridge, Mass.: Harvard University Press, 1970).

20. One studied, for example, in addition to Roman and Salic Law, such works as Otto Gierke's *Political Theories of the Middle Ages* (Cambridge: Cambridge University Press, 1927) and his *Natural Law and the Theory of Society 1500 to 1800* (Cambridge: Cambridge University Press, 1950). One also read J. N. Figgis, *Studies of Political Thought from Gerson to Grotius 1414–1625* (Cambridge: Cambridge University Press, 1923) as well as work on the evolution of conciliarism into social contract theory.

21. Reform, therefore, does not mean improving procedures but amending the design, designating particularly relevant clienteles, and, as a consequence, realizing ever more equitable and efficacious combinations of principles with institutions. Stability and order are among the important outcomes of such judicious accomplishments, a result of appropriate and timely amendments of practice and the fine-tuning of principles. Such principles were by no means abstract but constituted fundamental elements in the discourses of democracy viz. liberty against arbitrary rule and authoritarianism, individualism versus collectivism, nationalism versus colonialism, socialism against capitalism, autonomy against domination, separatism versus integration, to name a few.

22. See Brian Barry, *Political Argument* (London: Routledge and Kegan Paul, 1965).

23. While stated in somewhat lofty terms, these are some of the essential ingredients of the old institutional analysis of politics, and for squaring the circle between private wants and public needs. Political science takes on some of the characteristics of its subject. That is, it is itself an open-ended discipline, always unfinished, always in process, and always in need of amendment.

24. The two models Institutionalism judged successful were the American federal experience and the British parliamentary system. Even a country with a democratic and

revolutionary tradition like France was held up as the prototypical case of institutional instability. Weimar Germany was the supreme example of constitutional failure. Scandinavian countries, save a mild interest in "socialist" Sweden, did not count for much.

25. See Hannah Arendt, *On Revolution* (New York: Viking Press, 1963). For a good statement of the liberal position, see in particular John Rawls, *A Theory of Justice* (Cambridge, Mass.: Harvard University Press, 1971).

26. This snapshot of institutionalism also indicates the kind of knowledge required by scholars. Whatever its faults, this, the "old" institutionalism, represented a powerful configurational synthesis. It afforded rigorous training in the history, ideas, and practices of democratic government and administration. The intellectual pedigree was formidable, from Bryce and Woodrow Wilson to Ernest Barker in England, Hans Kelsen and Charles McIlwain in the U.S., Carl Schmitt in Germany, Andre Siegfried and Maurice Duverger in France, Carl Friedrich, Herman and Sammy Finer (and a much younger Giovanni Sartori). All were, by present standards especially, extraordinarily learned. For them institutions were not just institutions. That is, they were not simply practical instrumentalities but embodiments of universal public principles and legal rights. Each specific ensemble of legislative, judicial, executive, and administrative practices could be considered in terms of their efficiency, but each was also a signifier for the values represented, and therefore not merely mechanisms for policy making, or a means of reconciling different views and preferences, although such matters were obviously crucial.

27. While cold war considerations were present, they were not predominant in the minds of younger scholars in that period.

28. The search for a "functional equivalent to Max Weber's Protestant Ethic virtually became a holy grail of developmental politics. See, for example, Robert N. Bellah's *Tokugawa Religion* (Glencoe, Ill.: The Free Press, 1957).

29. By the same token cold war and ideological issues more and more affected research priorities. If one needed to question the universality of Western forms of democracy, one's answers would suggest how, when, and where it could be made to work and where it might be vulnerable to authoritarian alternatives.

30. This was the general topic which became my own central interest in the context of Ghana, the first African country to come to independence by following this route. See David E. Apter, *Ghana in Transition*, originally published as *The Gold Coast in Transition* (Princeton: Princeton University Press, 1955, 1963, revised, 1972; London: Frank Cass, 2000).

31. In my own case it took on special relevance when I, near the end of my first year of graduate work, became interested in what then struck me as an extraordinary event, the transition of a then British colonial territory, the Gold Coast, to the independent state of Ghana. The comparative implications were clear enough: in Africa there was already a pattern of change from colonial rule to independence (as in India, Burma, and the then Ceylon), which in British territories took the form of nationalism directed into parliamentarianism. The event not only spelled the end to African colonialism and the beginnings of African liberation, but could not help having a profound impact on the lives and outlooks of African-Americans.

To do justice to such a subject required anthropological and cultural understanding of African societies, some good reckoning of the history of where they had come from, and considerable sociological awareness of the directions in which they were likely to go. As well, one's attention was drawn to the development of theories which drew their inspiration from that larger corpus of work dealing with transitions from preindustrial to industrialization in the West, and not least of all the kind of inquiry into the rise of modern capitalism which gave rise to the idea of development in the first instance. As for political science itself, what it provided, and indeed was best at, was its institutional sophistication not least of all in terms of the question of to what extent British parliamentary institutions could be adapted to social circumstances vastly different in every way from those to which they were indigenous.

32. Perhaps the most incisive contemporary critique of the field as then constituted was David Easton's *The Political System* (New York: Alfred A. Knopf, 1953).

33. For example, the Carnegie Corporation played a key role in nudging universities out of their disciplinary provincialism. Such bodies as the Social Science Research Council were far more sensitive to the importance of societal change and established grant programs and committees to provide opportunities for people in different fields and institutions to interact in ways that impacted directly on university research and teaching.

The SSRC, for example, not only sponsored committees concerned with developing research, it also stimulated reflexivity with respect to the enterprise itself. It gave support to those within political science concerned with such larger questions, not least of all in the Social Science Sub-Committee on Comparative Politics under the leadership of Gabriel Almond.

34. Role became a central conceptual building block in social analysis generally with role networks as the structural components of institutions. "Role play" became used in therapy as well. In political science it was incorporated particularly in studies of political socialization (Easton) and political psychology and ideology (Lane, Converse). Central to functional anthropology (Linton), role analysis became the key operational concept in so-called "structural-functional" sociology (Parsons and Merton). The functional and motivational attributes of role became central to the internal study of societies as well as comparisons between them, especially in terms of political beliefs. On the latter, see the now classic article by Philip E. Converse which continues to be widely used in many college and university courses, "The Nature of Belief in Mass Publics," in David E. Apter, *Ideology and Discontent*.

35. See, for example, Herbert Hyman, *Political Socialization* (Glencoe, Ill.: The Free Press, 1959); Robert Lane, *Political Ideology* (Glencoe, Ill.: The Free Press 1962); Richard E. Dawson and Kenneth Prewitt, *Political Socialization* (Boston: Little, Brown and Company, 1969); Fred I. Greenstein, *Personality and Politics* (New York: W. W. Norton, 1975); Charles F. Andrain, *Children and Civic Awareness* (Columbus, Oh.: The Charles E. Merrill Publishing Company, 1971); and Paul R. Abramson, *Generational Change in American Politics* (Lexington, Mass: D. C. Heath and Company, 1975).

36. See in particular Robert E. Lane, *Political Life* (Glencoe, Ill.: The Free Press, 1959); Fred I. Greenstein, *Personality and Politics*; and David C. McClelland, *The Achieving Society* (Princeton: D. Van Nostrand, 1961). Perhaps once a more important influence in political science than today, social psychology as a field has more or less given way to cognitive psychology. In the fifties and sixties it contributed to the development of the concept of role and role networks as in the work of Newcomb, Hartley, and Lewin's "field theory." It was of particular import especially in conjunction with studies of socialization, education, and political learning. It was also applied to so-

called "primitive" societies. See Michael P. Banton, *Roles, An Introduction to the Study of Social Relations* (New York: Basic Books, 1965).

37. In fact it had a diverse pedigree, which includes Bernard Berelson and Paul Lazersfeld, both of whom contributed to the field methodologically and empirically. More analytically minded figures such as S. N. Eisenstadt, Seymour Martin Lipset, Stein Rokkan, Mattei Dogan, Reinhard Bendix, Neil Smelser, and Juan Linz came to personify the field. For an interesting discussion of the role of Michels, see David Beetham, "Michels and His Critics," in *European Journal of Sociology* 22:1 (1981): 81–99. See also Robert Michels, *Political parties; a sociological study of the oligarchical tendencies of modern democracy*, trans. Eden and Cedar Paul (New York: The Free Press [1968, c1962]).

38. See Barrington Moore, Jr., *Social Origins of Dictatorship and Democracy* (Boston: Beacon Press, 1966).

39. See, for example, Seymour Martin Lipset, *Political Man* (Garden City, N.Y.: Doubleday, 1960); Reinhard Bendix and Seymour Martin Lipset, *Class, Status and Power* (Glencoe, Ill.: The Free Press, 1953); Bernard Berelson and Morris Janowitz, *Reader in Public Opinion and Communication* (Glencoe, Ill.: The Free Press, 1950); Reinhard Bendix, *Nation Building and Citizenship* (New York: John Wiley and Sons, 1964); S. N. Eisenstadt, *The Political Systems of Empires* (New York: The Free Press of Glencoe, 1963), and his *Political Sociology: A Reader* (New York: Basic Books, 1971); Stein Rokkan, *Citizens, Elections, Parties* (Oslo: Universitetsforlaget, 1970). See also Neil Smelser, *Handbook of Sociology* (Newbury Park, Calif.: Sage Publications, 1988).

40. It incorporated a good many ideas from anthropology and psychoanalytical theory (Freud most importantly, Erik Erikson, and others). In terms of psychoanalytical approaches the early contributions of Harold Lasswell were particularly important. See his *Psychopathology and Politics* (Chicago: University of Chicago Press, 1930).

41. Like its best practitioners, including political scientists such as Robert Lane, Heinz Eulau, and Samuel J. Eldersfeld, and psychologists like Angus Campbell, director of the Survey Research Center at the University of Michigan, Philip Converse had broader theoretical interests, the research for which was done was largely at ground level. On the whole, and except in the context of voting studies and the analysis of political parties (and exemplified by such figures as David Butler in England), comparative politics for some time resisted these tendencies until such figures as Jean Blondell, Stein Rokkan, Erwin Scheuch, and Rudolph Wildenmann began following suit, building up data archives at various European centers. Current emphases are on national election studies, micro-analysis of individual behavior, and cross-national electoral behavior. See Warren Miller, "Political Behavior, Old and New" in Goodin and Klingemann, *The New Handbook of Political Science*, pp. 294–303.

42. See, for example, Nelson Polsby, *Community Power and Political Theory* (New Haven: Yale University Press, 1963) and Aaron Wildavsky, *The Politics of the Budgetary Process* (Boston: Little, Brown, 1964). In a more comparative vein, see Arendt Liphardt, *Patterns of Democracy* (New Haven: Yale University Press, 1999); Robert Putnam's *The Belief Systems of Politicians: Ideology, Conflict, and Democracy in Italy and Britain* (New Haven: Yale University Press, 1973) and his *The Comparative Study of Political Elites* (Englewood Cliffs, N.J.: Prentice-Hall, 1976); Fred I. Greenstein,

Personality and Politics; and many others including James David Barber and Denis Lacorne.

43. See Joseph A. Schumpeter, especially his *Capitalism, Socialism and Democracy* (New York: Harper, 1947.)

44. It did not take long for pluralist theories to become comparative, their influence spreading to universities and research centers in Germany, Israel, Italy, Norway, and Japan, not to speak of France and Great Britain although in both of the latter countries institutionalism remained dominant for a considerable period of time.

45. One can see how these different ingredients fit together in the work of Robert Dahl who, in *A Preface to Democratic Theory* (Chicago: University of Chicago Press, 1956) identified models of democratic polity in terms of systemic formalism. Dahl located the dynamics of pluralist changes in power and accountability in *Who Governs?* (New Haven: Yale University Press, 1961) and *Pluralist Democracy in the United States* (Chicago: Rand McNally and Co., 1967). Both books applied elements of political sociology to political change in an American context, which challenged reigning sociological ideas about stratification and power. The political economy of pluralism was explicitly examined in *Politics, Economics, and Welfare* (New York: Harper and Row, 1953) in which Dahl, working with Charles E. Lindblom, showed the critical connections between the economic aspects of politics and equality, and between social welfare and the normative aspects of democracy; these different dimensions became the parts of a moral-prescriptive political system they called "polyarchy." Other important shaping influences were V. O. Key; David Truman, particularly *The Governmental Process* (New York: Alfred A. Knopf, 1951); and Joseph A. Schumpeter, especially his *Capitalism, Socialism and Democracy* (New York: Harper, 1947). Dahl and his putative descendants also challenged more elite sociological theories of stratification based on the work of Floyd Hunter and W. Lloyd Warner.

46. In addition to Lane's *Political Life*, see *Political Ideology* (New York: The Free Press of Glencoe, 1962).

47. See Ludwig von Bertalanffy, *General System Theory* (New York: George Braziller, 1968).

48. The more it did so the more it was resisted by those who preferred more behavioral and empirical approaches such as George Homans, Otis Dudley Duncan, Angus Cambell, Alex Inkeles, Warren Miller, the coup de grace perhaps delivered by Charles Tilly.

49. See in particular the pioneering work of Norbert Weiner, *Cybernetics* (New York: John Wiley and Sons, Inc., 1948).

50. For my own effort to trace the main theoretical resources available in such terms, see David E. Apter and Charles Andrain, *Contemporary Analytical Theory* (Englewood Cliffs, N.J.: Prentice-Hall, Inc., 1972). Focusing on the problem of choice, the selections indicate parameters of choice, including normative aspects, the problem of meaning, structural relationships embodied in roles and their interaction, and behavioral aspects, involving such matters as motivation and perception. These different met-discourses tended to emphasize one or more of these normative, structural, and behavioral dimensions.

51. It should be clear that the structuralism which falls under the general rubric of general systems theory differs substantially from the structuralism of Levi-Strauss and others in a continental tradition and which derives from a very different philosophical

and socio-linguistic tradition, bearing little resemblance to the sociological structuralism of Talcott Parsons in particular. Continental structuralism is strong precisely where structural-functionalism is weakest, most particularly in dealing with problems of meaning, intentionality, discourse, narrative, and indeed knowledge itself, not to speak of the power all these generate in terms of individual and collective action. Here again there were several important strands. One, the exact opposite of positivism, was the influence of Wittgenstein and his particular expression of hermeneutics. A second was critical theory, deriving from the Frankfurt School, particularly Horkheimer and Benjamin. A third was Sartrean existentialism. A fourth involving language, myth, and narrative theory, has a complex background including such quite contradictory figures as Nietzsche, Saussure, Bataille, Claude Levi-Strauss, Ricoeur, Bourdieu, Baudrilliard, and others.

52. See, for example, Carl G. Hemple, "Fundamentals of Concept Formation in Empirical Science," *International Encyclopedia of Unified Science*, ed. Otto Neurath, Rudolf Carnap, and Charles Morris (Chicago: University of Chicago Press, c1938– ?), vol. II, no. 7. See also Carl G. Hempel, "Symposium: Problems of Concept and Theory Formation in the Social Sciences," in American Philosophical Association, *Science, Language, and Human Rights* (Philadelphia: University of Pennsylvania Press, 1952). There was also a great deal of interest in the impact of science on society and the relations between them. See Bernard Barber, *Science and the Social Order* (Glencoe, Ill.: The Free Press, 1952). See also Michael Polyanyi, "The Growth of Science in Society," in *Minerva* 5:4 (1968): 533–45.

53. For early examples, see Robert Redfield, *A Village That Chose Progress* (Chicago: University of Chicago Press, 1950); A. R. Radcliffe-Brown, *Structure and Function in Primitive Society* (Glencoe, Ill.: The Free Press, 1952); and B. Malinowski, *Coral Gardens and Their Magic* (London: George Allen & Unwin, 1935) and *The Dynamics of Culture Change* (New Haven: Yale University Press; London: H. Milford, Oxford University Press, 1945). For greater emphasis on aspects of culture and its interpretive powers, see, for example, Victor Turner, *The Ritual Process* (Chicago: Aldine Publishing Company, 1969) and Clifford Geertz, *The Interpretation of Culture* (New York: Basic Books, 1972). See also Michael Banton, ed., *Anthropological Approaches to the Study of Religion* (London: Tavistock Publications, 1966) and Edmund Leach, ed., *The Structural Study of Myth and Totemism* (London: Tavistock Publications, 1967), the last dealing at length with the varied contributions of Claude Levi-Strauss.

54. See in particular A. R. Radcliffe-Brown, *Structure and Function in Primitive Society* (Glencoe, Ill.: The Free Press, 1952).

55. It was further adapted and amended by Robert Merton and Marion J. Levy Jr. in the form of "latent functional analysis " and "requisite analysis," respectively.

56. Perhaps the most interesting if short-lived "experiment" in these terms was the establishment of the Social Relations Department at Harvard under the influence and direction of Talcott Parsons.

57. Its main analytical strategy was top down, exhausting the level of explanation of the more inclusive collectivity, and then proceeding to subsystems, at all times using the same general categories and core systems-problems as self-maintenance predicaments at each level. Briefly put, such categories were paired polar opposites or binaries, clustering in varying degrees in integrative and complementary ways, or the opposite,

serving as sources of malintegration, tension, and conflict. In these terms all concrete systems represented different degrees of departure from a theoretical equilibrium point defined in terms of the reinforcing and mutually responsive interaction of cultural values, social systems and subsystems, and personality. Role was the central operational concept, and it was through the examination of roles that certain attributes like the functional specificity attributed to modern societies could be compared, for example, to functional diffuseness in premodern societies. Likewise with universalism and particularism. The relative extent to which these and similar "pattern variables" showed inconsistencies within societies or subsystems led observers to identify disequilibrating aspects of social and political life.

58. See also Edward Shils, "On the Comparative Study of the New States," *Old Societies and New States*, ed. Clifford Geertz (New York: The Free Press of Glencoe, 1963). The book was the product of the Committee for the Comparative Study of New Nations at the University of Chicago, one of several bodies primarily concerned with comparative theory and field research. Others included the Sub-Committee on Comparative Politics of the Social Science Research Council, directed by Gabriel Almond, and the Research Scholars Group of the Institute of International Studies at the University of California, Berkeley, and the Bureau of Applied Social Research at Columbia, to mention only a few.

59. Psycho-linguistics became of particular interest to those concerned with "value theory" in the social sciences, and the connections between language formation, "deep structures," and symbolic processes, including the power of messages, addressers and addressees, and using concepts of metaphor and metonymy, scholars in several fields borrowing liberally from such diverse figures as Roman Jacobsen and Noam Chomsky. More specifically, as with those studying the politics of particular regions of the world, linguistics contributed much to the understanding of what was fast becoming the problem of ethnicity and "identity" politics, a linguist like Joseph Greenberg of Stanford University practically rewriting the linguistic map of Africa at a time when such issues were mixed with questions of historical migrations, and debates among scholars about who were original ethnic occupants versus interlopers. As for structural linguistics, from Saussure to Levi-Strauss, it became particularly important in anthropology and a strand in the evolution of what today is known as "cultural studies." Today, for whatever reasons, neither analytically nor in terms of specific reference to political problems, both psycho-linguistics and linguistics occupy less important spaces on sociological and political science maps than they did ten or fifteen years ago.

60. In this context, institutionalism took on the virtues of its deficiencies, i.e., the close analysis of political institutions and how they worked. The more political science enlarged its range of concerns and became less parochial, the more structuralism in this sense became attractive.

61. Max Weber's "Politics as a Vocation," in H. H. Gerth and C. Wright Mills, *From Max Weber: Essays in Sociology* (New York: Oxford University Press, 1946), was widely read and discussed.

62. As indicated, a good many of these assumptions derived from prior assumptions made by historians, anthropologists, economists, and historical sociologists, and from Adam Smith to Marx, from Fustel de Coulanges to Durkheim, and from Weber to Walras. Paralleling these assumptions was the notion that democracy emerged with the evolution of formal-legal institutions that were an intrinsic part of the transition from

preindustrial to industrial society. The scholarly pedigree here includes Blackstone, Stubb's charters, social contract theorists, parliamentarianism, and Dicey's *Law and the Constitution*.

63. In my own experience such application to case materials led me to ideas about relationships between economic growth in somewhat unusual ways, such as growth creating the need for new information of a sort which would decline with an increase in hierarchy and coercion by the state. In this sense the information cost of coercion became crucial in accounting for regime change and, based as well upon empirical observations made in the case of Ghana, was stated more generally in the form of an inverse relationship between coercion and information. If correct, as a systems problem, the implication was that limitations on growth in authoritarian countries could only be rectified by a change to a more democratic state. At the time, too, examining the societal context of innovative change, it was also possible to predict functional polarization, and a growing gap between those being rendered functionally superfluous on the one hand and functionally significant on the other by the impact of innovative change on the economy. See David E. Apter, *The Politics of Modernization* (Chicago: University of Chicago Press, 1965). See also *Choice and the Politics of Allocation* (New Haven: Yale University Press, 1971). In effect, the validity of this idea has been affirmed both in the case of the U.S.S.R. and China.

64. "This diffuse character of political power explains the peculiar relevance to it of the gradient of drasticness (*sic*) of means. Since ability to use force in its relation to territoriality is one ultimate focus of power in this sense, the control of the use and organization of force relative to territory is always a crucial focus of the political power system, in one sense the crucial focus. It is this which gives the state its central position in the power system of a complex society." See Talcott Parsons, *The Social System* (Glencoe, Ill.: The Free Press, 1952), p. 126. For Parsons, power is essentially integrative.

65. In terms of the analytical pedigree, see Talcott Parsons, *The Structure of Social Action* (Glencoe, Ill.: The Free Press, 1949) and Talcott Parsons, Edward A. Shils, Kaspar D. Naegele, and Jesse R. Pitts, *Theories of Society* (New York: The Free Press of Glencoe, 1961). In terms of the overall framework of structural functional analysis, see Talcott Parsons and Edward A. Shils, eds., *Towards a General Theory of Action* (Cambridge, Mass.: Harvard University Press, 1951). On the economy, see Talcott Parsons and Neil J. Smelser, *Economy and Society* (London: Routledge and Kegan Paul, 1956). On society, culture, and social structure, see Talcott Parsons, *The Social System*. On method and conceptual schemes, see Talcott Parsons, Robert F. Bales, and Edward Shils, *Working Papers in the Theory of Action* (Glencoe, Ill.: The Free Press, 153).

66. See Robert Bellah, *Tokugawa Religion*.

67. David E. Apter, *The Politics of Modernization*.

68. See in particular Gabriel A. Almond and James S. Coleman, eds., *The Politics of the Developing Areas* (Princeton: Princeton University Press, 1960); see also Leonard Binder et al., *Crises and Sequences in Political Development* (Princeton: Princeton University Press, 1971); James S. Coleman, ed., *Education and Political Development* (Princeton: Princeton University Press, 1965); Joseph LaPalombara, *Bureaucracy and Political Development* (Princeton: Princeton University Press, 1963); and Lucian Pye, *Communications and Political Development* (Princeton: Princeton University Press, 1963).

69. See Gabriel Almond and Sidney Verba, *The Civic Culture* (Princeton: Princeton University Press, 1963). See also Sidney Verba and Norman Nie, *Participation in America, Political Democracy and Social Equality* (New York: Harper and Row, 1972), and Norman H. Nie, Sidney Verba, and John Petrocik, *The Changing American Voter* (Cambridge, Mass.: Harvard University Press, 1976).

70. Others, however, have developed this topic outside the field of functionalism and within a larger framework of pluralism, such as Putnam, Huntington, Kitschelt, Huber, Klandermans, Abramson, and Inglehart to name a few, some using fairly sophisticated statistical analysis. To take only one excellent example, see Paul R. Abramson and Ronald Inglehard, *Value Change in Global Perspective* (Ann Arbor: University of Michigan Press, 1995).

71. See Ralf Dahendorf, *Class and Class Conflict in an Industrial Society* (London: Routledge and Kegan Paul, 1959).

72. See, for example, Dieter Misgeld, "Critical Hermeneutics versus Neoparsonialism?" *New German Critique* 25 (Spring/Summer 1985).

73. Which may help explain why Thomas S. Kuhn's *The Structure of Scientific Revolutions* (Chicago: University of Chicago Press, 1962) made such an impact.

74. Such are the theories of ethno-methodology developed by Harold Garfinkle (a former Parsons student), and the attacks from those who preferred conflict theory such as Ralf Dahrendorf. See Ralf Dahrendorf, *Class and Class Conflict in an Industrial Society* (London: Routledge and Kegan Paul, 1959). Perhaps the final indignity was the expropriation of the term structuralism in French and continental versions. These ranged from the linguistically oriented concern of Levi-Strauss and his emphasis on the relationship between kinship, language, myth, and rationality to the philosophical Marxism of Althusser with its condemnation of bourgeois science as ideology to the inversionary theories of Foucault which turned social science into another form of hegemony.

75. Left political economy was mainly a critical theory focusing on the defects of bourgeois political economy, and the socially negative aspects of the market as social and moral as well as class and economic arbiter.

76. It attracted scientists who saw in Marxism an appropriate analogy to science itself. Indeed, for Althusser Marxism was science where all other theories were ideologies. See, for example, Louis Althusser, *For Marx*, trans. Ben Brewster (New York: Random House, 1970). See also Cornelius Castoriadis, *Political and Social Writings*, 2 vols. (Minneapolis: University of Minnesota Press, 1988).

77. Not to speak of the original influence of George Lukàcs. See Georg Lukàcs, *History and Class Consciousness*, trans. Rodney Livingstone (London: Merlin Press, 1971). For a general discussion of the Frankfurt School, see Martin Jay, *The Dialectical Imagination* (Boston: Little, Brown and Company, 1973). For the French School, see Denis Hollier, ed., *The College of Sociology (1937–9)*, trans. Betsy Wing (Minneapolis: University of Minnesota Press, 1988).

78. See Perry Anderson, *Arguments Within English Marxism* (London: Verso, 1980).

79. See, for example, Gavin Kitching, *Class and Economic Change in Kenya* (New Haven: Yale University Press, 1980).

80. See Immanuel Wallerstein, *The Modern World-System*, 3 vols. (New York: Academic Press, 1980).

81. See Alain Touraine, *Sociologie de l'action* (Paris: Éditions du Seuil, 1965).

82. See, for example, Jean-François Lyotard, *The Postmodern Condition: A Report on Knowledge*, trans. Geoff Bennington and Brian Massumi (Minneapolis: The University of Minnesota Press, 1984).

83. In terms of political economy, Marxism and neo-Marxism lent themselves to the comparative analysis of the dynamics of capitalism and the double hegemony of state domination and imperialism (Baran, Sweezy, Mandel, Frank). In terms of radical psychoanalysis, especially in application to colonialism, there was emphasis on a transformational need for cathartic violence (Fanon). In literature, the focus was on marginalized and stigmatized colonial others, subalterns, and "hybrids" (Spivak, Homi Baba). In sociology the emphasis shifted to social movements in which students replaced workers as the class with radical brains (Touraine), and a politics of third world exploitation (Leys, Mamdani). Perhaps the most lasting influence has been the work of Jürgen Habermas, especially his emphasis on intentionality, communicative action, public rationality, and public space, which provided a critical view of democracy and offered guidelines for its improvement, while departing from the earlier assumptions of the Frankfurt School—see in particular Jürgen Habermas, *The Theory of Communicative Action* (Boston: Beacon Press, 1981).

84. See in particular Frederic Jameson, *The Political Unconscious* (Ithaca: Cornell University Press, 1981). See also Terry Eagleton, *Criticism and Ideology* (London: New Left Books, 1976).

85. See in particular Sidney Tarrow, *Power in Movement* (Cambridge: Cambridge University Press, 1994). See also Charles Tilly, *From Mobilization to Revolution* (Readubgm, Mass.: Addison-Wesley, 1978) and David E. Apter, ed., *The Legitimization of Violence* (London: Macmillan, 1997).

86. See Ralph Miliband, *Parliamentary Socialism* (New York: Monthly Review Press, 1964) and Claus Offe, *Contradictions of the Welfare State* (Cambridge: MIT Press, 1984).

87. See Gabriel Almond and Sidney Verba, *The Civic Culture* (Princeton: Princeton University Press, 1963). See also Sidney Verba and Norman Nie, *Participation in America, Political Democracy and Social Equality* and Norman H. Nie, Sidney Verba, and John Petrocik, *The Changing American Voter*. Putnam, Huntington, Kitschelt, Huber, Klandermans, Abramson, and Inglehart, to name a few, have all dealt with different aspects of this topic, some using fairly sophisticated statistical analysis; one excellent example is Paul R. Abramson and Ronald Inglehard, *Value Change in Global Perspective* (Ann Arbor: University of Michigan Press, 1995).

88. Too often the result is analytical glibness. The term "culture" when borrowed by some political scientists, becomes at one and the same time a residual category and an independent variable. Nor does putting the word "political" in front of it help very much. A theory of political culture ostensibly can explain why, say, democracy is more likely to work in some settings better than others (Almond and Verba), or conflicts between the West and Islam (Huntington), but there are too many conditionalities for conclusiveness. Similarly with the word "society" which by putting the word "civil" in front of it (Shils) presumably takes on more explanatory meaning. This is not to demean such concepts or consider them of no use. The problem is that because they explain both too little and too much, they become popularized and drained of their utility.

89. Examples of this would be the work of Ralph Miliband, or in a different vein, Claus Offe.

90. His types of consensus models include, among others, electoral systems, pluralism and corporatism, federal and unitary, and constitutions and interest groups. See Arend Lijphart, *Patterns of Democracy* (New Haven: Yale University Press, 1999).

91. See in particular Geoffrey Garrett, *Partisan Politics in the Global Economy* (Cambridge: Cambridge University Press, 1998).

92. It was Theda Skocpol's work on comparative revolution and the evolution of the state. By elevating Weber over Marx in the context of comparative revolutions, and their implication for democracy and state formation, Skocpol shifted the focus from the class analysis characteristic of her mentor, Barrington Moore, to the historical state and its bureaucratic evolution. In so doing she came to represent a renewed interest in the historical and legal aspects of institutionalism, an emphasis which includes Stephen Skowronek, Rogers Smith, Bruce Ackerman, and many others. See Theda Skocpol, *States and Social Revolutions* (Cambridge: Cambridge University Press, 1979). See also Rogers M. Smith, *Civic Ideals* (New Haven: Yale University Press, 1997), and Bruce Ackerman, *Social Justice in the Liberal State* (New Haven: Yale University Press, 1980).

93. Rawls effected a deontological foundation for grounding political justice and its principled formation of fairness, justice, equality, and rights. See, for example, Peter Hall, *Governing the Economy* (New York: Oxford University Press, 1981).

94. The latter in effect brought the law back into the discussion by distinguishing between monist and dualist notions of constitutionalism. See Bruce Ackerman, *We the People* (Cambridge, Mass.: Harvard University Press, 1991).

95. For an interesting discussion of this point, see Alan Ryan, "John Rawls," *The Return of Grand Theory in the Human Sciences*, ed. Quentin Skinner (Cambridge: Cambridge University Press, 1985), pp. 108–9.

96. See John Rawls, *A Theory of Justice*; see also Michael Walzer, *Spheres of Justice* (New York: Basic Books, 1983); J.G.A. Pocock, *The Machiavellian Moment* (Princeton: Princeton University Press, 1975); Robert Nozick, *Anarchy, State, and Utopia* (New York: Basic Books, 1974), and Benjamin Barber, *Strong Democracy* (Berkeley: University of California Press, 1984).

97. One says rerediscovered because the radical generation was very much preoccupied with the state, whether capitalist or socialist, and particularly the relations of class to hegemony.

98. See Kenneth J. Arrow, *Social Choice and Individual Values* (New Haven: Yale University Press, 1951).

99. See Dennis Chong, "Rational Choice Theory's Mysterious Rivals," *Critical Review* 9: 1–2, p. 39. Among those important in developing the basic framework in addition to Arrow were Gerald Kramer, Anthony Downs, Gordon Tulloch, James M. Buchanan, Mancur Olson, Thomas Schelling, and William Riker. See in particular Anthony Downs, *An Economic Theory of Democracy* (New York: Harpers, 1957) and Kenneth J. Arrow, *Social Choice and Individual Values*.

100. I find it interesting, for example, to compare my own work on the then Gold Coast, *The Gold Coast in Transition*, which used a modified structural model, with Kathryn Firmin-Sellers, *The Transformation of Property Rights in the Gold Coast: An Empirical Analysis Applying Rational Choice Theory* (Cambridge: Cambridge University Press, 1996).

101. Olson argues that "the larger the group, the smaller the fraction of the total group benefit any person acting in the group interest receives, and the less adequate the reward for any group-oriented action, and the farther the group falls short of getting an optimal supply of the collective good, even if it should get some." See Mancur Olson Jr., *The Logic of Collective Action* (Cambridge, Mass.: Harvard University Press, 1965), p. 48. See also James Fearon and David Laitin, "Explaining Interethnic Cooperation,"*American Political Science Review*, December 1996: 715–35.

102. See, for example, Kenneth A. Shepsle, "Reflections on Committee Power," *American Political Science Review*, March 1987: 935–45; David Gauthier, *Morals by Agreement* (Oxford: The Clarendon Press, 1986); and Adam Przeworski, *Democracy and the Market* (Cambridge: Cambridge University Press, 1991).

103. See Donald P. Greeen and Ian Shapiro, *Pathologies of Rational Choice Theory* (New Haven: Yale University Press, 1994). It should be noted that the special issue of *Critical Inquiry* on rational choice has stimulated the kind of debates over science, rationality, and its limits, which characterized the broader questions of science debated within the framework of general systems theory in the earlier period. However, on the whole the replies of such luminaries as Ferejohn and Shepsle and others to Green and Shapiro seem relatively modest, given the broader claims of the approach itself.

104. Indeed, one of the chief differences between the "now" as compared with the "then" of political science is an explosion in method and inquiries into method in and of itself. Indeed, the evolution of statistical as well as mathematical modeling fits well with the political economy—institutionalism—rational choice combination.

105. But the problem has been very well discussed in Gary King, Robert O. Keohane, and Sidney Verba, *Designing Social Inquiry* (Princeton: Princeton University Press, 1994).

106. Indeed, most of the really interesting theoretical questions are now embedded in what might be called the analytic aspects of case studies, requiring interiority, depth, and the detailing of interaction between different networks, jurisdictions, and relationships, not to speak of attitudes, beliefs, and their complexity rather than oversimplification. One might call this a need for cases for comparison. Good examples include Atul Kohli, *Democracy and Discontent* (Cambridge: Cambridge University Press, 1990) and Timothy Mitchell, *Colonizing Egypt* (Cambridge: Cambridge University Press, 1988). A more comparative use of case materials is Joel S. Migdal, *Strong Societies and Weak States* (Princeton: Princeton University Press, 1988).

107. In these regards, see Bruce Ackerman, *Social Justice in the Liberal State.*

108. For an example of how an interpreter can use this type of translation to shatter the transparency of accepted common sense by means of a logic drawn from mythic narratives, see my *Against the State* (Cambridge: Harvard University Press, 1984); *Revolutionary Discourse in Mao's Republic* (Cambridge, Mass.: Harvard University Press, 1994); and *The Legitimization of Violence.*

109. See Robert Bates, "Area Studies and Political Science: Rupture and Possible Synthesis," *Africa Today* 44: 2: 123–31.

110. What may also happen, and as a result of professional practice, is further fragmentation. Already scholarship is localized , parochialized, and sectarian with each academic parish establishing boundaries within which the parishioners mainly follow only each other's works and read their footnotes, a field of specialized niches between which communication becomes less easy and there is little agreement about appropriate agendas, scholarly priorities, and academic employment.

CHAPTER 15

Interdisciplinarity at New York University

INNOVATION WITHOUT PLANNING

Mary Poovey

INSTEAD OF discussing "interdisciplinarity" in the abstract, this essay describes how one university—New York University—has enhanced its reputation partly by developing numerous and, in some cases, quite innovative interdisciplinary programs, centers, and institutes. I focus on a specific institution not only because it is the case I know best, but in order to make two theoretical points. The first is that within the U.S. university system, the term *interdisciplinary* has no determinate meaning. "Interdisciplinary" refers neither to a consistent way of combining disciplinary inquiry nor to a practice that somehow *transcends* discipline-specific research and teaching. Indeed, the problem of the relation, in specific institutional settings, between particular interdisciplinary programs or centers and the disciplines, as they are institutionalized in departments, remains one of the most vexed and vexing problems of contemporary university organization and management.

This observation leads directly to my second theoretical point. The term *interdisciplinary* has no determinate meaning because different universities "do it" in so many different ways. For this reason, only local histories, which focus on the specific conditions that led a university to institutionalize particular kinds of interdisciplinary ventures, can illuminate the range of practices that count as interdisciplinarity now. In focusing exclusively on NYU, I do not mean to imply that this university's situation is unique or that the conditions that led its administrators to implement so many interdisciplinary programs were not shared by other universities. I do want to insist, however, that we will only be able to approach an understanding of the aspirations and discontents conveyed by the term *interdisciplinarity* if we look carefully at the specific institutional conditions that have made various kinds of curricular innovation possible.

Given my theoretical commitments, it will come as no surprise that the story I offer of the last twenty-five years of interdisciplinary enterprises at NYU emphasizes local detail. I admit that I was led to this story—and, by extension, to the theoretical commitment to localism—despite my initial assumptions. When I began the research for this essay, I expected to discover what I assumed was a master narrative for the rise of interdisciplinary initiatives in American universities. I thought I would find out that NYU's enthusiasm for interdisciplinary programs and centers either echoed a society-wide recognition that the traditional disciplines were obsolete or constituted a response to the initiative of innovative faculty members, whose intellectual interests had taken them beyond the limitations of disciplinary research. Instead, I discovered that, with very few exceptions, the interdisciplinary ventures NYU has launched in the last twenty-five years were initiated by administrators, who wanted to save the university from ruin or to enhance its ability to attract tuition dollars. That administrators could use the clarion call of interdisciplinarity to accomplish these goals attests to the cultural currency of this term, despite its relative indeterminacy, and one might say that this confirms my initial assumption that the time for interdisciplinary work has simply come. That these initiatives were largely engineered from the top, however, makes the story considerably more complicated. At NYU at least, the forces that have led to the introduction of interdisciplinary programs have involved economics as much as a commitment to intellectual innovation.

INSTITUTIONAL CONDITIONS AND THE REVITALIZATION OF THE HUMANITIES

Originally named the University of the City of New-York, New York University was founded in 1831.[1] At least three of the factors that shaped the early-nineteenth-century university have continued to influence nearly every aspect of NYU—including its periodic promotion of interdisciplinary enterprises. The first is NYU's location in New York City, which has alternately embroiled the university in debilitating city politics, shackled it to the city's fiscal woes, and provided the university with the resources and rhetoric necessary to reanimate its educational mission. The second crucial factor is the heterogeneity of the university, which, in turn, expresses the founders' original commitments to promote useful knowledge for the shopkeepers and merchants of the city. In the nineteenth century, this heterogeneous university consisted of two arts and science units—an undergraduate and a graduate school (founded in 1831 and 1866, respectively)—and several professional schools—a law school (1835), a school of medicine (1841), a college of engineering and science (1854), a school of art and design (1856), and a college of dentistry (1865). In this century, Arts and Science formed a single school, with undergraduate and graduate divisions, but the number of professional schools has been expanded by the addition of a school of the arts, a school of business and public administration, a graduate school of public administration, a school of education, an institute of fine arts, a school of continuing education, and a school of social work (some of which also have undergraduate divisions).

While the coexistence of these units within a single university preserves the founders' original commitments, it has also generated a complex administrative structure that tends to produce both intended and unintended effects. The twentieth-century version of each of the schools is governed by its own set of deans, a remarkable percentage of whom have been scholars of international reputation, while the university as a whole is administered by a group of people, collectively referred to as Central Administration, whose members do not all hold advanced academic degrees. NYU's heterogeneity and administrative complexity have had at least four pronounced effects upon the university: first, faculty members in the Arts and Science division have always had at least the theoretical opportunity to teach with and learn from their colleagues in the professional schools and vice versa; second, whatever financial benefits were associated with exclusive commitment to a classical education in the nineteenth century and to purely practical degree programs in some decades of the twentieth century have eluded NYU; third, the complex administrative structure has sometimes allowed strong deans to initiate innovative programs and sometimes impeded such initiatives, depending, in part, on how much communication is occurring among the various parts of the system at any given time; and fourth, the fact that professional managers increasingly use a different language and sometimes have different goals from those of the academic deans has meant that, especially in the last two decades, academic initiatives have required a mediator capable of translating projects from an academic sociolect into language that makes sense to the managers of the university.

The third factor that has always played a determining role in the character of New York University is the nature, and sometimes the precarious state, of its financing. Because NYU's founders were committed to educating the city's merchants and shopkeepers, they did not emphasize the classical subjects that would have attracted a more elite (and wealthy) student population. Because NYU was founded as a nondenominational university, it never had the church-related financial support that many other nineteenth-century universities enjoyed. Because NYU was largely a commuter school before the late-1980s, it was unable to benefit from alumni loyalty as residential universities are typically able to do. And because its fortunes were initially wedded to the politics of New York City, NYU could not free itself from competing political interests for much of the century. As a consequence, NYU's financial base has always depended heavily on tuition and its endowment has typically been smaller than those of rival universities. As a result of its relative financial insecurity, NYU has been unusually responsive to local, national, and global developments. While its dependence on tuition has driven the university to the brink of bankruptcy more than once, it has also meant that university administrators have been encouraged to cultivate an entrepreneurial attitude that has periodically positioned them to take advantage of emergent trends in institutional finance or education.[2]

The history of NYU's commitment to interdisciplinary programs must be written in the light of these three large and continuously influential factors.

But there is no obvious or invariant correlation between any of these factors and interdisciplinarity at NYU. Instead, my research suggests that these large factors have typically been mediated through six additional conditions, all of which have had to be present in some form for any substantial initiative to succeed. These six conditions include: (1) a theme that could be used to focus the use of existing resources and recruitment efforts and that was consistent with the university's historical mission; (2) a vocabulary that could capture this theme and make it attractive to the president, the managers in Central Administration, the faculty, donors, and foundations; (3) an organizational structure that would enable administrators to take advantage of NYU's resources and to present the outcome as distinctive; (4) well-regarded or influential faculty members willing to put energy and imagination into new ventures; (5) the sponsorship of key figures in the administration (usually the president or, more recently, the deans or the Deputy Chancellor); and (6) physical space that could be reconfigured to house a new enterprise and signal its institutional presence. While a new venture at any university might require some combination of these or similar conditions, and while NYU undeniably benefitted from developments in U.S. society at large, this university's history makes initiatives both especially dependent on and responsive to the convergence of these conditions. In a general sense, that is, the three large factors that have dictated the character of New York University as a whole have produced an institution unusually eager to exploit opportunity, wherever it may arise. When these six conditions have converged—as they did in the mid-1970s and again in the decade between the mid-1980s and 1995—the university has launched significant numbers of *interdisciplinary* ventures. Interdisciplinarity at NYU, however it might seem to outsiders, is less the result of institutional planning or innovation within the disciplines than an expression of the university's continuing need to make the most of limited resources to promote and develop NYU.

Promoting New York University has most often mean expanding opportunities to make the university more visible. *Developing* the university has meant both attracting financial resources and improving the caliber of faculty and students. In the mid-1970s, promotion and development went hand-in-hand because administrators correctly perceived that they could raise outside funds by creating highly visible programs designed to improve the quality of academic areas that had already achieved distinction. That a remarkable number of these programs were interdisciplinary echoes an emphasis apparent in U.S. society as a whole and articulated in particular by nonprofit foundations: the paired ideas that "the humanities" were currently in disrepair and that, if "the humanities" could be strengthened, universities could help society recover from the excesses of the 1960s.[3] Between 1975 and 1978, NYU launched five such interdisciplinary humanities initiatives, all of which were able to attract foundation support: the Humanities Council of New York University (1975), the Poetics Institute (1976), the Center for the Study of Social Relations

(1976), the New York Institute for the Humanities (1977), and the Institute for French Studies (1978). In what follows I focus on two of the most successful of these programs: the New York Institute for the Humanities and the Humanities Council.

All of these programs were created, in part at least, to help NYU emerge from the severe financial crisis it experienced in the 1970s. The university took other measures to achieve economic stability, of course, including, most importantly, selling its Bronx campus in 1973. NYU had initially acquired this campus in 1894 in order to provide its undergraduates a liberal arts education in a residential setting. Instead of enhancing the university's ability to provide a scholarly education, however, the physical division of NYU into the downtown and Bronx campuses exacerbated fiscal deficits, created overlapping and sometimes competing faculty commitments and curricula, and led to administrative inefficiency. By 1960, the number of applicants to all parts of the university had decreased to a disastrously low level and it had become clear that redundant programs, especially at the undergraduate level, constituted an unmanageable drain on university resources. While a grant of $25 million from the Ford Foundation enabled NYU to initiate sweeping reforms in 1963, even internal improvements could not counter the effects of decreasing enrollments, rising costs, a reduction in federal funding, and the pervasive effects of the escalating financial crisis of New York City. When university administrators predicted annual deficits of nearly $10 million in 1969, President James Hester had no choice but to implement a new set of drastic reforms. In addition to mandating efficiency at all levels of university operation, these reforms included the sale, in 1973, of the beloved University Heights campus.[4]

For several reasons, the sale of the University Heights campus constitutes a traumatic episode in NYU's history. On the one hand, the loss of the Bronx campus represented the end of some administrators' dream that NYU could preserve its founders' commitments without really integrating professional training (and graduate instruction) with liberal arts instruction (for undergraduates). On the other hand, the sale of the Bronx campus forced what soon became a single faculty to accommodate two groups of professors whose expertise had diverged during the previous eighty years. Whereas the University Heights faculty had consistently focused on undergraduate teaching, the professors at the Arts and Science Graduate School at Washington Square had professionalized during the first half of this century, like other faculties at twentieth-century research universities (and like the faculties at NYU's professional schools). When the Arts and Science faculties merged in 1973, some members of the Heights faculty thus felt their pedagogical skills were devalued, while some members of the Washington Square faculty felt that the overall quality of their departments was diminished because their new colleagues did not enjoy a reputation for research and scholarly publication. While the merger was relatively rapidly completed, the resulting departments tended to lack the coherence, consistency, and seniority of leadership that might have enabled them to vie for power more effectively with the top-level academic administrators and the managers in Central Administration. This relative weakness of all Arts and Science departments, along with the special liabilities incurred by the science departments, which had not been able to equip major research laboratories, contributed significantly to the emergence of humanities-based interdisciplinary enterprises in the 1970s.

Along with the sale of the C. F. Mueller Company in 1976 and the successful completion of a Leadership Campaign, the sale of University Heights also laid the foundation for NYU's financial recovery in the 1980s. In order to sustain the recovery that began in 1975–76, President Sawhill decided to focus the university's rebuilding efforts on "islands of eminence" instead of trying to develop departments that would have required extensive outlays of funds. In practice, this meant strengthening those departments that contained recognized research scholars who might attract notice and students, while neglecting or even eliminating departments that did not. In general, it also meant privileging humanities departments—for reasons we will see—and initiating interdisciplinary enterprises that would use foundation grants to expand the ideology of "the humanities" throughout the NYU community.

In this first extensive foray into interdisciplinarity, "islands of eminence" provided the theme that guided administrators' ambitions for the university, and a cluster of terms related to "the humanities" supplied the requisite vocabulary. The university's structural heterogeneity, which permitted what Sawhill celebrated as "academic interdependence," contributed one part of the organization necessary for curricular innovation, for some of the programs implemented during these years used the idea of combined degree programs to forge a closer bond between "applied" subjects like dentistry, business, and medicine and "theoretical" or "uplifting" subjects like history and literature. Another part of the requisite organization, its outreach, derived from the university's definition of itself as part of the city. President Sawhill provided the administrative leadership for the two interdisciplinary ventures I examine in some detail. Richard Sennett, Professor of Sociology, and L. Jay Oliva, who had begun his career as a Professor of History, contributed the faculty leadership for the New York Institute for the Humanities and the Humanities Council, respectively. Even though adequate space was only available for the NYIH in 1978, most of the conditions necessary to implement such institutional initiatives were thus already in place by 1975.

Two related features distinguish the products of this mid-seventies convergence of conditions from their counterparts of twenty years later. The first is the pervasive influence of an expansive definition of "the humanities" on all of these enterprises; the second is the relative imprecision of the nature and agendas of the institutes themselves. In fact, the NYIH and the Humanities Council did not need to have explicitly defined agendas because the concepts associated with the term *humanities* tended to stress both the universal nature of values considered central to all educational enterprises and the potential relevance of any project that pursued ethical or cultural enrichment. As Professor of English James Tuttleton explained in 1974, the word *humanities* implied "all of those intellectual activities, appropriate to a university, that bear upon the question of what it means to be human."[5] In light of the assumptions implicit in the term, university administrators could also assume that they spoke for the community when they initiated humanities-based projects, and, in the absence of strong departmental or disciplinary advocacy, they could behave in an autocratic manner without having to question whether their assumptions about the value of particular projects were universally accepted.

President Sawhill had a personal interest in the humanities, but when he set out to float the university's "islands of eminence" on a sea of humanities initiatives, he was also echoing a concern voiced repeatedly in post-sixties America: the fear that society, and especially America's youth, had lost moral direction. Many government officials and university administrators had come to believe that a combination of factors was threatening to undermine American students' embrace of principles that should have been innate. A historian of the Humanities Council refers explicitly to this belief in describing the intention embodied in this organization: "NYU created the Humanities Council to teach the importance of the individual and moral and ethical values in all areas of learning and professions."[6] In his "Appropriations Request" to the Congressional Subcommittee of the Department of the Interior on Appropriations, Joseph Duffey, the Chair of the National Endowment for the Humanities, tried to explain why "the humanities" could help Americans revive the values modern society seemed ready to cast off. The humanities, Duffey explained, consist of "a mode of inquiry, a dimension of learning" that "resists closure" because of the peculiar form of curiosity it expresses: "As a mode of thinking, curiosity in the humanities has to be distinguished from other ways of exercising our minds. To me, the key distinction is the way such curiosity resists closure. Unlike technical problem-solving, which occupies much of our time in a busy and increasingly bureaucratized society, thinking about the questions of the humanities is not a way of reaching answers quickly. In fact, it might be said that learning in the field of the humanities is not chiefly concerned with answers to questions as much as sharpening the way we ask questions in the first place."[7] As this and similar comments from the period suggest, in 1978 few advocates of the humanities paused over the tension between capacities assumed to be innate and qualities actually manifested by U.S. citizens, nor did they tend to note the inequalities later critics charged the humanities with masking. Instead, government officials, foundation directors, and university administrators simply focused on strengthening the humanities, as if the values implied by that term could counteract prevailing trends.[8]

NYU administrators, especially President Sawhill, embraced the promise that such unproblematic accounts of the humanities held out because NYU seemed particularly susceptible to the fragmentation and utilitarianism Duffey associated with "a busy and increasingly bureaucratized society": its historical mission tended to privilege the kind of professional training the humanities disdained and its more recent history of forced consolidation and fiscal crisis jeopardized the university's commitment to specific humanities departments. As the historian of the Humanities Council explains, the combination of student interest in "job-oriented curricula," the fragmentation of humanities departments, the fiscal crisis of New York City (which presumably deterred some students from taking liberal arts courses), and the expectation of fewer appointments in NYU's Arts and Science school required the faculty "to look to itself to create new ideas on how to develop educational programs that responded to student needs."[9]

NYU also seemed particularly susceptible to the woes of modern society because the city from which it drew the vast majority of its students was experiencing a particularly virulent version of modernity's crisis: by the midseventies, New York City was on the verge of bankruptcy; escalating rates of homelessness, crime, and drug use were making living in the city—not to mention going to college there—seem untenable to many white, middle-class Americans; and almost none of the city's officials seemed able to propose a solution. To Sawhill, who realized that NYU needed to draw its intellectual sustenance as well as its students from New York City, one response to the fragmentation undermining the city was to try to extend the cohesiveness promised by Duffey's definition of the humanities to the broader intellectual community of New York City. With funding from the New York State Humanities Council and intellectual leadership from sociologist Richard Sennett, Sawhill hosted a conference in December 1976, entitled "The Future of the Intellectual Community in New York City." Over one hundred educators, business leaders, lawyers, artists, politicians, and writers attended the conference, which—not surprisingly—reached the conclusion that had provoked Sawhill to propose the conference in the first place: "the very variety and abundance of . . . resources [in New York City] have produced a fragmentation of intellectual life in the city which too frequently precludes close interchange between various groups."[10] In order to remedy this fragmentation and to enhance "close interchange" between New York intellectuals and select NYU faculty members, Sawhill began to host a series of dinners, discussions, and fund-raising initiatives, which soon provided the New York Institute for the Humanities much of its constituency and support.

Sawhill created the NYIH from the previously existing Center for Humanistic Studies. Sennett founded this center in 1975, as the next phase of a Humanities Study group he co-chaired with Lionel Trilling of the Columbia English Department; Sennett and Trilling in turn had organized the study group in the wake of a Rockefeller Foundation conference on "Humanities and Social Thought," which was also held in 1975. The Center for Humanistic Studies had two agendas: to sponsor "a series of programs including workshops, seminars, lectures, and a variety of less structured, informal meetings, all designed to promote the greater cohesion of the intellectual community and to develop new forms of interaction among diverse intellectual groups"; and "to extend the purview of humanistic studies into all areas of intellectual endeavor, including the social sciences." The greater purpose of the Center was to extend the programs' influence beyond the organization's immediate membership: "to enrich and strengthen the intellectual community in New York City, and to make the city's outstanding intellectual resources more accessible to the nation as a whole."[11] After the December 1976 conference, and with the participation of many of the nonacademics who attended Sawhill's dinners, the Center's study group expanded its series of ventures to include, in addition to the existing interest groups (the Humanities Study Group and the Committee on Psychiatry and the Humanities), a Committee on Work and American Society, a Committee for the Study of the Social Production of Texts, and committees on Psychoanalysis and the Visual Arts and Acting and Ritual in Everyday Behavior.[12]

On October 19, 1978, the newly renamed New York Institute for the Humanities held its formal opening in its new NYU quarters, the fifth floor of 19 University Place. By that time, the organization that began as the Center for Humanistic Studies had received funding from Ford, Rockefeller, and the National Science Foundation in addition to NYU and private donors; and, in September 1978, the National Endowment for the Humanities had awarded the NYIH a challenge grant of $350,000. In June of that year, Sawhill received word that the Exxon Educational Foundation was also awarding NYU $300,000 to support the NYIH. In 1978, the New York Institute for the Humanities had an annual budget of $150,000 and, although the Dean of the NYU Faculty of Arts and Sciences was a member of the NYIH Board of Advisors, then-dean Norman Cantor declared the Institute free of decanal control.

The NYIH's early success in raising funds from foundations confirmed the accuracy of a prediction made by some of Sawhill's top administrators in 1974. In a working paper entitled "Organization for Research at New York University in the Coming Decade," which was drafted for the 1975 NYU Goals Conference, the Vice Chancellor for Federal Relations, Sidney G. Roth, and Victor Medina, Assistant Director of the Office of Sponsored Programs, predicted that "basic disciplinary research support will continue probably at a reduced level; [and] that interdisciplinary research is likely to increase rather than fade away." To take advantage of foundations' willingness to support interdisciplinary over disciplinary research, Roth and Medina concluded, NYU "should identify and act upon these opportunities for faculty and student support."[13] This observation dovetailed with Sawhill's desire to cultivate the university's "islands of eminence" by devoting its resources to "problem-centered, as opposed to discipline-centered, programs of study," and, once this preference for interdisciplinary projects over departmental development was articulated alongside the mandate for "academic interdependence" in the NYU Goals Statement of 1975, it assumed the status of university policy.[14]

From its early days as the Center for Humanistic Studies, the New York Institute for the Humanities had worked closely with another interdisciplinary venture, which was also begun in 1975, the Humanities Council of New York University. Like the NYIH, the Humanities Council received foundation support from the beginning, in this case from the Andrew W. Mellon Foundation. Like the NYIH again, the Humanities Council was designed both to infuse the university with the values associated with the humanities and to develop connections between members of the NYU community and educators and business leaders outside the university. Unlike the NYIH, the Humanities Council was initially engaged in curricular innovation as well as noncurricular events. With financial assistance from Mellon, the Council sponsored cross-faculty, interdisciplinary seminars, and, in 1978, with the encouragement of the Council, the School of Medicine and the College of Dentistry began to require their students to take humanities courses as part of their formal training. In 1978, Sawhill boasted that the Humanities Council helped encourage "academic interdependence" through collaborative work by the fifty faculty members it drew from all parts of the university and through the thirty undergraduate seminars and colloquia the Council had thus far sponsored.[15]

The curricular component of the Humanities Council was soon curtailed, in part because the university instituted a Core Curriculum. By the mid-1980s, the Council had shifted its energies to events designed either to link NYU to other educational institutions or to enhance the university's visibility among area intellectuals. For example, beginning in 1983, the Council held summer sessions for New York City high school teachers staffed by NYU faculty, and in 1985, the Council began to host the Faculty Resources Network, which brings together faculty from institutions of higher education in Connecticut, New Jersey, and New York in order to promote faculty and curricular development through the sharing of resources. In 1989, the Council sponsored "The French Revolution and Its Modern Legacy: A Bicentennial Reappraisal"; in 1992, it participated in the citywide conference entitled "Democracy's Poet: A Walt Whitman Celebration"; and, also in 1992, the Council sponsored the Quincentenary series, "1492–1992: Crosscurrents of Culture." As one might expect from the magnitude and focus of these activities, the Humanities Council was consistently successful in attracting outside grants. As even this brief history suggests, the Humanities Council and the NYIH both benefitted from President Sawhill's commitment to building the university by supporting "islands of eminence" and "academic interdependence," and they both mobilized the vocabulary of "the humanities" to host a range of programs, seminars, and high-profile colloquia. Both organizations benefitted from Sawhill's support in more explicit ways, as well: he not only hosted the conference that helped produce the New York Institute for the Humanities, but he was also one of the five members of the Institute's original Executive Committee; along with Vice President L. Jay Oliva and Leslie Berlowitz (who became Director of the Humanities Council), Sawhill also helped prepare the proposal that secured Mellon funding for the Humanities Council. Sawhill's priority in these ventures reflects the effects of NYU's administrative complexity: because the schools were (and are) separate but governed and financed by a single administrative unit, programs or centers that cross the boundaries between schools and divisions require administrative support for fund-raising initiatives. Both the NYIH and the Humanities Council also involved NYU faculty, of course: Sennett helped plan the Intellectuals conference, he promoted the idea for the NYIH, and he became its first director; and, even though the Humanities Council was directed by a member of Central Administration, it did engage members of the faculty in planning and teaching courses. Finally, both organizations consolidated their institutional identities through the physical space they occupied.

Both organizations encountered problems as well. As largely administrative initiatives, designed partly to attract funds to the university and partly to increase NYU's visibility in local and national circles, the New York Institute for the Humanities and the Humanities Council have historically had uncertain, even tenuous relationships with both NYU faculty and the university's educational mission. Neither of these organizations was ever intended to be primarily an academic program, in the sense of providing courses, degrees, or research opportunities for graduate or undergraduate students: the NYIH was always intended to encourage "mutual education" among the "already-educated"; and, as we have just seen, the Humanities Council ceded its curricular efforts to the Core Curriculum in 1980. Nor was either of these institutions primarily intended to support or enhance the NYU faculty as a whole, even though individual faculty members did benefit from course development funds (in the case of the Humanities Council), and fellowships and intellectually stimulating dinners (in the case of the NYIH). Judged in terms of at least one of their organizers' common goals—to increase the university's visibility—both interdisciplinary ventures undeniably enjoyed a great deal of success. By contrast, judged in terms of what individual faculty members or—in the case of the New York Institute for the Humanities—foundations increasingly wanted, either enterprise could be—and was—found wanting. The complaints that surfaced relatively early about these two organizations help us understand the limitations of the university's mid-seventies venture into this particular variant of interdisciplinarity.

It is predictable that disgruntled faculty members would complain that the organizations were too exclusive and too closely associated with an administration too neglectful of departmental needs and academic issues. Somewhat less predictable is the fact that only a few faculty members were even aware of these initiatives. Professor Robert Raymo, who was Graduate Dean of Arts and Science when the two organizations were created, says that most NYU faculty members were so involved in department rebuilding that the activities of these two interdisciplinary and cross-school initiatives went unremarked.[16] Because neither organization was involved in the university curriculum in any sustained way, the impact of both on the university community was bound to be indirect. Lectures by such international luminaries as Michel Foucault were no doubt intellectually stimulating for those who attended, and the Humanities Council's colloquia and conferences undoubtedly fostered intellectual exchange, but the effect of these interdisciplinary ventures was inevitably limited by their relatively marginal status in the university as a whole.

Another complaint, which foundation program officers began to voice by the end of the 1970s, is equally telling. In January 1980, Loren Baritz, the Director of the NYIH, bitterly informed the Institute's Executive Committee that he had applied to numerous foundations for support, only to be repeatedly rebuffed because most foundations were no longer willing to sponsor an enterprise as unspecific and non-productive as the NYIH committees and seminars. Baritz's discouraging conclusion reflects on the growing discrepancy between research in the humanities disciplines, the bulk of which has always been pursued through individual, often solitary, effort that (to cite Duffey) resists rather than seeks closure, and the expectations of foundations, which increasingly wanted all sponsored research to be organized like research in the sciences— that is, collectively and with a predictable outcome in mind. At the same time, the reluctance of foundations to support the NYIH after 1980 also reflects an emergent social phenomenon, sometimes miscast as anti-intellectualism, which was directly antithetical to the capacious sense of the humanities that animated the 1970s. Whereas combating the kind of fragmentation that Sawhill had found in the New York intellectual community had seemed important in the mid-seventies and whereas an unproblematized version of the humanities had seemed capable of leading this campaign, by the end of the decade, worries about fragmentation had been superseded by a ringing endorsement of specialization, both in funding agencies like foundations and within the university disciplines themselves. At the same time, and as one expression of this specialization in particular humanities disciplines (literary studies), theorists had begun to interrogate the ability of "the humanities" to generate universally desirable values. Partly as a consequence of the increasing specialization within disciplines, moreover, and partly as a result of the pervasive distrust of claims about universality, projects that administrators had once been able to cast as having universal appeal no longer seemed to engage both theoretically sophisticated university professors and members of a public increasingly distrustful of work that seemed arcane or nonproductive. Whereas the Humanities Council remained relatively successful in raising funds after the end of the

1970s because it directed its energies to the kind of topic-centered single events that could be promoted to particular audiences and foundations, the New York Institute for the Humanities had to curtail its early ambitions as its funding base shrank to the university and private donors. Both organizations still exist today, in scaled-back versions of their former selves, but neither the NYIH nor the Humanities Council promotes its activities by reference to values considered sufficiently universal to link the disciplines, much less to attract participants in increasingly specialized walks of life.

THE INTERNATIONAL AGENDA AND FACULTY RECRUITMENT

If concern for "the humanities" governed the majority of NYU's interdisciplinary ventures in the mid-seventies, a new slogan—"internationalism"—inspired a raft of new initiatives in the 1980s and 1990s. Whereas "the humanities" had promised universal values to a city perceived as fragmented, "internationalism" was intended to unite an entire globe made newly accessible by the end of the Cold War and the rise of digital technology. As we will see, this new rhetoric, audible at national as well as local levels, was just one of the conditions necessary for the successful initiation of NYU's new academic enterprises. Despite "internationalism's" apparent inclusiveness, however, we will also see that all of the university programs created during these years bear some mark of the academic specialization that was already on the horizon by 1980.

By the late 1980s, NYU was a radically different kind of institution than it had been in the mid-seventies. Most important, even though the university was still disproportionately dependent on tuition, its fiscal health was remarkably robust. Because of the university's presidents' astonishing ability to raise money, the sale of valuable real estate, and New York City's emergent economic boom, NYU had begun to enjoy an unprecedented period of economic prosperity by the late 1980s.[17] No longer a commuter school that drew its population from students who did not want to leave the city but who were not admitted to Columbia, NYU had become a residential university by 1987, and it attracted applicants of increasingly high caliber from all over the world.[18] For the first time in its history, the expansionist agenda that President Sawhill had disdained was undertaken on an almost university-wide scale. Improvements were made to buildings, dormitory space was expanded, and an explicit plan to improve the research quality of the Arts and Science faculty was undertaken by C. Duncan Rice, the Dean whom President Brademas appointed in 1985.

In 1991, L. Jay Oliva, who had moved from the NYU History Department into the administration under President Hester, became president of the university. Because of his long experience at NYU, Oliva was able to conceptualize the university's rapid transformation as part of an evolution, which, as he envisioned it, would enable NYU to become "the quintessential global university."[19] In January 1995, Oliva assigned Rice the task of realizing this goal when he appointed him Vice Chancellor. Sylvia Baruch, who had long worked with Oliva in Central Administration, became Deputy Chancellor when he assumed the presidency. Partly because of her own extraordinary talent, and partly because she had Oliva's ear, Baruch exercised immense influence during this period, working closely not only with Oliva but also with Rice and nearly all of the faculty members involved in launching new ventures.

Just as the interdisciplinary initiatives undertaken in the 1970s required a convergence of the six conditions I have identified, so did the interdisciplinary programs launched in the 1980s and 1990s. Whereas fiscal constraint mandated a focus on "islands of eminence" in the earlier period, however, relative prosperity permitted a more aggressive and ecumenical form of opportunism in the later period. Rice remembers that the charge he was initially given as dean was relatively unspecific; it was simply "to improve the research performance and visibility of the [Arts and Science] faculty."[20] To carry out this charge, Rice sought both to build individual departments that already contained established scholars and, in cases where a given department was not strong enough to attract prominent recruits, to offer "intellectual footholds" in other divisions or schools to entice faculty members to come. As Rice described his strategy, it was "to pick up the potential for strength wherever it lay. If the potential for strength was to rebuild a political science department, let's say, or to build an excellent and traditional economics department, then we would do that. . . . But if, on the other hand, there were different kinds of opportunities, like using the building of anthropology as a way of strengthening certain area studies activities . . . we'd be totally delighted with that too." Rice described his efforts to "leverage" the appeal of the university as a whole as creating "synergy" between Arts and Science and the professional schools. "If the Law School was trying to recruit somebody from a university of very, very high standards, like, say, someone from Michigan or Harvard, you could envision this kind of person not wanting to change schools, particularly if changing law schools meant moving downwards in the pecking order. However, such people, we felt, could at times be attracted by giving them, not necessarily a joint appointment, but an intellectual foothold in an Arts and Science faculty. . . . The other direction . . . was that there were certain kinds of people who might be attracted to Arts and Science only if they felt there was a professional school. . . . We were trying to use joint school units, so to speak, to leverage the attraction of the university, rather than simply relying on one school at a time."[21]

As these descriptions suggest, Rice's efforts to rebuild departments, along with his reliance on terms like *synergy* and *leveraging*, sometimes—although not always—tended to encourage interdisciplinarity, if for no other reason than that many of the faculty members NYU wanted to recruit were used to working across academic divisions at their home institutions. Along with other deans, moreover, Rice also actively encouraged new interdisciplinary ventures in the 1980s as a way of recruiting or retaining valuable faculty members who could help raise the standard of research and attract better students. Among these ventures, two deserve special attention: the Neural Science Center, which was created in 1987, and the Program in Culture and Media (1982) with its affiliated Center for Media, Culture, and History (1990).

In the formation of these two enterprises we once more see the convergence of the six conditions I identified in the first section of this paper as well as the coincidence of this convergence with larger national trends. With themes and language drawn from the presidents' and deans' emphasis on internationalism and faculty excellence, these projects also relied on the specific features of the organization that allowed for what Rice called "synergy": the coexistence of Arts and Science and the professional schools offered a distinctive "vertical" approach to problems because it facilitated student, faculty, and professional engagement in specific problems or research areas. Like each of the interdisciplinary projects I have already discussed, the Neural Science Center and the Program in Culture and Media/Center for History, Culture, and Media also enjoyed strong administrative support, with the former depending primarily on Rice and Baruch, and the latter being instigated by Annette Weiner, Chair of Anthropology, then Dean of the Graduate School under Rice. Partly because the university had become more complex by the mid-eighties, partly because its faculty had gained considerable strength relative to the administration, and partly because research in the individual disciplines had become more specialized, the interdisciplinary centers and programs created in these decades depended more heavily on faculty leadership than had the NYIH and the Humanities Council. In this regard, the Neural Science Center benefitted from the presence of Professor of Psychology Anthony Movshon, and the Program in Culture and Media depended on the university's recruiting of anthropologist Faye Ginsburg to develop the initiative in ethnographic film. Finally, as both Movshon and Ginsburg emphasized to me, acquiring space was critical to the two programs' success: the Center for Neural Science currently occupies four floors in a centrally located building just off Washington Square, and the much smaller Program in Culture and Media shares space with the Anthropology Department on Waverly Place, where the Program offers students the opportunity to work with sophisticated production and editing equipment, use of a screening room, and extensive video and film materials.

While the six conditions present in the 1970s also converged in the mid-eighties, more than just NYU's financial condition had changed in the intervening decade. By 1985, a language that stressed universal values was no longer capable of attracting scholarly consensus or external funding. Throughout U.S. higher education, academic projects tended to be more specialized, in focusing more narrowly on specific problems; more theoretically self-conscious, in subjecting their methodologies to the kind of scrutiny associated with a heightened sensitivity to race, class, gender, and sexuality and with post-structuralism; and more product-oriented, as an expression of the speed-up of scholarly production the digital revolution facilitated and as a response to students' need for marketable skills in the recovering global economy of the 1980s. Because Rice's campaign to improve the research profile of the NYU faculty coincided with these national changes, the interdisciplinary projects he and his colleagues supported were inevitably more specialized, more theoretically self-conscious, and more product-oriented too.

As Arts and Science Dean, Rice initially directed his attention to rebuilding the sciences, which had generally been neglected in the wake of the merger of the two campuses. Because he believed that scientists were raising the most important questions of the day, Rice soon began to float ideas for inter-disciplinary, cross-school ventures that would enable him to direct resources to this division. Among Rice's ideas for research was a project on the brain.[22] Coincidentally, a group of faculty members interested in brain function from a variety of disciplinary perspectives had already been meeting for some time to discuss the problem of training graduate students in this area. Coincidentally again, Anthony Movshon, a promising young researcher in psychology, received an offer from MIT, and Rice seized the opportunity to retain Movshon, advance his campaign to improve the science departments, and strengthen connections between Arts and Science, the Courant Institute of Mathematical Sciences, and the Medical School by initiating an Arts and Science–based center for brain research. Because any all-university project needed Central Administration support, Rice enlisted Sylvia Baruch to help develop the Neural Science Center. With Baruch translating Rice's language of "synergy" and "leveraging" into the fiscal and thematic terms the president and Central Administration appreciated, with Movshon providing imaginative and capable leadership, with external funding from numerous granting agencies, and with the university willing to consolidate the Center in a single location, the Center for Neural Science was created in 1987. Almost immediately, the university's willingness to risk so many resources in a single enterprise paid off. The Center was successful from its inception, both in attracting prominent researchers from a variety of departments and in raising substantial funding for research. It was also successful in producing the cross-school alliances and the "verticality" that Rice had envisioned in its highly visible research projects and curricular opportunities: the CNS linked faculty, graduate student, and undergraduate research to work being pursued in the Courant Institute and the Medical School; it also soon offered both advanced graduate degrees and a rigorous, highly competitive undergraduate major.[23]

While Rice and Baruch were the prime administrative movers behind NYU's commitment of resources to CNS, they were not the only administrators to launch interdisciplinary initiatives in this period. In 1985–86, Annette Weiner joined forces with Brian Winston, a distinguished film scholar and documentary filmmaker who was then chair of Cinema Studies, to initiate a program in ethnographic film. This program drew on Weiner's disciplinary training as an anthropologist and the distinction of NYU's Tisch School of the Art's Departments of Film and Television and Cinema Studies, and it complemented both the international agenda, which President Brademas was already promoting, and NYU's historical engagement with members of the New York community (in this case filmmakers, scholars, and the community engaged in documentary and cross-cultural films). Needing a leader for the project and not finding one on the NYU faculty, Weiner and Wilson called on Faye Ginsburg, who was completing her Ph.D. in CUNY's Anthropology Department and teaching at the New School. Weiner cobbled together a three-year adjunct assistant professorship in the Anthropology Department for Ginsburg and encouraged her to look for funds. With the help of the Curricular Development Challenge Fund and money from the New York Council for the Humanities, the Program in Ethnographic Film got off the ground in 1986. By 1992, the program had shifted its emphasis from the history, theory, and production of ethnographic film to a range of questions centered on the interpretation and screen representation of culture. Its change of name to the Program in Culture and Media, reflects this shift in focus.[24] Ginsburg, by then a tenured professor in Anthropology, proved to be a resourceful fund-raiser. Along with fellow faculty in six other departments and with financial assistance from the Rockefeller Foundation and the UN Environmental Program, Ginsburg launched not only the internationally recognized, graduate certificate-granting Program in Culture and Media, but also the Center for Media, Culture, and History, which sponsors visiting faculty fellows, a regular faculty seminar, and an extensive program of scholarly film screenings.

The interdisciplinary enterprises created in the mid-eighties were more obviously linked to faculty research interests than were the NYIH and the Humanities Council. Because they were in part at least fulfillments of Rice's faculty-building initiative, the CNS and the Program in Culture and Media were explicitly designed to enhance and showcase the expertise of individual faculty members. As outgrowths of faculty interest, moreover, these 1980s initiatives also reflected the increased specialization, theoretical self-consciousness, and product-orientation that had come to characterize most academic work by the middle of this decade. While the CNS brought together researchers from a wide range of disciplines, for example, it offered opportunities for each person to use his or her disciplinary expertise instead of seeking a common method that would transcend disciplinary differences. When the Program in Ethnographic Film became the Program in Culture and Media, its participants explained the change of name with a theoretically sophisticated account of the changes that their foundational assumptions about "culture" had undergone.[25] And both the CNS and the Program in Culture and Media are designed to produce all kinds of products, from scholarly publications to research data to ethnographic films to graduate students credentialed to conduct sophisticated research and produce original films.

The decade between the mid-1980s and the mid-1990s saw the creation or reconstitution of additional interdisciplinary centers, programs, and institutes, some—like Africana Studies—prompted by a combination of student, administrative, and faculty demand, and others—like American Studies—initiated by a dean, then developed by a faculty committee charged with hiring a director. After 1991, however, when Oliva assumed the presidency and Rice became Vice Chancellor, the majority of new initiatives, whether within departments, between departments, or across schools, bore the stamp of the theme that acquired national prominence in the late 1980s and that Oliva adopted for his presidency: internationalism. The national resonance of this term can be attributed to the end of the Cold War and the fall of the Berlin Wall, although NYU's commitment to internationalism may predate these events; some remember this emphasis being current as early as Hester's presidency, while others associate it with Brademas or Oliva.[26] Whatever its origins, "internationalism," like "the humanities" before it, derived its power to animate NYU's ambitions from the salience this concept acquired among U.S. educators and foundation executives. As early as 1993, the Rockefeller Foundation had identified "transnationalism" as the next great area of academic concern, and the 1995 publication of the four-color glossy promotional with which Oliva announced NYU's "global vision" for the twenty-first century followed hard on the heels of a conference on "The Internationalization of Scholarship" sponsored by the American Council of Learned Societies in the fall of 1994. Citing the end of the Cold War, "the consequent relaxation of some long-standing barriers to travel, access, and colleagueship," and "rapid advances in electronic scholarly communication," the leaders of the conference also credited "the internationalization of scholarship" to the emergence of "new scholarly perspectives (postmodernism, multiculturalism)" in the humanities and the social sciences.[27] Participants in the conference concluded that, while American educators displayed "a strong reaffirmation of the importance of scholarship which increases our understanding of particular cultures and human communities across the world ... resources to take advantage of [increased opportunities for international scholarship] have decreased."[28]

Administrators at NYU made the theme of internationalism their own by stressing once more the university's location in New York City, which they now represented as "the greatest international entrepot in the world."[29] Already populated by a student body and a faculty drawn from all over the world, already the sponsor of numerous international programs and centers, NYU was now to become "an even greater magnet for global scholarship" by devoting to internationalism the resources that other universities had yet to supply.[30] To spearhead the university's commitment to internationalism, in 1995 Oliva announced the creation of a new interdisciplinary venture, the Institutes for

Advanced International Studies, which was to be organized and directed by Tony Judt of the NYU History Department. As Rice explained, the approach to internationalism epitomized by this new institute was to mark a significant departure from the additive model that had thus far characterized most universities' approach to the subject. In the past, Rice explained, "we plotted international activities and saw our strength in them as a sign of superior cosmopolitanism, but they were simply added on to our existing work and in general remained separate from it. One of the most exciting signs of our times is that we have reached a point where that approach is no longer adequate, either for students or for scholars. We have lived into a decade where we cannot afford to have our internationalism be a peripheral. It has become a part of a mindset that tilts every aspect of the University's life."[31]

In order to "tilt[. . .] every aspect of the University's life," internationalism had to be "mainstreamed," as feminist ideas had been mainstreamed in the 1980s, and it also had to be showcased, in an institute devoted explicitly to international themes and cooperative projects.[32] By 1995, plans for the institute that was to showcase NYU's commitment to internationalism were already well underway, for as early as 1991, Sylvia Baruch had enlisted Judt's help in devising a plan for just such an international institute.[33] In response to Baruch's overture, Judt came up with a plan that would advance Rice's charge to enhance faculty research and further the university's global agenda at the same time. Adapting the short-term visitor plan already in place in the Law School's international law program, Judt proposed inviting international scholars to attend regular seminars with NYU faculty and graduate students. Seeking to avoid some of the criticisms directed at the NYIH but to reproduce the intellectual exchange that institute fostered, Judt proposed two kinds of programs: one permanent program was to emphasize a geographical area (Europe), and the other was to emphasize a theme, which would be pursued for a few years before being replaced by another, related theme. In keeping with Oliva's commitment to undergraduate education, Judt also devised ways to extend the institute's scholarly work beyond its seminars and lectures; each visiting scholar was to teach an undergraduate course or class during his or her residence, and NYU faculty participants were to develop courses that incorporated the work they did at the institute. Finally, Judt insisted that the proposed institute be located in space dedicated specifically to it, so that it could house its fellows in offices whose proximity would encourage informal exchange.

For a variety of reasons, the Institutes for Advanced International Studies did not materialize in the exact form Judt envisioned. Whatever the reasons (and they are numerous and complex), by the end of the academic year 1995–96, the proposed Institutes for Advanced International Studies had been replaced by two separate institutes, which, taken together, contained most of the thematic and organizational features Judt had outlined in 1994. On the one hand, the Remarque Institute, which is directed by Judt, focuses on Europe; on the other, the International Center for Advanced Studies, directed by Thomas Bender, is devoted to a single theme for a specified period of time. Both institutes offer fellowships of varying lengths to NYU faculty members, to international visitors, and to graduate students. Both institutes offer regular seminars to foster intellectual exchange. Both institutes are housed in the newly renovated Judson Hall, renamed the King Juan Carlos I Center. And both institutes are resolutely interdisciplinary, with Remarque having thus far drawn participants from history, sociology, political sociology, anthropology, and various literatures; and, in its first year, ICAS having included fellows from political science, history, art history, philosophy, and economics.

Provisional Conclusions

It is difficult to know how widely one can generalize from observations about a single university. The story of NYU's engagement with interdisciplinary enterprises does highlight one complex theme, however, which seems important to any attempt to understand the history and the future of U.S. universities. This involves questions about who initiates change, especially the kind of far-reaching change that challenges the traditional disciplines. In the history I have given here, change has typically been initiated by university administrators, but these initiatives succeeded in large part because they dovetailed with the priorities of foundations, which were able to offer crucial financial support. The reliance of NYU's administrators on foundations points not only to the historical relation between this university's goals and outside funding sources but to the reliance of all U.S. universities on extra-university support. Between the mid-1940s and the mid-1990s, the bulk of this support came from the federal and state governments, with foundations playing an important, but supplemental role.[34] Since the mid-1990s, by contrast, as the proportion of both federal and state contributions to the overall operating budgets of universities and colleges declined, increasing numbers of universities have begun to seek corporate funding as well.[35] Given the connection between interdisciplinary programs at NYU and their foundation funding sources, one can only worry that as universities accept more corporate funding, corporations—not university administrators or faculty or foundation advisory committees—will have the power to initiate curricular change. Some kinds of interdisciplinary programs will surely result from such initiatives, as the new biotechnology programs suggest, but it is by no means clear that corporations will consider using these programs to promote or develop individual universities more important than using them as incubators for specific products.

I would like to be able to generalize what I learned about NYU to another theme with important implications for the future of U.S. universities—the relationship between interdisciplinary programs and the traditional disciplines. Every time I try to do so, however, I find that I cannot even generalize about this tension within NYU. The specific personalities involved in each program or department and the particular conjunctures of social and economic conditions seem so various—and so important—that deriving general principles is impossible. It is clear to me that the idea of interdisciplinarity carries hopes and fears about the way that universities will be able to produce knowledge in the future, but it is not clear from this one case what these hopes and fears are—even at NYU. In order to understand the fantasies that various scholars invest in "interdisciplinarity," as well as how this idea relates to larger social investments in themes like globalism, I think we need more studies like the one I have provided here. Without a better picture of the local conditions and forms in which specific interdisciplinary programs have flourished or failed, we will be more likely to project our own hopes and fears onto this capacious idea than to reach greater clarity about it.

NOTES

Research for this essay was conducted in the New York University Archives, with the expert assistance of Nancy Cricco; in the Archives for the New York Institute for the Humanities, where I enjoyed the help of Scott Hughes; and with the assistance of Lynda Smith, of the Office of the Dean of the Faculty of Arts and Science. In addition, I conducted personal or telephone interviews with the following individuals: Leonard Barkan (Director of New York Institute for the Humanities, Professor of English and University Professor); Sylvia Baruch (past Deputy-Chancellor); Thomas Bender (Director of ICAS; Professor of History and University Professor; past Dean for the Humanities, Arts and Science); Jess Benhabib (current Dean of Arts and Science); Faye Ginsburg (Director, Program in Culture and Media; Director, Center for Media, Culture, and History; and Professor of Anthropology); Tony Judt (Director of Remarque Institute; Professor of History; and past Dean for the Humanities, Arts and Science); Anthony Movshon (past Director of the Center for Neural Science and Professor of Psychology); Fred Myers (Chair and Professor of Anthropology); C. Duncan Rice (past Dean of Arts and Science, past Vice Chancellor of NYU and currently Principal at Aberdeen University, Scotland); Robert Raymo (past Dean of the Graduate School and Professor of English); Andrew Ross (Director of American Studies and Professor of Comparative Literature); George Sorter (University Professor and Professor of Accounting, Stern Business School); and Catharine R. Stimpson (current Dean of the Graduate School, Arts and Science). Throughout this project, I have also been ably assisted by Eileen Bowman, who transcribed interviews and tracked down missing pieces of information. Sylvia Baruch, Thomas Bender, Nancy Cricco, Faye Ginsburg, Nancy Greenberg, Dorothy Nelkin, Robert Raymo, and Joan Scott kindly read an early version of the essay and offered valuable suggestions. I am very grateful to everyone who provided time, expertise, and memories for this project. While I could not have written this essay without the assistance of all these individuals, I remain responsible for the interpretation I advance here.

1. The best history of NYU's first 150 years is Thomas J. Frusciano and Marilyn H. Pettit, *New York University and the City: An Illustrated History* (New Brunswick:

Rutgers University Press, 1997). On the founding of NYU, see chapter 1. The university changed its name to New York University in 1896.

2. For a discussion of NYU's recent success in fund-raising, see Kenneth R. Weiss, "NYU Earns Respect by Buying It," *Los Angeles Times*, 22 March 2000, A1.

3. It is worth citing Samuel Weber's observation that "wherever the humanities have imposed themselves as an issue of academic discussion, at least in the United States, it has been in a context of crisis." Weber notes that the Rockefeller Foundation sponsored a conference in April 1978 to assess the crisis that was associated with the humanities in the mid-seventies. See "Ambivalence: The Humanities and the Study of Literature," in *Institution and Interpretation* (Minneapolis: University of Minnesota Press, 1987), p. 135. My thanks to Joan Scott for reminding me about this essay.

4. In March 1973, the City University of New York agreed to pay NYU $61.9 million for the University Heights Campus (Frusciano and Pettit, pp. 241–43).

5. "A Proposal for an NYU Institute for the Humanities," p. 1, contained in a memo to Sawhill from Tuttleton (September 26, 1978); NYU Archives, Sawhill Papers.

6. [Anon.], "History," in "Finding Aid" to Humanities Council files, p. 3; NYU Archives.

7. Speech by Duffey in 1978 to the U.S. House of Representatives for Fiscal Year 1979, pp. 5–6. NYU Archives, Sawhill Papers.

8. Weber points out that pre-1980s discussions of the "crisis" in the humanities tended to emphasize either the relationship between the humanities and the sciences or the tension within humanities disciplines between particularistic descriptions and the derivation of general laws. See "Ambivalence," pp. 135–37.

9. "History," p. 1. The authors of this document do not address the contradiction between their observation that students were self-selecting out of humanities courses and their claim that the new educational programs were designed to meet student needs. Presumably the faculty—or, quite possibly, the administration—claimed the prerogative to decide what students needed, even when students failed to want what they were declared to need.

10. "The New York Institute for Humanistic Studies," Draft (October 5, 1977), p. 1; NYU Archives, Sawhill Papers.

11. "Draft," p. 2. In 1978, when the NYIH applied for the NEH grant, its leaders described its foundational principles as follows: "First, an intellectual community should be more than an academy; it should include businessmen, lawyers, doctors, diplomats, labor leaders, architects, and other professionals. Second, 'the humanities' take a particular form in an urban setting. Third, New York has both unique needs and resources for forming a community of humanists. The aim of the Institute is to create an intellectual culture which is urban in the best sense—diverse, open, and complex" (Project Grant Application to NEH, p. 1). In keeping with the NEH's grant category (Public Programs), the composers of this application emphasized the NYIH's ability both to contribute to urban renewal by making New York intellectuals available as a talent pool for the City and to lead other cities to similar projects (Project Grant Application, pp. 1–2).

12. "Draft 2" of "New York University: The Humanities Institute: A Prospectus" (July 29, 1977), pp. 6–9; New York University Archives, Sawhill Papers.

13. "Organization for Research at New York University in the Coming Decade," NYU Archives, Sawhill Papers, p. 7.

14. Sawhill suggested that a problem-centered program of study was one of the topics to be considered at the conference; see "Goals Conference: Selected Issues / Workshop E: Academic Planning III—Techniques," NYU Archives, Sawhill Papers.

15. *NYU Annual Report* 1976–77, p. 4; NYU Archives, Sawhill Papers, NYU.

16. Personal interview, June 4, 1999.

17. The fund-raising talents of some of NYU's presidents are legendary. James Hester, president from 1962 to 1975, is said to have raised one million dollars a week during one three-year period; and John Brademas, president from 1981 to 1991, raised $110 million in just two years. See Nathan Glazer, "Facing Three Ways: City and University in New York Since World War II," in *The University and the City*, ed. Thomas Bender (New York: Oxford University Press, 1988), p. 281; and Frusciano and Pettit, chapter 15.

18. The story of NYU's transformation from a commuter school to an international university has yet to be written. One measure of the change is its ability to house its students. In 1987, NYU was able to house 40 percent of its students in university-owned buildings; this represented a 150 percent increase since 1981 (see Frusciano and Pettit, pp. 254–55).

19. L. Jay Oliva, "Our Vision for the 21st Century," in *New York University: The Global Vision* (1995), p. 3. This glossy promotional brochure was produced by the NYU Press Office.

20. Telephone interview, June 1, 1999. Rice was remarkably successful at achieving this goal. During his tenure as dean, he appointed about 200 faculty members—"some from industrial labs and great foreign universities such as Oxford, Sydney, Rome—and the overwhelming majority coming from the faculties of Harvard, Columbia, Michigan, Yale, Princeton, and the California system or from Ph.D. programs at those and other outstanding American universities" (Virgil Renzulli, "Rice to Devote Full Time to Vice Chancellor's Duties, Leading University's Global Initiative," *NYU Today* [10/14/95], p. 1).

21. Telephone interview, June 1, 1999.

22. Memo to "Small Group of Deans" (January 8, 1991), p. 1; NYU Archives, Rice Correspondence.

23. I describe Baruch as the "translator" because that is the term she uses to describe herself. Baruch attributes the conviction that "*the* most interesting intellectual questions of the day were being faced in the sciences" to Rice, but she also notes that she and Rice focused on neural science primarily because they recognized in Anthony Movshon "a very bright, young, energetic [faculty member who was] willing to work" for the Center (personal interview, May 28, 1999).

The Neural Science Center is probably the most profitable interdisciplinary program at NYU. In its Annual Planning Report for 1999, CNS reports that during the past five years, "CNS faculty have obtained $30,224,381 of total external funding. The indirect costs from federal funds *alone* (NSF and NIH) amount to approximately $8,000,000" ("Annual Planning Report, Center for Neural Science, May 1999," p. 3; compliments of Professor Anthony Movshon). Baruch quite correctly points out that by the time that the CNS was founded in 1987, neural science was no longer, strictly speaking, an interdisciplinary enterprise (personal interview, May 28, 1999). While neural science draws on contributions by physiologists, anatomists, chemists, behavioral scientists, mathematicians, computer scientists, and psychologists, and while the CNS enlists faculty associates and affiliates (in addition to its core faculty) from eight NYU departments, neural science had developed into a discipline in its own right by the mid-1980s. Even though it is still called a "center," the NYU Neural Science Center became a department in 1993–94.

24. A history of the Program in Culture and Media can be found in Faye Ginsburg and Toby Miller, "Certifying Culture and Media: Anthropology Meets Cinema Studies," *Media International Australia* 82 (November 1996): 66–72. See also Ginsburg, "Institutionalizing the Unruly: Charting a Future for Visual Anthropology," *Ethnos* 63:2 (1998): 173–201.

25. See Ginsburg and Miller, "Certifying Culture and Media," pp. 66–72.

26. John Sexton, Dean of the NYU Law School, is also mentioned in conjunction with the international agenda, although it did not originate with him. Sexton did help devise an organizational model that could facilitate internationalism. This scheme involved bringing scholars from other parts of the world into the NYU Law School for short residential periods during their own universities' recesses. The desired outcomes of these brief visitorships were the creation of an international community of law scholars, the development of the Global Law Project at NYU, and the emergence of a new language for discussing legal issues across national boundaries.

27. "The Internationalization of Scholarship: Report on the Fall 1994 CAO [Conference of Administrative Officers] Retreat," *ACLS Newsletter*, vol. 4, no. 3, second series (Winter–Spring 1995), p. 1. Tom Bender reports that he found this report and passed it along to Sylvia Baruch, who then took the initiative at NYU.

Alberta B. Arthurs reports on the Rockefeller Foundation's turn to internationalism in "The Foundation of Knowledge: Reflections on Rockefeller Fellowships," paper delivered to the Consortium of Humanities Centers and Institutes (December 12, 1998), p. 7. My thanks to Faye Ginsburg for giving me a copy of this address.

28. "The Internationalization of Scholarship," p. 5. On May 3, 1995, Sylvia Baruch sent copies of this article to Duncan Rice, Philip Furmanski, and Thomas Bender in preparation for a meeting the four administrators were to have on May 10. The subject of this meeting, as Baruch's memo states, was "The Future of the Institutes." By May 1995, the "institutes" the meeting was designed to discuss would have been the two institutes specifically developed to advance the global agenda: the Remarque Institute and the International Center for Advanced Studies.

29. Rice, "Our International Mission," in *New York University: The Global Vision*. Oliva also used "entrepot" to describe NYU, calling the university "an entrepot between New York City and the international community" ("Our Vision," p. 3). I find it somewhat surprising that both administrators emphasized distribution rather than production, whether they cast the city or the university as the "entrepot," but this may have dovetailed with their desire to stress the exchange of ideas and culture instead of claiming credit for originating knowledge and culture.

30. Oliva, "Our Vision," p. 6. By 1995 NYU had already dedicated or attracted resources to several prominent international institutes and centers. The Institute of French Studies had been founded in the 1970s, as had the Hagop Kevorkian Center for Near Eastern Studies. In addition, by the mid-1990s, NYU boasted the Center for Latin American and Caribbean Studies, the Center for European Studies and the New Europe, the program in Africana Studies, the Skirball Department of Hebrew and Judaic Studies, the Russian-American Press and Information Center, the Center for Japan–U.S. Busi-

ness and Economic Studies, La Maison Française, Deutsches Haus, the Alexander S. Onassis Center for Hellenistic Studies, Casa Italiana Zerilli-Marimo, and the Lewis L. and Loretta Brennan Glucksman Ireland House.

31. Rice, "Our International Mission," p. 11. In my telephone interview with Rice, he called this "a kind of step change in the way in which one saw international cooperation. You know, this was no longer just exchanges or studying international things, where the subjects of study were international; the idea was to put an international component into practically everything we were doing" (telephone interview, June 1, 1999).

32. Rice credits the women's movement with having taught him "that a subject may not be most quickly institutionalized by teaching it through a separate department" ("Our International Mission," p. 13).

33. As Baruch remembers the conversations that preceded the launching of Judt's institute, they involved herself, Duncan Rice, and Judt, then herself, Rice, and Bender (personal interview, May 28, 1999). Tom Bender remembers two vectors converging in the idea for the institute: one came from Sylvia Baruch, who had already superintended the successful launch of CNS and the resurrection of the Courant Institute for Mathematical Sciences and who contributed expertise about organizational matters; the other came from Duncan Rice, who was being encouraged by Tony Judt to devote resources to the study of Europe but who wanted to expand the focus of any international institute beyond Europe (personal interview, May 19, 1999).

34. For a discussion of universities' financial dependence on the U.S. government, see R. C. Lewontin, "The Cold War and the Transformation of the Academy," in *The Cold War and the University: Toward an Intellectual History of the Post-War Years*, ed. Noam Chomsky et al. (New York: New Press, 1997), esp. pp. 12–33.

35. See Eyal Press and Jennifer Washburn, "The Kept University," *Atlantic Monthly* (March 2000): 39–54.

PART FOUR

The World in Pieces: Political Philosophy and World Governance

CHAPTER 16

Political Theory and Moral Responsibility

Jean Bethke Elshtain

THE STORY OF the revival of moral inquiry in political theory is, in large part, an account of the fate of political theory itself. The rising and falling, waxing and waning of the fortunes of political theory—an unabashedly normative enterprise—goes a long way toward alerting us to how political science takes up, or manages to avoid or evade, certain moral questions, including the relationship between our theories and our practices; between freedom and responsibility; between the political actor and the ordinary citizen; and so on.

Political theory in the American academy involves the stitching together of certain texts. Those of us who teach political theory know the drill. Inevitably there will be an undergraduate course in political theory or philosophy entitled "Ancient and Medieval Political Theory." As well, one invariably finds a listing for "Modern Political Theory." Modern political theory usually begins with Machiavelli and takes the student and instructor through Marx and Mill. Perhaps he or she gets into the twentieth century at some point. Ancient political theory is primarily reading of Plato and Aristotle. Medieval thinkers get, at best, cursory nod. Indeed, "religious thinkers," for the most part, are excised. American political thought is a separate course and is sometimes not even placed within the realm of political theory, but, rather, seen as a task for "Americanists."

The story of how political theory is to be defined is a story of contestations *within* political theory. What texts are in, what are out? Academic political theory is also a story of debates about how to interpret canonical texts.[1] But whatever their answers to textual questions or modes of interpretation, political theorists come together to engage in a contest of another sort, one that pits political theory against political science.[2] That debate has very much to do with the question at hand for the purpose of this volume, namely, is a rethinking of moral inquiry underway in the American academy, and, if so, what is the nature of that rethinking? This question can neither be posed nor asked apart from a concrete consideration of a particular tradition of discourse. When I was studying political theory as a graduate student of political science, I learned from the political science side of things that the goal was a commitment to neutral, scientific objectivity. To this end, values were expunged as a central feature of political study. The ideal was a value-free enterprise with the values of the researcher bracketed as "biases" and the values of research subjects reduced to calculations of opinions, attitudes, and preferences that were not themselves of great epistemological value. This was an enterprise called behaviorism or behavioralism. It was an enterprise whose assumptions and objectives included the presumption that there are discoverable uniformities in political behavior; that these regularities are akin to the laws of physics; and that they provide the grounding for explanatory theories in political science which are verifiable (or falsifiable) empirically and have predictive value. This effort, according to its enthusiasts, shared the scientific rigor of its counterparts in the physical and natural sciences.[3]

In order for political science to take on this particular status, it was necessary to separate utterly ethical evaluation from empirical explanation. A wedge was driven between so-called descriptive and so-called evaluative or normative statements. The goal of behavioralist explanation was neither the understanding of human beings and their social and political world, nor the interpretation of that world of self and others, but the construction of verifiable hypotheses with the power to predict. In order to predict, one needed behavioral regularity that followed an inexorable logic; behavior, in other words, must be caused. The test of lawlike generalizations within political and social life was implicit within a logic of explanation that assumed the possibility of prediction and regularity, according to behaviorists. The aim was to strip away the "apparent" complexities of political life and action and to get rid of anything untidy. Then, and only then, could one engage in a search for law-likeness in political life. Thus, all resonant themes and moral issues must be expunged from view before the analyst begins work, or contested issues may be incorporated, but in an anemic way, as the "biases" one brings to one's research.

Within the epistemological presumptions of behavioralist political thinking, to describe and to evaluate, to state what is and to state what ought to be, are two entirely separable activities. Those who mixed the two were considered fuzzy-minded, impressionistic, and incapable of rigorous analysis. A bifurcation, then, between descriptive and evaluative statements was essential to behavioralist inquiry. Laborers in the mainstream vineyard assumed that in statements other than those which could not be falsified—so-called analytic statements that entail a non-falsifiable correspondence between subject and predicate by definition, for example, "all married women are wives"—the political analyst was presented with a problem of linking or establishing a relationship between subject and predicate that could be explored and adjudicated for thorough empirical investigation. The investigation that ensued would demonstrate—or so the assumption went—a correlation between the subject of the statement and its predicate. The nearer the investigator came to a correlation of 1.0, the closer he or she was presumed to be to the truth and the greater the power of the statement, couched as a hypothesis, to predict. The researcher was required to reduce or to bracket ambiguity, imprecision, complexity, and ambivalence, in order to come as close as possible to symmetry between naming (the subject) and meaning (the predicate which expresses the truth of the statement). The result was a simplistic verificationist theory of meaning, one in which meaning is ground so fine—as a "predicate" carrying a very lightweight truth—that it is stripped of the power to persuade or to compel.

The theory of meaning embedded in mainstream behavioralist political inquiry claimed as a central presumption that the meaning of synthetic statements—a synthetic statement, by contrast to an analytic, might be, for example, "all married women are happy"—is exhausted, once a relationship between the subject and predicate has been established via correlations. Yet, even before such tests begin, the hypothesis has been impoverished by the reduction of rich, reactive terms central to human social relationships to a series of stipulative definitions. In the words of Charles Taylor, "[t]he profound option of mainstream social scientists for the empiricist conception of knowledge and science makes it inevitable that they should accept the verification model of political science and the categorical principles that this entails. This means, in turn, that a study of our civilization in terms of its inter-subjective and common meanings is ruled out. Rather, this whole level of study is made invisible.[4]

Early challenges to this position came from a number of different fronts. For example, from the epistemological side, thinkers such as Peter Winch, Charles Taylor, Steven Lukes, and Alasdair MacIntyre questioned the coherence of the verificationist theory of meaning. In an important work that appeared in 1967, Julius Kovesi in *Moral Notions* offered an especially compelling critique of the presumptions undergirding behavioralist political inquiry. He argued that the presumptions with which the behavioralists began inevitably yielded normative implications for persons and for politics, for there is no such thing as "mere" description. Description, Kovesi insisted, is always from point of view and hence is always evaluative: it cannot help but be moral in some sense, or secrete moral notions and ideas.[5]

We describe situations on the basis of those aspects of the situation we deem relevant or important. In this way we are always in a world of interpretation, for we are always evaluating under a certain description. Thus, the most important contrast is not between description and evaluation, but between "description from the moral point of view as opposed to other points of view"(63). Kovesi argued that the description was always to a purpose. That purpose may, and often does, remain hidden from view—embedded in a series of tacit prior commitments the analyst or researcher has not acknowledged and therefore sees no need to defend. Other critical hammer blows of this sort were struck.

The behavioralist reaction to some of these early challenges was to reaffirm even more vehemently the separation between description and evaluation, between statements of fact and statements of value. In the behavioralist world, opinions and values were presumed, first, to be rationally indefensible and, second, to be related to facts and descriptions in much the way that clothing and accoutrements are related to an unadorned department store mannequin. A window decorator begins with this unadorned mannequin and dresses or undresses it as he or she sees fit. In much the same way, the behavioralist would have the political analyst add values to the objective facts. These facts, like so many immobile, silent mannequins, remained unaltered through such external operations.

Ramifications of behavioralist presumptions floated into moral theory as well. A link between political inquiry and moral imperatives was presumed explicitly by classic theorists in the history of political thought; however, behavioralist political science tended to divide politics from moral considerations. But those raising challenges to behavioralism by focusing on moral dilemmas demonstrated the ways in which the bifurcation between description and evaluation simply did not work. This is an example that I used. Imagine that a group of persons are gathered around listening to a description of a brutal event in which young children are tortured systematically by sadistic adults. The account is replete with details of the desperate cries of the children and the impervious cruelty of their torturers. One of those who hears this tale of terror and tragedy is a behavioralist political scientist who accepts the dichotomy between description and evaluation. He insists, once the speaker has recounted the tale in all its graphic horror, that the group now be queried as to whether the actions of the torturers are to be approved or not. Would such a demand make sense? Remember, this situation was characterized by the speaker on the basis of those aspects considered relevant. These included the details of the suffering of children at the hands of torturers, described as brutal and sadistic. The *description* of events constituted an evaluation from what Kovesi called the moral point of view. A person devoid of a moral perspective would have described these events in different language—in language not designed to arouse compassion, sorrow, moral indignation, and outrage from the listener.

Kovesi, and other critics of behavioralism, then, gestured toward a world of "thick" moral concepts, a world in which morality isn't slathered like butter on bread but is there in the baking of the bread itself, is a constituent ingredient. They reminded us of the dense imbrication of moral notions and responses with something that seems as "mere" (as in "mere description" or "mere rhetoric") as the words we use to describe and the words we use to persuade.

If we place these considerations within the context of contemporary political inquiry, we find that those analysts who adopt a moral point of view from which to describe and thereby evaluate political reality, characterize social reality in language very different from that deployed by analysts who presume they have at their disposal a neutral language of description. For critics, precisely the obverse of the behavioralist claim pertains: we evaluate the world *through* our descriptive notions. In Kovesi's language, "moral notions describe the world of evaluation"(161).

There was, of course, a moral theory to which behavioralism was committed. Those who adhered to the view that moral notions, opinions, biases, and beliefs could be stated apart from description and research methods and findings; that such notions are indefensible rationally; and that they can be bracketed after they have pushed the researcher toward certain questions, adopted tacitly a theory known as *emotivism*. Emotivism is an account of moral notions compatible with behavioralist presumptions. The emotivist holds that such terms of moral evaluation as *good* or *bad* are purely emotive, i.e., these terms stand "for nothing whatever" and merely "serve as an emotive sign expressing our attitude . . . and perhaps evoking similar attitudes in other persons."[6]

According to the emotivist, that which we call *good* depends on our values or biases. Should individuals commend a course of action to us as good, they are merely recounting their biases or tastes—none of which comprises an evaluation for which reasons can be adduced and given. Should my own taste happen to concur, I will likely accept the commendation as good. But suppose, a critic might challenge, I am confronted with a moral dilemma. One day I find myself sequestered with a sadist who delights in lighting a fire to tails of captured stray dogs. Wishing to draw me into the enterprise of maltreating and abusing animals, this person tells me, "It is good to torture helpless creatures and to make them feel pain." Why is it good? Because this individual feels it to be, and "feels good" when engaging in the torture of animals thus commending these actions to others, so that they, too, might feel good.

How am I to respond to these claims? I could try to get out of the problem by declaring the puppy torturer a psychopath whose views must perforce be ignored. But perhaps the torturer's behavior betrays no sign of irrationality. Indeed, the person is calm and cool throughout. All that is left me, if I am a consistent emotivist, is the reply: "Well, you have your opinion as to what is good, and I have mine. Personally, I do not feel it is good to torture animals. My feelings are different from yours, so why don't we agree to disagree, and I'll leave now, if it's all the same to you."

Emotivists presume that no epistemologically valid argument for or against a social structure or set of social arrangements could be formed from a moral point of view that requires powerful terms—injustice, fairness, exploitation, discrimination—just in order to *describe* the situation. The emotivist might oppose obnoxious practices but this would be taken as his "biases." To the extent my biases matched up with his we would have a political agreement. The emotivist or value neutralist insists that he does take up values, remember, but these are, by definition, indefensible rationally. Critics of emotivism argue that the problems presented by questions of bias or values cannot be dealt with simply by admitting to one's biases and claiming that one has set them aside for the purpose of research. For this response does not touch the heart of the matter, namely, an epistemology that requires severing fact from value in the first place. The problem, then, was more complex and fundamental by far than any charge, or embrace, of bias. It was that every explanatory theory of politics supports a particular set of normative conclusions. To proffer an explanatory theory the analyst must adopt a framework that sets the boundaries of the phenomena to be investigated. Some factors of social life will be incorporated and others will be expunged from view before research begins. The framework compels choices, celebrates some interests, excludes others, and precludes seeing the political world under an alternative characterization.[7]

Although behavioralism has been on the wane for twenty years, the sense of intensive epistemological contestation I have just conveyed offers the reader insight into arguments that most often pitted advocates of behavioralism against political theorists.[8] Political theorists were the most likely members of departments of political science to be philosophically trained and engaged explicitly with politics and ethics, including questions of politics and moral responsibility.

Several books published in the early 1970s helped to set political theory on a new and more robust course. Among them are political theorist Sheldon Wolin's *Politics and Vision* and philosopher John Rawls's *A Theory of Justice*.[9] Wolin's accomplishment was to put before us a rich tradition of political theory and to show the deep and abiding questions it raises about freedom, responsibility, justice, order, equality, and political action itself. Rawls's work made much the bigger impact, in part because he offered up a powerful antidote to both behavioralism and the thin, ethical theory of emotivism with which it had been associated. But the Rawlsian strategy was to play out the revival of moral inquiry at a very lofty level. Staying with the metaphor of the social contract, Rawls posited an original position in which essentially beings generated principles of justice behind a veil of ignorance.[10] Rawls's project spawned a renewal of public ethics and all sorts of subfields emerged rather quickly, including so-called discourse ethics or communicative ethics of the sort associated with Jürgen Habermas. In the meantime, continental philosophy made huge inroads and one began to hear words like anti-foundationalism, post-modernism, and post-structuralism. Indeed, some have even suggested that we have come full circle, for in the most extreme forms of post-modernism ethics is, once again, depleted or forsaken as central to our understanding of politics. Interestingly enough, the primary political category for most post-modernists is "power," rather than "justice."

In reducing all of life (not just all of politics) to a series of power plays, some post-modernists reproduce the ardent claims of founders of modern political science who insisted that politics was about "who gets what, where, and when" *tout court* and that larger issues of freedom, justice, and fairness were so much icing on the cake of the "real stuff" of power. If anything, strong post-modernists tend to see human beings as "wholly constructed," creatures with no substantive identity nor inner life, hence beings much more at the behest of the reigning "constructions" (ideologies, ideas, etc.) of the day than did behavioralists who presumed that, because they couldn't talk "scientifically" about anything other than behavior, had to limit their claims to that. (Although in sustaining that claim, they imported lots of other concomitant ideas, as I have already argued.)

But it would be to take on far too much to survey this entire realm of inquiry. What I propose to do instead is to assume a revitalization of moral inquiry, and to go on to suggest that one problem with much of that moral inquiry, at present, is that it remains too tightly bound to certain academic struggles and issues, emerging as a terribly abstracted enterprise. That is one issue. A second, related concern is a strand in political theory and philosophy practiced by thinkers who long ago gave up on the behavioralist severing of political from moral inquiry. They embraced, instead, what I here want to call *the heroic temptation*, a tendency inherent in the tradition of political theory itself.[11]

A heroic dimension has long been part of the moral aspect of political theory. From Plato's ideal city in speech, to Rousseau's perfect republic where the general will reigns supreme, to Marx's classless society, to Mill's happy realm of rational, liberal choosers, political theorists have often taken as their task clearing away the debris of the old and making room for a brand new and much better, if not perfect, way of life.

The political enterprise was a matter of remaking the world as it is for a world that is to come: a world to be made radically different, better, if not perfect. One problem with political theory as a systematic plan for overcoming the old in favor of the new, often proffered as a "few simple maxims" (Mill's phrase) that would, if followed, usher in a cleaned-up social and political universe, was that it made the day-to-day humanly possible work look rather boring, distinctly unheroic, hence not particularly interesting and not something to be sustained by human agents and interpreted and understood by political theorists. The heroic urge, then, is a systematizing temptation, a desire to bring all of social and political life under the umbrella of a grand schema of one sort or another, or to reel all of life in on the line of one thread or strand. It is this tendency that separates a political philosopher, like Rawls, from a political theorist, like Wolin. Rawls, the philosopher, aims to abstract from the concrete and the particular in order to establish tradition and context-free norms or rules to which any disinterested person might subscribe. Wolin, the political theorist, while not abandoning the aspiration for commonalities or "the universal," claims that our understandings are tradition-dependent in vital ways and, certainly, that political theory and action cannot be made to subscribe to a few ahistorical norms, no matter how elegantly couched. To call the one approach "monistic," and the other "pluralistic," would be to oversimplify, of course, but these terms do designate the tendencies embodied in the positions I here associate with Rawls and Wolin, respectively.

A second, important political theorist who urged theorists to forsake the ground of systematicity (and ideology), for there are real dangers inherent in visions of perfect freedom, or equality, or "positive liberty" that turn on naive views of a perfectible human nature and utopian claims about the perfectibility of political life, was Isaiah Berlin. When I was in graduate school in the late 1960s, it was in vogue to make light of these warnings, and Berlin was accused of being a faint-hearted compromiser with the status quo. But he understood that debates about moral claims can never be settled definitively in a political world. Part of what it means to recognize moral claims is to recognize, at one and the same time, the contestability of these claims.[12] As one recent observer put it:

> Berlin uttered a truth, much against the current of the age, that remains thoroughly unfashionable and fundamentally important . . . [he] cuts the ground from under those doctrinal or fundamentalist liberalisms—the liberalism of Nozick or Hayek no less than of Rawls or Ackerman—which suppose that the incommensurabilities of moral and political life, and of liberty itself, can be smoothed away by the application of some theory, or tamed by some talismanic formula. . . . It is in taking its stand in incommensurability and radical choice as constitutive features of the human condition that Berlin's liberalism most differs from the Panglossian liberalisms that have in recent times enjoyed an anachronistic revival. Unlike these, Berlin's is an agonistic liberalism, a stoic liberalism of loss and tragedy. For that reason alone, if there is any liberalism that is now defensible, it is Berlin's.[13]

Although I am not primarily concerned with debates about, or within, liberalism, the basic contention—that we cannot smooth away moral conflict—is vital and either overlooked or glossed over in much political thought. That, or the moral universe, is made to look too simple as a battle between individualists, on the one hand, or communitarians, on the other, as one major contestation has been posed, and parsed, in recent years.

As we near the end of this bloodiest of all centuries, political theorists are struggling to find ways to deal with a multiplicity of moral claims that must be adjudicated both within ourselves and within our societies, and to do so in a way that does not presuppose a final harmony of purposes, ends, virtues, and identities. There must be something in common, if human beings are to hold together a way of life as an ongoing and relatively humane enterprise. But to try to forge too overweening a unity out of human plurality is to fall into the heroicizing mode, on the level of theory, and, all too often, to promote one version or another of antidemocratic politics, on the level of practice.

Two exemplary thinkers and political actors who illustrate the approach to moral inquiry and political theory I have in mind as an alternative to abstract systematicity, on the one hand, and antinominian refusal to make any strong moral claims, on the other, are the American reformer and social thinker Jane Addams, and philosopher, playwright, and current president of the Czech Republic, Václav Havel.

Havel begins by rejecting ideology and the heroic and utopian urgency it bears when he writes: "The idea of manufacturing a paradise on earth did not triumph, and it will be very difficult now for it to do so. Such a notion could only feed the arrogant minds of those who are persuaded that they understand everything, that there are no longer any higher, mysterious institutions above them, and that they can give directives to history."[14] Havel recognizes that our practices can never be made perfect any more than our theories can explain all that wants explaining or help us to understand all that requires understanding. But nevertheless he insists that it is the very murkiness and ambiguity of the world that demands our very best effort, an effort he describes as "a commitment to live in truth."

That commitment for Havel is inescapably shaped by a loss of metaphysical certainties in modernity coupled with an equally sure and certain insistence on our continuing need for a "higher horizon," for "a transcendental or super-personal moral authority which alone can check the human will to power, an anthropocentric arrogance that threatens the human 'home.'" Havel insists that one must begin from the bottom, from the humbly respected boundaries of the natural world, rather than from behind a veil of ignorance where one enacts a project of justice as a noumenal moment.

As well, a primary challenge to all post-totalitarian, postideological political thought and action is to avoid what Havel calls "pseudo-ideological thinking," thinking of the sort that separates the words we use from the realities they purport to describe, leading to what he calls "evasive thinking." He offers a wonderful example of this tendency—a tendency to disarticulate words from concrete referents, to leap-frog too quickly from the particular to the universal. A stone window ledge has come loose, fallen from a building, and killed a woman. The response of the communist regime (mired in ideological thought, of course) is to assure everyone that window ledges "ought not to fall" but look, after all, what wonderful progress we have made in so many areas and, what is more, we must always think about mankind itself and "our prospects for the future." A second window ledge falls and kills someone else. There is another flurry of reports about the overall prospects for mankind—rosy, as it turns out, as socialism spreads and workers' states proliferate! In the meantime, ledges fall and particular people in real local places are killed. The prospects of mankind are, Havel warns, "nothing but an empty platitude if they distract us from our particular worry about who might be killed by a third window ledge, and what will happen should it fall on a group of nursery-school children out for a walk."[15] Language, and not only language, is degraded if hollow platitudes deflect our attention from concrete worries and dangers.

Where the ideologist mystifies and a certain sort of universalist tries to unify, the thinker and actor devoted to what Havel calls "politics without cliché" tries to demystify and diversify, to look at the messy, complex realities of *this* situation, here and now, as that which requires our attention and calls forth our very best and clearest attempts at thick description laden with moral notions. For politics is a sphere of concrete responsibility. Its antithesis is an all-purpose, grandiose leap into the universal that too easily promotes a vapid (because unbounded) "responsibility" for everything everywhere. As well, a politics beyond cliché is one in which the political theorist and political actor refuses what Havel calls a "messianic role," an avant-garde arrogance that knows better and knows more than anyone else. Authentic political hope, by contrast, draws us away from systems that do our thinking for us and heroes that do our acting for us to what Havel calls a politics of "hope and reality." His hope is that human beings, in taking responsibility for a concrete state of affairs, might "see it as their own project and their own home, as something they need not fear, as something they can—without shame—love, because they have built it for themselves."[16]

Seventy years before Havel's writings first became available to English-speaking readers, Jane Addams penned her classic of American autobiography, *Twenty Years at Hull-House.*[17] Interestingly, Addams's reputation as a writer and thinker plummeted rather sharply, even before her death, and there has been no revival. She isn't a "systematic" thinker. She relies on stories and parables. These and other criticisms put her beyond the ken of political theory. But her work bears another look as an example of political theory as the morally aware and concrete activity I here endorse. Addams understood that political and social life cannot be written about save from one's own standpoint. But that standpoint need not be confined: it could radiate from a particular point (say, her father's den in Cedarville, Illinois) to a wider world beyond (the Italy of Mazzini). She describes her deep fellowship with her own father and her dawning understanding when he explained why his visage, at a particular day, was particularly solemn: Mazzini had died. Young Jennie Addams protested: But Mazzini wasn't even an American! Her father explains and does so in a way that affords her intimations, even a "solemn realization," of a genuine relationship" made possible with strangers—strangers who become part of a loose community of international fellowship. Her father helps her to understand through analogy by comparing the American abolitionist struggle to Italians fighting Hapsburg oppression.[18]

ADDAMS argues that we are called into the moral life through bonds of affection when we are children: not through abstract formulae and nostrums. We seek to imitate an "adored object." We struggle to live up to expectations. We seek companionship and fellowship. Hopefully, the circles of fellowship widen as we grow. But this is always done through example and by moving from the particular toward the universal without losing the tethering to the particular in the process. Hers is a dense, thick moral theory that relies heavily on stories and descriptive power to bear the moral point, so to speak. Stories are intrinsic to her method of social diagnosis: this is, in an interesting way, a method that enabled her to combine empirical observation—telling the facts—with strenuous moral lessons and claims. Let one example suffice:

> I recall one snowy morning in Saxe-Coburg, looking from the window of our little hotel upon the town square, that we saw crossing and recrossing it a single file of women with semicircular heavy wooden tanks fastened upon their backs. They were carrying in this primitive fashion to a remote cooling room these tanks filled with a hot brew incident to one stage of beer making. The women were bent forward, not only under the weight which they were bearing, but because the tanks were so high that it would have been impossible for them to have lifted their heads. Their faces and hands, reddened in the cold morning air, showed clearly the white scars where they had previously been scalded by the hot stuff which splashed if they stumbled ever so little on their way. Stung into action by one of those sudden indignations against cruel conditions which at times fill the young with unexpected energy, I found myself across the square, in company with mine host, interviewing the phlegmatic owner of the brewery who received us with exasperating indifference, or rather received me, for the innkeeper mysteriously slunk away as soon as the great magnate of the town began to speak. . . . It was doubtless in such moods that I founded my admiration for Albrecht Dürer, taking his wonderful pictures, however, in the most unorthodox manner, merely as human documents. I was chiefly appealed to by his unwillingness to lend himself to a smooth and cultivated view of life, by his determination to record its frustrations and even the hideous forms which darken the day for our human imagination and to ignore no human complications. I believed that his canvases . . . were longing to avert that shedding of blood which is sure to occur when men forget how complicated life is and insist upon reducing it to logical dogmas. (73–75)

The complexity of these passages is stunning. The word portrait Addams paints, unforgettable. One sees the bowed over women, their faces and hands laced by scalding brew as they make their way, tediously, laboriously, back and forth, on a snowy wintry day in Saxe-Coburg. All this for beer! One peers head-on at a bitter process and, from this defining moment, one is catalyzed to protest and to thought, to philosophic reflection that refuses to take refuge in the excising comforts of systematicity.

In giving up God-likeness and mastery, Havel and Addams hold on to the vitality of the moral act in the here and now. This, I would argue, is the form an authentic revitalization of moral inquiry in political theory will hopefully take. Political thinking in the American academy has suffered from the penury and niggardliness of behavioralism and its various offspring, and, as well, from an overly grand tradition of political and ethical theorizing. It has suffered

from the fact that political theory as a tradition has been constituted and recon-
stituted through a set of nigh invarying texts. But political theory and moral
inquiry from the ground up shifts the terrain and leads us into a realm in which
we refuse to freeze history and politics into a set of categories that yield what
I and others have called "narratives of closure." These are narratives—theories—in which everything is known in advance, all the categories are specified,
and all the possibilities are laid out. A genuine revival of moral inquiry shifts
us away from narratives of closure to narratives of possibility capable of entering into and helping us to see the vitality and importance of everyday life and
small events and their connection to wider streams of life and thought.

Michael André Bernstein, in his book *Foregone Conclusions*, writes against
apocalyptic history: "Beliefs, ideas, values and people are tested best in the
daily, routine actions and habits of normal life, not in moments of extraordinary
crisis, and because foreshadowing can only point to a single, inerrantly dramatic, rather than typical, quotidian resolution, it must privilege the uniquely
climactic over the normative and repeatable."[19] By foreshadowing, Bernstein
refers to reading the past from the stance of a present moment, whether a
described historic moment or a theoretical moment and seeing everything as
leading almost inevitably to that very moment. Hence, his retelling of an old
Russian joke during the Brezhnev era: "Q. What is the great world historical
event of 1875? A. Vladimir Ilych Lenin turned 5!" There is a way in which
political theory has given shape and form to events, precisely through a kind
of foreshadowing with the past, or at least particular highly dramatic moments
within it, leading to the promise of a new and more glorious present. It is
very difficult to give up this frame of mind. It is, if anything, even more
difficult to offer up a defense of the quotidian. To quote Bernstein again,
"The kind of ethics for which I am contending can better be enacted than
formalized, and any adequate description must itself contain sufficient local
depth and resonance to make vivid the lived world in which particular actions
take place."[20]

Now that the dust has settled on the behaviorist and anti-behaviorist debates,
now that foundationalism and anti-foundationalism have been rehearsed and
re-rehearsed, perhaps we will be open to a humbler and more political enterprise. Some will argue that to try to offer up the very best sense one can of
particular voices, moments, and movements, not in a still life, but in the stream
of life, is to lose political theory altogether. But I think it just may be the way
for political theory to find itself and to embrace a new identity as we enter the
next century. This would lend support to a politics of experimentation, but
from deep seriousness of purpose; a politics of wariness and skepticism that
nevertheless encourages and even requires faith, trust, and hope. Such a revival
of moral inquiry strips the political theorist herself of any privileged role in the

discussion. But that's all right. One engages then as a citizen among citizens, a neighbor among neighbors, a friend among friends.

Let me return to Havel and give him the final word. Havel argues that a central task of political philosophy for our time lies in recognizing what has happened at this century's end for what it is. What has happened is the definitive collapse of an attempt to rebuild human society on some overarching Weltanschauung. What has been undermined is the comforting myth that we have transparent and direct instructions and relations. Europe, Havel has argued, has entered the long tunnel at the end of the light. One might say the human race has entered the long tunnel at the end of the light. The problems which lie before it could not be more exigent and will not be dealt with in a kind of lightning flash. One must continue to think political thoughts and to do political deeds, not knowing how the story ends, nor with any finality of who or what is its author. The last word shall be Havel's: "Genuine politics, politics worthy of the name, and in any case the only politics that I am willing to devote myself to, is simply serving those close to oneself: serving the community, and serving those who come after us. Its deepest roots are moral because it is a responsibility expressed through action, to and for the whole, a responsibility that is what it is—a 'higher' responsibility, which goes out of a conscious or subconscious certainty that our death ends nothing, because everything is forever being recorded and evaluated somewhere else, somewhere 'above us,' and what I have called 'the memory of Being, an integral aspect of the secret order of the cosmos, of nature, and of life, which believers call God and to whose judgment everything is liable. Genuine conscience and genuine responsibility are always, in the end, explicable only as an expression of the assumption that we are being observed 'from above,' and that 'up there' everything is visible, nothing is forgotten, and therefore earthly time has no power to wipe away the pangs brought on by earthly failure: our spirit knows that it is not the only one that knows of these failures. If there is to be a minimum chance of success, there is only one way to strive for decency, reason, responsibility, sincerity, civility, and tolerance: and that is decently, reasonably, responsibly, sincerely, civilly, and tolerantly."[21]

NOTES

1. Thus one finds Straussians pitted against non- or anti-Straussians. Straussians follow the interpretive mode and method of the late Leo Strauss. Other major contenders at the moment include post-modernists and Habermasians. But there is great variety in interpretive styles.

2. I would be loathe to give the impression of a war unto death here, and certainly many political theorists and political scientists have maintained diplomatic relations throughout the years. Few political theorists disdain altogether empirical research;

rather, it is a particular epistemology that precludes so-called "normative" questions that draws their fire. The discussion that follows is about this debate and should not be construed as an attack on empirical research *per se*.

3. What is at stake, then, is a reductive scientism versus those who refuse such a reduction. It is also important to note that the American, academic appropriation (at least in political science departments) of the positivist tradition was, for the most part, philosophically naive. The great positivist thinkers—the early Wittgenstein (if he really belongs here—a disputed matter), Ayer, Hempel, and others—would scarcely recognize, and certainly would not call their own, what behavioralism did to, or with, positivism as a philosophical tradition that aimed to protect certain moral commitments by taking them out of disputations over "the facts of the matter." They were, in other words, insulating moral commitment from both ideology and religion. But, in the process, moral norms themselves took a beating and got ever more "privatized." For a *locus classicus* of the behavioralist revolution, see David Easton, "The Current Meaning of 'Behavioralism' in Political Science," *The Limits of Behavioralism in Political Science*, ed. J. C. Charlesworth (Philadelphia: American Academy of Political and Social Science, 1962; 1983). Easton is one of the makers of the behavioralist triumph in political science—and one of its most intelligent spokesmen.

4. Charles Taylor, "Interpretation and the Sciences of Man," *The Review of Metaphysics* 26 (1971): 4–51 (see especially p. 33).

5. Julius Kovesi, *Moral Notions* (London, UK: Routledge & Kegan Paul, 1967), p. 63.

6. Quoted in W. H. Hudson, *Modern Moral Philosophy* (Garden City, N.Y.: Doubleday, 1970), p. 125.

7. Portions of the material discussed thus far, including several of the examples, appeared in my piece, "Methodological Sophistication and Conceptual Confusion: A Critique of Mainstream Political Science," in *The Prism of Sex: Toward an Equitable Pursuit of Knowledge*, ed. J. Sherman and E. Beck (Madison: University of Wisconsin Press, 1980), pp. 229–52.

8. Rational choice theory is now the dominant mode embraced by those committed to one form or another of emotivism. The model to which rational choice practitioners aspire is macro-economics.

9. Sheldon Wolin, *Politics and Vision* (Boston: Little, Brown, 1970); John Rawls, *A Theory of Justice* (Cambridge, Mass.: Harvard University Press, 1971).

10. Thanks to Fred Dallmayr for his helpful suggestions in this regard.

11. Rawls, with his grand, systematic theorizing a la German idealism, perhaps belongs in this camp, although he has come down to *terra firma* in his more recent works.

12. Berlin's most recent statement of his basic insights appears in *The Crooked Timber of Humanity* (New York: Vintage, 1992).

13. John Gray, "The Unavoidable Conflict," *Times Literary Supplement*, 5 July 1991, p. 3.

14. Václav Havel, *Toward a Civil Society* (Prague: Nakladatelstvi Lidove Novinyi, 1994), p. 23.

15. Václav Havel, *Open Letters* (New York: Knopf, 1991), p. 11.

16. Václav Havel, *Summer Meditations* (New York: Knopf, 1992), p. 128.

17. Jane Addams, *Twenty Years at Hull-House* (New York: Macmillan, 1910, o.p.). Available currently in an edition edited by Henry Steele Commager, drawings by Norah Hamilton (New York : New American Library [A Signet Classic], 1961).

18. This story appears in *Twenty Years at Hull-House*, Chapter I, "Earliest Impressions," p. 21.

19. Michael André Bernstein, *Foregone Conclusions* (Berkeley: The University of California Press, 1994), p. 89.

20. Bernstein, *Foregone Conclusions*, p. 121.

21. Václav Havel, "Paradise Lost," *New York Review of Books*, 9 April 1992, pp. 6–7.

CHAPTER 17

A "Moral Core" Solution to the Prisoners' Dilemma

Jane Mansbridge

IN THE LAST century, we have created a world that is threatened by nuclear proliferation, environmental disaster, and at least a temporary weakening of movements and institutions designed to protect the most vulnerable. Which of the *ideas* developed in the same hundred years holds out the most hope for helping save us from ourselves?

My candidate is the idea of the "free-rider problem" (or "collective action problem"), formulated by game theorists as the "prisoners' dilemma." This idea, I contend, takes the next major theoretical step beyond Hobbes, and deserves to become as well known as the laws of supply and demand. This central idea is effectively supplemented by poststructural critiques and by deliberative understandings of democracy.

THE PRISONERS' DILEMMA/FREE-RIDER PROBLEM

Game theory, the approach that led to the discovery of the prisoners' dilemma, was developed toward the end of World War II. The mathematician Johann von Neumann, whose name graces a drive at the Institute, played a central role in its development. Within this new discipline, two game theorists in 1952 discovered the "prisoners' dilemma" as a strategic interaction.[1] This interaction has a structure such that, in contrast to the market, each individual rationally acting on self-interest produces an outcome that is worse—often disastrously worse—than what the same actors could have produced by acting cooperatively.[2]

The logic is this: Whenever a good produced collectively is structured so that those who avoid contributing to the good nevertheless cannot be excluded from its benefits (they can "free ride" on the others' contributions), it *always* pays each individual to avoid contributing (presuming that contributing is costly to the contributor). Yet the more individuals avoid contributing (the more they "defect" instead of "cooperate"), the worse the outcome for everyone will be.

"The tragedy of the commons" is one version of this dilemma. When land is divided up into private plots, all the farmers experience the good and ill effects of their own efforts on their own plot. Non-contributors are excluded from the benefits. But when land is held in common, each farmer has an interest in taking but not giving. Each, for example, has an interest in putting another cow on the common grazing land. If everyone does this, the commons soon becomes overgrazed and all the cows starve. When the good is structured (like a commons) so that no one can be excluded from its benefits, it will be in the interest of each to free-ride on the forbearance or contribution of others. The commons then erodes, is not provided in the first place, or is provided less than would be the case if non-contributors could be excluded from the benefits.[3]

I sometimes ask my students to engage in the following free-rider experiment. We postulate that they each have $100. They can contribute either none or all of that $100 to the common pool. (Specifying only these two choices keeps the logic simple). The pool will double what it receives and distribute that amount back to the class. However, it will distribute the doubled receipts equally among the students without regard to who has and who has not contributed (non-contributors cannot be excluded from the benefits). Each individual makes a contribution of either $0 or $100 anonymously, by writing the choice on a paper that is folded before handing in, so there can be no social pressure to contribute. If everyone in the class contributes $100, each individual will walk out of the class with $200. If all but one contribute, the one who does not contribute will leave the class with both her original $100 and her equal share of the doubling of what everyone else has contributed (almost $200)—a total of almost $300. Of course, if everyone employs that strategy, no one gives anything, the pool receives nothing, nothing is doubled, and no one gains anything from the available resource of a pool that will double whatever it gets. In this case, as in all prisoners' dilemma/free-rider problems, the circumstances and payoffs are arranged so that it is always in each individual's narrow interest to "defect" (not cooperate, not give, or not forbear from taking), but the more people follow that course the worse it is for everyone.

Hobbes's war of all against all was a version of this dilemma, and the Leviathan his answer to it. Peace benefits everyone, Hobbes realized, but it is to no one's interest to disarm unilaterally. When the state has the monopoly of violence, it can force all to disarm, and all benefit. This logic of the prisoners' dilemma/free-rider problem, however, lets us see that far more human interactions than mutual violence fit the pattern, and far more responses than state power are available to solve it. Examples of these problems run the gamut from environmental pollution to being a good "citizen" in your department. In an example from politics, each negative campaign advertisement helps the individual politician but harms the reputation of politicians as a group. Nuclear proliferation has a similar structure. So many instances of the structure abound that in 1980 Arthur Stinchcombe entitled a review essay "Is the Prisoner's Dilemma All of Sociology?"[4]

Far less widely accepted, but the major contention of this essay, is the recognition that the Leviathan, or state power, is a highly inefficient way of solving prisoners' dilemma/free-rider problems. Far better is a combination of deep social ties and commitment to principle supported by a minimum of external coercion. Indeed, most societies with common land, common forest, common fisheries, or a need for common defense have historically dealt with the inherent free-rider problem by using *both* the sense of duty that a tight-knit community inculcates in its members *and* the sanctions available to such a community.

A subordinate problem, as game theorists recognize, is that communities must provide incentives to their individual members to agree on what one's duty is and to pay whatever costs are involved in administering the punishment for noncooperation. The subordinate problem is made infinitely easier when the proper duties have been established far in the past, thus lowering current costs of agreement, and when the corollary duty to punish misbehavior has been established through traditional patterns of socialization, and when the institutions through which punishment is legitimately levied—from gossip circles to a state—have been established and perceived as legitimate for as long as anyone can remember. When modernization or other shocks weaken traditional forms of socialization, feelings of duty and institutional legitimacy, or when new needs (including new understandings of justice) arise that cannot easily be assimilated into the traditional forms, the old restraints on narrow self-interest tend to unravel.

MORAL CORE, COERCIVE PERIPHERY SOLUTIONS

In the early stages of game theory, the theorists who modeled the prisoners' dilemma and free-rider problem proposed only solutions based entirely on self-interest. Some suggested setting up a state that would punish free-riders. Some suggested dividing as many commons as possible into private property, thus eliminating the problem of non-excludability. Others came to see that when an interaction is iterative (it happens over and over), each can punish another's noncooperation by refusing to cooperate the next time around ("tit for tat").[5] More recently, others have seen—and here we begin to depart from the self-interest assumption of traditional game theory—that when participation in the interaction is voluntary, when some participants for some reason *want* to cooperate even against their self-interest, and when the participants have access to markers (such as reputation) that help them identify the cooperators, the cooperators will choose only other cooperators with whom to accrue mutual gains, and the noncooperators will be left with only one another and no mutual gains.

The most recent breakthrough departs even further from game theory's usual assumption of self-interest to craft what I call "moral core, coercive periphery" solutions. In many prisoners' dilemma/free-rider problems, the new logic suggests, the *most* efficient solutions—which will win in competition with other solutions—require two features. First, they are based primarily on individuals' internalized moral values (the "moral core"). Second, they are supported by sufficient coercion to deter defectors (the "coercive periphery"). Most of the work in these solutions is done through cooperation rooted in moral values—among them, internalized concern for the common good. This moral core must, however, be supplemented by at least a minimal level of coercion. Otherwise, the competitive successes of first a few and then a growing number of noncooperators will gradually erode most individuals' moral commitments to advancing the common good.

John Braithwaite provides examples of moral core, coercive periphery solutions from the nursing home, pharmaceutical, and mining industries.[6] The CEOs in those industries do not usually want to tie little old ladies to their beds, put badly tested drugs on the market, or send their workers down into unsafe mines. But the structure of competition is such that if they don't do these things, a competitor will. By offering the product cheaper, the unscrupulous competitor will eventually put the "good guy" out of business. So it makes sense for the CEOs themselves to create regulations for the common good, backed up by institutions that punish those who do not go along. *Most* of the work of adherence to the regulations will then be done by individual moral values—internalized concern for the good of others. A *little* work, around the edges, will be done by a coercive apparatus designed to keep potential defectors in check.

In these situations, the bigger the moral core and the smaller the coercive periphery, the more flexible and genuinely responsive to a problem the solution can be. Most of the individuals affected will promote the common good because they believe in the goal—healthy and happy old ladies, well-tested drugs, safe mines. They will do what they can to promote that goal for internal reasons, not because they are forced to do so. The law books, accordingly, will not need to fill every loophole or plan for every contingency. The committed individuals will have an incentive to monitor and sanction those who look for loopholes in the law or disobey it with little concern for the common good.

If two societies are competing with one another, the society that can solve its cooperative problems at the lowest cost will win, all other things being equal. A society composed primarily of citizens who believe they *should* not put another cow on the common, who believe they *should* volunteer to defend their country, and who believe they *should* cooperate in other instances of nonexcludable goods will do better than societies whose citizens act only upon self-interest. These commitments to norms of practice can sometimes be maintained only by tradition, but as societies change and tradition weakens, they must often be maintained by appealing to deeper standards of justice. The most efficient society's practices would engage the willing cooperation of all participants.[7] To maintain a concern with the common good in situations of contest, a polity must have institutions that are generally perceived as making legitimate decisions that promote some relatively consensual version of the common good.

A polity cannot, however, depend for solutions to collective action problems wholly on its citizens' concern for the common good. Crucially, it must also be able to enforce these decisions through coercion backed by legitimate authority. Most people in most societies are neither full saints nor full sinners. If people, distributed along a spectrum from the holy to the psychopath, live in a society with no coercion to back up its moral core, the highly sinful will at some point take advantage of some of the large majority of well-meaning citizens. If they do well from their sin, some of the slightly less sinful will be tempted to do the same. If these prosper, some of the even less sinful will notice their success and be tempted in turn. Commitment to the common good will, in game theory terms, "unravel." It may take only minimal coercion to prevent this unraveling. But without any coercion, the group will find it hard, year after year, to sustain cooperation when those who refuse to cooperate prosper in comparison to those who cooperate.

Throughout much of its history, the United States seems to me to have had a citizenry that came closer than in most other countries to meeting the criteria of cooperation sustained primarily by inner commitment and minimally by coercion. Frequent stranger-to-stranger interaction in this new country did spawn many and glorious forms of con artistry, attested to in fictions from Mark Twain's *Huck Finn* to George Roy Hill's movie "The Sting" (starring Paul Newman and Robert Redford), and by ample folklore about "wooden nickels," "snake oil," and "selling the Brooklyn Bridge." Nevertheless, the overall level of mutual trust, based on the predictable trustworthiness of others, seems to have been far higher than in European contexts with equally high rates of stranger-to-stranger interaction. In 1848, when Louis Brandeis's father came to the United States, he wrote back to Prague in astonishment that in New York, a city of 400,000 people, "housewives set out a pitcher every evening on the doorstep with 3 or 4 cents and in the morning find as much milk as they have paid for. Isn't that idyllic?"[8] Perhaps some combination of Judeo-Christian tradition, a positive-sum economy, a viable level of material well-being, and a relatively legitimate democratic government produced this level of stranger-to-stranger trust.[9] Whatever the causes, it seems that at least some of the business of the country in the nineteenth century was transacted in a context of relatively high mutual trust, based on actual trustworthiness.

Many recent works have pointed out how important trust and trustworthiness are to efficient economic transactions.[10] Francis Fukuyama, for example, has argued that both the U.S. and Japan can reap the economic gains of relatively high levels of mutual trust. Yet Fukuyama misses a crucial distinction between the two countries. In Japan, mutual trust among businesses is undergirded by dense social and reputational networks that generate obvious and often immediate sanctions for betrayal. In the U.S., by contrast, many social and economic interactions involve strangers. In laboratory experiments set up so that not cooperating is in each individual's self-interest but against the collective good, about 35 percent of American college students usually cooperate, even in one-shot anonymous interactions in which by defecting they can take away $10 or so more than otherwise and their defection will be known only to themselves. The percentage of cooperators decreases as the stakes rise. But cooperation grows from 85 to 100 percent when the participants can talk together and promise one another to cooperate.[11] Toshio Yamagishi's experiments demonstrate that Japanese students tend to give less money to the common pool than American students.[12] Although we tend to think of the Japanese as being group-minded, the group relevant to most Japanese is the close-knit reputational group. The American student seems more likely to make a cooperative move in an interaction with a stranger.

In the United States as in many postindustrial countries, generalized interpersonal trust (as measured by survey questions asking, "Generally speaking, would you say that most people can be trusted or that you can't be too careful in dealing with people?") has declined greatly since it was first measured in the 1950s, although it has rebounded somewhat recently. In Japan, however, trusting answers have been rising. In the most recent survey Japan has actually overtaken the United States. At the same time, trust in government in the United States has also been declining. Although it is not yet as low as Japanese respondents' trust in their parliament, it is lower than Japanese trust in their bureaucracy.[13] Our declining trust in government may simply be a move toward realism after the heady romance with government that followed World War II. But the decline in generalized interpersonal trust since 1950 may be undermining the moral core that makes possible cooperative transactions backed by only minimal sanctions.[14]

The U.S. and European economic systems have evolved without a full analytic understanding of their necessary underpinnings in internalized moral commitments to the common good. Paul Hirsch has suggested that capitalism requires, while itself undermining, the moral values generated by precapitalist societies.[15] But this is an oversimplification. Market societies certainly legitimate a particular form of self-interest. But they also, paradoxically, undermine classic envy. They do not undermine what is best called covetousness—my wanting what you have. Market societies probably increase covetousness. Markets do, however, undermine envy—my preferring that you lose what you have even if I gain nothing thereby. Markets often undermine an us-versus-them mentality. They replace zero-sum, peasant thinking, based on fixed amounts of land, with positive-sum thinking based on the creation of value through exchange.[16]

STRANGER-TO-STRANGER MORALITY

At least in the United States, market relations have been combined with habitual *stranger-to-stranger* interactions. The U.S. economic system seems to have evolved on the basis of a set of moral values and institutions that undergird smoothly functioning stranger-to-stranger relations. By contrast, the economies of more traditional societies seem to have evolved on the basis of institutions and moral values appropriate to more tightly knit communities where economic, social, and political relations can be secured by reputational and local sanctions. When the traditional bases for those local sanctions and reputational networks disappear, chaos and cutthroat action appear in their stead.

To much of the world in the year 2000, the alternatives appear to be fundamentalist morality or market amorality. Few analyses make clear that for stranger-to-stranger markets to be efficient, they must usually be sustained both by the intervention of legitimate governments and by predictable, trustworthy, individually internalized moral values on the part of most of those with whom one will choose to deal. In the last decade some previously libertarian exponents of the free market have come to appreciate the central role of a legitimate state in maintaining economic efficiency. The greater efficiency of moral core, coercive periphery solutions has not, however, been widely recognized. Nor is it widely recognized how hard it is to sustain both legitimate government and the internalized values that make possible moral core, coercive periphery solutions in stranger-to-stranger settings. Both institutional designers and normative theorists have a big job ahead of them.

Trust is not impossible to create. On the institutional front, it does not depend on a history of choral societies reaching back to the twelfth century. Current thinkers are making progress in understanding the kinds of institutions that can help develop trustworthiness and hence justified trust. Richard Locke, at MIT, reports that in Southern Italy and Northeast Brazil, areas thought lost to any mutual trust not monitored by individual families or the Mafia, certain local mayors and other political actors have begun to forge bonds of trust through open democratic deliberation and negotiation among traditional adversaries. Elinor Ostrom has also helped design in different countries institutional arrangements that promote cooperation through effective monitoring and sanctions.[17]

The next step is normative: coming to understand better the different possible moral and normative underpinnings of effective cooperation. Because earlier generations of normative theorists did not have access to the theoretical tools provided by the prisoners' dilemma/free-rider problem, they misunderstood the relation between individual self-interest and the common good when the common good takes a nonexcludable form. Nor did these theorists conceive of the subordinate problem as constructing a morality for strangers.

Consider the ancient Greek theorists. Plato posed what might be considered an early form of the prisoners' dilemma problem in Glaucon's question, which sparks the main inquiry in *The Republic*. Glaucon asks why one should pursue the good if one possessed the ring of Gyges, which makes its bearer invisible and therefore impervious to sanctions. Plato concluded that doing good produces the deepest form of happiness. He assumed, however, that some could approach real knowledge of the good. Moreover, he addressed himself to the problem of "the good," not the "common good,"[18] perhaps expecting that if enough individuals aimed at the good, the common good would follow.

Aristotle wrote often of the "common advantage" or "common interest." He wrote less often of the "common good," although Thomas Aquinas would translate him that way. In one passage that became famous in post-thirteenth-century Europe, Aristotle contrasted monarchies, aristocracies, and democracies, in which the rulers care about the common interest, to the tyrannical forms of these governments, in which the rulers care only about their private interests. But apart from this passage, he rarely addressed the relation between self-interest and the common good. He may have assumed that these were to a large degree congruent.[19]

In strong contrast with the Greeks, theorists in the Middle Ages continually stressed the opposition between private advantage and the common good.[20] First, Roman canon law stated as doctrine that "the common good is to be preferred over the private good." Second, Augustine and his successors understood sin as the choice of that "part, which belongs privately to itself" over "the whole which is common." These two strands fed a tradition, culminating in the work of Thomas Aquinas, that, unlike the Greeks, saw private and public good as often fundamentally opposed.[21]

The seventeenth century began to turn the medieval theory on its head. The market theorists who preceded Adam Smith stressed continually the congruence of public and private interest.[22] As Albert Hirschman has shown us, these arguments shored up the moral base of capitalism as a way of counteracting the passions that lead men, among other things, to war. They promoted the virtues of self-interest as a path to peace through *la douce commerce*.[23] By the eighteenth century, Shaftesbury, Butler, Hutcheson, Maxwell, and many others were proclaiming the congruence of self-interest and the common good.[24] Alexander Pope rhymed this conclusion in couplets: "Thus God and Nature link'd the gen'ral frame,/And bade Self-love and Social be the same."[25] Thomas Jefferson wrote his Overseer of Slaves that "providence has made our interests and our duties coincide perfectly."[26]

The Greek theorists got it wrong if and when they thought that understanding what was naturally right for you would produce the common good. The medieval theorists got it wrong when they thought that only surmounting sin (the part that puts private good first) would produce the common good. The eighteenth-century theorists got it wrong when they imagined a congruence of self-interest and the common good. None understood that in some contexts self-interest is perfectly congruent with the common good, and in other contexts—e.g., when noncontributors cannot be excluded from the good—self-interest is not at all congruent with the common good.

David Hume came the closest to parsing out the prisoners' dilemma/free-rider logic in his example of the two farmers who would not help each other harvest their corn, thereby losing both their harvests "for want of mutual confidence and security."[27] But even Hume could get no further than arguing, we now see incorrectly, that mutual cooperation was in each individual's *remote self-interest.*[28] A century later Alexis de Tocqueville described with a reporter's detachment the American doctrine that he called "self-interest rightly understood": "[T]hey endeavor to prove that it is the interest of every man to be virtuous. I shall not here enter into the reasons they allege, which would divert me from my subject; suffice it to say that they have convinced their fellow countrymen."[29] Tocqueville was wise not to enter into those reasons, for he could not have sustained a plausible argument for them. Perhaps he suspected that. Neither Hume nor Tocqueville could explain—because it is impossible to explain—how an individual motivated only by narrow self-interest could see as in that self-interest cooperation in a free-rider situation unsecured by reputation or other sanction. It is neither in my "remote" self-interest nor in my self-interest "rightly understood" to cooperate in a situation structured like a prisoners' dilemma or free-rider problem unless (1) my self-interest already includes the good of others or adherence to principles of cooperation, (2) my behavior will influence others' behavior, or (3) voluntary selection or other institutions specifically reward my cooperative behavior. When a nonexcludable good provides opportunities to free-ride on others' efforts, simply being a member of a community that benefits from its members' contributions does not provide sufficient incentive for a narrowly self-interested individual to contribute.

Specifying analytically the subcategory of nonexcludable goods within the larger category of the common good reveals the inadequacies of earlier accounts of the relation of the common good to individual goods. This analysis clears the way for genuine solutions to the many situations structured this way in everyday and political life. If the "moral core" argument is correct, however, those solutions in today's world will have to depend on a morality that will hold among strangers, a morality that can be internalized, and a morality robust enough to withstand the erosion of tradition, the temptations of anonymity, and the challenges of relativism.

THE POSTSTRUCTURAL CRITIQUE

Suppose we agree, on the basis of this analysis, that in order to achieve some nonexcludable good (for example, protection for the most vulnerable against the worst effects of global capital) we need mutual pacts reinforced with some relatively legitimate coercion but based primarily on commitment to the common good. We have first, as has already been discussed, the obvious problem of how to create that commitment and coercion in a world of strangers. We also have the second, and deeper, problem that any system of norms that produces the needed commitment will marginalize, exclude, and probably harm those who have little power to influence these norms. Any system of legitimation that makes coercion normatively acceptable will marginalize, exclude, and probably harm those who have little power to influence that system of legitimation.

Systems of domination and subordination reach deep. They influence the very words with which we think. When I speak in this academic context,[30] the language in which I voice my ideals plays a subtle role in marking as subordinate that part of me that I and others experience as female. The gestures that I have made my own, the very way I tilt my head, mark me as a woman— subordinate for that reason no matter what I do. Similarly, the way I speak, gesture, and so forth, as well as the paraphernalia of the room at the Institute in which I speak, mark me as a member of an intellectual elite in a nation whose language and culture are sweeping the world—dominant for that reason no matter what I do. Any concept of the common good that I help to forge cannot be neutral in these interstices of power.

I know, from my encounters with "virtue," with "fraternity," with the *polis* conceived in contrast to the household, that the very concepts of political morality that I grasp as I try to forge my own and others' commitments to the common good are pervaded with meanings which subtly point out that I and other women are in some ways not quite right for this task. I know, from my encounters with "sisterhood" in the feminist movement, that the solidarity around a common good that in my first years of enthusiasm I thought bound all women together in shared sorrows and joys, was without my realizing it deeply inflected by the experiences of white, middle-class American, heterosexual women in a way that became brutally clear as Black feminists and lesbians began to point it out.

What is true of norms—that they are deeply embedded in existing structures of domination and subordination, that they are never simply "there," or neutral, but are both contested and continually doing their active work of domination and subordination—is, if anything, even more true of systems that legitimate coercion.

Bonnie Honig argues for the "perpetuity of political contest" and against theories of politics that aim at final resolution. She argues that "every politics has its remainders." We cannot hope for a consensus that pleases everyone equally or a vote in which there are no losers. Every settlement leaves some individuals at least comparatively less powerful. Every settlement thus engenders resistances.[31] If we recognize the permeation of all norms and all systems of coercion by larger structures of domination and subordination, we cannot adopt a purely instrumentalist approach to social engineering, expecting that the structures we institute to solve collective action problems will do their work neutrally. We must recognize that any normative system or system of coercion will always reinforce some existing forms of domination and subordination, and will probably institute others.

Systems of norms and systems of coercion must therefore be subject to perpetual contest. Michael Walzer has helped us all think seriously about the way any social critic is embedded in the norms and values of her own society.[32] That embedded position insures some blindness to the way the very values and institutions that make possible organization around a common good also deeply privilege some as against others.

Can we live with a concept of the common good that acknowledges its inevitable noncommonality? Can we ask individuals to make personal sacrifices in the name of moral commitments that they acknowledge are by their nature flawed?

I think we can. Doing so requires an extension of our already acute sense of fallibility to encompass the inevitability of our implication in systems of domination and subordination. Such recognition need not produce paralysis. If we overthrew all existing norms and sanctions, or refused to develop new norms and sanctions to handle the collective action problems that threaten us most today, most of the currently disadvantaged would probably be far worse off—particularly if the alternative were one or another form of raw power, either market power or the power that grows from the barrel of a gun.

The challenge, then, will be continually to rearticulate existing systems of mutual trust to let in new players and formulate new rules, while retaining punishments, rewards, and signalling mechanisms sufficiently reliable to defend the trustworthy and trusting against major losses. The challenge will be to conceive and institute systems of decision sufficiently legitimate and stable to carry the weight of social trust but sufficiently open to accept, even encourage, far-reaching criticism. The challenge will be to develop moralities that can be internalized and that work among strangers, but are open enough to contest that they do not rigidly support existing structures of domination and subordination.

DEMOCRATIC THEORY

Here is where the third source of hope comes in, in the progress over the past twenty-five years in democratic theory.

One of the great achievements in democratic theory in the last twenty-five years has been bringing to fruition, indeed to dominance, the idea of "deliberative" democracy. Shortly after World War II, Hanna Arendt—and later Sheldon Wolin and others—promoted a politics of the common good that explicitly distinguished itself from the dominant U.S. understanding of politics as entirely about who gets what, when, and how—that is, interest group pluralism. In Europe, Jürgen Habermas developed his theories of the public sphere, distinguishing between "communicative action," aimed at understanding, and "strategic action," aimed only at winning. More recently, Michael Walzer has distinguished the political sphere as, ultimately, the sphere of persuasion.[33]

Empirical political scientists have joined political theorists in the project of making deliberative democracy work. James Fishkin, a theorist, has persuaded the BBC in England and various foundations elsewhere to fund experiments with "deliberative opinion polling," an alternative to the usual telephone survey, in which a representative sample of citizens conducts hearings, talks together for several days, and comes to a decision on a controversial policy matter.[34] Empirical political scientists such as Benjamin Page have begun to judge television and newspaper reports on the basis of their deliberative contributions.[35]

Now that normative theorists and empirical political scientists are finally coming together on a conception of politics that includes deliberation, and now that so many countries are trying to establish democracies in their different cultures, a next step must be to explore ways in which democratic deliberation can keep alive the contest and critique necessary for continued scrutiny of various contenders for the title of the common good.

The work on prisoners' dilemmas is founded on an unproblematic concept of the common good—one in which all gain or lose potentially equally, and in which the benefits of cooperation are relatively obvious, as are the benefits of noncooperation. Often unnoticed, many moments in democratic politics approximate these conditions. Discussions in town meetings over how to get the best price for a roof on the firehouse, and in Congress over how to reduce cost overruns in the military, have much of this character. The only citizens in the polity who will lose from a good decision in these circumstances are potential non-cooperators, who want to make more money from the appropriation than they would have made, say, in a free market. Legislators of all stripes long for decisions like these, in which few if any lose, and in which their votes will please everyone. But most decisions that come before legislators, even decisions that seemingly involve only "efficiency," do produce winners and losers. There is always the question, for example, of how the gains from efficiency should be distributed. Equally? On the basis of proportional contribution? On the basis of a previously negotiated agreement reflecting the existing distribution of power? In addition, many decisions that benefit most nevertheless hurt some. In these circumstances it becomes hard to describe any outcome as furthering an unambiguous "common good." Democratic deliberation then comes to have two goals: to provide continuing criticism of existing understandings of the common good while at the same time maintaining, through the engagement of the deliberators, commitment to that common good.

Many who have participated in a small group of committed actors have had the experience of maintaining both of these somewhat contradictory goals simultaneously. Critical, probing discussions with strong feelings on different sides can eventuate in decisions that represent both new understandings of what is best for the whole and an uneasy combination of negotiated side payments that make some willing to bear losses both for the good of a unified decision and because gains on other issues have made the losses bearable. Calling the result "the common good" has little of the simplicity of either the good in a prisoners' dilemma or the good described in much traditional literature on the subject. Yet the result can command loyalty and even sacrifice. Commitment to a decision in which one has participated and realistic acceptance of the necessary tensions in that decision can combine with willingness to sacrifice for the group even as all members of the group continue to scrutinize this and other decisions with a wary eye. Deliberation done well should validate ongoing tensions and also provide ways of surmounting those tensions for specific decisions. A free press and free association only begin the list of the institutional and cultural background conditions necessary to promote the kinds of critical deliberation that democracy ideally requires.

The human race today is still a long way from understanding how to deliberate and negotiate well. We have not yet even fully articulated the normative criteria for judging good and bad democratic deliberation. Similarly, we are still far from understanding how to institute good democratic coercion. And we have not yet even fully articulated the normative criteria for judging good and bad democratic coercion. But in the last twenty-five years I believe we have arrived at the point at which many normative theorists agree that democracies require both deliberation and coercion, and most empirical political scientists agree that democracies practice both deliberation and coercion. To the degree that this agreement prevails, it is a major advance over the situation when I entered the profession, when most political scientists defined politics as power, neglecting persuasion almost entirely, and most normative theorists defined democracy as persuasion, neglecting legitimate power almost entirely. If this agreement can stick, in the next twenty-five years both normative theorists and empirical political scientists may learn to work together on these problems, recognizing that political problems usually require *both* moral commitment *and* coercion, and that neither commitment nor coercion are analytically or morally simple.

USING THE NEW LOGIC

Several years ago Jesse Jackson, a preacher by training and at heart, traveled around the nation's schools telling schoolchildren to leave their guns at home. Not surprisingly, his preaching did not work. Anyone following his advice without other assurances would become the "sucker" in a classic prisoners' dilemma. If others brought guns, the cooperators would be defenseless. These young cooperators need the protection of some coercion aimed at punishing the gun-slinging defectors. But a system based only on coercion is also doomed to fail. Any self-respecting youngster can defeat metal detectors at the door and the school's security guard. The most effective system depends mainly on persuasion—Jackson's preaching, the parents' explaining, and the students' internalizing commitment to the larger good of a disarmed school—but backs up the processes that produce moral commitments with a good security force. At the moment, neither Jesse Jackson nor the school's security force, nor the students themselves, realize that they are enmeshed in a form of prisoners' dilemma, a version of the tragedy of the commons. Without this logic at their command, they do not see how to articulate persuasion with coercion. Coercion tends to drive out persuasion, just as extrinsic motivation tends to drive out intrinsic. But as coercion expands to fill more and more of the field, it simply fails.

The students are not alone in not yet having this logic. The U.S. Senators asked to sign a bill for public education, or a chemical weapons ban, or the Law of the Sea, do not have the analytic tools to see that the problems to which these solutions are addressed involve nonexcludable goods. They reject the coercion required to implement these solutions instead of trying to reduce the coercion to the lowest possible minimum by fostering agreements based on principles of fairness that most can accept. Even my own discipline of political science has not yet begun to develop these ideas. The rest of the world certainly does not yet have them in its analytic arsenal.

With luck, in the next hundred years the logic of the prisoners' dilemma/ free-rider problem will become as well known as is now the logic of supply and demand. Throughout the history of human exchange, prices have often risen when supply was low and fallen when supply was high (so long as demand remained the same and the community or individual moral standards did not intervene). But through most of history the actors affected by this dynamic, although grasping the underlying logic well enough to begin to hoard after a bad harvest, did not have the analytic framework for understanding its implications. Since the seventeenth century, theorists and practitioners of economics have developed the logic of supply and demand, refined it, come to understand its limitations, and observed its implications in practice. Today in every Western country every educated person understands, in a general way, the logic of the concept. If the price of bread goes up, an explanation that harvests recently produced less wheat makes sense of the phenomenon.

Yet, as the logic of supply and demand becomes more readily accepted around the globe, so too spreads the free-market logic that consumers in the aggregate (not workers and not the poorest consumers) benefit from restrictions on cartels and government abstinence from regulation. Along with this conceptual framework spreads the idea that acting on self-interest is not only congruent with, but promotes, the common good.

By contrast, the logic of the prisoners' dilemma/free-rider problem delimits one important set of instances, found in all aspects of everyday life, in which self-interest is not simply congruent with the common good. In these instances, without social intervention, without thought, without human beings acting together to create both internal commitments to duty and external institutions that punish defections, individuals acting on self-interest will destroy the common good. In the cases of nuclear proliferation and environmental pollution they may also destroy all of humanity.

The next decades loom before us like a minefield through which the human race must pick its way most delicately. As capitalism spreads across the globe, creatively destroying not only inefficient modes of production but also traditional moral systems, and as countries try to develop forms of democracy that produce decisions with legitimacy in their own culture and historical settings, normative political theory and empirical political science can have a positive role in helping to shore up collective moral commitment to the common good and sustaining that moral commitment with appropriate forms of democratic coercion. The key, I believe, is to remember that both moral commitment and coercion are necessary to solve these omnipresent prisoners' dilemma/free-rider problems. We cannot sustain the one without the other.

NOTES

1. Merrill Flood and Melvin Dresher discovered the interaction; A. W. Tucker gave it the name "prisoners' dilemma" (see Russell Hardin, *One for All: The Logic of Group Conflict* [Princeton: Princeton University Press, 1995], p. 32). Like Michael Taylor, I place the possessive apostrophe after the "s," indicating that the problem is a collective one as well as an individual one (Michael Taylor, "Rationality and Revolutionary Collective Action," *Rationality and Revolution*, ed. Michael Taylor [Cambridge: Cambridge University Press, 1988]).

2. In a prisoners' dilemma, two prisoners have been convicted of a small crime and are being detained in two separate cells, unable to communicate with one another. They are correctly suspected of having committed a far larger crime, but there is insufficient evidence to convict. Each is offered the following deal: If he gives evidence that will convict his partner, he will get off free but his partner will receive a very harsh sentence. If both remain silent—that is, in the language of this theory, if they "cooperate" with one another, each remaining silent—they will each receive only a small sentence. If one cooperates with his partner, remaining silent against the authorities, but the other "defects" against his partner, giving evidence to the authorities, the one who defects will go scot free, sending his partner off to years in jail. If both defect on one another, each squealing to the authorities, each will get a very harsh sentence, mitigated only slightly by having turned state's evidence.

3. See Mancur Olson, *The Logic of Collective Action* ([1965] Cambridge, Mass.: Harvard University Press, 1971) for the basic logic and for the concept of "free-riding"; see Garrett Harding, "The Tragedy of the Commons," *Science* 162 (1968): 1243–48 for the commons; see Russell Hardin, *Collective Action* (Washington/Baltimore: Resources for the Future/Johns Hopkins Press, 1982), p. 25 ff, for the recognition that the prisoners' dilemma and the logic of collective action have the same underlying structure. More recently Hardin has argued that the deeper structure is simply that of exchange, in which cooperation for mutual gain requires each individual to forgo the greatest gains she could demand; see Hardin, *One for All: The Logic of Group Conflict* (Princeton: Princeton University Press, 1995), pp. 32 ff.

4. Arthur L. Stinchcombe, "Is the Prisoners' Dilemma All of Sociology?" *Inquiry* 23 (1980): 187–92.

5. See Robert Axelrod, "The Emergence of Cooperation Among Egoists," *American Political Science Review* 75 (1981): 306–18, and *The Evolution of Cooperation* (New York: Basic Books, 1984).

6. Ian Ayers and John Braithwaite, *Responsive Regulation: Transcending the Deregulation Debate* (New York: Oxford University Press, 1992).

7. John Rawls, *A Theory of Justice* (Cambridge, Mass.: Harvard University Press, 1971), p. 15 and passim. See also Michael Walzer, *Spheres of Justice* (New York: Basic Books, 1983).

8. Adolph Brandeis, quoted in Josephine Goldmark, *Pilgrims of '48* (New Haven: Yale University Press, 1930), p. 201. Other travelers, such as Martineau, Butler, Bryce, and Trollope, reported similar phenomena (e.g., Jane Louise Messick, *The English Traveller in America 1785–1835* [New York: Columbia University Press, 1922], p. 114).

9. Mansbridge, "Altruistic Trust," *Trust*, ed. Mark Warren (Cambridge: Cambridge University Press, 2000).

10. Francis Fukuyama, *Trust* (New York: The Free Press, 1995).

11. Robyn Dawes et al., "Cooperation for the Benefit of Us," *Beyond Self-Interest*, ed. Jane Mansbridge (Chicago: University of Chicago Press, 1990).

12. Toshio Yamagishi, "The Provision of a Sanctioning System in the United States and Japan," *Social Psychology Quarterly* 51 (1988): 265–71.

13. Susan Pharr in Joseph Nye et al., *Why People Don't Trust Government* (Cambridge, Mass.: Harvard University Press, 1997).

14. We do not know if declining trust is caused by declines in trustworthiness or simply by more negative perceptions. We have no measures of trustworthiness over time.

15. Fred Hirsh, *Social Limits of Growth* (Cambridge, Mass.: Harvard University Press, 1976).

16. George M. Foster, "Peasant Society and the Image of Limited Good," *American Anthropologist* 67 (1965): 293–315, and "The Anatomy of Envy: A Study in Symbolic Behavior," *Current Anthropology* 13 (1972): 165–202.

17. See Richard Locke, "Strategies of Cooperation in a Rent-seeking World," forthcoming, and Elinor Ostrom, *Governing the Commons* (Cambridge, Mass.: Cambridge University Press, 1990).

18. Although the search is not complete, in the computerized *Thesaurus Linguae Grecae*, I have found instances in which Plato used the phrase "the common good"

(*koinon agathon*), in an even broadly political sense (contra claims by, e.g., Richard Flathman, *The Public Interest* [New York: Wiley, 1966], pp. 53, 56, 57). I would like to thank John Kirkpatrick's significant help in this work.

19. In this passage (*Politics* 1279b7–10) Aristotle used the words *koinon sumpheron*, meaning "common advantage" or "profit," and *koinon lusiteloun*, meaning "common profit, gain, or advantage," and deriving from the word for "taxes." In the *Politics*, Aristotle used the phrase *koinon agathon*, meaning "common good," only twice, but *koinon sumpheron*, meaning "common advantage" and "common interest" seven times. Although the "good" described by *agathon* does not usually mean benefit, interest, or advantage, at one point Aristotle used *sumpheron* and *agathon* seemingly interchangeably (*Politics* 1279a13–14), and at another point wrote, "What is good (*agathon*) in the political field, that is, the general advantage (*koine sumpheron*), is justice" (*Politics* 1282b17–18). For more on the language of Plato, Aristotle, Cicero, Augustine, and Aquinas on the common good, see Mansbridge, "On the Contested Nature of the Public Good," *Private Action and the Public Good*, ed. Walter W. Powell and Elisabeth Clemens (New Haven: Yale University Press, 1998).

20. Ewart Lewis, *Medieval Political Ideas* (London: Routeledge and Kegan Paul, 1954), vol. 1., p. 214.

21. See Thomas Eschmann, "A Thomistic Glossary on the Principle of the Preeminence of a Common Good," *Medieval Studies* 5 (1943): 123–66, for canon law, Augustine and Aquinas. Aquinas did, however, consider the common and private good congruent both on a higher and more mystical plane and, less convincingly, on the grounds that because one is "part" of the common good it is in one's interest to pursue it; see Mansbridge "On the Contested Nature of the Public Good."

22. E.g., "The advancement of private persons will be the advantage of the publick." Joseph Lee, "A vindication of a regulated enclosure" (1656), quoted in Joyce Oldham Appleby, *Economic Thought and Ideology in Seventeenth-Century England* (Princeton: Princeton University Press, 1978), p. 62.

23. Albert O. Hirschman, *Exit, Voice, and Loyalty: Responses to Decline in Firms, Organizations, and States* (Cambridge, Mass.: Harvard University Press, 1970) and "The Concept of Interest: From Euphemism to Tautology," in *Rival Views of Market Society* (New York: Viking, 1986).

24. Milton L. Myers, *The Soul of the Modern Economic Man: Ideas of Self-Interest, Thomas Hobbes to Adam Smith* (Chicago: University of Chicago Press, 1983).

25. "An Essay on Man," Epistle III, lines 317–18, in Pope [1733], *Pope's Poetical Works*, ed. Herbert Davis (New York: Oxford University Press, 1966).

26. Letter (1819) in *Jefferson's Farm Book*, ed. Edwin Marry Betts (Princeton: Princeton University Press, 1953), p. 43. Jefferson was, chillingly, referring to his orders to allow female slaves not to work in the fields during the last days of their pregnancies, because the offspring were worth more monetarily as saleable property than the agricultural goods that the few days' work in the fields would produce.

27. David Hume, *A Treatise on Human Nature* [1739–40], ed. L. A. Selby-Bigge, 2nd edition, ed. P. H. Neddish (Oxford: Oxford University Press, 1978), pp. 520–21.

28. Hume postulated, for example, a "remote" interest in "the preserving of peace and order in society" (*A Treatise on Human Nature*, p. 545).

29. Alexis de Tocqueville, *Democracy in America* [1835–40], trans. Henry Reeve and Phillips Bradley, 2 vols. (New York: Vintage, 1954), vol. 2, p. 130; see also p. 132.

As he formulates the same theory earlier, "the personal advantage of each member of the community . . . consist[s] in working for the good of all" (129).

30. This paper was originally a talk given before the scholars gathered to celebrate the 25th anniversary of the School of Social Sciences at the Institute for Advanced Study.

31. Bonnie Honig, *Political Theory and the Displacement of Politics* (Ithaca: Cornell University Press, 1993).

32. Michael Walzer, *The Company of Critics: Social Criticism and Political Commitment in the Twentieth Century* (New York: Basic Books, 1988).

33. Hannah Arendt, *On Revolution* (1963; reprint, New York: Viking, 1965); Jürgen Habermas, "Hannah Arendt's Communications Concept of Power" (1976), *Philosophical-Political Profiles*, trans. Frederick G. Lawrence (Cambridge, Mass.: MIT Press, 1985); Habermas, "Further Reflections on the Public Sphere," *Habermas and the Public Sphere*, ed. Craig Calhoun (Cambridge, Mass.: MIT Press, 1992); Habermas, "Three Normative Models of Democracy," *Democracy and Difference*, ed. Seyla Benhabib (Princeton: Princeton University Press, 1996); Sheldon Wolin, *Politics and Vision* (Boston: Little Brown, 1960); Wolin, "Fugitive Democracy," in *Democracy and Difference*; and Michael Walzer, *Spheres of Justice*, esp. pp. 304–6. See Mansbridge, "Using Power/ Fighting Power: The Polity," in *Democracy and Difference* for arguments that democratic legitimacy requires power (as coercion) as well as persuasion.

34. James S. Fishkin, *Democracy and Deliberation* (New Haven: Yale University Press, 1991). Joshua Cohen and Joel Rogers, *Associations and Democracy* (London: Verso, 1995) and Amy Gutmann and Dennis Thompson, *Democracy and Disagreement* (Cambridge, Mass.: Belknap Press, 1996) give specific, policy-relevant advice about how to make the democratic process more deeply deliberative.

35. Benjamin I. Page, *Who Deliberates? Mass Media in Modern Democracy* (Chicago: University of Chicago Press, l996).

CHAPTER 18

Reinterpreting Risk

Michael Rustin

"Risk" has become a fashionable concept in social theory. The idea of "risk society," developed most notably by Ulrich Beck and Anthony Giddens, is part of an influential attempt to redefine the agenda of left-of-center politics.[1] Although it has sought to identify a new progressive agenda of its own (for example, around the issues of environmental danger, gender equality, and information), its greatest significance lies in its attempted displacement of earlier social democratic concerns with issues of scarcity, distribution, and justice. The redefinitions offered by these theorists of "reflexive modernity" have been tested by the theoretical contributions to the political project of New Labor in Britain.[2]

The essential thesis of "risk society," as it is outlined in both Beck's and Giddens's writings, is the idea that a new hierarchy of problems now facing humanity has substantially replaced the agendas of the "old" Social Democratic, and *a fortiori* Communist, past.[3] The argument is that the distributive struggle over goods, mainly material goods, characteristic of industrial society is now being displaced by a potentially more universal struggle against "bads" of which ecological dangers are the most significant. Beck argues that industrial society is being transformed by changes whose essence can be found in the fact that they are not planned and thus generate continuing turbulence. What were once considered "externalities" and "side-effects" have become the main action. At the same time, it is argued that social structures—classes, families, nations, religious communities—which used to contain and structure social identities and antagonisms are being undermined by exposure to "globalizing" forces made effective by deregulated markets, by the weakened power of national governments, and by the reach of the new communication technologies. These "traditional" social memberships are dissolving in a process of individualization, from which are emerging new kinds of individual and collective subjects. Knowledge (mainly scientific knowledge) is deemed to be the driving force of these changes, but the knowledge-driven character of change also contains, according to Beck and Giddens, a "reflexive" democratic potential. The diffusion of knowledge and information, and the processes of "de-traditionalisation" and "disembedding," as Giddens calls them, has undermined formerly hierarchical structures of authority, even those of science. The democratic processes implied by the "modernization of modernization," at least in potential, will—it is argued—allow new individual and collective subjects to participate in shaping their world. Two models for this ideal of democratic reflexivity are the ecological movements, who pit themselves against the dangers of nuclear power and acid rain, and the feminist movement, which articulates new identities and claims of women. A concomitant change is said to occur at the level of the self-construction of individual identity (an explicit "feminization" of the social agenda) where the potential for self-discovery through intimate relationships is not prescribed by tradition. The culture of therapy is held up by Giddens as a leading aspect of a new freedom.[4]

By framing this argument in terms of a shifting hierarchy of issues (related to a more general change from material to post-material values), the authors acknowledge that some of the old problems (inequality, injustice, material scarcity) remain. Yet the new frame allows them to insist that these issues no longer count for very much, and should no longer dominate a progressive or modernizing political agenda. The tendency among both intellectuals and politicians who hold this position is not to argue with or to refute the older terms of analysis in any detail but to bypass these positions and make them appear passé. I have elsewhere described this as a strategy of "turning a blind eye," to the realities of capitalism.[5] Nor does this new theory stop with the reevaluation of social issues: it also seeks to displace a core enlightenment idea that the main constraints on human freedom derive from the obduracy of nature. Instead, these dangers are now located in an environment transformed by human action, especially by the interventions of science and technology. Ills no longer derive principally from the maldistribution of goods and harms, but from the unpredictable effects of humanly created hazards; remedy for harms is to be found not in specific, structured forms of social agency (such as social classes and their institutions) but in the more diffused "reflexive" power of active citizens mentioned above.

To a certain extent, this theory tries to establish an absolute break with both previous theories and prior eras: risk is presented as a new societal condition, succeeding in time the earlier era of distributive politics and bureaucratic state regulation, but otherwise unconnected with it. This claim is based in a kind of historicism—justification by reference to what is modern or historically appropriate—without methodological justification. In fact, many of the important "risks" to which contemporary citizens are vulnerable, notably in the flexible and insecure labor market, are the direct consequence of the defeat and breakup of the postwar settlement and the social guarantees that it achieved for employed people. Whilst this is abstractly pointed to as the effects of "globalization," its more tangible explanation in the renewed power of the market is glossed over, since the properties of capitalism are deemed politically off-limits as a topic. It is argued that "risks" are different from historic "bads" in that they are no longer being distributed as structured social inequalities.[6]

A HISTORY OF RISK

The theorists of risk society claim that both the substantive conditions they name and the framing vocabulary they use give appropriate definition to a changing "late modern" environment. But there is something curiously unhistorical about this definition of "risk society" as a novel one. Substantively, although an argument can be made that there are new kinds of risk to which contemporary mankind is liable, it is hard to see such risks as greater, or even different in quality, from those already experienced in the course of the twentieth century. And so far as the frame of reference is concerned, it can be shown that the idea of "risk," far from being new to social theory, has been foundational to modern social organization, and indeed to the Welfare State itself.

How far is the claim plausible that mankind is now beset by dangers of a kind different from those experienced in the past? Is it possible that risks are now generated mainly by social action rather than the forces of nature, and therefore require a new kind of reflexive response? The reality is of course more complex. The twentieth century saw a series of massive catastrophes that were the direct result of human activity rather than the result of human impotence in the face of nature. Among these we can count the two World Wars, the Great Depression and its dire political consequences, the Holocaust, the purges and famine of the Stalin period, the famine of postwar China, and the colonial wars of the postwar period. Numbers of continuing wars and collapses of civil order in the developing world can be added to this list. All of these were man-made catastrophes, and largely unforeseen. Even earlier, nineteenth-century famines—as Amartya Sen and Jean Drèze have demonstrated[7]—were largely failings of social and economic organization rather than natural catastrophes. The victims of these disasters were subject to risks little different in their impact upon them, or in their human origin, than the risks which our "risk theorists" deem to be novel features of the late twentieth century. It is therefore hard to understand why, given this terrible history, risk should be deemed a new condition.

To explain, we might consider that the ways of thinking about "objective risks" to human well-being have changed. But this does not really help us: not only were objective risks incurred, and their disastrous consequences suffered, for millions of men and women, throughout the previous century, but the language and terminology of "risk" was widely deployed. Thus not even the conceptualization of risk as a new intellectual phenomenon holds true; it has for a century been a standard, even at times a dominant idiom, of policy-making fundamental to the construction of the mature industrial capitalism of the post–Second World War period.

Consider, for example, two leading builders and theorists of the postwar settlement in Britain, Beveridge and Keynes, who each explicitly made the idea of risk and risk management central to their thought. Beveridge's plans for the welfare state were intended as a universal system of insurance against the normal risks of injury, ill-health, old age, poverty, and unemployment. Beveridge won popularity for his program because of the intended universality of its scope. The idea that the struggle for redistribution dominated the politics of the previous era, as Beck and Giddens suggest, gives too much weight to class-based values and neglects to note that these programs were largely framed in universalist and populist terms, even if only as a condition of their political success. This was true both of the achievement of democratic rights and liberties in the nineteenth and early twentieth centuries, and of social and economic entitlements in the middle part of this century.[8] Universalism is not an invention of the 1990s.

For Keynes, too, "risk" was a central concept. Keynes observed in *The General Theory* that

> there has been a chronic tendency throughout human history for the propensity to save to be stronger than the inducement to invest. The weakness of the inducement to invest has been at all times the key to the economic problem. Today the explanation of the weakness of this inducement may chiefly lie in the extent of existing accumulations, whereas, formerly, risks and hazards of all kinds may have played a larger part. But the result is the same. The desire of the individual to augment his personal wealth by abstaining from consumption has usually been stronger than the inducement to the entrepreneur to augment the national wealth by employing labor on the construction of durable assets. (Papermac edition, pp. 347–48)

Here already, at the center of Keynes's great text of 1936, is set out the shift from risks that derive from natural hazard to risks that are a product of social and economic organization. Keynes set out to modify the economic environment such that the risks perceived by investors would no longer be too high to generate the full use of the available factors of production, and in particular labor. The Keynesian program was one in which governments managed the environment of economic risk to the general benefit, whilst primary economic initiative and risk-taking remained in the hands of entrepreneurs.

The precondition for this attention to insurance against risks of various kinds, and to their planned management within the economy, had been the earlier studies in the "science" of risks and probabilities developed as a subcategory of modern statistical science which made it possible to conceive of risk as calculable and thus susceptible to precaution and insurance. Keynes was himself a leading theorist of probability. The strategies of risk management, which I shall argue underpinned the postwar order, were founded on this intellectual revolution whose intellectual background has been described by Hacking and Gigerenzer, among others.[9]

Keynes is not, of course, the only example of the prior usage of the concept of risk. The language used by Max Weber early in the twentieth century, and by neo-Weberian sociology since then, to characterize the conflict and competition of capitalist democracy is also implicitly a language of probabilities and risks. The "life chances" through which stratified differentials of power and opportunity are measured are probabilities, not outcomes which are determined and predictable for each individual. Classes are understood to be formed by perceptions of the probable outcomes of competitions in which a variety of resources are deployed. Social policies designed to mitigate inequality and poverty were formulated with reference to average conditions and life-risks, assessed by statistical means.

Similarly, the model of "Fordism" developed by Michel Aglietta and the Regulation School in France, and by Piore and Sabel in the United States, among others, characterizes structures whose principal objective was the management of economic and social risk seen in systemic terms.[10] The model of "organized capitalism," developed in the late 1980s in Britain by Scott Lash and John Urry, provides a convergent explanation of many of the same phenomena.[11] The emergence of "corporatist" systems of planning, the incorporation of trade unions into the conflict-management system of large manufacturing firms, and the emergence of welfare programs guaranteeing a measure of security to citizens, were devices designed to manage the risks of the new systems of mass production. The need for stable demand, for a fit and competent workforce, and for a measure of negotiated cooperation in the factories, followed from the scale and scope of investment in mass manufacturing technologies. One "risk" to which corporations were exposed by these new technical systems was of severe losses of output and profit due to industrial disruption. Sabel and Piore have shown how trade unions served, at least for a time, as useful mediatory instruments in negotiating the workforce into compliance with these new technologies.

The remarkable success of the Great Boom of 1950–75, producing higher average rates of economic growth than at any time in economic history, was a result of the fact that its organizing compromises were a device for managing risks for both sides of the institutionalized class conflicts.[12] A key reference point for most social actors in the period was the catastrophic inflation that had followed the Great Crash of 1929 and the Depression of the 1930s. The benefits for working people of employment and steadily rising incomes, and of the systems of social and industrial protection which were then created in most industrial societies, were obvious. But the goal was to ensure that most social groups benefitted from a sustained economic expansion. Different aspects of this settlement were designed to manage different kinds of risk. For example, the Bretton Woods arrangements were designed by Keynes to manage not only the risks of international financial instability, which in the 1920s and 1930s had produced both hyperinflation and recession, but also the political threat from the East and competition from domestic Communist Parties in

Europe. Thus welfare states were introduced across Europe as much by the parties of the center-right, maintaining their popular constituency against the competition of the left, as by social democrats directly serving the interests of their class constituencies.

This model of cooperative risk-management also enables us to explain the emerging instability of this compromise, as the incidence of risks to the great social blocs that made it up came markedly to differ. Given a measure of economic security, and the growth of higher levels of aspiration, the working population came to demand a higher price for its compliance with industrial discipline. Mass production systems turned out to be vulnerable to industrial disruption, once employees acquired the self-confidence and sense of security to flex their industrial muscle. A relatively small number of strategically placed employees could disrupt large flows of output and the supply chains on which they depended. At the macro-level, demands for higher levels of wages and social expenditure began to pose inflationary pressures, and although the systems of negotiation then set in place contained these to a degree, average profit-levels fell significantly during the late sixties and early seventies. The effects of the exogenous stimuli of the Vietnam War, and the large oil-price rises following the assertion of bargaining power of the oil producers, raised tensions to a high level, as testified to by the discussion of social anxieties which became current in the late 1960s and 1970s: "system overload," "ungovernability," "legitimation crisis," and the like.[13]

The emergence of "post-Fordist" methods of production,[14] and the spatial reorganization of production both within the industrial countries and on a global scale, were arguably a response by capital to the unacceptable levels of risk to which the "Fordist" system exposed the corporate sector. The spatial decentralization of production was a means to spread and reduce risks. For example, whereas the dockworkers in a large port such as London or Liverpool could successfully hold up the modernization of dockwork (and the consequent loss of employment) through the threat or reality of disruption, concerted industrial action became much less feasible once dock-working was dispersed to many smaller ports—often without strong trade-union traditions—all around the coast. Diversification of energy sources to counter the monopoly power of the coal miners, and the conservative preference for a dispersed system of road freight over the more centralized modes of railway transport are other examples of the deliberate reduction of risks to capital. "Flexible specialization" is similarly a form of risk management. Under this system, specific products can be matched more precisely to demand for them, and investments undertaken in anticipation of uncertain demands for products could be reduced.

Even financial markets show evidence of the success of these systems of stabilization—and of the pressures for change when they became less stable in the 1970s—as Peter Bernstein documents in *Against the Gods: The Remark-*

able Story of Risk.[15] Bernstein describes the state of high volatility and low growth in capital markets between 1926 and 1945, where the standard deviation of annual total returns (income change plus change in capital values) was 37% per year while returns averaged only about 7% per year. He then points out how, in the postwar period

> [a] renewal of speculative fever and unbridled optimism was slow to develop, despite a mighty bull market that drove the Dow Jones Industrial Index from less than 200 in 1945 to 1000 by 1966. From 1946 to 1969, despite a handsome return of over 12% a year and a brief outburst of speculative enthusiasm in 1961, the standard deviation of total returns was only one-third of what it had been from 1926 to 1945.

In the turbulence of the early seventies, things changed again. From the end of 1969 to 1975, the average return on shares dropped to half of what it had been from 1946 to 1969, whilst the annual standard deviation, Bernstein's measure of volatility and thus of risk, nearly doubled to 22%. Interest in risk management in the financial markets was a product of that experience, and has probably contributed to the wider interest in risk as an idea. The huge growth in the scale and diversity of financial markets can thus be seen as a set of devices for spreading and off-loading risks.[16]

There are other spheres in which strategies of risk management were central in the postwar era. The management of international currencies, and the evolving apparatus of GATT, regional trading blocs, G7, and all the other institutions of international economic management are good examples. Another is the Single European Currency, the Euro, one of whose objects is to take away the risks of fluctuations in currency values, so effectively exploited by speculators in 1992. The threat of nuclear disaster, one of the original sources of anxiety about global risk, generated baroque theories and strategies of risk management such as deterrence theory, and the fail-safe arrangements put in place after the Cuban Missile Crisis (in which process the two sides in the Cold War learned to cooperate). Nuclear arms treaty negotiation became a distinct specialism of foreign policy, whose avowed purpose was risk management.

The programs of the new right in the years of Reagan and Thatcher can also be understood as a response to two, connected, kinds of perceived risks. One was the threat posed by Communism in the Third World, especially in the years after the U.S. defeat in Vietnam. The other was the threat of subversion or revolution closer to home, in such countries as Portugal, Chile, and Italy. Western governments in the 1980s saw themselves as battling to save the market society from its enemies both at home and abroad. Once the global victory of capitalism was assured by the fall of the Berlin Wall in 1989, the radical right lost some of its influence over Western governments, and more pragmatic attitudes to the balancing and management of risks reasserted themselves, for example, in the politics of the New Democrats and the Third Way.

Parties like the A.N.C. in South Africa, or the P.D.S. in Italy, were allowed to assume power, events that would not have been tolerated by the United States before 1989.

Whatever explains the salience of "risk" in contemporary political discussion, it is certainly not that risks for most citizens are greater than they were, nor that theories which calculate and manage risk have only just been invented. Both risks, and theories of risk management, have been with us for some time. What then does explain this new intellectual fashion?

RISK AS A PROBLEM OF DEFINITION

To answer this question, attention needs to be given to the ways in which the discourse of risk frames the problems and harms which it seeks to explain. All theories which identify social harms are selective, offering some explanations and remedies whilst excluding others. Risk theory is no exception. The concept of risk draws attention to potential and universal dangers, rather than to immediate and particular ones. Its essence is its lack of specificity, its preference for what the psychoanalyst Wilfred Bion referred to in another context as "nameless dread." The advantage of "hailing" (as Althusser once put it) the prospective subjects of political action in this way is that the constituencies thus constituted are almost boundless as it is proposed that everyone is in equal danger. Because the term "risk" derives from the language of insurance, and the probability theory which underpins it (as we suggested above), it encodes an idea of a liability to harm which is ideally both calculable and assignable to individuals. It thus connects with, and rhetorically enforces, the "individualizing" of social problems.

In the hands of these risk theorists, this concept has evoked a universal—if individualized—condition of risk at the expense of the more specific normative dimensions typical of an earlier lexicon of social problems. A "risk" is something one might want to avoid or lessen, but it is not *ipso facto* something one might be entitled to protest against. A counterview has come from Mary Douglas and Aaron Wildavsky,[17] who have demonstrated that "risks" are culturally constructed and differ within different locations in the social structure; that their definition is both highly normative and sociologically highly specific. Zigmunt Bauman has perceptively drawn attention to the fact that "risk" may for some even represent a positive value. His account[18] of the changes in experience and consciousness associated with post-modernity suggests that an earlier phase of regulated and managed society may have been experienced as offering insufficient freedom and opportunity for individuals to define their own life-course. A measure of "risk" can in these circumstances come to seem an enhancement of life, as growing children and adolescents sometimes embrace risk as a benefit of their freedom from parental or other social control. The changed balance between risk and security, which was made to seem desirable for many by the conservative governments of Margaret Thatcher, can be understood in these terms. The 1997 election of the New Labor government represented a widespread desire to rebalance the climate of risk in the opposite direction, in an alternation between dominant mentalities of a kind described by Albert Hirschman.[19] One has to understand what alternative vocabularies are being displaced by risk analysis to recognize that the issues of definition involved in the supposed transition to a "risk society" may be of as much consequence as the substantive new kinds of harm which the theory of risk society seeks to name.

The evolution of the radical political tradition has involved a migration of conditions of life deemed undesirable or harmful, from the category of unavoidable misfortune to the category of remediable injustice. T. H. Marshall's social democratic theory of citizenship, with its Whiggish progression from legal recognition and protection of the liberties of the subject to political enfranchisement, and thus to social and economic entitlements, is one of the best-known versions of this story. Remediable injustices are held to include poverty, absence of educational opportunity or achievement, inequality, lack of access to fulfilling work, and damage to the natural environment. Claims of this kind have been made on behalf of collectivities, as well as on behalf of individuals. Inhabitants of a specific place, fellow-employees, and members of a family or of a church sometimes claim rights in virtue of their common identities.

What are the implications of substituting a critique of "risks" for the more conventional frameworks of social goods and ills which have hitherto dominated radical politics if not all aspirations to an improved way of life, to a particular idea of social relationship, or to definite normative principles? A "risk" after all, is simply that: something that an individual might prefer not to face. There is a link between the abstractness of the specification of "risks" and "harms" in risk society theory, and the reluctance by its theorists, and New Laborites and Third Wayers more generally, to attend to the structural and systemic properties of capitalist market societies. Indeed, the aim seems to be to displace attention from the more definite material and social risks which late capitalist societies continue to generate.

In fact, citizens are increasingly preoccupied by insecurity, as they are urged to regard secure lifetime employment as a thing of the past. "Flexibility" in work patterns is celebrated, for example, by Charles Leadbeater.[20] In Britain and the U.S., inequalities are much greater than they were twenty years ago. In the UK, New Labor has barely begun to claw these back. Whilst aspirations to high standards of education and health care are high, the reality in Britain (and the U.S.) is of considerable scarcity and insufficiency in both spheres. The powerlessness which the idea of "risk society" conjures up is not so much a condition of the general environment as a displaced reflection of governments' impotence in the face of global markets. It is therefore not surprising that to refocus such concerns has been an explicit purpose of this argument.

Risk society theory does of course identify new kinds of risk, generally seeking to shift attention from the material and social domain to the environment—from the red to the green part of the political spectrum. Global warming and the uncertain consequences of genetic modification are currently the most significant of these perceived risks. (Barbara Adam has developed an important theoretical argument that it is the disruptions of "timescapes" inherent in genetic modification that constitutes its deepest threat to well-being.)[21] Whilst these new risks need close study, they should not divert attention from more traditional radical concerns for material and social being. The actual harms attributable to either of these "new" risks are still minute compared with the devastations that continue to be brought about by poverty, backwardness, the breakdown of law, and war. But even if it were reasonable to give priority to future risks of infinite harm (e.g., from nuclear weapons, climate change, or generic modification) over present sources of material harm, it seems that the same social systems are implicated in the causes of each. Risk society theorists have sought to shift political attention away from earlier critiques of capitalism even though any serious consideration of environmental danger points immediately back to the need to contain and control the operation of markets as one of its primary causes: increased energy consumption is an outcome of the expansion of the world's industrial economy; applications of GM technology are being promoted most vigorously by corporate agriculture. Environmental anxieties require that market society be examined and regulated in new ways, not a decision to declare the operations of global capitalism as outside mainstream political debate.

REFRAMING THE ARGUMENT

The implication of Ulrich Beck's theory of risk society (and Anthony Giddens's parallel reflections) has been to insist on the need for a radical revision of left-of-center political perspectives. The old politics of material benefits and distributive conflict have to be replaced, they argue, by a new universalism, a mobilization of a dispersed democratic community to assert control over potentially uncontrollable global forces, in particular those of technology and science. The continuing salience of environmental conflicts in recent years, and the vigor of environmental activism compared with many traditional forms of political protest, indicate that this argument has identified important realities. The insistence on the qualitative difference of this new environment, even if exaggerated, has had its benefits in provoking new thought. The arrival of the concepts of globalization and individualization at the center of social debate certainly has defined new agendas, and drawn a useful line under earlier nation- and collectivity-based frameworks for political action which had outlived some of their usefulness.

But it is another matter whether the risk society theorists are justified in insisting on the need for a wholesale paradigm shift in social thinking. I have argued that, at all events, the emergence of a new climate of risk needs to be understood in the context of the earlier success of elaborate structures of social risk management that were the achievements of the post–Second World War period. Defined in this way, many risks have *reemerged* as consequences of deregulation, of an *unbalancing* of powers formerly locked into negotiated settlements. The demand for a wholly new agenda, sometimes defined by Giddens and Beck as "post-socialist," is confusing, since the major agency leading the global transformations which they theorize remains the system of capitalism.[22] A distinction needs to be drawn between the manifest failures of many of the programs and strategies drawn up by Marxists and social democrats in their long confrontation with capitalism, and the continuing validity of their analyses of its dynamics as a system.

Beck and Giddens have "invented" the discourse of risk as the rallying call for new post-socialist kinds of democratic politics.[23] In contrast to their approach, which has defined "risk" in substantive terms as a new kind of social fact, is that of the late Niklas Luhmann, whose *Risk: A Sociological Theory*[24] (the German edition is dated 1991) came out around the same time as Beck's *Risk Society*. Luhmann views risk as the outcome of rational calculation of future dangers (what he calls the need for "time-binding") fully embedded in the practice of most "modern" social institutions. In his view, the origins of the modern conception of risk lie in the development of commerce, when merchants advancing capital decided on the probable risks of different voyages and enterprises—a concept already well illustrated by the character of Antonio in Shakespeare's *Merchant of Venice*. For Luhmann, the calibration of risks is the essence of capitalist enterprise, and of all those activities that are shaped or influenced by its spirit.

Luhmann's sociological theory holds that all institutions devise their own communicative codes through a process he refers to as "autopoiesis." Through these they encode those elements of the environment with which they interact, as determined by their calculations of risk. The law, the institutions of government (bureaucracy), politics, and science each have their own coding procedures and distinct strategies for managing the "risks" that their differentiated functions engender. "Risks" today may be generated in one sphere (the economy), and transferred to another (the political). Political action in modern democracies is in fact routinely concerned with managing and balancing the risks incurred by different actors within the economic sphere, deploying the powers of the state for this purpose: farmers, consumers, employees, house-buyers, exporters, importers, trade unions, employees in the financial sector, for example, all call on governments to improve their advantages and minimize their disadvantages in the market. In this sense too, risks may be said to pass from one part of the political system to another. For example, as "new social movements" respond to the existence or construction of new kinds of risk (environmental damage, the extinction of a species) they generate pressures on established political parties and on their governments to respond to these anxieties. Thus, insofar as modern society is the outcome of purposeful action undertaken within differentiated social institutions, it consists of the generation and management of risks within and between these systems.

What Luhmann's theory explains, as Beck's does not, is the relentless drive to the calculation of risks embedded in modern social institutions. Whereas the theorists of individualization describe a world of individuals threatened by turbulent environments, Luhmann sees a world of self-reproducing, differentiating, and expanding systems regulating and programming their individual members to act in prescribed ways. Although individuals are to varying degrees capable of reflexiveness, of deciding on their own strategies and routines of life, it is a mistake, according to Luhmann, to overestimate their capacity to shape the systems of which they are a part.

Luhmann's is a more pessimistic vision, continuous with that of Weber and Foucault, in seeing individuals more as programmed than programmers. "Risk" becomes in his terms less a condition of hazard to which individuals are subject than a programmed assessment by an institution or system of the significance, for its own self-reproducing routines, of some encountered aspect of its environment. Thus "risk" exists both for the cardiac patient and the cardiology unit, but it is most clearly defined and acted on through the medical routines of the latter. An examination is a moment of risk for the student who takes it, but is also an elaborated set of procedures maintained by a system.

Luhmann sees the systemic, autopoeitic process of constructing, calculating, and managing "risks" as a generalized one, an immanent form of rationalization of everything, one might say. But one can see this process as having its particular drivers in the shaping power of the capitalist economy that insists on a common commensurable measure of value being applied to every form of life. It is this insistence on a common measure, on surrogates and equivalences being found for the univocal and one-dimensional measures of value represented by economic surpluses, which explains how it is that even in an ostensibly more differentiated social system, with more specialisms of every kind, variety appears to diminish, not increase.

Late modern capitalism is thus driving institutions of all kinds to more deliberately calculated routines of risk-management. Global markets impose these routines on competing firms, requiring that they develop state-of-the art forms of self-monitoring and performance measurement. Governments, anxious about the competitiveness of their national economies and about the burden of their public sectors upon it, have been busy inventing parallel methodologies for their own spheres of operation. New Labor in Britain has been as insistent on this "modernization" of government as its Conservative predecessor. Whilst this has involved some increased accountability to electors (devolution in Scotland and Wales), equally significant has been the drive to improve the upward accountability of public service organizations and professions. This process of public sector modernization, like the privatizations earlier pioneered by Thatcher, seems now be taking place across the European Union. In these respects Britain seems to function as a European relay for modes of management thinking developed initially in the corporate sector worldwide, and then transferred to the sphere of government.

There are many instruments in this process of what is called "increased accountability" and "risk management" in the public sector. These include an obligation to compete in various marketplaces (e.g., by compulsory tendering), the exposure of performance standards by league tables or the results of inspections, and the imposition of quality standards. Michael Power has memorably described this system of increased regulation and accountability as "the audit explosion."[25] Perhaps the most important risks to which individual citizens are now being exposed are those of being over-processed by the various organizations to which they are attached. These systems require, according to Luhmann, that every aspect of activity must be rendered calculable and accountable, lest they fail to cope adequately with the systemic "risks" to which they are subject. If individuals are more exposed to risk, it is because organizations deliberately ensure that they should be, making use of such heightened individual accountability to assure their own survival. The process of globalization includes the extension of these pervasive forms of regulation, ultimately driven and legitimated by the imperatives of competition. Individualization also needs to be redefined in this light, as in part a "regime of power": disciplines of self-improvement imposed by institutions, internalized within the self, and amounting at times to a psychic Taylorism.

Luhmann's conservative, system-oriented approach gave him an understanding of the continuities inherent in social constructions of risk which were obscure to his more politically radical contemporaries. As pointed out above, the radical risk theorists were limited by their desire to shock the traditionalists of the old left, a position that has often left them short-sighted.

CONCLUSION

The debate about risk society demonstrates that the enlightenment brought about by social science arrives in many forms. Ulrich Beck and Anthony Giddens have helped to construct a new political agenda, which has been in its own way productive. Zigmunt Bauman, Mary Douglas, and Aaron Wildavsky have drawn attention to how risks are subjectively perceived, rather than how they are produced. Bauman sees that there may be oscillations between periods in which citizens are more risk-averse, and others in which they positively enjoy risks; a perspective which helps us to understand the shifts that have occurred in this century in dominant attitudes, and the governmental responses, to risk. Douglas and Wildavsky, on the other hand, see responses to risk as socially determined by the different positions of social actors in structures of opportunity and membership—Douglas's "grid" and "group" dimensions of social solidarity. They see much of the agitation against environmental and other risks as emerging from a particular kind of social vulnerability. Useful in their approach is their recognition that the way in which social problems are framed by social actors is itself a social fact of importance, and may even be more significant than the actual problems that the actors identify. Niklas Luhmann, no opponent of capitalist democracy, nevertheless identifies in his analysis of the social system deep continuities in its drive to the prescription and regulation of every form of life. It is paradoxical that where the radical theorists identify turbulence and unpredictability as the principal risks of late modernity whilst generally being in favor of democratic participation, Luhmann the conservative, in principle inclined to favor order, describes a society in which it is an excess of order and not its opposite that seems to constitute the principal risk to human well-being.

The enlightenment brought by social science is thus not well aligned with political intentions. Arguments that largely ignore capitalism have nevertheless unwittingly drawn attention to its pervasive power. Arguments that demonstrate the drive to regulation of modern social systems have clarified the constraints and limits to voluntary social action more profoundly than its democratic advocates. Social science does produce illumination, but in paradoxical and unintended ways. This seems an appropriate conclusion to have drawn from the analysis of the unexpected and disruptive phenomena of risk.

NOTES

1. See Ulrich Beck, *Risk Society* (London: Sage, 1992); *Ecological Politics in an Age of Risk*, trans. Amos Weisz (Cambridge, Mass. : Polity Press, 1995); *The Reinvention of Politics: Rethinking modernity in the global social order*, trans. Mark Ritter (Cambridge, UK: Polity Press, 1997). For Giddens, see Anthony Giddens, *The Consequences of Modernity* (Cambridge UK: Polity Press, 1990); *Beyond Left and Right* (Cambridge, UK: Polity Press, 1994); and also Ulrich Beck, Anthony Giddens, and S. Lash, *Reflexive Modernization* (Cambridge, UK: Polity Press, 1994).

2. Anthony Giddens, who became Director of the London School of Economics and Political Science just after the election, produced a book, *Beyond Left and Right*, which attempted to translate his theoretical work into a kind of proto-political manifesto, pointed in the direction of New Labor. It defined itself as "post-socialist," in a way that is fully consistent with Blarite practice if not declaration.

3. I have written a more detailed critique of the arguments of these two writers in my "Incomplete Modernity: Ulrich Beck's *Risk Society*," *Radical Philosophy* 67 (Summer 1994); and "The Future of Post-Socialism," *Radical Philosophy* 74 (Nov.–Dec. 1995), pp. 17–27.

4. See Anthony Giddens, *Modernity and Self-Identity* (Cambridge, UK: Polity Press, 1991); and *The Transformation of Intimacy* (Cambridge, UK: Polity Press, 1992).

5. M. J. Rustin, "The Future of Post-Socialism." It should be noted that Giddens's most recent writing, *The Third Way and Its Critics* (Cambridge, UK: Polity Press, 2000), does suggest some attempt to reconnect to earlier social democratic agendas.

6. In fact, however, there are very few risks of which this is true. Richard Wilkinson's work has showed that the incidence of ill-health and rates of mortality are closely linked to the level of material inequality, not only in that the worse-off in terms of income are also likely to suffer more illness, and die sooner. But also, remarkably, in that the steeper the income gradient and the greater the degree of inequality, the worse-off the poor are, and the worse the average standard of health is for all citizens. Observing the effects of natural disasters and civil wars, of natural catastrophes such as earthquakes, of access to education, informal and cultural goods, the normal laws of distribution seem to apply—the better-off are more likely to be able to buy immunity or escape from hazard than the poor. The current fashion for the idea of risk may be due to the fact that some modern hazards (e.g., global warming) seem to threaten even the citizens of Hampstead or Cambridge, but in reality the latter have kept, and even increased, most of their relative advantages. See Richard Wilkinson, *Unhealthy Societies: The Afflictions of Inequality* (London: Routledge, 1996).

7. Jean Drèze and Amartya Sen, *Hunger and Public Policy* (Oxford: Oxford University Press, 1989).

8. T. H. Marshall's (1950) model of evolving citizenship rights made clear the successive universalist extensions of this idea. See his *Citizenship and Social Class* (Cambridge: Cambridge University Press, 1950).

9. Ian Hacking, *The Taming of Chance* (Cambridge: Cambridge University Press, 1990). Gerd Gigerenzer et al., *The Empire of Chance: How probability changed science and everyday life* (Cambridge: Cambridge University Press, 1989).

10. See Michel Aglietta, *A Theory of Capitalist Regulation: The US Experience* (London: Verso, 1979) and M. J. Piore and C. F. Sabel, *The Second Industrial Divide* (New York: Basic Books, 1984).

11. Scott Lash and Josh Urry, *The End of Organized Capitalism* (Cambridge, UK: Polity Press, 1987).

12. See P. Armstrong, A. Glyn, and J. Harrison, *Capitalism Since 1945* (Oxford: Basil Blackwell, 1991).

13. On this, see Jürgen Habermas, *Legitimation Crisis*, trans. Thomas McCarthy (Boston: Beacon Press, 1975); J. O'Connor, *The Fiscal Crisis of the State* (New York: St. Martin's Press, 1973); and Claus Offe, *Contradictions of the welfare state*, ed. John Keane (Cambridge, Mass.: MIT Press, 1984).

14. For the definition of this idea, see Ash Amin, ed., *Post-Fordism: a reader* (Oxford: Basil Blackwell, 1994).

15. Peter Bernstein, *Against the Gods: The Remarkable Story of Risk* (New York: Wiley, 1996).

16. The primary sources of capital in these markets are institutional—the savings and profits of pension funds, corporations, local government, and so on. The managers of these funds are charged with ensuring the highest returns compatible with relatively low risks. Although those operating the financial systems inhabit a rather peculiar space that allows much scope for the impulse to gamble on a huge scale, and where incomes

and profits are thus exceptionally high, the goal of the whole system is to insure against risk in every possible way, not to increase it.

17. Mary Douglas, in her *Risk and Blame* (London: Routledge,1992), has developed a powerful neo-Durkheimian model of types of social solidarity, based on variables of membership (group) and opportunity (grid). She and Aaron Wildavsky have deployed this to demonstrate how risk is defined and within different kinds of social order. See Mary Douglas and Aaron Wildavsky, *Risk and Culture* (Berkeley: University of California Press, 1982).

18. Bauman notes, in criticism of Mary Douglas, that "risk" is indeed semantically distinctive. "Unlike 'danger,' 'risk' belongs to the discourse of gambling, that is to a kind of discourse which does not sustain clear-cut opposition between success and failure, safety and danger, one which recognises their co-presence in every situation, thereby straddling the barricade which separates them in the discourse of 'order' which the term 'danger' comes from and represents. 'Risk' signals that moves are not unambiguously safe or dangerous (or at least, that what is the case is not known in advance)— that they differ only in the proportion in which safety and danger are mixed. 'Risk' is also referred to what the gambler does, not to what is done to him. 'Risk,' therefore, more than the danger it allegedly 'simply transcribed', is resonant with the postmodern view of the world as game, and the being-in-the-world as play." Zigmut Bauman, *Postmodern Ethics* (Oxford: Basil Blackwell, 1993), p. 200 n. 14.

19. See Hirschman's *Exit, Voice, and Loyalty* (Cambridge, Mass.: Harvard University Press, 1970); *The Passions and the Interests* (Princeton: Princeton University Press, 1977); and *The Rhetoric of Reaction* (Cambridge, Mass.: Harvard University Press, 1991).

20. See Charles Leadbeater, *Living on Thin Air* (London: Viking Press, 1999).

21. Barbara Adam, *Timescapes of Modernity* (London: Routledge, 1998).

22. One might nevertheless argue that the "Third Way" has been politically productive, making possible a break with the previous conservative ascendancy in Britain and Germany.

23. Giddens and Beck's theory of globalization and individualization, as key aspects of late modernism, restates the perspectives of mass society advanced by the Frankfurt School. Although their perspectives are politically engaged and activist, the characterization of states of risk as universal and unpredictable, and the rejection of earlier forms of structured resistance as irrelevant and outdated, constructs a world of atomized individuals, weak in the face of global uncertainties and turbulence.

24. The English edition is *Risk: A Sociological Theory*, trans. Rhodes Barrett (New York: A. de Gruyter, 1993).

25. See Michael Power, *The Audit Explosion* (London: Demos Press, 1994), and his *The Audit Society* (Oxford: Clarendon Press, 1997).

CHAPTER 19

Retrotopia: Critical Reason Turns Primitive

Istvan Rev

> A map of the world that does not include Utopia is not even
> worth glancing at. [. . .] Progress is the realization of Utopia.
> —Oscar Wilde, *The Soul of Man Under Socialism*

FROM THE beginning of the 1980s, reform economists in Poland and Hungary
started to forecast drastic increases in inflation and predicted that rising prices
would spin out of control. Inflation was also used as a metaphor, denoting
everything to which it was still not possible to refer by name: planning, centralization, one-party rule, the market, private property. These coded, Cassandra-
like forecasts, predicting the coming of doomsday, were meant to warn the
party leadership that unless serious and comprehensive reform measures were
taken, the socialist economy, indeed the whole system, might find itself irrepa-
rably damaged. A conventional anti-inflation policy, with price controls, quotas, and subsidies, promised to be very costly and dangerous, likely resulting
in a host of domestic crises ranging from shortages to resource depletion. Faced
with stagnant growth, rising inflation, and hidden unemployment (much of the
workforce was still artificially employed, a fraying last thread of legitimacy
contained in socialist rhetoric), conventional measures seemed just too dangerous. To certain reform economists and a growing number of Western-trained
or Western-oriented economic technocrats (for the most part, freshly returned
from American business schools), a successful model for fighting inflation was
emerging from the West in the form of monetarism. There was not much else
at the time one could import from American business schools (in fact, not
much else one could adopt from social science debates in the West); an East
European reading of the philosophy of monetarism became the theory and
remedy of the times.

The spread of monetarism—at least in the beginning—did not seem to
threaten the remnants of the socialist credo. It did not necessitate any resettle-
ment of property rights, the abolition of one-party rule, or even stripping the
national economies of their facade of central planning. In fact, a more independent body within the monetary sphere gave hope to party leaders that they
would not be held solely responsible for growing inflation; the central bank
and the financial sphere would serve as a buffer zone to absorb all blame.

The annual failure, beginning in the early 1980s, of the optimistic and self-assured inflation predictions by Party economists resulted in the extension of credit to the forecasters of economic doom not only by the wider public, but even by publicly optimistic but ever more uncomfortable party officials themselves. This in turn allowed self-styled monetarist and neo-conservative reformers to gain both credibility and influence. The opportunities to implement neo-conservative policy grew. The only trouble was that, when they looked around, they were unable to find the ground on which to test their proposed remedy: the commercial environment needed for the introduction of monetarist policy—an independent central bank, working financial institutions, real merchant banks, a money market—were all lacking. The monetarists may have had the medicine, but a subject on whom the treatment would be tested was yet to be born. And in order to create the conditions for such a birth, there was no escaping privatization or a self-regulated market. Property rights—a taboo in a socialist economy—had to be reconsidered as well. Herein lay the secret of the end of the 1980s, hidden even from the progressive but unimaginative reformers.

From this perspective, the demise of the socialist system came about as an attempt to create the environment for the application of a particular economic system and philosophy. Simply put, according to the logic of this story, Communism had to die because it proved antithetical to the existence of those institutions necessary to the measures that were supposed to save it.

But this is only a partially serious story, one that would tell of the victory of the West—a rather uninteresting victory at that.[1] But there was no victory. Instead, the key to understanding the sudden and unexpected collapse—as Karl Polányi would say—lay in the Communist reformers' "ignorance of the wider implications of the development they were facing."[2] As nobody, including critical social scientists, was able to foresee what was coming, no one could stem the tide or save what could have been saved (if there had still been anything to save) from Communism. (If any member of the Politburo would have guessed at the time of Gorbachev's election to the post of the general secretary of the Bolshevik party where that choice might lead, history might have taken a slightly different course.)

Instead of there being a victory for anyone, the system committed a not-so-dramatic suicide. Communism melted like butter in late, tired summer sunshine. Even in its demise, Communism fooled the people one more time by denying them the experience of their sovereignty. Still, this simplistic story is not meant only as a joke. It is my firm belief that, in the second half of the 1980s, the only things available to be borrowed from the West were those mainstream—and by then outdated economic—policies, and some important ideas from late liberalism. And this impoverished choice proved to be a fortunate state of affairs: there was no need to exterminate Communism, no pressing need for a bloody fight, no need for a victory of any kind, and little room for either daring political debates or for adventurous post-communist experiments.

In a sense, the Fall happened at a uniquely lucky moment. Had Communism collapsed some twenty years earlier, at a time of lively dialogue between the New Left of the West and the emerging democratic critics of the East, it would have been quite difficult—unlike in 1989—to reach a quick agreement at the round tables in Warsaw and Budapest. This dialogue involved organizations such as the *Praxis* group (the journal was published between 1964 and 1975), the Lukács school, the rediscoveries of Lange, Kalecki, and Karl Korsch, Lucian Goldmann, the critical sociologists, Polish revisionists such as Kolakowski, Pomian, Baczko, Bauman, and Czechs like Karel Kosik with his Dialectics of the Concrete. A body of New Left work had begun to be published, among them Barrington Moore's *The Social Origin of Dictatorship and Democracy* and his "Revolution in America?" review in the *New York Review of Books*; Andre Gunder Frank and Samir Amin's dependency theory; Franz Fanon's *Les damnés de la terre*; *Althusser's Pour Marx*; the late publications of the Frankfurt School; Abbey Hoffman's *yippee manifesto*; Régis Debray's *Revolution in the Revolution?*; Herbert Marcuse's *One-Dimensional Man*; Marshall Sahlin's *The First Affluent Society*; Norman O. Brown's *Love's Body*; and Theodore Roszak's *Where the Waste-Land Ends?* May 68 had happened in Paris, Rudy Dutschke in West Berlin, SDS and Haight-Ashbury in the U.S., etc. It would have even been rather difficult to get the parties belonging to different persuasions of the opposition to sit next to each other at the same table to stare down the perplexed Communists.

The 1980s agreement among members of the East European opposition took place in a world-wide wasteland of critical social science thinking. This wasteland was due primarily to changes that had taken place in their understanding of the concept of progress. The startling nature of this change should be set in context: only a few years earlier, Stalin's stage theory of the modes of production was an integral part of university textbooks, and W. W. Rostow's *The Stages of Economic Growth* was the currency of the most enlightened socialist economic history and reform economy monographs (naturally, no one mentioned the subtitle of Rostow's book, which happened to be "A Non-Communist Manifesto"). But then, "[t]he progress-oriented historical viewpoint [had] totally disappeared because the historical movement is now toward capitalism from socialism. The crisis also finds its expression in the whole decline of stage-oriented historical theory in general."[3] This decline left no utopia[4] for the future, only the continuation of time after Communism.

The critique of stage-theory came about as a critique of modernization. Already at the time of Hrushchev's famous *dagnat'i peregnat*, "to reach and surpass," both existing Socialism and its East European New Left critics fell into slow but terminal trouble. Anti-modernization theories began in the first third of the 1960s and came from a direction broadly defined as the Western radical, anticapitalist New Left. They were directed at both the capitalist West (signified by self-regulating markets, the welfare state, imperialism, inequality, and the center's exploitation of the periphery) and—in an "anti anti-communist" fashion[5]—against certain features of the socialist East (such as centralization, bureaucratic exploitation, and liberalism posing as socialist centralization). The New Left arguments about the divorce of modernization from progress, of progress from the future, of mechanization from modernity, and development from utopia all dealt a decisive blow to the socialist alternative which until then had been firmly connected to the engine of progress. In a sense—and one could see this already in the growing predominance these theories gave to anthropology—radical utopia was replaced in the world of Stone Age Economics (Marshall Sahlins); La Société began to be defined contre l'état (Pierre Clastres).

THE Cold War was fought with two parallel ideologies taken to be each other's mirror images: scientific communism and modernization theory. Both were universalistic in aspiration, expansionist in practice, and each had a firm belief in the inevitability of technical progress that would determine social, political, and cultural outcomes. Communism assumed its own certain future prosperity; modernization theory assumed the arrival of affluence (Kenneth Galbraith's *The Affluent Society* was published in 1958). Cold war discourses aimed at justifying the present by means of the anticipation of the future, on the basis of a conviction according to which those who shape the perception of the future firmly rule the present. Until the first third of the 1960s, the Left argued that—with the help of ex-ante regulation (i.e., planning), as opposed to ex-post regulation (i.e., the market)—the unlimited potential for technical progress attributed to Communism would insure the elimination of economic and social injustice. Socialism understood itself to be only on the way to becoming itself and thus the regime could exonerate itself from responsibility for the excess of terror, the shortage of goods, and other sorts of failures.

Another way to put this is that until the middle of the 1960s, the main currents of leftist utopia were intimately connected with the belief in development, technical progress, and modernization. Belief in the inevitability of technical, economic, and social development—in the genetic program of history—formed the basis of the idea of historical progress that lead inevitably to Communism with its technical superiority over previously extant social formations.

[N]obody can doubt that for all or most of the last 1,000 years before 1800, economic evolution consistently took place in the same direction . . . Capitalism, while no doubt providing the historic condition for economic transformation everywhere, in fact made it more difficult than before for the countries which did not belong to the original nucleus of capitalist development or its immediate neighbors. The Soviet Revolution of 1917 alone provided the means and the model for genuine world-wide economic growth and balanced development of all peoples.[6]

So stated Eric Hobsbawm, with firm conviction. And Man, according to Ernst Bloch, the author of *Geist der Utopie*, is essentially Utopia-minded and believes in a perfect world anticipating the future with undying hope. Thus for Bloch, "Marxism is wholly future-oriented: it recognizes the past only in so far as it is still alive and is therefore part of the future. . . . According to this philosophy the significance of being is revealed only in acts directed towards the future."[7] Bloch, who until his last years was loyal to the Communist Party of the GDR and, even during the great purges, to Stalin (but who in the summer of 1961, at the time of the erection of the Wall between the two parts of Berlin, happened to be in the Western zone and decided to stay there—proving that one's whereabouts define one's loyalty), reasons again in *Das Prinzip Hoffnung* in the following way: "Der Mensch ist dasjenige, was noch vieles vor sich hat. . . . Er steht immer wieder vorn an Grenzen, die keine mehr sind, indem er sie wahrnimmt, er überschreitet sie . . ." ("Man is he who has much before him. . . . He is always reaching boundaries that are boundaries no longer: as he perceives them, so he passes beyond them.")[8]

The antimodernist critique of the radical movements of the 1960s was foremost directed against the perceived irrationality of Western democracies derived from the perceived irrationality of the market, where "claims to reason . . . function as strategies, as tools to accumulate power," and where "[t]he dream of reason was itself a strategy for domination."[9] But by giving up the progressive project of the Left and projecting the communal utopia backwards to a romanticized pre-modern time—to the societies of, for example, the Trobrian Island, of Ticopia, of Tierra del Fuego, of upper Xingu, of Indian Chieftainships, and to worlds characterized by Potlatch—the Left became vulnerable and eventually helpless, although this did not become evident for some time to come. For the 60s were the heyday of the post–World War II Left, the recovery of critical social theory, the days of student protest, of the American civil-rights movement, anticolonial wars, national liberation movements in Algeria, Africa, and, especially, a time of the myth of Latin American radicalism—Cuba, Bolivia, Vietnam, and the birth of the Third World. It was difficult to understand the full meaning and tragic consequences of the anthropological turn of the Left. In retrospect however, it is not too difficult to argue that critical Left social science thinking wounded itself mortally in exactly these times.

THE East European Left—especially the critical sociologists—became particularly receptive to the antimodernist, anthropologically informed retrotopia, in part as a direct consequence of the special characteristics of East and Central European modernization. During the nineteenth and twentieth centuries, in almost all the countries of these regions, modernization, progress, technical development, and industrial growth were achieved via state-controlled processes which neglected to similarly strengthen society. As a consequence of this so-called inorganic development, capitalism in this part of the world was seen as "simulated capitalism." Such was the title of a collection of essays published in 1917 by a self-made, self-taught, self-styled sociologist in Hungary;[10] according to Leopold, simulated capitalism is a type of economic system that lacks capitalist content. As a consequence, "a make-believe society emerges with a disproportionate bureaucracy and armaments . . . with a paralyzed concentration and regional centralization."[11]

From the beginning of the twentieth century, both the anticapitalist Left and populist Right in East and Central Europe saw capitalism as a stranger to its part of the world. While the historically minded apologists aimed at legitimizing socialism in Eastern Europe—with its top-heavy state and general centralization—as a natural outcome of specific autochthonous historical trends, critical sociologists tried to explain socialism by reference to the unfortunate, non-Western peculiarities in the past of Central and Eastern Europe. Iván Szelényi traced the roots of this type of East European development back to the sixteenth century, describing a "Junker road to Socialism" that connected protracted serfdom and landed estates to collectivization of agriculture and the economic development of "under-urbanization."[12]

In the 1960s, the virtues not only of the countryside and the periphery but also of peasantry were reinvented both East and West—although the strong pro-peasant leftist tradition in some of the Central European countries also dated to the beginning of the twentieth century. The rediscovery of the same peasantry doomed to extinction by the intervening post–World War II modernization theory and classical Communist ideology was welcome among the critical Marxists in the communist East and radical circles of the West as a corollary of the anthropologically rooted critique of modernization. The leftist intellectuals, disappointed by the consumerist aspirations of the white-collar workers, were forced to find new subjects in new places for their radical aspirations. The people of the ghettos, the Black Panthers, the hippies and yippies out-migrating from the cities, the homeless of the Third World, and the peasantry of the peripheries provided new promise. Throughout the decades of communism there had been a subterranean flirtation between critical Marxism and romantic antistatist, antibureaucratic, anticapitalist populism; Dimitrie Gusti, the leader of the Romanian village research movement in the 1920s and 1930s, still had important influence in the 1950s and 1960s. His most remarkable student, Henri H. Stahl, perhaps in spite of his Marxist persuasion, remained an undaunted believer in peasant self-government, communal villages, and commons. Between 1958 and 1965 he published a three-volume synthesis on traditional village communities; a translation of the entire work appeared in French and a synoptic version also appeared in English.[13] Narodniks had deep roots in Russian soil and countryside movements; Sociography of the village was a continuous preoccupation of progressive social scientists in both Russia and Hungary. (Incidentally, in 1910 my grandfather won the gold medal in the second village-sociography essay-competition of the Galliei Circle, whose treasurer he became at the time when Karl Polanyi served as president.) At the beginning of the 1960s, interest in the fate of the Russian village-commune, the *Obshahina*, was reborn.

In the first half of the 1960s, East European sociologists had their profession decriminalized. Owing to the populist, pro-peasant tradition, they were under-standably enthusiastic about the republication of A. V. Chayanov's *Peasant Farm Organization* (edited by D. Thomer, B. Kerblay, and R. E. Smith) and Theodor Shanin's studies on Russian and Soviet peasant economy, works si-multaneously influential in romantic, anticapitalist Left circles in the West. The publication of these and other books of similar persuasion resulted in a new interest in the German *Mark*, the *mir*, the *obshchina*, and the *zadruga* not as historical organizations of the past but as models for alternative integrating structures vis-à-vis modern industrial and market organizations.[14] The anti-modernist radicals re-created a new critical tradition, rediscovered new sacred texts, and built a new Pantheon with old saints such as Rosa Luxemburg (who believed that Latin America was still free space for nonbureaucratic socialist experiments), Leon Trotsky, Mao, and Georg Lukács. They created links be-tween imaginary processes in the Third World and mythical heretical leftist intellectuals who in large part came from the East. As a bridge was also being built by Western critical intellectuals toward radical traditions of the East, the dialogue between social science counterparts was a natural outcome. (The dia-logue was, however, somewhat asynchronic: the Westerners read Eastern works from the past, while the Easterners also read contemporary works by Western critical authors.)

DESPITE the original intentions of the critique to discredit Western capitalism (and the practice that followed it in some peripheral and unfortunate parts of the world), in the end it turned against socialism. And not only against existing socialist regimes, against which it was employed by the internal democratic opposition in the East; the critique unexpectedly pulled the carpet out from beneath the critics themselves.

The *nomenklatura* of the socialist regimes was naturally and understandably uncomfortable with the ideas of the New Left, and tried to silence them. The radical project posed a real danger for the stabilized, and stabilizing, law-and-order real-socialists; the last thing they wanted was any upheaval similar to that caused by the Western radical movements. The antimodernist rhetoric of the sixties went headlong against the canons of existing socialism which as-sumed that—at least internally—history was nearing its end: only a small in-crease in economic growth remained to be accomplished. The new ideas had subversive potential. The new pantheon included serious and dangerous heretics like Luxemburg, Trotsky, Lange, Bakunin Kropotkin, Kolontai, Emma Goldman, and Alexander Berkman. The discovery of the young Marx and his *Economic-Philosophical Manuscript*, with its possible anthropological interpretation, posed ideological and political challenges for which the socialist regimes were unprepared. But the strong antimarket, anticapitalist, antiimperialist, antidemocratic, anti-Western ideas of the radical New-Left—together with the appeal of the anti–Vietnam War movement in the U.S. and the Cuban revolution—were just too seductive. In spite of all the efforts to the contrary by the socialist officials, these ideas found their way even into the language of the official socialist ideology and propaganda.

In a strange way, the urge to change the discourse, the will to abandon belief in technical determinism, and the inevitability of technical progress in favor of an anticonsumerist rhetoric did not come from the realization that the East would not be able to achieve, let alone surpass, the standards of the developed West. In fact, both the hard-line Stalinists and the romantic, antibureaucratic believers in Socialism with a human face feared that affluence, the materialist Canaan, was already too near the horizon. Before the end of the 1950s, official socialist propaganda had been cautious enough not to set a fixed date for the arrival of the Communist heaven in which everyone would be able to satisfy their needs. A fixed date risked the regime's taking responsibility for its unfulfilled promises. But at the end of the 1950s, socialism ran itself fatally aground.

Reacting to the Chinese "great leap forward" (a modernization plan based ironically, but understandably, on small-scale, rurally based, so-called "people's steel mills" that employed village peasants), a seven-year-plan was adopted at the twenty-first congress of the Soviet Communist Party. According to the plan's forecast, by 1965 the Soviet Union would surpass the per capita GDP of the United States both in industry and agriculture. In November 1958, Czechoslovakia declared that it would, in a very few years, reach the level of the most developed capitalist countries. The German Democratic Republic in turn decided to surpass the German Federal Republic in per capita consumption of the most important consumer goods in two or three years. In February 1960, the agricultural development conference of the European socialist countries held in Moscow declared that "in the socialist countries, all the necessary preconditions are given that are needed to achieve the highest standard of living in the world in a few years."[15] In Hungary, the Central Planning Office worked out a twenty-year-plan in 1960. According to its preamble, "fulfilling the target figures of the plan would make it possible to satisfy all those consumption needs that, according to the standpoint of contemporary science, are enough for both the spiritual and physical well-being of humans. . . . The suggested level of consumption is around the saturation point."[16] The eighth congress of the Hungarian Socialist Workers' Party declared that "in 1980, per capita consumption will be higher in Hungary than in the most developed capitalist countries of the Earth."

In September 1961, commenting on the draft program of the Communist Party of the Soviet Union, one of the official poets of Hungary, Mihály Váci, published a polemical article. The official artist, who was a member of the Central Committee of the Hungarian Workers' Party, envisioned the 'final defeat of the material world,' talked about 'the final attack, the near victory over nature,' and asked the not so poetic question: 'what can we do when the distance between needs and satisfaction will irrecoverably disappear?' (Vaci, 1961: 579–80; cited in Berend, 1983: 196). The party poet tried to solve the problem of how to mobilize for further efforts when the population has nothing better to do than just 'lie lazily snoring on the sandy beaches of Communism.' The article provoked a debate, referred to later on as the 'refrigerator socialism controversy,' with more than 130 interventions and contributions about alienation, self-serving cars and self-serving satisfaction, the horror of holiday houses, petty bourgeois mentality, the terror of the market, the return of capitalism, the death of communal values, and so forth.

Economic reforms were ended in the Soviet Union around the time when, according to the seven-year-plan, the country should have surpassed the standard of the United States. The New Economic Mechanisms were reversed in Hungary by the end of the 1960s, when economic reforms were already dead in Czechoslovakia, Poland, and East Germany. By the time the post–World War II boom was over in the West, the East gave up the plan to outsmart it economically. I am tempted to argue that the communist parties did not give up the reforms only to protect central planning. They did not only fear the market as a more or less self-regulating institution that might make the centralized state superfluous, but feared the outburst of consumerism: that the bourgeois would step out of the simple disguise of the proletar. The finality of the Marxist theory of modes of production, and the Stalinist idea of a finite number of "social formations," proved to be dangerously rigid, especially if fixed dates were attached. The same communist officials who, a few years earlier, saw the launching of the first Sputnik in 1957 as proof of the basic axiom of the communist ideology—namely, that the constant development of the forces of production would inevitably lead to the advance of Communism, the ultimate stage of human history—had by the end of the 1960s given up one of the most important claims of the leftist utopia of the Left: that a technically developed economy inevitably creates social relations that lead to the solution of economic inequality, banishing social injustices forever.

IT WAS natural that works by economic anthropologists with a strong antimarket bias were the first to be translated into Polish, Hungarian, and Russian in the 1960s. Sahlins, Eric Wolf, Service, Dalton, Bohannan, Godelier, and Malinowsky had a liberating impact on the thinking of an increasingly active and sophisticated group of native social science thinkers. Marcel Mauss's *Essai sur le don* was not only widely read but provided a model for the critical sociologists. The discovery of the theory of the gift was timely: the roots of the second economy—first in the form of the agricultural household plot, then the *kaláka*, the reciprocal labor-exchange of quick family-house building— were just becoming visible to sociologists in search of anticentralist "coordinating mechanisms." Reciprocity promised to provide a spontaneous, voluntary, civic network of solidarity against the atomizing consequences of centralization; the second economy offered the vision of self-protected enclaves outside the sight of the center.

The housing industry offered a clear example of this change in perception. At the beginning of the 1960s, when the first modern housing estates were built in the socialist cities, the new constructions were still surrounded by the aura of progress and modernization. Rhetoric to the effect that housing factories meant cheap, widespread, working-class housing still had the ring of credibility.[17] But by the end of the decade, the situation had changed dramatically. Although Radovan Richta published his pro-modern best-seller about the so-called "scientific-technical revolution" in 1966,[18] after 21 August 1968–that is, after the invasion of Czechoslovakia—existing Socialism lost all chances to ever acquire a human face. The housing estates had quickly lost all of their aesthetic qualities if they ever had any and, rather than being a symbol for an egalitarian future, they became the terrain of a state redistributive policy that favored those already more privileged. As Konrád and Szelényi demonstrated, there was nothing inherently just or equalizing about redistribution; in fact it could serve the interest, even the material interest, of the redistributor.[19]

In 1968, the first method-of-sociology textbook was published in Hungary. The first sentence of the book—although it seemed a completely neutral, matter-of-fact sentence—was a programmatic statement: "Sociology is an empirical discipline."[20] What the sentence intimated was that the duty of sociologists was not to speculate about, but to investigate society, to reveal the facts of the real world and make them available for both the society at large and for party officials in the position to implement change. (No wonder that this boring book became an instant best-seller.)[21] At the same time, sociography was resurrected in Hungary. A book-series was begun entitled *The Discovery of Hungary*. And indeed, most of the works that it published were based on empirical research, mostly in the form of fieldwork, that also maintained sociography's preoccupation with ethical problems and its distrust of formalized theories with

> their insistence that conflicts were not merely problems to be solved, difficulties to be overcome, but represented an authentic form of existence . . . [The metaphorical language and the indefinable terms were] rooted in the prevailing undifferentiated form of social discourse which mixes types of discourse that would, in other parts of the world, constitute the separate

genres and appropriate languages of poetry, fictional narrative, social science, politically agitating pamphlets, or meditative essays. Not only was the discourse undifferentiated, but the roles of the participants as well. This role evolved historically, the role of the intellectual, obligatory for all who wish to join in the discourse. . . . Overt and covert censorship from all sides hedged in public discourse and suggesting that all utterances possessed an almost magic force, capable of evoking and realizing the reference of the words used.[22]

Sociology in other East Central European countries also was reborn under the spell of interwar sociography and its perceived mission of the critical intellectual. In Romania, for example, between 1934 and 1938, 2,563 researchers were sent into 114 villages to systematically survey the remnants of the traditional Romanian countryside. One of the most interesting and longer lasting outcomes of the fieldwork was Stahl's monograph on the village Nerej that was written for the aborted Sociological World Congress that would have taken place in 1939 in Bucharest.[23] Stahl discovered in mid-twentieth-century Vrancea, an isolated part of Romania, free villages with communal property that he presented not simply as an archaic and anachronistic formation, but as a contemporary alternative.[24]

The late 60s critical social scientists also discovered that families in villages had managed to reinvent archaic, time-saving construction techniques that enabled them to finish building their houses before the authorities woke up and denied them building permits. Sociologists found there second and even third economies of family-house building that were parasitically dependent on the socialist first economy, but also on local solidarity, labor-exchange, self-help, and the advantages of small-scale operations (this at a time when small was considered beautiful).[25] The square-house of the socialist countryside turned up as a "counter-utopia," allegedly an ingenious alternative to the deceptive and inhuman rhetoric—and practice—of socialist planning.[26] In the hands of the critical sociologist it became a social and ethical emblem.

In the 1980s the "world system-local response dialogue" still focused on the role of the East European villagers' central role in the formation of national identity.[27] In 1981, Iván Szelényi generalized the lessons of both socialist urbanization and resistance against it in his essay, "Urban Development and Regional Management in Eastern Europe." One of the longer subtitles of the paper, "The new-working class takes revenge: the silent revolution of the East European peasant-workers against the exploitative policy of the socialist redistributive regional management," a title that echoes the title of one of the most famous sociographical works on the peasants from the interwar period, I. Kovacs's *The silent revolution*—sums up not only his new theoretical framework, but some of the more important consequences the critical sociologists of the East had derived from their antimodernist readings.

Though the virtues of the peasant alternative economies seemed to be something that the sociologists "discovered" anew in the sixties and the eighties, even earlier historiography of East and Central European sociology prefigured the affinity of those critical thinkers for retrotopia:

> [The] refusal to follow the rules of academic sociological description characterizes the tradition of sociography in many Central European countries, especially Poland, Hungary, and Rumania. The authors combined in themselves the interest and methods of poets and politicians, social philosophers and journalists, reformers and researchers. They thought of themselves as parts of an important social movement within contemporary society. . . . The necessity and impossibility of a normal, i.e., Western form of peasant *embourgeoisement* in these countries could be adequately expressed only in the metaphorical language of these sociographers who spoke of sickly processes, half-hearted and awkward *embourgeoisement*, silent revolution, escape.[28]

Szelényi, in his "Footnotes to an Intellectual Autobiography," written to his collected essays in July 1989—after Imre Nagy's reburial and at the time of the collapse of Communism—argues for a "Garden Hungary," and for a "revolution of quality," expressions borrowed from László Nemeth, one of the most influential retrograde populist dreamers of the interwar period, who according to Szélenyi, "was stigmatized as an utopian but was in fact the only real *realpolitician*, whose vision of the future would have meant a much more feasible future for the Hungarians than what the Communists have proposed."[29]

East Europeans, especially Hungarian social scientists, discovered the Hungarian-born Karl Polányi at the very end of the 1960s. *Dahomey and the Slave Trade, an Analysis of an Archaic Economy* was the first of his works translated into Hungarian in 1972 (with an exceptionally denunciatory foreword by Tamás Szentes, who was misread and hailed in the West as one of the few East European supporters of dependency theory). Two books of collected essays followed, but not *The Great Transformation* which, apart from selected chapters published in restricted circulation, has never been published in Hungary. Polányi directed attention to *antipepontos*, a term used by Aristotle in his *Nicomachean Ethics*. Antipepontos, in Polányi's no-doubt oversimplified (mis?)-reading is the predisposition of a community to share the burden, and is similar to what anthropological literature calls reciprocity; it is an essential element in keeping and reproducing the community in antiquity.[30] According to Aristotle—in Polányi's reading—reciprocity is as natural as *autarkheia*. Proof of this had been rediscovered in the socialist economy of small-scale peasant subsistence farming, or in the household plots of the members of agricultural co-operatives. In *The Great Transformation*, Polányi describes different integrating principles of the economy. His third principle is house-holding. "Looking back from the rapidly declining heights," writes Polányi, we must concede that Aristotle's famous distinction of house-holding proper and money-making, in the introductory chapter of his *Politics*, was probably the most prophetic pointer ever made in the realm of the social sciences; it is certainly still the best analysis of the subject we possess. Aristotle insists on production for use as against production to gain as the essence of house-holding proper; yet accessory production for the market need not, he argues, destroy the self-sufficiency of the household . . . the sale of the surpluses does not necessarily destroy the basis of householding. . . . In denouncing the principle of production for gain "as not natural to man," as boundless and limitless, Aristotle was, in effect, aiming at the crucial point, namely the divorce of a separate economic motive from the social relations in which these limitations inhered.[31]

From Polányi's interpretation of Aristotle, East- and Central-European critical social scientists distilled the idea that household and market production could coexist, that one is able to produce for gain at the same time as one produces for use. As long as this coexistence prevails, man (woman too, perhaps, Aristotle uses the neuter term) is able to exercise control over the sphere of the economy. The family farm and the household plot of the cooperative members are not only means of peasant subsistence—reasoned the Central- and East-European critical intellectual—but sites of an alternative economic and social integration. Preoccupation with survival techniques of the peasantry became the most fashionable research program of the Central-European sociologist. This led to the exposé of the shadowy world of the second economy, and to the cracks in the wall of the socialist construct. It became current to say that "real life" flourished only in those spaces protected from the gaze of the centralizing authorities whose ambition it was to pretend that they were capable of being, and seeing, everywhere. The popularity of these research programs derived in part from the aporia in which social scientists found themselves. If one had been educated in Marx's modes of production or, in less fortunate cases, in Stalin's ideas of social formations, social and economic development was necessarily based on technological progress. There was no way to transcend either highly developed capitalism—Rostow's "stage of high mass consumption"[32]—or the centralized state of existing socialism from the perspective of which capitalism turned out to be a transitional historical formation. But when the marriage of Communism with technical utopianism was over, modernism seemed to be dead without the possibility of resurrection. In this logic *there was no escape forward*; a different trajectory had to be discovered.

The 1970s socialist countryside seemed to provide an alternative if not to socialism at least to the existing post-Stalinist model of socialist economy and centrally organized society. In Hungary, it was the supposed ingenuity of the peasantry that formed the basis of the post-1956 relative well-being of the

population, of "goulash-communism," and of the seeds of the supposed socialist welfare state.[33] Sociologists, especially representatives of the older sociographical tradition, interpreted the survival and resurfacing of these peasant
economic techniques as a sign of the existence of a "late- or post-peasantry."
Others saw these peasants as representatives of a "new working-class, occupying two worlds while living and working in two different types of settlement."[34] Others discovered sure signs of the continuation of a stifled process
of *embourgeoisement* interrupted by the Communist takeover.[35] These later
theories expected that the development of the peasant economy could lead to
a widening market, small-scale production, the establishment of a class of
socialist entrepreneurs, and even to long-term changes inside the state-
controlled industrial sector of the socialist economy. The subcontracting system in industry, introduced after the beginning of the 1980s in the Hungarian
firms, fueled these romantic expectations.[36] Analysts predicted a slow, peaceful
change that however would not affect a basic logic of the socialist system in
the shorter-run. Szelényi, for example, was still predicting in 1989 that the
hegemony of socialist redistribution would remain in place for another fifteen–
twenty years, as nobody in their right mind would be able to come up with a
program of large-scale mass privatization that would affect the strongholds of
the socialist industry. Instead, the state would help "the original accumulation"
of capital inside the socialist mixed economy so as to allow a sufficiently
sturdy stratum of small- or smaller-scale entrepreneurs to emerge. The mistake
of the reform economists of the 1970s and 1980s—one that Szelényi's argument intended to correct—was that they concentrated their efforts on changing
the socialist sector, trying to introduce market measures in the terrain under
the strict rule of the planner, rather than on strengthening the second economy,
the birthplace of the future.[37]

THERE WERE some social scientists in East and Central Europe—myself included—who tried to base less an economic than a political theory on the
romanticized reading of the history of the peasantry. Influenced by E. P. Thom-
son's *The Moral Economy of the English Crowd*, James Scott's *The Moral
Economy of the Peasant*, John Gaventa's *Power and Powerlessness*, Hobsbawm's *Primitive Rebels*, George Rude, and Eugene Genovese, these scholars
engaged in an effort to explore the history and possibility of covert, everyday
resistance under Socialism. In 1985, I wrote a paper entitled "The Advantages
of Being Atomized," in which I tried to prove that despite the overall centralizing ambitions of the state, in fact as their consequence, it became relatively
easy and cheap to resist the socialist regime. I deliberately mixed-up individual
escape attempts with mass movements and, after extensive archival research,
I came to a very similar conclusion to that of James Scott in his *Weapons of
the Weak*, though without first reading his book. I argued that the post-Stalinist
changes were mostly the consequences of an ongoing fight in the countryside,

that the 1956 Revolution could not be understood without connecting it to that previous hidden war, and that almost all the 1956 reforms were nothing but the legalization of already existing secret practices in diverse parts of the society.[38] Only in 1994 was I able to understand the dangers of that scholarly and critical program; I added a postscript written to the original text:

> Back in 1985, it was decidedly unclear that such ideas could lead to efforts aimed at legitimizing a political program diametrically opposed to my original intentions at the time of writing. After the collapse of Communism certain groups aspiring to political power that try to find legitimacy in the peasantry, the people, the folk, *das Volk*, point to the peasantry and its alleged continuous, transhistorical resistance to every oppressive regime. The "people" is uncorrupted as it was willing and capable of waging an ongoing, secret war of liberation even during the darkest days of Communism. Only the peasant is clean—since he was the only one who had a strategy against the centralizing state. The work of the disappeared Communist becomes complete only when others, the peasants, the historian who is analyzing the fife of the peasantry, or the politician of the 1990s who would like to make use of the peasantry of the 1950s, start to think with the mind of the former authorities, use their language, when they read a conscious, real resistance into unreflected, everyday life. When from the perspective of the collapse of Communism, the historian starts to speak about the past of concerted political actions of the millions worked out in secret, behind closed kitchen doors, then he or she finishes the great, heroic work of Communism. What the Communist regime was unable to accomplish itself—because it proved unable to persuade the peasant that eating, seeding, harvesting, just living one's life were direct unequivocal political acts—comes to fruition with the help of the historian. When the historian speaks about the national liberation movement, countrywide anti-communist war, then he or she becomes an accomplice in the post-mortem victory of the Communists.[39]

But the retrotopian attitude did not die out at the time of the transition. Latter-day nationalist politicians and serious historians still frame their findings in such narratives.[40] Communism might be over but the primitive utopia, as imagined by anthropology, lives on.

REDISTRIBUTION first arrived in East and Central Europe through readings of Karl Wittfogel's ideas about Oriental Despotism and the Asiatic mode of production, first published in 1957.[41] This is how Polányi, relying on Thurnwald, introduces the concept of distribution, i.e., redistribution, in *The Great Transformation*:

> Distribution has its own particular history, starting from the most primitive life of the hunting tribes. . . . But the distributive function increases with the

growing political power of a few families and the rise of despots. The chief receives the gifts of the peasant, which have now become "taxes," and distributes them among his officials, especially those attached to his court. . . . This development involved more complicated systems of distribution. [and Polyányi elaborates:] Redistribution . . . has its long and variegated history which leads up almost to modern times. . . . Obviously, the social consequences of such a method of distribution may be far reaching. . . . Whether the redistribution is performed by an influential family or an outstanding individual, a ruling aristocracy or a group of bureaucrats, they will often attempt to increase their political power by the manner in which they redistribute the goods.[42]

According to the logic of *The Great Transformation*, centrally planned and executed actions were needed to defend both the society and even the economy from the devastating and self-destructive mechanism of the allegedly self-regulating market: "Regulation and the markets, in effect, grew up together . . . a network of measures and policies was integrated into powerful institutions designed to check the action of the market relative to labor, land and money. Paradoxically enough, not only human beings and natural resources, but the organization of capitalistic production itself had to be sheltered from the devastating effects of a self-regulating market. . . . While laissez-faire economy was the product of deliberate state action, subsequent restrictions on the laissez-faire started in a spontaneous way. Laissez-faire was planned, planning was not."[43]

On the basis of Polányi's insights, the socialist system could be presented "under a new description." The first such attempt was *The Intellectuals on the Road to Class Power* by Konrád and Szelényi, first distributed in manuscript form and then published in samizdat in Hungary. The authors tried to present the socialist system as a new, more advanced form of redistribution, a "rational redistribution" as compared to the "traditional redistribution" of Asiatic despotism. János Kornai, the economist, influenced by Polányi, worked out his own system of coordinating mechanisms, and started to use the term "bureaucratic coordination" in the sense of Polányi's redistributive integration. Other sociologists concentrated on the constraining potential of redistribution, and argued that, properly employed, redistribution could diminish inequality, and compensate for the handicaps of the most underprivileged strata, or groups, or even classes of the society.[44]

As it became clear that certain groups within the society were able to gain additional income on the market, Szelényi and his colleagues introduced a revision to Polányi's original ideas about redistribution. Szelényi argued that second-level mechanisms (redistribution in a market economy the market in a redistributive economy) have a leveling effect, such that the market could compensate for the inequality caused by the very mechanism of redistribution.

Szelényi wrote: "[T]he interest of the powerless and the dispriviledged can be best served with increasingly transactive (and consequently marketlike) relationships in the economic system." This is to say, contrary to Polányi, that there is nothing inherently unequal in the market, as there is nothing inherently equal in redistribution.[45] This insight was based mostly on empirical research about the housing market, and influenced by the surprising fact that the less privileged were able to counteract the injustices of redistribution with the help of their participation in the "markets" of the second and third economy. Equipped with these empirical facts, some sociologists advocated the widening of the sphere of the market (the market of these non-market-economies, like the secondary and tertiary economies) not only in order to help nonredistributive, noncentralized, not-so-socialist alternatives, but to decrease economic and social inequality.

At this point, the tension grew between the two groups of sociologists, one advocating redistribution, the other arguing for the market as a mechanism for the attainment of social justice. Both felt that the other had become the ally of the inhuman bureaucratic state. The economic reformers fighting for the diminishing role of the state considered the pro-redistribution sociologists politically blind, whereas the pro-redistributors saw their pro-market colleagues as enemies of the underprivileged and traitors to the traditional cause of critical sociology.[46] Szelényi and his colleagues decided to make further revisions to their thesis. Now they argued that under certain conditions, the second-level mechanism might contribute to further inequality: the market might favor those who were supported by the system of redistribution, redistributors could double-dip by leveraging power in the redistributive economy to gain unfair advantage in the marketplace.[47] By distinguishing between "economic" and "welfare" redistribution, they now argued for the need of "third-level mechanisms" that would compensate for both the inequalities of redistribution and those of the market.[48] They hoped that this theory of third-level mechanisms—a further revision of Polányi's idea that came closer to the original than the previous revision—would be able to bridge the gap between the pro-redistribution sociologists and the economic reformers. Their efforts turned out to be futile. The expected change, the Collapse, came from a completely unexpected direction. It turned the romantic utopia into one tragicomically outdated.

FROM the end of the 1960s, certain insights drawn from the antimodernist critique of the New Left and the empirical data collected by the sociographically influenced group of East- and Central-European sociologists seemed to match one another. There was an apparent overlap between a theorized primitive utopia and the results of fieldwork. This overlap provided both a critical research program, guidelines for an ideology, and a pragmatic plan of action. The sociologists felt that in the womb of existing socialism there lay growing an alternative both to socialism and capitalism that the Western New Left was trying unsuccessfully to find. They hoped that this nearly invisible but potent process would gradually transform the socialist system, that reform would provide more breathing and living space for the protagonists of the second and third economies, and that the widening sphere would restore the dignity of life and work as well as revitalize self-help and solidarity at the level of the local community. They hoped, in sum, that it could serve as the basis for the rebirth of civil society. Such hopes were fueled by Konrád's *Antipolitics*,[49] and by Václav Havel, who in his famous and naive essay "The Power of the Powerless" wrote:

> It would appear that traditional parliamentary democracies can offer no fundamental opposition to the automatism of technological civilization and the industrial-consumer society. . . . In a democracy, human beings may enjoy many personal freedoms and securities that are unknown to us, but in the end they do them no good, for they too are ultimately victims of the same automatism. . . . But to cling to the notion of traditional parliamentary democracy as one's political ideal and to succumb to the illusion that this "tried and true" form is capable of guaranteeing human beings enduring dignity and an independent role in society would, in my opinion, be at least shortsighted. . . . I see a renewed focus of politics on real people as something far more profound than merely returning to the everyday mechanism of Western (or if you like, bourgeois) democracy. . . . In other words, are not these informal, non-bureaucratic, dynamic and open communities that comprise the "parallel *polis*" a kind of rudimentary pre-figuration, a symbolic model of those more meaningful "post-democratic" political structures that might become the foundation of a better society?[50]

According to Havel, the "parallel *polis*" meant "an opposition to the automatism of technological civilization," to "traditional parliamentary democracy," and everything else associated with progress in modern Western thinking. (It is just a small, unintended historical irony that Havel is now presiding over the most successfully Westernized of the post-communist transformations, the paradise of American tourists.)

There seemed to be no hope for real political change, no hope for change coming from the sphere of politics, only hope vested in the supposedly self-protected corners of the villages, the "small-circles of freedom." The critical sociologists hoped that if change could come, it would mean the end of heavy state intervention, even the end of the rule of politics.

For a moment, at the time of the Collapse, the sociologists supposed that more legality, greater freedom, and democracy would favor the previous actors of the second economy, that East- and especially Central-Europe once more could become an experimental laboratory, as large-scale privatization and the immediate introduction of real market institutions seemed unimaginable. It was not easy to see that the world of the second economy was entirely dependent on the sphere of the first, that success in the second was a function of shortages and inefficiency in the first, that the market of the second was not really self-perpetuating, and that the skills it had valued would become obsolete in the economy of the self-regulating market. Nor did they see that survival techniques were individualistic, indeed individualizing, the opposite of any form of solidarity. In the meantime, without much thought or reason, and without either party exactly knowing what they were doing, the technocratically minded part of the *nomenklatura* formed an alliance with the self-styled Western-oriented economic reformers who did not think much of the obscure preoccupations of the critical sociologists. This alliance, referring to common sense and economic necessity, began the process of privatization, and introduced certain neo-conservative and monetarist measures. There was not much resistance, as most of the people were busy working in the second economy and did not understand that the measures being introduced would deal it a fatal blow; trying to survive Communism, they missed the moment of transition.

The majority of the population could not, did not, contribute much to the design of the new system. The sociologists, too, were busy trying to reconcile their research and political programs with the new realities. Their failures on this front were not only ideological, but scholarly. The changes that occurred were not the ones they had worked for either as social scientists or reformers. Real processes falsified research programs. With resignation they diagnosed the end of the Left alternative that went into a terminal spin exactly at the moment they discovered it. The mid-sixties attempts to find a new beginning were, in fact, the beginning of the end.

IT IS rather unfortunate that serious academic research does not pay sufficiently close attention to events that happen as a consequence of a lack of foresight. According to mainstream reasoning, there is nothing to explain in such cases as social processes cannot be predicted in a scientifically sound way: every day the car runs over another dog, and one cannot foretell which dog will be next. Seldom does anyone dare say that something happened exactly as a consequence of the silence *ante eventum*. The academic world usually does not see any causal relationship between silence and event. Conversely, I have to admit that it is rather difficult to prove that something did not happen exactly as a consequence of it having been predicted beforehand, for according to rational suppositions there is no connection between prediction and occurrence of an event. The nonoccurrence of an event is seen as proof of the nonexistence of the connection between the prediction and the nonevent. It is risky to state then that there is a causal relationship between prediction and the nonoccurrence of an event on the basis that the prediction proved to be untenable *post eventum*.

The German Institut für Demoskopie Allensbach carried out a retrospective survey in February and March 1990 in East Germany. The Institute wanted to know whether the East Germans had foreseen the fall of the Wall. According to the poll, more than 68% of the East Germans answered—even in retro-spect—that they had misread the signs. According to the researchers, the fact that thousands of East Germans fled to Western embassies only a few days before the collapse of the Wall shows clearly that the East Germans did not have a clue about the very near future: had they been able to foresee what would happen, they would have stayed at home waiting for the spontaneous Fall. But would it have happened in that case? Was not the lack of foresight a necessary—if not sufficient—precondition for what was to come? Cannot we say that the preoccupation with the primitive utopia, with the second economy, and the supposed everyday resistance of the peasantry in fact did *contribute* to the collapse of Communism? The silence of the social scientists, Kremlinol-ogists, economists, and sociologists turned out to be a history-forming force. The self-inflicted wound of the critical social scientist, their turn away from any form of progress or alternative utopia, played a very important role in ending the system against which they had been fighting. There are times (is this not always the case?) when the real service social scientists render is their silence and their ignorance.

When writing about the consistent policy of Tudor and early Stuart statesmen, who aimed to prevent the process of enclosures from turning into a degenera-tive process, Polányi asks the following question: "Why should the ultimate victory of a trend be taken as a proof of the ineffectiveness of the efforts to slow down its progress?" And he states with enviable modesty:

> The rate of change is often of no less importance than the direction of the change itself; but while the latter frequently does not depend upon our voli-tion, it is the rate at which we allow change to take place which may well depend upon us. . . . For at this rate, mainly, depending on whether the dis-possessed could adjust themselves to altered conditions without fatally dam-aging their subsistence, human and economic, physical and moral; whether they would find new employment in the fields of opportunity indirectly con-nected with the change. The answer depends in every case on the relative rates of change and adustment. The usual 'long-term' considerations of eco-nomic theory are inadmissible; . . . 'long-term' considerations of economic theory are effect of a change is deleterious, then, until proof to the contrary, the final effect is deleterious.[51]

NOTES

1. "[T]he Cold War is over, the West won. [. . .] The Soviet Union . . . has collapsed." This is not a factual, retrospective historical statement, but these words were spoken by Daniel Patrick Moynihan in 1984 before Gorbachev took office. Daniel Patrick Moy-nihan, "The Soviet Union Is a Failed Society in Need of Clear Policy," *US Buffalo News*, 15 October 1984.

2. Karl Polányi, *The Great Transformation* (Boston: Beacon Press, 1957), p. 89.

3. S. Itshitsuka, "The Fall of Real Socialism and the Crisis in Human Sciences," *Social Justice* 27:3 (1994). Quoted in Jeffrey C. Alexander, *Fin de Siècle Social Theory* (London: Verso, 1995), p. 48.

4. "[B]y the exercise of a little imagination the 'u' can also stand for the Greek prefix *eu*—'good,' 'well'—and then we get 'good place,' 'ideal place.'" M. I. Finley, "Utopianism Ancient and Modern," in *The Use and Abuse of History*, ed. M. I. Finley (London: Chatto and Windus, 1975), p. 178. The essay was originally, and not surprisingly, published in K. H. Wolff and B. Moore, eds., *The Critical Spirit: Essays in Honor of Herbert Marcuse* (Boston: Beacon Press, 1967).

5. See Todd Gitlin, *The Sixties* (New York: Bantam Books, 1989).

6. Eric Hobsbawn, "From Feudalism to Capitalism," in *The Transition from Feudalism to Capitalism* (London: Verso, 1978), pp. 162 and 164. This essay was originally published in *Marxism Today* in 1962.

7. See Leszek Kolakowski, *Main Currents of Marxism*, vol. 3 (Oxford: Oxford University Press, 1981), pp. 421–34.

8. Frankfurt: Suhrkamp Verlag, 1959, pp. 284–85.

9. Jeffrey C. Alexander, *Fin de Siècle Social Theory*, p. 3.

10. Lajos Leopold, *Szinlelt Kapitalizmus* (Budapest, 1917). An essay drawn from this book was republished in *Medvetánc* 8:2–3 (1988), pp. 321–55.

11. György Lengyel, "Economic Sociology in East-Central Europe: Trends and Challenges," *Replika* (Special Issue, 1996), p. 37.

12. "Urban Development and Regional Management in Eastern Europe" (1981), in Iván Szelényi, *Új osztál, állam, politika* (Budapest: Europa, 1990), pp. 303–50. My critique of this deterministic *Weltanschauung* was published as "When was the Original Sin committed? Local autonomy or centralisation," *International Journal of Urban and Regional Studies* (1984).

13. Henri H. Stahl, *Contributi la studiul satelor devalmare Romanesti*, 3 vols. (Bucharest, 1958–1965). In English: *Traditional Romanian Village Communities*, trans. Daniel and Holley Coulter Chirot (Cambridge: Cambridge University Press, 1980).

14. Even Mexico and the Mexican *ejido* had a role to play in this story, partly because of the chapters Eric Wolf devoted to the Mexican revolution in his *Peasant Wars of the 20th Century*. Mexico and Central Europe had not been so close to one another since the time of the Habsburg emperor, Maximilian.

15. See *Társadalmi Szemle* (Social Review), 1960:2, p. 10.

16. This quote is take from Iván T. Berend, *Gazdasági Útkeresés 1956–1965* (Economic Exploitation 1956–1965) (Budapest: Magvető, 1983), pp. 194–95.

17. Recently I happened to see a few documentary films about the first housing estates from the middle of the 1960s, and it was not only in the official propaganda that one was able to find aesthetic qualities in those early housing projects. The harsh horizontal and vertical lines still sent one back to echoes of a Mondrian painting, or the puritanism of the Bauhaus with its modernist, Left commitment, or the constructivism of the 1910s and 1920s—especially from Soviet Russia—and an affinity to the minimalist programs of art in the 1960s.

18. *Civilisation on the Crossroad*, published in Prague in 1966 and translated into Hungarian in 1967 as *Válaszúton a Civilizáció* (Budapest: Kossuth).

19. Konrád György and Szelényi Iván, *Az új lakótelepek szodológiai problémái* (Budapest: Akadémiai, 1969).

20. Cseh-Szombathy Lázló és Ferge Zsuzsa, *A szociológiai felvétel módszerei* (The methods of sociological survey) (Budapest: Közgazdasági és Jogi, 1968), p. 5.

21. See Péter Somlai, "Szociológia és Társadalom Magyarországon" (Sociology and Society in Hungary), in *Arat a Magyar* (The Hungarian is harvesting) (Budapest: MTA Szociológiai Kutató Intézete, 1988), p. 345.

22. Anna Wessely, "The Cognitive Change of Sociology," *Replika*, special issue (1996): pp. 16–17.

23. *Nerej, un village d'une région achaique*, Monographies Sociologiques dirigée par H. H. Stahl (Bucharest, 1939).

24. See his "Traditional Romanian Village Communities." A collection of his essays was published in Hungarian: *A régi román falu öröksége* (The heritage of the traditional romanian village) (Budapest, 1992).

25. On the sociological problems of socialist housing-policy and "its discontents," see: J. Hegedüs and I. Tosics, "Lakáspolitika, lakáspiac" (Housing-policy, housing-market), *Valóság* 7 (1971); J. Hegedüs and I. Tosics, "Housing Claws and Housing Policy: Some Changes in the Budapest Housing Market," *International Journal of Urban and Regional Research* 7:4 (1983); I. Tosics, "Dilemmas of Reducing Direct State Control" (paper presented at the IRCHP Conference, Gavle, Sweden, 1986); J. Dávid, "A magánlakásépítés formái és feltételei" (The forms and preconditions of private housing-construction), *Valóság* 10 (1980); and J. Kenedi, *Do it yourself: Hungary's Self-help Economy* (London: Pluto, 1981). On labor-exchange, see Endre Sik, "The Survival of an Institution of Survival: The Reciprocal Exchange of Labour in Modem Times" (paper presented at the Conference on Trends and Challenges of Urban Restructuring, Rio de Janeiro, 1988).

26. See Rajik Lászlo, "The anti-utopia of the 'square-house'" (lecture given as part of the "Anti-utopia" lecture series, Budapest, 1976).

27. See, for example, Katherine Verdery, *Transylvanian Villages* (Berkeley: University of California Press, 1983) and Gail Kligman, *The Weeding of the Dead* (Berkeley: University of California Press, 1988).

28. Anna Wessely, "Cognitive Change," p. 16. She quotes from Révai József, *Marximus, népiesség, Magyarság* (Budapest: Kossuth, 1955), pp. 300–303.

29. *Új osztály, állam, politika*, pp. 468–69.

30. On the probable meanings of *antipepontos*, and on Aristotle and economics in a more general sense, see Moses Finley, "Aristotle and Economic Analysis," *Past and Present* 47 (1970), pp. 3–25. According to Finley, Polányi misread Book V of the *Nicomachean Ethics* and Book I of the *Politics*. For Polányi's take, see: Karl Polányi, "Arisztotelész felfedezi a gazdaságot" (Aristotle discovers the economy), *Az Archaikus Társadalom és a gazdasági szemlélet* (The archaic society and the economic attitude) (Budapest, Gondolat, 1976), p. 170. An English edition can be found in K. Polányi, M. Arensberg, and H. P. Pearson, eds., *Trade and Market in Early Empires* (Glencoe, 1957).

31. *The Great Transformation* (Boston: Beacon Press, 1957), pp. 53–54.

32. The logic of Rostow's stage theory owed a lot to Friedrich List's classification. See List's *Das nationale System der politischen Oekonomie* (Stuttgart, 1841).

33. This development was interpreted by some Western scholars and journalists as if the peasantry, and to a certain extent the society in general, had won a postmortem noncapitalist victory after the 1956 Revolution, forcing the regime to accept growing individual autonomy, access to the market, and toleration of the second economy. The modest enrichment of the peasantry, an achievement of only relative success in light of the devastating agricultural policy of the pre-1956 Stalinist era, was interpreted as more or less conscious resistance, a liberation movement of the society. Atomized, individualistic escape attempts were sometimes interpreted as collective self-defense; individual economic techniques were consciously confused with reciprocity; labor-exchange with signs of altruism and the restoration of the meaning and decency of human work and solidarity. The best analysis of the resistance and survival techniques of the socialist peasantry can be found in works by Pál Juhász. See his *Adalékok a háztáji és kisegítő gazdaság elméletéhez* (Notes to a theory of the household and subsidiary economy) (Budapest: Szövetkezeti Kutatóintézet Évkönyve, 1975).

34. See, for example, I. Márkus, "Az utóparasztság arcképéhez" (Towards a portrait of the post-peasantry), *Szociológia* 1 (1973).

35. Iván Szelényi, R. Manchin, P. Juhász, B. Magyar, and B. Martin, *Socialist Entrepreneurs: Embourgeoisement in Rural Hungary* (Cambridge, UK: Polity Press, 1987). The title of the later Hungarian edition of the book was characteristic: *Harmadik út? Polgárosodás falun* (The Third-way? Embourgeoisement in the countryside).

36. See the studies of the American sociologist David Stark: "Rethinking Internal Labor Markets: New Insights from a Comparative Perspective," *American Sociological Review* 4 (1986); and "Markets Inside the Socialist Firm: Internal Subcontracting in Hungarian Enterprises" (paper presented at the annual meeting of the American Sociological Association, Washington, D.C., 1985). Such hopes were not confined to Hungary, not even to the East European socialist countries As late as 1989, when changes were well under way in Eastern Europe, Cornell sociologist Victor Nee (a colleague of David Stark who in turn had worked with Iván Szelényi at Wisconsin) published a paper in the *American Sociological Review* with the title that paraphrases Polányi: "A Theory of Market Transition: From Redistribution to Markets in State Socialism." His paper quotes Stark as claiming that "[t]he boundaries of the second economy and the relative proportions of its legal, illegal, and alegal parts are products of contestation between state and society—a continuously changing outcome of a struggle in which society attempts to create and maintain a sphere of activity relatively autonomous from the state." About China, Nee says that "market opportunities open up alternative avenues of socioeconomic mobility. Thus changes in the structure of opportunities give rise to entrepreneurship as an alternative to bureaucratic advancement in state socialism. . . . Changes in distribution will flow from changes in power, incentives, and opportunities. The processes are interdependent and occur simultaneously. Overall, the theory of market transition predicts that direct producers gain in power relative to redistributors in those sectors of the socialist economy that experience a shift from redistribution to market allocation." Victor Nee, "A Theory of Market Transition," *American Sociological Review* 54 (October 1989), pp. 663–81.

37. Iván Szelényi, "Notes to an intellectual autobiography," pp. 464–69.

38. My article was published in *Dissent* (Summer 1987).

39. "Az Atomizálás előnyei, post scriptum," *Replica* 23–24 (1996), p. 157.

40. See, for example, Gábor T. Rittersporn, "Das kollektivierte Dorf in der bauer-lichen Gegenkultur" (paper presented at the conference Stalinismus vor dem Zweiten Weltkrieg, Munich 1996).

41. For philological correctness, I have to note that the term and the theory originate with Lajos Magyar, a Hungarian-born Sinologist, an acquaintance of Polányi, and a victim of the Stalinist purges in Moscow, who had to die because of the interference between Chinese history and the Stalinist Soviet Union.

42. *The Great Transformation*, pp. 47–55. Thurnwald's quote is taken from *Economics in Primitive Communities* (1932).

43. *The Great Transformation*, pp. 68, 76, 132, and 141, respectively.

44. See János Kornai, "Bürokratikus és piaci coordináció" (Bureaucratic and market coordination) *Közgazdaségi Szemle* 9 (1983), pp. 1025–38. For the latter, see, for example, Zsuzsa Ferge, *A Society in the Making* (White Plains, NY: Sharpe, 1976).

45. Iván Szelényi, "Social Inequalities in State Socialist Redistributive Economies," *International Journal of Comparative Sociology* 19 (1978), p. 63. See also Iván Szelényi and Róbert Manchin, "Szociálpolitika az államszocialmusban" (Social Policy in State Socialism) *Új osztály, állam, politika*, pp. 203–58.

46. About the debate between the two camps, see Iván Petõ and István Rév, "Dupla vagy semmi" (Double or nothing), unpublished manuscript, 1982.

47. See Nee, "A Theory of Market Transition," p. 679.

48. Szeldny and Manchin, "Szociálpolitika."

49. George Konrád, *Antipolitics* (New York: Harcourt, Brace, 1984). Konrad was an essayist-turned-sociologist who became president of the International PEN. He is one of the important theoreticians of East-European civil society.

50. In Václav Havel et al., *The Power of the Powerless*, ed. John Keane (New York: A. E. Sharpe, 1985), pp. 91–92, 95.

51. Polányi, *The Great Transformation*, 1957:36–8.

CHAPTER 20

International Society: What Is the Best that We Can Do?

Michael Walzer

PREFACE

I finished a first draft of this essay in 1999, just before the NATO bombing campaign against Serbia began—a campaign that provides a striking example of the failure of international society. A double failure in that case: its political agencies were not able to respond in a timely fashion to the disaster of the former Yugoslavia, and then they were not able to find a more immediately effective form of military intervention. The problem both times wasn't one of organization but of political will, and I won't have much to say here about how to solve it. No doubt there are organizational structures that lend themselves to strong action in a crisis. But these structures can as easily produce reckless and cruel acts as wise ones, and so we need to limit their powers. And then, properly limited, they may not act at all. This dilemma is an old one; it arises as often in economic as in political and humanitarian crises; and my way of dealing with it—which, as readers will see, is to multiply structures and agents in the hope that somewhere, somehow, someone will do the right thing—will certainly seem inadequate. I concede immediately that I cannot produce an organizational chart showing how a decision to act rightly in international society would be deliberated, decided, and then resolutely carried out. There is no solution of that kind; we have to think instead of political arrangements as if they were strategies—for avoiding as well as for coping with crises. That's what I will try to do; doing it doesn't answer to the urgency of the daily news, but these days nothing could.

• • •

IMAGINE the possible political arrangements of international society as if they were laid out along a continuum marked off according to the degree of centralization. Obviously, there are alternative markings; the recognition and enforcement of human rights could also be measured along a continuum, as could democratization, equality (among countries or individuals), welfare provision, pluralism, and so on. But I think that focusing on centralization is the best way of opening a discussion of international politics and the quickest way to reach the key political and moral questions, above all the classical questions: What is the best or the best possible regime? What constitutional goals should we set ourselves in an age of globalization?

My plan is to present seven possible regimes or constitutions or political arrangements. I will do this discursively, without providing a list in advance, but I do want to list the criteria against which the seven arrangements have to be evaluated: these are their capacity to promote peace, distributive justice, cultural pluralism, and individual freedom. Within the scope of a single essay, I will have to deal briefly and summarily with some of the arrangements and some of the criteria. This is especially regrettable since the criteria turn out to be inconsistent with, or at least in tension with, one another. So my argument will be complicated, and could be, no doubt it should be, much more so.

• • •

IT IS probably best to begin with the two ends of the continuum, so that its dimensions are immediately visible. On one side, let's say the left side (though I will raise some doubts about that designation later on), there is a unified global state, something like Kant's "world republic," with a single undifferentiated set of citizens, identical with the set of adult human beings, all of them possessed of the same rights and obligations. This is the form that maximum centralization would take: each individual, every person in the world, would be connected directly to the center. A global empire, in which one nation ruled over all the others, would also operate from a single center, but insofar as its rulers differentiated between the dominant nation and all the others, their rule would necessarily be mediated, and this would represent a qualification on its centralized character. The centralization of the global state is unqualified. Following Hobbes's argument in *Leviathan*, I want to say that such a state could be a monarchy, oligarchy, or democracy; its unity is not affected by its political character. By contrast, unity is certainly affected by any racial, religious, or ethnic divisions, whether these are hierarchical in nature, as in the imperial case, establishing significant inequalities among the groups, or merely functional or regional. Division of any sort moves us rightwards on the continuum as I am imagining it.

At the far right is the regime or the absence-of-regime that political theorists call "international anarchy." This phrase describes what is in fact a highly organized world, but one that is radically de-centered. The organizations are individual sovereign states, and there is no effective law binding on all of them. There is no global authority or procedure for policy determination, and there is no encompassing legal jurisdiction for either sovereigns or citizens. More than this (since I mean to describe an extreme condition), there are no smaller groups of states that have accepted a common law and submitted to its enforcement by international agencies; there are no stable organizations of states working to generate common policies with regard, say, to environmental questions, arms control, labor standards, the movement of capital, or any other issue of general concern. Sovereign states negotiate with each other on the basis of their "national interests," reach agreements, and sign treaties, but the treaties are not enforceable by any third party. State leaders watch each other nervously, and respond to each other's policies, but in every other sense, the centers of political decision-making are independent; every state acts alone. I don't mean this as an account of our own situation; I am not describing the world as it is in 2000. But we are obviously closer to the right than to the left side of the continuum.

The strategy of this essay will be to move in from the two sides. I will be moving toward the center, but from opposite directions, so as to make clear that I am not describing a developmental, purposive, or progressive history. The different regimes or arrangements are ideal types, not historical examples. And I don't assume in advance that the best regime lies at the center, only that it doesn't lie at the extremes. Even that assumption needs to be justified; it isn't obvious; so I had better turn immediately to the twin questions: What's wrong with radical centralization? What's wrong with anarchy? The second of these is the easiest, since it is closer to our own experience. Anarchy leads regularly to war, and war to conquest; conquest to empire; empire to oppression; oppression to rebellion and secession; and secession leads back to anarchy and war again. The viciousness of the circle is continually reinforced by inequalities of wealth and power among the involved states, and by the shifting character of these inequalities (which depend on trade patterns, technological development, military alliances, etc.). All this makes for insecurity and fear not only among the rulers of states but also among their ordinary inhabitants, and insecurity and fear are, as Hobbes taught us, the chief causes of war.

But would an international society, however anarchic, all of whose constituent states were republics be drawn into the same circle? Kant argued that republican citizens would be far less willing to accept the risks of war than kings were to impose those risks on their subjects—and so would be less threatening to their neighbors (*Perpetual Peace*, First Definitive Article).[1] We can certainly see evidence of that unwillingness in contemporary democracies, though it has not always been as strong as it is today. At the same time, it is qualified today by the willing use of the most advanced military technologies— which don't, indeed, put their users at risk though they impose very high costs on their targets. So it may be the case, as the Kosovo war suggests, that modern democracies won't live up to Kant's pacific expectations: they will fight, only not on the ground.

A rather different argument has been made by some contemporary political scientists: that, at least in modern times, democratic republics don't fight *with one another*. But if this is so (and here too the Kosovo war might be considered a counterexample), it is in part because they have had common enemies, and have established multilateral forms of cooperation and coordination, alliances for mutual security, that mitigate the anarchy of their relations. They have moved, so to speak, to the left along the continuum.

But I don't want to dismiss international anarchy without saying something about its advantages. Despite the hazards of inequality and war, sovereign statehood is a way of protecting distinct historical cultures, sometimes national, sometimes ethnic/religious in character. The passion with which stateless nations pursue statehood, the driven character of national liberation movements, reflect the somber realities of twentieth-century international society, from which it is necessary to draw moral and political conclusions. Sovereign power is a means of self-protection, and it is very dangerous to be deprived of this means. So, the *morally* maximal form of decentralization would be a society in which every national or ethnic/religious group that needed protection actually possessed sovereign power. But for reasons we all know, which have to do with the necessary territorial extension of sovereignty, the mixing of populations on the ground, and the uneven distribution of natural resources above and below the ground, dividing up the world in this way would be (has been) a bloody business, and once the wars start, the divisions that result are unlikely to be either just or stable.

The problems at the other end of the continuum are of a different kind. Warfare as we know it would be impossible in a radically centralized global state, for none of the motives for going to war would any longer operate: ethnic and religious differences and divergent national interests, indeed, every kind of sectional interest, would simply cease to exist. Diversity would be radically privatized. In principle, at least, the global state would be constituted solely and entirely by autonomous individuals, free, within the limits of the criminal law, to choose their own life plans and their own associates.

In practice, however, this constituting principle is unlikely to prevail, and it is a mistake to construct ideal types that are entirely fictional; they have to fit an imaginable reality. It just isn't plausible that the citizens of a global state would be, except for the free choices they make, exactly like one another, all the collective and inherited differences that we now live with having disappeared in the course of the state's formation. Surely disagreements about or, at least, diverse understandings of, how we ought to live, would persist; and these would be embodied, as they are today, in ways of life, historical cultures and religions, commanding strong loyalties and seeking public expression. So let me redescribe the global state. Groups of many different sorts would continue to exist and shape the lives of their members in significant ways, but their existence would be largely ignored by the central authorities; particularist interests would be overridden; the public expression (or, at least some public expressions) of cultural divergence would be repressed.

The reason for the repression is easily explained: the global state would be much like contemporary states, only on a vastly greater scale. If it were to sustain itself over time, it too would have to command the loyalty of its citizens and give expression to a political culture distinctly its own. It would have to look legitimate to everyone in the world. Given this necessity, I don't see how it could accommodate anything like the range of cultural and religious difference that we see around us today. Even a global state committed to toleration would be limited in its powers of accommodation by its prior commitment to what I will call "globalism," that is, centralized rule over the whole world. For some cultures and religions can only survive if they are permitted degrees of separation that are incompatible with globalism. And so the survival of these groups would be at risk; they would not be able under the rules of the global state to sustain and pass on their way of life. This is the meaning I would give to Kant's warning that a cosmopolitan constitution could lead to "terrifying despotism" (*Theory and Practice*, Part III)[2]—the danger is less to individuals than to groups. A more genuine regime of toleration would have to make room for cultural and religious autonomy, but that would involve a move rightwards on the continuum.

Once again, however, I want to acknowledge the advantages that lie on the continuum's far left side, though in this case they are more hypothetical than actual, since we have much less experience of centralization than of anarchy. But we can generalize from the history of centralized states and suggest that global distributive justice might be better served by a strong government that was able to establish universal standards of labor and welfare and to shift resources from richer to poorer countries. Of course, the will to undertake egalitarian reforms might well be absent in the world republic—just as it is in most sovereign states today. But at least the capacity would exist; the European Community provides some modest but not insignificant examples of the redistributions that centralized power makes possible. At the same time, however, the strength of the single center would make it impossible for nations, ethnic groups, and religious communities (as we know them today) to win any significant independence from it, even if they sought independence not in order to maintain inequalities from which they benefit but only to preserve their cultural traditions. Once again, centralization carries with it the threat of tyranny.

•   •   •

Now let's move one step in from the left side of the continuum, which brings us to a global regime that has the form of a *pax Romana*. It is centralized through the hegemony of a single great power over all the lesser powers of international society. This hegemony sustains world peace, even if there are intermittent rebellions, and it does this while still permitting some degree of cultural independence—perhaps in a form like that of the Ottoman *millet* system, under which different religious groups were granted (partial) legal autonomy. The autonomy is not secure, since the center is always capable of canceling it; nor will it necessarily take the form most desired by a particular group.

It isn't negotiated between equals but granted by the powerful to the weak. Nonetheless, arrangements of this sort represent the most stable regime of toleration known in world history. The rulers of the empire recognize the value (at least, the prudential value) of group autonomy, and this recognition has worked very effectively for group survival. But the rulers obviously don't recognize individual citizens as participants in the government of the empire, they don't protect individual rights, and they don't aim at an equitable distribution of resources among either groups or individuals. Imperial hegemony is a form of political inequality that commonly makes for further inequalities in the economy and in social life generally.

I have to be careful in writing about imperial rule, since I am a citizen of the only state in the world today capable of aspiring to it. That's not my own aspiration for my country, nor do I really think that it's possible, but I won't pretend to believe that a *pax Americana*, however undesirable, is the worst thing that could happen to the world today (it may be the worst thing that could happen to America), and I have been an advocate of a more activist American political/military role in places like Rwanda and Kosovo. But a role of that sort is still far from imperial hegemony, which, though we might value it for the peace it brought (or just for an end to the massacres), is clearly not one of the preferred regimes. It would reduce some of the risks of a global state, but not in a stable way, since imperial power is often arbitrary and capricious. And even if empire protects communal autonomy (which it doesn't always do), it can be very dangerous to individuals, who are often trapped in oppressive communities.

Now let's move in from the right side of the continuum: one step from anarchy brings us, I think, to something like the current arrangement of international society (hence this is the least idealized of my ideal types). We see in the world today a series of global organizations of a political, economic, and judicial sort—the United Nations, the World Bank, the International Monetary Fund, the World Trade Organization, the World Court, and so on—that serve to modify state sovereignty. No state possesses the absolute sovereignty described by early modern political theorists like Bodin and Hobbes, which makes for anarchy in its strongest sense. On the other hand, the global organizations are weak; their decision mechanisms are uncertain and slow; their powers of enforcement are difficult to bring to bear and, at best, only partially effective. Warfare between or among states has been reduced, but overall violence has not diminished. There are many weak, divided, and unstable states in the world today, and the global regime has not been successful in preventing civil wars, military interventions, savage repression of political enemies, massacres, and "ethnic cleansing" aimed at minority populations. Nor has global inequality been reduced, even though the flow of capital across borders (labor mobility too, I think) is easier than it has ever been—and, according to theorists of the free market, this ought to have egalitarian effects. All in all, we cannot be happy with the current state of the world; indeed, the combination of (many) weak states with weak global organizations brings disadvantages from both directions: the protection of cultural difference is inadequate and so is the protection of individual rights and the promotion of equality.

Let us take another step in from this same side, toward greater centralization. I don't think that this brings us to, say, a United Nations with its own army and police force or a World Bank with a single currency. In terms of intellectual strategy, we would do better to reach arrangements of that kind from the other side. Consider instead the same "constitutional" arrangements that we currently have, reinforced now by a much stronger international civil society. Contemporary political theorists have argued that civil society can serve to strengthen the democratic state. Certainly, associations that engage, train, and empower ordinary men and women serve democracy more effectively than they serve other regimes, but they probably strengthen any state that encourages rather than suppresses associational life. Would they also strengthen the semi-governmental international organizations that now exist? I am inclined to think that they already do this in modest ways and could do so much more extensively.

Imagine a wide range of civic associations—for mutual aid, human rights advocacy, the protection of minorities, the achievement of gender equality, the defense of the environment, the advancement of labor—organized on a much larger scale than at present. All these groups would have centers distinct from the centers of particular states; all of them would operate across state borders; all of them would recruit activists and supporters without reference to nationality. And all of them would be engaged in activities that governments also ought to be engaged in—where governmental engagement is more effective when it is seconded (or even initiated) by citizen-volunteers. Once the volunteers were numerous enough, they would bring pressure to bear on particular states to cooperate with each other and with global agencies; and their own work would enhance the effectiveness of the cooperation.

But these associations of volunteers coexist in international civil society with multinational corporations that command armies of well-paid professional and managerial employees and threaten to overwhelm all other global actors. The threat may be exaggerated—these corporations haven't yet entirely escaped the control of the nation-state—but it isn't imaginary. And I can describe only an imaginary set of balancing forces in an expanded civil society that doesn't yet exist: multinational labor unions, for example, and political parties operating across national frontiers. Of course, in a global state or a world empire, multinational corporations would be instantly domesticated, since there would be no place for their multiplication, no borders for them to cross. But that isn't an automatic solution to the problems they create; similar problems arise in domestic societies. We still need a *politics*, not an organizational chart, and international civil society provides the best available space (or the most easily imagined space) for the development of this politics.

Best available, but not necessarily sufficient for the task: it is a feature of the associations of civil society that they run after problems; they react to crises; their ability to anticipate, plan, and prevent lags far behind that of the state. Their activists are more likely to minister heroically to the victims of a plague than to enforce public health measures in advance. They arrive in the battle zone only in time to assist the wounded and shelter the refugees. They struggle to organize a strike after wages have already been cut. They protest environmental disasters that are already disastrous. Even when they predict coming troubles, they have too little power to act effectively; they are not responsible agents, and their warnings are often disregarded precisely because they are seen as irresponsible. As for the underlying, long-term problems of international society—insecurity and inequality above all—civil associations are at best mitigating factors: their activists can do many good things, but they can't make peace in a country torn by civil war or redistribute resources on a significant scale.

• • •

I WANT now to take another step in from the left side of the continuum, but before doing that it would probably be useful to summarize the steps so far. Since this next one, and the one after that, will bring us to what seem to me the most attractive possibilities, I need to characterize, perhaps try to name, the less attractive ones canvassed so far. Note first that the right side of the continuum is a realm of pluralism and the left side a realm of unity. I am not happy with that description of right and left; there have always been pluralist tendencies on the left, and those are the tendencies that I identify with. Still, it is probably true that unity has been the dominant ambition of leftist parties and movements, so it doesn't make much sense, on this occasion anyway, to fiddle with the rightness and leftness of the continuum. Starting from the right, then, I have marked off three arrangements, moving in the direction of greater centralization but doing this, paradoxically, by adding to the pluralism of agents. First, there is the anarchy of states, where there are no effective agents except the governments that act in the name of state sovereignty. Next, we add to these governments a plurality of international political and financial organizations, with a kind of authority that limits but doesn't abolish sovereignty. And after that, we add a plurality of international associations that operate across borders and serve to strengthen the constraints on state action. So we have international anarchy and then two degrees of global pluralism.

On the left, I have so far marked off only two arrangements, moving in the direction of greater division but maintaining the idea of a single center. The first is the global state, the least divided of imaginable regimes, whose members are individual men and women. The second is the global empire, whose members are the subject nations. The hegemony of the imperial nation divides it from the others, without abolishing the others.

The next step in from the left brings with it the end of subjection: the new arrangement is a federation of nation-states, a United States of the World. The strength of the center, of the federal government, will depend on the rights freely ceded to it by the member states and on the direct or indirect character of its jurisdiction over individual citizens. Defenders of what Americans call "states' rights" will argue for a mediated jurisdiction. Obviously, the greater the mediation the more this arrangement moves rightward on the continuum; if the mediation disappears entirely, we are back at the left end, in the global state. To make sense of this federal regime, we need to imagine a surrender of sovereignty by the particular states and then a constitutionally guaranteed functional division of power, such that the states are left with significant responsibilities and the means to fulfill them—a version, then, of the American system (different, no doubt, in many of its features), projected internationally. A greatly strengthened United Nations, incorporating the World Bank and the World Court, might approximate this model, so long as it had the power to coerce member states that refused to abide by its resolutions and verdicts. If the UN retained its current structure, with the Security Council as it is now constituted, the global federation would be an oligarchy or perhaps, since the General Assembly represents a kind of democracy, a mixed regime. It isn't easy to imagine any other sort of federation given the current inequalities of wealth and power among states.

These inequalities are probably harder to deal with than any political differences among the states. Even if all the states were republics, as Kant hoped they would be, the federation would still be wholly or partly oligarchic, so long as the existing distribution of resources was unchanged. And oligarchy here represents division; it drastically qualifies the powers of the center. By contrast, the political character of the member states would tend to become more and more similar; here the move would be toward unity or, at least, uniformity. For all the states would be incorporated into the same constitutional structure, bound, for example, by the same codes of social and political rights. And they would be far less able than they are today to ignore those rights; citizens who think themselves oppressed would quickly appeal to the federal courts and presumably find quick redress. Even if the member states were not democracies to start with, they would become uniformly democratic over time.

As a democrat I ought to find this outcome more attractive than I do; the problem is that it's more likely to be reached and sustained by pressure from the center than by democratic activism at (to shift my metaphor) the grass roots. My own preference for democracy doesn't extend to a belief that this preference should be uniformly enforced on every political community. Democracy has to be reached through a political process that, in its nature, can also produce different results. Whenever these results threaten life and liberty, some kind of intervention is necessary, but they don't always do that, and when they don't the different political formations that emerge must be given room to develop (and change). But could a global federation make its peace with political pluralism?

It is far more likely to make its peace with material inequality. A federal regime would probably redistribute resources, but only within limits set by its oligarches (once again, the European Community provides examples). The greater the power acquired by the central government, obviously, the more redistribution there is likely to be. But this kind of power would be dangerous to all the member states, not only to the wealthiest among them. It isn't clear how to strike the balance; presumably that would be one of the central issues in the internal politics of the federation (but there wouldn't be any other politics since, by definition, nothing lies outside the federation).

Constitutional guarantees would serve to protect national and ethnic/religious groups. This seems to be Kant's assumption: "In such a league, every nation, even the smallest, can expect to have security and rights . . ." (*Idea for a Universal History with a Cosmopolitan Intent*, Seventh Thesis).[3] In fact, however, only those groups that achieved sovereignty before the federation was formed would have a sure place within it. (This might be an argument for the maximal development of international anarchy before any attempt is made to form a federation—except that no one can determine the timing of federalist opportunities.) So there would have to be some procedure for recognizing and securing the rights of new groups, as well as a code of rights for individuals without regard to their memberships. Conceivably, the federal regime would turn out to be a guardian of both eccentric groups and individuals—as in the United States, for example, where embattled minorities and idiosyncratic citizens commonly appeal to the central government when they are mistreated by local authorities. When such an appeal doesn't work, however, Americans have options that would not be available to the citizens of a global union: they can carry their appeal to the UN or the World Court, or they can move to another country. There is still something to be said for division and pluralism.

Now let's take another step in from the right side and try to imagine, what may be impossible, a coherent form of division. I have in mind the familiar anarchy of states mitigated and controlled by a threefold set of nonstate agents: organizations like the UN, the associations of international civil society, and regional unions like the European Community. This is the third degree of global pluralism, and in its fully developed (ideal) version, it offers the largest number of opportunities for political action on behalf of peace, justice, cultural difference, and individual rights; and it poses, at the same time, the smallest risk of global tyranny. Of course, opportunities for action are no more than that; they bring no guarantees; and conflicts are sure to arise among men and women pursuing these different values. I imagine this last regime as providing a context for politics in its fullest sense (and conflict is included in that fullness) and for the widest engagement of ordinary citizens, with citizenship understood in the most highly differentiated way.

Consider again the troubling features of the first six regimes: in some of them it is the decentered world and the self-centered states inhabiting it (whether the states are strong or weak) that threaten our values; in others it is the tyrannical potential of the newly constituted center that poses the danger. So the problem is to overcome the radical decentralization of sovereign states without creating a single all-powerful central regime. And the solution that I want to defend, the third degree of global pluralism, goes roughly like this: create a set of alternative centers and an increasingly dense web of social ties that cross state boundaries. The solution is to build on the institutional structures that now exist, or are slowly coming into existence, and to strengthen all of them, even if they are competitive with one another.

So the third degree of global pluralism requires a United Nations with a military force of its own capable of humanitarian interventions and a strong version of peacekeeping—but still a force that can only be used with the approval of the Security Council or a very large majority of the General Assembly. Then it requires a World Bank and IMF strong enough to regulate the flow of capital and the forms of international investment and a World Trade Organization able to enforce labor and environmental standards—all these, however, independently governed, not tightly coordinated with the UN. It requires a World Court with power to make arrests on its own, but needing to seek UN support in the face of opposition from any of the (semi-sovereign) states of international society. Add to these organizations a very large number of civic associations operating internationally, including political parties that run candidates in different countries' elections and labor unions that begin to realize their long-standing goal of international solidarity, as well as single-issue movements aiming to influence simultaneously the UN and its agencies and the different states. The larger the membership of these associations and the wider their extension across state boundaries, the more they would knit together the politics of the global society. But they would never constitute a single center; they would always represent multiple sources of political energy; they would always be diversely focused.

Now add a new layer of governmental organization—the regional federation, of which the European Community is only one possible model. We can imagine both tighter and looser structures (but tighter is probably better for the control of global markets and multinational corporations), distributed across the globe, perhaps even with overlapping memberships: differently constituted federal unions in different parts of the world. This sort of thing would bring many of the advantages of a global federation but with greatly reduced risks of tyranny from the center. For it is a crucial feature of regionalism that there will be many centers.

• • •

To appreciate the beauty of pluralist arrangements of this kind, one must attach a greater value to political possibility, and the activism it breeds, than to the certainty of political success. To my mind, certainty is always a fantasy, but I don't want to deny that something is lost when one gives up the more unitary versions of globalism. What is lost is the hope of creating a more egalitarian world with a stroke of the pen—a single legislative act enforced from a single center. What is lost is the hope of achieving perpetual peace, that is, the end of conflict and violence, everywhere and forever. What is lost is the hope of a singular citizenship and a singular identity for all human individuals—so that they would be autonomous men and women, and nothing else.

I must hasten to deny what the argument so far may suggest to many readers: I don't mean to sacrifice all these hopes solely for the sake of what is today called "communitarianism"—that is, for the sake of cultural and religious difference. That last is an important value, and it is no doubt well-served by the third degree of pluralism (indeed, the different levels of government allow new opportunities for self-expression and autonomy to minority groups hitherto subordinated within the nation-state). But difference exists alongside peace, equality, and autonomy; it doesn't supersede them. My argument is that all these values are best pursued politically in circumstances where there are many avenues of pursuit, many agents in pursuit. The dream of a single agent— the enlightened despot, the civilizing imperium, the communist vanguard, the global state—is a delusion. We need many agents, many arenas of activity and decision. Political values have to be defended in many different places so that failure here can be a spur to action there, and success there a model for imitation or revision here.

But there will be failures as well as successes, and I need to mention and at least briefly worry about three possible failures—so as to stress that all the arrangements, including the one I prefer, have their dangers and disadvantages. The first is the possible failure of peacekeeping, which is also, today, a failure to protect cultural or religious minorities. Wars between and among states will be rare in a densely webbed international society. But the very success of the politics of difference makes for internal conflicts that tend toward and sometimes reach "ethnic cleansing" and even genocidal civil war. The claim of all the strongly centered regimes is that this sort of thing will be stopped, but the price of doing this, and of maintaining the capacity to do it, is very high. The danger of all the decentered and multi-centered regimes is that no one will stop the awfulness. The third degree of pluralism maximizes the number of agents who might stop it or at least mitigate its effects: individual states acting unilaterally (like the Vietnamese when they shut down the killing fields of Cambodia); alliances and unions of states (like NATO in the Kosovo war); global organizations (like the UN); and the volunteers of international civil society (like Doctors Without Borders). But there is no assigned agent, no singular responsibility; everything waits for political debate and decision—and may wait too long.

The second possible failure is in the promotion of equality. Here too the third degree of pluralism provides many opportunities for egalitarian reform, and there will surely be many experiments in different societies or at different levels of government (like the Israeli kibbutz or the Scandinavian welfare state or the European Community's redistributive efforts or the proposed "Tobin tax" on international financial transactions). But the forces that oppose equality will never have to face the massed power of the globally dispossessed, for there won't be a global arena where this power can be massed. What there will be, or could be, is very different: many organizations that seek to mobilize the dispossessed and express their aspirations, sometimes cooperating, sometimes competing, with one another.

The third possible failure is in the defense of individual liberty. Once again, the pluralism of states, cultures, and religions—even if full sovereignty no longer exists anywhere—means that individuals in different settings will be differently entitled and protected. We can (and should) defend some minimal understanding of human rights and seek its universal enforcement, but enforcement in the third degree of pluralism would necessarily involve many different agents, hence many arguments and many decisions, and the results are bound to be uneven.

Can it possibly be the case that a regime open to such failures is the most just regime? I only want to argue that it is the political arrangement that most facilitates the everyday pursuit of justice under conditions least dangerous to the overall cause of justice. All the other regimes are worse, including the one on the far left of the continuum for which the highest hopes have been held out. For it is a mistake to imagine Reason in power in a global state—as great a mistake (and a mistake of the same kind) as to imagine the future world order as a millennial kingdom where God is the king. The rulers required by regimes of this kind don't exist or, at least, don't manifest themselves politically. By contrast, the move toward pluralism suits people like us, all-too-real and no more than intermittently reasonable, for whom politics is a "natural" activity.

Finally, I must insist that the move toward pluralism really is a *move*. We are not there yet; we have "many miles to go before we rest." The kinds of governmental agencies that are needed in an age of globalization haven't yet been developed; the level of participation in international civil society is much too low; regional federations are still in their beginning stages. Reforms in these institutional areas, however, are rarely sought for their own sake. No one is sufficiently interested. We will strengthen global pluralism only by using it, by seizing the opportunities it offers. There won't be an advance at any institutional level except in the context of a campaign or, better, a series of campaigns for greater security and greater equality for groups and individuals across the globe.

NOTES

An earlier version of this essay was given as the Multatuli Lecture at the Catholic University of Leuven and published in the journal of the European Ethics Network, *Ethical Perspectives*, December 1999. A different version appeared in *Dissent*, Fall 2000.

1. Immanuel Kant, "Eternal Peace" (often called "Perpetual Peace"), *The Philosophy of Kant*, ed. Carl J. Friedrich (New York: Random House [The Modern Library], 1949).

2. Immanuel Kant, "Truth and Practice Concerning the Common Saying: This May Be True in Theory But Does Not Apply to Practice," *The Philosophy of Kant*.

3. Immanuel Kant, "Idea for a Universal History with a Cosmopolitan Intent," *The Philosophy of Kant*.

AUTHOR NOTES

DAVID APTER is the Henry J. Heinz II Professor Emeritus of Political Science and Sociology at Yale University.

KAUSHIK BASU is Carl Marks Professor of International Studies and Professor of Economics at Cornell University.

JUDITH BUTLER is Chancellor's Professor of Rhetoric and Professor of Comparative Literature at the University of California, Berkeley.

NICHOLAS DIRKS is Professor of Anthropology at Columbia University.

JEAN BETHKE ELSHTAIN is the Laura Spelman Rockefeller Professor of Social and Political Ethics at the Divinity School of the University of Chicago.

PETER GALISON is the Mallinckrodt Professor of the History of Science and Physics at Harvard University.

CLIFFORD GEERTZ is Professor Emeritus in the School of Social Science at the Institute for Advanced Study.

WOLF LEPENIES is Rektor of the Wissenschaftskolleg in Berlin.

JANE MANSBRIDGE is the Adams Professor of Political Leadership and Democratic Values in the John F. Kennedy School of Government at Harvard University.

ANDREW PICKERING is Professor of Sociology and Director of the Program for Studies of Science, Technology, Information and Medicine at the University of Illinois, Urbana-Champaign.

MARY POOVEY is Professor of English and Director of the Institute for the History of the Production of Knowledge at New York University.

ISTVAN REV is Director of the Open Society Archives at the Central European University.

RENATO ROSALDO is Lucie Stern Professor of Social Science and Professor of Anthropology at Stanford University.

MICHAEL RUSTIN is Dean of the Faculty of Social Sciences and Professor of Sociology at the University of East London.

JOAN W. SCOTT is Harold F. Linder Professor of Social Science at the Institute for Advanced Study.

WILLIAM H. SEWELL, JR. is Max Palevsky Professor of History and Political Science at the University of Chicago.

QUENTIN SKINNER is Regius Professor of Modern History and Pro-Vice Chancellor of Christ's College at the University of Cambridge.

CHARLES TAYLOR is Professor Emeritus of Philosophy at McGill University.

ANNA TSING is Professor of Anthropology at the University of California, Santa Cruz.

MICHAEL WALZER is UPS Foundation Professor of Social Science at the Institute for Advanced Study.

GAVIN WRIGHT is the William Robertson Coe Professor of American Economic History at Stanford University.